April 19th, '18

To my good Friend Mi...

We Foond that Lindbergh
marker today! And, we had
a GREAT DAY wandering soothwest
down the Fox River Valley —
Yorkville to WEDRON!!

Enjoyed the day Mike!

Yoor Friend,
Bill Mon...

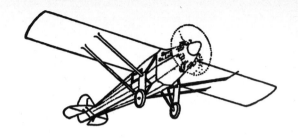

THE SPIRIT *of* ST. LOUIS

Charles A. Lindbergh

SCRIBNER CLASSICS

SCRIBNER
1230 Avenue of the Americas
New York, NY 10020

ISBN 0-684-85277-2

To **A. M. L.**

*Who will never realize
how much of this book she has written*

ACKNOWLEDGMENTS

IN WORKING OVER LATER DRAFTS of the manuscript for *The Spirit of St. Louis*, I have used the facilities of several organizations and received assistance from many friends. I wish to express my deep appreciation to the following:

For reading part or all of the manuscript, and for criticism, suggestions, and assistance, which have been of tremendous value: Carl B. Allen; Dana W. Atchley; Betsy Barton; Jeanne A. Biltz; Harold M. Bixby; Kenneth Boedecker; Juno L. Butler; George T. Bye; Eva L. Christie; Michel Detroyat; Hope H. English; Margaret B. Evans; Paul W. Fisher; Judith S. Guild; Harlan A. Gurney; Elisabeth Habsburg; Donald A. Hall; J. G. E. Hopkins; Charles H. Land; Emory Scott Land; Kenneth M. Lane; Anne Morrow Lindbergh; Evangeline Lodge Land Lindbergh; Frank A. Lindbergh; Jon M. Lindbergh; Land M. Lindbergh; Lauren D. Lyman; Constance Morrow Morgan; Esther B. Mueller; Grace Lee Nute; Paul Palmer; Wesley Price; Dorothy E. Ross; Linda L. Seal; H. Robinson Shipherd; John Hall Wheelock.

For refreshing my memory and/or supplying information needed in various chapters: James T. Babb; Gregory J. Brandewiede; Paul E. Garber; Harry F. Guggenheim; John H. Towers; Willard R. Wolfinbarger.

For secretarial assistance: Dorothy M. Austin; Marta A. Brodie; Patricia Carey; Christine L. Gawne; Jeannette Greene; Gladys Leahey; Irene Leahey; Barbara Mansfield; Katharyne Toner; Anne M. Wylie; Jean W. Wylie.

For research facilities and technical and historical data: The Institute of the Aeronautical Sciences; The Minnesota Historical Society; The Missouri Historical Society; The National Aeronautic Association; The New York Public Library; The Smithsonian Institution; The Yale University Library.

For newspaper articles, extracts, and information: *Aftonbladet*, Stockholm; The Associated Press; *Chicago Sunday Tribune*; *The Denver Post*; *Le Figaro*, Paris; *und Handels-Zeitung*, Berlin; International

News Service; *Los Angeles Times; The New York American; New York Herald Tribune; The New York Times; The New York World; La Prensa,* Buenos Aires; *St. Louis Globe-Democrat; San Diego Independent; San Diego Sun; San Diego Union; San Francisco Chronicle; The Sunday Star,* Washington, D. C.; *The Times-Picayune,* New Orleans; The United Press Associations.

For the use ot lines from "The Builders" by Henry Wadsworth Longfellow: Houghton Mifflin & Co.

For hours which might otherwise have belonged to them: Jon, Land, Anne, Scott, and Reeve.

CHARLES A. LINDBERGH

MEMBERS OF

The Spirit of St. Louis

ORGANIZATION

HAROLD M. BIXBY
HARRY F. KNIGHT
HARRY H. KNIGHT
ALBERT BOND LAMBERT
J. D. WOOSTER LAMBERT
CHARLES A. LINDBERGH
E. LANSING RAY
FRANK H. ROBERTSON
WILLIAM B. ROBERTSON
EARL C. THOMPSON

PREFACE

IN GENERAL, this book is about flying, and an aviator's life, in the beginning third of the 20th century. In particular, it describes the planning and execution of the first nonstop airplane flight between the continents of America and Europe. It has been fourteen years in the writing. Started in the city of Paris, during the tense prewar winter of 1938, its manuscript was completed on the shore of Scotts Cove, off Long Island Sound, in the hardly more tranquil year of 1952.

The chapters that follow have been drafted and revised under conditions ranging from the uncertainty of a fighting squadron's tent in the jungles of New Guinea, to the stable family life of a Connecticut suburban home, and under such diverse daily influences as accompany noonday, midnight, and dawn. On top of a manuscript sheet I often marked down my location at the moment of writing or revising. Glancing through old drafts, I now pick out, more or less at random, the following geographical positions: aboard S.S. *Aquitania,* en route Cherbourg to New York; Army and Navy Club, Washington, D.C.; with the Marines on a Marshall atoll; in a bomber, returning from the North Magnetic Pole; General Partridge's residence at Nagoya, Japan; in a house trailer on the Florida Keys; on an air base in Arabia; parked on a roadside in the Italian Alps; camped in Germany's Taunus mountains; at the Carrels' island of St. Gildas.

Because the writing began more than eleven years after the last incident described took place, and because detailed records were not available at the time and later could not be transported everywhere the manuscript traveled, I have drawn heavily on memory for early drafts.

Searching memory might be compared to throwing the beam of a strong light, from your hilltop camp site, back over the road you traveled by day. Only a few of the objects you passed are clearly illuminated; countless others are hidden behind them, screened from the rays. There is bound to be some vagueness and distortion in the distance. But memory has advantages that compensate for its failings. By eliminating detail, it clarifies the picture as a whole. Like an artist's brush, it finds higher value in life's essence than in its photographic intricacy.

Records, on the other hand, illuminate the corners with which they are concerned, and surround your mind with their contemporary problems. They are relatively specialized, sometimes contradictory, and often incomplete. They restrict your perspective by bringing you too close to the area they cover. But they offer pay in precision for what they lack in breadth. I have rearranged and rewritten later manuscript drafts under the light of documents culled from attics, files, and libraries.

Throughout the following chapters I have digested conversations and press articles in order to avoid tedious detail. In telegrams I have used the originals where they were available, and approximated from memory where they were not. Since it is impossible to describe exactly the wanderings of the mind, I have placed flashbacks out of sequence to attain impressionistic truth. All incidents in this book are factual, and I have tried to put them into words with accuracy. The engine log and navigation log of the *Spirit of St. Louis* were stolen by some member of the crowd that overran fences and guards at Le Bourget. Therefore the log entries which form chapter heads in Part II have been filled in from performance curves and other records. The figures used are close to those marked down in flight, but there is certainly some variation.

When the *Spirit of St. Louis* flew to Paris, aviation was shouldering its way from the stage of invention onto the stage of usefulness. Enthusiasts still talked about "the conquest of the air." Rules for safety were sometimes just the reverse of today's. When a pilot encountered fog, he turned his eyes to the earth instead of to his dials, and the quality of his senses was as important as that of his mind. The ability of an aircraft to make an emergency landing in a small pasture warranted a considerable reduction in its cruising speed; while the advantage of a cockpit forward, from the standpoint of vision, was more than offset by the advantage of a cockpit aft, from the standpoint of crash. But the monoplane had become a serious threat to the biplane's superiority. Instrument-flying techniques were being developed by the more progressive pilots. And promises of radio communication gave airmen cause for hope.

Along with most of my fellow fliers, I believed that aviation had a brilliant future. But my vision, extravagant as it seemed at the time, fell short of accomplishments now achieved with aircraft, by their pilots, engineers, and executives. Speeds, ranges, altitudes, powers, sizes, economies, and destructive capabilities today have shattered limiting factors of a quarter century ago. Science has transformed the frail craft of Le Bris, Lilienthal, and the Wright brothers into metal, and loaded them with cargoes varying from orchids to atomic bombs. Thousands of men, women, and children now cruise each day above the racing pilot's speed of 1927. Agencies all over the world sell tickets to cross the ocean at steamer-travel prices. Airlines have flown billions of passenger miles between fatalities. Engines have changed their horsepower ratings from hundreds into thousands. Military crews fly regularly above what the world's altitude record used to be.

Technically, we in aviation have met with miraculous success. We have accomplished our objectives, passed beyond them. We actually live, today, in our dreams of yesterday; and, living in those dreams, we dream again. Our visions of the future now embrace rocket missiles and supersonic flights. We speculate on traveling through space as we once discussed flying across oceans. But, unlike the early years of aviation, our dreams of tomorrow are disturbed by the realities of today. In this new, almost superhuman world, we find alarming imperfections. We have seen the aircraft, to which we devoted our lives, destroying the civilization that created them. We realize that the very efficiency of our machines threatens the character of the men who build and operate them.

Together with people outside the field of aviation, we find ourselves moving in a vicious circle, where the machine, which depended on modern man for its invention, has made modern man dependent on its constant improvement for his security—even for his life. We begin to wonder how rocket speeds and atomic powers will affect the naked body, mind, and spirit, which, in the last analysis, measure the true value of all human effort. We have come face to face with the essential problem of how to use man's creations for the benefit of man himself. But this leads beyond the scope of my story, which ends on May 21, 1927, when we were still looking forward to the conquest of the air.

C. A. L.

CONTENTS

ACKNOWLEDGMENTS   vii

PREFACE   ix

PART I · THE CRAFT

I. *The St. Louis-Chicago Mail*   3

II. *New York*   51

III. *San Diego*   79

IV. *Across the Continent*   134

V. *Roosevelt Field*   148

PART II · NEW YORK TO PARIS

VI. *New York to Paris*   181

AFTERWORD   493

APPENDIX

THE LOG OF THE *Spirit of St. Louis*   503

THE CRUISER *Memphis*   517

DECORATIONS, AWARDS, AND TROPHIES
by ESTHER B. MUELLER   517

THE RAYMOND ORTEIG PRIZE   530

ENGINEERING DATA ON THE *Spirit of St. Louis*
by DONALD A. HALL   531

SPECIFICATIONS AND GENERAL DESCRIPTION
OF THE WHIRLWIND ENGINE
by KENNETH M. LANE   545

We   547

OTHER BOOKS, MAGAZINE ARTICLES, AND PRESS ACCOUNTS   547

GLOSSARY   549

LIST OF ILLUSTRATIONS

The flights of the *Spirit of St. Louis* (Map)   514

Three-view drawing of plane   541

Performance curves   542–544

Plan and elevation (partly sectional) of a biplane   559

HALFTONE SECTION

Lambert Field

Curtiss Jenny — JN4-D

De Haviland — DH-4

The wreck of Capt. Lindbergh's mail plane

At the Ryan Airlines factory, San Diego

Wright Whirlwind J-5C engine

The *Spirit of St. Louis* over Coronado Strand, California

Capt. Lindbergh, in the pilot's seat

Start of the truck-tow from Curtiss Field, May 21, 1927

The cockpit of the *Spirit of St. Louis*

On Roosevelt Field

The Mercator's charts

A typical scene on a field where the *Spirit of St. Louis* landed

Headlines from a variety of newspapers appearing between May 21 and
December 15, 1927

The *Spirit of St. Louis*, after landing at Croydon

Farewell to St. Louis

·PART I·

THE CRAFT

THE ST. LOUIS—CHICAGO
MAIL

SEPTEMBER, 1926

NIGHT ALREADY SHADOWS the eastern sky. To my left, low on the horizon, a thin line of cloud is drawing on its evening sheath of black. A moment ago, it was burning red and gold. I look down over the side of my cockpit at the farm lands of central Illinois. Wheat shocks are gone from the fields. Close, parallel lines of the seeder, across a harrowed strip, show where winter planting has begun. A threshing crew on the farm below is quitting work for the day. Several men look up and wave as my mail plane roars overhead. Trees and buildings and stacks of grain stand shadowless in the diffused light of evening. In a few minutes it will be dark, and I'm still south of Peoria.

How quickly the long days of summer passed, when it was daylight all the way to Chicago. It seems only a few weeks ago, that momentous afternoon in April, when we inaugurated the air-mail service. As chief pilot of the line, the honor of making the first flight had been mine. There were photographs, city officials, and handshaking all along the route that day. For was it not a milestone in a city's history, this carrying of the mail by air? We pilots, mechanics, postal clerks, and business executives, at St. Louis, Springfield, Peoria, Chicago, all felt that we were taking part in an event which pointed the way toward a new and marvelous era.

But after the first day's heavy load, swollen with letters of enthusiasts and collectors, interest declined. Men's minds turned back to routine business; the air mail saves a few hours at most;

it's seldom really worth the extra cost per letter. Week after week, we've carried the limp and nearly empty sacks back and forth with a regularity in which we take great pride. Whether the mail compartment contains ten letters or ten thousand is beside the point. We have faith in the future. Some day we know the sacks will fill.

We pilots of the mail have a tradition to establish. The commerce of the air depends on it. Men have already died for that tradition. Every division of the mail routes has its hallowed points of crash where some pilot on a stormy night, or lost and blinded by fog, laid down his life on the altar of his occupation. Every man who flies the mail senses that altar and, consciously or unconsciously, in his way worships before it, knowing that his own next flight may end in the sacrifice demanded.

Our contract calls for five round trips each week. It's our mission to land the St. Louis mail in Chicago in time to connect with planes coming in from California, Minnesota, Michigan, and Texas — a time calculated to put letters in New York City for the opening of the eastern business day.

Three of us carry on this service: Philip Love, Thomas Nelson, and I. We've established the best record of all the routes converging at Chicago, with over ninety-nine percent of our scheduled flights completed. Ploughing through storms, wedging our way beneath low clouds, paying almost no attention to weather forecasts, we've more than once landed our rebuilt army warplanes on Chicago's Maywood field when other lines canceled out, when older and perhaps wiser pilots ordered their cargo put on a train. During the long days of summer we seldom missed a flight. But now winter is creeping up on us. Nights are lengthening; skies are thickening with haze and storm. We're already landing by floodlight at Chicago. In a few more weeks it will be dark when we glide down onto that narrow strip of cow pasture called the Peoria air-mail field. Before the winter is past, even the meadow at Springfield will need lights. Today I'm over an hour late — engine trouble at St. Louis.

Lighting an airport is no great problem if you have money to pay for it. With revolving beacons, boundary markers, and floodlights, night flying isn't difficult. But our organization can't buy such luxuries. There's barely enough money to keep going from month to month.

The Robertson Aircraft Corporation is paid by the pounds of mail we carry, and often the sacks weigh more than the letters inside. Our operating expenses are incredibly low; but our revenue is lower still. The Corporation couldn't afford to buy new aircraft. All our planes and engines were purchased from Army salvage, and rebuilt in our shops at Lambert Field. We call them DHs, because the design originated with De Haviland, in England. They are biplanes, with a single, twelve-cylinder, four-hundred-horse-power Liberty engine in the nose. They were built during the war for bombing and observation purposes, and improved types were put on production in the United States. The military DH has two cockpits. In our planes the mail compartment is where the front cockpit used to be, and we mail pilots fly from the position where the wartime observer sat.

We've been unable to buy full night-flying equipment for these planes, to say nothing of lights and beacons for the fields we land on. It was only last week that red and green navigation lights were installed on our DHs. Before that we carried nothing but one emergency flare and a pocket flashlight. When the dollars aren't there, you can't draw checks to pay for equipment. But it's bad economy, in the long run, to operate a mail route without proper lights. That has already cost us one plane. I lost a DH just over a week ago because I didn't have an extra flare, or wing lights, or a beacon to go back to.

I encountered fog, that night, on the northbound flight between Marseilles and Chicago. It was a solid bank, rolling in over the Illinois River valley. I turned back southwest, and tried to drop my single flare so I could land on one of the farm fields below; but when I pulled the release lever nothing happened. Since the top of the fog was less than a thousand feet high, I decided to climb over it and continue on my route in the hope of finding a clear spot around the air-mail field. Then, if I could get under the clouds, I could pick up the Chicago beacon, which had been installed at government expense.

Glowing patches of mist showed me where cities lay on the earth's surface. With these patches as guides, I had little trouble locating the outskirts of Chicago and the general area of Maywood. But a blanket of fog, about 800 feet thick, covered the field. Mechanics told me afterward that they played a searchlight upward and burned two barrels of gasoline on the ground in an effort to attract my attention. I saw no sign of their activities.

After circling for a half hour I headed west, hoping to pick up one of the beacons on the transcontinental route. They were fogged in too. By then I had discovered that the failure of my flare to drop was caused by slack in the release cable, and that the flare might still function if I pulled on the cable instead of on the release lever. I turned southwest, toward the edge of the fog, intending to follow my original plan of landing on some farmer's field by flarelight. At 8:20 my engine spit a few times and cut out almost completely. At first I thought the carburetor jets had clogged, because there should have been plenty of fuel in my main tank. But I followed the emergency procedure of turning on the reserve. Then, since I was only 1500 feet high, I shoved the flashlight into my pocket and got ready to jump; but power surged into the engine again. Obviously nothing was wrong with the carburetor — the main tank had run dry. That left me with reserve fuel for only twenty minutes of flight — not enough time to reach the edge of the fog.

I decided to jump when the reserve tank ran dry, and I had started to climb for altitude when a light appeared on the ground — just a blink, but that meant a break in the fog. I circled down to 1200 feet and pulled out the flare-release cable. This time the flare functioned, but it showed only a solid layer of mist. I waited until the flare sank out of sight on its parachute, and began climbing again. Ahead, I saw the glow from a small city. I banked away, toward open country.

I was 5000 feet high when my engine cut the second time. I unbuckled my safety belt, dove over the right side of the fuselage, and after two or three seconds of fall pulled the rip cord. The parachute opened right away. I was playing my flashlight down toward the top of the fog bank when I was startled to hear the sound of an airplane in the distance. It was coming toward me. In a few seconds I saw my DH, dimly, less than a quarter mile away and about on a level with me. It was circling in my direction, left wing down. Since I thought it was completely out of gasoline, I had neglected to cut the switches before I jumped. When the nose dropped, due to the loss of the weight of my body in the tail, some additional fuel apparently drained forward into the carburetor, sending the plane off on a solo flight of its own.

My concern was out of proportion to the danger. In spite of the sky's tremendous space, it seemed crowded with traffic. I shoved my flashlight into my pocket and caught hold of the parachute risers so I could slip the canopy one way or the other in case the plane kept pointing toward me. But it was fully a hundred yards away when it passed, leaving me on the outside of its circle. The engine noise receded, and then increased until the DH appeared again, still at my elevation. The rate of descent of plane and parachute were approximately equal. I counted five spirals, each a little farther away than the last. Then I sank into the fog bank.

Knowing the ground to be less than a thousand feet below, I reached for the flashlight. It was gone. In my excitement when I saw the plane coming toward me, I hadn't pushed it far enough into my pocket. I held my feet together, guarded my face with my hands, and waited. I heard the DH pass once again. Then I saw the outline of the ground, braced myself for impact, and hit — in a cornfield. By the time I got back on my feet, the chute had collapsed and was lying on top of the corn tassels. I rolled it up, tucked it under my arm, and started walking between two rows of corn. The stalks were higher than my head. The leaves crinkled as I brushed past them. I climbed over a fence, into a stubble field. There I found wagon tracks and followed them. Ground visibility was about a hundred yards.

The wagon tracks took me to a farmyard. First, the big barn loomed up in haze. Then a lighted window beyond it showed that someone was still up. I was heading for the house when I saw an automobile move slowly along the road and stop, playing its spotlight from one side to the other. I walked over to the car. Several people were in it.

"Did you hear that airplane?" one of them called out as I approached.

"I'm the pilot," I said.

"An airplane just dove into the ground," the man went on, paying no attention to my answer. "Must be right near here. God, it made a racket!" He kept searching with his spotlight, but the beam didn't show much in the haze.

"I'm the pilot," I said again. "I was flying it." My words got through that time. The spotlight stopped moving.

"You're the pilot? Good God, how ─ ─ ─ "

"I jumped with a parachute," I said, showing him the white bundle.

"You aren't hurt?"

"Not a bit. But I've got to find the wreck and get the mail sacks."

"It must be right near by. Get in and we'll drive along the road a piece. Good God, what went wrong? You must have had *some* experience! You're sure you aren't hurt?"

We spent a quarter hour searching, unsuccessfully. Then I accompanied the farmer to his house. My plane, he said, had flown over his roof only a few seconds before it struck the ground. I asked to use his telephone. The party line was jammed with voices, all talking about the airplane that had crashed. I broke in with the statement that I was the pilot, and asked the telephone operator to put in emergency calls for St. Louis and Chicago. Then I asked her if anyone had reported the exact location of the wreck. A number of people had heard the plane pass overhead just before it hit, she replied, but nothing more definite had come in.

I'd hardly hung up and turned away when the bell rang— three longs and a short.

"That's our signal," the farmer said.

My plane had been located, the operator told me, about two miles from the house I was in. We drove to the site of crash. The

DH was wound up in a ball-shaped mass. It had narrowly missed a farmhouse, hooked one wing on a grain shock a quarter mile beyond, skidded along the ground for eighty yards, ripped through a fence, and come to rest on the edge of a cornfield. Splinters of wood and bits of torn fabric were strewn all around. The mail compartment was broken open and one sack had been thrown out; but the mail was undamaged — I took it to the nearest post office to be entrained.

The Illinois River angles in from the west. Lights are blinking on in the city of Peoria — long lines of them for streets; single spots for house and office windows. I glance at the watch on my instrument board — 6:35. Good! I've made up ten minutes since leaving St. Louis. I nose down toward the flying field, letting the air-speed needle climb to 120 miles an hour. The green mail truck is at its usual place in the fence corner. The driver, standing by its side, lifts his arm in greeting as my plane approaches. And for this admiring audience of one, I dive down below the treetops and chandelle up around the field, climbing steeply until trembling wings warn me to level off. Then, engine throttled, I sideslip down to a landing, almost brushing through high branches on the lee-ward border.

The pasture is none too large for a De Haviland, even in daytime. We'll have to be doubly careful at night. If a pilot glides down a little fast, he'll overshoot. To make matters worse, a small gully spoils the eastern portion of the field for landing, so we often have to come in with a cross wind.

I taxi up to the mail truck, blast the tail around with the engine, and pull back my throttle until the propeller is just ticking over. The driver, in brown whipcord uniform and visored cap, comes up smiling with the mail sack draped over one arm. It's a registered sack, fastened at the top with a big brass padlock. Good! The weight of that lock is worth nearly two dollars to us, and there was registered mail from Springfield and St. Louis too. Those locks add an appreciable sum to our monthly revenue.

I toss the sack down onto aluminum-faced floor boards and pass out two equally empty sacks from St. Louis and Springfield. A few dozen letters in, a few dozen letters out, that's the Peoria air mail.

"No fuel today?"

"No, plenty of fuel," I answer. "I've had a good tail wind."

It's a relief to both of us, for twenty minutes of hard labor are required to roll a barrel of gasoline over from our cache in the fence corner, pump thirty or forty gallons into the DH's tank, and start the engine again. That is, it takes twenty minutes if the engine starts easily; an indefinite time if it doesn't.

Leaving the engine idling, we walk over to inspect the field-lighting equipment which has been improvised for the night landings of winter. Since the Robertson Aircraft Corporation keeps no mechanics at intermediate stops between St. Louis and Chicago, all the assistance we have comes from the mail truck drivers. They help us with refueling and starting, keep the wind sock untangled, and hold on to a wing when taxiing is difficult. For whatever the pilot can't do alone, he has to call upon them. It's not part of their work; they get nothing for it, but they're always ready to give us a hand. Now we'll have to depend on them to arrange the lights for our night landings.

Electric floodlights cost too much, so our Corporation bought flares instead. The first shipment has just arrived. The driver unlocks a plank box near the gasoline barrels and takes out a long, cylindrical flare. On one end there's a spike that can be stuck into the ground to hold it upright, like a piece of Fourth-of-July fireworks. We selected a type that would burn for nearly two minutes — long enough if lighted at the right moment, and much less expensive than the larger ones.

I show the driver where it should be placed with different directions of wind—always on the leeward end of the landing strip, with a curved sheet of tin behind it for a reflector and to keep the intense light from blinding the pilot as he glides down. A flare is not to be set off, I tell him, unless he sees the plane's navigation lights blink several times. On moonlit nights we can economize by not using one at all.

I'm an hour and ten minutes behind schedule, taking off. The trees at the far end of the field have merged into a solid clump in thickening dusk, have lost their individual identity. The moon, just past full, is rising in the east. I didn't notice it before I landed, but now it seems to be competing with me for domination of the sky — just the two of us, climbing, and all the world beneath.

I welcome the approach of night as twilight fades into brilliant moonlight. The day has been crystal clear and almost cloudless; perfect for flying. It's been almost too perfect for flying the mail, for there's no ability required in holding your course over familiar country with a sharp horizon in every quarter. You simply sit, touching stick and rudder lightly, dreaming of the earth below, of experiences past, of adventures that may come. There's nothing else to do, nothing to match yourself against. There hasn't been even an occasional cloud near enough to burrow through. Skill is no asset. The spirit of conquest is gone from the air. On such an evening you might better be training students. It's an evening for beginners, not for pilots of the mail—no tricks of wind, no false horizons. Its hours were shaped for beauty, not for contest.

The last tint of pink disappears from the western sky, leaving to the moon complete mastery of night. Its light floods through woods and fields; reflects up from bends of rivers; shines on the silver wings of my biplane, turning them a greenish hue. It makes the earth seem more like a planet; and me a part of the heavens above it, as though I too had a right to an orbit in the sky. I look down toward the ground, at the faintly lighted farmhouse windows and the distant glow of cities, wondering what acts of life are covered by the weird semidarkness in which only outlines can be seen. Around those points of light are homes and men—family gatherings, parties, doctors at births and deathbeds, hope and despair, youth and age. That line of six glowing dots — is it a bar-room, church, or dance hall? And all those myriad lights, all the turmoil and works of men, seem to hang so precariously on the great sphere hurtling through the heavens, a phosphorescent moss on its surface, vulnerable to the brush of a hand. I feel aloof and unattached, in the solitude of space. Why return to that moss; why submerge myself in brick-walled human problems when all the crystal universe is mine? Like the moon, I can fly on forever through space, past the mail field at Chicago, beyond the state of Illinois, over mountains, over oceans, independent of the world below.

Suppose I really could stay up here and keep on flying; suppose gasoline didn't weigh so much and I could put enough in the tanks to last for days. Suppose, like the man on the magic carpet, I could fly anywhere I wanted to — anywhere in the world — to the North Pole or to China or to some jungle island if I wished. How much fuel *could* a plane carry if its fuselage were filled with tanks? But Fonck tried that out in his big Sikorsky biplane, only a few days ago, and crashed—crashed into flames on a New York field, taking off for a nonstop flight to Paris. Why does fuel have to be so heavy? If gasoline weighed only a pound per gallon instead of six, there'd be no limit to the places one could fly — if the engine kept on running.

If the engine kept on running! The schooled habit of periodic instrument readings brings me back to the mechanics of human flight. One can't be following a satellite's orbit and watching these dials at the same time. I return abruptly to earthly problems of temperature, oil pressure, and r.p.m. I contended for a moment, but the moon has won. Independent of the world? Only as long as the engine runs smoothly and the fuel holds out. I have fuel enough for another two hours at most. But long before that I'll have to be down at Chicago; my DH safely in the hangar; the mail sorted, resacked, and most of it in the cockpit of an eastbound transcontinental plane, headed for the Alleghenies and New York City.

I'm annoyed at the thought of landing. It's a roundabout method anyway, this flying the mail to Chicago to get it east. Why shouldn't we carry it direct to New York from St. Louis? True, there aren't enough letters in that wilted sack to pay for a direct service, but the mail will grow in volume as aircraft improve and people learn to use them. The more time we save, the more letters we'll get. If we flew direct, we could wait until the business day closed before collecting St. Louis mail, and still land at New York City before offices opened the next morning. Such a service would really be worth the cost of extra postage. We might even be able to fly from St. Louis to New York nonstop, eventually. Not with these salvaged Army DHs — they can't reach Chicago against a headwind without refueling — but with new planes and new engines — — —

The lights of a small city emerge behind my right wing — Streator. Ottawa is ahead and a few miles to the left. I make a mental note of my position, glance at the instruments, and let the plane bore its way on toward Chicago.

Those new Lairds the Northwest pilots are flying, for instance — they have only half the power of our DHs, but they're faster and they carry a bigger load. And there's that Wright-Bellanca. It has taken off with an incredible weight on some of its test flights. With three planes like the Bellanca we could easily carry the mail nonstop between St. Louis and New York, and on clear nights possibly two or three passengers besides.

But the cost — it would take ten or fifteen thousand dollars to buy just one Wright-Bellanca. Who could afford to invest so much money in a single airplane, to say nothing of the three that would be needed for a mail route? Our Corporation has a hard enough time to keep going with the DHs, and they cost only a few hundred dollars apiece.

I grow conscious of the limits of my biplane, of the inefficiency of its wings, struts, and wires. They bind me to earth and to the field ahead at Chicago. A Bellanca would cruise at least fifteen miles an hour faster, burn only half the amount of gasoline, and carry double the pay load of a DH. What a future aviation has when such planes can be built; yet how few people realize it! Businessmen think of aviation in terms of barnstorming, flying circuses, crashes, and high costs per flying hour. Somehow they must be made to understand the possibilities of flight. If they could see the real picture, it wouldn't be difficult to finance an airline between St. Louis and New York, even at the price of three Bellancas. Then commercial pilots wouldn't have to fly old army warplanes or make night landings with flares instead of flood-lights.

If only I had the Bellanca, I'd show St. Louis businessmen what modern aircraft could do; I'd take them to New York in eight or nine hours. They'd see how swiftly and safely passengers could fly. There are all kinds of records I could break for demonstration — distance, altitude with load, nonstop flights across the country. In a Bellanca filled with fuel tanks I could fly on all night, like the moon. How far *could* it go if it carried nothing but gasoline? With the engine throttled down it could stay aloft for days. It's fast, too. Judging from the accounts I've read, it's the most efficient plane ever built. It could break the world's endurance record, and the transcontinental, and set a dozen marks for range and speed and weight. Possibly — my mind is startled at its thought — I could fly nonstop between New York and Paris.

New York to Paris — it sounds like a dream. And yet — if one could carry fuel enough (and the Bellanca might) — if the engine didn't stop (and those new Wright Whirlwinds seldom do stop; they aren't like our old Liberties) — if one just held to the right course long enough, one should arrive in Europe. The flying couldn't be more dangerous or the weather worse than the night mail in winter. With fuel enough, a pilot would never have to land in fog; if he got caught, he could simply keep on going until he found clear weather. Navigation? — over the Atlantic and at night, boring through dark and unknown skies, toward a continent I've never seen? The very thought makes me rise to contend again with the moon — sweeping over oceans and continents, looking down on farms and cities, letting the planet turn below.

Why shouldn't I fly from New York to Paris? I'm almost twenty-five. I have more than four years of aviation behind me, and close to two thousand hours in the air. I've barnstormed over half of the forty-eight states. I've flown my mail through the worst of nights. I know the wind currents of the Rocky Mountains and the storms of the Mississippi Valley as few pilots know them. During my year at Brooks and Kelly as a flying cadet, I learned the basic elements of navigation. I'm a Captain in the 110th Observation Squadron of Missouri's National Guard. Why am I not qualified for such a flight?

Not so long ago, when I was a student in college, just flying an airplane seemed a dream. But that dream turned into reality. Then, as a two-hundred-hour pilot barnstorming through the country for a living, the wings of the Army Air Service seemed almost beyond reach. But I won them. Finally, to be a pilot of the night mail appeared the summit of ambition for a flyer; yet here I am, in the cockpit of a mail plane boring through the night. Why wouldn't a flight across the ocean prove as possible as all these things have been? As I attempted them, I can — — — I will attempt that too. I'll organize a flight to Paris!

I sit contemplating my decision. The magnitude of the undertaking overwhelms me for a time. This idea which has come upon me, this vision born of a night and altitude and moonlight, how am I to translate it into an actual airplane flying over the Atlantic Ocean to Europe and to France?

The important thing is to start; to lay a plan, and then follow it step by step no matter how small or large each one by itself may seem. I haven't enough money to buy a Wright-Bellanca. Could any other plane make the flight — the Fokker, or the new Travel Air? They might not cost as much. Maybe I could raise the money in St. Louis. I can put up some myself. Other people might be willing to take part when they realize all the things that could be done with a Bellanca. Then there's the Orteig prize of $25,000 for the first man to fly from New York to Paris nonstop — that's more than enough to pay for a plane and all the expenses of the flight. And the plane would still be almost as good as new after I landed in Europe. In fact, a successful trip to Paris wouldn't cost anything at all. It might even end up a profitable venture.

There must be men of means with enough vision to take the risk involved. The problem is to find them, and to get them to listen to my plan. Maybe the Wright Aeronautical Corporation itself would back the project. What could be a better advertisement for their plane and engine than a nonstop flight across the ocean? New York to Paris nonstop! If airplanes can do that, there's no limit to aviation's future.

The Chicago beacon flashes in the distance. In ten minutes I must land.

2

It's too late to think more about ocean flights tonight. I crawl into bed, angle cornerwise for room, and kick the blanket underneath my toes – – – But can a plane really carry enough gasoline to fly nonstop between New York and Paris? What made Captain Fonck's Sikorsky crash? Had he demanded too much of wings on air; was the frail structure simply overloaded; or did he make an error in piloting technique, as expert witnesses suggested?

From gallant start to tragic ending, all kinds of things went wrong. The tail skid slipped off the dolly, according to newspaper reports, while the big machine was being moved, before dawn, from its hangar to the runway's end. That damaged the center rudder, which had to be repaired. The press columns stated that not long afterward, in swinging the plane around, some auxiliary landing structure was bent and had to be straightened out again. After the take-off was started, about halfway down the runway, one of the auxiliary landing gears came loose and dragged up a cloud of dust. The plane swerved, straightened—engines still wide open. It reached the end of the runway without gaining speed enough to fly, and crashed—in flames. Fonck and his copilot, Lawrence Curtin, escaped from the wreckage almost uninjured, but Jacob Islamoff, the navigator-mechanic, and Charles Clavier, the radio operator, lost their lives.

"Fonck should have stopped the take-off." "It was too late to stop." "He should have lifted the tail up sooner." "The plane was too heavily overloaded." "Someone released the auxiliary landing gear too soon." Newspaper accounts are so conflicting that it's hard to judge the causes of the crash. All one can be sure of is that the flight ended in failure, quarreling, and death. In fact, quarreling blighted the project for weeks before its end. How many pilots were to be carried? Who was "in" at the beginning? Who had the right to go along? Accusations alternated with threats to withdraw, to remove financial support. A contract was argued back and forth. Members of the crew were quickly changed.

Think of the weight those wings were asked to lift—more than 28,000 pounds. But the big Sikorsky had taken off beautifully on its lighter load tests. There was good reason to believe it could carry enough fuel for the Paris flight. Probably the auxiliary landing gear dragging was what held it on the ground. I should think Fonck would have cut his switches the moment the gear broke loose. But who am I to judge his crisis-action while I lie snugly here in bed? Fonck had to decide in seconds what his critics have had days to talk about. And what pilot is immune to errors? We all commit them, as every honest man will say. Usually our errors don't end in a crash. But when a man is unlucky, does that make him more to blame?

There's another thing I don't understand about the Fonck project. A plane that's got to break the world's record for nonstop flying should be stripped of every excess ounce of weight. But descriptions of the great biplane said that its cabin had been luxuriously finished in red leather, and that it even contained a bed. There were long-wave and short-wave radio sets, and special bags for flotation in case of a landing at sea. Four men were in the crew. It certainly doesn't take four men to fly a plane across the ocean. The newspapers said that presents were being carried for friends in Europe, and a hot dinner to be eaten in celebration after the landing in Paris. One of the last things to be placed on board

before the attempted take-off was a gift of buns—French crois-
sants.

Well, if I can get a Bellanca, I'll fly alone. That will cut out the
need for any selection of crew, or quarreling. If there's upholstery
in the cabin, I'll tear it out for the flight. I'll take only the food I
need to eat, and a few concentrated rations. I'll carry a rubber
boat for emergency, and a little extra water.

Now I've got to stop thinking about it. I must get a few hours'
sleep.

3

The alarm clock's shattering ring seems to reach down through
a dozen layers of blankets. It's a drugged awakening. This is the
worst part of the air mail—getting up before daybreak. For a few
moments I almost believe that flying isn't worth such a terrific
effort to overcome bodily desire. If I reset the clock, maybe I
could sleep for ten minutes more. I reach out for it. But this
morning there's something of exceptional importance, something
that should make me jump quickly out of bed to start the day. It's
not like other mornings. Consciousness wakes first, then memory.
Oh, yes, this is the dawn of a new life, a life in which I'm going
to fly across the ocean to Europe!

While I'm dressing, on the drive to the mail field, and all during my southbound flight to St. Louis, I turn over one plan after
another in my mind. Where can I get a modern airplane? How can
I get accurate figures on cruising speed, take-off run, and fuel
consumption? Who can give me information about the Wright-
Bellanca—how soon can one be bought, how much will it cost,
how many gallons of gasoline can it lift?

I probably won't be very successful if I simply go to the Wright
Corporation and say that I want to use a Bellanca airplane for a
flight to Paris. They'd ask immediately what references I could
furnish. Without either cash in hand or well-established references
to show, they'd have little interest in my ideas. Aviation is full of
promoters and people looking for a job. Ideas are free for the
taking, and almost every pilot has some plan he'd like to carry

out — if someone else will furnish the money. An aviation executive has to look at banking references. If he doesn't, his company will soon go broke. Even if I could persuade the Wright Corporation that the value of a New York-to-Paris flight would justify taking the chance involved, they'd probably want to have their Bellanca flown by a better-known pilot. After all, there are lots of pilots much more experienced than I.

No, I'll have to present the Wright Corporation something more substantial than an idea. I'll have to get other people to go into the project with me — men with both influence and money. Then I'll be in a different position when I negotiate for a plane. I can say that I represent a St. Louis organization which intends to purchase an airplane for the New York-to-Paris flight, and that we are considering, among others, the Bellanca. That ought to impress the Wright Corporation. That would just reverse our positions: then they'd be trying to sell their product to me instead of my trying to sell an idea to them. If I have proper backing, maybe I can get a reduction in price. Possibly the Wright Corporation would go into partnership with us. And if they won't, I can try other manufacturers — Fokker, and Huff-Daland, for instance.

Above everything else looms the question of finance. I have a few thousand dollars, invested for me by my mother in Detroit. This includes childhood savings, small amounts sent home from my pay as a flying cadet, and profits from my years of barnstorming. It's a reserve I've built up slowly and carefully to safeguard my flying career — to cover a crashed plane, or a bad season. I've depended on that reserve to let me stay in aviation. If I spend it on an unsuccessful venture – – – Well, a financial reserve isn't quite as important as it used to be. Now that I'm an experienced pilot, I can always get some kind of a job flying. I can afford to take some risk with that money. But all my money put together would pay for only a fraction of a Bellanca. How does one organize a major flying project? How did Commander Byrd get money for his polar expedition? Who finances De Pinedo on his flights?

For the St. Louisians who might be interested in taking part, I have two major arguments. First, I'll show them how a nonstop

flight between America and Europe will demonstrate the possibilities of aircraft, and help place St. Louis in the foreground of
aviation. Second, I'll show them that a modern airplane is capable
of making the flight to Paris, and that a successful flight will cover
its own costs because of the Orteig prize. Then, of course, as additional talking points, there are all the records one could break
and the places one could fly with a plane like the Wright-Bellanca.
But where shall I start? To whom shall I go with my project? I
have friends in the city, but most of them are aviators too, and
men in aviation seldom have much money.

As I cruise back over the route to St. Louis, practical thinking
alternates with a feeling of awe toward a project of such magnitude — a flight over the whole Atlantic Ocean — a flight through
air, between the very hemispheres of earth! How can I do, why
should I dare, what others, more experienced and influential, have
either failed to do or not attempted? Difficulties seem insurmountable. Wasn't my classmate, Lieutenant Gathercoal, lost on a flight
across Lake Michigan last year? That's a minute body of water
compared to the Atlantic Ocean. According to the last news I had,
they never found a trace of him. But of course he was flying an
OXX-6 engine. For reliability, you can't compare an OXX-6 with
a Whirlwind.

4

Lambert Field lies in farming country about ten miles northwest of the St. Louis business district. A pilot, flying high above its
sodded acres, sees the Missouri River in the distance, bending
north and then east to spew its muddy waters into the clearer
Mississippi. The city nestles vaguely in its pall of smoke, a different textured patch contrasting with fields and forests. Southward,
wooded foothills step up toward the distant Ozark Mountains.

Lambert Field is named after Major Albert Bond Lambert,
who commanded a school for balloon pilots during the World
War, and who is among the most active leaders in Midwestern
aviation. Selected for the site of the National Air Races in 1923,
it was enlarged to present size by planking over a little stream

which cut through the eastern end. There are no runways, but the clay sod is good surface for any size of aircraft during summer months. In freezing weather, gusty winds and deepening ruts make operation difficult.

Lambert Field's major commercial activity is carried on by the Robertson Aircraft Corporation, built and managed by the Robertson brothers, Bill, Frank, and Dan. A little, stove-heated office, two frame warehouses for airplane and engine parts, and half of a civilian hangar, house its operations. The Corporation's major income results from the sale of reconditioned Army training planes, engines, and spares — all placed on the market at extraordinarily low prices.

Except on week ends, when the National Guard Squadron comes out in force, there are seldom more than a half-dozen pilots on the field, and the chief activity consists of training students. One can always make a few extra dollars and build up flying time by instructing. Besides there is no better way to learn the tricks of air and aircraft.

Those of us who instruct know Lambert Field as a child knows the details of his home and yard. We know the erosions on its shallow slope, the downdraft over Anglum, the depressions where drain tiles have caved in. In every azimuth there's a reminder of some past incident of flight. One pushes his plane out of a hangar that housed the Curtiss Navy racer. (It left its source of sound somewhere in the air behind as it flashed around the pylons.) At this spot, just beyond the line, George Harmon was killed when his pilot stalled on a left chandelle. (I helped cut him out of the wreckage — unconscious but still alive. He died on the road to the hospital.) Against an east wind, one takes off over the cornfield where Captain Bill spun in after his National Guard Jenny's engine failed. (By some miracle he wasn't hurt, and climbed out of the crash before we reached him.) There's where Smith and Swengrosh died when they lost a wing in a loop. There's where Frank Robertson and Pres Sultan clipped the top from a big cottonwood tree, without even cracking a spar. (The trunk was eight inches in diameter where their Jenny snapped it off.) On the side of that ditch is where Bud Gurney broke his arm in a parachute spot-landing contest. The pigpen by the white farmhouse is where O. E. Scott once nosed over.

How Scotty loves to tell that story! His engine cut on take-off. He wasn't high enough to turn. Straight ahead lay the pigpen, and in it he landed. Muck caught his wheels and whipped him upside down. He found himself hanging on the safety belt, his head two or three feet above a stinking wallow, "with all those pigs squealing and nudging in around me, just as though I was one of 'em!"

Scotty is manager of the field, and its oldest and most cautious pilot. He owns an OX-5 Standard with wings that haven't been re-covered for so many years that you can poke your finger through their varnish-stiffened fabric. When weather is good his plane is always on the line, ready to carry any passenger who'll pay five dollars for a ride. Scotty is also pilot of the new Travel Air which was bought last year by Harold Bixby, a St. Louis banker who became interested in aviation. With an OXX-6 engine, deep blue fuselage, and shining, nickel-plated struts, it's the most modern and attractive plane in our hangars.

Scotty has let me fly the Travel Air several times, and introduced me to its owner. To us on the field it's more than a symbol of better aircraft to come. It's a link with the powerful business world. Bixby is one of the men who run the great city of St. Louis, yet he looks on flyers as something more than acrobats and dare-devils. Judging from a more stable viewpoint, he too believes that aviation has a future. His Travel Air, resting on the line, is like a signpost assuring us that the road we follow leads toward fertile lands.

Since Bixby bought his plane several of the city's businessmen have started flying. There's Harry Knight the broker, who's taking lessons. And Earl Thompson the insurance executive, with his golden-winged Laird. I've given him a little instruction now and then. Thompson is the kind of man who'll listen to my ideas. I've often talked to him about aviation, and he knows that I can fly. I'll telephone tomorrow for an appointment. Meanwhile, I'll get a pad of paper and outline a plan of action.

ST LOUIS — NEW YORK — PARIS FLIGHT

Action

1. Plan
2. Propaganda
3. Backers
4. Equipment
5. Co-operation of manufacturers
6. Accessory information
7. Point of departure
8. Advertising

Advantages

1. Revive St. Louis interest in aviation
2. Advertise St. Louis as an aviation city
3. Aid in making America first in the air
4. Promote nation-wide interest in aeronautics
5. Demonstrate perfection of modern equipment

Results

1. Successful completion, winning $25,000 prize to cover expense
2. Complete failure

Co-operation

1. Plane manufacturers
2. Motor manufacturers
3. Weather Department
4. State Department
5. Newspapers
6. Steamships

Equipment

1. Raft (sail)
2. Rockets
3. Clothing (waterproof)
4. Condensed food
5. Still (water)

Maps

1. Prevailing winds
2. Coast and interior
3. Islands
4. Steamship travel

Landmarks

1. Islands
2. List of coast towns
3. Index to towns
4. Characteristic names
5. Characteristic terrain

That list will do for a start. I'll add to it, improve it, and clarify it as time passes.

I've begun work on my propaganda, too. That shouldn't be difficult, because fact and adventure are both on my side. I feel sure there's a tremendous future for the commerce of the air. I reread the first paragraph I've drafted.

St. Louis is ideally situated to become an aviation city. – – – We have one of the finest commercial airports in the United States, and we will undoubtedly become a hub of the national airways of the future. Some day airliners on their way from New Orleans to Chicago, and from Los Angeles to New York, will be landing on our airport. – – –

That should interest people, especially the businessmen. And I've started working on the schedule and cost of an air-mail line to New York by way of Indianapolis, Columbus, and Pittsburgh. Even with DHs we'd be able to make the eastward trip within twelve hours, including time for stops. With a Bellanca – – – well, that's what this propaganda's for. I must show what can be accomplished with aircraft like the Bellanca.

5

I push the bell button at No. 1 Hortense Place, and step back on the porch to wait. Earl Thompson said he could see me at once at his office or spend an evening with me at his house the next week. I chose the latter. It seemed less likely that one could sell a flight across the ocean at an office desk. Besides, time builds dignity and thought.

A maid shows me to the living room. Mr. Thompson comes in. We shake hands. He motions me to a chair. I feel uncomfortable in the soft upholstery. I don't seem to fit into a city parlor. It would be easier to talk on the flying field. There, the sound of engines and the contours of wings would surround my arguments with factual elements of flight. When one sees a plane suspended in the sky, it's more difficult to use such words as "impractical" or "can't be done." Now I've got to sit inside a carpeted and curtained room and believe as well as convince another, that an airplane can take me, without landing, between New York and Paris.

"Mr. Thompson," I start out, "I've come to ask your advice about a project I'm considering."

He smiles and nods encouragement.

"You've heard about the Orteig prize of $25,000 for a nonstop flight between New York and Paris," I continue. "I think a modern plane can make that flight. I'd like to try it. It would show people what airplanes can do. It would advance aviation, and it would advertise St. Louis."

I go on to explain that I want to get a group of businessmen behind me to finance the project and give me the prestige I'll need in dealing with aircraft manufacturers.

"I can furnish $2000 myself," I say. "But the right kind of plane will probably cost at least ten thousand."

Mr. Thompson's face becomes serious. "What kind of plane would you get for that flight, Captain?" he asks.

"I think the Wright-Bellanca could probably make it," I tell him.

"But the Wright-Bellanca is a land plane — and it has only one engine, hasn't it?" His voice is as disturbed as his question. "You aren't thinking of flying over the ocean in a single-engined airplane, are you? I think it's a very interesting idea, but I'd want you to have a flying boat, or a plane with enough engines so you wouldn't have to land in the water if one of them stopped. Have you considered using a three-engined Fokker, like Commander Byrd's?"

I was afraid of that. Businessmen are always conservative. But at least he's taking my idea seriously.

"Well," I argue, "a flying boat can't take off with enough fuel, and a trimotored Fokker would cost a huge amount of money. I don't know what they sell for; but I'm afraid it would be at least $30,000 and it might be considerably more. Besides, I'm not sure three engines would really add much to safety on a flight like that. You see the plane would be overloaded with fuel anyway. There'd be three times the chance of engine failure; and if one of them stopped over the ocean, you probably couldn't get back to land with the other two. A multiengined plane is awfully big and heavy. [This is my trump card.] You know Fonck had three engines, but that didn't help him any when his landing gear gave way. A single-engined plane might even be safer, everything considered."

"Well, you know a lot more about airplanes than I do," Mr. Thompson says. "But I don't like the idea of a single engine out over the ocean. If you really want to make that flight, I think you ought to consider getting a trimotored plane, like a Fokker."

We spend the entire evening talking about aircraft and the New York-to-Paris flight. Mr. Thompson is definitely interested. He's encouraging, but cautious and greatly concerned about the risks involved. After all, his business is insurance. He has to be conservative.

6

"There's a Fokker man here. He's up with Major Robertson, talking about a St. Louis agency."

I'm eating late breakfast at Louie De Hatre's lunch stand, after bringing in the Chicago mail. At the counter one learns immediately about everything new that has happened on the field—new arrivals, new accidents, new business. The possibility of a Fokker agency is real news. Just think of having one of those big tri-motored monoplanes on the line. They have seats for ten passengers, besides the crew. Who would be chosen for the pilot? What kind of flying would it do? There are rumors that a St. Louis company is ready to place an order.

For me, this news has special meaning. Here's a chance to get some accurate information about performances and costs. I've got to be careful, though. I haven't yet mentioned my plans to anyone on the field. I watch the white door to Major Robertson's little office until he emerges with the stranger — a fair complexioned, stocky man in city clothes. They stroll down to the lunch stand, talking; and here we are introduced. Pilots, mechanics, and students gather, sit on benches, lean against walls, listening to stories of Tony Fokker's genius, the safety of multiengines, the efficiency of thick airfoils. The Fokker salesman's "line" is good.

A phone call comes for Major Robertson. The Fokker man and I walk over toward the hangar.

"When you have time, I'd like to talk to you for a few minutes about a project we're considering here in St. Louis," I tell him.

"How about right now?"

His attitude makes it clear that he's not losing any opportunity to size up the aviation situation at Lambert Field. Business radiates from posture, tone, and dress.

"I'm going to ask you to hold what I talk about in confidence until we get further along with our plans," I start out.

"Certainly." He nods assent.

"A group of men here in St. Louis are thinking of buying a plane for the New York-to-Paris flight," I say. "We've been considering a Fokker. We'd like to have any information you can give us."

"What kind of information do you want?"

He's looking at me intently now. I mustn't show the slightest uncertainty.

"Well, we'd like to know whether you can build a plane that

can carry enough fuel to make that flight. We'd like to know how much it would cost, and how soon it could be delivered."

"I can answer all of those questions," the salesman tells me, in a tone which implies courtesy without enthusiasm. "The Fokker Company happens to have made a study of a flight from New York to Paris. Mr. Fokker can design a plane with enough range to reach Paris with a good reserve of fuel. The company can deliver it by next spring, if the order is placed now. It would cost about $90,000."

I try to keep my face as expressionless as his, but my mind whirls. *Ninety thousand dollars!* That's hopeless. I can never raise such an amount. I haven't even thought in such figures.

"Of course," he goes on, fastening his eyes on mine again, "the Fokker Company would have to be satisfied with the competency of operating personnel before they would be willing to sell a plane for such a flight."

I pass over the last statement, as though it didn't apply to me.

"That's much more than we planned on," I say. "I didn't know Fokkers cost that much. The figure I heard quoted was – – –"

The salesman doesn't wait for me to finish, "Oh, our standard trimotors are much less. A plane for long range would have to be specially built, you see. It would need a larger wing, and extra tanks in the fuselage. The landing gear would have to be beefed up. It would be a different airplane entirely." He speaks with even voice and measured words. He knows he has something to sell, and he's not going to strike an easy bargain. "The Fokker Company's reputation would be at stake," he adds. "You should plan on *over* $100,000 for such a project. In fact, you should have almost unlimited financial backing."

I pause for a moment. He's probably sounding me out, trying to bracket the figures he can work with. Maybe if I do a little sparring – – –

"We've also considered using a single-engined plane," I tell him. "How much would it cost to build a single-engined Fokker with enough range for – – –"

The salesman breaks in again. "Our Company would not be

interested in selling a single-engined plane for a flight across the ocean," he says definitely.

I feel embarrassed, as though I were an adolescent boy broaching an ill-considered venture to a tolerant but disapproving parent. But I think he's wrong about multiengines in this case. Anyway, I'm not going to give up yet.

"We thought a single-engined plane might be just as safe as one with three engines when it's heavily overloaded. [What am I talking about — "we"? I'm the only one who believes that.] If one engine stopped on a Fokker, how far could you go on the other two?"

"There would be dump valves on the fuel tanks, of course," he answers. "If an engine stopped, you would simply dump enough fuel to keep flying on the other two. That's why Mr. Fokker believes in three engines."

"But if an engine failed on take-off, or several hundred miles out over the ocean, could – – – "

"Mr. Fokker wouldn't consider selling a single-engined plane for a flight over the Atlantic Ocean."

The salesman's voice is sharpening. He's still courteous; but I can see that he has formed his estimate, and rejected me as an important prospect. I slip away as soon as I can, and walk out through the little town of Anglum, along the narrow dirt road, to farm lands beyond. I need time, alone, to think.

I don't want a trimotored plane. Besides costing more, a big plane isn't as efficient, and it would need a crew. I'd rather go alone. I inquired about it more at Thompson's insistence than because of my own interest. But the blunt statement that the Fokker Company won't sell a single-engined plane for my project wasn't what I expected from their sales representative. I've never known a salesman before this to question what a plane was going to be used for, if you had enough money to buy it. If you cracked up and killed yourself, that was your responsibility. It didn't mean there was anything wrong with the plane.

Well, the two men I've talked to about a New York-to-Paris flight are both prejudiced. One of them looks on the risk from the standpoint of an insurance executive. The other wants to sell and promote multiengined airplanes. But Earl Thompson is interested in the flight — that's the important thing; and there are other companies besides Fokker.

Flying to Chicago on the mail route in the evening, I decide to build up my backing in St. Louis, and then try to purchase the Wright-Bellanca. The Wright Corporation will certainly have confidence in its own engine; and since they don't make a multiengined plane, they should be in sympathy with my arguments against one.

Next week I have an appointment to talk to Major Lambert.

7

Major Lambert sits at his desk, alert, serious, looking at me through thick eyeglasses. His gray hair is thinning where he parts it in the center. He's immaculately dressed.

"That's quite a flight, Slim. Do you really think it can be done?" he asks.

"Yes sir, I believe it can; but I'm going to be sure of my facts before I go much farther in laying plans. That's where I need help. I want to tell the manufacturers that responsible people are behind me. If they know my backing is sound, they'll give me all the information I want about costs and performances. Otherwise, they may think it's not worth while spending the time. I want to be in a good position to trade on prices, too. If I can say you're one of the men who's interested in this project, it will be a tremendous help --- I won't make any commitments without getting your approval."

I lay my cards, face up, on the table, and explain the difficulties I'm confronted with.

Major Lambert, good old-timer that he is, doesn't raise any question about flying boats or multiengines. He has lived through too many years of aviation to be fooled by popular ideas of safety. He knows there's danger involved in all flying.

"If you think it's a practical venture, and if you can get the right fellows together, I'll take part, Slim," he says. "You can count on me for $1,000.

A thousand dollars! That's the first real money I've gotten. I'll put in $2,000 of my own; that's a total of $3,000. And Mr. Thompson is with me, even though he hasn't promised any definite amount. I hadn't planned on asking for money yet. Major Lambert just volunteered that thousand dollars. How like him — no halfway measures. He's either with you or he isn't, and it doesn't take him long to decide.

Whom shall I go to next? Driving back to the field in my halfowned, secondhand Ford coupé, I feel that my New York-to-Paris flight is emerging from the stage of dreams: I have an organization under way. Now it's time to talk to Bill Robertson. I haven't said anything to him yet about my plans. I want to bring him something more tangible than an idea. He has enough on his hands keeping the mail route going without trying to finance a New York-to-Paris flight. A lot of people think he'll go broke flying the mail. They'll call him a wild man if he talks about flying the ocean too.

8

"Wheeuuu-u-u-u---." Major Bill Robertson whistles as he turns toward me on his swivel chair. "That's *some* flight, Slim. Do you really think it can be done? How many miles *is* it from New York to Paris?"

"It's about thirty-five hundred," I answer. "I know it's a long way, but I think the Bellanca can do it, and I'm going to find out."

"It doesn't seem possible to put that much gasoline in an airplane. Say, a plane like that could sure carry a lot of mail, couldn't it? How much does a Bellanca cost?"

"I don't know, Bill; but my guess is about ten thousand dollars."

"Wheeuuu-u-u-u; that's a *lot* of money. Where are you going to raise it, Slim?"

"That's what I'm working on now," I tell him. "Major Lambert says he'll put in a thousand dollars. Earl Thompson is interested, and I can put in two thousand myself. I haven't asked anybody else."

"Say, you're lucky to get Major Lambert interested. That'll help a lot. Did he really say he'd put up a thousand dollars?"

"He said he would if I could get enough of the right kind of men together."

Bill hesitates, and then goes on.

"We'll help as much as we can, Slim, but you know we aren't in a position to put up much money. We're losing dollars every day right now. I've got to go down to the bank and try to raise some more."

"I know, Bill. I didn't come to you for money. You can help in two other ways. I want to be able to say that the Robertson Aircraft Corporation is in the group that's behind me; and I need your permission to arrange the mail schedule so I can get away for two or three days at a time when it's necessary."

"You can say we're behind you if that will help any," he says. "But I don't know about the schedule. You know the Post Office won't take excuses. The mail's just got to go through. Can Phil and Nellie handle it alone? Suppose one of them goes down. We wouldn't have a reserve pilot. You three are the only ones who know the route."

"I think we can keep the route running all right, Bill. The biggest danger is weather. But you can telegraph me if a plane goes down and I'll take the first train back. If I have to be away too much, we'll train another pilot."

"Well, be awfully careful, Slim. We mustn't get into trouble with the Post Office. Be sure and fix it up with Phil and Nellie. And keep me posted where you are. Say, that flight ought to be worth a lot for advertising. Have you thought about getting some company to back it? Say, why don't you talk to the *Post-Dispatch*? They might be willing to put up enough money to cover the whole thing. You could paint the paper's name on the fuselage. Say, it would be great advertising for them. I know one of the editors. Why don't we go down and talk to him?"

Bill is bubbling over with enthusiasm. You can see how he managed to finance the mail route. Once he gets behind an idea, he makes you believe anything is possible.

I'm not too happy about the *Post-Dispatch* suggestion. There's something wrong about flying a billboard to Paris; it's too much like blocking out a mountain vista with an advertisement for beer. Still, if I want to make the flight, I've got to look into all possibilities. One must establish alternatives before he can choose. And Bill's had a lot of experience raising money. He knows that if you set your sights too high the bullets fall short.

"You make the appointment," I tell him.

"Fine, Slim, fine. I'll try to make it this week. Say, that's *some* flight, isn't it?"

I start out the door, and pause.

"How's the boy, Bill?" I ask.

It's a standing joke with the mail pilots. We tell each other that the Major's arms lengthen two inches every time he talks about his baby. Major Bill leans back in his chair, laughs, and stretches his arms out as far as they'll go.

9

I stand in the doorway of the Anglum post office, reading an Associated Press dispatch.

BYRD TO FLY ATLANTIC

POLE CONQUEROR PREDICTS OCEAN CROSSING NEXT YEAR

BRIDGEPORT, CONN., Oct. 28 (AP).— Conquering the Atlantic Ocean by air from New York to London or Paris in a heavier-than-air machine would be accomplished next summer, Lieut. Commander Richard E. Byrd declared here tonight, intimating that he himself would attempt the journey.

The American naval officer, who commanded the first successful expedition to fly to the North Pole, said that he could make no announcement of the exact plans for an expedition which he admitted were being formulated at present.

That's formidable competition. Commander Byrd is a keen and able officer. It's not long ago that I met him here in St. Louis, and heard him speak. He's experienced in organization; and he knows how to get financed. Maybe he can put a bigger wing on his North-Pole Fokker, and carry enough fuel to fly from New York to Paris.

And what about those French pilots who say they are going to win the Orteig prize by flying from east to west? For weeks there have been newspaper rumors to the effect that they were ready to take off. And the other American projects — I've read reports about two or three of them. A lot of people want to be first to make the nonstop New York-Paris flight. It looks as though my idea will end as it began — a dream.

10

"The *Post-Dispatch* wouldn't think of taking part in such a hazardous flight. To fly across the Atlantic Ocean with one pilot and a single-engine plane! We have our reputation to consider. We couldn't possibly be associated with such a venture!"

Major Robertson and I sit uncomfortably in front of the editor's desk. He hasn't even asked us any questions. The *Post-Dispatch* is not impressed either with the advertising value of a flight to Paris or with my plan for making it. There's nothing else to say. We get up, shake hands, and leave.

"I'm surprised, Slim. I didn't think they'd feel that way about it. I think they're losing a good bet." Bill's face is as long as though the mail were unreported. "Well, we'll have to try somebody else," he continues. "I just *know* there are people who'll get behind that flight. We've got to find them, that's all. Say, I wonder if – – – " His face brightens. He's off on a new idea. You have to admire Bill Robertson. He doesn't stay down for long. No matter how hard he's hit, he bobs back up like a cork in water.

"I'm going to talk to the Wright people before we proposition anybody else," I interject. "I want to know just what the Bellanca can do, and how often Whirlwind engines fail. If I'd had accurate data, I could have put a better argument up to that editor. It's time for me to make a trip east."

11

A student is waiting for me when I get back to the hangars —
a Catholic Father, who has become a personal friend. He arrived
at Lambert Field one day last summer and announced that he
wanted to take flying lessons. It was a great surprise to all of us
pilots, for he's close to sixty years of age, and we look with doubt
on any prospective student over thirty.

I had taken Father Hussman up in an OX-5 Standard and
turned the stick over to him, simply because instructing was my
job. His handling of the controls was just as bad as I'd expected.
But how he loved to fly! I learned that he didn't care much
whether he soloed or not. He wanted to climb up above the earth
and look down on its farms and villages, over its horizons, to see
the great winding lengths of its rivers, and handle the controls of
the plane he was in — wallow, slip, or skid as it might. He couldn't
afford to fly often; but every week or two he came out to the field
for another hour in the Standard. And he wasn't a fair-weather
flyer. If it was windy or raining, he'd still go up with you if you'd
take him, as though he wished to know God's earth and air in all
their phases.

It's cold, overcast, and blustery this afternoon. We have a
hard time getting the OX-5 started, even with five gallons of hot
water in the radiator. Ground is soft after the morning's thaw.
Water oozes slowly into tire tracks. It's not a day for student landings and take-offs. I suggest that we do an hour's air work, and the
Father happily agrees. The wind's northwest, blowing kitty-corner
downfield from the hangars. I take off with it on our tail to keep
from rutting the sod any more than necessary. Besides, the engine's
not revving up too well, and I don't like the downdrafts on the
higher, western border. With an OX-5, one doesn't clear the electric wires by many feet even in the best of weather.

The Father has his hand on the stick, and his feet on the
rudder. He's studying my movement of controls; but he's touching
them so lightly I can barely feel the pressure he exerts. No need to

worry about him "freezing." We clear the ditch by a man's height, and start climbing the cornfield slope beyond. I lift both hands above my head as a signal to the Father to take complete command. It's time for him to learn what rough air is like. He fights stick and rudder while wings rise and drop. I motion a left turn into wind, twist against my belt, look back, and laugh. It usually helps a student if you laugh when flying is hard. The Father smiles back. He's all right. He doesn't need any assurance. He's perfectly content to be bouncing around, and now he's not doing such a bad job. I put my right hand to my cheek to signal that he's skidding slightly, and then let him alone to fly in whatever way he will. He doesn't want to be trained in precision like an ordinary student. I pull on my goggles, button my jacket around my throat, and sink down into my cockpit. The next hour is his. – – –

How *am* I going to contact the Wright Corporation? No friend of mine knows anyone in the organization, even indirectly. It won't make a very good impression if I just arrive at the reception desk and say I want to talk to one of the officers. There are probably dozens of people asking for interviews each day — salesmen, job hunters, and promoters. "What is your business?" the girl at the desk would ask. And how she'd look at me if I told her that I wanted to fly the Wright-Bellanca from New York to Paris! She'd class me as another "aviation bug," and sit me down with half a dozen others in the waiting room. I'd receive scant courtesy — if I got an interview at all.

I've got to remember that New York isn't St. Louis. Here in St. Louis I'm well known in aviation circles. I can get a good reference from anyone connected with Lambert Field. But I'm unheard of in New York and at Paterson, New Jersey, where the Wright Aeronautical Corporation has its plant.

(I motion the nose down. We're still quite a way from stalling, but if the Father ever does solo, he's got to be more careful.)

I can write a letter to the Wright Corporation in dignified business language, mentioning our St. Louis group, our interest in the Paris flight, and our wish to discuss purchasing the Bellanca. I can say, casually, that I plan to be in New York in the near future, and that I will phone for an appointment. That's a better procedure. It would probably get me by the girl at the desk.

But the Corporation might be cautious and write back for more definite information, for banking references, and for the names of my partners in the enterprise. That would be the worst thing that could happen. I could only say that three responsible men in St. Louis are interested in my plan for a flight to Paris, and have more or less committed themselves to take some part provided I can get together a large enough group to finance the project adequately. Such a statement wouldn't make a very good impression.

I might not get any reply to my letter. That happened once, when I applied for a pilot's job. I spent hours framing and reframing my paragraphs. But weeks passed and an answer never came. Big companies receive hundreds of letters a day. I've got to get the Wright Corporation really interested in my project before I arrive; and it's going to take more than a letter to do that.

(The stick is shaking. I look back at the Father. He slants his hand downward behind the windshield, and raises his eyebrows. He wants to dive. Oh yes, we're above the Catholic school. He has friends down there. I nod. He'll enjoy it, and his dive won't be much more than a steep glide. He won't clip any branches with our wings. We bank, skid a little, and nose down. I signal to ease the throttle back. Black-gowned figures run outdoors, spread over the lawn and gravel driveway, look up, and wave. We're fully two hundred feet high when we level off and start to climb again. Now the Father heads west, toward the Missouri.)

I might telegraph the Wright Corporation. A telegram carries an impression of importance and urgency. But I'd like to do something more out of the ordinary. Why not *telephone* the Wright Corporation all the way from St. Louis? It would probably cost at least five dollars, but a long-distance call would carry a prestige which no letter or telegram, signed by an unknown pilot, could possibly have. Besides, like whistling in the dark, it would add to my own confidence. There's so much unreality about this dream of a nonstop flight to Paris that a little whistling may help. I'll tell them that I'm coming to Paterson to discuss buying the Bellanca for the New York-to-Paris flight. A long-distance phone call and a two-thousand-mile train trip ought to impress them enough for a starter.

(Now, we must head back toward the field. The Father's hour is almost up, and it's my turn to fly the mail tonight.)

12

It looks as though I'll have to entrain the mail. Yes, trees ahead disappear in fog and twilight. I open the throttle and bank sharply right, away from the Illinois River. Peoria is only a ten-minute flight away, but there's not a chance to get there. I take up a compass course back toward Springfield. The ceiling south is lowering too, with the night, and it's getting hazy. I let the pro-peller turn a hundred revolutions fast — better to save every minute of twilight. If I miss the cow pasture at Springfield, a forced landing under a parachute flare will be hazardous in reflecting haze and on frost-softened ground. Oblong lights appear, here and there, beneath me as farmhouse doors fling open at the roar of my engine. I pull up to 500 feet. The radius of lights contracts. The ground fades. I nose down to 400 feet. A wisp of cloud burrows in below me. I drop down to a hundred feet above the treetops.

In the distance, on my left, the cloud layer glows dimly. That's Springfield. One of these roads I'm angling across leads to the mail pasture. It's too dark to tell exactly where I am. I press the button on my stick which turns on the compass light — about 185 degrees. That's approximately the right heading. The card is swing-ing too much to read accurately. I release the button and look down. The compass light, too faint to be seen by day, has blinded my eyes to dimmer details of the night.

A bright light appears between my right wings. I bank toward it. Yes, it's the "beacon" that boy put up and wrote to us about.

"Your mail planes fly over my house every day," he'd said in his letter, "so I have fixed up an electric light in our yard. Maybe it will help you when the weather is bad this winter. I will keep it lit every night."

We'd circled overhead once or twice to thank him. Now, his hundred-watt beacon is of real value. I shift course five degrees and watch for the straight row of lanterns that will mark our mail field. We have no electric lights there. There's no power line nearby. But we've arranged with the mail-truck driver to hang a half dozen lanterns on fence posts along the southern border.

Four lanterns are still burning when I find the pasture. Fortunately the wind's north — or at least it was at dusk. I leave the lanterns a quarter mile to my left, let them angle back sixty degrees toward my tail, bank around steeply, and pull back to half throttle – – – hold a hundred feet – – – quarter throttle – – – stick back a little – – – down to fifty feet – – – up slightly on power – – – stay right of the telephone poles along the western edge – – – keep left of the gulley that cuts through from the east. South and north there's nothing but the fence lines. Night's black brush has swept over posts and poles, trees and earth, leaving no contrast between them to help a pilot's eye — only four dim points of light, a yard above the ground, and several farmhouse windows for horizon.

Too high — close throttle — left rudder — right stick — slip — straighten – – – remember, the size of Springfield's pasture is less than forty acres – – – A burst of engine – – – ten feet above a lantern – – – blackness – – – keep the tail up – – – ready with the throttle – – – Bump — let her bounce once — stick forward — back – – – a little power – – – good — almost three-point that time – – – let her roll – – – how near is the fence? – – – a slow ground loop – – – taxi back toward the lanterns.

There's nobody on the field, of course, and not a car on the dirt road alongside. I pull up close to the fence corner, swing into wind, cut switches, turn off the fuel valve, unsnap the belt, and climb out of my cockpit. The ground is starting to freeze — a sharp ridge dents the sole of my sheepskin moccasin. We've had a telephone installed on one of the poles — a party line. I wait until the receiver is clear of voices, and put in a call for the post office.

"This is the flying field — Pilot Lindbergh. I've got to entrain the mail. Peoria's closed in."

"We'll send a truck out. Is there anything else you need?"

"That's all, thanks, but could you notify St. Louis?"

"We'll get a wire right off."

The Springfield post office knows its business.

I walk out along the fence line, gather up the lanterns, and station them around my plane. From the looks of the weather, it's not likely that I can take off before sunrise. If I drain the engine and tie my DH to the fence, I can ride to town on the mail truck and get a night's sleep. But then it would take two men, at least, to start up tomorrow morning, even if I pour boiling water into the radiator. Once a Liberty cools off, it's a devil's job to get it running again. And you can't ask help from just anybody who comes along — it takes training to handle either throttle or propeller. I'd probably have to phone for a mechanic to be flown up from Lambert Field. No, I'll stay with the plane, and start the engine every twenty minutes. That will keep it warm. And the ceiling might lift after midnight; then I could get through to Chicago in time to take the southbound mail. But in that case, I'll need more gasoline. There's plenty to keep the engine warm through the night, but not enough, after that, to fly to Chicago. We haven't got extra fuel cached at Springfield. I walk back to the pole box and phone the oil company.

"This is the air-mail pilot at the flying field. I'm down in weather and low on fuel. Can you send a truck out about an hour before daybreak?"

"Sure. How much'll you need?"

"My plane will take about eighty gallons of gasoline, and the driver better bring a five-gallon can of oil."

"You don't want the truck out now?"

"No, I'll probably have to idle the engine all night, and I want to fill the tank just before I take off. If the weather starts to clear, I'll call again."

"Okay. We'll be there about four o'clock."

It feels good to move around after spending so much of the

day in office, car, and cockpit. The air is sharp; my flying suit, comfortably warm. I walk out into the pasture's darkness. Why shouldn't I telephone the Wright Corporation tomorrow, from Chicago? I could make an appointment, fly the mail to Lambert Field the next morning, and take the afternoon train east. Or why not take the train right on through from Chicago? It's closer than St. Louis — there'd be both time and money saved. No, I'll have to go back to St. Louis for my clothes. It wouldn't be good technique to present myself at the Wright Corporation's offices in boots, breeches, and a three-day-old shirt. But what do I have to wear after I get back to St. Louis? A captain's uniform is the only good suit I own, and one just doesn't wear an officer's uniform on personal business. My blue serge business suit goes back to college days; besides it's shiny and worn, and never did fit very well. It's good enough for visiting friends in St. Louis, but I want something better than that for a conference with the Wright people. I'll need a felt hat and an overcoat, and I haven't either one. All the successful businessmen I know wear felt hats and overcoats — they give an impression of dignity and influence.

Car lights skim along the road and stop opposite my plane.

"Hello there!"

"Hello!" I shout.

"Need any help?" Figures appear in the lantern light.

"No, thanks very much." I hurry back over the fifty yards I've covered.

"Want a ride to town?"

"No, I've got to stay with the plane."

"Engine trouble?"

"Weather."

"Hell, you're not going to stay here all night are you? The weather won't get any better."

"You're the air-mail pilot, aren't ya?" another man breaks in. "You fellers can have your job. I wouldn't fly one of them things for a million dollars."

"I feel just like my dad. He says he just a' soon fly in one of 'em as long as he can keep one foot on the ground. Haw-haw-haw!"

That joke comes out wherever an airplane lands, and the teller always expects you to laugh with him.

"Man, I wouldn't think of going up in one of 'em. I get dizzy looking down from my barn roof. How does it feel to be a aviator? You fellers sure live with your life in your hands."

"My uncle saw a airplane fall once. They was two fellers in it. The passenger, he got killed right off. The pilot wasn't dead, though. He was just all smashed up—bones busted and bleeding all over. They took him to a hospital. I guess he died too, a couple days later."

"D'ya have a radio set on board?"

"No, mail planes don't carry any radio."

"I never could understand how these things stay up in the air." One of the men pokes a wing with his finger.

"How fast can you make this machine go?"

"It can do about a hundred and twenty miles an hour at full throttle," I reply.

"Jesus Christ! Say, that's two miles a minute. How'd you like to travel two miles a minute, Bill? That would take you from the farm to town in about two minutes, wouldn't it?"

"Hell, it takes longer than that to get started."

"Do you s'pose people'll ever travel around in airplanes like they do in automobiles?"

Lights are coming along the road from the south. It's probably the mail truck. I leave my new friends, and go round and unstrap the hatch to the mail compartment.

The truck pulls in through the gate.

"Well, it isn't often you do us the favor of stopping at Springfield for the night."

I know that voice — it's Mr. Conkling, the postmaster. I jump down off the fuselage, and we shake hands. He's a big man, getting on in years.

"Tie your plane down and come in for supper with us," he says.

"I'd like to," I tell him, "but I can't leave it that long. The engine would freeze up."

I hand the mail sacks over to the driver as we talk.

"Well, can't we send you something to eat?"

"No, thanks. I'm not hungry."

I'm used to going without meals, and I don't want to bother him to make another trip out from town. Postmaster Conkling climbs back into the truck. He's one of the few people who understand an air-mail pilot's life. He accepts my statement, offers what help he can, and doesn't argue about problems of the storm and night.

"Good-by and good luck," he calls. "We notified both St. Louis and Chicago that you got down all right. Let us know if you need anything."

The truck grinds off, and the car of visitors follows. I'm alone on the field, in the night. The time is quarter past seven.

I'd better start the engine before it gets too cold — if I can start it. You're never sure with a Liberty; it's really a stunt for one man, and a very dangerous stunt if he doesn't watch himself. The trick of handling a propeller is to make your muscles always pull away from it. If you lean against a blade, on contact, you're asking for some broken bones. I put a lantern on the ground next to my cockpit, and line the other three up in front and a little to the left of the propeller. I hang my pistol and belt around a strut, chock the wheels, tie the stick back with my safety belt, check switches, give the engine three primer shots, retard spark, close throttle, run back to the propeller, catch one blade with my left hand, scrape over frozen ground with my moccasins as I pull a cylinder through compression. It takes all the strength I've got — the oil's beginning to thicken. How fast an engine cools in winter!

One – – – two – – – three – – – four blades through. Leave the fifth sixty degrees below horizontal. Back to the cockpit. Throttle one-half inch open. Switches on. Back to the propeller — ten feet to the right side. Got to watch this; I should have two men pulling on my arm, and a mechanic in the cockpit. Run – – – grip the blade – – – throw my weight against it – – – angle forward to clear its bone-shattering strength – – – let go – – – catch balance – – – back for another try. There's a "ping" this time – – – the blade moves

forward – – – stops as I trip away – – – No action on the third
blade. On the fourth she hits — one cylinder — two – – – the engine catches. I stumble as the blade jumps from my hand — break
the fall with my arm and shoulder. I scramble up and around the
wing to my cockpit — Ease on throttle — A roar from the engine
— she's safe now. I unsnap the belt from the stick, and climb into
the pilot's seat.

I'll idle at 800 r.p.m. for five minutes; then switch her off for
twenty. Might as well turn on the exhaust heater — that will keep
my feet warm, even in an open cockpit. Now if I had a Bellanca,
with its closed cabin, it would be easy to spend the night on a field.
I could go to sleep between engine starts — sleep twenty minutes
— idle the engine five minutes — sleep again. I could carry an
alarm clock for such emergencies.

But how about flying the mail in a closed cabin on a foggy
night? You can't see well through glass; it merges with haze, and
reflects every light on the ground. In rain you can hardly see
through it at all. And suppose you got into a little sleet, what then?
No, you just couldn't fly through bad weather in a closed cabin.
And if you should crack up in a Bellanca, the engine would be right
in your lap. There's hardly any structure between it and the cockpit
to protect you; you wouldn't have a chance in a bad crash. It
would be still worse with a fuel tank in the fuselage, for the New
York-to-Paris flight. You'd be like the filling in a sandwich — your
knees against the fire wall, your back against the gasoline. Suppose
the landing gear failed. Suppose a tire blew. Suppose a cylinder
started missing as you took the air – – –

It's 7:35. I have nine hours to pass before dawn.

The time is half past three. The fuel truck should soon be
here. It's too cold to stay in my cockpit with the engine off. I climb
out and walk back and forth in front of the wings. A glow still
spreads over the clouds above Springfield, but there's not a farmhouse light to be seen; the last one went out hours ago. – – – How
long will the grease last on a Wright Whirlwind's rocker arms?

Suppose a valve should stick, out over the Atlantic Ocean? — — — I'd have to be in the air for nearly forty hours between New York and Paris. How long can an engine run without attention? How long can a pilot stay awake? It seems ages since I got out of bed yesterday morning; actually it's less than twenty hours.

13

"If you want a really good suit, you'd better have it tailor-made."

Captain Littlefield and I stand at the side of a National Guard Jenny. It's Sunday morning, and our training maneuvers are getting under way. I've selected the most neatly dressed officer in the squadron for advice on clothing.

"A tailored suit looks better, and it lasts longer," he goes on. "It's worth the extra cost. I know a good tailor in the city. He won't charge too much, and he can make up a suit for you in a week. I'll give you his address after we come down."

We climb into our cockpits. There'll be a half hour's formation flying; then the squadron is scheduled to break up for individual acrobatics. We taxi out into the field and take off. My two wingmen follow close — Captain Young with Sergeant Wecker, Lieutenant Hutchinson with Sergeant Gerding. We set course for St. Louis. People will look up and tell each other that the National Guard is overhead. It's good advertising, and helps bring us new recruits.

There's Forest Park below, winding roads among its trees — that's where the flying field used to be. Now we're up to three thousand feet, above the center of the city. I bank toward open country to the north. There's the Missouri-Mississippi junction — perfect landmark for a pilot lost in haze. You can't miss the earth's great landmarks, if you can see the earth at all. Rivers, mountains, coastlines, point your way. It's by them I'll have to find France, and Paris, if I can finally get a plane to make the flight.

Now formation training is over. I wobble my wings to signal a breakup. Wingmen peel off to either side. Stick back, right, full rudder, throttle open — our Jenny snaps over, upside down — — —

a half loop – – – a roll right – – – a roll left – – – a vertical reversement. We're too low for more: bank toward Lambert Field and
climb. We'll do one spin before our landing. A flying wire starts
to vibrate in the inner bay. It's amazing what those thin steel cables
stand in acrobatics — tons of strain on their metal threads. When
wings and wires hold their shape through loops, spins, and barrel
rolls, they can surely carry the fuel load I'll need for a flight to
Paris.

14

1 overcoat, blue
1 hat, gray felt
1 pair gloves, fur lined
1 scarf, silk
2 pair sox, wool
1 necktie, silk
1 suitcase, leather

I read, upside down, the items on the clerk's sales slip. He
hasn't filled in the prices yet. Good Lord, that's going to run close
to a hundred dollars, and there's still my suit to pay for. Shoes
and shirts are about the only things I can economize on. The ones
I wear with my uniform will do.

I don't like to spend money on such intangible assets as clothes.
But if I'm really going to fly to Paris, I must be willing to put
everything I've got into the project — time, energy, money, even
my position as chief pilot on the air-mail line. I'll hold back only
enough to pay for room and board until I can get a new start flying
if I fail. It bothers me to think that I'm buying these clothes just
to make an impression on the Wright Corporation — they won't
add a penny's worth to my ability as a flyer. I'm actually spending
money on an overcoat just to wear it through the front door! I'll
probably take it off before I even sit down. And the silk scarf and
the felt hat — I haven't the slightest use for them. I hate to do
things just to make an impression. But right now that may be as
essential to my Paris flight as a plane itself will become later.

I've decided to get my traveling outfit all in order before I telephone the Wright Corporation. Once I start, I must keep pushing my project constantly. It would be bad tactics to let a week or ten days pass between my phone call and arrival.

15

It's been a warm afternoon for November. Three of us stroll down the road to Bridgeton — Love, Mendenhall, and I. Mendenhall is a newcomer to the field.

"Slim, the doctor says I can start flying again next Monday," Love announces suddenly. He's not given to talking very much, and he has a habit of heaving an important statement into conversation like a rock.

"That will help a lot, Phil," I say. "Are you sure it's all right?"

"Would have been all right a week ago," he answers. "These surgeons are just cautious."

Love crashed last year in Georgia, on a cotton-dusting job — passed out in the cockpit of a Huff-Daland — left a perfect imprint of his teeth on a tubular steel crossbar of the fuselage. (He now carries a four-inch length of that crossbar in his pocket to prove it.) They thought he was dead at first, then dying. But the surgeons straightened out his face bones, put a silver plate beneath his flesh, and he pulled through. His face began bothering him again this fall and, after X rays, another operation was advised. While he's been recovering from it, Nelson and I have taken all the mail flights.

"Phil," I ask, "when your face is really all right again, do you suppose you and Nellie could handle the mail route for three or four days? I've got to make a trip to New York."

"Sure, Slim. Any time. I'll be all right next week, I tell you."

We reach the crossroad, and stop at the corner barbecue stand. "Hello, there!"

It's the auto mechanic from Bridgeton. Small of stature, in oversize, grease-smeared clothes, he extends his hand, smiling. He makes a living working by himself in his red-painted board garage a block or two away. He keeps so busy that we don't see much of him — only a wave of the arm or a shout of greeting as we drive past his junk-cluttered yard. Occasionally he comes over to Lambert Field to repair or tow off a stalled car.

Mendenhall steps over to the counter and asks the salesgirl for some candy and a package of cigarettes. Tires scrubbing along the roadside draw my eyes. A stocky, flashily dressed man jumps out of a sport-model car and walks hurriedly to the counter. He shoulders past Mendenhall rudely, and demands immediate attention.

"Say, how about taking your turn?"

The stranger mutters a reply I can't understand, but its meaning mirrors in his round, surly face. Mendenhall, larger of build, shoves him aside. At this, three more stocky men spring out of the car — tough-looking fellows.

"Hey, none of that!" Love moves forward to intercept them.

"Phil!" I call. But it's no use. If there's going to be a fight, red-headed Phil Love will be in it. He's forgotten his face, forgotten everything but the one-sided mêlée that's forming. "Watch that face," the surgeon told him. "One blow will make it pulp." Now he's heading into a scrap where he's almost sure to get that blow. And I guess I'm committed too.

But the stranger doesn't wait for his cohorts. His hand goes down, brushes back his coat; there's the shine of a nickel-plated gun.

"Put it back!"

It happened so fast I didn't see the draw. The little auto mechanic is standing in front of me, a horse pistol in his hand, pointing straight into the stranger's belly.

"That kind of thing doesn't go here," he says quietly, but with a tenseness that's in keeping with his finger on the trigger.

Everyone has stopped moving. The nickel-plated gun slips back into the pocket which its muzzle never left. Now I notice that the mechanic's left hand is holding his jacket open to show, pinned carelessly to his vest, a deputy sheriff's badge. None of us knew he had it.

"Let's get going!" he says.

The four men climb back into their car. Tires claw angrily on gravel. They speed out of sight around a bend in the road to St. Charles.

Pistol and badge have disappeared. The little mechanic smiles and shrugs his shoulders.

"Probably some gangsters from St. Louis," he remarks calmly. As far as he's concerned, the incident is over.

The salesgirl, rather shakily, gives Mendenhall change from his dollar. We say good-by and start back toward the hangars.

"Phil, damn it, you can't afford to get into a fight. You haven't got a chance with that face of yours."

"I know it, Slim," he says. "But that was going to be four to one. It made me so mad I forgot all about my face."

16

"I want to put in a call for the Wright Aeronautical Corporation at Paterson, New Jersey — — — Yes, anybody who answers." I've never talked that far over the phone before. I hope the connection's good.

"Hold the line, please."

I wish the operator didn't say it so casually — almost as though I were making a local call. I hear clickings, buzzings, snatches of words and numbers. I've got my new suit and suitcase, and everything ready to pack.

"Here's your party."

Within a minute — that's fast work. Another girl's voice comes on.

"Wright Aeronautical."

"I'd like to speak to one of your officers, please," I tell her, trying to hide all trace of excitement in my voice.

"What officer do you want?" she asks.

"One of your executive officers."

"Which executive officer?" Her voice is insistent, and a little annoyed now. Somehow I've got to break through this.

"I am calling on long distance from St. Louis, Missouri. I want to talk to one of the Wright Corporation's executive officers

— on business." I say it slowly and firmly to impress her. Apparently it does.

"Hold on a minute, please."

The next voice is a man's.

"I'm calling from St. Louis," I repeat. "My name is Charles Lindbergh. I represent a group of men here who are interested in buying a plane for the New York-to-Paris flight. I'd like to talk to you about the Bellanca, and I want to get some information about your engines. When would it be convenient for you to see me in Paterson?"

"Did you say you're calling from St. Louis, Missouri?" the officer asks.

"That's right."

He's impressed, as I thought he'd be. My phone-call money is well spent.

"We'll be glad to see you any day," he says. "Just let me know when you get to New York, and we'll set the hour."

·II·

NEW YORK

NOVEMBER, 1926

IT'S FOURTEEN YEARS since I've been in New York. I was a child then, and I don't remember much about it. I stand in the great, columned entrance of the Pennsylvania Station and look up and down Seventh Avenue. I've checked my suitcase. I'm going to walk around the city before I look for a hotel. Tomorrow morning I'll make an appointment with the Wright Aeronautical Corporation. I wonder if I'll have to take a ferry across the Hudson, or if I can get a train direct to Paterson, New Jersey.

2

The Wright factory has all the appearances of a successful business organization. As I step in through the door I feel that my new hat, overcoat, and tailored suit are paying off. The girl at the desk glances at my card, and smiles. Yes, she's been told to expect me. So far, so good. I am exactly one minute ahead of my appointment.

"Won't you leave your hat and coat in the corner?" She motions toward a well-filled rack, and calls a number on her phone. "'Captain Lindbergh is here," I hear her saying to someone on the wire.

"This way, please."

The girl leads me down a corridor to a room near the end. An executive rises from his desk in greeting.

"You've just come from St. Louis, Captain?"

"I arrived in New York yesterday," I tell him.

"I understand you're interested in the Wright-Bellanca," he says. "Sit down, won't you?"

"Yes, sir. I'd like to have all the information you can give me about the Bellanca. We're also interested in Whirlwind engines."

"I can get all the data you want on Whirlwind engines, but at the moment we can't quote a price on the Bellanca. We're negotiating to sell both the plane and manufacturing rights to the Huff-Daland Company. You see, the Wright Corporation never intended to manufacture aircraft. We built the Bellanca to show how a Whirlwind could perform in a modern plane — it was really a demonstration of our engine. Of course if the deal doesn't go through, we may still be interested in selling the plane. But don't you think a three-engined ship would be better for a flight across the ocean?"

The multiengine problem again! I didn't expect it from the Wright people.

"Not necessarily," I say. "It seems to me there are a number of advantages to a plane with one engine. How often does a Whirlwind fail in flight?"

The executive laughs. "You've got me there. We think our engines are pretty good. We haven't got exact figures, but they seem to be averaging about nine thousand hours to a failure — — — Still, we don't believe in taking chances, and you're better off with three than with one."

"How soon do you think you'll know whether the Bellanca is for sale?" I ask.

"You'd better talk to Giuseppe Bellanca about that. I've arranged for you to meet him. You may want to talk to the Huff-Daland people, too. But wouldn't you like to take a trip around our factory while you're here in Paterson?"

We walk through lines of lathes, under belts and spinning wheels. Metal shavings twist off hardened tool points and fall to the floor. Hand trucks, stacked with finned and contoured castings, pass us by. I see it all with my eyes, but my mind is on the Bellanca and my flight to Paris.

"How long can a Whirlwind engine stay in the air without any servicing?" I demand.

"I don't believe we know exactly," the executive replies. "The rocker-arm bearings would be the limiting factor. When they run dry, they get sluggish and stick. They'd keep going for a good many hours; but for a long flight, we probably ought to find some way of greasing them in the air – – – This is our foundry."

We continue on, past tempering ovens, down the engine overhaul line, out to the deafening test stands.

"We run our engines here till they break down," the executive explains, "to see what parts fail first."

3

"My plane is fully capable of flying nonstop from New York to Paris." Giuseppe Bellanca leans forward intently from a lounge in the Waldorf-Astoria. "I should like very much to have it make the flight."

Bellanca is a serious, slender man — straight black hair, sharp-cut features, medium height. One feels, in his presence, genius, capability, confidence. Here there'll be no feinting for position, no cards held back. What he says, you can believe.

"It will only be necessary to put a big gasoline tank in the cabin," he tells me.

"Is the landing gear strong enough to take off with such a load of fuel?" I ask.

"Yes; I have built the landing gear especially strong. There should be no trouble about taking off," he says.

"How many hours do you think your plane could stay in the air without refueling, if the pilot kept it throttled down to minimum flying speed?" I ask.

"I believe it could stay up for more than fifty hours, Captain Lindbergh. That would break the world's endurance record."

"It might be a good idea to try to break the endurance record, as an engine test, before starting out on a nonstop flight over the ocean," I suggest.

"I think that would be wise," he replied. "The plane is fully capable of it."

"If we can't buy the Bellanca you're flying now, how soon could you build another one?"

"It would not take long if I have a factory, Captain Lindbergh. But now I have no factory. I cannot tell. If I must organize a factory, it takes much longer – – – But I think there is a good chance that the sale of the plane we have built can be negotiated for such a purpose. I hope so. A successful flight to Paris would be of great value."

It's clear that in Giuseppe Bellanca I have a friend. He's as much interested in the New York-to-Paris flight as I am. And he knows the problems of financing an enterprise — he's going through these himself. He doesn't change his attitude at all when I tell him that our St. Louis organization isn't yet complete. We talk about cruising speeds, fuel requirements, take-off distances. He has at his finger tips the answers to practically everything I want to know.

"Well, I think I have all the information I need," I say finally. "I must take the train west tonight. Thank you very much for all your help."

We get up, shake hands.

"I hope you have success with your organization, Captain Lindbergh," he tells me in parting. "I hope you are able to buy my plane."

Well, now I've made contact with the Wright Corporation, and with Bellanca. When I return to St. Louis, I'll have more than an idea to sell. I'll be able to tell about an airplane that's able to make the flight, and a designer who's anxious to have his plane bought for that purpose. Then, if I can raise enough money, I'll take the train back to New York and make a cash offer to whoever owns the Wright-Bellanca.

4

As soon as I reach Lambert Field, I send Bellanca a telegram:

WESTERN
UNION

GIUSEPPE BELLANCA   ANGLUM MO.
PASSAIC NEW JERSEY

IMPORTANT TO KNOW SOON AS POSSIBLE WHETHER PLANE
CAN BE PURCHASED FOR ST. LOUIS TO PARIS FLIGHT STOP
WOULD GREATLY APPRECIATE YOUR KEEPING ME POSTED ON
DEVELOPMENTS.

LINDBERGH

It's essential to keep my project alive. I must press action wherever I can, show people that I mean business when I talk about a flight across the ocean. This will leave the next move up to Bellanca.

After lunch I drive in to the city to tell Mr. Thompson and Major Lambert about my eastern trip.

5

Days pass, while I call at Anglum's little railroad station, only to find that no answer from Bellanca has come in. Then, on the morning of December 4th, the station agent hands me a message:

WESTERN
UNION

PASSAIC N.J. 1006AM 12-4-26
CHAS. A. LINDBERGH
ANGLUM MO.
SORRY LONG UNAVOIDABLE DELAY WILL BE GLAD TO HELP
YOU IN ANY WAY TO OBTAIN PURCHASE OF WRIGHT BELLANCA
AND PREPARE SAME FOR PARIS FLIGHT BUT IF UNABLE TO
BUY WRIGHT BELLANCA I OFFER THREE MOTOR PLANE FOR
TWENTY NINE THOUSAND DOLLARS WHICH IS EXCEPTIONALLY
ADAPTED FOR PARIS FLIGHT

BELLANCA

Good Lord! I thought Bellanca was one man who wouldn't advocate multiengines. How am I going to raise $29,000 when I haven't been able to raise $10,000? And even if I had the money, how many months would it take to build a new, trimotored plane?

I'm still turning this problem over in my mind, unsuccessfully, when a telegram arrives from one of the officers of the Huff-Daland Company, indicating that negotiations for purchase of the Wright-Bellanca have been broken off. So I wire the Wright Corporation:

WESTERN
UNION

```
WRIGHT AERONAUTICAL CORP.            ANGLUM MO.
PATERSON NEW JERSEY                  DEC. 9, 1926
ESSENTIAL TO KNOW SOON AS POSSIBLE WHETHER WRIGHT
BELLANCA CAN BE PURCHASED FOR ST. LOUIS TO PARIS
FLIGHT
                                     LINDBERGH
```

6

Four days have passed since I telegraphed the Wright Corporation. This morning I sent another message. This reply arrives:

WESTERN
UNION

```
PATERSON N.J.   349 PM   12-13-26
C. A. LINDBERGH
ANGLUM, MO.
RETEL NINTH THIRTEENTH REGRET THAT WE DO NOT DESIRE
AT THIS TIME TO HAVE WRIGHT BELLANCA USED FOR
TRANSATLANTIC FLIGHT SUGGEST FOKKER OR HUFF DALAND
THREE ENGINE PLANES
                        PETERSON WRIGHT AERO
```

Well, that's definite enough. But since Bellanca has offered to build a three-motored plane, he must have found a factory. If he has a factory, he can build another single-motored plane both faster and cheaper. If I can raise enough money, I might still be able to get a Whirlwind-powered Bellanca before summer. It's money I've got to find now. After that comes the question of a plane. I'll wire Bellanca anyway, just to keep in contact and let him know my interest is still keen:

WESTERN
UNION

ANGLUM MO.
GIUSEPPE BELLANCA
PASSAIC NEW JERSEY
WRIGHT CORPORATION REFUSES SELL BELLANCA STOP WHEN
COULD YOU DELIVER SIMILAR SINGLE ENGINE PLANE FOR
PARIS FLIGHT AND WHAT WOULD PRICE BE
                                        LINDBERGH

7

For days, nothing has flown on Lambert Field except our mail planes. Turbulent winds, and mud alternating with frozen ground, have brought student training to a standstill. Barnstorming petered out with November. I've had plenty of time to work on my Paris project, and I've gotten nowhere. Bellanca hasn't replied to my latest telegram. Aside from Mr. Thompson and Majors Robertson and Lambert, I've found no one willing to take part in financing a flight across the ocean. The men I've talked to who are interested don't have enough money. Those who have enough money consider the risk too great — if not for their bank accounts, then for their reputations. I've not been able to convince them that flying the ocean is no more dangerous than a winter on the mail. They want no share in the criticism they think would come from sending a young pilot to his death.

Possibly I could raise money by popular subscription. Maybe I could get a thousand people in St. Louis to contribute ten dollars each. I could offer to return their investment with a profit, from the Orteig prize, if I succeeded. But to raise small amounts from many people is tedious and uncertain. I'd have to publicize the project, set up an organization, keep records, write a lot of letters. And time is passing. It's not many weeks to spring. Maybe I could raise some money in Chicago. But I don't know any businessmen in Chicago. To whom could I go for a start?

I must have walked five miles this afternoon, over frozen roads, thinking of the Paris flight and hunting for new ideas on which to build a successful organization. I was walking like this yesterday, and the day before, and the day before that. Walking has become a regular habit in my life.

The winter is almost half over. Each day makes my failure more complete. In France and in America, aircraft for the trans-oceanic flight are being built and tested, while I do nothing but lay plans and talk. If I'm not careful, I'll be in a class with those erratic and often-to-be-avoided people who have wonderful ideas and accomplish nothing with them. I must make a final effort or give up my dream. I'll ask Love and Nelson to take over the mail schedules completely for a few days. Then I'll lay my Paris project before every businessman in St. Louis I can get an appointment with.

8

"Slim, you ought not to be running around worrying about raising money. You've got to put all your attention on that flight if you're going to make it."

"I'm talking to Harry Knight in his brokerage office at Fourth and Olive Streets. I've come to ask his advice in regard to other businessmen I might approach with my project, and in the hope that he'll take some part himself. Harry Knight is president of the St. Louis Flying Club. I met him three or four times on the airfield last summer when he was taking flying lessons from Cloyd Clevenger. He's a stocky, abrupt young man in a brown suit, not much older than myself. He doesn't believe in wasting too much time by being tactful. I fully expected to be turned down at once, or put off with one of those evasive, business executives' statements about wanting to think the matter over. But:

"Let me talk to a friend of mine in the bank," he continues. "Maybe we can take care of the financial end for you. How much money is it going to take?"

His words strike like the flash of an airfield's beacon on a stormy night. Then I'm not lost — here's help, someone to share responsibility.

"If we can get the plane and engine manufacturers to stand part of the expense, I think $10,000 would be enough," I tell him. "If we can't get them to take part, it might cost as much as $15,000 to buy the plane and engine, and make the flight."

"You're talking about a single-engined plane. Wouldn't a trimotor be better for that kind of flight?" he asks.

I start in with my old arguments again:

"It would cost $29,000 to get a trimotored plane from Bellanca. The Fokker Company wants $90,000 for one of theirs. And I don't know how long it would take to build one. Multiengined planes are more complicated; there are more things likely to go wrong with them. Besides, the greatest danger lies in weather, and in take-off with a full load — not in engine failure — Whirlwind engines are averaging 9000 hours to a failure. As a matter of fact, I think I'd rather make the flight with one engine than with three, to say nothing of the difference in cost. A big ship is hard to handle in thick weather — — —"

Knight suddenly swings around in his chair, and picks up the telephone.

"Get me Harold Bixby at the State National Bank," he says — — — "Bix, how about coming over here for a few minutes? — — — sure you can — — — okay — — — in my office."

"He's only a block up the street," Knight tells me after hanging up, " — Fourth and Locust. You know he's president of the Chamber of Commerce."

Within ten minutes Bixby knocks on the door. He's a man you like right away — smiling and full of humor. But his penetrating brown eyes size you up and warn you that you'd better pass inspection. You know you can depend on Harold Bixby, and that if he can't depend on *you* he won't be around you very long.

Harry Knight outlines my project for flying an airplane from St. Louis to New York to Paris.

"You think a plane with a Whirlwind engine can make a flight like that?" Bixby asks.

"Yes sir," I answer. "Bellanca says his can make Paris from New York with a good reserve of fuel."

"How much does a Bellanca cost?"

"I don't know," I answer. "But I'm not sure I can buy one." I tell about my trip to New York and my talks with the Wright Corporation and Bellanca.

"You'd have to have a new plane built, then?" Knight asks.

"It might work to put an oversize wing on an existing fuselage," I tell him. "That shouldn't add very much to the cost. Besides, there's not time to do a lot of building. I want to be ready to start as soon as the weather breaks next spring."

"Why wouldn't the Wright Company furnish an engine for the advertising they'd get?"

"They might," I reply, "but I don't think we can count on it. They didn't make any offer in that direction when I was at Paterson. Of course then I wasn't in a very good position to trade. If I can show them we mean business, I think we can at least get a reduction in price."

"You said you already have some money lined up. Who's in this project with you?"

"Yes sir. I can put in two thousand dollars myself. Major Lambert has promised to put in a thousand. Earl Thompson and Bill Robertson say they'll take part, but I haven't talked to them about amounts."

"Slim, don't you think you ought to have a plane with more than one engine for that kind of flight?" Bixby asks.

Harry Knight laughs. "That's what I asked him, Bix; but he doesn't think it would be much safer."

"Suppose one of the engines cuts out halfway across the ocean," I put in. "I couldn't get to shore with the other two."

"No, but you might be able to stay up long enough to find a ship you could land beside," Bixby argues.

"I can't see myself circling around over the water looking for a boat," I say. "You know, I don't believe a flight to Paris would be any more dangerous than a winter on the mail line. If one of our DH engines cuts on a bad night, it's pretty serious too — and we've only got rebuilt Liberties. None of the lines coming in to Chicago has multiengine planes, you know — except when Ford makes those experimental runs. A pilot can't fly at all without taking *some* risk. I've weighed my chances pretty carefully – – –"

Bixby breaks in. "Yes, you've only got a life to lose, Slim. But don't forget, I've got a reputation to lose."

"The Army's 'round-the-world' planes had only single engines," I say, searching desperately for new arguments.

"Yes, but half of them didn't make it," Bixby counters. "And they had the whole government behind them." Then, instead of following through the opening I've given him, he adds, "You let us think about this for a day or two, and talk to some of our friends. If you're going to make the flight, we've got to get started right away. Come down and see me next Wednesday. How about ten a.m., at my office?"

"Any time at all. I'll be there at ten."

I can hardly believe what I'm hearing. I hoped, at most, to get a pledge for another thousand dollars. I never dreamed of finding anyone with sufficient interest to suggest taking over the entire financial burden.

I say good-by and start driving toward Lambert Field.

9

It's snowing on the Springfield pasture. I've just flown through an area of sleeting rain. I taxi slowly to the fence corner. Wings rock with gusts of wind.

"Here's Chicago weather. It don't look so good," the Springfield mail truck driver says, handing up a folded sheet of paper. It doesn't look so good here either. I've just measured the ceiling at three hundred feet, and darkness isn't far away. I wait until the driver starts unbuckling the mail hatch, and then throw his message over the far side of my cockpit, unread. The slipstream blows it away. Chicago reports are so unreliable that I don't want to condition my mind with them. I'd rather judge weather ahead as I fly.

Then I won't push too far on a clear report or land too soon on a bad one. Chicago has a habit of saying that the ceiling is high when clouds are on the steeples, and that it's "zero zero" when the night is plenty good enough to fly.

We pilots once held a conference on these reports, and Nelson was appointed to investigate their origin.

"Those Chicago fellows just look out the window before they call Springfield," he told me when I next saw him. "If they can see a few blocks down the street, they say the weather's good. But if a little haze fuzzes up the lamps, they say it's all closed in. I tried to explain what we needed, but I don't think it did much good."

"Why don't we tell them to save the money they spend on phone calls?" I suggested.

"No," he answered, "you know as well as I do that we need those reports. Don't discourage them. Maybe some day they'll get better."

Yes, Nellie is right. At least we've got the principle of weather reports established. And one thing is certain: they can't get any worse.

I know there's bad weather ahead tonight. The Transcontinental went down at Bellefonte, and Love had to entrain the southbound mail. If Love couldn't take off in daylight, there's not much chance of my getting through in darkness. But maybe I can make Peoria. And then it's just possible that the ceiling will lift enough between there and Chicago to let me squeeze underneath. When clouds leave us room above the treetops we always start with the mail, regardless of how far we think we can go. Often we get through apparently impassable barriers of storm and fog, now that we've got a few beacons turning on our route. But whether we get through or not, the Corporation is paid for the poundage we take off with.

Somehow I've got to get back to St. Louis in time to make another ten o'clock appointment with Harold Bixby tomorrow morning. I can take a train from Springfield or Peoria; and if I do get through to Chicago, I'll start at daybreak on a southbound ferry flight. The chances are that I won't get ten miles north of Springfield tonight, in the snow and haze.

Flakes of snow melt against my cheeks as I open the throttle to take off.

Is something wrong with the engine? I glance at instruments. No, the needles are all in place. Still – – – It's like that first, vague, uncomfortable feeling which precedes the outward manifestation of an illness. I cut the left switch; then the right. The engine vibrates, spits, and sputters, with the right switch cut. I turn back toward Springfield's pasture. It's not over five minutes since I left.

The mail truck driver is waiting for me. He knew I might return. I bank, land, taxi, and stop the engine.

"Too thick?" he calls, stomping up and down to keep his feet warm.

"No, it was lifting a little. My engine started cutting out," I answer as I crawl forward through the wings. "Put a stone behind the wheels, will you, so she doesn't blow backward."

Wind is howling through the flying wires.

"Okay. Want to entrain the mail?" he asks.

"Let me look at these distributors first."

I find the trouble immediately — a loose spring.

"Hang up the lanterns and wait here twenty minutes," I tell the driver. "I want to try again."

He nods, gives me a hand pulling through the propeller, waves me off the field.

Twenty miles north of Springfield it stops snowing. Thirty miles north, the stars are out and there's not a cloud in the sky.

I lose almost half an hour refueling at Peoria. It takes longer to do everything in winter weather, outdoors. For a time it looked as though we couldn't start the Liberty at all.

I find Chicago cloud-covered; but visibility is good, and the ceiling has lifted to at least five hundred feet.

"Think you're a mail pilot, don't you?" Love, feet apart, hands in pockets, stands beside my fuselage as I climb down. His DH rests silently behind its chocks, half hidden in the darkness.

"Oh, it was a little thick; but nothing to worry about," I answer, making the most of his embarrassment. He'll find out soon enough that I've come in with clearing skies. "Where's Nellie?"

"He's got enough sense to know a plane shouldn't fly in this kind of weather," Love says, in a special tone he reserves for condemnation. "He said nobody'd be fool enough to come into Maywood tonight — — — He's damn well right, too, if you want'a know what I think about it."

"The mail must go, Phil — post office orders."

"All right, just keep it up and we'll be looking for a new chief pilot one of these days. What kind of flowers do you like best?"

"Wild flowers."

An extra puff of steam from Love's nose is my only acknowledgment.

Everett, our Chicago mechanic, is grinning. He has that crewman's intuition which tells him whether a flight has been tough or not. He feels pretty sure I've come through without much trouble. "We'll have to leave one of these planes out tonight," he remarks.

This is the moment to lay down my joker. "Oh, I'm going to ferry back just as soon as we can refuel. We don't want *two* planes up here at Chicago. Phil, do you think you can get down in the morning if the weather's better?"

"Slim, are you crazy? You're not going back into that stuff tonight!" Love is starting to get angry.

Everett looks at me and stops grinning.

"Just stand by and watch," I say. "Nothing stops a mail pilot, you know. But I want supper first. Phil, how about taking me over to a restaurant?"

There's no answer. We climb into the car and drive off across the snow. I see right away that Love wants an argument. There are times when nothing makes him happier.

"Slim, when are you going to sew up my bearskin flying suit?" he demands.

That flying suit has been a bone of contention between us ever since I borrowed it one night, weeks ago, and had to jump from my plane in a storm — the second DH I've lost. It was too dark to see the ground, so I had no choice of landing places, and my parachute dropped me right on top of a barbed-wire fence. The wires eased my fall against the ground, but they put a foot-long rip in Love's flying suit.

"Phil, you ought to be so glad I'm alive that you wouldn't even think about asking me to sew it up," I answer.

"Well, if I get rheumatism in my leg and can't fly the mail, it's your responsibility," he ends up as we enter the restaurant.

Eight – – – nine – – – ten – – – eleven – – – flash. That makes three beacons in sight on the airway ahead — all installed at government expense; by spring our entire airway will be lighted. I subtract fifteen degrees from my heading to cut across to the Springfield leg. It's as easy to fly by night as by day, with the sky clear, and flashing lights to show me where I am. "You big Swede," is all Love had said when we stepped out after dinner, and looked up to brilliant stars. He was a little mad because I wouldn't let him take the ferry flight back. But I've got to see Harold Bixby in a few hours.

I climb to five thousand feet and throttle down. Why hurry to complete this trip? I have no mail. No one at St. Louis will be waiting. No one there even knows I'm in the air; I told Love and Everett not to send any message of my departure. There are the lights of Joliet, and Lockport, and a dozen villages whose names I do not know. I have the cockpit heater turned full on, but it's so cold that my finger tips pain slightly inside their silk-lined gauntlets. And if I lean into the slipstream, my forehead feels as though a nail were being driven through it.

10

"Do you mind waiting? Mr. Bixby is still in conference. He'll be through in just a few minutes."

The secretary smiles and leaves. It's ten oclock. I sit down in a corner chair at the State National Bank of St. Louis. A teller, behind his lightly barred window, is counting out bills for one of the customers. Stacks of greenbacks are piled neatly on a shelf at his left. Fifty dollar, twenty dollar, ten dollar — the denomination of each sheaf is marked on a paper band around it. There must be *more* than fifteen thousand dollars in those stacks. If I owned that pile of paper I could fly to Paris. In exchange for those printed slips, manufacturers would give me an airplane, an engine, and fuel enough to fly across the ocean.

I have an idea. If I can translate that idea into paper, I can translate the paper into reality and action. The idea and the action I understand. The paper stage which intervenes forms my major difficulty. I glance sidewise at the people waiting with me. They must be facing problems similar to mine. That middle-aged lady, what has she to sell — shop, café, or beauty parlor? And that man in the creased, striped suit? You want a sales agency? A factory? An airplane to fly across the ocean? A bank is like a courthouse. You go in to state your case, to bring your plea before the judges. A poor risk? The verdict is against you. Appeal to someone else or be condemned. Good business? You get the decision, a written order requiring the compliance of other men. Take this pile of paper; go ahead. These slips, worthless in themselves, signify that this bank, this nation stands behind you.

I shift in my chair. My clothes bind; my collar sticks around my neck. I feel out of place. Mine is not a business proposition. How can a bank afford to back a flight across the ocean? I want to take off a heavily overloaded airplane with one engine, fly through unknown weather, over thousands of miles of land and water where a single crack in an oil line would mean a crash. I want to — — —

"Hello Slim! I'm sorry I had to keep you waiting. I've been jammed up this morning."

Bixby slips in through one of those waist-high mahogany, semiprivate gates. I stand to shake hands.

"Slim, you've sold us on this proposition of yours," he says. "It's a tough job you're taking on, but we've talked it over and

we're with you. From now on you'd better leave the financial end
to us." His cheeks wrinkle back in confidence as he speaks. "If
you can keep costs down to the figures you gave us, we believe
we can swing the deal. You put in your two thousand dollars.
We'll telephone Major Lambert and Earl Thompson and Bill
Robertson, and arrange whatever organization we need. That will
be our part of the partnership. You concentrate on the plane and
getting ready for the flight. We want to be sure it's a practical
proposition. Don't get obligated before we meet again. But let us
know as soon as you have something definite lined up."

I stop, start, and turn automatically as I drive back to Lambert
Field. I'm conscious of neither time nor distance. Then I'm really
going to fly to Paris! It's no longer just an idea, no longer simply
a plan in my mind. I feel like a child on Christmas morning, seeing all that he's longed for suddenly piled, dazzling, before him,
not knowing which object to pick up first. My most difficult problems are solved — organization and finance.

As soon as I get to my room, I change into boots and breeches
and start walking over frozen country roads. Definite plans must
be laid and immediate action taken. Now I must find a plane. I'll
sound out all the builders of aircraft in the United States. The
Travel Air Company at Wichita is producing a monoplane along
the general lines of the Wright-Bellanca — National Air Transport pilots have been talking about it all winter. The fuselage is
rather large and heavy for a record-breaking flight, but I'm no
longer in a position to ask for perfection. There's a possibility that
it might do. Also I've read of a high-wing monoplane built by a
company named Ryan, out in San Diego — Pacific Air Transport
is using it on their mail route up and down the coast. It doesn't
weigh as much as the Travel Air, and according to published figures
has unusually good performance. The Travel Air Company is
nearer. I'll telegraph them first and ask whether they'd consider
building a plane for the St. Louis - Paris flight.

11

I wake soon after dawn. There's much to be done. As I fry potatoes and eggs for breakfast, I list items to be covered on this new day of the new life I've entered. For it is a new life; I'll now bend every thought and effort toward one objective — landing at Paris. All else is secondary.

First, I'll call Earl Thompson and Major Lambert and tell them of my conferences with Knight and Bixby. I'll tell Bill Robertson as soon as he arrives at his office. Then I'll write to Mother and say that I've got to withdraw a large amount of money from my account in Detroit. We'll have to select and train another pilot for the mail route. It will be difficult in winter; but most of the beacons are now installed, and days are getting longer. Love and Nelson can take bad-weather flights until the new man is broken in. Love will act as chief pilot while I'm away. I must notify Major Wassall that I'll be absent from the Guard for weeks or months. Other officers will have to take over my duties. I'll get in touch with the Department of Commerce and the Weather Bureau in Washington, and find out from the State Department what arrangements I must make to land an American plane in France.

12

A reply comes back quickly from Travel Air. They won't accept the order. The speed and definiteness with which they've turned me down is depressing. I expected at least some interest on their part. Shall I try the Ryan Company next? Probably I'll receive a similar answer from them. They're new and small, and not well known. But I'll try them. And then I'll send wires to Curtiss and Boeing and Douglas and Martin. I'll sign the messages "Robertson Aircraft Corporation." Major Bill gave me permission to do that, and I'll get more consideration. I walk over to the Anglum station, and write out another telegram.

```
            WESTERN
            UNION

RYAN AIRLINES INC.                      ANGLUM MO.
SAN DIEGO CALIFORNIA                    FEB. 3 1927
CAN YOU CONSTRUCT WHIRLWIND ENGINE PLANE CAPABLE
FLYING NONSTOP BETWEEN NEW YORK AND PARIS STOP IF
SO PLEASE STATE COST AND DELIVERY DATE
                       ROBERTSON AIRCRAFT CORP.
```

13

```
            WESTERN
            UNION

SAN DIEGO CALIF.
FEB. 4, 1927
ROBERTSON AIRCRAFT CORP.
ANGLUM MO.
CAN BUILD PLANE SIMILAR M ONE BUT LARGER WINGS
CAPABLE OF MAKING FLIGHT COST ABOUT SIX THOUSAND
WITHOUT MOTOR AND INSTRUMENTS DELIVERY ABOUT THREE
MONTHS

                            RYAN AIRLINES
```

Six thousand dollars! With the engine, that would make about ten thousand. It's well within my budget. How reliable is the bid? Does the Ryan company understand what it's offering to undertake? Has it engineers who can follow through with this promise? But here, at least, is interest and quick action.

```
            WESTERN
            UNION

RYAN AIRLINES INC.                      ANGLUM MO.
SAN DIEGO, CALIFORNIA                   FEB. 5, 1927
COMPETITION MAKES TIME ESSENTIAL CAN YOU CONSTRUCT
PLANE IN LESS THAN THREE MONTHS STOP PLEASE WIRE
GENERAL SPECIFICATIONS
                       ROBERTSON AIRCRAFT CORP.
```

I read over the message I've printed out, and push it across the counter, with a five-dollar bill, to Anglum's telegraph operator. He counts the words, thumbs through a huge catalogue of figures, and hands back my change. I pocket it, pull on gauntlets, button my coat, and tramp out into the snow.

14

WESTERN
UNION

```
SAN DIEGO CALIF.
3 PM FEB. 5, 27
ROBERTSON AIRCRAFT CORP.
ANGLUM MO.
GAS CAPACITY THREE HUNDRED EIGHTY GALLONS CRUISING
SPEED ONE HUNDRED MILES PER HOUR LOADING ONLY
TWELVE AND HALF POUNDS PER FOOT AND TWENTY POUNDS
PER HORSE POWER STOP CAN COMPLETE IN TWO MONTHS FROM
DATE OF ORDER IF NECESSARY STOP WILL REQUIRE FIFTY
PERCENT DEPOSIT
                                    RYAN AIRLINES
```

Three hundred and eighty gallons! That's a tremendous load of gasoline for a two-hundred-horsepower engine. And one hundred miles per hour is excellent cruising speed.

Two months — — — that would let me start tests sometime in April. I could still be ready to take off when the weather breaks in spring.

15

"I've never heard of the Ryan Company."

"Do you think they can build a plane with enough performance, Slim?"

Bixby and Knight are looking at the two telegrams I've laid before them.

"All I know is that Ryan mail planes have a pretty good reputation," I answer.

"Well, I certainly wouldn't turn them down because we haven't heard of them," Knight tells me. "They probably haven't heard of us either. What kind of plane do they make?"

"It's a high-wing monoplane, like Bellanca's, only it's got an open cockpit, and the span is shorter," I reply.

"At least they're anxious to build us a plane," Bixby says. "That puts them ahead of the other companies we've tried. Do you want to go out to California and talk to them, Slim?"

"I don't know any other way to find out what the Ryan people can do," I reply. "I can't very well size them up until I see them."

"Well, we'd better move right up on it then. How soon can you start?"

"Within a week. I don't know how long I'll be away, of course. If we decide to buy a plane, I'll stay in California while it's being built – – – I'll take care of my own expenses on this trip."

"No, you won't," Bixby says. "We're in this with you. We'll split up on all those things."

16

"Here's a telegram for you." A Robertson mechanic hands it to me as I jump down from the front cockpit of my training plane, on Lambert Field. I tear the envelope open and read:

```
                    WESTERN
                     UNION
PASSAIC N.J.  1110 AM  2-6-27
CHAS. A. LINDBERGH
ROBERTSON AIRCRAFT CORP.
ANGLUM MO.
SORRY DELAYED AS HAVE BEEN OUT OF TOWN STOP WILLING
TO MAKE ATTRACTIVE PROPOSITION ON THE BELLANCA
AIRPLANE FOR PARIS FLIGHT STOP SUGGEST YOU COME
NEW YORK SOON POSSIBLE SO WE CAN GET TOGETHER IN
QUICKEST MANNER STOP WIRE ME CARE COLUMBIA AIRCRAFT
CORPORATION 5104 WOOLWORTH BUILDING NEW YORK
                                    BELLANCA
```

Bellanca must have organized a new company, and bought his one existing plane from the Wright Corporation. His message came just in time; in two more days, I would have left for California. In another week, I might have signed a contract with Ryan Airlines.

Then the Wright-Bellanca is at last available; and now I have the financial backing to buy it. I'll be ahead of everyone else. I'll have the best plane for the flight, and plenty of time to test it before weather clears in the spring. I'll get big fuselage tanks put in, fly nonstop to St. Louis, fill them up, and break the world's endurance record — I'll try for forty-eight hours, at least, without landing. After that, we'll have the Whirlwind torn down and in-spected to see if any parts show excessive strain or wear; and at the same time we'll give the plane a final going over. Then I'll be ready to take off for Paris whenever conditions are best. Mean-while I'll assemble equipment for the flight. I'll study methods of long-range navigation. How does a pilot locate his position over the ocean — by day — by night? How accurate is a sextant sight? How can one measure drift above water? – – – But it's difficult to concentrate on such items. The future is too broad and full. Life is overflowing.

I wire Bellanca that our St. Louis organization is complete, and that I'm coming to New York, as he suggests.

17

"Captain Lindbergh, I want you to meet Mr. Levine, Chair-man of the Board of Directors of the Columbia Aircraft Corpora-tion – – – And this is Mr. Chamberlin, our pilot."

Bellanca, smiling and pleasant, introduces me. We shake hands. I'm in the Corporation's offices in the Woolworth Building, New York City.

"So you want to buy our Bellanca?"

Mr. Levine's eyes size me up as he speaks.

"Yes sir. That depends, of course, on the price. We want to buy a plane for the New York-to-Paris flight," I tell him.

"We will sell the Bellanca," he says. "It is the best you can get for that flight. But who is in your organization at St. Louis?"

"There are a number of men. There's Mr. Bixby of the State National Bank. There's Mr. Knight of the brokerage firm of Knight, Dysart, and Gamble. There's Major Lambert, after whom the airport is named. There's Major Robertson, president of the Robertson Aircraft Corporation – – – "

I can see that Levine is impressed by my partners.

"You have your money all raised?" he asks.

"No, only part of it," I answer. "We're not going to raise much money until we know what plane we're going to buy. We can raise the money all right, but we think the manufacturer ought to contribute something too. A flight to Paris would be worth a lot in advertising."

"We would contribute to such a flight," Levine tells me. "We would give you a good price on the Bellanca. It is worth $25,000. For that flight, we will sell the plane for $15,000. That would be a contribution of $10,000."

Fifteen thousand dollars! I thought I could cover the entire project for that amount — fuel and tests included. "That's considerably more than we expected to pay," I say. "Is it the lowest price you'd consider?"

"Fifteen thousand dollars is cheap for our Bellanca," he replies. "We could not take less. Remember it is the only existing plane capable of flying from New York to Paris! It needs only gasoline tanks. It can start whenever you are ready."

Levine won't budge from his price. Bellanca and Chamberlin extol the virtues of their plane, but take no part in the business negotiation.

"You never seem to load it down too much," Chamberlin asserts. "The wing keeps right on lifting, and it has wonderful stability."

"I designed the fuselage like an airfoil to give more lift — and the wing-strut fairings too," Bellanca breaks in.

"It can easily break the world's record for nonstop range," Chamberlin continues.

"Yes," says Bellanca. "A flight from New York to Paris would set a new world's record for distance. But, Captain Lindbergh, I like your plan of making an endurance flight first with my plane. It would be a good test of the engine. Also it would give us important data on fuel consumption – – – I feel sure my plane can break the endurance record."

"For a plane like ours, fifteen thousand dollars is a low price," Levine repeats.

"I'll have to go back to St. Louis before I can give you a definite answer," I say finally. "I'll have to talk to my partners."

18

Then the Bellanca is for sale. At a high price, but it's for sale. I can still make the flight for less than twenty thousand dollars — considerably less. "Don't turn it down if it costs a little more than you expect," Bixby and Knight had said. "Come back and we'll talk it over."

Success seems in my grasp as I board the train for St. Louis. This is the eleventh day of February. The next time I head westward I'll be at the controls of the world's most efficient airplane. It's only necessary to get a cashier's check, return east, and then I'll have possession of the Wright-Bellanca.

19

"What would you think of naming it the *Spirit of St. Louis*?"

Bixby's question strikes vaguely through my ears. I'm staring at the shredded and color-stained figures on a slip of paper in my hand — FIFTEEN THOUSAND DOLLARS. This slip can be traded for the Wright-Bellanca, and this slip is mine — "Pay to the order of Charles A. Lindbergh" it says on the back.

The *Spirit of St. Louis* – – – it's a good name. "All right, let's call it the *Spirit of St. Louis*." My eyes go back to the check. "I didn't know you were going to make this out to me personally," I say.

Bixby laughs. "Well Slim, Harry and I decided that if we couldn't trust you with a check, we ought not to take part in this project at all."

"When do you plan on starting back to New York?" Knight asks.

"I'll take the train this afternoon," I tell him.

"We'll start setting up a *Spirit of St. Louis* organization while you're away," Bixby says. "Let us know as soon as you can when you'll be here with the plane. How long do you think it will take to put the tanks in?"

"Maybe I can fly back while the tanks are being made," I

reply. "They can be installed later on. I'll try to land the Bellanca on Lambert Field within a week."

"Grand. We'll be out to meet you – – – Good luck!"

20

"We will sell our plane, but of course we reserve the right to select the crew that flies it."

I stand, dumfounded, in the Columbia Aircraft Corporation office. The fifteen-thousand-dollar cashier's check lies alone and conspicuous on Mr. Levine's polished desk top.

"You understand we cannot let just anybody pilot our airplane across the ocean," he continues.

I feel more chagrined than angry. Here's a point there can be no trading over.

"I'm afraid there's been a misunderstanding," I say. "We wouldn't be interested in such an arrangement. This is a St. Louis project. We'd naturally want to work with you very closely in running tests and planning for the flight; but if we buy a plane, we're going to control it, and we'll pick our own crew."

"The Columbia Aircraft Corporation cannot afford to take such a chance with our airplane," Levine replies. "We would select a good crew. Your organization in St. Louis would have all the credit for the flight, all the publicity."

"As far as I can see, we'd be paying $15,000 for the privilege of painting the name of St. Louis on the fuselage," I tell him. "If you'd stated these terms when I was here before, it would have saved me a two-thousand-mile train trip. Is the Bellanca for sale or isn't it? If it is, we can close the deal. If it's not, I want to look for another plane. There's no use wasting any more time."

"Yes, yes, it is for sale," he insists, "but why will not you let us select the crew? We know better than anybody else how to fly the Bellanca, how to take care of it. It would be wise for you to let us manage the flight to Paris. You should think it over. What I tell you is best."

"There's no use thinking it over," I state definitely. "We'll co-operate with you in every way we can, but we either buy the plane outright or we don't buy it. Will you accept this payment, or must I find another plane?"

I pick the check up from the desk top. Levine's eyes follow it.

"You are making a mistake," he argues. "You are making a mistake. The Bellanca is the only airplane built that is capable of flying between New York and Paris."

"I'm sorry," I reply; "but if you won't sell outright, the sooner I start looking for another plane the better." I start out the door.

"Wait — — — call me up tomorrow."

"There's no use waiting," I tell him, "unless you'll reconsider your terms."

Levine hesitates. Then, "Call me up tomorrow — at eleven o'clock," he says.

I walk aimlessly through Manhattan streets, looking up at skyscrapers, staring into goods-filled windows. After supper I go to a motion picture theater to pass time — — — But I can't lose myself in the story. Shootings and love affairs from a Hollywood stage don't replace my vision of the Bellanca. Behind trivial and fantastic escapades on the screen, I see wings, and engines turning.

21

It's eleven o'clock. I close the phone booth door and call my number. The reply comes at once.

"Good morning," Levine says. "Well, have you changed your mind?"

I hang up the phone too angry to reply, step outside, and stride up Madison Avenue. It's overcast, cold, and windy. Crevices in the sidewalk hold filthy chunks of ice. Taxis surge at the traffic lights. Crowds of people, with problems of their own, flow by, filter through traffic, seep in and out of stores. Brisk walking, and the cold February air, gradually clear my mind.

Fokker, Wright, Travel Air, Columbia — one company after another has turned me down. If I go out to San Diego, will the

Ryan offer collapse too? With money in hand to buy a plane, I thought my major difficulty past. But now it seems a greater problem is to find one. This is the third week of February. Even if Ryan can build a plane in two months, it would be late April before I could be back in New York, ready to take off for Paris. The Bellanca is here, now. It can start on any date its pilot chooses. Levine may already have decided to let Chamberlin make the New York-to-Paris flight. Instead of being ahead, I'm behind all my competitors — so far behind, in fact, that they don't even consider me in the running. Most of them don't know I exist.

It is reported that Lieutenant Commander Davis is well along with his plans for a New York-to-Paris flight, and that Major General Patrick, Chief of the Army Air Corps, has authorized the Huff-Daland Company to sell him a stripped-down, three-engined bomber — which is probably already built. It has been announced that Commander Byrd is going to try for the Orteig prize in a new trimotored Fokker — so he must have found financial backing of close to $100,000. There are rumors that Sikorsky is building another multiengined biplane for Captain René Fonck. Several transatlantic planes may be undergoing final tests in Europe — the French have been pretty secretive about their projects. All I can offer my partners is the possibility that some as yet unknown manufacturer of aircraft, maybe Ryan, will build a plane in which, during late spring or summer, I could try the New York-to-Paris flight. I never did have a business proposition. Now it can hardly be called even a sporting venture. Someone is almost certain to take off before my plane is built. Of course taking off doesn't necessarily mean reaching Paris. And there's always the Pacific Ocean. I don't think anybody is preparing for a transpacific flight.

22

"Let's stick to the Paris flight, Slim," Harry Knight is saying. "That's the idea we started out with."

I'm back at 401 Olive Street, after the dreary train trip from New York.

I have just suggested that it might be wise to give up plans for flying the Atlantic and concentrate on a transpacific flight. "No one is working on a Pacific flight," I say. "We'd have plenty of time to prepare — to build a plane — to run our tests. We might be able to work up another prize like Orteig's. It would be a longer flight, an even greater demonstration of aviation's capabilities."

But Knight and Bixby have no thought of quitting. Until this moment I didn't realize how firmly they stand behind me. I went to them hoping only for financial aid, and here I've found real partners in the venture.

"We'll put the money back in the bank," Bixby says, "and it will be ready when you need it. You may decide that Ryan can do a pretty good job. Let's stay with this Paris flight. We're not whipped yet."

·III·

SAN DIEGO

FEBRUARY, 1927

THE RYAN AIRLINES factory is an old, dilapidated building near the waterfront. I feel conspicuous driving up to it in a taxicab. A couple of loafers stare at me as I pay my fare. There's no flying field, no hangar, no sound of engines warming up; and the unmistakable smell of dead fish from a near-by cannery mixes with the banana odor of dope from drying wings. What a change in weather! It was sleeting when I left St. Louis. Here, on the 23rd of February, palm leaves flutter in warm wind and sun.

I open the door to a small, dusty, paper-strewn office. A slender young man advances to meet me — clear, piercing eyes, intent face. He introduces himself as Donald Hall, chief engineer for Ryan Airlines, Incorporated. Another young man moves up beside him. He is Walter Locke, in charge of the purchasing department. Within a few minutes, A. J. Edwards, sales manager, arrives — genial, stockily built.

B. F. Mahoney, president of the company, is broad-shouldered, smiling, young — in his late twenties, I judge.

"Before we get down to talking business," Mahoney says after shaking hands, "we'd like you to see what we're doing in the factory."

He opens a door at the back of the office and we step down onto the factory floor. One of the workmen is welding a steel tube in place on a fuselage skeleton in front of us. A half-dozen men are scattered about, splicing cables, drilling holes, installing instruments and levers, attending to the infinite details of aircraft construction.

"Here's Hawley Bowlus, our factory manager." A lanky fellow with curly, brown hair extends his hand. Workmen glance up from their jobs — sizing me up, no doubt, as a prospective customer. Another plane sold? A few more weeks of pay secure? A small aviation company like this must live from hand to mouth.

"This is Bert Tindale, shop superintendent. Mr. McNeal, here, has charge of final assembly. Mr. Anderson does our welding. Mr. Morrow is our fitting expert, and Mr. Rohr takes care of tanks and cowlings." We shake hands as the introductions are made.

"Our fuselages are all tubular steel," Mahoney explains. "We use wood wing-spars and ribs."

We climb upstairs, past a gold-pigmented fuselage, to a big loft of a room on the second, and top, floor. Two men are fitting ribs to spars of straight-grained spruce. Another is brushing into a cotton-clothed aileron its second coat of dope.

"Captain Lindbergh, this is Mr. Fred Ayers. We depend on him for all our covering and finishing." Mahoney thumps his fingers on a rudder's fabric while we exchange greetings. "Look at that construction," he continues, pointing to the framework. "It's strong and it's simple. You can hardly believe how much that wing will lift – – – Well, you've seen about all of our establishment. Shall we go back to the office and talk things over?"

We start downstairs. I count the fuselages under construction — two in framework stage, one about ready for its wing — not much business to keep a factory going.

"Mr. Mahoney has just bought full ownership of Ryan Airlines," the sales manager confides to me. "We'll probably change the name to the 'B. F. Mahoney Aircraft Corporation.'"

"Where do you test your planes?" I ask.

"Our flying field is at Dutch Flats," Edwards answers. "It's out on the edge of the city. We put the wing on a truck and tow the fuselage behind."

"The field isn't very big," Mahoney adds, "but it gets by, and it's convenient. We'll take you out there later on. You'll want to meet Harrigan and Kelly; they're our pilots."

"Have a chair." We sit down on desks and tables. There's a moment of silence.

"Well, we'd like to build your plane," Mahoney says. "What do you think of our proposition?"

"Your telegram quoted a price of $6000, without engine," I reply. "How much would that make the cost, complete?"

"We quoted the price that way because we didn't know what you'd want in the way of engine and equipment," Mahoney tells me. "It includes standard instruments and oversize fuel tanks. If we put in a J-4 Whirlwind and use our regular instruments, the completed price would run between nine and ten thousand dollars. If you want one of the Wright Corporation's new J-5 engines, it would run $10,000 or better. We can't give an exact figure until we know what you want us to put in."

"I'd much rather fly a J-5," I say. "They develop a little more power, and their rocker-arms are enclosed. I want a metal propeller, and I've got to have a turn and bank indicator. Maybe a fuel-flow meter would pay for its weight. And I'd like to carry an earth-inductor compass; I understand it's easier to hold a course with one of them. I'll need good instruments — the best we can get."

"That's just it," Mahoney answers. "There's no way for us to make an estimate. I'll tell you what we'll do. We'll give you the engine and all the extra equipment we buy for just what it costs us. We're interested in this flight too. We won't take any commission on the extras."

"That's fair enough. How about performance? Are you sure you can build a plane that will take off with enough fuel for the flight?"

"We've spent quite a bit of time studying the problem since you wired us you were coming out here," he replies. "We know it's a tough job, but we believe we can do it. We'd put a big tank in the mail compartment, and add a few feet to the wing span. But you'd better talk to Donald Hall about that. He made the calculations."

"If we place our order with your company, will you guarantee to give us a plane with range enough to fly from New York to Paris?"

Mahoney shifts his weight uncomfortably on the table.

"I don't see how we can do that," he says. "The risks are too high. It isn't as though we were a big company with a lot of money in the bank. We aren't going to make any profit on this plane anyway, and we can't afford to take a loss – – – the price doesn't leave us any margin for a guarantee. We'll put everything we've got into it. We'll do the best we can. But at $6000 we can't go overboard on guarantees."

"How soon could you start building the plane?" I ask.

"We'd put some of our workmen on it as soon as you place the order," Mahoney replies.

"Do you feel sure we could depend on delivery in two months?"

"We think we can build it in less time, but I wouldn't want to promise."

It's increasingly obvious that the answer to my problem lies in Donald Hall, the engineer. My decision as to whether the Ryan company is capable of building a plane with the performance I need must depend primarily on my estimate of him.

"I think the next step is for me to talk to your engineer about some of the details of construction."

"All right," Mahoney agrees. "You probably won't want us around. Why don't you and Hall go off somewhere together?"

2

Hall and I are in his bare but spacious drafting room next to the wing loft.

"Now we can't use the standard Ryan fuselage," he says. "Also, the wing span will have to be considerably increased so as to reduce the wing loading for take-off and increase the aspect ratio for range. That means we'll have to move the tail surfaces aft to maintain satisfactory stability and control. And that means the engine will have to be moved forward. When it comes right down to it,

I've really got to design a completely new fuselage structure to meet your requirements. We will have to design a different type of landing gear while we're about it," he continues. "The M-2 type of gear would be too heavy when it's designed to go with the longer wing span and to take the load you're going to carry. Here's the type of landing gear I favor for your airplane – – –"

Hall begins to sketch.

"It won't take long to build, and one like this is structurally sound. The loads are efficiently carried to the fuselage, and the wheels are outside of the slipstream — that will cut down the drag." A slightly lopsided monoplane is taking form on the sheet of paper in front of us. "My preliminary calculations indicate that ten feet will have to be added to the wing span to get the airplane off the ground in a reasonable distance with a full fuel load," Hall goes on. "That will increase the range too, of course – – – Say, you know the Clark-Y is a good airfoil – – – The main gas tank will have to be located under the wing, in the fuselage, with its center of gravity close to that of the airplane. Now, where are we going to put the cockpits for you and the navigator?"

"I only want one cockpit," I reply. "I'll do the navigating myself."

"You don't plan on making that flight alone, do you?" Hall looks at me, rather startled. "I — I thought you'd need somebody to navigate and be relief pilot. I — I thought it would be much too long for one pilot."

"I've thought about it a good deal," I tell him, "and I believe the chances of success are better with one pilot than with two. I'd rather have extra gasoline than an extra man."

Hall's mind picks up the idea instantly: "Well, of course that would be a big help from the standpoint of weight and performance — particularly range. That would keep the length of the fuselage down to a more reasonable figure. It would probably save about 350 pounds. That's at least fifty gallons more fuel, including tank weight. That would give you a good reserve. I was worried about the reserve you're going to have – – – But are you sure one pilot, alone, can make a flight like that? It's going to be something like forty hours in the air, you know. Say, exactly how far is it between New York and Paris by the route you're going to follow?"

"It's about 3500 miles. We could get a pretty close check by scaling it off a globe. Do you know where there is one?"

"There's a globe at the public library. It only takes a few minutes to drive there. I've got to know what the distance is before I can make any accurate calculations. My car's right outside."

We climb into a rusting, black Buick roadster and head downtown.

"It's 3600 statute miles." The bit of white grocery string under my fingers stretches taut along the coast of North America, bends down over a faded blue ocean, and strikes — about at right angles — the land mass of Europe. It isn't a very scientific way of finding the exact distance between two points on the earth's surface, but the answer is accurate enough for our first calculations.

"I assumed that the airplane ought to carry fuel for 4000 miles in still air," Hall says. "Maybe that isn't enough. You may want to follow the ship lanes. Suppose you run into a head wind – – –"

"I'm going to fly straight," I tell him. "I don't plan on detouring at all. What's the use flying extra hours over water just to follow the ship lanes? If I run into a head wind, I'll turn back and try again. If the plane can make 4000 miles in still air, that's plenty. That's 400 miles reserve plus whatever tail wind I pick up. I won't start without a tail wind."

Hall is figuring on the back of an envelope again.

"Maybe we'd better put in 400 gallons of gasoline instead of 380," he concludes.

3

"We quoted a price of $6000 without engine, and we're going to deliver a plane that will do the job for that price. If it takes a different fuselage and landing gear, we'll build them."

Mahoney leans forward in his office chair. He speaks slowly, seriously. Hall has just finished describing the changes he wants to make in the Ryan M-2 design in order to achieve a range of 4000 miles.

"We can't afford to waste any money," Mahoney says; "but don't forget that the company's reputation goes along with this plane ――― Can you make those changes and still get it built in sixty days?"

"It will be a real job; but I think we can if — if the men will put in a lot of overtime," Hall replies.

"All right, let's get under way as fast as we can." Mahoney turns to me. "You give us the order, and we'll start," he says. "That will make $10,580, with a J-5 engine — special equipment extra, at cost."

4

WESTERN
UNION

SAN DIEGO CALIFORNIA
FEB. 24 1927

HARRY H. KNIGHT
401 OLIVE ST.
ST. LOUIS, MO.
BELIEVE RYAN CAPABLE OF BUILDING PLANE WITH
SUFFICIENT PERFORMANCE STOP COST COMPLETE WITH
WHIRLWIND ENGINE AND STANDARD INSTRUMENTS IS TEN
THOUSAND FIVE HUNDRED EIGHTY DOLLARS STOP DELIVERY
WITHIN SIXTY DAYS STOP RECOMMEND CLOSING DEAL

LINDBERGH

I check wording and hand my telegram to the girl in the office. I'm ready to cast my lot with the Ryan organization. I believe in Hall's ability; I like Mahoney's enthusiasm. I have confidence in the character of the workmen I've met. This company is a fit partner for our organization in St. Louis. They're as anxious to build a plane that will fly to Paris as I am to fly it there.

5

```
WESTERN
UNION
                                    ST. LOUIS, MO.
                                    FEB. 25, 1927
C. A. LINDBERGH
CARE RYAN AIRLINES, INC.
3200 BARNETT AVE.
SAN DIEGO, CALIF.
YOUR WIRE STOP SUGGEST YOU CLOSE WITH RYAN FOLLOWING
TERMS - - -
```

It's from Harry Knight: the deal is closed. The chafing, frustrating weeks of hunting, first for finance and then for a plane, are over. I can turn my attention to the flight itself — to the design and construction of the plane, to outfitting it with instruments and emergency equipment, to studying navigation and the weather conditions I'm likely to encounter along the route I follow.

Aside from the loss of time, there are great advantages in building a new plane instead of buying a standard model. Every part of it can be designed for a single purpose, every line fashioned to the Paris flight. I can inspect each detail before it's covered with fabric and fairings. And by knowing intimately both the strengths and weaknesses of my plane, I'll be able to tax the one and relieve the other according to conditions which arise. By working closely with the engineer, I can build my own experience into the plane's structure, and make the utmost use of the theories he expounds.

6

"There are several items we've got to decide on before I can go ahead with the design."

Donald Hall and I sit down on the long, curving beach at Coronado Strand. It's pleasantly warm in the morning sun.

"Where are we going to put the cockpit?"

"I'd like to have it behind the gas tank — about where it is in the M-2," I reply.

"But then you couldn't see straight ahead," he argues. "The tanks would be directly in front of you. I thought you would want to sit behind the engine so as to have the best possible vision."

"You know we always look out at an angle when we take off," I tell him. "The nose of the fuselage blocks out the field straight ahead, anyway. Some of the mail pilots even have their windshield painted black to cut down reflection at night. I don't need straight forward vision – – – "

"I'm not referring to take-off," Hall says. "I know the engine blocks out forward vision like a barn door while the airplane is in a high angle of attack attitude — I've done a little piloting myself. I'm thinking of forward vision in normal flight."

"There's not much need to see ahead in normal flight," I reply. "I won't be following any airways. When I'm near a flying field, I can watch the sky ahead by making shallow banks. Why don't we leave the cockpit in the rear, and fair it in? All I need is a window on each side to see out through. The top of the fuselage could be the top of the cockpit. A cockpit like that wouldn't add any resistance at all. I think we ought to give first consideration to efficiency in flight; second, to protection in a crack-up; third, to pilot comfort. I don't see why a cockpit in the rear doesn't cover all three. Besides, I don't like the idea of being sandwiched in between the engine and a gas tank the way you are up forward. If you crack up you haven't got a chance in a place like that. A compass won't work as well, either, close to the engine. I've got to have an accurate compass on this flight."

"All right. The cockpit goes in the rear, then," Hall says. "You're going to be the pilot. I'll depend on your judgment about things like that. I wouldn't want to sit in front of a big gas tank myself. You remember what happened to the old British-type DH-4s, or flying coffins, with the pilot between the engine and the gas tank, and the observer aft? They were built in this country during the war, for the Army. I recall the 1919 transcontinental air

race, with about forty DH-4s among other types starting. Seven
of them cracked up in forced landings. All seven pilots died, and
all seven observers lived – – – Say, an enclosed cockpit that doesn't
have any projections from the fuselage ought to increase the cruising speed two or three miles an hour. We might pick up an extra
hundred miles of range that way – – – But what are you going to
use the airplane for later on? The passenger arrangement won't be
as good with the pilot behind."

"I know it won't be as good a passenger plane," I reply, "but
if we're going to break the world's record for distance, we've got
to put range above everything else. I haven't even thought about
what to do with the plane after I land at Paris; and I'm not
going to until I get there – – –"

"Okay. Now what night-flying equipment do you want to put
in the plane?"

"None. Those things are nice to have, but we can't afford the
weight."

"How about a parachute?"

"Same answer," I reply. "That would cost almost twenty
pounds."

Hall makes some notes on his pad. "Well, if you don't have
to carry those things, it will make it a lot easier for me," he says.
"Say, I'm not satisfied with the size of the M-2 tail surfaces. They
ought to be bigger for a heavy-load take-off, and to get good
stability in cruising flight. The trouble is I just don't have time to
design new tail surfaces and get the plane built in two months."

"Do you think it would be dangerous to use the M-2 surfaces?"
I ask.

"No, not for an experienced pilot," Hall replies. "But I'd
rather do a first-class job all the way around. The stability just
won't be as good as I'd like to have it."

"Wouldn't bigger surfaces cut down the range?"

"A little, but not very much."

"Let's put everything into range," I say. "I don't need a very
stable plane. I'll have to be watching the compass all the time

anyway. I don't plan on going to sleep while I fly. Besides, we can't afford to spend time on anything that isn't essential."

"All right; that's decided then. Now it's time to talk about range."

We agree to eliminate from our calculations the uncertainties of wind along the route, and to plan our reserves on the basis that it will neither hinder us nor help. We conclude that the minimum requirement for fuel will be enough to fly between New York and Paris over the great-circle route in still air. Of course to do that in actual practice requires a theoretical reserve. An engine in flight doesn't operate with perfect settings, and a pilot doesn't navigate with perfect accuracy, or plan on landing with his tanks dry. We decide that the plane should be designed around a theoretical range of 4000 miles, as Hall originally suggested.

"Well, Charlie, I think we can freeze the design now," Hall tells me. "I'll make a preliminary layout of the general arrangement and show it to you. There isn't going to be much left of the M-2 design, except the wing ribs and the tail surfaces. I want to start on the weight and balance analyses, and I'll have to follow them with the wing and fuselage stress analyses. Then I've got to get the drawings of the wing and fuselage structures out as fast as I can so the shop can start work."

7

The drafting-room door knob rattles. We've got the lock turned. There are loud bangs.

"Don't you fellows ever quit work?" Mahoney asks as I let him in. "Say, where do you keep the key to this door? I might want to get in here some night."

"There isn't any key," Hall tells him, "at least not since I've been working here. We use a hacksaw blade to get in — just slip it through the crack there, and push."

Mahoney laughs and shakes his head. "I've brought up the paper," he says. "There's an article you may want to see. Well, I've got to be downtown in fifteen minutes. Good night."

WANAMAKER BEHIND NEW YORK-PARIS FLIGHT

WILL FINANCE BYRD VENTURE

WITH $100,000

May Race with Fonck

NEW YORK, March 2.—Rodman Wanamaker, who once financed a project to fly the Atlantic ocean which was prevented by the war, will back Commander Byrd's attempt to fly non-stop from New York to Paris next spring. A huge three-engined Fokker monoplane, now under construction, is to be used for the trip. It is expected that the machine will be ready by May, which is the earliest month weather conditions will be suitable for a transatlantic flight.

In carrying out his project, Commander Byrd will make use of the most advanced instruments and navigational devices known to science.

(This is the most definite and comprehensive story about the Paris flight I've seen. I continue reading.)

This spring may see a race between American and French pilots for the honor of being first to fly between New York and Paris. The Sikorsky Company announced recently that a big plane was being built for the Atlantic flight. Although company officials would not comment, it is reported that the pilot will be Capt. Rene Fonck, the French ace who crashed on Roosevelt Field on an attempted take-off for Paris last September.

A number of American pilots, including Commander Noel Davis, are known to be planning on competing for the Orteig prize of $25,000 which will be awarded to the first aviator to fly between New York and Paris without stopping. Charles A. Lindbergh, a St. Louis mail pilot, has filed the latest entry, according to the National Aeronautic Association. He will pilot a single-engined Ryan monoplane, and plans to make the flight alone.

On the European side of the ocean, it is understood that transatlantic planes are being constructed in France, England, and Italy.

I fold the paper and stand up.

"We'd better go get some supper." I say it firmly.

Donald Hall straightens on his stool. Pencil lines curve and angle delicately over the face of his drafting board's white sheet. A fuselage is taking outline form. He's been sitting on that stool since early morning, with no break except for quick meals and a few trips downstairs to talk to Bowlus and the workmen. It was the same yesterday, and the day before.

"You've been here long enough," I tell him. "A fellow can work so hard that he loses time, you know."

"I *have* to get these drawings done, Charlie," he explains. "They're holding everything up. Bowlus can't start work on the plane until he gets them. All he can do is assemble some of the material and order a few parts." Hall hangs his T square on its nail and stretches his body stiffly. "I've got to have some sleep tonight, though, and I think I can finish the first drawing in the morning."

We close windows, turn off lights, make sure all factory doors are locked, and climb into his roadster.

"Don, don't you think you ought to set a regular pace at this work?" I suggest, while we're eating at the café counter. "A fellow can't think as clearly without sleep."

"I know. I'll get some rest as soon as I get ahead of the shop," he says vaguely. "Say, we ought to have some kind of ventilation in the cockpit if you're going to fly with the windows closed." Then, pulling his mind away from design with obvious effort, he comes back to my question. "I'll go for a hike through the mountains this week end. Did you ever hike through the mountains? It's the best way of getting a rest I know. Last summer, I went hiking up in the — — — Say, do you want gauges on your gasoline tanks, Charlie?"

"No. That would mean extra pounds, and they never seem to work. I'll measure fuel consumption with my watch."

8

How does one navigate along a great circle, crossing 3600 miles of earth and ocean? I've never made an over-water flight before. In fact, I've never really done any long-distance flying at all. Not one of the planes I've piloted in the past was capable of five hundred miles nonstop without a strong tail wind. My navigation has always been carried out on maps which I checked with landmarks on the ground. There were lakes, towns, bends in rivers, and railroad tracks to tell me when I was on my route or how far I'd drifted from it. At night, on the mail, there were familiar lights below. Flying the Atlantic will be different. I'll have to use navigation like that of ships at sea. I'll have to change my heading by time and theory instead of by railroad tracks and rivers. How do ship captains find their destined harbors after sailing for weeks out of sight of land? Of course they take sextant sights on the sun and stars. Why can't I do that too? And they have radio to help them. Maybe I can carry a set in the *Spirit of St. Louis* — if it's not to heavy. How does one lay out a great-circle route? Does it require much knowledge of mathematics? Where can I find out about such things?

I could undoubtedly get the information I need from some of the naval officers stationed at San Diego, but I hesitate to ask them for advice. There's enough skepticism about my flight now, without adding to it by showing how inexperienced I am in the technique of long-distance navigation. Most men already look at me askance when they hear of my plans, and shake their heads when they learn that I intend to go alone. They say I'm attempting the impossible, that I'm too young to realize what I'm undertaking, and that someone with authority should stop my flight. That attitude, if carried far enough, might even affect the officers of the Ryan Company and the workmen in the shop. It could put my partners in St. Louis in a false position of responsibility. It could add greatly to my problems, and cause all kinds of trouble. No, it's essential to maintain an atmosphere of experience and capability concerning every detail of my flight. I can't afford to inquire openly about such an elementary procedure as the construction of a great-circle course. Well, San Diego is an ocean port. There'll be ship chandlers on the waterfront, where stocks of charts are carried. I'll go there first and see what I can buy.

9

"I want a set of charts covering the North Atlantic Ocean," I tell the clerk. He looks up in obvious surprise.

"The *Atlantic*? Sorry, we supply only Pacific shipping. You might get Atlantic charts at San Pedro. We've never had a request for them before."

That means a trip up north. I'll try to borrow one of the Ryan Company's monoplanes.

10

The store at San Pedro has drawers of charts that apparently cover all the earth's salt water.

"I think these are what you want."

The salesman pulls out two oblong sheets. They're Mercator's projections and — yes, I'm in luck — they extend inland far enough to include New York and Paris. Then, like stumbling over a nugget of gold, I see a gnomonic projection covering them both. "A great circle on the earth's surface translates into a curve on a Mercator's chart, but it becomes a straight line on a gnomonic projection" — I remember learning that in the Army's navigation class. Why? Because all maps are distorted in one way or another. You can't just skim the surface off a globe and flatten it out neatly on a table.

Rummaging around still farther, I locate a time-zone chart of the world, a chart of magnetic variation, and others showing prevailing winds over the Atlantic for April, May, and June. I buy them all.

For crossing the continent to St. Louis and New York, I know of nothing better than the Rand McNally railroad maps one can buy at any first-class drugstore, for fifty cents per state.

11

Donald Hall has cleared off a table for my use in his drafting room. It's a dusty, uninspiring place, with damp-spotted walls and unshaded light bulb hanging down on a wire cord from the ceiling's center. Divergent factory noises mingle with the odors of dope and fish, and on rainy days a bucket has to be placed on the floor to catch dripping water. But there's enough room to spread out sheets of charts and drawings; and, locked in, we work in relative seclusion.

My navigating problems have begun to clarify. I found, printed on the charts I bought, ample instructions for laying out my great-circle route. With the instruments Hall loaned me, I drew a straight line between New York and Paris on the gnomonic projection. Then I transferred points from that line, at hundred-mile intervals, to the Mercator's projection, and connected these points with straight lines. At each point, I marked down the distance from New York and the magnetic course to the next change in angle. I chose hundred-mile intervals as convenient distances to work with because, wind and cruising speed considered, it seems likely that the *Spirit of St. Louis* will cover about that distance each hour. Since there's no way to be sure, one might as well choose a convenient figure. Now, I have my route inked in and its time zones measured off. The distance scales at exactly 3610 miles.

I stand looking down at the completed chart. It's fascinating, that curving, polygonic line, cutting fearlessly over thousands of miles of continent and ocean. Independent of the world it seems — just as I was independent of the world that moonlit night in September when I conceived this flight to Paris. It curves gracefully northward through New England, Nova Scotia, and Newfoundland, eastward over the Atlantic, down past the southern tip of Ireland, across a narrow strip of England, until at last it ends sharply at the little dot inside of France marked "Paris."

What freedom lies in flying! What godlike power it gives to man! I'm independent of the seaman's coast lines, of the landsman's roads; I could as well have drawn that line north to the Arctic, or westward over the Pacific, or southeast to jungles of the Amazon. I'm like a magician concocting magic formulae. The symbols I pluck from paper, applied to the card of a compass held straight by rudder and stick, will take me to any acre on the earth where I choose to go.

But laying out that course seems too simple to justify building my entire project on its accuracy. After all, when everything else has been done, when the *Spirit of St. Louis* has been built, tested, and paid for, when I've made the final take-off from New York with enough fuel in the tanks to reach Paris, then success, reputation, life itself will depend on the correctness of that curving black line and the numerals I've marked along its edges. I'd feel better if I could get some check on my work, some confirmation of my figures and my angles.

The public library downtown has texts on navigation that give detailed instruction about spherical mathematics. I decide to lay a second route across the ocean by trigonometry. But it's not as easy to find great-circle latitudes and longitudes through logarithmic formulae as it is to pick them off charts. Even after I learn the procedure, it takes a long time to work out each position, and there are thirty-six of them in all. After spending several days at this task, I reach a point in the Atlantic twelve hundred miles beyond the coast of Newfoundland. My mathematical route and my charted route coincide so closely that it seems time wasted to continue with the calculations. I have satisfied myself that the headings I marked on the Mercator's projections are correct; and there are other problems which demand attention.

Now that I have my courses laid out properly, I must be sure I can hold them — over the ocean — over fog — at night — and with unknown wind drifts.

Should I buy a sextant and study celestial navigation? But could I handle a sextant at the same time I'm flying a plane? That at least is something I can ask the naval officers on North Island — no one expects an airplane pilot to know much about celestial navigation. I can also ask them about the radio sets they use. The next question is how to make contact with the Navy.

12

"You might get a sun-line, but I don't think you can hold a sextant steady enough to take a bubble sight at the same time you fly the plane. You ought to carry a navigator on a flight like that."

A blue-uniformed officer has come to see the *Spirit of St. Louis.* Insignia and stripes of gold mark a rank I do not know. But here's a source of information I can tap.

"How much do your aircraft radios weigh, and how far can you get direction with a loop?" I ask.

"I can't answer those questions," he tells me. "Radio isn't my specialty. But why don't you come out to North Island and visit us? I'll introduce you to the experts there."

13

I find that naval radios are much too heavy for my single-engined plane, and that their value on a flight like mine is doubtful. The more I study the problem, the more I realize that I'll have to rely on dead reckoning for my navigation, and that a successful flight will depend primarily on the reserve of fuel the *Spirit of St. Louis* can carry. After I tell Hall the result of my studies, we decide to increase the tank capacity to 425 gallons — we'll trade radio and sextant weight for extra gasoline. What I lose in navigational accuracy I hope to gain twice over in total range.

"How difficult would it be to design the landing gear so I could drop it in flight?" I ask.

"We could do that. Of course it would weigh a few pounds more," Hall tells me. "But you'd crack up landing, Charlie!"

"Not badly. It might get the prop, but if I landed on sod, I don't think the fuselage and wings would be damaged much — with a light load. If the margins are close, it might make the difference between success and failure. It might even save the plane."

"Well, that would give us a lot of extra range," Hall says. "But suppose you had to turn back after you cut loose the gear?"

We discuss methods of dropping a landing gear from the air,

so that it would break free cleanly without danger of injuring any part of the plane. Hall's not happy about the idea, and neither am I. We decide to put it in the back of our minds, as an emergency reserve, in case more accurate performance calculations prove disappointing.

I have divided my reserves for the flight into two categories. The first I class as reserves for success; the second, as reserves for failure. I depend on my reserves for success to land me on the aerodrome at Le Bourget. I depend on my reserves for failure to let me live if I can't get through to Paris, and, if possible, to save my plane. They will be kept in the background.

Extra fuel is my greatest reserve for success. With it, I can ride through night and detour storms. Prevailing westerly winds form a reserve which costs me nothing. And the long coast line of Europe — I can be hundreds of miles off course when I strike it, and still reach Paris.

The ability to turn back is my greatest reserve for failure. For more than a thousand miles after I leave New York I'll be within easy reach of land. If weather becomes too thick, if I encounter head winds, or if some fluctuating gauge or engine roughness indicates danger, I can turn back and start the flight again. Here, too, the amount of fuel I carry may be of top importance.

But suppose my engine fails over the Atlantic, what emergency equipment shall I take with me? Is it wise to carry *any* equipment for a forced landing on the ocean; or would that simply be a self-deceiving gesture — actually a detriment to safety? Under such conditions, could anything I carry save my life? It's a problem to which I can find no clear-cut answer. Safety at the start of my flight means holding down weight for the take-off. Safety during my flight requires plenty of emergency equipment. Safety at the end of my flight demands an ample reserve of fuel. It's impossible to increase safety at one point without detracting from it at another. I must weigh all these elements in my mind, and attempt to strike some balance. In each instance, I'll try to buoy life with hope, no matter how faint that hope may be.

I decide to buy a small, black-rubber raft that's displayed in the window of a sporting-goods store downtown, which stripped of its oars, weighs only ten pounds. Should I carry a rubberized sheet to keep out wind and spray when I'm in the raft? No, I can use fabric from the wing for that. I'll need a knife for cutting. I mark it down on my list. A big knife with a fixed blade would be best in emergency, held by a cold or injured hand. Of course if I land in the ocean, I'll get soaked, and it's doubtful that I'll ever get dry again. I must dress to stay as warm as possible in wet clothing. That means wool material, no cotton or leather — except my shoes.

Even if a ship did pass nearby, it could hardly see a little raft floating in the waves. Suppose it passed at night — I ought to take some flares. At best, it's not likely that I'd be found quickly, so I'll have to carry some water and some food. Water weighs an awful lot — eight pounds a gallon, plus container. I've heard that a man named Armbrust has invented a device that condenses moisture from the breath, which can be drunk again — possibly I can buy one.

14

A stamp collector has offered me a thousand dollars to carry one pound of mail to Paris in the *Spirit of St. Louis!* I reread his letter: yes, a single pound. He has seen newspaper notices about my project. I don't understand it; I don't see why anybody is willing to pay so much money for a few souvenir envelopes and stamps. A thousand dollars would help our financing quite a lot; and maybe there are other ways of earning money that I haven't thought about. But the principle involved — I've determined to hold down every ounce of excess weight. If I once start compromising, I won't know where to stop. Still — one pound — a thousand dollars — — — I'll write to my partners about it.

15

LEGION BACKS DAVIS NEW YORK-PARIS FLIGHT

PLANE TO HAVE 4,600 MILE RANGE

MARCH 14.—Lieut. Commander Noel Davis plans to take off from Mitchell Field, Long Island, in June for a non-stop flight to Paris. He will fly a Keystone Pathfinder biplane with additional fuel tanks in the fuselage which will give a flying radius of fifty-four hours. The big ship will be powered with three Wright Whirlwind engines.

The plane to be flown by Commander Davis will be christened "The American Legion." Members of the Legion will contribute to the cost of the flight, which will be about $100,000.

Commander Davis, who is one of the most experienced aviators and aerial navigators in the United States, will not leave anything to chance. He will use a sextant of his own invention - - -

The Huff-Daland Company must have changed its name to Keystone. I wonder if Davis's *American Legion* is the stripped-down bomber that General Patrick authorized the company to sell — redesigned for an extra engine in the nose. Every few days a new article about the progress of New York-to-Paris projects appears in the paper. I'm clearly in a race against time, with odds against me.

The construction of the *Spirit of St. Louis* moves along as fast as Hall can produce drawings from his board. Bowlus starts work on less important items without waiting for drawings. Everyone is taking a personal interest in my flight; hours of overtime labor have become normal and voluntary. Hall often goes to the factory at five o'clock in the morning to inspect the previous day's progress before the men arrive. Work on other planes has almost stopped. It's less than three weeks since I arrived in San Diego, yet skeletons of the fuselage and wing have taken form.

I've completed my general plans of navigation. My study brings out four critical points on the flight: First, my take-off with full tanks of fuel. Second, my check-out on the coast of Newfoundland. Third, my landfall on European shores. Fourth, my landing at Le Bourget. I can only be sure of covering two of these points in daylight. The most important is the take-off — I must be able to see for that. The next is to locate my position accurately before starting over the ocean.

I'll take off from New York at daybreak. That will give me sunlight for my overloaded hours, and put me over Newfoundland before dusk. It should let me strike Ireland before nightfall of the second day. I'll have to find Paris and land on Le Bourget after dark. Of course I'll be a little tired by that time; but I'll have a lightly loaded plane. And there's the moon — if weather and competition don't interfere too much with my take-off date, I can arrive above Europe when it's close to full. I think I could even locate my position at night if I make a landfall in clear weather, under a full moon. The third week in June would be an ideal time to start — the longest days of the year, and brilliant moonlight.

Hall is busy computing more accurate performance curves. He now estimates the theoretical range of the *Spirit of St. Louis* to be 4100 miles, at the most economical cruising speeds. Even with no help from wind, that would put me over Paris with 500 miles of fuel in my tanks — a reserve to ease the mind of any pilot.

To get maximum range, of course, throttle and mixture controls must be correctly set. It would help a lot if I had an instrument in the cockpit which would show my exact consumption of gasoline with each different adjustment of the engine. I've tried to get such an instrument both through the Army and through commercial companies, without success. Apparently there is no satisfactory fuel-flow meter for aircraft. So I'm designing one myself. It's light and simple, and maybe it will work.

16

NUNGESSER TO FLY ATLANTIC

FRENCH ACE ANNOUNCES
PARIS TO NEW YORK FLIGHT
THIS SUMMER

PARIS, March 26.—Captain Charles Nungesser, one of the top aces of the World War, said today that he would pilot a French-built plane across the Atlantic this summer. He will be accompanied by Lieut. Coli, the famous one-eyed airman, as co-pilot and navigator. M. Coli has been working on plans for a transatlantic flight for the last two years. The machine they expect to use will have a single 450-horsepower engine, and carry 800 gallons of gasoline.

I lay the evening paper down on the restaurant counter. That makes the fourth New York-Paris project besides my own, to be definitely announced — Byrd, Fonck, Davis, Nungesser. And Chamberlin is almost certainly getting the Bellanca ready. He's in the best position to be first to start. I wonder if he'll try to break the world's endurance record before taking off for Paris. I pay the waitress for my supper, and start on a walk along the waterfront.

17

WESTERN
UNION

ST. LOUIS MO. MAR. 28, 27
CHARLES A. LINDBERGH
CARE RYAN AIRLINES INC.
SAN DIEGO, CALIF.

CHANGES IN WING AREA AND LOADING APPROVED STOP
COMMITTEE ADVISES THAT THEY HAVE A RUMOR THAT YOU
INTEND TO DROP LANDING GEAR WHICH THEY DO NOT
APPROVE PLEASE ADVISE

                        HARRY H. KNIGHT

That means our formal entry has just been accepted by the Contest Committee of the National Aeronautic Association —

they administer the rules for the Orteig prize. I mailed our application a month ago, but the committee wanted more definite information than I could furnish then about the plane I was going to fly, and my intended point of take-off from New York. Sixty days must elapse between a pilot's entry and his flight, according to the regulations. That means I won't be eligible until the end of May. If I start before that, and get to Paris, we'll lose twenty-five thousand dollars!

I send a return wire, saying that I do not intend to drop the landing gear, and that the *Spirit of St. Louis* will be ready for its test flights sometime in April.

18

When the Whirlwind engine arrives from Paterson, we gather around the wooden crate as though some statue were to be unveiled. It's like a huge jewel, lying there set in its wrappings. We marvel at the quality of cosmoline-painted parts. Here is the ultimate in lightness of weight and power — two hundred and twenty-three horses compressed into nine delicate, fin-covered cylinders of aluminum and steel. On this intricate perfection I'm to trust my life across the Atlantic Ocean.

The inner organs of this engine — its connecting rods, cams, gears, and bearings — will be turning over many hundred times each minute — sparks jumping, teeth meshing, pistons stopping and reversing at incomprehensible speeds. And I'm demanding that this procedure continue for forty hours if need be, for all the 3610 miles between New York and Paris! It seems beyond the ability of any mechanism to withstand such a strain, yet — I force myself back to reality — Whirlwinds are flying on the mail lines for thousands of hours between failures. And this engine, the Wright Corporation says, has had a special inspection.

19

It's early April. Word has gotten around San Diego about the plane we're building for a flight across the Atlantic Ocean. Two or three reporters have come to talk to me about it. Short articles

have appeared in the city's papers. Each week brings more visitors
to our factory. This afternoon several naval aviation officers from
North Island stop by. Since I have my preparations well in hand,
I take time off to show them various parts of the *Spirit of St. Louis,*
and tell them about the flight I'm planning. As they leave, they
invite me to give an address at the Naval Air Station some evening,
on the subject of long-distance aerial navigation. Imagine! The very
men to whom I'd have gone for advice, had I not feared making a
display of my ignorance, asking *me* to give *them* a lecture on navigation! Do I have enough knowledge and ability now to do this?
As far as the use of dead reckoning on the flights between San
Diego and Paris is concerned, I've studied it intensively, and laid
out my charts with detailed care. If I confine myself to these items,
I'll be on solid ground. And these men from North Island can give
me much assistance in the future. There's little to lose and much
to gain by accepting.

20

The lecture turns out to be less difficult than I expected. The
naval officers are as fine a group of men as I've ever met —
courteous, genial, intelligent. They are greatly interested in my
plans; and since none of them has studied such a long flight before,
I find myself in the enviable position of a speaker who knows his
subject better than anyone else present.

"Why did you select a monoplane for the trip?" one of the
officers asks.

"It's more efficient than a biplane, there's more room in the
wing for gasoline, and it can carry more ice," I tell him.

"What kind of charts do you intend to use?" a lieutenant commander queries.

"The same as you carry on ships at sea, after I leave the coast
line," I answer.

"Suppose you strike a wind change in the night, and it drifts
you far off course?"

"A navigating error wouldn't be too serious; this flight isn't like shooting for an island. I can't very well miss the entire European coast."

They all laugh at that.

"When do you plan on starting?"

"I hope to leave San Diego sometime in April," I reply.

"Ideally, I'd like to take off from New York in June, when the moon is full. That would give me a minimum of darkness."

As I outline the reserves I'm establishing and the high performance we expect to obtain from the *Spirit of St. Louis,* even the skeptics apparently begin to feel that the flight may be within realms of possibility — not a purely suicidal venture.

21

PARIS PLANE TESTED

AMERICAN LEGION SHOWS HIGH SPEED IN SURPRISE FLIGHT

BRISTOL, PENN., Apr. 9.—Lieut. Commander Noel Davis took his Keystone Pathfinder biplane, the American Legion, off on its maiden flight here today, with Lieut. Stanton H. Wooster at his side as co-pilot. The speed with which his big ship has been constructed was a surprise to everyone who has been watching the progress of the various transatlantic flight projects. It threw consternation into the camps of his rivals.

"The plane handles beautifully," Commander Davis said. "But we want to test it thoroughly: we are not going to leave anything to chance."

Meanwhile, construction is progressing rapidly on the trimotored Fokker with which Commander Richard E. Byrd expects to make a non-stop flight between New York and Paris next month. Commander Byrd's plane will be christened the "America" – – –

Commander Byrd emphasized the fact that the flight is to be made solely in the interests of aeronautic science and international good will – – –

On the Ryan factory floors the workmen are out to set a record in construction time — they're reading the papers too. They know how desperately I want to be in New York by the end of April. They have been watching the reports about Nungesser's final preparations in France, about Byrd's transatlantic Fokker, about Chamberlin and the Bellanca, about Davis and Wooster. Every expedition is ahead of me. A single day's delay might make the difference between success and failure, and they are determined that the responsibility for such a disappointment won't lie with the man in the shop. Each of them is striving to do a quicker and better job on the *Spirit of St. Louis* than he's ever done before. No pains are too great, and no hours too long; lights sometimes burn in the factory all through the night. Donald Hall worked for one stretch of thirty-six hours, without sleep. The only good-natured grumbling I've heard in the shop was when Hall sent down drawings that called for fuselage fairings to an accuracy of one thirty-second of an inch. Then Superintendent Bert Tindale remarked that he'd never before been asked to hold such accuracy. But I saw him working there the rest of the afternoon with a scale on which the inches were divided into thirty-seconds.

22

In this second month of construction I have plenty of free time. Instruments and emergency equipment have all been ordered, and, except for a few items, have arrived. Practically all the details of my plans are laid. I've considered every contingency I can think of that might arise during the flight — how much weather to push through, how to locate my position on the European coast, what to do if I have to land at sea, how to find Paris if I make my landfall after dark, and a hundred other possibilities. I've studied wind roses over the North Atlantic for April, May, and June until I practically know them all by heart — especially those disturbing, short blue arrows that indicate the percentage of head winds.

I make a point of spending part of each day at the factory. In good weather I often go out to Dutch Flats and fly one of the company's machines. None of them has a Whirlwind engine; but they perform well with their wartime Hispanos, and they teach me the characteristics of high-wing monoplanes.

23

ENDURANCE PLANE SMASHES WORLD'S RECORD

CHAMBERLIN AND ACOSTA MORE THAN TWO DAYS IN AIR

NEW YORK, April 14.—The world's endurance record for aircraft returned to the United States yesterday when two weary aviators, Clarence D. Chamberlin and Bert Acosta, landed their Bellanca monoplane on Roosevelt Field, Long Island, after 51 hours, 11 minutes, and 25 seconds aloft. They exceeded by nearly six hours the previous endurance record which was established in August, 1925, by two French Army officers, Drouhin and Landry, at Etampes.

WANT TO FLY ATLANTIC

Tired but happy, both flyers are anxious to be the first to make the New York to Paris flight, across the Atlantic Ocean. Giuseppe Bellanca, the designer, said his plane could be made ready for the ocean flight within three days, but that much more time would be used for careful preparation.

Charles A. Levine, chairman of the Columbia Aircraft Corporation, which plans on building Bellanca Aircraft, said that preparations would be rushed to permit the Bellanca to be the first plane to complete the New York to Paris flight – – –

Well, that's the record I've hoped to break. Maybe I still can break it. In the *Spirit of St. Louis* I'll have the extra pilot's weight in fuel. Other things being equal, that should give me a fifty-gallon advantage over the Bellanca. But as far as the New York-to-Paris flight is concerned, there's no use blinding myself to reality. Almost

everyone else would have to fail before my project can succeed —
and everyone else seems to be getting along wonderfully well. I
was too far behind in starting. I probably won't even fly my plane
through to New York, to say nothing of taking off for Paris.

I've already purchased charts and begun laying out a transpacific flight by way of the Hawaiian Islands. I could land on all
five continents, and fly around the world. That might be even more
worth while and interesting than the flight from New York to Paris.
Of course navigation would be difficult. I'd need either directional
radio or a navigator to be sure of striking the small, mid-ocean
islands; but the longest nonstop distance would be less than 2,500
miles. I'd have over a thousand miles extra fuel range to turn into
equipment weight. And I've heard of an electrical engineer in Los
Angeles who thinks he can build an aircraft radio set that has reliability and long range, with a weight of less than forty pounds.
I'm going to get in touch with him this week.

24

AMERICA CRASHES ON TEST FLIGHT

BYRD, BENNETT, AND NOVILLE INJURED, FOKKER PILOTING CRAFT AT TIME

NEW YORK, April 16.—The big trimotored Fokker monoplane which Commander Richard Evelyn Byrd and his crew
were preparing for the transatlantic flight
between New York and Paris crashed at
Teterboro airport at 6:00 o'clock this
afternoon. The machine was coming in for
a landing after its first trial flight when it
overturned, injuring three of the four
members of its crew. Damage to the plane
itself was serious, but can be repaired
according to Anthony J. Fokker who was
at the controls during the landing, and the
only one uninjured.

The accident may force Commander
Byrd to abandon his plans for a trans-
oceanic flight this spring — — —

Tony Fokker has cracked up! Every member of the Byrd crew has been injured. I can hardly believe the sentences my eyes are reading. Much as I want to be the first to start for Paris, I don't wish my competitors hard luck. Crashed planes and flyers in hospitals impair all of aviation, and destroy the joy of flight. Apparently the Fokker just nosed over on the field. Its tail hadn't been loaded down enough. The nose structure, holding the center engine, collapsed and crushed Floyd Bennett's leg.

That's one of the things I don't like about big planes, and forward cockpits. If a small plane, like the *Spirit of St. Louis,* with the cockpit in the rear, noses over, the pilot isn't likely to be hurt at all.

25

The third week of April is crammed with the endless details which precede the completion of a new airplane. An atmosphere of tension and expectancy pervades the entire factory. Mahoney remarks dryly that there's no use thinking about producing other machines until the *Spirit of St. Louis* is out of the way — as though he himself hadn't ordered the construction of my plane rushed ahead of everything else. Each workman has some finishing touch to add before he's ready to call his job completed. They all sign their names on the front wing-spar, before the fabric covering is added, "to ride along on the flight for good luck."

I am working on lists for the flight arrangements I must make at every stop, from San Diego through to Paris. I open my little black notebook, and read them again:

TO BE ARRANGED FOR:

San Diego Take-Off

> Stop mail: leave address
> Pack and address suitcase
> Wire day of arrival to Knight and Wassall
> Notify papers
> Start motor at:
> Take off at:

St. Louis Arrival

Taxi to position near N.G. hangars
Arrange for care of plane
Arrange for guard
Wire Ryan Airlines
Arrange for quarters
Arrange for servicing
Total gal. gas —
Total gal. oil —
   (Chamois gas, screen oil)
Arrange final flight details
Wire for necessary arrangements at N.Y.
Complete St. Louis business
Arrange for future mail and express

St. Louis Take-Off

Notify papers and C. M. Young
Wire Roosevelt Field, Weather Bureau,
   Wright, Pioneer, N.A.A.
Notify papers
Start motor at —
Take off at —

N.Y. Arrival

Arrange for care of plane
Arrange for guard
Wire St. Louis and Ryan Airlines
Arrange for quarters on field
Arrange for weather reports, motor overhaul,
   instrument check
Light code

N.Y. Take-Off

Notify papers
Have time of take-off wired to St. Louis and
   Ryan Airlines

Paris Arrival

Arrange for care of ship
Arrange for guard
Cable St. Louis, Ryan Airlines, Wright Aero,
    Mother, Standard Oil, Union Oil
Arrange for clothes
Arrange for quarters

I've completed about all the arrangements I can before I'm ready to start. San Diego and St. Louis won't be difficult. I have plenty of friends in both places. New York and Paris will be the problems. I don't know anyone I can count on for help in either city.

As to my personal and emergency equipment, it's all purchased — flying suit, canteens, Army rations, rubber raft, pump, repair kit, flares — everything I can think of I may need that comes within the weight allowance I've set. At first I couldn't find any red flares. Then I bought four of the kind railroads use for danger signals. I've got each one sealed up watertight in a piece of bicycle inner tube. I opened one of the cans of Army rations as a test. Inside were three bars of a dry, chocolatelike concoction. The taste is awful. You'd have to be pretty hungry to eat the stuff; but for me, that's probably an advantage.

26

NUNGESSER TO TAKE OFF
SUNDAY ON OCEAN FLIGHT

PARIS, Apr. 19.—Captain Charles Nungesser, the great French ace, announced that if weather conditions are favorable, he will take off from Le Bourget Airdrome at daybreak Sunday morning on a nonstop flight for New York – – –

If Nungesser is ready to start on Sunday, the Bellanca is the only American plane that can beat him to the take-off. I wonder what has been holding Chamberlin back. Maybe this next article will throw some light on the question:

MAIL PILOT TO NAVIGATE
BELLANCA ON PARIS FLIGHT

NEW YORK, Apr. 19.—An announcement issued at the offices of the Columbia Aircraft Corporation stated that Lloyd W. Bertaud had been chosen as navigator for the Bellanca monoplane on its projected non-stop flight between New York and Paris. Bertaud has been an air-mail pilot for two years, and has the reputation of being one of the best night flyers on the eastern division.

The other man in the plane will be either Acosta or Chamberlin. "The choice will not be made until the last minute before the flight," Mr. Levine said, "and it will then be determined by lot. Both pilots will appear upon the field in flying togs. Their names will be written separately on slips of paper. One slip will be drawn. The name on it will decide the flyer."

The selection of Bertaud came as a surprise to followers of the New York to Paris projects. After their successful record-setting endurance flight, it was thought that Chamberlin and Acosta would fly the plane over the Atlantic together.

It is now estimated that the Bellanca will take off within the next ten days. ‑ ‑ ‑

Well, I'm not going to let these press reports worry me. There's nothing I can do to push construction faster. I'll fly my plane through to St. Louis as soon as its tests are over. Then, my partners and I will get together and lay our final plans.

27

"Major Young is in San Diego. He wants to see you while he's here." Mahoney has knocked on our drafting room door to give me the news. Major Clarence M. Young commands my Reserve Squadron at Richards Field, in Kansas. Shot down while flying a bomber over Italy's Austrian front during the war, he returned from prison camp to enter a law practice in Des Moines. Two weeks of active duty in summer help keep him in training as an officer and pilot. I gave him some instruction in the Air Service's latest techniques last year, since I had just graduated from Kelly; and we formed a personal friendship. He was recently appointed chief of the Air Regulations Division of the government's new Aeronautics Branch of the Department of Commerce. Now he's coming to see me and my *Spirit of St. Louis*. I'll ask him about the new regulations for civil aircraft. In the past, all a man needed to fly a plane was the money to buy one and the ability to get it in the air; now both pilots and aircraft must be licensed. The *Spirit of St. Louis* will have to carry a registration number painted on its wings.

"I'll see that your applications are acted on right away, Charlie. We want to get a number on your wings before you take off for Paris, and we certainly want you to be a licensed pilot when you land in Europe."

Major Young is inspecting the cockpit of my plane, and I've asked him about the licenses I need for a transoceanic flight. He has a dry sense of humor that leaves one a little uncertain as to when he's serious and when he's not.

"We'll give you an N-X license," he continues. "That will let you do about anything you want to."

"What's an N-X license?" I ask.

"N is the International-Code letter assigned to the United States. Planes flying outside the country have to carry it for identification. X stands for experimental. It authorizes you to make modifications without getting government approval. Of course you can't carry passengers with an X license; but I guess you won't want to do that anyway." He glances at the huge gas tank bolted in where passenger seats would ordinarily be. "You won't have any trouble about licenses."

28

In another week the *Spirit of St. Louis* will be ready for flight. I'll make the light-load tests from the Ryan Company's field at Dutch Flats. Its a smooth, grassless area, like a dry lakebed, boxed in by roads and telephone wires. It will do while the tanks are only partly filled with fuel, but we'll have to make our heavy-load tests elsewhere; for them, I'll need clear approaches and three or four thousand feet of run.

Several weeks ago Hall suggested that we use the parade

grounds on the abandoned Army post at Camp Kearney. This afternoon he and I drove out to look them over. The conditions are almost ideal for our purpose. There's a long, level strip available for a runway, lying almost exactly parallel to prevailing winds. The mountains are far enough back to be out of the way for landing, and there's nothing at all to clear on take-off — no trees, houses, or telephone wires, not even a fence. The end of the field rolls off gradually into a series of hills descending to the sea.

Out here there won't be a crowd to distract us while we're running tests; and this is important. If we don't talk about our plans in advance, we may not be bothered by newspaper reporters and photographers. The press has become a problem in recent weeks. The big associations in New York have asked San Diego papers to cover my activities in more detail. What started as a pleasant relationship with local journalists now involves elements of tension. On the one hand, a reasonable amount of publicity will be an important asset to this project. On the other hand, I begin to realize that the distraction created by newspapers could cause its failure. We have to concentrate our attention on the tests and the accuracy of data we obtain. A slight error can cause a crash. One makes errors more easily when onlookers get in the way, and ask questions, and smoke cigarettes near fumes of gasoline. Also, plans often go wrong; and the less said about them in advance, the better. People who talk a lot about what they're going to do seldom accomplish their predictions.

If we run our tests at Camp Kearney, we may be able to get them over with before the newspapers find out what we're doing. Very few people realize that a field suitable for flying exists here; and if some reporter notices that the plane is gone from its hangar on Dutch Flats, he'll think it's in the air on a test flight, or else over at Rockwell Field on North Island.

The only serious disadvantage of the old parade grounds is the innumerable stones that lie scattered over its surface. Many are larger than a man's fist, and might cause a tire to blow on take-off or landing with one of the heavier fuel loads. However, we can pick up the biggest ones.

29

NUNGESSER PLANE COMPLETES TESTS

Bellanca Made Ready For Take-Off

DROUHIN ENTERS CONTEST

Fonck Sails for America

APRIL 22.—Competition in the New York to Paris flight contest has intensified with the entry of M. Drouhin, the French aviator whose duration flight record of 45 hours 11 minutes and 59 seconds was broken recently by Bert Acosta and Clarence Chamberlin. Drouhin has been running secret tests with a Farman biplane.

Capt. Charles Nungesser's Levasseur plane, the White Bird, is undergoing a final check after its successful test flights of the last several days. Capt. Nungesser says he does not plan on taking off Sunday morning as announced, but that he hopes to get away by the end of the month.

Two other French contestants are known to be preparing planes for the transatlantic flight. M. Tarascon will fly a Bernard-Marie-Hubert plane, with a Gnome-Rhone-Jupiter engine. M. Coste plans to pilot a Breguet, with a Hispano-Suiza engine.

Meanwhile, the work of repairing Commander Byrd's Fokker monoplane, America, is under way. It should be completed in from two to three weeks, according to estimates made by officials of the Atlantic Aircraft Corporation.

The Bellanca is being re-equipped with instruments. Tension and uncertainty still exists in regard to whether Chamberlin or Acosta will be chosen to make the flight, in addition to pilot-navigator Bertaud. When asked about this, Mr. Charles A. Levine, owner of the plane, said he could not decide until just before the take-off.

"I want both boys to have their heart in their work up to the last moment," he said, "and if one of them was chosen now, the other would probably be sore."

Work on the plane is being rushed, and a secret take-off is thought likely within the next several days. – – –

If events had only let me come to San Diego a month earlier,
I too could now be ready for the Paris flight. In three or four more
days we'll haul the *Spirit of St. Louis* to the flying field and
assemble fuselage to wing.

30

WESTERN
UNION

SB26025 GOVT.
WASHINGTON DC 22 212P

CHARLES A. LINDBERGH
CARE RYAN AIRLINES INC.
SAN DIEGO CALIF.

YOUR LICENSE NUMBER EXPERIMENTAL TRANSATLANTIC SHIP
IS N DASH X TWO HUNDRED ELEVEN STOP TRANSPORT
LICENSE WILL BE MAILED TOMORROW CARE ROBERTSON
AIRCRAFT ANGLUM MISSOURI

E. KINTZ

That's from the Department of Commerce. Now we can paint
the license numbers on the wings and tail. It may save me time
and a lot of trouble later on. Telegrams are coming in fast these
days, and they're all helpful. My plans are meshing together
smoothly.

WESTERN
UNION

PATERSON N.J.
APRIL 22, 1927

WHEN USING FIRST CLASS AVIATION GASOLINE THERE IS
NO CARBURETOR INTAKE ATTACHMENT NECESSARY STOP AFTER
ARRIVING EAST WE WILL FIT ENGINE WITH CARBURETOR
AIR HEATER IF FOUND DESIRABLE STOP SENT PROOF COPY
INSTRUCTION MANUAL AIR MAIL YESTERDAY

HARTSON WRIGHT AERONAUTICAL CORP.

That's good. I was concerned about the cold of altitude and
night. If I don't have to use a carburetor air heater, it will save
several pounds of weight.

```
                    WESTERN
                    UNION
                                        HOLMSTEAD
                                        PENN.

      RYAN AIRLINES
      SAN DIEGO, CALIF.

      15.5 DEGREES SETTING PROBABLY NECESSARY ON YOUR
      MONOPLANE TO GET TAKEOFF WITH HEAVY LOAD FUEL
      ECONOMY WILL BE IMPROVED ON HIGHER PITCH SETTING
      STOP IF TAKEOFF IS SATISFACTORY WITH 15.5 SETTING
      SUGGEST TRY 16.5 AS THIS WILL IMPROVE FUEL ECONOMY.

                      STANDARD STEEL PROP. CO.
```

It's a good suggestion. We'll try it out. The higher the pitch, the more the range.

31

BELLANCA IN CRACK-UP

CHAMBERLIN'S SKILL SAVES GIRLS

NEW YORK, April 24.—The Bellanca transatlantic monoplane narrowly escaped disaster, following its christening ceremonies today, when part of the landing gear tore loose on take-off. Clarence D. Chamberlin, the pilot, was making a flight with two little girls, age nine and fifteen, on board. The girls had climbed happily into the cabin a few minutes after breaking a bottle of ginger ale over the nose of the plane and naming it the "Columbia." - - -
Only Chamberlin's great skill as a pilot saved what might have been a serious accident. He landed so gently on the one sound wheel that only minor damage was sustained by the Bellanca. - - -

Landing on one wheel and a wing tip with a lightly loaded plane isn't very dangerous when a pilot is well acquainted with his craft. It's not likely to cause much of a crack-up, and it has been done a great many times. The newspapers always make it seem a good deal worse than it really is. But suppose that landing-gear strut had broken loose on a transatlantic take-off, after the big fuselage tanks had been filled to the neck with fuel — then there would have been a real crash. Gasoline would have splattered all over the place, as it did last year from Fonck's Sikorsky. And the engine, after pulling full power for several hundred feet of roll, would probably have been hot enough to cause ignition.

Both Bellanca and Sikorsky are top designers. Then why did the landing gears fail? Is some strain caused by these heavily loaded take-offs being overlooked in engineering calculations? May there also be a hidden weakness in the *Spirit of St. Louis?* I must talk to Donald Hall about it.

32

WESTERN
UNION

EXTRA NL
NEW YORK, N.Y.
APR. 25

CHARLES A LINDBERGH
CARE RYAN AIRLINES INC.
SAN DIEGO CALIF.

YOUR TELEGRAM TWENTY FOURTH RECEIVED ARE HAPPY TO
LEARN YOU HAVE CHOSEN MOBILOIL B FOR YOUR FLIGHT
STOP GASOLINE HAS BEEN RECEIVED STOP HAVE ADVISED
ST. LOUIS REGARDING MOBILOIL SUPPLIES ON YOUR
ARRIVAL THERE STOP GLAD TO OFFER ALL POSSIBLE
ASSISTANCE BOTH HERE AND ABROAD STOP BEST WISHES FOR
SUCCESS

VACUUM OIL COMPANY E. J. SNOW

That's another problem off my mind. At first, I didn't know how to handle the fueling of the *Spirit of St. Louis* in New York. It would be easy enough to get some dealer to send his truck out to the field — a four-hundred-gallon sale would bring such service quickly. But I found I could buy special gasoline in the West that would give me a little more range per gallon. I've bought 500 gallons of this fuel for my New York-to-Paris flight, from the Standard Oil Company of California. The company would arrange to ship it east in barrels, they said; but who would handle the shipment for me in New York? The Vacuum Oil Company offered to do so free of charge, and this telegram was sent from their New York office in final confirmation.

The big oil companies and their agents have always gone out of their way to help develop aviation. A barnstorming pilot can usually get a truck sent out to his field for as little as a twenty-gallon sale of fuel; and if he wants it, the driver will give him a ride back into town, where the local oil dealer is a ready source of information about the community, its hotels and stores.

I had hoped to get gasoline and oil free for my flights eastward from San Diego. There's plenty of precedent for that, and I felt that the advertising value to the companies whose products I use should be sufficient compensation. But both Standard and Vacuum stood pat on their prices. I'd have to pay their regular charge. However, all the service I need will be furnished at no extra cost. That's been the case with every item connected with the *Spirit of St. Louis*. I've had assistance for the asking, but no product without paying for it.

33

This morning we hauled the *Spirit of St. Louis* to Dutch Flats. By taking off the landing gear on one side, it was easy enough to move the fuselage through the big doorway of the factory's ground floor; but the wing in the loft created an unexpected problem. When Hall concluded that ten feet should be added to the standard M-2 span, no one thought about getting a forty-six-foot wing out of the room where it was built. For a time it looked as though we'd have to tear out a section of the wall; but careful measurement showed that we could get by if we tipped the wing over at an angle and removed the loft's double doors.

Such a delicate structure required careful handling. Fortunately an empty boxcar was standing on the railroad siding next to the factory, and all hands turned out to push the boxcar into a position which would form the first step downward from the loft. Then, with a contractor's derrick, we maneuvered the wing onto the car top, and from the car top down to a waiting truck. The workmen who weren't tugging at guy ropes or steadying the panel, stood watching from open doors and windows as though some child of theirs were going away to war. Their part was done. For them, the flight had started. For two months theirs has been the active part, while I stood by watching their craftsmanship. Now, the roles are reversed, and I'll have the field of action. Now, the success of their efforts depends upon my skill; and my life, upon their thoroughness.

34

DAVIS AND WOOSTER KILLED

AMERICAN LEGION CRASHES
ON TAKE-OFF

HAMPTON VA., April 26.—Lieut. Commander Noel Davis and Lieutenant Stanton H. Wooster lost their lives today in the last of the trial flights of the huge trans-Atlantic plane in which they were to attempt a flight to Paris next week.

The tragedy occurred when the machine was carrying almost the equivalent of its full load for the trans-Atlantic trip. Those on the ground saw a huge splash as the big machine came down in an area of marsh land, not far from Langley Field.

Both Commander Davis and Lieutenant Wooster were exceptionally skillful aviators. They had planned on taking off for the transatlantic flight to Paris within the next few days. - - -

Davis and Wooster killed! My God! Every one of the big multi-engine planes built for the New York-to-Paris flight has crashed — Fonck's Sikorsky, Byrd's Fokker, and now Davis's Keystone! Four men have lost their lives, and three have been injured. Even the Bellanca has had a crack-up. What happened? Did an engine cut out on take-off? Maybe the plane was just overloaded beyond its ability to climb.

That's another example of how dangerous it is to have a cockpit forward. If the cockpit had been aft, the way it is in the *Spirit of St. Louis,* the chances are that nobody would have been even injured, since the fuselage wasn't badly crushed and the gasoline didn't catch on fire.

<h1 style="text-align:center">35</h1>

This morning I'm going to test the *Spirit of St. Louis*. It's the 28th of April — just over two months since I placed our order with the Ryan Company, and exactly sixty days since business formalities were completed and work on the plane began. What a beautiful machine it is, resting there on the field in front of the hangar, trim and slender, gleaming in its silver coat! All our ideas, all our calculations, all our hopes lie there before me, waiting to undergo the acid test of flight. For me, it seems to contain the whole future of aviation. When such planes can be built, there's no limitation to the air. In a few minutes I'll make the first take-off — for I plan to run all tests myself.

Today, reality will check the claims of formula and theory on a scale which hope can't stretch a single hair. Today, the reputation of the company, of the designing engineer, of the mechanics, in fact of every man who's had a hand in building the *Spirit of St. Louis,* is at stake. And I'm on trial too, for quick action on my part may counteract an error by someone else, or a faulty move may bring a washout crash.

"Off! Throttle closed."

I'm in the cockpit, still unfamiliar and strange in spite of the hours I've spent sitting in it on factory and hangar floors. John van der Linde, chief mechanic, turns the propeller over several times.

"Contact!"

"Contact!"

He swings his body away from the blade as he pulls it through. The engine catches – – – picks up quickly as I crack the throttle — 800 revolutions per minute, every cylinder hitting, oil and fuel pressures normal, the temperature already up. I check controls, moving them from one position to another in a last attempt to get their feel. This is considerably different from any cockpit I've been in before. The big fuel tank in front of me seems doubly large, now that I'm actually to fly behind it.

I open the throttle slowly – – – 1000 – – – 1200 – – – 1400
– – – wide. The fuselage trembles with power, and I feel the wheels
crowd up against their chocks. I cut first one magneto and then
the other — not a miss or a jerk in the engine — each gauge tells
its proper story.

I signal the chocks away. A young mechanic named Douglas
Corrigan ducks under the wing to pull them out. The *Spirit of St.
Louis* rolls lightly over the baked-mud surface of the field. How
strange it is to taxi with such a wide wheel tread! I glance again at
the wind sock on the hangar, at instruments, valves, and levers,
at the field ahead, at the sky above — and open the throttle.

Yes, my cockpit is a little blind; but I can see ahead well
enough by leaning to one side. I've never felt a plane accelerate so
fast before. The tires are off ground before they roll a hundred
yards. The plane climbs quickly, even though I hold its nose well
down. There's a huge reserve of power. I spiral cautiously upward — 500 feet – – – 1000 – – – 2000 feet. I straighten out and
study my instruments – – – nose up – – – nose down – – – they're
all working properly – – – the liquid inclinometer shows nicely a
dive or climb. I circle over the factory, watching little figures run
outdoors to see the machine they built actually flying overhead. I
rock my wings, and head across the bay.

Now I'm over North Island, looking down on big naval hangars,
planes on the line, and flying boats at anchor in the harbor. Both
the Army and the Navy have establishments down there, with a
huge landing area in between. The Naval Air Station is on one
side and Rockwell Field is on the other. I'm perfectly safe now,
even if the engine stops. One *couldn't* overshoot North Island in a
forced landing.

But I have no time for gazing over the earth. There are tests
to run, and men waiting anxiously for the reports I'm to bring back.
Ailerons ride a bit too high. The fin needs slight adjustment. I note
these items down on my data board, and push the stick over to
one side. The wing drops rather slowly. The ailerons on the *Spirit
of St. Louis* aren't as fast as those on the standard Ryan. But we

expected that. Hall made them short to avoid overstraining the wing under full-load conditions, and he gained a little efficiency by not carrying them all the way out to the tip. The response is good enough for a long-range airplane.

I straighten out, pull into a stall, and let go of the stick. The nose drops and has no tendency to come back up. The dive steepens and the right wing slants lower until I force the plane back to level flight again. I take my feet off the rudder, and steer with stick alone. The fuselage veers the opposite way to the ailerons. It's clear that stability isn't a strong point with the *Spirit of St. Louis*. But we didn't design the plane for stability. We decided to use the standard tail surfaces to save construction time, and possibly gain a little extra range.

What top speed can I make? That's one of the crucial tests. If the *Spirit of St. Louis* has enough speed and can take off with enough load, I can fly nonstop to Paris. Otherwise I can't. I drop down to one thousand feet, level off, and open throttle. The indicator starts to climb: 100 – – – 115 – – – 120 – – – 128 miles an hour, jumping up and down over several graduations in turbulent air. A hundred and twenty-eight miles an hour is encouraging too. If time over the measured course checks with the needle, then the speed exceeds Hall's calculations by three and a half miles. I throttle down and head toward the white houses of San Diego. That's enough for the first flight. There's no use doing more until ailerons and fin are adjusted.

A Navy Hawk fighter dives down from higher altitude to inspect, at close range, the strange creature which has dared invade its skies. Almost instinctively I bank for position in mock combat. Of course the Hawk has greater speed, but the *Spirit of St. Louis* can turn in a shorter radius. We spiral, zoom, and dive for several minutes, while we try to get imaginary guns on one another. Then I break off, and take up course again for the Dutch Flats field.

I do two or three stalls on the way back to get the feel of my plane and practice for its landing.

"How's the control, Charlie?"

"Good enough, but she needs some adjustment." I let my engine idle for a minute or two while I describe the results of the flight.

"Say, you ran only a hundred and sixty-five feet before your wheels left the ground — only six and one-eighth seconds." Hall is enthusiastic over the performance.

"What was the stability like?" he asks.

"Not very good," I tell him.

"I was afraid of that, Charlie. You know I wanted to put on bigger tail surfaces — — — we can still do it, but — — — "

36

SAN DIEGO, APRIL 29, 1927

LINDBERGH ESCAPES CRASH

PLANE NEAR COLLISION

Captain Charles A. Lindbergh, former airmail pilot, narrowly escaped disaster when the plane he is grooming for a transatlantic flight almost collided with a Curtiss Hawk fighter from North Island. Lindbergh was putting his plane through its first tests preparatory to taking off for St. Louis tomorrow night on a non-stop flight which will put him in that city Sunday afternoon — — —

I read the morning paper as I eat breakfast. Well, it's news to me. I've had narrow escapes in flying, but that's one I didn't know about. And the statement that I'm going to start home tomorrow is just more fiction. I've told everybody that I have several days of tests to run.

37

This is May 4th, the day of my final speed and load tests. A morning fog is lifting when I take off and head toward the Army's three-kilometer speed course along Coronado Strand. It's 5:40 a.m. My plane has been ready since sunrise. As I climb over San Diego Bay, I find it still half covered with low, rolling clouds which obscure the buoy markers I must use. The sun is not high enough to burn them off quickly. Inland, mountains are clear. Seaward, I can see most of North Island through breaks in fog. I decide to drop in at Rockwell Field and try out the roughness of its surface. I'd like to use it as my departure point from San Diego.

I slip down on the final glide, nose high and left wing low — that gives me perfect forward vision. Then I straighten out just before my wheels touch. Bumps and hummocks are worse than I expected. The *Spirit of St. Louis* gets a good shaking up, landing and taxiing — it won't strain anything with a load of less than thirty gallons in the tanks, but taking off with enough fuel for the flight home will be a different matter. I'll need two hundred and fifty gallons to give me the reserve I want to carry.

Several officers are waiting on the line as I taxi in. They saw my plane coming down, and want to inspect it at close range. There's still much skepticism among most of them about my flight; but they extend a hearty welcome, and invite me to spend the morning and stay for lunch.

"Thanks, but we've got to run tests today. I'll have to take off as soon as the fog clears."

"Well, how about coming over to the club while you're waiting?" they insist.

"I'd like to, but I'd better size up the field first. I want to take off with a fairly heavy load when I leave for St. Louis, and some areas are probably a little smoother than others."

"We'll drive you over it."

"Thanks, but I'd rather walk. I can get a better idea of what it's like."

They laugh and wave me off.

"We'll look over your plane until you come back. Let us know if there's anything we can do to help."

I want to dig my heels into the surface, see the height of grass on my legs, and study contours of earth by zigzagging back and forth across them. If Rockwell Field turns out to be too rough, even for a medium load, then I'll have to take off for St. Louis from Camp Kearney. My decision will depend largely on the tests we're to make this afternoon, and the length of run the plane requires.

When I return to the hangars, the day is beginning to feel warm and the clouds are fading away. A mechanic swings my propeller, and another holds a wing-strut as I taxi out from the line. I do a chandelle off the field, to show how well the *Spirit of St. Louis* performs, and head toward the speed course. The buoys are still obscured by patches of mist, so I return to Dutch Flats and let an hour pass.

When I reach the bay on my third flight there's no trace of fog. I fly once over the speed course to locate its markers. Then, at a distance of about two miles from the nearest one, I turn back, nose down to fifty feet above the water, and push my throttle wide open, adjusting the stabilizer for neutral load on stick. One mile of level flight before striking the first marker is what we agreed on. At times, when the plane hits turbulent air, the indicator jumps to over 130 miles an hour. I press my stop watch as the first buoy streaks by under the wing. I can't see the next, but I know it's dead ahead. Now the third buoy is in sight, a black dot in the distance. I press my watch again as I pass above it, throttle back, and climb several hundred feet while I fill in the time on my data board. One flight back over the buoys in the opposite direction, two more round trips to average with the first, and the high-speed runs are finished.

Now I'll fly to Camp Kearney for the load tests. On my way I note down the relation of air speed to engine revolutions, so Hall will have several check points for his curves. By the time I'm over the parade grounds there's only one more test to make before we start putting fuel in the tanks for the load take-offs. I pull the throttle back to 1500 r.p.m. and let needles steady – – – 96 miles an hour: that's pretty good. I take a pencil from my pocket and pick up the data board – – – The nose rises – – – a wing drops – – – I reach for the stick – – – a gust of air snatches the data board from my hand and carries it through the open window! All the figures I've collected this morning go fluttering down toward a brush-covered hill below! I bank sharply and watch the board, flashing as it catches sun, land in the branches of a thick bush about two hundred yards from the edge of a clearing. Now it's only a white spot among brownish-green leaves.

The clearing looks big enough to land on with one of the company's Hisso-Standards. I circle around for several minutes, locating in my mind the exact position of the data board. When I'm sure I can spot its bush again, I fly back to Camp Kearney and land. In spite of loose stones, the surface is smoother than that of Rockwell Field. But wheels bang up and down uncomfortably at times.

Donald Hall, A. J. Edwards, and several mechanics are waiting beside a gasoline truck parked on a corner of the parade grounds. And there's Mahoney, a little to one side, leaning against his car. (Benjamin and Franklin are his given names, but nobody dares use them.) Apparently the secrecy of our plans has been well kept, for there isn't a newspaperman in sight. Hall's face lengthens when I tell what happened to the data board. Either it will have to be retrieved or all the morning's tests must be run again. Mahoney sends a mechanic to the nearest telephone, with orders to have one of the Hisso-Standards sent over from Dutch Flats. Meanwhile we'll fill the center wing-tank with gasoline for our first load test. After that, we'll add fifty gallons for each flight, until Hall gets enough measured points to check his theoretical curves.

The Hisso-Standard arrives in a half hour. The pilot and some of the mechanics want to go with me to help hunt for the board, but I decide it's wiser to take the plane alone. The clearing where I must land is small, and there's not enough wind to cut down landing speed appreciably. The weight of even one more man might cause a crack-up.

When I arrive over the brush patch again, I find the data board still clearly visible. I stall down into the clearing and stop rolling with several yards to spare. Leaving the engine idling, with a stone under each wheel of the plane to keep it from creeping forward, I crawl in through thick and scratchy bushes to where I think the board should be. After hunting for several minutes without result, I remove my coat, spread it on top of some branches, return to the clearing, and take off again in the Standard.

As soon as I'm in the air, I see my coat to be at least fifty yards from the data board. My sense of direction certainly went wrong that time. Maybe I should have brought a compass. I land again, but am still unsuccessful in my search; so I leave the coat in a new location and take off once more. This time, coat and data board are only twenty feet apart. I land, pick them both up, and head back to Camp Kearney.

The *Spirit of St. Louis* is ready for its first load flight when I arrive. Hall takes charge of the data sheets as though they contained directions to a lost gold mine. We're several hours behind schedule, and anxious to finish tests before any major change in weather. A quartering wind has already sprung up — close to seven miles an hour, we estimate. The late take-off, the delay at Rockwell Field waiting for fog to clear, and the time spent regaining my data board, have eaten up the morning. Now we'll have to work fast to finish before dark.

The first two or three take-offs are easy. The *Spirit of St. Louis* runs only a few yards farther than with no extra load at all. But as we keep putting in fifty-gallon increments of gasoline, the run lengthens and the wheels jerk up and down over loose stones until I wonder how tires can be built to stand the strain. When I'm ready for the 300-gallon test, the wind has dropped to zero and the sun is almost touching the horizon. My plane is off the ground in twenty seconds; but the tires took a terrific beating, and the landing is even rougher than the take-off.

"Charlie, your wheels were clear in one thousand and twenty-three feet!" Hall tells me. His curves are checking out.

"Do you want us to put in fifty gallons more?" the chief mechanic asks.

"It's too late for another flight today," I say, looking toward the west.

"I don't think you ought to take a heavier load across those stones anyway," Mahoney says. He's out in front, examining tires and landing gear.

"Do we need any more check points?" I ask.

"I—I'd like to get one for three hundred and fifty gallons," Hall replies, hesitantly. "But Charlie, if you think the surface is too rough, we can probably get by with what we've got. The wheel bearings were smoking a little, you know," he adds.

"It's landing with all that gasoline that worries me," Mahoney argues. "I'm for calling it enough."

I had intended to take off with loads up to 400 gallons; but if I keep on, and a tire blows, it may wreck our whole project. After all, one can carry tests so far that instead of adding to safety they increase the over-all danger. I'll probably never land with as much as 300 gallons again, so as far as that part of the test is concerned I've already exceeded any future requirements. True, I'll have to take off with 125 gallons more at New York, but the field there will certainly be smoother—and it will be close to sea level; the parade grounds at Camp Kearney are at an altitude of five hundred feet. I think Mahoney is right; we'll call it enough.

Twilight is thickening. We stake the *Spirit of St. Louis* down and leave it under guard. The tanks can be drained tomorrow morning.

When I get back to the city, I telegraph my partners that the tests are satisfactorily completed, and that I'll be ready to start east within forty-eight hours. I had originally planned on running a series of gasoline consumption checks before leaving California. But I'll save at least a day by doing that on my flight between San Diego and St. Louis. As yet I haven't been able to make my fuel-flow meter work. It looks as though I might as well discard it.

38

The *Spirit of St. Louis* is standing ready in its hangar. My plans are complete. All San Diego details have been attended to: my bills are paid; my bank account is closed. The rubber boat is lashed down tightly in the fuselage. Tires are pumped to just the right pressure. The center wing-tank is full. It's early morning on the 8th of May. For two days I've been waiting on weather. A general storm area hovers over the Rocky Mountains and the Southwest, making even a daylight flight a questionable venture. And I want to fly to St. Louis through the night.

39

NUNGESSER OVER ATLANTIC

DUE IN NEW YORK
TOMORROW

PARIS, May 8.—As the sun rose above the horizon this morning, Captains Charles Nungesser and François Coli started their heavily overloaded Levasseur biplane, the White Bird, rolling over the ground at Le Bourget Aerodrome for the start of their transatlantic flight westward to New York.

There was a breath-taking moment during the long take-off, when Captain Nungesser tried to lift his machine, but failed. He was successful, however, on the next attempt, and the white plane rose slowly, to disappear into the western sky. - - -

That's the first time a plane loaded for the New York-Paris flight has actually taken off the ground. Nungesser and Coli are in the air with full tanks. They're experienced men. They should land in New York tomorrow. I spend most of the day studying charts and data I've assembled for the westward, Pacific flight. It's the route beyond Honolulu that concerns me most; there's probably not even a radio station on the pin-point islands I'll have to strike. And can I find beaches hard enough and long enough for landing and take-off? Maybe we'll have to put pontoons on the *Spirit of St. Louis*. But with pontoons, could my plane get off the water with enough fuel to reach Honolulu?

40

NUNGESSER SIGHTED OFF CAPE RACE

WHITE BIRD REPORTED BY DESTROYER

FRENCH AIRMEN REACH NOVA SCOTIA

OCEAN PLANE SEEN OFF PORTLAND

TRANSATLANTIC FLYERS OVER BOSTON

CROWD AT BATTERY WAITS ANXIOUSLY

NUNGESSER, COLI LOST

PARIS FEARS WORST

NAVY READY FOR SEARCH

It's May 9th. Step by step newspaper headlines have followed Nungesser and Coli from their take-off at Paris to the city of Boston, only to have them vanish like midnight ghosts. Now no one seems to be sure that they were *ever* sighted after their plane left the coast of France. Only one thing is definite: the *White Bird* is down somewhere short of its goal, on land or on sea, for time has exhausted its fuel.

Accidents, delays, and tragedies have combined to leave only the Bellanca poised for the New York-Paris flight. And now, 2500 miles farther westward, my *Spirit of St. Louis* is built and tested.

I've gone down to the Weather Bureau at the Federal Building each afternoon to talk to its chief, Dean Blake, and to look over maps and forecasts. Each time it has been the same story — a low-pressure area covering the route I want to follow — mountaintops in clouds — low visibility in passes — heavy rain — local reports of ice and hail. Three days wasted on account of weather, waiting for the clouds to clear. Why does flying have to be so dependent on the eyesight of a pilot? After all, the *Spirit of St. Louis* is perfectly capable of traveling through that storm area if only I could see well enough to hold my course and keep out of icing regions. The clouds are harmless enough in themselves. I wait here helplessly simply because of an area of opaque air.

Aviation will never amount to much until we learn to free ourselves from mist. The gyroscopic turn indicator is a step in the right direction, but it will take much more than that — better instruments, and radio, and possibly some way of dissipating fog above an airport. Experiments are being made in all three fields, but the answers are years away — interesting to speculate about, but useless for getting me to St. Louis. What I really need is a pair of spectacles to see through fog. If I had a device like that, how simple the entire flight would be!

Possibly I can get through anyway if I fly by daylight. Most of my friends advised against an overnight flight to St. Louis. Even in perfect weather, they said, flying over the mountains at night was taking too much chance. But for me, the experience of 800 miles of darkness will be the best training I can get for my far more difficult flight across the ocean.

I've never flown through an entire night. To do so should give me a familiarity with the *Spirit of St Louis* I can obtain in no other way. I want to find out how accurately I can hold my course between sunset and sunrise, without any check points on the ground. And there's another consideration. A nonstop overnight flight across deserts, mountains, and prairies to St. Louis will do much to answer the people who talk about my lack of experience in long-distance flying, and who say that my New York-to-Paris project must be stopped. My partners in St. Louis have been subjected to several attempts to stop the flight — rather weak attempts, to be sure, which have had no effect on my friends; but I want to give them something with which to argue back, and no argument can be as good as a successful trip of the kind I'm planning.

Today, I visit the Weather Bureau with more hope than usual, for the low-pressure area has shown signs of moving eastward. When it's gone far enough, I'll follow in its wake across the continent, and possibly across the ocean too. Dean Blake spreads out meteorological charts again. I can tell by the expression on his face that good news awaits me. Flying conditions should soon be favorable, he says. I can probably take off tomorrow and expect fair weather all along my route. I should even have a tail wind most of the way! We study the charts carefully. Then I thank him and say good-by for the last time. I'll go to bed early tonight.

The Bellanca hasn't started yet, and Byrd's Fokker isn't ready. If I follow close on the tail of this storm, I may get to New York before the weather permits anybody else to leave for Paris. But that will mean cutting out the St. Louis ceremonies my partners have planned. We intended to christen the plane, and Bixby wrote that the Chamber of Commerce wants to hold a big luncheon while I'm there, to promote aviation and increase interest in the air mail, the National Guard squadron, and my flight to Paris. We've already given up the idea of setting a new endurance record — that would have brought a lot of attention to our city. How will my partners feel about my using Lambert Field as little more than a refueling point en route to New York? It really isn't fair to them. After all, I'm flying a St. Louis plane. It's a St. Louis project. I planned the flight to be from St. Louis to Paris, with a stopover at New York. To spend only a few hours in my home city is not enough. And yet if I'm to be successful, I can't waste time on ceremonies.

·IV·

ACROSS THE CONTINENT

MAY 10–12, 1927

THIS IS THE day of take-off, May 10th. I pack a small suitcase, which I'll lash to the left side of the fuselage, beside my seat. Since the fuel tanks will be only slightly over half full for a 1500-mile flight, I can afford the luxury of carrying a suitcase. I'll need business clothes both in St. Louis and New York. After that I'll leave everything behind except what I wear.

I stop for a few minutes to say good-by to the men in the factory, and to tell them again what a grand job I think they've done on my plane. They're as pleased as I am about the performance of the *Spirit of St. Louis*.

"Send us a wire when you get to Paris," someone calls out as I leave.

From the factory I drive to Dutch Flats and fly over to North Island, where a gasoline truck is waiting for me. Hall and I have lunch with some of the officers. Afterward we walk around the Air Station, looking at planes and equipment, and I take one of the Navy's new Hawk fighters up for a twenty-minute acrobatic flight. I don't want to start east too early, for I plan on meeting daybreak over Kansas. That's far enough from St. Louis to hold down my angular correction if I've drifted many miles off course. Also, it will give the sun a chance to burn morning mists away.

At 3:15 I return to my plane. I've set 4:00 as departure time. That will leave nearly three hours of daylight during which I can turn back or land if anything goes wrong.

There's no need to ask anyone to telephone the newspapers when I take off. Their reporters and photographers are already on the field. It looks as though I won't have to bother much about adequate publicity from now on.

I wish my earth-inductor compass was working, but a bearing froze on one of the test flights and we can't get parts out here to repair the damage. The Pioneer Instrument Company telegraphed that they'll have a new compass ready in New York when I arrive. They're also going to put in a newer type of liquid compass for me. The one in my cockpit now has excessive deviation; but it's good enough for my trip across the country. In a compass, I prefer steadiness to accuracy of reading. As long as the deviation chart is correctly made out, it's easy to subtract or add a few degrees to one's magnetic course.

At 3:40 I crawl into my flying suit. It's uncomfortably hot in this California sun, but I can't very well put the suit on while I'm in the air — and I'll certainly need it over the mountain ranges tonight.

"Let me know what your fuel consumption is when you get to St. Louis," Hall says. "I want to get another check on those curves."

We start and warm up the engine. It's a few minutes early, but why wait longer in the heat? I wave good-by, taxi into position, and ease the throttle open. As I pick up speed, I hold the tail low to put as much load as possible on the wings and reduce strain on the landing gear.

The *Spirit of St. Louis* is in the air soon after its wheels start clattering over the hummocky portion of the field. The take-off wasn't as difficult as I expected. It's 3:55 Pacific. I make a mental note of the time, check instruments, pull the throttle back slightly, and begin a wide, climbing turn to the left. Two Army observation planes and a Ryan monoplane have taken off with me as an escort. Colonel Graham, the Commanding Officer at Rockwell Field, is in one of the observation planes. Hall, Bowlus, Harrigan, and A. J. Edwards are in the Ryan. We circle North Island, the factory, and the city of San Diego. Then, leaving ocean and bay behind, I set my compass heading for St. Louis.

The coastal range of mountains is only a few miles eastward, lying about at right angles to my route. I cross over valley orchards, and climb with bush-green foothills — using just enough power to keep a safe altitude above their crests.

What a hopeless place for a forced landing! I look down on boulder-strewn mountain sides. The few bushes on that summit must root in crevices of rock. There's not a level area in sight to which I could glide in emergency. A pilot has to trust his engine above terrain like this. Of course I could have spiralled to greater height, and then held a gliding angle to some valley clearing; but in another twenty miles I'll be over desert on the eastern side. I want to make a fast flight to St. Louis. Why lose time safeguarding my plane through a few minutes of daylight when I'm to spend the entire night above canyons, lava beds, and cliffs?

At 4:30 the escorting planes dip their wings and turn back toward San Diego. To my right is Superstition Mountain; to my left, the San Jacinto peaks. Ahead, the coastal range breaks down into sharp-shadowed desert ridges.

A great valley stretches out before me, sun-scorched, sage-flecked, veined with dry, stony creek beds. Soft desert colors merge into one another until I'm not sure whether the sands are more yellow or pink. In the middle of this valley is the Salton Sea — a pale blue wash which seems to have neither depth nor wetness. My course lies directly across it, toward the crinkled Chocolate range beyond. Men have died of thirst traversing such burning wastes on foot or muleback. I glance at the two canteens hanging beside me in the cockpit. Suppose I'm forced down in the desert. Have I enough water to take me out?

I pass the winding Colorado River at 5:45, on course, and continue eastward above lengthening shadows and the weird rock formations of the Southwest. As Dean Blake predicted, I have a tail wind.

Sunset finds me over purple valleys, dusk-filled canyons, and silhouetted cliffs of Arizona, climbing steadily toward night. There are threads of steel on the ground below, barely visible in gathering twilight — tracks of the Santa Fe, and my last check point of day. I try out the magnetos — not a skip or jerk on either one. I run my eyes over the instruments — all readings are normal. My altitude is 4900 feet.

It's getting cold. I draw on boots, then mittens. Three and a quarter hours out, now. The altimeter is up to 8,000 feet, and I'm still climbing to stay well above the ridges. Ground details are obscured by a haze which has been forming since sunset. The moon is almost overhead, several days from full — and there's still some light in the west. If the sky doesn't become cloud-covered, I won't encounter full darkness until the later night.

I can't see far ahead now; but below me, the general contours of earth are perceptible in outline. When my eyes parallel the rays of the moon, its vision seems added to mine, as though I gained a satellite's perception. I run my flashlight over the instrument board — several of the dials are not luminous, and must be checked with a separate source of light. Every needle is in place. I fill out the log, and settle back in my cockpit.

The engine jerks! – – – again! – – – again! – – – the danger sign I know so well. It splutters – – – jumps – – – begins to vibrate. I grip the stick and glance toward earth I'm over mountains — bare ones — no trees. That's all I can tell. Haze is thicker: but I still see outlines with the moon. I ease back on the throttle, and throw my flashlight on the instruments. Fuel pressure is up — that's not the trouble. The engine shakes the entire plane. I pull the mixture control back, slowly, to its stop. The coughing goes on.

A forced landing — over mountains — at night – – – is it all finished, then — the flight to Paris, all our plans? There's a possibility, just the barest possibility, that I can stall down into some area of moonlight without crashing my plane beyond repair. But I'm over one of the wildest regions of Arizona, with close to 200 gallons of gasoline in my tanks. I stare at the earth. There's not a single light on its surface, not a ranch-house window to break this desperate solitude of night. Thousands of feet below I see a huge desert slope, curving up the side of a mountain. It bears no trees — the greenish-yellow shading vouches that. Is it strewn with lava? Is it veined with creek beds? Is it studded with petrified logs? Are there ridges and cliffs, eroded by rain? The dim light gives little hint of texture, but I can feel the surface there below — I've seen such mountain slopes before. My mind pictures it — cut by arroyos, spattered with stones, without a level spot where wheels can roll. Of course I'm lucky to see anything at all — suppose there were no moon, or that the sky were overcast?

I'm losing altitude slowly. In spite of its coughing and sputtering, the Whirlwind is still putting out some power. I may be able to stay in the air another quarter hour. Should I turn back now and try to find a better place to crash? No, there are only more mountains behind, and I remember vague outlines of canyons. I'll be better off where I am.

I bank slowly toward the valley, trying to estimate my altitude above ground, trying to perceive some detail of the surface to tell me what I really have to face. Which way is the wind? Probably still northwest — there's no way of being sure – – – But if I land toward the northwest, that's down slope! No, there's another place in that great scoop of earth, a place where I can land up the slope and into the wind — if it hasn't changed.

I'm still several thousand feet high. I glance at my altimeter. The needle hasn't moved much since I last looked. The forced landing, apparently, won't be immediate. I may be able to stay in the air for a long time.

There's nothing more to do about the ground. I won't be able to see any surface details until I'm much lower, and I've already decided on the general area where I'll land. I turn my eyes to the instruments again. What *can* the trouble be? It sounds like fuel mixture, but I've tried the mixture control in different positions without success. Three pounds pressure — that's normal; besides, wobbling the hand pump doesn't do any good. Is it ignition? How can it be ignition when the engine runs as well — or as badly — on one magneto as on the other? Is there water in the carburetor? But we strained every drop of fuel, carefully, and I've just drained the Lunkenheimer trap. Is something broken in the engine? Nothing I can do about it if there is.

I open the throttle wide and pull it back again. The coughing decreases slightly. I open the mixture control cautiously. That helps too. Lord only knows why it didn't help before. Yes, the engine is definitely running better. I keep circling. I'm no longer losing altitude. *Can it be that I won't have to land?* Will some miracle keep my Whirlwind going while I circle between these mountain ridges through the night? Of course I'll stay up as long as I can — nothing would be gained by crashing sooner than I have to. Each minute makes my fuel load a little lighter, reduces my landing speed some fraction of a mile. Each minute separates me that much farther from the earthly impact that's almost certain to be crushing to my body and my plane.

I keep working with mixture control and throttle, moving first one and then the other to the position which reduces shaking most. By just the right jockeying of these levers I find that I climb slowly, gaining back part of the altitude I've lost. I was down to 7,000 feet above sea level at the lowest point – within two or three thousand of the ground, as near as I could judge. Now, I'm up to 7,500.

Should I try to spiral until daybreak? Should I take up my heading east across the Rockies, toward sunrise and level Kansas plains? Should I turn back toward California where I know the skies are clear, and try to find the air field on North Island? I glance at the clock — 8:07. It seems hours, yet it's been only fifteen minutes since the missing started.

Against the wind, San Diego is close to five hours of flight behind me. I'd have to pass over all those weird formations of the desert, where a forced landing might well be equal to a fatal crash. And even if I reached the ocean, there's the possibility of a coastal fog at night.

If I fly eastward, I've got Rocky Mountain crags to pass, but I'll cut almost an hour off night by flying toward dawn. In eight hours at most I'll meet the rising sun over that gigantic landing field, Kansas.

Staying where I am holds little appeal; though if my engine fails completely, I'd be better off.

Twenty minutes have passed since the missing started — a third of an hour lost, circling around. The Whirlwind is running better now. I feel confidence returning. Maybe my trouble is caused only by altitude and the cold air of night. If so, there is still hope. I'll use more power and watch the mixture control carefully. I stop spiralling and take up my St. Louis course, setting the throttle at 1750 revolutions a minute, climbing steadily to get above the mountain peaks. The missing increases as I gain altitude, but I want to clear those ridges with an extra margin. I should hold at least 10,000 feet.

Of course — a new thought enters my mind — I might turn south toward the Mexican border, where mountains are lower and where the air is probably warmer. I have plenty of fuel in the tanks. But that would destroy the check on navigation which is my main object in this flight. It's extremely important to see how far off route I am when the sun rises. If serious errors have crept into my navigational techniques, I must learn about them before I start across the ocean. The fuel-consumption data I hoped to obtain is already thrown off — spiralling, climbing, and using an extra hundred r.p.m. to keep the engine warm make it almost valueless. But I can run another test on that during the flight from St. Louis to New York — not as good, but accurate enough for my requirements. What I need now is a check on navigation. So I'll try to hold to the route I laid out in San Diego.

I've left the broad valleys behind. Below, I see only steep sides of mountains, sheering into narrow, night-locked ravines. There's not even a spot fit to crash on. But the use of more power is working. The engine sometimes runs for several minutes between coughing spells.

I'm over 13,000 feet now. I wonder if it's the Continental Divide — that long, snowcapped ridge, reaching to outer limits of the moonlight. I clear summits by about 500 feet. Those big dark patches, farther down, may mark the timber line.

The Rockies are behind. Mountains melted quickly into foot-hills, and foothills have rolled out into level plains. I see the lights of four villages, stringing north and south. They're probably tied together by a railroad. I ease my stick forward to lose altitude and reach a warmer air. Soon I'll be over the panhandle of Oklahoma, if I've not drifted north of route.

Twelve o'clock, San Diego time. I'm about halfway to Lambert Field. The *Spirit of St. Louis* has been in the air for better than eight hours. That's much longer than any flight I ve made before. Haze is thicker. The moon is low in the west. I'm down to 8000 feet. The Whirlwind runs smoothly now, with the throttle well advanced. I'll have a carburetor heater put on at New York. The warning I received tonight may save my life over the North Atlantic, flying in still colder air.

The moon is setting at – – – 1:20 by the clock. I no longer see outlines on the ground; but scattered lights, here and there, give perspective to night's growing blackness.

Stars are fading in the sky ahead — the first sign of morning. I've spanned deserts and mountains during hours of night, but the sun has flown all around the world — over the Pacific, over Asia and Europe, across the Atlantic which I am soon to meet; and now we're about to come together above Kansas plains. I feel sleepy. That's normal with the dawn.

East's horizon sharpens. A tinge of pink precedes the birth of day. I see outlines of fields below — straight-edged shades, one darker than another; and here and there is a ravelled line which marks a creek bed. I'm somewhere over Kansas. That's almost certain. But where? How far off course? In a few more minutes I'll know.

A red disc bumps up the sky's edge. A barn roof glints sharply at my plane. Spinning windmills point northwestward. Oil derricks are scattered around ahead. The ground is clearly lit. Now to find where I am on the map. There's the smoke of a train. Tracks come angling in from the northwest, and run on toward a small city several miles away, under my right wing. I unfold the map of Kansas.

About forty minutes ago, in early dawn, I crossed a fairly large river. If I haven't drifted off my route, it must have been the Arkansas. If so, I'm more than three hours ahead of schedule, in spite of the time I lost circling that Arizona valley, and I should be seventy-five or eighty miles east of Wichita. Finding my position will be a matter of elimination. For the moment I can eliminate all railroads which don't run northwest and southeast. There's another roadbed that enters my field of vision from east of north, converging with the first on the same little city. I try to find a line of ink that corresponds to it. And there's a third railroad, with straight miles of track coming in from the east and bending sharply southwest. Such straight lines and definite angles should be distinctive even in the state of Kansas. But I see no printer's counterpart in the area where I think I ought to be.

Could I have drifted south to the Cimarron, or to the Arkansas' west fork? I begin searching farther from my estimated position. My eyes jump up and down across the map. Soon I find the pattern I'm looking for — the same lines, the same angles, villages and towns where villages and towns should be. The track on my right connects Cherryvale with Parsons, Kansas.

Yes, my location is definite. There must have been a strong tail wind during the night; and I've held a higher r.p.m. than I intended. But I'm nearly fifty miles south of my route! I had expected to come out closer than that. Of course I've been nine hours in unknown wind drifts. That's an average of only five miles an hour toward the south. And it won't make much difference to my time — the corrective angle is too small. But I hope to hold a better course across the ocean.

Well, the flight has been successful. That's the important thing. In less than three hours I'll be at St. Louis. And if anything *should* go wrong now, there are landing fields everywhere below. Soon I'll circle Lambert Field; and then, if my partners agree, after one night of rest, I'll take off for the flight over the Alleghenies to New York. That's a short trip, compared to the one I'm finishing. Tomorrow I may be on Long Island, the starting point for Paris. And then – – – But I won't let my mind go any farther; there's still too much to be done. It's better to concentrate on one step at a time.

To the south are Ozark foothills. The Missouri River winds below. I barnstormed that town on my left, last year. And thirty miles up this tributary valley lies a narrow pasture, in between hills, from which I carried passengers in an area where no plane had dared land before. Then I wasn't even thinking about a flight across the ocean.

I mark down instrument readings for the last time. In a few minutes more I'll be landing. I see the outline of Lambert Field. Now buildings begin to show. There are the twin, round-roofed "air race" hangars. There, the black hangars of my National Guard squadron. Now I see Robertson Aircraft's shops and office, at first screened off by trees. There's Louie's lunch shack, closer to the line — all as I left them two and a half months ago. How green the field has become! It was a muddy brown in February.

I push my stick forward and open the throttle. A minute or two of full power won't hurt the engine — it's had plenty of running-in. Here at my home field, after a record flight from California, I can indulge in that luxury. I want everyone to see how fast the *Spirit of St. Louis* is, and how wonderfully it climbs.

Several men are standing in front of the National Guard hangars as I approach. It's only eight o'clock, local time. I wonder who'll be first to spot my plane. The air speed needle touches 160 miles an hour. That's fast enough; I won't push the nose down more — no use putting too much strain on the wings. Figures run out of buildings as I flash overhead. Fifty feet off the ground now. I ease the stick back slightly – – – twenty feet – – – ten – – – five – – – over the center of the field – – – I pull up steeply in a climbing turn – – – three hundred feet – – – seven hundred – – – a thousand – – – fifteen hundred. Lambert Field never saw a plane with such a combination of range, speed, and climb.

I circle once, and point my nose toward St. Louis — I promised to fly over the business district before landing. The city shows clear today, its streets like ruled lines. The west wind has carried off the usual pall of smoke.

There's the bump of office buildings that marks the downtown section. There's Harry Knight's brokerage firm. There's Bixby's State National Bank — I nose down and fly close to the flagpoles, so everyone there will hear my engine. I'll have to head for the Mississippi if I have a forced landing; but after my night over the mountains, flying within gliding distance of a river in daylight seems the height of safety.

The *Spirit of St. Louis* touches ground at 6:20 California time — fourteen hours and twenty-five minutes from take-off. No man ever traveled so fast from the Pacific coast before. I taxi up in front of the National Guard hangars. Every person in sight is walking or running toward my plane. Bill and Frank Robertson come up to welcome me, and a half-dozen pilots and mechanics — all old friends. Several St. Louis reporters are on hand. I climb out of my cockpit.

"When did you leave San Diego, Slim?"

"Say, you must'a made pretty good time!"

"What was the weather like?"

"How's the engine?"

"Did you come all the way nonstop?"

Soon we're walking over to Louie's shack for breakfast.

"Here's your transport-pilot's license," Bill Robertson says, handing me a Bureau of Aeronautics envelope. "You've got number 69."

"Just fits you," somebody remarks. "Right side up or upside down — the same."

"Any news from Nungesser and Coli?" I ask.

"There's a report that a British ship picked them up at sea," one of the newspapermen replies. "But we can't get confirmation."

"Has the Bellanca taken off yet?"

"No. The last report is that they're going to take off Saturday, if the weather's good enough."

"What's holding them up?"

"Don't know; but have you heard about the warning from the State Department?"

"No. What is it?"

"Our Embassy in Paris sent a cable saying it might be misunderstood if an American plane lands in France before there's definite word about Nungesser and Coli."

"Has the government put any restriction on taking off?" I ask.

"No. That's apparently up to the pilots. There weren't any restrictions issued, just the warning."

"The Bellanca is going to make the flight anyway," somebody else says. "What do you think you'll do, Slim?"

"I don't know. I'll have to find out exactly what the situation is," I answer. "I'll go through to New York at least. If Nungesser and Coli are lost, it seems to me it's up to the rest of us to carry on what they attempted."

Louie keeps a collection of photographs of aviators tacked to his lunch-stand walls — on one wall the flyers who are alive, on another the flyers who are dead. Every now and then someone slips into the stand when Louie is away and mixes up the photographs. We pilots check occasionally, just to be sure we are on the right wall. This time nobody has changed my picture — or maybe Louie looked over his collection and straightened it out before I landed.

While we're eating Louie's ham and eggs, Harold Bixby and Harry Knight arrive. Soon my other partners begin phoning and assembling. I show them the *Spirit of St. Louis,* tell them about the flight, and of the results of our tests in San Diego. We go off together to discuss plans.

"How long can you stay in the city, Slim?" Bixby asks.

"We've got a half-dozen dinner invitations for you," Harry Knight adds, laughing. "A lot of people would like to hear about your flight."

"I'll stay as long as you want me to," I answer. "But I think I ought to go right on to New York. If I don't, somebody else will beat us to the take-off. Unless this storm holds them down, the Bellanca crew will probably start before I can anyway. But they may not get through the first time they try."

"That's what we thought you'd say, Slim. It's going to disappoint a lot of people, but you're right. Now that we're really in the running, we're not going to let a couple of dinners hold us down. We had some things lined up for you tomorrow, but we'll cancel them all. You'd better stay here and get some sleep tonight. Why don't you come out to my house? Take off in the morning if you want to. How's the plane?"

"Couldn't be better," I answer. "All it needs is some grease on the rocker arms and a little gas."

How could one have better partners? They always understand my problems, and they're always behind me when I need help. If I'm not the first to land at Paris, it certainly won't be their fault.

"How's the Spirit of St. Louis Organization coming along?" I ask.

"Fine. We've got some new members, too," Bixby tells me. "Harry Knight's father is with us. Frank Robertson is in with Bill, of course. E. Lansing Ray joined up — he runs the *Globe-Democrat*. Doc Lambert got his brother, J. D. Wooster Lambert, to come in. We're moving along pretty fast. Don't you worry about finances. You just leave them to us, and we'll leave the flight to you."

·V·

ROOSEVELT FIELD

MAY 12–20, 1927

I TAKE OFF from Lambert Field at 8:13 a.m., and set course for New York City. The sky is clear. My route takes me directly over the Missouri-Mississippi junction. Illinois grain fields ripple in a northwest wind. The *Spirit of St. Louis* has grown with those crops: I conceived the flight last fall when the wheat was planted. Now I'm getting under way with the green blades of spring.

Land below is rolling. Shadows of white, fluffy clouds slide across alfalfa, corn, and wood lot. I've caught up with the tail of the storm that delayed my San Diego take-off. Will the Allegheny Mountains be clear? Maybe I started too early. Maybe I can't get through to New York today. But I've got to follow as closely as I can on the area of bad weather. If only it will hover over the Atlantic and hold my competitors on the ground for two or three days more, I'll have the engine checked, the compasses in, and the *Spirit of St. Louis* refueled.

There's Columbus already, and I'm only three and a quarter hours out. This is the way the mail should fly from Lambert Field to New York.

The sky has become overcast. Mountainsides above me slant into heavy clouds, their rocks and forests merging with the mist. Clearings are scarce. Hogback ranges push valleys down to creek beds that are hardly visible through the leaves. Now I follow a pass with the railroad; now I squeeze over a saddle in a ridge. That village of square, gray, dreary houses must be part of a coal mine. I'm over Pennsylvania. I crossed the Monongahela River, south of Pittsburgh, fifty-five minutes ago.

It's the end of the seventh hour, 3:15 St. Louis time. Manhattan Island lies below me — building-weighted, wharf-spined, teeming with life — millions of people in that river-boundaried strip of brick and concrete, each one surrounded by a little aura of his problems and his thoughts, hardly conscious of earth's expanse beyond. What contrast to the western spaces I have crossed! I feel cooped up just looking at it.

Ahead, beyond those suburbs on Long Island, lies the field from which I'll start for Paris. Will it be Curtiss, Roosevelt, or Mitchel? How long a run will I have? What obstacles must I clear? For weeks I've tried vainly to get that information; now I'll soon have the answers to my questions.

That looks like a line of hangar roofs. Yes, there's a field beside them, and a second — and a third, not far away. The one on the right must be Mitchel, for its planes are painted olive drab. I bank to circle all three, while I study size and surface.

Mitchel is better kept than the others; after all, it's an Army field. But, except near the center, the sod looks rough as I pass over it — a bit like North Island. And Curtiss, where I'm about to land, is much too small for a heavy-load take-off. Roosevelt is large enough, and it's the only one that has a runway — a long, narrow affair, laid out approximately east and west. If the wind blows in the direction of that runway when I want to start, Roosevelt will be the best. Yes, I'll take off from either Roosevelt or Mitchel. I can't decide which until I've walked over them several times and found out whether I can get permission to use the one I prefer. Byrd and Chamberlin must have made satisfactory arrangements for their tests and overloaded take-offs. Whatever solution they found will probably do for me.

I circle over Curtiss. It has peak-roofed wooden hangars to the north and west. Beyond them are scattered houses — the outskirts of Mineola. A short but rather steep slope, clearly visible from my thousand feet of altitude, separates Curtiss from Roosevelt Field. The west end of the long runway is just beyond it. A dozen or so planes are on the line—Jennies, Standards, Orioles, painted in all the colors of the rainbow.

There must be two or three hundred people down there looking up at me. I glance at the wind sock, bank steeply around, and throttle back. It's 3:31 Central Standard time.

A number of men with cameras have scattered out onto the field. Some of them right where I want to touch my wheels. I gun the engine, bank out of the way, and slip down to land at an angle with the wind. Almost as soon as my plane comes to a stop it's surrounded by newspaper photographers. I shout at them to keep clear of the propeller, but no one pays attention. Two men are trying to get a picture of me in the cockpit. Others are in front, at the sides, and behind the plane. Heavy motion-picture cameras on their tripods are pointing at me. I've never seen such excitement and disorder around aircraft. Why can't they wait until I taxi to the line and stop my engine? I'd put the *Spirit of St. Louis* wherever they want it for background, angle, and light, just as I did yesterday at Lambert Field. They'd have better pictures, it would save a lot of time, and I wouldn't have to worry about anyone getting hurt.

Several mechanics come out to guard my propeller and lead me to a place on the line in front of one of the hangars. I cut switches, and someone chocks my wheels. A crowd packs around my cockpit, pushing and shouting. A man who obviously has some authority works his way through it with difficulty.

"I'm Casey Jones — — — airport manager." Welcome in eye and voice accompany his extended hand.

Casey Jones, the famous Curtiss test pilot! What aviator hasn't heard of him?

"We've got one of the hangars ready for you," he continues.

"You've made a fast flight." His glance sweeps around my cockpit, over instruments and controls.

Another man comes up beside him, slender, moustached: "I'm Dick Blythe," he says. "I represent the Wright Aeronautical Corporation. They've instructed me to offer you all the help they can give."

"I won't need a whole hangar," I tell them — "just room enough for my plane. I'd like to have an expert mechanic check over the engine. It hasn't had much time in the air, but I want to be sure that – – –"

Blythe doesn't wait for me to finish. "We've got the best Whirlwind men in the country right here waiting," he says. "I think you know Ken Boedecker. He's one of the corporation's field service representatives. And this is Ed Mulligan. He's assigned exclusively to your plane, as long as you need him. I haven't told you about myself yet. I handle public relations. And along that line, how about letting the camera boys get a picture of you in front of the plane? Some of them have a deadline to make."

There's a milling about as I climb down from my cockpit. Several men are making notes on pads of paper. They must be reporters. Space is cleared with difficulty, and I take position, as requested, with one hand on the propeller of the *Spirit of St. Louis*.

Each moment I feel more uncomfortable. It's not like San Diego or St. Louis. These cameramen curse and jostle one another for position, while they take pictures from every conceivable angle. Some stand up, others kneel or crouch; a few even lie on the ground to point their lenses at me. They take photographs head on, photographs from the quarter, photographs from the side, distant shots, close-ups, motion pictures, and stills.

"Smile!"

"Look this way, will ya?"

"Shake hands with somebody."

"Say something."

"God damn it, stop yer shovin'!"

"Hey, there's Chamberlin and Bertaud."

"Start talkin' to each other."

"Christ, get out of the way!"

They must have enough pictures to last forever. I start to leave.

"Wait a minute. Gotta get a close-up."

"Hold it."

"Just one more."

They crowd nearer. Cameras come within three or four feet of my face. I turn away and begin walking toward the nearest hangar. Photographers run in front. Reporters close in around me; there must be a dozen of them.

"When're you going to start for Paris?"

"Tell us something about your flight from California."

"Did ya have any close calls?"

"What do you think about Nungesser?"

"What does yer mother say about all this?"

There's no use asking the questions because I don't get a chance to answer any of them. Somebody slaps me on the back, hard. Somebody else pulls sideways on my arm.

"Now fellows," Blythe breaks in, "let's get this organized so it's fair to everybody."

"Look! There's the *America*."

We all glance up. A big trimotored Fokker drones overhead.

"That's the first time it's been over here."

"Byrd must be about ready to go again," somebody says.

I slip into the side door of a hangar while Blythe is making arrangements for the interview. Mechanics push the *Spirit of St. Louis* into one end, in front of two Orioles and a Waco. We stretch a rope across the entrance and leave the sliding doors open so people can see my plane, while at the same time it's protected from the fingers of their curiosity. The crowd outside is increasing; and when people are interested enough to come to the field, it would be unfair to confront them with closed hangar doors — that's not the way to build up aviation.

Now I've got to get the final conditioning of my plane under way; but it's past six, Eastern daylight time — too late to accomplish much today.

"I'll want to phone about my compass in the morning," I start out saying.

"You won't have to bother about that," Boedecker tells me. "Hey, come over here a minute." He beckons to a man looking in through the near window of my cockpit.

"This is Brice Goldsborough, from the Pioneer Instrument Company. He can fix you up on anything about instruments. Just tell him what you want. He's got your earth-inductor compass here, all ready to put in."

To my amazement, I find that all the organizations I planned on contacting have their representatives right here on Curtiss Field, ready to do whatever they can to help me.

Another man steps up. "I'm from the Vacuum Oil Company. My name is Umlauf. When do you want your gasoline and oil sent out? We've got it all ready for you."

A hand grips my arm. It's Dick Blythe.

"Captain, I've got the press representatives all together now. They're waiting for you in the hangar office. But a few photographers didn't get a picture when you landed. They want you to stand in front of the plane again and give them another chance."

"Good Lord, haven't they got enough photographs?" I ask. "I want to get down to business."

"I know," Blythe replies, "but they say it will only take five minutes, and that they won't ask for any more. They didn't think your ship was so fast — that's why they're late. They probably stopped to get a drink along the road. I think you ought to do it," he argues pleasantly. "It will keep them in good humor, and if you don't, some of them may lose their jobs. New York editors are pretty tough."

I stand in front of the *Spirit of St. Louis* again, feeling awkward and foolish, with dozens of people staring at me and girls giggling, while the pictures are being taken. Instead of "a few" photographers who arrived late for my landing, there are more than before.

Pictures over at last, I find the reporters waiting in a large office at the side of one of the hangars. There must be twenty or thirty of them, standing, leaning, draped on desks and chairs — all looking at me intently. In between them are scattered more photographers, with flash bulbs attached to their cameras. The questioning starts at once.

"When are you going to take off for Paris?"

"My engine needs servicing, and I'm having new compasses installed," I answer. "After that's done, I'll take off as soon as the weather clears up enough."

"Do you think you'll take off in the morning?"

"No, I don't know yet when I'll start. It may be several days. I won't leave until everything is right."

"What kind of navigation are you going to use?"

"Dead reckoning."

"You're not carrying a sextant?"

"No."

"How about a radio?"

"I'm not carrying one."

"Why not?"

"They're heavy, and they're not very well developed," I explain. "The best information I can get indicates that they cut out when you need them most."

"Well, Byrd and Chamberlin are going to carry radios, and sextants too."

"I looked into it rather carefully, and decided I'd rather have extra gasoline."

"What are you going to do about that State Department warning?" a reporter asks.

"I'll follow whatever requests the government makes," I answer.

Questions about my plane and flights are covered quickly.

Then subjects are raised which I feel are too personal or too silly to discuss.

"Do you carry a rabbit's foot?"

"What's your favorite pie?"

"Have you got a sweetheart?"

"How do you feel about girls?"

After the interview, a reporter from one of the tabloids tells me that his editor wants to purchase the exclusive story of my flight, and that it's worth several thousand dollars! That's a huge amount of money for a little writing. Here's a chance to build up our cash reserve. I reply that I'll think the proposition over, and suggest that we talk about it more tomorrow. If there's going to be an exclusive story, my partner, E. Lansing Ray, should have first right to it for his *Globe-Democrat*; but we could sell the rights outside of St. Louis to someone else. I'll phone Bixby and Knight and ask for their advice.

It's dark by the time I reach my room at the Garden City Hotel. I wanted to stay on the field, but there's no place to sleep, and the hotel isn't far away.

2

During supper my newly made friends bring me up to date on the New York-to-Paris flight developments. Everything centers on Curtiss and Roosevelt Fields. Mitchel Field has dropped out of the picture — partly because it's military and partly because of its size. The runway on Roosevelt Field is close to a mile long — it's really the only place for a heavily loaded take-off. Byrd has a lease on the field, but I can probably get permission to use the runway when he doesn't need it himself. His trimotored Fokker is now in the hangar at the far end of Roosevelt. Its rebuilding has just been completed, after the crack-up at Teterboro. Byrd and Noville weren't injured very badly, but Floyd Bennett is still in the hospital. Chamberlin's Bellanca is on Curtiss Field, only a few hundred feet away from the *Spirit of St. Louis*.

"Why hasn't the Bellanca taken off yet?" I ask.

"Weather and personnel trouble," Blythe tells me. "The route forecasts have been bad, and there's been a lot of squabbling going on. You've probably read about some of it. Acosta withdrew, you know. He's going to fly with Byrd."

"Don't think it was Giuseppe Bellanca's fault though, or Clarence Chamberlin's," one of my friends adds. "The plane would have been off long ago if the decision had been up to them."

The Wright Aeronautical Corporation is in the enviable but difficult position of having its Whirlwind engines in all the New York-to-Paris planes. Consequently the corporation must maintain strict neutrality as far as Byrd, Chamberlin, and myself are concerned. Its engineers and mechanics have been instructed to help put each engine and plane in the best possible condition, as a matter of policy. The corporation's interest doesn't end with the engine, Boedecker explains, for the engine is no better than its installation; and if something goes wrong with a plane that forces it to land in the ocean, the engine will probably get the blame regardless of the real cause. As long as its Whirlwinds are going on the Paris flight, the Wright Corporation intends to get them there—engine, installation, plane, and all.

During the last few days, Blythe tells me, newspaper interest has become intense. Several editors think that the New York-to-Paris flight will be the story of the year. With a long record of crashes, with four men killed, two missing, and three injured, and with three planes waiting only on weather or minor adjustments before taking off for France, the journalistic atmosphere has reached fever heat.

Before I arrived at St. Louis yesterday, New Yorkers had paid relatively little attention to my project. The fact that I was an unknown pilot, that I planned to fly alone, and that my plane was being built by a small company over two thousand miles away, had thrown them off guard. But when I landed on Lambert Field, nonstop and overnight from California, their attitude underwent a rapid change. Then my swift, though shorter, flight through to New York caused me to be viewed with different eyes. My critics are confronted with the fact that the *Spirit of St. Louis* has now been more thoroughly tested in long cross-country flights than either the *America* or the *Columbia*. The trim lines of my plane, the solo crossing of the continent, my actual presence here among them, create extraordinary elements of competition and suspense, and give new impetus to old arguments — both lay and professional. Engineers argue about whether wings can take off so heavily loaded. Pilots question the ability of a man to fly 3,600 miles alone. There are a few who believe I have the best chance of all, but most say that mine is a fool's venture.

"What do you think of that?"

I read the clipping placed beside my fork:

THINKS NUNGESSER TRIED TOO MUCH

HALIFAX, N.S., May 10 (AP).—Captain Charles Nungesser made "the mistake of endeavoring to fly his machine the entire distance himself," in the opinion of Major A. S. Shearer of the Royal Canadian Air Force, who arrived here from Ottawa yesterday in company with J. L. Ralston, Minister of National Defense. The Major said he considered it a physical impossibility for one man to pilot an airplane across the Atlantic for forty hours ---

"Well, I've stayed awake over forty hours more than once, working pretty hard most of the time too," I say. "I don't see why I shouldn't be able to fly that long, sitting down."

After supper we drive back to Curtiss Field. "What's the latest news on Nungesser and Coli?" I ask.

"Same story. One headline says they've been picked up; the next says they haven't. That sells papers. There are reports that their plane was heard over Newfoundland by a dozen people last Monday. It will probably be denied in the next editions. Some of the French papers printed an account of the *White Bird*'s landing at New York. They even quoted Nungesser's first words to the American press."

Mulligan has the cowlings off when we arrive, and is working efficiently and quietly on my engine. Boedecker pulls off his coat and starts working too. Blythe goes out to talk to reporters. I putter around the plane. I'm going to take out the six dry batteries to save weight; the instrument board lights are too bright anyway, and I can carry an extra flashlight in my pocket.

"You've certainly got the rival camps stirred up," Blythe tells me when he comes back. "The press boys say it looks as though mechanics are going to work all night on both the Fokker and the Bellanca."

"How about the Fokker?" I ask. "Is Byrd ready to go?"

"They're all damn secret about their plans, but he'll probably be tied up for a few days with tests."

"Do you think the Bellanca will try a morning take-off?"

"There are rumors to that effect," Blythe replies, "but the Weather Bureau says conditions over the Atlantic are pretty bad."

"As far as I'm concerned, that's fine," I say. "I hope the weather stays bad until I get my engine checked and compasses swung. Then I'd like to follow this storm right on across the ocean, the same way I followed it from San Diego."

3

LINDBERGH HERE, READY
FOR SEA HOP

CHAMBERLIN AND LINDBERGH
SET TO GO

It's the morning of May 13th. Blythe has brought the New York papers to my room. I stare, slightly dazed, at the headlines. My name is in huge print on all front pages. I glance down the columns:

Bellanca Plane, Spurred by Lindbergh's Arrival, Is Ready to Go

---

Spirit of St. Louis and America Join Their Rival Here for the Hop-Off

---

WEATHER AT SEA STILL BAD

SHIPS HUNT NUNGESSER

What promises to be the most spectacular race ever held—3,600 miles over the open sea to Paris—may start tomorrow morning. Three transatlantic planes are on Curtiss and Roosevelt Fields, within a short distance of each other, ready to take the air. - - -

"When will they go and who will be the first away?" was the question on everyone's lips.

Observers at the field look to Lindbergh as a dark horse in the race. He arrived yesterday afternoon, ahead of schedule, after a fast seven and a quarter hour flight from St. Louis. The trim, slender lines of his silver-coated monoplane impressed pilots and mechanics alike. - - -

"You've taken the show," Blythe says. "The boys don't know how to size you up. They can't laugh off your flight from California. At any other time that would be a big story in itself."

"How's the weather?" I ask.

"Still bad."

"Let's get some breakfast."

When we arrive at the hangar on Curtiss Field, I find a crowd already assembled to see the *Spirit of St. Louis*. Mulligan comes up to me with a piece of cowling in his hands.

"Where's the propeller?" I inquire.

"Over at the Curtiss Company," he tells me. "We found a crack in the spinner. They're fixing up a new one for you."

"They said they wouldn't send a bill for the work," Boedecker adds, "so we didn't wait to ask you if it was all right. Outside of that, your engine's checked and set to go. Mulligan and I worked most of the night on it — thought you might want to run some tests today – – – I'd like you to meet Ken Lane, chief airplane engineer for Wright — just got in this morning. He'll be in charge of the corporation's interests over here from now on."

It's extraordinary. Here's the Curtiss Company, one of the Wright Corporation's chief competitors, repairing my spinner for nothing. Everywhere I turn it's the same way. Bellanca and Chamberlin stop by to wish me well. Commander Byrd comes to my hangar to extend a welcome, and to offer me the use of Roosevelt Field for my take-off. He's spent much more effort and money than I have in preparing for the Paris flight, and he must be just as anxious as I am to be first to land on Le Bourget; yet he gives me the use of his runway, free of charge—and he says I'm welcome to his weather information too.

"The press boys want another interview and some more photographs," Blythe tells me. "They want a picture of you, Byrd, and Chamberlin, together. How about it, Commander?"

Byrd smiles and nods.

I work on the *Spirit of St. Louis* most of the morning, with mechanics and instrument experts. Mulligan is installing a carburetor air heater on the Whirlwind; we have concluded that all my trouble over the mountains, on the flight between San Diego and St. Louis, was caused by cold air. After lunch I walk to Roosevelt Field to go over the runway, foot by foot. The surface has a tendency to softness, and I wish it were a little wider; but on the whole, it will give me a longer and better take-off run than I expected to find anywhere around New York.

Now I must take Brice Goldsborough on a flight to check my compasses. That will be fun. It will surprise everyone to see how quickly the *Spirit of St. Louis* can take off and climb. A car bumps out over the field to pick me up, and a motorcycle police-man escorts us back to the hangar, where two more uniformed officers are stationed at the doors. Inside, Blythe hands me another group of papers. "You won't like these very much," he says.

FLYIN' FOOL HOPS TODAY

A big front-page picture of myself is below the tabloid head-lines. I'm the "flyin' fool," and I'm supposed to be ready to take off for Paris at any moment! Didn't I tell the reporters that I wouldn't leave until the weather was right and my compasses were swung? All they had to do was look in through the door of the hangar if they didn't believe me. Well, I suppose they think this makes a better story. And here's another article, just as bad:

Flying Kid Will Write From Paris

--- The Kid Flyer sauntered --- to Cur-tiss Field --- in his pocket was a tooth-brush and a comb ---
    Asked about his mother, Mrs. Evangeline Lindbergh, a teacher of chemistry in Cass Technical High School, Detroit, the young aviator said: "Mother is a flying enthusiast --- No, of course I'm not going to wire her before I take off. It would be too hysterical, as if I were worrying or thought she was. - - - And I'm not going to tell what Mother's address is. Reporters might worry her too much." Meanwhile, news-papermen in Detroit found Mrs. Lind-bergh who steadfastly refused to make a statement. ---

Now, I don't carry a toothbrush in my pocket, and what I said about my mother was very different from that — I wish the Detroit reporters would leave her alone.

Depending on which paper I pick up, I find that I was born in Minnesota, that I was born in Michigan, that I was born in Nebraska; that I learned to fly at Omaha, that I learned to fly at Lincoln, that I learned to fly at San Antonio, in Texas. I'm told that my nickname is "Lucky," that I land and take off by looking through periscopes, that without them I can see only downward from my cockpit, that I carry "devices" on my plane which will enable me to "snatch a snooze" while steering a "beeline" for Paris.

4

There are knocks on the door of my bedroom, in the Garden City Hotel. Conversation stops.

"Telegram, sir!" I give the bellboy a dime and tear open the yellow envelope.

CAPT. CHARLES A. LINDBERGH   DETROIT MICH.
CURTISS FIELD, LONG ISLAND, N.Y. MAY 13, 27

ARRIVE NEW YORK TOMORROW MORNING
       MOTHER

Good Lord! I know what's happened: it's the newspapers. She's been reading the stories that say I'm likely to crash on take-off, like Fonck and Davis, or be lost at sea, like Nungesser and Coli. She's coming to Long Island to see if I need advice or help – – – No, it's not as definite as that. She's coming to be near me in this period of danger. Probably the Detroit reporters have been phoning her every hour. But Curtiss Field is the last place where she should be. I don't want to leave her to the tabloid press when I take off for Paris; and before that, I should concentrate every minute on my preparations. I'll telephone – – – no, her train's already left.

I begin to realize there's another reason, besides being first to Paris, why I should get away from New York. Every day I stay here will draw more of my attention from my plane and preparations. My problems are already shifting from aviation to reporters, photographers, business propositions, and requests for autographs. Now I must arrange to meet and care for my mother when she arrives in this chaotic place.

It wouldn't be so bad if I could go off quietly for an hour by myself — if I could walk over the field alone and feel earth beneath the soles of my shoes while I let the wind blow confusion from my mind. But the moment I step outside the hangar I'm surrounded by people and protected by police. Somebody shouts my name, and immediately I'm surrounded by a crowd. Even at the hotel, newspapermen fill the lobby and watch the entrance so carefully that I can't walk around the block without being followed. There's never a free moment except when I'm in my room. It detracts from the health of one's body and prevents real clarity of thought. That's why Lane, Mulligan, Blythe, and I are sitting here together. That's why I phoned room service to send our supper up on trays. I'm tired of shaking hands, and writing my name on slips of paper, and being poked and stared at. I want to spend a normal hour for a change.

I put the telegram in my pocket. The waiter leaves. Conversation begins again.

"There are more damn crazy ideas floating around this place than I've ever heard before."

"Did you talk to that fellow with the gray beard? Says he's invented some way to get more power out of a gallon of gas."

"Sure, I told him the Curtiss Company might be interested. Thought it would keep him out of the way for a day or two."

"That guy with the high speed engine is the tough one to shake off."

"Say, did I tell you about the man who's got a young dancer on his string? She's worked out an act to symbolize the flight between New York and Paris. He wants to get her out here in costume and have her photographed doing a split on the propeller of the *Spirit of St. Louis*."

"A what?"

"A split."

"What's that?"

"It's a stage stunt. You know — when they slide one leg out front and the other back, and set down in between."

"On a propeller?"

"Yeh — horizontal."

"I should think it would be pretty difficult."

"Well, we're not going to make the test."

The phone rings. It's another weather report. The Atlantic is still partly covered with areas of fog and storm, and there's not much sign of improvement.

"You ought to visit the New York Weather Bureau, Captain," Blythe says. "Doc Kimball could give you a lot of dope. He's working out charts for Byrd. you know. The boys all say he's good."

"I'd like to do that tomorrow," I answer. "Do you suppose he'll be there Saturday? I've got to get my passport and visa lined up too. I wonder if ——— "

The door bursts open and two men stride into my room carrying press cameras. We all jump from our chairs. There's a moment of silence.

"Say, who do you think you are?" Lane is the first to regain his voice.

"We represent the New York ———. We're here to get a picture of 'Lucky Lindy' shaving and sitting on the bed in his pajamas."

"Well, where I come from, it's customary to knock before you walk into somebody's bedroom!"

The men grin, look at me, start adjusting their cameras.

"No! ——— Get out." We practically push them from the room.

It may be bad public relations, but I'm not going to have my private life invaded to *that* extent. I feel fighting mad about the incident.

Blythe laughs. "You'll find a lot of 'em like that around here," he says.

We lock the door.

5

My mother spent one day with me, and left. She felt she had to have that day, she told me. The stories in the newspapers and the phone calls from reporters in Detroit disturbed her so greatly that she had to see me before I took off — just to see me — to talk to me — to make sure I really wanted to go and felt it was the right thing to do. Then, she said, she would return home. She had never meant to stay, because she knew that would take my attention from the flight.

This is Monday evening, May 16th. The *Spirit of St. Louis* is ready to take off, but my route to Paris is still covered with fog and storm. These have been the most extraordinary days I've ever spent; and I can't call them very pleasant. Life has become too strange and hectic. The attention of the entire country is centered on the flight to Paris, and most of all on me — because I'm going alone, because I'm young, because I'm a "dark horse." Papers in every city and village are headlining my name and writing articles about me. Newspaper, radio, and motion-picture publicity has brought people crowding out to Curtiss and Roosevelt Fields until the Nassau County police are faced with a major traffic problem. Seventy-five hundred came last Saturday, the New York *Times* said. On Sunday there were thirty thousand!

And mail has started coming to the field, addressed to me. First a few letters arrived, then dozens; now I have more than a hundred envelopes stacked in my room. I've opened only a few. The writers want me to send autographs, want to give me advice, want to show me inventions, to offer me business propositions, to share with me their viewpoints on religion. One or two dreamed that Nungesser and Coli are still alive, and sent vague directions for finding them. What to do with all this mail is a problem. I don't like to sit down at a desk and answer letters; but anyway, I'm not going to worry about that before my take-off.

Up to date, our project has been successful beyond my wildest dreams. We've brought the attention to St. Louis that we planned. We've helped focus everybody's eyes on aviation and its future. We've shown what kind of flights a modern plane can make; and my reputation as a pilot has been established. The New York *Times* is going to buy the story of my flight and syndicate it throughout the country. All this is very satisfactory. But there are disturbing elements too. The way the tabloid people acted when my mother came, left me with no respect for them whatever. They didn't care how much they hurt her feelings or frightened her about my flight, as long as they got their pictures and their stories. Did she know what a dangerous trip her son was undertaking? they asked. Did she realize how many older and more experienced aviators had been killed in its attempt? They wanted her to describe her sensations for their readers. They demanded that we embrace for their cameras and say good-by. When we refused, one paper had two other people go through the motions, and substituted photographs of our heads for theirs — composite pictures, they call them. I decided then that I wouldn't write about my flight for the tabloid press no matter what they'd pay me.

Then there was that unnecessary incident with the press on the field, last Saturday. I had taken first Mulligan and then Boedecker up to check my engine in flight, and on the last landing I'd broken my tail skid, simply because some photographers got in the way again. The most annoying thing was that, instead of having a penalty to pay for violating the field regulations, the cameramen got a more valuable picture — and the reporters had "a better story." That seemed to be all they cared about. As far as I could tell, the fact that I damaged my plane to keep from hitting somebody didn't bother them a bit. Most reporters omitted that from their accounts. "So terrific was his speed that in landing he slightly damaged the machine's tail skid. Undismayed by this accident, which he considered trivial, Lindbergh hopped out wearing a broad smile: 'Boys, she's ready and rarin' to go!' he said." That's how one of the next day's articles went. These fellows must think I'm a cowpuncher, just transferred to aviation. Now they're calling me "a lanky demon of the air from the wide open spaces."

Such statements make "good stories," and the fact that they're not true causes little disturbance to the press. Accuracy, I've learned, is secondary to circulation — a thing to be sacrificed, when occasion arises, to a degree depending on the standards of each paper. But accuracy means something to me. It's vital to my sense of values. I've learned not to trust people who are inaccurate. Every aviator knows that if mechanics are inaccurate, aircraft crash. If pilots are inaccurate, they get lost — sometimes killed. In my profession life itself depends on **accuracy**.

6

Dr. Kimball is a grand person. He had his latest weather map spread out when I visited his bureau in New York City, and he went to no end of trouble explaining its details to me. He was disturbed about my intention to follow the great-circle route rather than the ship lanes. He said he couldn't get enough information that far north to forecast the weather properly. I explained that I'm willing to take a chance on weather in order to save distance; and that if the weather proves too bad I can change my course to the southward after I'm under way. Dr. Kimball may be disturbed, but I'm pleased by the forecasts he can give me. I hadn't counted on getting much information about weather over the ocean.

On the strength of Dr. Kimball's forecasts of continuing poor conditions, I've accepted a number of invitations to visit private homes. Today I had lunch with Colonel Theodore Roosevelt, Jr., at Oyster Bay. He showed me some of his father's books and trophies, and gave me several letters of introduction to friends of his in Europe. "You've got to meet Ambassador Herrick when you're over there," he said. "He's a wonderful fellow — good friend of mine."

Those letters create a problem, because I couldn't very well refuse to take them after all the hospitality the Colonel had extended, and the trouble he went to in writing them; and they may be of great help to me in France. But I turned down a thousand dollars rather than carry a pound of mail, and my partners in St. Louis decided they wouldn't ask me to carry anything on the flight. "If you get yourself and your plane across the ocean, that's enough," they said. I'm taking one letter for Postmaster Conkling of Springfield — I couldn't say no to him — and one letter for my friend Gregory Brandewiede, who worked with me laying out the mail route. That's all — except for the messages of introduction.

I found a local doctor waiting to talk to me when I returned to the field. He was concerned about the effects of fatigue and eyestrain on my flight. He had brought me a small first-aid kit, and a pair of colored spectacles for protection from the sun. I don't think I'll need either one, but I slipped them into my map pocket because his arguments were good. You feel grateful to men like that. They help wherever they can, and they don't expect anything for it.

Some of my best hours, here on Long Island, have been spent showing off the *Spirit of St. Louis*. Charlie Lawrance came to look it over — he's president of the Wright Aeronautical Corporation and one of the men who developed the Whirlwind engine. René Fonck stopped by, and Al Williams, and Tony Fokker; they were legendary figures to me a week ago. C. M. Keys and Frank Russell of the Curtiss Company came to see me, and Chance Vought and Grover Loening. One day Harry Guggenheim arrived with his wife — he runs the big fund that's promoting aviation.

During the last day or two I've let a number of reporters sit in my cockpit while I explained the working of instruments and controls. Now that I know the New York press representatives better, I'm finding a few with standards of value I respect — men like Owen and Lyman of the *Times,* Gould of the *Post,* and Allen of the *World.* They don't try to build up a supersensational story. They make a real effort to get at facts, and to keep the articles they write in balance with the subjects covered. They're interested in the fundamental problems of my flight — in such things as wing loading on take-off, fuel consumption, cruising speed, and my plans for measuring wind drift over water. Time is well spent in answering their questions.

Bill MacCracken, Assistant Secretary of Commerce for Aeronautics, has flown up from Washington. I asked him about navigation lights for the *Spirit of St. Louis.* The new federal regulations require lights on night-flying aircraft, but I've left them off, wiring and all, to save weight and complication.

"Could I have permission to fly without lights, on this particular trip?" I inquired.

MacCracken smiled. "Well, you probably won't encounter

much night traffic up where you're going," he said. "I think we can give you a special dispensation, just this once."

7

With every day that passes here in New York, I realize more fully that, aside from a plane with performance enough to make the flight, my greatest asset lies in the character of my partners in St. Louis. Byrd has been delayed by elaborate organization, and by Wanamaker's cautious insistence on a "scientific" test program for the *America*. Bitter dissension has broken out in the Bellanca camp; there still are arguments about who is to go, the route to be followed, and whether or not to carry a radio along. According to the papers, Levine has notified Bertaud that he is "not wanted as navigator" on the transatlantic flight, and Bertaud has obtained a court injunction to restrain the plane from taking off without him. Of course the press is playing all this up in headlines. But my partners haven't interfered with my plans in any way. They've stuck to Bixby's original proposition that they'll take care of the finances, and leave the technical end of the flight to me. "Let us know when we can help you," is all they've said; and they sent one of my fellow Guardsmen, Lieutenant Stumpf, through to New York to act as an aide.

Earlier this week I phoned Harry Knight and told him that if I'm going to be first to Paris I'll probably have to start before I'm eligible for the $25,000 Raymond Orteig prize. The sixty days specified in the contest rules haven't yet passed since my entry was accepted. Knight didn't even stop for a moment to consider. "To hell with the money," he replied. "When you're ready to take off, go ahead."

8

This is Thursday afternoon, the 19th of May, exactly one week since I landed in New York. The sky is overcast. A light rain is falling. Dense fog shrouds the coasts of Nova Scotia and Newfoundland, and a storm area is developing west of France. It may be days, it may be — I feel depressed at the thought — another week or two before I can take off. I wouldn't be so concerned about weather if the moon weren't already past full. Soon it won't be any use to me.

I've been ready to take off since daybreak Monday, watching every report and sign of weather, listening to every rumor about my competitors' plans. The newspapers have kept us on edge about it all, and it's difficult to pull out any plums of fact from the hot cake of fiction that they print. Byrd's test flights seem to have been going well, but he has several more to run. On the one hand, he has stated repeatedly that he is going to complete all his scheduled tests, and that he won't be rushed into taking off for Paris. On the other, one of the morning papers says that "Commander Richard Byrd and his aides yesterday stowed aboard their ship, the *America,* enough food to last the three flyers for a month and announced themselves ready to hop off at a moment's notice." That sounds more like a reporter than like Byrd; but one is never certain.

The status of the Bellanca varies with the day's editions. In one paper the headlines say: "BERTAUD BARS BELLANCA TRIP BY INJUNCTIONS"; in another they announce: "BERTAUD TO REMAIN IN BELLANCA CREW." The first paper says that controversial developments indicate "there is very little prospect the *Columbia* will take off when the others do, if at all," while the second tells its readers that "Bertaud announced early this morning that he would withdraw the injunction today."

As for me, one of the morning's subheadlines reads: "Flyin' Fool Adopts Mystery Air, Indicating Quick Take-off – – – " Actually, nothing could be further from the fact. Weather reports were so discouraging that I left the *Spirit of St. Louis* under guard and drove off with my friends Lane, Blythe, Stumpf, and Mahoney. Mahoney has just arrived, by train, from San Diego. We visited the Wright factory at Paterson, and then Guy Vaughan's home — he's vice president and general manager. Tonight we'll go to a theater in New York to see "Rio Rita," back stage — Dick Blythe arranged for that. It ought to be great fun.

"Shall we call Doc Kimball for another report?" Lane asks, as we drive east on 42nd Street.

"Yes," I say, "I think we'd better."

With the forecasts we've had, pavements shiny wet, and the tops of skyscrapers lost in haze, it's probably a waste of time to call for a final check on weather; still, I'm not going to miss any chance. We park our car at the curb, and wait while Blythe goes into an office building to phone the Bureau. When he comes out I know by his face and gait that he has news for me.

"Weather over the ocean is clearing," he announces. "It's a sudden change." Unmindful of the rain, he stoops to outline the situation to us through the car window. The low-pressure area over Newfoundland is receding, and a big high is pushing in behind it. "Of course conditions aren't good all along your route," Blythe continues. "They say it may take another day or two for that."

But there's a chance I'll be able to take off at daybreak. Thoughts of theater and stage vanish. The time has come, at last, for action.

We start immediately for the flying field. Will the *America* and *Columbia* crews be there, getting ready too? They probably had this weather report some time ago. I can't fly over to Roosevelt Field tonight — the haze is too thick, and the ceiling too low. We'll put about a hundred gallons of gasoline in the tanks before taking the *Spirit of St. Louis* out of its hangar. But most of the fueling will have to be done after daybreak, when my plane is in take-off position at the runway's end. That gives Byrd a big advantage. His Fokker can be taxied from its hangar to the take-off position, regardless of haze or fog. Of course if he starts tomorrow he'll have to cancel his christening ceremonies; they're scheduled for Saturday. But if the weather's right, and if his plane is ready, I don't think he'll let a christening hold him back. If I'd only had a little warning, I could have flown over to Roosevelt this afternoon. Now it's much too late. How many hours can I sleep and still be in my cockpit with the shades of dawn?

At Queensboro Plaza we stop for a quick dinner and to lay plans for the night. Lane offers to take charge of fueling and putting my plane through a final inspection; Boedecker, Mulligan, Umlauf, and other friends will help. And there's the recording barograph to be fastened inside my fuselage by Carl Schory; he represents the National Aeronautic Association. Somehow we'll have to locate him before morning. The barograph marks time and altitude on a slowly revolving cylinder of paper. Without it, the record of my flight won't be officially accepted.

"You'd better prepare yourself for some unpleasantness in France," one of my friends tells me while we sit eating. "I was talking to a fellow who just came back from Europe last week. He says the feeling over there isn't very friendly toward Americans. He thinks our embassy in Paris is right — that no American ought to make the flight so soon after Nungesser and Coli have been lost. It won't be like Curtiss Field when you land; but I don't think you'll have any serious trouble."

On reaching the air field, I'm surprised to find no sign of preparation in the Byrd or Chamberlin camps. It seems, as I inquire further, that everyone else is waiting for confirmation of the reports of improving weather; after all, they're only indications of a clearing sky. Odds are against a daybreak start for Paris. The Weather Bureau's message is bracketed with reservations.

But isn't this the opportunity I've been wishing for? Isn't it a chance to prove my philosophy of flying the mail? Often a pilot can get through when weather reports are bad. Sometimes he's forced down when they're favorable. He can always turn back and try again. We've completed many a flight with the St. Louis mail when we'd never have taken off if we'd waited for more than "indications" of clearing weather; and that was over a route of less than three hundred miles.

If I wait for confirmation of good weather all the way to

Europe, I may be the last rather than the first to leave. Dr. Kimball will be extremely cautious about saying the time is opportune, knowing that life and death are involved in his decision. My competitors can wait for him to give the word to go, if they want to. I'll take that responsibility on my own shoulders, where it belongs. I'll be ready at daybreak, and decide then whether or not to start.

9

With plans made and work quietly under way, I leave for my hotel to get whatever sleep the night still holds for me. But rumors of activity in my hangar have already spread, and reporters are waiting in the lobby. Several people come up and demand autographs while I'm answering questions. One man asks me to sign a motion-picture contract — he talks about guaranteeing $250,000. Another wants me to make a series of appearances on the stage — he speaks of $50,000. I've never thought in figures of that size; and now I've got to keep my mind free for the problems of my flight. I say that I can't make any plans for the future until after I reach Paris.

The time is close to midnight when I finally reach my room and lie down. There are only two and a half hours to sleep — if I'm to have everything ready for a dawn take-off — but that's enough to help a lot. Even an hour's sleep can separate the 19th from the 20th of May. I've learned, flying the mail, that any sleep at all has value — that minutes or even seconds add to wakened strength.

I let my head sink into the pillow and my mind relax. All my work is done, all arrangements made. Competent men have charge of the final servicing of the _Spirit of St. Louis_. I need think of nothing more until I wake. One of my friends is outside in the hall, guarding the door. He's going to keep everyone away, and get me out of bed at 2:15.

Now I must sleep. I ought to have been in bed three hours ago — that was a serious slip in plans; a pilot should be fresh for the start of a record-breaking transoceanic flight. Your mind doesn't work as well when it's short of sleep. I've let myself be caught off guard at a critical moment. But how could I have foreseen the sudden change in weather? This morning it looked as though I'd have to wait days before the fogs broke up. Dr. Kimball must have had new reports from ships and points along the coast. After all, my route's not organized for flying forecasts; what meteorological stations there are were set up to serve sailors and farmers, not pilots of the air. Their interest in weather is connected with the surface of the earth rather than with the sky itself.

Well, this is one of the emergencies that fill a flying life. You try to avoid slips like this, but you know they come now and then, and you keep reserves to meet them. I can get by without sleep. I've done it on the mail run – – – But how much better it is to start a day fully rested — how much keener you are — how much more you enjoy the art of flying — and I want to enjoy my trip to Paris — to be fresh for the overloaded take-off — to appreciate the lands and seas I pass – – –

If only the weather is good in the morning. If only there's a little wind along the runway, not across it. I can't take off with a strong cross wind, heavily loaded. How much cross wind should I attempt to take off with — what angle — what velocity? If only the runway were a little wider and the field a little longer – – – If only there's a west wind – – – I wish I could get a good sleep before starting – – – or that I could put it off for one more day – – – But a pilot should never turn down a break in weather – – – weather's too fickle – – – especially over the North Atlantic – – – if I let a day of good weather pass, someone else will probably start ahead of me – – – Chamberlin with the *Columbia* – – – or Byrd with the *America* – – – Now I've drawn even with them at last – – – no, I'm ahead of them – – – I won't give up that advantage – – – I won't lose it for the sake of a little sleep – – – there's still time for some rest – – – over two hours – – – it's a long time – – – they'll call me at 2:15 – – –

There are loud knocks on the door. It opens. A man steps inside — the one I posted in the hall to see that my rest was undisturbed. Has something gone wrong? Weather changed again? Trouble at the field? Is someone else starting ahead of me? Drowsiness leaves; I rise up on my elbow; he comes over and sits on the edge of the bed.

"Slim, what am I going to do when you're gone?" he asks.

Good Lord! Is that why he came in at such a time? — to ask *that* question? "I don't know," I say. "There are plenty of other problems to solve before we have to think about that one." After all, I'll be in Paris tomorrow if everything goes well — yes, it's after midnight — and if everything doesn't, time will make it obvious enough what to do. I tell him I've got to get some sleep, and he goes away. But all desire to sleep has left. I'm wide awake. When I have only two and a half hours to lie here before flying over the ocean — no, it's two hours now — why can't I be left alone?

Two more hours and I'll start the day of my flight to Paris — unless weather turns bad again. I wish it would turn bad; then no one could leave. Then I'd get a full night's rest before my take-off. I'm not eligible for the Orteig prize yet anyhow, and I won't be for another week. Why couldn't my entry have been accepted sooner? It's a shame to miss getting that money because competition makes me leave a week too soon. A few more days of bad weather would be worth $25,000 plus a good night's sleep. I could stand another week of crowds and newspapers for that. Besides, I'm getting on toward the end of the $15,000 I asked my partners to raise. There's only $1,500 left — only ten percent of what I started with. But everything is paid for — plane, equipment, personal expenses. Now I must sleep. Time is passing — good Lord, it's half past twelve.

Why did that fellow have to ask such a fool question, just as I was dozing off? Maybe I won't sleep at all. That's a bad start for flying over the ocean — a full day without sleep before the take-off.

But would I have slept anyway, even if my friend hadn't come in? I'm not sure. Usually when I lie down tired I fall unconscious in an instant. After a day's work in open air I need only to shut

my eyes and all problems leave my mind. The days in New York
have been tiring — there's no question about that — but tiring in
an unhealthy sort of way. If I had been working on the plane,
pouring fuel in the tanks, and walking over the field to watch its
surface, I'd now be asleep. That's what I would have been doing
except for the newspapers, and the crowds they've brought. But I
wanted publicity on this flight. That was part of my program.
Newspapers are important. I wanted their help. I wanted headlines. And I knew that headlines bring crowds. Then why should
I complain? The excesses are what bother me — the silly stories, the
constant photographing, the composite pictures, the cheap values
that such things bring. Why can't newspapers accept facts as they
are? Why smother the flavor of life in a spice of fiction?

Well, I'll be away from it all in the morning — this same
morning, if the weather breaks. It will all be gone once I'm in the
air, left behind. Somehow I must stop my mind from rambling. It's
already 1:15. There's only an hour left. But did I make a mistake
in telling Lane to fill all the gasoline tanks? I'll have to get 450
gallons into the air. It's more than Hall designed the plane for —
the tanks came out 25 gallons oversize. I'll gain 160 miles' more
range; but at a cost of 150 pounds of extra load — as though I
weren't asking enough of wing and engine anyway. I'm saving a
few pounds on oil — that will help. When we found how little oil
the Whirlwind used between San Diego and New York, Lane and
I decided we could cut from 25 gallons down to 20 for the flight
to Paris. That takes 35 pounds off the extra 150.

No reserve in flying is more valuable than a reserve of fuel;
but how much weight can an airplane lift? When does it just refuse
to climb? Suppose the *Spirit of St. Louis* can't climb with its load
— that's what happened to the *American Legion*. And Fonck
couldn't get off the ground at all with his Sikorsky. The papers
quote some engineer who declares that all three New York-to-
Paris flights are doomed; and they say that the president of the
American Society for the Promotion of Aviation agrees with him.
But Chamberlin and Acosta got the Bellanca off with a full load

for their endurance flight, and Nungesser got the *White Bird* into air at Le Bourget.

One-forty on my watch — almost time to dress. No, I won't get any sleep tonight, but I'll lie and rest a few minutes more. The night is past; the new day has begun; and with it, revived hope, interest, life. I feel fresher, ready for the start, anxious to get away. Will there be a wind at daybreak? What changes have these two hours brought to sky?

10

Frank Tichenor and Jessie Horsfall drive me to the field — they're publisher and editor of *Aero Digest*. We arrive a little before 3:00. Clouds are low. It's hazy, and light rain is falling. There's a small crowd outside my hangar, and several Nassau County police officers are standing at the door.

"Didn't my message get through, Slim?" Lane asks.

"No. What was it?"

"We've found a way to haul your plane up over the rise to Roosevelt Field," he tells me; "you won't have to fly it. We've got a truck standing by. I said to let you sleep until just before daybreak, and we'd have everything set for you to take off. Say, the Curtiss boys have been a real help; they've been working with us all night. Well, as long as you're here, you might tell us what you think about the weather. I don't like to take your plane outside in this rain."

"Is anybody else getting ready to start?" I ask.

"It doesn't look like it," Mahoney answers. "Byrd is going to run some more tests. There have been lights in the Bellanca hangar, but not enough activity to indicate a take-off. They seem to be still tied up by that injunction."

"What are the last reports on weather?"

"Still not too good - - - but it's improving."

I slip out through the big, half-open door, and stare at the glowing mist above Garden City. That means a low ceiling and poor visibility — street lights thrown back and forth between wet earth and cloud. The ground is muddy and soft. Conditions certainly aren't what one would choose for the start of a record-breaking flight. But the message from Dr. Kimball says that fog is lifting at most reporting stations between New York and Newfoundland. A high-pressure area is moving in over the entire North Atlantic. The only storms listed are local ones, along the coast of Europe.

Clearing along the American coast, clearing over the Atlantic, only local storms in Europe. What does a low ceiling matter at New York? If clouds here leave room to slip beneath, I'll start at daybreak. If I can't get through, I can turn back. I order the *Spirit of St. Louis* taken to Roosevelt Field, and tanks topped off regardless of the rain.

Mechanics tie the plane's tail skid to the back of a motor truck and wrap a tarpaulin around the engine. Reporters button up their raincoats. Men look out into the night and shake their heads. The truck starter grinds. My plane lurches backward through a depression in the ground. It looks awkward and clumsy. It appears completely incapable of flight — shrouded, lashed, and dripping. Escorted by motorcycle police, pressmen, aviators, and a handful of onlookers, the slow, wet trip begins.

It's more like a funeral procession than the beginning of a flight to Paris.

·PART II·

NEW YORK TO PARIS

NEW YORK TO PARIS

THIRTY REVOLUTIONS LOW! The engine's vibrating roar throbs back through the fuselage and drums heavily on taut fabric skin. I close the throttle and look out at tense faces beside my plane. Life and death lies mirrored in them — rigid, silent, waiting for my word.

Thirty revolutions low — a soft runway, a tail wind, an overload. I glance down at the wheels. They press deeply, tires bulging, into the wet, sandy clay.

The wind changed at daybreak, changed after the *Spirit of St. Louis* was in take-off position on the west side of the field, changed after all those barrels of gasoline were filtered into the tanks, changed from *head* to *tail* — five miles an hour *tail*!

A stronger wind would force me to the other end of the runway. But this is only a breath; barely enough to lift a handkerchief held in the hand. It's blowing no faster than a man can walk. And if we move the plane, it may shift again as quickly as it did before. Taking off from *west* to *east* with a tail wind is dangerous enough — there are only telephone wires and a road at the far end of the field — but to go from *east* to *west* would mean flying right over the hangars and blocks of houses beyond — not a chance to live if anything went wrong. A missing cylinder and – – – "Hit a house. Crashed. Burned." – – – I can hear the pilots saying it — the end of another transatlantic flight.

And there's no time. There's no time to move the plane — so small, so delicate, so heavy — two and a half tons on those little tires, with all the fuel in. It would have to be towed, and towed slowly, five thousand feet over the muddy runway. We'd have to send for a tractor; I couldn't taxi — the engine's too light — it would overheat — the fuel tanks would need topping off again — hours lost — night would fall on the Irish coast. I'm already late — it's long past dawn — and the weather reports say *clearing*.

My cockpit quivers with the engine's tenseness. Sharp explosions from the exhaust stacks speak with confidence and precision. But the *Spirit of St. Louis* isn't vibrant with power as it's always been before. I'm conscious of the great weight pressing tires into ground, of the fragility of wings, of the fullness of oversize tanks of fuel. There is in my plane this morning, more of earth and less of air than I've ever felt before.

Plane ready; engine ready; earth-inductor compass set on course. The long, narrow runway stretches out ahead. Over the telephone wires at its end lies the Atlantic Ocean; and beyond that, mythical as the rainbow's pot of gold, Europe and Paris. This is the moment I've planned for, day and night, all these months past. The decision is mine. No other man can take that responsibility. The mechanics, the engineers, the blue-uniformed police officers standing there behind the wing, everyone has done his part. Now, it's up to me.

Their eyes are intently on mine. They've seen planes crash before. They know what a wrong decision means. If I shake my head, there'll be no complaint, no criticism; I'll be welcomed back into their midst, back to earth and life; for we are separated by something more than the few yards that lie between us. It seems almost the difference between the future and the past, to be decided by a movement of my head. A shake, and we'll be laughing and joking together, laying new plans, plodding over the wet grass toward hot coffee and a warm breakfast — all men of the earth. A nod, and we'll be separated — perhaps forever.

Thirty revolutions low! "It's the weather," the mechanic said when I climbed into the cockpit. "They never rev up on a day like this." But his encouraging words failed to hide the apprehension in his voice and eyes. Now, the expression on his face, out there behind my silver wing, shows more clearly than any words what is passing through his mind. He's gone over the engine piece by piece, helped tear it down and put it back together. He feels sure that every part is perfect, and firmly in its place. He's squirmed into the tail of the fuselage to inspect structure and controls. He knows that wheel bearings are freshly oiled; that air pressure is up; that tires are rubbed with grease to keep the mud from sticking. He's double-checked the thousand preliminary details to a flight. His work is done, done with faithfulness and skill. Now he stands there helplessly, intent, with tightened jaw, waiting for my signal. He feels responsible for the engine, for the plane, for me, even for the weather that holds the revolutions low.

I lean against the side of the cockpit and look ahead, through the idling blades of the propeller, over the runway's wet and glistening surface. I study the telephone wires at its end, the shallow pools of water through which my wheels must pass, and the top-heavy black column of smoke, rising from some source outside the field, leaning indifferently in the direction of my flight. A curtain of mist shuts off all trace of the horizon.

Wind, weather, power, load — how many times have I balanced these elements in my mind, barnstorming from some farmer's cow pasture in the Middle West! In barnstorming a pilot learns to judge a field so accurately that he can tell from the size of his passenger, and a tuft of grass tossed to the wind, just where his wheels will leave the ground, just how many feet will separate them from the boundary fence and trees beyond. But here, it's different. There are no well-established standards from which to judge. No plane ever took off so heavily loaded; and my propeller is set for cruising, not for take-off. Of course our test flights at San Diego indicate that it *will* take off — theoretically at least. But since we didn't dare try a full load from Camp Kearney's stony ground, the wings now have to lift a thousand pounds more than they ever carried before — five thousand pounds to be lifted by nothing more tangible than air.

Those carefully laid performance curves of ours have no place for mist, or a tail wind, or a soft runway. And what of the thirty revolutions lost, and the effect of moisture on the skin? No, I can turn to no formula, the limits of logic are passed. Now, the intangible elements of flight — experience, instinct, intuition — must make the final judgment, place their weight upon the scales. In the last analysis, when the margin is close, when all the known factors have been considered, after equations have produced their final lifeless numbers, one measures a field with an eye, and checks the answer beyond the conscious mind.

If the *Spirit of St. Louis* gathers speed too slowly; if the wheels hug the ground too tightly; if the controls feel too loose and logy, I can pull back the throttle and stop — that is, I can stop if I don't wait too long. If I wait too long — a few seconds will decide — well, another transatlantic plane crashed and burned at the end of this same runway. Only a few yards away, two of Fonck's crew met their death in flames.

And there's the added difficulty of holding the wheels on the runway while sitting in a cockpit from which I can't see straight ahead. A degree or two change in heading could easily cause a crash. The runway is narrow enough under the best of conditions; now – – – with the mud – – – and the tail wind – – – and the engine not turning up – – –

I lean back in the wicker seat, running my eyes once more over the instruments. Nothing wrong there. They all tell the proper story. Even the tachometer needle is in place, with the engine idling. Engine revolutions are like sheep. You can't notice that a few are missing until the entire flock is counted. A faint trace of gasoline mixes with the smell of newly dried dope — probably a few drops spilled out when the tanks were filled. I turn again to the problem of take-off. It will be slow at best. Can the engine stand such a long ground run at wide-open throttle, or will it overheat and start to miss?

Suppose I *can* hold the runway, suppose I *do* get off the ground — will fog close in and force me back? Suppose the ceiling drops to zero — I can't fly blind with this overload of fuel; but the wheels have doubtful safety factors for a landing. Shall I cut the switch and wait another day for confirmation of good weather? But if I leave now, I'll have a head start on both the Fokker and the

Bellanca. Once in the air, I can nurse my engine all the way to Paris — there'll be no need to push it in a race. And the moon's past full — it will be three weeks to the next one; conditions then may be still worse.

Wind, weather, power, load – – – gradually these elements stop churning in my mind. It's less a decision of logic than of feeling, the kind of feeling that comes when you gauge the distance to be jumped between two stones across a brook. Something within you disengages itself from your body and travels ahead with your vision to make the test. You can feel it try the jump as you stand looking. Then uncertainty gives way to the conviction that it *can* or can't be done. Sitting in the cockpit, in seconds, minutes long, the conviction surges through me that the wheels *will* leave the ground, that the wings *will* rise above the wires, that it *is* time to start the flight.

I buckle my safety belt, pull goggles down over my eyes, turn to the men at the blocks, and nod. Frozen figures leap to action. A yank on the ropes — the wheels are free. I brace myself against the left side of the cockpit, sight along the edge of the runway, and ease the throttle wide open. Now, in seconds, we'll have the answer. Action brings confidence and relief.

But, except for noise and vibration, what little effect the throttle has! The plane creeps heavily forward. Several men are pushing on wing struts to help it start — pushing so hard I'm afraid the struts will buckle. How can I possibly gain flying speed? Why did I ever think that air could carry such a weight? Why have I placed such reliance on a sheet of paper's curves? What possible connection is there between the intersection of a pencil's lines in San Diego and the ability of *this* airplane, *here, now,* to fly?

The *Spirit of St. Louis* feels more like an overloaded truck than an airplane. The tires rut through mud as though they really were on truck wheels. Even the breath of wind is pressing me down. A take-off seems hopeless; but I may as well go on for another hundred feet before giving up. Now that I've started, it's better to make a real attempt. Besides – – – it's just possible – – –

Gradually, the speed increases. Maybe the runway's not too

soft. Is it long enough? The engine's snarl sounds inadequate and weak, carrying its own note of mechanical frustration. There's none of the spring forward that always before preceded the take-off into air — no lightness of wing, no excess power. The stick wobbles loosely from side to side, and slipstream puts hardly any pressure against rudder. Nothing about my plane has the magic quality of flight. But men begin stumbling off from the wing struts. We're going faster.

A hundred yards of runway passes. The last man drops off the struts. The stick's wobbling changes to lurching motion as ailerons protest unevenness of surface. How long can the landing gear stand such strain? Five thousand pounds crushing down upon it! I keep my eyes fixed on the runway's edge. I *must* hold the plane straight. One wheel off and the *Spirit of St. Louis* would ground-loop and splinter in the mud. Controls begin to tighten against the pressure of my hand and feet. There's a living quiver in the stick. I have to push hard to hold it forward. Slight movement of the rudder keeps the nose on course. Good signs, but more than a thousand feet have passed. Is there still time, still space?

Pace quickens – – – turf becomes a blur – – – the tail skid lifts off ground – – – I feel the load shifting from wheels to wings. But the runway's slipping by quickly. The halfway mark is just ahead, and I have nothing like flying speed – – – The engine's turning faster — smoothing out — the propeller's taking better hold — I can tell by the sound. What r.p.m.? But I can't look at instruments — I must hold the runway, not take my eyes from its edge for an instant. An inch off on stick or rudder, and my flight will end.

The halfway mark streaks past – – – seconds now to decide — close the throttle, or will I get off? The wrong decision means a crash — probably in flames – – – I pull the stick back firmly, and – – – *The wheels leave the ground.* Then I'll get off! The wheels touch again. I ease the stick forward — almost flying speed, and nearly 2000 feet of field ahead – – – A shallow pool on the runway – – – water spews up from the tires – – – A wing drops — lifts as I shove aileron against it — the entire plane trembles from

the shock — — — Off again — right wing low — pull it up — — —
Ease back onto the runway — left rudder — hold to center —
must keep straight — — — Another pool — water drumming on the
fabric — — — The next hop's longer — — — I could probably stay in
air; but I let the wheels touch once more — lightly, a last bow to
earth, a gesture of humility before it — — — Best to have plenty of
control with such a load, and control requires speed.

The *Spirit of St. Louis* takes herself off the next time — full
flying speed — the controls taut, alive, straining — and still a
thousand feet to the web of telephone wires. Now, I *have* to make
it — there's no alternative. It'll be close, but the margin has shifted
to my side. I keep the nose down, climbing slowly, each second
gaining speed. If the engine can hold out for one more minute — — —
five feet — — — twenty — — — forty — — — wires flash by underneath —
twenty feet to spare!

Green grass and bunkers below — a golf links — people looking up. A low, tree-covered hill ahead — I shallow-bank right to
avoid it, still grasping the stick tightly as though to steady the
plane with my own strength, hardly daring to drop a wing for the
turn, hardly daring to push the rudder. The *Spirit of St. Louis*
seems balanced on a pin point, as though the slightest movement
of controls would cause it to topple over and fall. Five thousand
pounds suspended from those little wings — 5000 pounds balanced
on a blast of air.

The ground's farther underneath; the plane's climbing faster —
I'm above the trees on the hilltop! Plenty of height, plenty of
power — a reserve of it! Two hundred feet above the ground. Now,
if the motor starts missing, there are places I might land — level
fields between the hills and highways. The landing gear would give
way, and the fuel tanks would burst; but if I cut the switch, at least
there's a chance that the fuselage would skid along and not catch
fire.

Now I'm high enough to steal glances at the instrument board.
The tachometer needle shows 1825 r.p.m. — no sign of engine
overheating. I move the throttle back slowly — a glance at the
terrain ahead — a glance at the tachometer in my cockpit — 1800

– – – 1775 r.p.m. Pull the stabilizer back a notch. The air speed's still over 100 miles an hour – – – I throttle down to 1750 – – – the tail stays up – – – the controls are taut! Then the curves are right. If the *Spirit of St. Louis* can cruise at 1750 r.p.m. with this load, I have *more* than enough fuel to reach Paris.

On the instrument board in front of me, the earth-inductor compass needle leans steeply to the right. I bank cautiously northward until it rises to the center line — 65 degrees — the compass heading for the first 100-mile segment of my great-circle route to France and Paris. It's 7:54 a.m. Eastern daylight time.

The curtain of mist moves along with me. I can see three miles ahead — no more. Even at that distance details merge with haze. What lies beyond the curtain? Will it lift to show a clear horizon when I reach Long Island Sound, or will it turn into a solid bank of fog? The last report said weather along the coast was clearing; but a number of stations still reported fog. Suppose I've taken off an hour too soon, before the rising sun has warmed the mists away; suppose – – –

I pull the map of New York State from its cloth pocket at my side. The worse the weather, the more necessary accurate navigation will be. I must get a check on the compasses, watch for landmarks, make sure that the places I fly over on the earth's surface correspond to the symbols crossed by the black-inked line on my map.

The great landscaped estates of Long Island pass rapidly below: mansion, hedgerow, and horse-jump giving way to farms and woodlands farther east. I hold my plane just high enough to clear treetops and buildings on the hills. By flying close to the ground, I can see farther through the haze. That finger of water on my left is part of the bay-broken shore line of the Sound — it must be at least five miles away. Then visibility to the north is improving. The clouds look a little higher, too.

I'm in the air with full tanks and a following wind. The engine has withstood its test of power. It's throttled down, turning smoothly and easily. The *Spirit of St. Louis* is no longer an unruly mechanical device, as it was during the take-off; it's no longer balanced on a pin point, as it was over the golf course; rather, it seems to form an extension of my own body, ready to follow my wish as the hand follows the mind's desire — instinctively, without commanding.

I settle back in the cockpit, running my eyes carefully over the instruments, between glances at the ground — letting each one transmit the full significance of its message: oil pressure 56 pounds; oil temperature 34°; fuel pressure 3½ pounds – – – A little close to the treetops — ease back on the stick – – – Tachometer 1750 r.p.m.; air speed 105 m.p.h. – – – Off heading a bit — 3 degrees left rudder. Altitude 200 feet; time 8:07 a.m. Fifteen minutes out and all readings normal. I shift from center wing-tank to nose tank. Fifteen minutes flying on each of the five fuel tanks should leave enough air space to stop overflow, and every drop of gasoline must be saved.

There's Smithtown Bay, under my left wing. I'm a mile or two southeast of course — partly due to turning right, around that hill by the golf links. I won't correct my heading until I reach Connecticut's shore. That will give me a better check on the compasses.

As I look out, a newspaper plane banks steeply and heads back — probably trying to get a scoop on the others. I hadn't noticed them during the first few minutes after take-off. Then, as they drew in closer, cameras sticking out of cockpits and cabin windows, I was startled to find that I was not alone in the air. It never occurred to me that newspaper companies would hire planes to follow the *Spirit of St. Louis* on its way to Paris. At another time their presence wouldn't bother me so much, but now I wish they'd all go away. They seem out of place, not part of this flight. I can visualize their reporters and photographers at the end of the runway, back on Roosevelt Field, gathered around a flaming mass of

wreckage. But I've left all that behind, with the mud and the telephone wires. Now the air, the clouds, the sky — these elements are
mine.

The *Spirit of St. Louis* rocks slightly — turbulent air! I glance
up at the heavily loaded wings. Bumps are light, but the tips flex
up and down too far for comfort. I'm passing over Port Jefferson
and its harbor full of boats. Air's usually rough where land and
water meet — but suppose it gets really turbulent! My muscles
tense as though my own arms were stretched out in the wings,
helping to hold up the load. Can structure stand a sharper blow?
I feel in my shoulders — in my body — in my mind — that the
reserve of strength is low.

I fly through uneasy seconds until Long Island's coast is behind.
Then, within 1000 yards of the shore line, air smooths out like
glass. And at almost the same moment, the pilot of the last escorting plane, a Curtiss Oriole, gives his wing a farewell dip, and turns
back toward land.

I'm alone at last, over the first short stretch of sea on the route
to France. The surface is calm. There's hardly a sign of movement
beneath the oil-smooth sheen of its skin. It's only 35 miles to the
Connecticut shore, but I've never flown across that much water
before. The Sound comes as an advance messenger, welcoming and
at the same time warning me of the empire that lies ahead—of the
trackless wastes, the great solitude, the desertlike beauty of the
ocean.

Haze thickens behind me until the coast line becomes lost.
There's not a boat in sight. Only a few spiraling gulls and dark
bits of refuse on the water show that land is near. I'm the center
point in a circle of haze moving along with me over the glassy
water — gray haze over gray water, the one mirrored in the other
until I can't tell where sea ends and sky begins.

I relax in my cockpit — this little box with fabric walls, in which I'm to ride across the ocean. Now, if all goes well, I won't move from it for a day and a half, until I step out on French sod at the airport of Le Bourget. It's a compact place to live, designed to fit around me so snugly that no ounce of weight or resistance is wasted. I can press both sides of the fuselage with partly outstretched elbows. The instrument board is an easy reach forward for my hand, and a thin rib on the roof is hollowed slightly to leave clearance for my helmet. There's room enough, no more, no less; my cockpit has been tailored to me like a suit of clothes.

A pilot doesn't feel at home in a plane until he's flown it for thousands of miles. At first it's like moving into a new house. The key doesn't slip in the door smoothly; the knobs and light switches aren't where you put your hand; the stairs don't have proper spacing, and the windows bind as you raise them. Later, after you've used the key a hundred times, it fits at once, turns easily in the lock. Knobs and switches leap to meet your fingers on the darkest night. The steps touch your feet in perfect timing; and windows slide open with an easy push. My test flights in California, the long hours of night above deserts and mountains of the Southwest, the swift trip over the Alleghenies to New York, have removed the feel of newness from the *Spirit of St. Louis*. Each dial and lever is in proper place for glance or touch; and the slightest pressure on controls brings response. My ears have become accustomed to the radial engine's tempo. It blends with the instrument readings and the clearing mist to instill a feeling of confidence and hope.

I'm glad this flight to Paris hasn't become a race. Now I can set my throttle for range instead of speed, hoarding gallons of gasoline for that worried hour when extra fuel means the saving of a flight. I never wanted to race across the ocean. There are hazards enough without adding human competition.

What advantages there are in flying alone! I know now what my father meant when he warned me, years ago, of depending too heavily on others. He used to quote a saying of old settlers in Minnesota: "One boy's a boy. Two boys are half a boy. Three boys are no boy at all." That had to do with hunting, trapping, and scouting in days when Indians were hostile. But how well it applies to modern life, and to this flight I'm making. By flying alone I've gained in range, in time, in flexibility; and above all, I've gained in freedom. I haven't had to keep a crew member acquainted with my plans. My movements weren't restricted by someone else's temperament, health, or knowledge. My decisions aren't weighted by responsibility for another's life. When I learned last night that the weather was improving, I had no one to consult; I needed only to order the *Spirit of St. Louis* readied for daybreak. When I was sitting in my cockpit, on the muddy runway, in the tail wind, there was no one to warp my judgment with a "Hell, let's try it!" or, "It looks pretty bad to me." I've not been enmeshed in petty quarreling and heavy organizational problems. Now, I can go on or turn back according to the unhampered dictates of my mind and senses. According to that saying of my father's, I'm a full boy — independent — alone.

My eyes run over the instruments again. At 1750 r.p.m. the engine should stand a little leaning out, even at the low altitude of 150 feet. I open the mixture control cautiously, ready to jam it shut at the slightest sign of roughness.

New England's tree-covered hills harden from the northern haze — a different shade of gray, then blue, then green, then filled with depth and texture. Scattered ships and launches ply back and forth offshore. I fold up the map of New York on my knees, and pull out one of Connecticut. The first state is passed; the first salt water crossed. It gives me a feeling of speed and accomplishment far out of proportion to the actual miles I've covered.

As I approach shore, near the Connecticut River's mouth, wing tips tremble again. For some reason it bothers me less than before. Possibly the air isn't quite as rough. Possibly I feel that the structure passed its crucial test over Long Island. It may be my knowledge that the plane is already a few pounds lighter; or simply

optimism springing from a successful start. At any rate, the bumps
no longer cause an ache in my armpits.

Inland, there's not much room between green hills and clouds.
I climb slowly to 500 feet, and push out the periscope. It's a
home-made device, built by one of the workmen in the factory at
San Diego — just two flat mirrors, set at the proper angle, in a
tube that can be extended from the left side of the fuselage. The
field of vision isn't large, but it shows the country directly ahead
well enough to warn of a higher summit, and to assure me that no
factory chimneys or radio towers lie on my line of flight. I don't
have to lean over to one side for a better view. I can take off my
goggles and sit quietly in the center of the cockpit. On such a long
flight it's important to avoid fatigue.

Hills are rising. To the north, they penetrate the clouds. Will
the next ridge close off my route? Shall I turn south along a valley,
and try to follow the coast line eastward? That would take extra
fuel, but it would be cheaper than doubling back if I push on too
far. If the ceiling drops another hundred feet, I'll have to turn
back. But there's no certainty that I can get through along the
coast. The cloud level there may be still lower. And such detouring
would complicate navigation. It would keep me from getting an
accurate check on my compasses before I reach the ocean. No,
I'll hold straight on course as long as I see a layer of open air
ahead, no matter how thin it is.

After all, I mustn't be too disappointed if I have to turn back.
I've never counted on reaching Paris on the first try. I planned on
starting several times if need be. Suppose fog blankets the entire
area ahead? Well, I'll throttle down and try for the world's endurance record; I'll pick out a course from Roosevelt Field around
New York. And if clouds hang thick and low at night, I'll circle
the lights of Garden City.

I cross the Thames River between Norwich and New London. Over the valley, the ceiling is higher. Ahead, the haze is clearing, and the cloud base is lifting rapidly. I angle five degrees northward to pick up my great-circle route.

THE SECOND HOUR

Over New England

TIME — 8:52 A.M.

WIND VELOCITY	0 *m.p.h.*	VISIBILITY	*5 miles*
WIND DIRECTION	—	ALTITUDE	600 *feet*
TRUE COURSE	51°	AIR SPEED	102 *m.p.h.*
VARIATION	13° *W.*	TACHOMETER	1750 *r.p.m.*
MAGNETIC COURSE	64°	OIL TEMPERATURE	38° *C.*
DEVIATION	1° *E.*	OIL PRESSURE	59 *lbs.*
COMPASS COURSE	63°	FUEL PRESSURE	3.5 *lbs.*
DRIFT ANGLE	0°	MIXTURE	1
COMPASS HEADING	63°	FUEL TANK	*Fuselage*
CEILING	2000 *feet*		

One hundred miles behind me; 3,500 miles to go. The *Spirit of St. Louis* is about 100 pounds lighter. I mark down the instrument readings on my log, turn off the fourth and on the fifth gasoline tank, and reset the earth-inductor compass.

Rhode Island is already beneath me. How these northeastern states are crowded together! I'm accustomed to the great distances of the West, where an inch on the map represents many miles on the ground, and where railroads are often an hour's flight apart. Here in New England, states seem the size of counties, and maps are drawn on so large a scale that it takes no time at all to cross them.

I look down on small fields spread out in stream-fed valleys and sloping toward heavily wooded hills. They're filled with cattle, gray boulders, and moist green crops of spring — so unlike the big farms of my Mississippi Valley, with their straight miles of fence lines, "square with the world." Here, there's no direction, no sense of north, south, east, and west. The tumbled-down stone walls run every which way, with hardly a right-angle corner in sight. What a job it must be to work out a disputed boundary. And what a hopeless place for a forced landing if my motor should fail! There's not a single field where I could get down without crashing.

Highways and villages are everywhere. I can't keep count of them on the map. And the railroads are too close together to make good check points — it's hard to tell one from another. The engines leave long trails of smoke that hang motionless until they slowly fade in air — no wind down there. Columns of smoke from factory chimneys spread out lazily in whatever direction they desire, as undisciplined as the stone walls of the fields. I wish the wind would rise a little and blow from the west — blow me along on my route over the ocean.

There's Providence under my left wing. And on my right the intricate channels of Narragansett Bay spread out as far as I can see. The Massachusetts line runs through the city's eastern suburbs. Only an hour and a quarter since take-off, and I'm unfolding the map of the fourth state. The *Spirit of St. Louis* has flown over the whole of Rhode Island in the time it takes to walk a single mile. The Atlantic Ocean lies less than thirty minutes away — *and the sky is clearing*. The dull stratus layer overhead has become mottled with lighter patches. In the distance, dazzling white strips between gray bunched clouds show where the sun is breaking through.

Clearing along the North American Coast. Thirty-five hundred miles to Paris; nearly fifty hours of fuel in my tanks. New England, Nova Scotia, Newfoundland, the Atlantic Ocean — I'll pass above them — and then Ireland, England, and France! No plane ever flew with such range before. Open skies ahead, the world turning below: when it turns to Paris, I shall land.

The sky line under the wing seems to be dividing. Below the straight but still vague line of the natural horizon, a darker irregular line has formed — the Atlantic coast! There, above it, is the great ocean itself — real, wet, and endless — no longer simply an idea or a blue tint on paper.

I slip Massachusetts into the map pocket, and pull out my Mercator's projection of the North Atlantic. What endless hours I worked over this chart in California, measuring, drawing, rechecking each 100-mile segment of its great-circle route, each theoretical hour of my flight. But only now, as I lay it on my knees, do I realize its full significance. A few lines and figures on a strip of paper, a few ounces of weight, this strip is my key to Europe. With it, I can fly the ocean. With it, that black dot at the other end marked "Paris" will turn into a famous French city with an aerodrome where I can land. But without this chart, all my years of training, all that went into preparing for the flight, no matter how perfectly the engine runs or how long the fuel lasts, all would be as directionless as those columns of smoke in the New England valleys behind me. Without this strip, it would be as useless to look for Paris as to hunt for buried treasure without a pirate's chart. Twenty miles after passing the Massachusetts coast, it says, change course to 71 degrees magnetic. Proceed in that direction for 100 miles; then change course again, this time to 74 degrees. Allow for whatever wind is blowing, and in another hour you will be approaching the shore of Nova Scotia. With one more change of course, you will strike land near the mouth of St. Mary Bay — provided the instructions have been interpreted correctly and followed accurately. After the thirty-seventh instruction has been carried out, you will see the city of Paris lying ten miles ahead. Circle a tall tower near the center of the city, take up a course to the northeast, and within ten minutes you will find a great aerodrome called Le Bourget!

THE THIRD HOUR
Over the Atlantic
TIME — 9:52 A.M.

WIND VELOCITY	0 *m.p.h.*	VISIBILITY	*Unlimited*
WIND DIRECTION	—	ALTITUDE	150 *feet*
TRUE COURSE	56°	AIR SPEED	107 *m.p.h.*
VARIATION	15° *W.*	TACHOMETER	1760 *r.p.m.*
MAGNETIC COURSE	71°	OIL TEMPERATURE	40° *C.*
DEVIATION	1° *E.*	OIL PRESSURE	58 *lbs.*
COMPASS COURSE	70°	FUEL PRESSURE	3.5 *lbs.*
DRIFT ANGLE	0°	MIXTURE	1
COMPASS HEADING	70°	FUEL TANK	*Nose*
CEILING	4000 *feet*		

Cape Cod, a low, bluish hook of land, dents the horizon to my right. Back of my left wing, the smoke of Boston darkens clouds. Rapidly fading out of sight behind me is the coast line of the United States.

Looking ahead at the unbroken horizon and limitless expanse of water, I'm struck by my arrogance in attempting such a flight. I'm giving up a continent, and heading out to sea in the most fragile vehicle ever devised by man. Why should I be so certain that a swinging compass needle will lead me to land and safety? Why have I dared stake my life on the belief that by drawing a line on paper and measuring its azimuth and length, I can find my way through shifting air to Europe? Why have I been so sure that I can hold the nose of the *Spirit of St. Louis* on an unmarked point on that uniform horizon and find Nova Scotia, and Newfoundland, and Ireland, and finally an infinitesimal spot on the earth's surface called Le Bourget?

The first real test of navigation is at hand. For more than two hours, I'll be out of sight of land. There'll be no rivers or cities with which to check my course. When I left the coast of Massachusetts, I was on the great-circle route to Paris. When I strike the coast of Nova Scotia, I'll know exactly how many degrees I've deviated from it. Between the two there's nothing but the black line on my chart and the waves of the ocean beneath my plane.

This will be a check on theory, and on my ability to hold a compass heading over water. If I'm close to course at Nova Scotia, I should be close at Ireland too.

It's about 250 miles from Massachusetts to the Nova Scotian coast, and just under 2000 miles from Newfoundland to Ireland. If I multiply my error in miles by eight when I strike land, the result will indicate roughly how far off I'll be when I reach the shores of Europe — if my navigation across the ocean is neither much better nor much worse. Ten miles off at Nova Scotia would equal eighty miles at Ireland.

There are neither whitecaps nor wind streaks on the water — just hold the compass course; no need to compensate for drift. I nose down closer to the low, rolling waves – – – a hundred feet – – – fifty feet – – – twenty feet above their shifting surfaces. I come down to meet the ocean, asking its favor — the right to pass for thousands of miles across its realm. The earth released me on Long Island; now I need approval from the sea.

It doesn't seem a hostile ocean. It has rather a cold hospitality. There will be a polite relationship between us; it will hold a flattened surface while I fly on and on, with no rising hill or mountain top a hazard to my flight. I'll have only the air to contend with, the wind, fog, and storm. If I can combat my own element, I'll have nothing to fear from the sea. It will even help me a little, ruffling its surface or waving a flag of spray in warning of the changing tricks of wind.

A cushion of air lies close to the water. On it, wings glide more smoothly; the tail lifts higher, the waves flash by, and a plane races along with lessened effort. I drop down till my wheels are less than a man's height above the rollers. The *Spirit of St. Louis* is like a butterfly blown out to sea. How often I used to watch them, as a child, on the banks of the Mississippi, dancing up and down above the water, as I am dancing now; up and down with their own fancy and the currents of air. But a touch of wing to water, and they were down forever, just as my plane would be. I saw dozens of them floating, broken and lifeless, in eddying currents near our shore. Why, I used to wonder, had they ever left the safety of the land. But why have I? How similar my position has become!

Miles slip by quickly as I skim over the ocean farther from New York, closer to Paris; the haze clearing, the clouds lifting. Then, a fishing smack, appearing off my starboard wing, reminds me that I'm flying below mast-top level. I let the *Spirit of St. Louis* rise a few feet, and keep a sharper eye on the periscope.

Only once before have I been so far out over the ocean that I couldn't see land. I was eleven years old then. My mother and I were on board a ship, southbound for the Panama Canal. What a contrast! Even the lifeboats were bigger than my plane! There were long decks to walk on, dozens of people to talk to, three hot meals a day, and a stateroom at night. No one was concerned about fog or storm, aside from the inconvenience of staying under shelter. One morning, a flying fish landed on the deck; and the deck was no higher than my cockpit, now, above the waves. I look out on both sides of my plane; but there's no flash of wings, no splash in water. Maybe flying fish don't live in northern seas.

Flying next to the water grows tiresome. I climb up a hundred feet and search the horizon for signs of life. There are still a few fishing boats in sight. When I'm high, I can settle back comfortably, touching stick and rudder just enough to keep the compass needle centered. When I'm low, I have to keep a firmer grip on controls, and rivet my attention to the space between wheels and water.

The cockpit brightens suddenly, flooded with sunlight and warmth. I squint up through the oblong window overhead. I'm flying under a dazzling blue field of sky surrounded by gray-bottomed clouds and hemmed in by glacial mountains of blinding white. Ahead are the foothills—smaller cumulus masses, rising on each side of widening valleys; and beyond, closer to the horizon, lies a flat blue plain of limitless open sky.

THE FOURTH HOUR
Over the Atlantic
TIME — 10:52 A.M.

WIND VELOCITY	10 *m.p.h.*	VISIBILITY	*Unlimited*
WIND DIRECTION	*NW.*	ALTITUDE	*50 feet*
TRUE COURSE	57°	AIR SPEED	*104 m.p.h*
VARIATION	17° *W.*	TACHOMETER	*1725 r.p.m.*
MAGNETIC COURSE	74°	OIL TEMPERATURE	*41° C.*
DEVIATION	1° *E.*	OIL PRESSURE	*57 lbs.*
COMPASS COURSE	73°	FUEL PRESSURE	*3.5 lbs.*
DRIFT ANGLE	5° *R.*	MIXTURE	*1.5*
COMPASS HEADING	68°	FUEL TANK	*R. Wing*
CEILING	*Unlimited*		

I mark down a third set of instrument readings on the log sheet. At 16 gallons per hour, about 300 pounds of fuel have been consumed. The plane's almost a barrel's weight lighter. I think of upending a barrel of gasoline next our tractor on the farm — more weight than I can lift has been taken off the wings. I ease the throttle back to 1725 r.p.m., and lean out the mixture again. The air speed drops to 104 miles an hour. I have to pull the nose up a trifle — enough to warn me against reducing power further.

There are ripples on the water — a northwest breeze. That's too much from the side to be of value. What I need is a west wind; or better, one from the southwest. Now, I'll have to head into the drift. I reach down and offset 5 degrees on the earth-inductor dial. A side wind's not a good omen. With a large high-pressure area over the ocean, I had hoped for a tail wind on this portion of my route. What does it mean, this unexpected direction? Is it only temporary, or is it warning of a storm ahead?

I think of previous flights when clear skies ended against solid walls of cloud. Time and again, barnstorming or flying the mail, I've found my route blocked tightly by unexpected weather. But then it was usually a case of returning to the last flying field I'd passed over, or picking out some nearby pasture on which to spend the night. Now, there are no pastures below, no airports close behind. If I turn back, I'll have to go all the way to Long Island for another start. Even if I could find a field large enough for my overloaded plane along the New England coast, to land there would mean the failure of a nonstop flight.

I'm a little tired. The sun beating in through the window overhead makes the cockpit uncomfortably hot. Shall I take off my blanket-lined flying suit? I can wriggle out without too much trouble; but to put it on again while I'm piloting would be a tremendous effort, and I'll surely need its warmth tonight. Well, I can at least pull down the zipper and get some cool air around my chest. Why didn't I think of that before?

My legs are stiff and cramped. But that won't last more than three or four hours. The dull ache will get worse for a time, and then go away altogether. I've experienced the feeling before. It begins after about three hours of flying, and ends at about seven. After the seventh hour, my muscles will cease complaining of their restrictions and accept the mission they've been given to fulfill. I wish the desire for sleep could adapt itself to a long-distance flight as easily.

It would be pleasant to doze off for a few seconds. But I mustn't feel sleepy at this stage of the trip! Why, I'm less than a tenth of the way to Paris; it's not yet noon of the first day. There's still the rest of today and all of tonight, and tomorrow, and part — maybe all — of tomorrow night. After that I can think about being tired, not before. The *Spirit of St. Louis* is doing its job. I've got to do mine. I must stay alert, and match quality of plane and engine with quality of piloting and navigation. I'd be ashamed to have anyone know I feel tired when I'm just starting.

I sip some water from the quart canteen hanging at my side. Below it, wedged between seat and fuselage, are five sandwiches in their brown paper bag; but I'm not hungry. It's probably wise not to eat, anyway — easier to stay awake on an empty stomach.

I'll climb up two or three hundred feet and stop looking ahead for boats. There's not much danger of hitting one, but the idea is a mental hazard, and watching the periscope mirror is an added strain. Also, the concentration required in flying close to the rollers is too much effort. It no longer clears my mind as it did an hour ago. I want to sit quietly and rest. I must replace some of the energy I've expended. The lack of sleep I feel now, at eleven o'clock in the morning, is a grain of sand compared to the mountain that will tower over me when dawn breaks tomorrow. Past dawns I've flown through come forward in memory to warn me what torture the desire for sleep can be.

To the night pilot, dawn should be a harbor of safety, an experience of beauty. Each ray of light in the eastern sky brings out new contours on the ground — the smoothness of a sloping hillside where his plane might land; the danger of a stump-studded valley. A cloud flames for him like a lighted torch. Barns, fields, and fence lines spring from darkness. But when a pilot is fatigued, dawn may become as painful and dulling to his senses as an infected wound. Beauty is unseen; safety, unappreciated. He wishes only for the sun to rise and bring wakefulness and strength. I think of dawns on the mail route, after a late flight the night before. They brought moments when I almost felt that flying was not worth while — moments when only pride kept me from landing in some pasture, cutting my engine, and slumping back in my cockpit to sleep. But those moments were always at dawn. I awoke with the sunrise. This is different. It's much more serious. I want to sleep in broad daylight, before noon of the first day.

In glancing from compass to water and out to the horizon where land should soon appear, my eyes fasten on a band of mud sticking to the right wing's lower surface — brown and clumpy. One of the wheels threw it up during take-off. I want to reach out, scrape it off, and polish the fabric; but it's an arm's length too far away. Now, I'll have to look at it helplessly during all the rest of the flight — a step from my cockpit, on the ground — distant as Paris. What inadequate standards of measurement man uses — so many feet and inches to the engineer — a stride to the mechanic with a sponge — let's see, it's almost thirty-three hundred miles to that mud for me, the pilot in this cockpit. Why should I have to carry its extra weight and resistance all the way across the ocean? Why tear leaves from a notebook to save weight, and then be weighted down with *mud*?

There's another band of mud on the left wing. I remind myself that at most it's only a few ounces, that its roughness can't slow the plane down more than a fraction of a mile an hour, and that mudguards to protect against it would cost more in weight and resistance than the mud itself. But when one is tired, small items draw undue attention – – – If it takes thirty-three hours to get to Paris, it will take thirty-three hours to get that mud off the wings – – – Thirty-three hundred miles to Paris – – – "Things equal to the same thing are equal to each other" – – – an indisputable law, one learns in school – – – There's something wrong about these "laws" packed up in nutshells — they only work near the shell. If one tries to use them too far away from it – – – well, it certainly isn't thirty-three hundred miles to that mud – – – but six feet doesn't fit the distance either – – –

I'm half asleep! I cup my hand into the slipstream and deflect fresh air against my face. Check the instruments — that will help. The periscope's still out. I slide it back into the cockpit. There's been no ship for many miles, and I'm too high to strike a mast anyway. I can at least save its resistance.

The air-speed indicator shows no difference with the periscope retracted; but on such a long flight that should save a gallon or two of fuel. Possibly it will compensate for the mud. A pound of resistance saved is worth several pounds of weight. Besides, there's the principle involved. From the start, I've planned this flight on the basis that nothing can be wasted, that no detail is too small to be considered. I've made my own flying boots out of light material. I've bought small flashlights for my pocket, so that two would weigh no more than one of ordinary size. I've cut unneeded areas from my charts to gain some extra ounces.

There's an intangible value in striving for perfection — a value that can't be measured on such material standards as pounds of weight or resistance. When I was a child in grade school, I learned a verse which comes to mind when logic says I'm spending too much time on details:

> "In the elder days of Art,
>   Builders wrought with greatest care
> Each minute and unseen part;
>   For the Gods see everywhere."

THE FIFTH HOUR

Over Nova Scotia

TIME — 11:52 A.M.

WIND VELOCITY	*15 m.p.h.*	VISIBILITY	*Unlimited*
WIND DIRECTION	*NW.*	ALTITUDE	200 *feet*
TRUE COURSE	58°	AIR SPEED	103 *m.p.h.*
VARIATION	20°	TACHOMETER	1725 *r.p.m.*
MAGNETIC COURSE	78°	OIL TEMPERATURE	42° C.
DEVIATION	0°	OIL PRESSURE	57 *lbs.*
COMPASS COURSE	78°	FUEL PRESSURE	3.5 *lbs.*
DRIFT ANGLE	10° *R.*	MIXTURE	1.5
COMPASS HEADING	68°	FUEL TANK	*L. Wing*
CEILING	*Unlimited*		

It's noon of the first day. Four hundred miles from New York. Three thousand two hundred miles to Paris.

Land ahead! A huge green mass extends back to a hilly horizon. While I've been dreaming along in warm sunlight, with eyes on instruments and nearby sea, Nova Scotia has crept in unobserved. I glance at the clock — eight minutes after twelve. Time has leapt a quarter hour in a moment.

Nova Scotia! That strange northern country of school-day geographies. What an out-of-the-way place it had seemed, hanging there precariously on the eastern edge of Canada, green and cold against the pink tint of New Brunswick. I could never fully realize that it lay no farther north than Maine. I thought of it as a semiarctic land. And here it is, Nova Scotia itself — no longer an outline on the page of a thumb-marked book. The low, grassy coast, curving in under my right wing, is backed by growths of spruce and

pine. The scarcity of farms and stump land marks a rugged, frontier country of the north, a country where terrain, climate, and
forest are still battling hard against man's axe and plow.

I forget about being tired. Here's a vital point in the flight.
How accurately have I held my course? I climb higher, approaching the tidal flats. Altitude will help to locate my exact position.
When you fly low, you see only the individuality of landmarks — a
single village, the mouth of a river, a rocky cape jutting out to sea.
You gain intimacy but lose perspective. You may read the signs on
store fronts, wave at children in back yards, see birds startled from
tree branches, and guess the size of the lighthouse keeper's family
from the washing on his line; but there are probably a dozen river
mouths, capes, and villages on your map, and when you don't know
your position, no single one is likely to give the secret away. On
the other hand, flying high you see the entire geographical community. The village takes its place between the river and the cape,
and nowhere else on your map will there be a relationship quite
the same. If any doubt remains in your mind, a bend in the river
two or three miles upstream — an eighth-inch on the map — will
take all uncertainty away.

From a thousand feet, it's not difficult to find lines on my
chart corresponding to those formed by the shore below — a
peninsula on my left, a cape on my right, a tongue of the sea
stretching inland far ahead. I've made my landfall at the mouth of
St. Mary Bay, about six miles southeast of course. I've covered
440 miles in four hours and nineteen minutes. That's an average
of 102 miles an hour.

Laying out charts at San Diego, I'd decided that an error of
5 degrees would mark reasonably good navigation. Now, I've held
within 2 degrees of the great circle on my chart — less than half
the error I allowed for. Six miles off, at Nova Scotia, equals less
than 50 miles at Ireland. I'll be well satisfied if I can hold that
close to route.

This first test makes me feel in my bones what before I've
based only on theory and the experience of others — that the
swinging card of a compass can actually lead me safely across an

ocean to the shores of a foreign country beyond, and that lines and figures on a chart, if properly translated, will turn into the substance of real earth below.

Striking Nova Scotia has another significance. When I was planning this flight to Paris, I established three dividing lines in my mind before which I would, under certain circumstances, turn back; but beyond which I'd continue, "burning bridges behind me." The first of these lines lay across the runway on Roosevelt Field. When my wheels finally left the ground, that bridge was burned. Then, it was too late to pull the throttle back and stop.

Now, I've set fire to the second bridge. It spanned the Nova Scotian coast. I decided that if Nova Scotia were covered with fog, so that I could find no landmark on the ground with which to check my course, I'd turn back to Long Island. But if the Nova Scotian coast were clear, and my compasses proved well swung — if I had held reasonably close to course during the first 440 miles of flight — then I'd go on, even if all the rest of North America and the Atlantic Ocean were blanketed with fog.

The third dividing line lies about halfway across the ocean — depending on both wind and weather. Before I reach it, if mechanical trouble develops — if engine roughens or oil pressure drops or a fuel tank springs a leak — I'll turn back, hoping to reach an American shore and find some place to land without too bad a crash. But after I pass that line, regardless of what may happen, I'll continue on toward Europe.

The country under my plane is spotted with forests, lakes, and marshes. Gray boulders wart up everywhere — in woods, on hilltops — one sees them even under water where it's shallow. The lakes are smooth as glass — not a breath of air blowing across them. It won't make any difference which way I land if the engine fails.

A forced landing! Years of barnstorming with rebuilt Army planes and engines have trained me to keep that possibility always in mind. You never know, with such equipment, when an engine will stop running. Unconsciously my eyes are always searching for the place I'd choose to land should failure come at this particular moment.

I study the ground. It's certainly bad country for a forced landing. There's not a farmer's field in sight. It would be best to stall down into a lake. The *Spirit of St. Louis* would sink, of course, but there wouldn't be a fire. A swamp might not be too bad, and there are a lot of them.

I landed in a swamp in Minnesota, four years ago, with my old Jenny. A local storm had covered the city of Shakopee, for which I was headed. I'd tried to fly in underneath it, but the rain was too heavy — a real cloudburst. So I circled over country nearby, flying under a thick cloud layer, close to the ground, waiting for the storm to blow past. The visibility in places was less than half a mile. I flew into a heavy shower before I saw it through the mist. One cylinder cut out. I banked toward a clover field. Two more cylinders stopped firing. I had to land at once, either in a woods or in a swamp. I was less than 200 feet high, and there was nothing else within gliding range. I chose the swamp, and stalled down onto it. The wheels slithered along about thirty feet and sank to the spreader-bar. The cockpit jumped. My belt jerked tight. I found myself hanging upside down, looking at several tall blades of grass.

It's not easy to get out of an open cockpit when you're hanging upside down. You don't just unsnap the safety belt. Pilots have broken their necks doing that. It's one thing to fall a yard or two onto your feet, and quite another to fall that distance onto your head. You have to support your weight by hanging onto something with one hand while you release your safety belt with the other. My quick-release mechanism had jammed that day, and it resisted my single-handed attempt to open it. So I hung suspended until I loosened the buckles which held one end of the belt to the pilot's seat. Even then it required some acrobatics to get straightened out with the world again.

My plane wasn't damaged much. It was well splashed over with black mud, but all I needed to put it back in flying condition was a new propeller and a little cord and dope to bind up a crack in the spreader-bar. But that Jenny had only a little over ten gallons of gasoline in its tank when I landed. The *Spirit of St. Louis* has — let's see — I'm four and a half hours out — almost 400 gallons. My tanks would surely burst today if I stalled down onto a swamp. I'd be lucky if I didn't have a fire.

Well, there's no swamp or lake within gliding range now. If the engine cut out I'd land in that patch of young pines; their supple trunks and thick green boughs would break the shock of impact. I know of several pilots who landed on treetops without getting hurt badly.

Sitting comfortably at my drafting board in San Diego a few weeks ago, I decided that a forced landing was a possibility I'd prepare for and then forget. But old habits aren't so easily thrust aside. After hours of flying, a pilot's mind wanders along uncharted courses of its own fantasy, rushing back at intervals to check instruments, to make resolutions, to decide some pressing detail of his flight; and then, duty over, it slips unobtrusively off again, to be found in the most unexpected places. A forced landing is the thing I wish above all else to avoid; but my mind takes fiendish pleasure in planning one — on hills, in marshes, in tree clumps, it visualizes the best technique to use, carrying me along in its excursions until my ears can almost hear the motor cough, and my body feel the tearing impact of the wheels and wings.

THE SIXTH HOUR

Over Nova Scotia

TIME — 12:52 P.M.

WIND VELOCITY	30 *m.p.h.*	VISIBILITY	*Unlimited*
WIND DIRECTION	*WNW.*	ALTITUDE	*700 feet*
TRUE COURSE	60°	AIR SPEED	101 *m.p.h.*
VARIATION	22° *W.*	TACHOMETER	1700 *r.p.m.*
MAGNETIC COURSE	82°	OIL TEMPERATURE	42° *C.*
DEVIATION	0°	OIL PRESSURE	57 *lbs.*
COMPASS COURSE	82°	FUEL PRESSURE	3.5 *lbs.*
DRIFT ANGLE	10° *R.*	MIXTURE	1.5
COMPASS HEADING	72°	FUEL TANK	*Nose*
CEILING	*Unlimited*		

The wind is rising. I'm already crabbing fifteen degrees into its drift. Hills ahead roll up to a mountain range. I open the throttle fifty revolutions, and begin climbing. The *Spirit of St. Louis* gains altitude easily, considering its heavy load.

My course takes me over a saddle in the range. Wings flex in moderate turbulence as I pass between summits. Then, ground drops steeply on the eastern side, to another land of hills, lakes, and forests.

I wonder if my plane has been reported over Nova Scotia. That little village of wooden houses back on the coast, half a mile west of my landfall — a plane would be no ordinary sight to people living there. Maybe their local newspaper carried an article about the New York-to-Paris flight. Some of them must have heard my engine overhead and looked up to silver wings against the sky. Did anyone think to send a message back over wires to the United States, saying a plane had reached the shores of Nova Scotia?

One o'clock; it's lunch time in New York. It's lunch time in St. Louis, too, though there's an hour's difference by the sun; people eat earlier in the Mississippi Valley. My friends are probably sitting at their midday meal, speculating about where I am at this moment. What a contrast between my cockpit, high over Nova Scotian wilds, and the silvered settings of a city table! What amazing magic is carried in an airplane's wings — New York at breakfast; Nova Scotia at lunch. There hasn't been time enough between to prepare my mind and body for the difference. How can breakfast-to-lunch in time equal New York-to-Nova Scotia in distance? Flying has torn apart the relationship of space and time; it uses our old clock but with new yardsticks. If I'd watched fresh-sown wheat spring to a harvest since the dawn, it would hardly be stranger than this experience.

Lunch time! I drop my hand to the bag of sandwiches, but I'm not hungry. Why eat simply because it's lunch time? A drink of water will be enough. Mustn't take too much, though — can't afford to waste water — suppose I'm forced down at sea!

In hanging up the canteen, I let my map slide toward the window. One corner flutters in a puff of air. I jerk it away with a start. Suppose my chart blows out, as my data board blew out of the cockpit on that test flight in California? My key to Paris would be gone; I'd have to turn back and start again — turn back for lack of a sheet of paper. "On course, plenty of fuel, all readings normal; but the chart blew out the window." What an explanation that would make! No, the chart must never get close to a window.

But why not put the windows in? Why didn't I put them in before? Why have I wasted their streamlining value for these five hours of flight? They're in their rack, an arm's reach behind me. I carried them because they were worth more than their weight in fuel. They're included in the performance curves as extra gallons of gasoline would have been included. They'll smooth out the flow of air along the fuselage. Smoother flow means less resistance; less resistance means more speed; and more speed will result in additional miles of range.

I open the cockpit ventilator and start to slip the left window into place, when I realize that a new factor has to be considered, one of those factors engineers can't measure with their curves yet one on which all performances must rest — the condition of the pilot. Windows would cut down the flow of air through my cockpit. They'd form a barrier between me and elements outside my plane. They'd interfere with the crystal clarity of communion with water, land, and sky. They'd insulate me from a strength I'll need before my flight is done, and which, for some reason, cannot penetrate their thin transparency.

No, I'll leave the windows in their rack, waste the miles of range they offer. I'll sacrifice their efficiency to mine. It's a new experience. Always before, I've had a reserve of energy and skill on which my plane could draw, as during an overloaded take-off, or to compensate for instability or lack of forward vision in fuselage design. Now, for the first time, I'm taking a favor from my plane. It makes the *Spirit of St. Louis* seem more a living partner in adventure than a machine of cloth and steel.

Below, spreading across a narrow dirt road and a winding creek, is the largest Nova Scotian farm I've seen. Its eastern pasture is almost level, with only scattered rocks and stumps. As I look at it, my mind divides into two personalities who argue back and forth:

"It was a mistake not to put dump valves in the tanks. Now if you could dump 300 gallons of fuel, you could probably stall-in there with nothing worse than a blown tire and a bent propeller. You *might* get down with no damage at all."

"Yes, but we considered all that at the factory while the plane was being built. You know how much time we spent studying the problem. Dump valves might have leaked. No one was quite certain how to make them. And there'd be all the extra mechanism to go wrong. Suppose one of them opened halfway across the ocean. Suppose seepage filled the cockpit with fumes of gasoline. Besides, dump valves would have meant more weight and more resistance. You remember we decided to sacrifice everything to take-off and range — those were the danger points of the flight."

"But the rubber boat, and the red flares, and the emergency rations, and the extra gallon of water — we didn't sacrifice them. They're all here in the fuselage right now — thirty pounds of them. That's worth more than a half hour's flight when the tanks are low – – –"

The sky has been filling slowly: first, a few stray cumulus clouds, blinding in the sunlight; then flocks of them, with a higher layer drifting in above until now there's less blue than white and gray. A solid mass blocks out the north — tremendous, dark, and foreboding. Angular streaks of gray break the horizon ahead into segments — rain squalls. I hope that doesn't mean an area of storm over the rest of Nova Scotia and Newfoundland.

The *Spirit of St. Louis* is already bumping. Lakes and ponds down below are wave-roughed and lined with wind streaks. White beaches of foam have formed against islands and leeward shores. It takes a gale to whip up water like that — forty or fifty miles an hour.

For the last quarter hour, the wind has been blowing directly across my route, mounting constantly in velocity. I should be crabbing toward it at an angle of 25 degrees to compensate for drift. But that would leave my plane pointing into the great black body of the storm. I won't change my heading for the time being. I'll let wind drift me where it will. If the storm area is large, and the wind continues strong northwest, it will take me to the coast where ceilings should be higher, or blind flying safer. If the storm is small, the wind may shift again in a few more miles and blow me back on course. Winds which arise suddenly on the edge of storms often change just as suddenly and blow in another direction.

For five hours, the danger of turbulence has hardly entered my mind. I left it behind with the last gentle bumps over New England. It was crowded out by the warm sunlight, the majesty of the ocean, and the smooth, gliding flight above the waves. The slight trembling I felt over the Nova Scotian coast, and crossing the mountain range, was pleasant rather than alarming. But now, as I approach these storm clouds, air is really getting rough. Wing tips flex with rapid, jerking movements, and the cockpit bumps up, down, and sideways. I buckle my safety belt. Of course the *Spirit of St. Louis* is some 500 pounds lighter than on take-off; but with a ton of fuel left on board, its structure is still dangerously overloaded. A violent gust might easily snap a spar or fitting. I throttle the engine to 1625 r.p.m., and let air speed drop to 90 miles an hour.

The wings were never designed for such a wrenching! I feel as though the storm were gathering my plane in its teeth as a dog picks up a rabbit. If only I had a parachute! But there's no use wishing for things I don't have. A few minutes ago I wanted dump valves; now it's a parachute. After all, I can't carry everything.

I considered carrying a parachute, but decided against it. A parachute would have cost twenty pounds — a third of an hour's fuel — enough food and water for many days adrift. And it would be useless over the ocean. Without a rubber boat, no one could live long in icy northern waters. It would be better to stay with the plane, even if it crashed.

Over Long Island and New England, I flew too low to use a parachute. By the time I get to Europe, the wings will be so lightly loaded that I won't have to worry about turbulence of air. And the *Spirit of St. Louis* will be able to land so slowly that I could stall it down almost anywhere and walk away. No, the only portion of the route where I might need a parachute is right here in Nova Scotia, and possibly for an hour or two over Newfoundland. Even here, it would take quick work to get out of my cockpit from an altitude of 1500 feet if a wing gave way.

I'm not much higher than Lieutenant Smith was when he lost a wing looping his National Guard Jenny. He never did get clear of his plane. As the highest ranking officer on the field when the accident happened, I'd taken charge of the wreckage. I found Smith's parachute strung out on the ground beside the fuselage when I reached his broken body. His foot, shoe leather torn in struggle, had apparently caught between the cockpit's rim and an angular fuselage-to-center-section wire. He must have pulled the rip cord just before he hit, in the desperate hope that the 'chute would billow out and jerk him free.

Smith's observer had gotten clear of his cockpit. He must have been 800 feet high when I saw his figure sail out through the air. But there was no sign of a parachute's white canopy. I'd stood glued to the ground as I watched wing, plane, and man — fabric fluttering, and wires screaming toward the earth — all in a single vista of the eye. An extra kick — a ten-pound pull — would save a life. If only my hand could have traveled with my vision!

The observer hit first — in a cornfield. His body bounced six feet back into the air. Then plane and body struck together, leaving only the wing and bits of lighter structure in the sky. We never knew what happened to the observer. Some thought he was dazed by fear and couldn't locate the pull-ring, for he was a young and inexperienced airman. It was one of his first flights. But I've found senses more acute when falling down through space. If he'd been dazed, he couldn't have jumped so quickly. I think his head hit some part of the plane's structure, and that he was unconscious during the seconds that passed before his death.

Parachutes hadn't done those flyers any good, even with open cockpits to jump from. The *Spirit of St. Louis* would fall faster than that Jenny, with a wing off, and it would take extra seconds to squeeze out edgewise past a door. Besides, I'll soon have to drop lower to stay underneath the clouds. Everything considered, I was right when I decided not to bring a 'chute along – – – and yet, I'd feel better if I had one.

Logic's not enough to calm my senses. They know what it's like to feel fittings snap in air — the physical jolt — the mental shock — the tautening of brain and muscle. A wing on *my* plane once crumpled; but *then* I had a parachute. It was during a combat maneuver in Texas, not far from Kelly Field. Our pursuit squadron of SE-5s had located the "enemy" and nosed down to attack. Lieutenant Blackburn, our instructor, was in command. We had three units of three planes each. I was flying left wing in the top unit, with Cadet Love leading and Lieutenant McAllister on my right.

Our "enemy," a De Haviland observation plane, was cruising below us, some 5000 feet above the ground and over a layer of broken clouds. It was piloted by Lieutenant Maughan of "Dawn-to-Dusk Flight" fame. We pursuit pilots reached a pretty high speed in our dive. After Love pulled up, McAllister and I closed in to confirm the "kill." Then we pulled up too. I'd kicked left rudder, as I hauled back on the stick, into what I thought was empty sky.

Then it happened. I heard the snap of parting metal and the jerking crunch of wood, as my forehead bumped the cockpit's cowling and my plane cartwheeled through the air. I yanked the throttle shut as muscles tensed body back in place. There, canted sidewise, less than a dozen feet away, was the fuselage of another SE-5. Our wings were ripped and locked together.

For an instant, after that first crashing bump, both planes seemed to hang motionless in space. I saw McAllister reach for his safety belt and half rise in his seat. Then we began to rotate in the air. A trailing edge of the broken top wing folded back over my cockpit and vibrated against my helmet, shaking sight from my eyes and thought from my brain — except for the imperative idea of clearing the wreckage with my parachute.

By that time I had the rubber safety band removed and my belt unbuckled. Wires were howling; wooden members snapping; my cockpit had tipped toward the vertical. Our planes were revolving like a windmill. I pushed past the damaged wing, hooked my heels on the cowling, and kicked backward into space.

How safe the rushing air had seemed when I cleared those planes — like a feather bolster supporting me. I fell flat, face upward, for a time. My hand was on the rip cord but I didn't dare pull it, for the planes were right above me, spinning, and spewing out a trail of fragments to the sky. McAllister was nowhere in sight. Either he was caught in the wreckage or he'd cleared it sooner and was falling below me.

Then my feet had angled upward, and I'd turned sidewise, and flattened out again, face down. I remember twisting my head around to look at the planes. They were more than a hundred feet to one side, and gradually sliding farther away. I hit a cloud; sank into it; pulled the rip cord.

My parachute had no more than flowered out when I was below the cloud layer. The wrecked planes plummeted past me, and McAllister's 'chute came swinging down out of the mist above.

McAllister and I were close to 2000 feet high when our SE-5s, still locked together, hit the ground and burst into flames. Fighters from the other two pursuit units were diving and zooming all round us. They'd broken formation the moment they saw us collide, and followed us down through air. I'd been watching the disintegrating wreckage so intently that my eyes were blinded to other objects in the sky. Now I had time to look around, I realized that every cadet and instructor within sight was either there or headed toward us. Every few seconds, a pair of wings saluted by — too close for comfort.

We were over an area of mesquite and cactus, but angling with

the wind toward a plowed field which was ideal for parachute landings. Being lower than McAllister, I had to slip my 'chute a little
to reach it. I wasn't able to keep standing after my feet touched
the ground; but my landing was soft — across a shallow, furrowed
ditch.

I lost a vest-pocket camera and my goggles on that descent.
And I'd forgotten to hold onto my rip cord. You always got
razzed for losing the rip cord.

"What! You threw away your rip cord? And *you* want to be
an aviator?"

But such things were too trivial to worry about as I gathered
up my parachute. Being alive was what counted. McAllister was
trudging toward me. Planes were chandelling around the edges of
the field. Several DHs landed on the plowing. Everyone was happy
because no one had been killed. Lieutenant Maughan laughed, and
claimed two of the "enemy" brought down. Two DHs were sent
over from Kelly, rear cockpits empty, to carry us home. Two fresh
SE-5s, with parachutes, were placed on the line at our disposal;
and in slightly over an hour we were back in air again — members
number twelve and thirteen in the Caterpillar Club — that exclusive and unorganized group of flyers whose lives have been saved
by the silkworm's product.

Suppose I hadn't had a parachute on that flight! It might easily
have been the case — our class was the first to go through Kelly
equipped with them.

The first squall isn't a large one. I can see right through its
mist of rain. Hills and lakes beyond are only thinly veiled in white.
But with each succeeding squall, clouds grow darker, rain is
heavier, and lightning flashes down on trees and rocks. Finally, I
give up my course and turn eastward, to skirt the edges of the
more violent storms. I weave in and out, flying now through a
cloudburst, now under a patch of open sky; returning to my heading, and then leaving it again rather than drill through the heart of
a storm. Water lashes over the wings, turns the propeller into a

whitish disc of vapor, trickles along silver surfaces, eddies behind screw heads and fittings; seeps into my cockpit, splashing over flying suit and charts, moistening my lips, freshening the air I breathe.

Rain beats down against the wind-scraped lakes, until it seems to rebound a foot or two in air and then fall back again. Water glistens up from narrow dirt roads and shines on farmhouse roofs. Smoke is ripping away from the chimney of a backwoods sawmill I skim over. At times I can barely see the outline of the ground. Then I fly still lower, just clearing the top of a hill, nosing down into the valley beyond, watching the seething branches of spruce and pine, holding myself in readiness to turn sharply back if cloud and summit meet ahead. Can the ignition system stand such drenching? I haven't tested the *Spirit of St. Louis* in a cloudburst. I don't dare check the magnetos now; but not a single cylinder has missed.

There's no way of telling what lies beyond the rain's gray curtain; but each lake and little pond I pass signals its story of the storm. Waves mark the wind's velocity; ragged streaks of foam point out its direction. From northwest to southwest and up to west again it shifts, veering back and forth with each new squall. Gradually, as I watch, the wind swings southward, until at last it blows southeast, and then begins to die. From northwest to southeast — it's a good omen; that's the way the wind should veer if the storm area is small.

THE SEVENTH HOUR

Over Nova Scotia

TIME — 1:52 P.M.

WIND VELOCITY	10 *m.p.h.*	VISIBILITY	15 *miles*
WIND DIRECTION	*SSE.*		*outside of*
TRUE COURSE	61°		*squalls*
VARIATION	23° *W.*	ALTITUDE	900 *feet*
MAGNETIC COURSE	84°	AIR SPEED	100 *m.p.h.*
DEVIATION	0°	TACHOMETER	1675 *r.p.m.*
COMPASS COURSE	84°	OIL TEMPERATURE	40° *C.*
DRIFT ANGLE	5° *L.*	OIL PRESSURE	58 *lbs.*
COMPASS HEADING	89°	FUEL PRESSURE	3.5 *lbs.*
CEILING	1500 *feet,*	MIXTURE	1.5
	broken	FUEL TANK	*Fuselage*

Six hundred miles out. Three thousand miles to go. The columns of figures on my log sheet look impressive. When they grow six times that long, I should be over Paris. Squalls are lighter, and patches of blue sky are larger. "Clearing along the North American coast," the weather report stated; and clearing it really seems to be.

But I've got to be cautious about too much optimism. I'm at a point in my flight where I have the feeling of great accomplishment without having experienced the major strain of effort. In multiplying by six what I have done, I neglect the exponent of fatigue, and draw an arithmetical result from what is really a geometrical equation. Fatigue to a body is like air resistance to a plane. If you fly twice as fast (if you continue twice as long), you encounter four times the resistance (you become several times as tired). But elements of mind and body don't follow such clear, sharp curves of physics; they jump erratically to peaks, and back to depths, and then may strike an average for a time. The cool freshness of the rain, the concentration required in flying through the squalls, and the satisfaction of entering the seventh hour of my flight, have brought me to a peak of confidence and hope. Only 3000 miles, now, to Paris; and 40 hours of fuel remain in my tanks.

A wilderness lies beneath my wings — no road or field or cabin. Valleys are filled with the deep green of virgin timber. Flocks of duck rise out of lakes and marshes. I think of childhood nights on our farm, when I lay awake listening to my father's stories of hunting and trapping around such lakes as these. "There were thousands of duck," he had said, "so many that the sky was blackened." And there are thousands of duck below me, like a cloud's shadow drifting over land and water.

My grandfather must have found a country like this when he immigrated to America from Skåne in the southern part of Sweden. My father was only a few months old then. Traveling westward, the family settled on Sauk River's bank, in the new state of Minnesota. They built a log cabin in territory through which warpaths of the Chippewa and Sioux had run, only a few years before.

As soon as my father was old enough to carry a gun, it had been his job to keep the family supplied with meat. Since ammunition was scarce, his rounds were counted, and a bird demanded in return for each one fired. When he missed a shot, he tried to hit two birds with the next. My father had spoken of it casually, as part of his daily life in boyhood; but to me, it appeared a miraculous accomplishment — getting two duck in line to save one charge. Now, as I look down on this game-filled land, I understand his casualness better. It wouldn't be so difficult to kill two birds with one shot when they're as thick as that.

The rule was only for birds and small animals. On days when he brought back a deer, he wasn't asked to account for his ammunition. The woods here must be full of deer, too — and probably bear, porcupine, wildcat, and even moose. Envious of my father's boyhood, I often dreamed of such a country, and here it is, just outside my window — land of the pioneer: forests filled with game; dashing streams of crystal water.

Several small farms line the river ahead — fields walled in by timber. Cattle wade across the water, their shadows falling sharply on its surface. One of my father's stories was about fishing from a riverbank on the homestead. Sioux massacres in the Minnesota Valley and raids northward had left settlers' nerves highly tensed. It had been several years since the uprising, but fear remained in children's minds. Suddenly, my father saw shadows move along the edge of a pool upstream — Sioux warriors! He lunged backward into hazel brush as he looked up to see — no, not warriors, just farm cattle, like those below me now. Everybody feared the Sioux. They'd stretch a man to stakes and build a fire on his belly. They'd cram live children into kitchen ovens and let them roast. So the settlers' stories went.

Once, when my father was very young, a messenger arrived on horseback, warning all farmers to flee for their lives — Little Crow was on the warpath. Hogs and cattle were turned loose, doors locked, homes abandoned. My grandfather harnessed the oxen, and fled with his family to the fort at St. Cloud, about 40 miles away. It was crowded there, with so many people gathered in. There was little to do, and the men quickly grew restless. Two neighboring farmers decided to return to their homes, against the warning of the soldiers. They said the danger of Indians was exaggerated, and that their animals needed care. They left the town on horseback, and were never seen again — probably captured and tortured to death by Sioux, the settlers thought.

That made others at the fort more willing to accept the hardships of a refugee. Complaints lessened. The children even enjoyed their experience, my father said. There were new games to play, new sights to see. It was a welcome change from the isolated life on a homestead. Our family stayed on until my Aunt Linda was born. And what a commotion that caused — men standing around awkwardly outside, women running back and forth, children neglected for the day.

My grandparents were lucky. When they finally returned to their farm, they found everything as they had left it, except for the stock. It was a real job hunting through the woods for pigs and chickens, and rounding up the cows. Grandmother never did get all her chickens back — wild animals, of course.

The warlike Sioux were driven westward into the Dakotas. Red River oxcart trains creaked by the homestead with greater frequency. Father said you could hear them miles away. And more settlers came to set up farms. Only the friendly Chippewa remained — Indians of the forest. Their pointed, birchbark teepees often rose on the banks of Sauk River, near my grandfather's cabin. Many of my father's stories were about them. There was one I asked him to tell over and over again as I lay in bed, looking out at the stars.

They had been trading skins for firewater, those braves who came up to the log farmhouse and demanded food. My grandfather was away. My grandmother was busy baking bread and caring for the children. She had no use for drunken Indians. "Go away," she told them. "I've got nothing for you. See, the bread isn't baked yet." She opened the oven to show them. They muttered and argued for a time outside the door, while Grandmother went on with her work and the children peeked out at them. Finally, they decided to leave. But as they passed the woodpile, one of the braves grabbed my grandfather's axe and carried it off.

My grandmother took time to change her clothes before she ran after those Indians! She put on a silk dress which she had brought from Sweden, and guarded carefully through hard years of frontier life. She knew the importance of dignity in dealing with Indians; it would be unwise to confront them in soiled kitchen garments. When she caught up to them on the road, the brave refused to give up the axe. He shook it at her, scowled, and kept on walking with the others. She followed, arguing and threatening; until one of the squaws snatched the axe from the drunken warrior and laid it on the ground. My grandmother picked it up and returned to the farmhouse, to her work clothes and children, and to baking bread.

Why take such a chance for an axe? Well, that was another story. Grandfather Lindbergh had held a high position in Sweden. He was a leading member of the Riksdag, and a close friend of the King. But he'd gotten into political and business troubles, lost practically everything he had, and sailed to America to start a new life when he was over fifty years of age. In the small log cabin in Minnesota, our family was so poor that my grandfather sold a gold medal he'd been given in "the old country" to buy a breaking plow. Axes, like plows, couldn't be made on the farm; they cost real money, and real money was awfully hard to get. Besides, it was a special axe, weighted and shaped for my grandfather's single-handed use, for he had lost his left arm at the sawmill. He lost that arm trying to earn a little real money to buy things that couldn't be raised on the farm, such as salt, and kerosene, and tools.

Handling logs and lumber was heavy work for a man of my grandfather's age. But he had great physical endurance, and his services were valued. One day he stumbled, and fell against the spinning saw. Its teeth cut through his arm near the shoulder, and ripped open his back. The belt hurled him half way across the shed. The mill hands claimed that the gash was so deep they could see my grandfather's heart beating. They bound his wounds up crudely and sent for the minister, Reverend C. S. Harrison. Minister Harrison had my grandfather laid on some hay in the bottom of an oxcart and hauled him, bleeding terribly, over the rough roads to the family cabin. A man was started off on the only horse available, with instructions to get relays wherever he could and rush a doctor back. But the nearest doctor lived at St. Cloud — and he was not at home. The messenger eventually found him in a still more distant village, helping a young wife give birth to her child. Meanwhile my grandmother, the minister, and the friends who came to help expected Grandfather to die. They washed his wounds with cold water from a nearby spring, picked out rags and sawdust, and tried to stop the flow of blood.

Three days passed before the doctor arrived. He amputated the arm and stitched together the gaping hole in the back. My grandfather lived despite shock, infection, and loss of blood. Lying on his bed, in great pain, he demanded to see his left arm before it was buried in the garden. It was brought to him in a small, rough-board coffin. Taking the fingers in those of his right hand, he said slowly, in broken English, "You have been a good friend to me for fifty years. But you can't be with me any more. So good-by. Good-by, my friend."

It took months for my grandfather to recover. Then, he had special tools fashioned for his single-handed use. But farming and earning money were more difficult after that, and there were four young children to care for — my father, Linda, Juno, and Frank. Grandmother had to watch each penny spent. Her family couldn't afford to lose an axe.

Are there Indians in these forests too, here in Nova Scotia — teepees covered by branches? How much lies hidden under that blanket of green boughs. I can only guess as I fly over hills and valleys, now 50 feet, now 500 above the ground. There's no sign of life in the occasional clearings. There are no canoes in sight on the swiftly-flowing rivers. And the wild animals that live here probably took cover at the first terrifying sound of my engine.

In flying, you learn to know the external character, the geographical features of a country; but you have little contact with its inner life. You *see* the land below you, but you don't *feel* it around you; until you set foot on ground it remains a foreign soil. Here is a Nova Scotian hilltop, fifty feet away — so close that I can see the twigs on its bushes and the moss on its stones. Yet in another sense, a whole ocean lies between us. I can see pine needles on the boughs, but I can't smell their fragrance or feel them prickle on my skin as I push by. The branches are swaying, but I hear no sound of wind. Even if I were on a local flight, I couldn't land, for there's no level area that's solid, clear, and large enough to hold a plane. At times I feel as separated from the country below me as though I were looking through a giant telescope at the surface of another planet.

THE EIGHTH HOUR
Over Nova Scotia
TIME — 2:52 P.M.

WIND VELOCITY	15 *m.p.h.*	VISIBILITY	*Unlimited*
WIND DIRECTION	*SSW.*	ALTITUDE	600 *feet*
TRUE COURSE	64°	AIR SPEED	96 *m.p.h.*
VARIATION	25° *W.*	TACHOMETER	1650 *r.p.m.*
MAGNETIC COURSE	89°	OIL TEMPERATURE	39° *C.*
DEVIATION	0°	OIL PRESSURE	58 *lbs.*
COMPASS COURSE	89°	FUEL PRESSURE	3.5 *lbs.*
DRIFT ANGLE	5° *L.*	MIXTURE	2
COMPASS HEADING	94°	FUEL TANK	*Fuselage*
CEILING	*Unlimited*		

The edge of the storm recedes gradually toward the north. Huge cumulo-nimbus clouds, billows of white and gray, roll upward for thousands of feet, penetrating the highest stratus layers. On the ground, patches of old snow appear in hollows and on the north side of boulders. I left summer back on Long Island this morning. Only a few minutes ago, I flew through the showers of spring. Now, I'm over a land just emerging from winter. And my route continues to angle northward for more than a thousand miles.

Fog! I'm flying along dreamily when I see it — a narrow white band on the horizon to my right. *There's fog on the Nova Scotian coast!* It brings me to attention like ice water dashed in the face.

Fog — the most dreaded of all enemies of flight. Will Cape Breton Island and Newfoundland be hidden by a sheet of blinding white? Has the clearing sky made me too confident of weather; or is this a vanishing remnant of the morning mists?

If fog will only hold off a few hours more, if I can only check my course over Newfoundland, it won't matter what happens after that. I'll ask for nothing more until I reach the other side of the ocean. The 1900 miles of water can be covered with fog — I'll fly above it, or under it, or in it. Nothing else will matter if the coast of Newfoundland is clear.

But here I am, wishing for another favor. I got off with my overload of fuel; the mists of Long Island lifted; I struck the southwest coast of Nova Scotia close to course. The storm area is behind. Only high cirrus wisps are left to veil the sun. It's not likely that I can fly all the way to Europe without encountering fog. Why isn't this a good place to meet it, with my engine running perfectly and 3500 miles of fuel in the tanks?

I check the switch — no cylinders missing on the right magneto; none missing on the left. I open the throttle 50 r.p.m. and begin climbing, while my eyes search the ground for some landmark that shows on my map. It's important to know my exact position before venturing out over that sea of white.

I can find no check point on the ground. The best map of this country I could buy contains nothing but lightly tinted space and a few wriggling lines for rivers — the kind of wriggles a cartographer makes with his pen when he's been informed vaguely that a river runs somewhere through the area. But as I near the coast, what seemed a great fog bank from the distance turns out to be only a long, narrow strip hovering above shore. The ocean beyond is sparkling blue in sunlight. Even the strip of fog ends before I strike Chedabucto Bay, where the ocean wedges in to pry Cape Breton Island away from the mainland of Canada. It seems today that every door is flung wide open when I knock.

Air is crystal clear along Cape Breton Island's coast. Like Nova Scotia, the country is spotted with lakes, and its streams are white with rapids. The hills on my left, snow-patched and bleak, mount up toward higher ridges. Over barren mountains inland, a new cloud bank is forming.

Shall I subtract a few degrees from my heading to angle back toward the great-circle route? But with clouds thickening in that direction, it seems wiser to remain near the sea. There'll be plenty of time to correct my heading before I reach Newfoundland.

The earth-inductor compass needle leans right. I press left rudder, and glance up to the instrument board mirror to check my heading with the liquid compass. Ninety-four degrees, the mirror shows with the white numerals it reflects. But in it I also see the interior of a wooden hangar on Curtiss Field. An instrument specialist is twisted around grotesquely in the cockpit of the *Spirit of St. Louis,* pointing up at the compass he's just installed. I'm leaning against the fuselage, looking in through a window.

"That's the best place I can find for it," he's saying, unhappily. "But you'll have to read it through a mirror." The compass is fastened to the top of the fuselage, too close to my head, and the unfamiliar figures on it are printed backward for mirror reading. "It will give you a more accurate indication up there than any other place we can find. It will swing less in rough air - - - You sure haven't any extra room in here."

"I don't mind reading it through a mirror," I reply. "The most important thing is to have it accurate and steady."

"Okay. There she stays then. Who's got a mirror around here?"

"There's one in the office."

"That's too big. It ought to be about two inches square."

"Will this do?" It's a woman's voice. Several people are standing outside the rope across the hangar door. Among them is a girl, not much more than college age, neatly dressed. Her handbag hangs open, and she's holding up the small, round mirror from her compact. It's just the right size. We thank her, and stick it with a piece of gum to the instrument board, above the earth-inductor compass dial. One of the mechanics lifts the rope so she can see into the cockpit.

After that the girl disappeared, and I never saw her again. How much chance did she think her mirror had of reaching Paris? She must have read the prophesies that I'd crash on take-off, or from exhaustion half way across the ocean. Certainly she had no technical knowledge of aircraft and their capabilities. Was she among the few who maintained unreasoned confidence in my success; or was hers a gesture of compassion toward a man about to die — a man whose last hours could be brightened by the gift of a compact's mirror? Well, at least it's reflected my course successfully beyond Nova Scotian shores.

My eyes wander up to the taut, silvered wing outside my window. It's difficult to realize that the substantial element of air is rushing past that motionless surface at nearly a hundred miles an hour. One of the miracles of flying is that when you look out at your wings you see neither movement nor support. As you clasp your hand in the cockpit, there's nothing tangible to air — nothing to carry a finger's weight. There seems no reason whatever to keep you from plummeting earthward like a rock. It's not until you put your arm outside, and press hard against the slipstream, that you sense the power and speed of flight. Then air takes on the quality of weight and substance; and you begin to understand the invisible element which makes it possible for man to fly.

Barely a tremor of turbulence is left. The engine's even vibration, shaking back through the fuselage's steel skeleton, gives life to cockpit and controls. Flowing up along the stick to my hand, it's the pulse beat of the plane. Let a cylinder miss once, and I'll feel it as clearly as though a human heart had skipped against my thumb.

I push my fingertips against quivering, drum-tight fabric of the cockpit wall. The plane's entire structure is carried by this frail covering of cloth. Thousands of pounds are lifted by these criss-crossed threads, yet singly they couldn't restrain the tugging of a bird. I understand how giant Gulliver was tied so firmly to the ground. As he was bound to earth, I am held in air — by the strength of threads. Nine barrels of gasoline and oil, wrapped up in fabric; two hundred and twenty horsepower, harnessed by a layer of cloth — vulnerable to a pin prick, yet protecting an airplane and its pilot on a flight across an ocean, between the continents — suspended at this moment five hundred feet above a frigid, northern land.

My cockpit is small, and its walls are thin; but inside this cocoon I feel secure, despite the speculations of my mind. It makes an efficient, tidy home, one so easy to keep in order that its very simplicity creates a sense of satisfaction and relief. It's a personal home, too — nobody has ever piloted the *Spirit of St. Louis*, but me. Flying in it is like living in a hermit's mountain cabin after being surrounded by the luxury and countless responsibilities of a city residence. Here, I'm conscious of all elements of weather, immersed in them, dependent on them. Here, the earth spreads out beyond my window, its expanse and beauty offered at the cost of a glance. Here, are no unnecessary extras, only the barest essentials of life and flight. There are no letters to get off in the next mail, no telephone bells to ring, no loose odds and ends to attend to in some adjoining room. The few furnishings are within arm's length, and all in order.

A cabin that flies through the air, that's what I live in; a cabin higher than the mountains, a cabin in the clouds and sky. After much travail, I've climbed up to it. Through months of planning, I've equipped it with utmost care. Now, I can relax in its solitary vantage point, and let the sun shine, and the west wind blow, and the blizzard come with the night.

I become minutely conscious of details in my cockpit — of the instruments, the levers, the angles of construction. Each item takes on new values. I study weld marks on the tubing (frozen ripples of steel through which pass invisible hundredweights of strain), a dot of radiolite paint on the altimeter's face (whose only mission is to show where the needle should ride when the *Spirit of St. Louis* is 2000 feet above the sea), the battery of fuel valves (my plane and my life depend on the slender stream of liquid flowing through them, like blood in human veins) — all such things, which I never considered much before, are now obvious and important. And there's plenty of time to notice them. I may be flying a complicated airplane, rushing through space, but in this cabin I'm surrounded by simplicity and thoughts set free of time. Thirty hours? How inadequate a measure! I've lived through thousands of periods thirty hours long, yet none of them like this. Thirty hours to Paris! What a simple statement, when the entire ocean lies between; when there's a chasm of eternity to cross. Who could look at the sky, at the mountains, at the chart on my knees, at the motionless wings of my plane, and still think of time in *hours*? Here, in the *Spirit of St. Louis*, I live in a different frame of time and space.

How detached the intimate things around me seem from the great world down below. How strange is this combination of proximity and separation. That ground — seconds away — thousands of miles away. *This* air, stirring mildly around me. That air, rushing by with the speed of a tornado, an inch beyond. These minute details in my cockpit. The grandeur of the world outside. The nearness of death. The longness of life.

THE NINTH HOUR
Over the Atlantic
TIME — 3:52 P.M.

WIND VELOCITY	25 *m.p.h.*	VISIBILITY	*Unlimited*
WIND DIRECTION	*W.*	ALTITUDE	*500 feet*
TRUE COURSE	64°	AIR SPEED	94 *m.p.h.*
VARIATION	27°	TACHOMETER	1625 *r.p.m.*
MAGNETIC COURSE	91°	OIL TEMPERATURE	39° *C.*
DEVIATION	0°	OIL PRESSURE	58 *lbs.*
COMPASS COURSE	91°	FUEL PRESSURE	3.5 *lbs.*
DRIFT ANGLE	5° *R.*	MIXTURE	2
COMPASS HEADING	86°	FUEL TANK	*Fuselage*
CEILING	*Unlimited*		

The coast line stops wandering back and forth, and turns abruptly northwest — the end of Cape Breton Island. Soon I'll be over sea again, the third stretch of salt water on my route to France. First, Long Island Sound; then that calming bay of the ocean between Cape Cod and Nova Scotia; now, two hundred miles to Newfoundland; and after that — after that is the great body of the Atlantic.

I've been flying over land for most of four hours. The sea is as welcome a change as the coast of Nova Scotia was, and as the coast of Newfoundland will be by the time I reach it. The sea is no longer a stranger. I've passed over its surface for hundreds of miles. I no longer feel that I leave security behind and enter danger the moment I fly across its breakers. As I struck Nova Scotia, I will strike Newfoundland; and as I strike Newfoundland, I will strike Europe, close to course.

I nose the *Spirit of St. Louis* down to meet the sea, down toward the tundra, down over the wild and lonely shore, down so low that I can see dead weeds along the tide line and wetness of the pebbles on the beach. I level out at twenty feet above the water — above a rougher, greener, colder-looking ocean, with whitecaps breaking off to streaks of foam. Here, there's no need to push out my periscope. Here, there are no masts to break the solitude of a northern sea — no marks of human life along the coast, not even

a plank of wreckage rotting on the beach. My plane, surrounded
by uninhabited land and water, seems a tiny speck, easily lost forever in such a wild expanse.

The cloud layer which was forming in the north remains behind with the peaks of Cape Breton Island. Only a few high cirrus
wings sweep overhead. On each side, the sea's horizon presses knife-
edged against the sky. Now, it's time to angle back onto my great-
circle route. If I leave Newfoundland on my plotted course, accurate navigation will be simpler. Besides, I have a certain pride in
holding to that course if I can.

I look down at the Mercator projection on my knees. Fifteen
degrees subtracted from my heading would put me back on the
great circle by the time I reach Newfoundland's southern coast.
Still, there may be clouds on the mountains, as there were on Cape
Breton Island. Then I'd be better off to the eastward, where I could
follow up Placentia Bay and cross over the narrow neck of land at
its head into Trinity Bay, which opens to the ocean. That would
be the safest route from the standpoint of weather — unless I
detour far enough south to round Cape Race.

My flight plan argues against detours unless forced by weather
that I can't fly above or through — weather I actually see ahead.
But to strike Placentia Bay would require so slight a change in my
present heading that you could hardly call it a detour. You could
hardly measure the mileage it would add; and there'd be plenty of
time to get back onto the great circle during long hours of night
and day over the ocean. Besides, if I set my course for Placentia
Bay, and the mountains are clear, I can fly over the little city of
St. John's. Someone there will surely send a message back, to say
I have passed.

Those men back on the field at Long Island who worked all
night long that I might start — the mechanics who labored so faith-
fully over my plane — the engineers who checked final installa-
tions — they're probably all waiting for some word of my passing,
some sign that I haven't crashed. I think of the tense faces staring
at me before take-off. What relief a single line might bring to them:
"Silver monoplane headed eastward sighted above St. John's

at – – – " Let's see – – – three hundred miles to go – – – an hour's difference in time – – – it would be about 7:20 on Newfoundland clocks.

My partners in St. Louis have a right to know that when I start over the ocean all is well. They stood solidly behind me through discouraging days and nights. They're all waiting, back there in Missouri, anxious to hear that I cross the coast of Newfoundland safely and on time.

The men at the factory in San Diego who built the *Spirit of St. Louis* in those two record-breaking months — they're about starting the afternoon shift — it's four hours earlier out there. By this time they have heard that I got off the field with full tanks. They, too, will want to know where I am at nightfall.

My mother, teaching in Detroit — she's probably been at her laboratory desk all day, wondering and worrying, and trying unsuccessfully, with chemistry experiments, to curtain off in her mind a pilot and his plane. How well I remember the expression on her face that winter evening, five and a half years ago, when I told her I wanted to leave college and learn to fly. I was so anxious to get into aviation that I scarcely realized what parting meant to her. "All right," she said. "If you really want to fly, that's what you should do." "You must go," she told me later. "You must lead your own life. I mustn't hold you back. Only I can't see the time when we'll be together much again." Her prophecy came true. Hundreds of letters and packages have gone back and forth between us, but I haven't been home for more than a few days at a stretch since then. But we went barnstorming together in southern Minnesota in the summer; and she's flown back and forth between Chicago and St. Louis with me on the mail route, riding on the sacks. I know what a message of my welfare would mean to her tonight.

But the principles I laid down for this flight involve no waste, no luxuries, no following of shore lines. All extras must be held in reserve for adverse winds, or large areas of storm, or fog over Europe. I've already drawn enough on my reserves by detouring Nova Scotian squalls and leaving windows out. Misdirected sentiment could result in death. A message back from Newfoundland tonight is less important than to land in France tomorrow. Suppose I encounter head winds over the ocean. Suppose I miss the tip of Ireland and strike some European shore line after dark. Suppose the sky is overcast, screening off the moonlight so I can't see enough on the ground to locate my position. Suppose I have to fly all through a second night. I'll need each drop of fuel I can save. No, every decision must be made with one object, and one object only in view — to reach Paris. It will be little satisfaction for my friends to know that I left Newfoundland on schedule if passing hours bring no word that I am over France.

But suppose I have a forced landing on the ocean. There'd be an advantage in people knowing that I went down somewhere east of St. John's. It would add to my over-all safety as much as the rations and the rubber boat. If I can't charge a gallon of fuel to sentiment, I *can* charge it to safety. Not that there'd be much chance of rescue from those isolated northern waters; but no one would waste time searching for me along the coast as they searched for Nungesser and Coli. And at least they'd know that my flight was not a failure at the start, as so many predicted it would be. If it's definitely established that I've passed St. John's, then perhaps if any ships do happen up that way, they'll keep a sharper watch for a red flare by night or a silver wing by day.

I reset the heading on my compass, and turn the *Spirit of St. Louis* slightly toward the south.

Except for high cirrus wisps, the sky is uniformly blue. Instrument needles all point to their proper marks. My plans are laid. Now, for almost two hundred miles, until Newfoundland's coast appears, I'll have nothing to do but follow the compass and add one set of readings to my log. I twist around in the cockpit to a new and momentarily more comfortable position. And – – – sleep comes filtering in. It comes like that early turbulence of storm squalls, barely perceptible at first, satisfying to the body, alarming only in the warning it carries to conscious portions of the mind. Minute by minute it gathers strength.

Over Nova Scotia and Cape Breton Island, I hadn't noticed being tired. There was too much to think about, too much to see — the storms, the wind, the lakes and clearings. Before that, sleep would have been pleasant, like dozing off for an extra hour on a Sunday morning; but not too difficult to overcome. Now, it's getting really serious.

Why does the desire to sleep come over water so much more than over land? Is it because there's nothing to look at, no point different from all others to rivet one's attention to — nothing but waves, ever changing and yet changeless: no two alike, yet monotonous in their uniformity? Hold the compass needle on its mark, glance at the instruments occasionally; there's nothing else to do.

If I could throw myself down on a bed, I'd be asleep in an instant. In fact, if I didn't know the result, I'd fall asleep just as I am, sitting up in the cockpit — I'm beyond the stage where I need a bed, or even to lie down. My eyes feel dry and hard as stones. The lids pull down with pounds of weight against their muscles. Keeping them open is like holding arms outstretched without support. After a minute or two of effort, I have to let them close. Then, I press them tightly together, forcing my mind to think about what I'm doing so I won't forget to open them again; trying not to move stick or rudder, so the plane will still be flying level and on course when I lift them heavily.

It works at first; but soon I notice that the minute hand of the clock moves several divisions forward while I think only seconds pass. My mind clicks on and off, as though attached to an electric switch with which some outside force is tampering. I try letting one eyelid close at a time while I prop the other open with my will. But the effort's too much. Sleep is winning. My whole body argues dully that nothing, nothing life can attain, is quite so desirable as sleep. My mind is losing resolution and control.

But the sun is sinking; its brillance is already fading — night lies ahead, not day. This is only afternoon, yet I'm experiencing symptoms I've never known in the past until dawn was closer than midnight. If sleep weighs so heavily on me now, how can I get through the night, to say nothing of the dawn, and another day, and its night, and possibly even the dawn after? Something must be done — immediately.

I pull the *Spirit of St. Louis* up two or three hundred feet above the water, shake my head and body roughly, flex muscles of my arms and legs, stamp my feet on the floor boards. The nose veers sharply left, and I have to put my toes back on the rudder to straighten it out. I breathe deeply, and squirm about as much as I can while still holding the controls.

My body is shaped by the seat's design. My hand is tied to the stick and my feet to the rudder by cords of instability. Even the angles of my joints are fixed. But shaking clarifies my mind a little — enough to make new resolutions. I will *force* my body to remain alert. I will *force* my mind to concentrate — never let it get dull again. I simply can't think of sleep. I have an ocean yet to cross, and Paris to find. Sleep is a trivial thing, insignificant compared to the importance of this flight. It has no business bothering me now. It will interfere with my judgment, my navigation, my accuracy of flying. It can come later, after I land at Paris and have the *Spirit of St. Louis* put away safely in some hangar on Le Bourget. All this I tell myself savagely – – – and futilely. The worst part about fighting sleep is that the harder you fight the more you strengthen your enemy, and the more you weaken your resistance to him. The very exertion of staying awake makes you sleepier.

The cramped feeling in my legs has left, as I knew it would. Only dull aches in my back and shoulders remain. I would almost welcome sharper pain. It might help to stay awake. I'm like a man lost in a blizzard, feeling the weight of sleep on his shoulders as though his coat were made of lead, wanting nothing so much as to fall down in the softness of a snowbank and give way to irresponsible sleep, yet realizing that beyond such relaxation lies the eternity of death. But there's a difference. The man in the blizzard has an advantage. He can use his mind to force his body forward, and the movements of his body to keep his mind awake. While I, confined to this tailor-fitted cockpit, must stay awake by will of mind alone. How simple, the problem of the man in the blizzard. If only I

could take a dozen of his steps forward, if I could even stand upright for a few seconds, I could gain control of myself again.

I was caught in a blizzard once, in Minnesota. I'd thought I
was sleepy that night. But it was nothing; I was wide awake. I
never knew what the desire to sleep meant before this flight. Why
I could stand up in the blizzard; I could stretch; I could walk; I
could run, and swing my arms.

It was in midwinter. Deep snow had made roads impassable
except to man and horse. I was seventeen years old then, and I'd
just taken on a dealership for milking machines and farm engines.
Early that morning, I'd saddled one of my ponies and started out
for the little town of Pierz. It was a clear day, and sunny — about
five degrees above zero, Fahrenheit, when I left home. The ride to
Pierz took over three hours. All afternoon I'd talked to farmers
about their herds — about the time saved by mechanical milking,
about the best methods of putting teat cups on skittish cows. I'd
ridden from one barn to another, until evening found me almost
thirty miles from home.

Snow was falling lightly when I said my last good-by and
started back. The night was so black that I could hardly see the
road we were following. I'd pulled my fur hat down, buttoned my
sheepskin collar around my face, and almost gone to sleep in the
saddle, leaving navigation to my pony. I don't know how many
miles had passed when I was jolted to alertness. It was really a
change in rhythm more than a jolting. The pony's steps had become
stiff and slow. And as I noticed it, he stopped walking. Heel pressed
to flank moved him only a few feet forward. Then he stumbled,
stopped again, stood quivering — legs spread apart as though he
were afraid of losing his balance and toppling into snow. I dis-
mounted, spoke to him, and led him on. He could walk alone, but
my weight on his back was too much. It wasn't stubbornness. He
was a faithful pony. But he was getting old, and the day had been
long.

I'd made the rest of the way home on foot, some fifteen miles, my pony following behind. The first hour was easy enough, even pleasant as a change. Then, the heavy winter clothing began to bear down on my shoulders, and my felt-lined boots grew heavier with every step I took. The snow thickened with a rising wind, lashed against my eyes, drifted over the road, held back my plodding feet like desert sand.

Sometime after midnight the blizzard stopped, and it turned cold — that bitter cold in which a quickly drawn breath strikes into lungs with pain. I'd fisted my hands inside their mittens to keep the fingers warm. Hoar frost formed on the fur of my cap, on the wool scarf wound below my eyes. My pony's hoofs crunched into the silence of the night. As hours passed I lost consciousness of muscles moving. My legs swung back and forth like clock pendulums, as though they were part of a machine on which my upper body rode.

Oh how I wanted to lie down in a snowbank and sleep! Each drift carried an invitation. That night I did lie down. I commanded my legs to stop walking. It took a definite mental effort. I hooked the bridle reins over my arm, fell into the snow, and for two or three minutes let every muscle forget its responsibility; while the pony stood above me, head down, also resting. I could lie, and rise, and make my body walk, and stop, and walk again. I wasn't bound to a cramped position in a cockpit.

But I'm not in Minnesota. I'm in the *Spirit of St. Louis,* over the ocean, headed for Europe and Paris. I *must* keep my mind from wandering. I'll take it in hand at once, and watch it each instant from now on. It must be kept on its proper heading as accurately as the compass. I'll review my plans for navigation. Then, I'll concentrate on some other subject.

The first quarter of my flight is behind. There's a sense of real accomplishment in that fact. How satisfying it is to have 800 miles behind – – – No! that's the wrong tack. Sleep has crept up a notch. Anything that's satisfying is relaxing. I can't afford to relax. I must think about *problems* — concentrate on difficulties ahead.

Actually, I haven't quite reached the quarter mark. In another three hours, I'll leave Newfoundland behind and start out over nearly 2000 miles of ocean. If the wind keeps on increasing and swinging tailward, I ought to average over 100 miles an hour through the night. A strong tail wind would put me over Europe well ahead of schedule – – – No, I'm getting off course again — concentrate on difficulties. Suppose the wind shifts north or south during the night, and blows me hundreds of miles off route. (This ought to be a line of thought to stay awake on!) The night has always formed a gap in my plans for navigation. How many hours I've spent thinking about it! If the sky stays clear, I may be able to check my drift by wind streaks in the moonlight — if I fly low enough. But suppose it's overcast. I've already had my share of good weather.

"If you had a sextant, you could climb over the clouds and take a sight on the stars. Maybe you made a mistake not to carry one."

"I couldn't take a sight and fly the plane at the same time. The slightest turn throws the bubble off."

"You never really tried, you know. You took other people's word for that."

"Well, I took the advice of experts. What more could I do?"

"Most of the experts said you couldn't make this flight at all. You didn't believe *them*."

"I couldn't possibly use a sextant. The *Spirit of St. Louis* won't hold a straight course for two seconds by itself. Besides, there's the weight — you can't carry everything on a record flight. If we'd tried to carry every safeguard, the plane couldn't have gotten off the ground — dump valves, parachute, radio, sextant; it would be nice to have a four-engined flying boat as far as that's concerned."

"Ridiculous! The idea of comparing a sextant to a flying boat! A sextant doesn't weigh five pounds. With a flying boat you couldn't get off the water at all with enough fuel to fly nonstop from New York to Paris. And you *didn't* give up everything that wasn't essential. You've got thirty pounds of emergency equipment right behind you — the rubber boat and the flares, and the – – – "

There's no use going over the argument again. It's just thinking around in a circle, just making my mind more tired and confused. That isn't planning navigation. I must concentrate on navigation. That's what I started out to do. I made my decision weeks ago in San Diego. Now, right or wrong, there'll be no sextant sights. I'll have to get to Europe by dead reckoning, or not get there at all. I'll correct my heading for the wind at nightfall. If it's blowing in a different direction at daybreak, I'll estimate that it blew half the night in one direction, and half in the other.

My watch will give a general indication of my position as I approach Europe. If I sight land on or ahead of schedule, it will probably be Ireland, for Ireland lies farther west than any other country. If my landfall comes a little late, that may be caused either by a head wind holding me back from Ireland, or by a cross wind drifting me north to Scotland. If I fly for two or three hours beyond my estimated time of crossing, and still there's only sea ahead, I'll probably be south of route and over that portion of the ocean which extends eastward to the coast of France. In that case, I'll take up a northeast heading and hope to strike England or the Channel.

If I make a landfall in daylight, or even in clear moonlight, I'll know what country I'm over. Ireland has green mountains rising from a fjorded coast. Large islands lie westward of Scotland. Cornwall has a cliff-lined shore, and is so narrow that an airman can see across it. The French coast is lower; and it too has characteristic lines. From the heathered mountains of Scotland to the Pyrenees of Spain, each country is distinctive from the air. If there's any doubt in my mind, I'll drop down over the first village I come to and see in what language the store-front signs are written.

Suppose Europe is covered with fog, or I make my landfall after dark? Well, I'll simply hold my course until – – – until – – – There's trouble in the cockpit – – – I've been half asleep again, dreaming about my navigation. The compass needle's a full ten degrees right of the lubber line! I bank the *Spirit of St. Louis* back on course, and hold the needle firmly on its mark, gripping the stick as though hundreds of pounds of strength were required on controls instead of ounces.

Cape Breton Island is nearly a hundred miles behind. I've been staring out of windows at the horizon, dragging my eyes back to check the compass, making them look blearily at instruments, performing routine duties of flight mechanically and dully, and only because I know they must be done. Suddenly, I become aware of a difference – – – one of my senses is banging on a distant door, shouting for attention – – – there's an essential message I must have. It's like the moment of confusion that precedes alertness, when you've been startled from a deep sleep – – – who? – – – what? – – – where? And then life clarifies. Consciousness becomes a skull-encompassed prisoner again.

The ocean ahead has assumed a different texture, brighter, whiter — an ice field! It turns dazzling white in sunlight as it slides in beneath my wing. I feel that I'm entering the Arctic. Even those patches of snow on the bleak hillsides of Cape Breton Island did not prepare me for this change. I knew, of course, that my route lay north of the ship lanes, and that ships keep south because of floating ice; but I wasn't ready to be transported so quickly to a frozen sea.

Great white cakes are jammed together, with ridges of crushed ice pushed up around the edges, all caught and held motionless in a network of black water which shows through in cracks and patches as I pass. A quarter mile in from the field's edge, the sea smooths out, the waves disappear, and there's not a sign of movement among the blocks of ice. As far as I can see ahead, the ocean is glaring white. Despite the noise and vibration of the engine, I feel surrounded by the stillness of a Minnesota winter — the frozen silence of the north. I feel a trespasser in forbidden latitudes, in air where such a little plane and I have no authority to be.

The brilliant light and the strangeness of the sea awaken me — make my mind the master of my body once again. Any change,

I realize, stimulates the senses. Changing altitude, changing thought, even the changing contours of the ice cakes help to stay awake. I must look for differences, and find ways of emphasizing them. I can fly high for a while and then fly low. I can fly first with my right hand and then with my left. I can shift my position a little in the seat, sitting stiff and straight, slouching down, twisting sidewise. I can create imaginary emergencies in my mind — a forced landing — the best wave or trough to hit — the stinging wetness of the ocean. I can check and recheck my navigation. A swallow of water now and then will help. And there's the hourly routine of fuel tanks, heading, and instrument readings. All these tricks I must use, and think of others. Similarity is my enemy; change, my friend.

THE TENTH HOUR
Over the Atlantic
TIME — 4:52 P.M.

WIND VELOCITY	25 *m.p.h.*	VISIBILITY	*Unlimited*
WIND DIRECTION	*WSW.*	ALTITUDE	150 *feet*
TRUE COURSE	73°	AIR SPEED	95 *m.p.h.*
VARIATION	29° *W.*	TACHOMETER	1600 *r.p.m.*
MAGNETIC COURSE	102°	OIL TEMPERATURE	38° *C.*
DEVIATION	0°	OIL PRESSURE	59 *lbs.*
COMPASS COURSE	102°	FUEL PRESSURE	3.5 *lbs.*
DRIFT ANGLE	0°	MIXTURE	2.5
COMPASS HEADING	102°	FUEL TANK	*Nose*
CEILING	*Unlimited*		

Nine hours of fuel burned. That means about 800 pounds less load. The plane feels lighter and more buoyant too, and the stick is vibrant with power, responding to the slightest pressure from my hand, bringing me closer to the ice, climbing farther from it, following as though with pleasure my slightest whim. I pull the throttle back to 1600, lean the mixture out another half point, and resume my study of the ice cakes. Here is a land where no man has ever been before, which no human eyes but mine will ever

see — solid, like earth — impermanent, like cloud — so close —
so far away — so strange — — —

I've always been fascinated by stories of the Arctic seas. Just
over a year ago I tried to join Wilkins' polar expedition. He
planned on basing his airplanes in Alaska, and exploring the great,
unknown area north of the northern, ice-packed coast.

I nose down, catching up to the shadow of my plane, which
has been gliding fleetly on ahead. The largest cakes are fifty or
sixty feet across. I could bounce my wheels on them with a half-
inch movement of the stick. At moments I forget I'm in a plane.
It's as though the wings and thinly covered framework no longer
suspend me in air or separate me from the ice I skim across. I feel
I could reach down and plunge my hand into freezing water, or
close my fingers on a chunk of ground-up ice. I'm conscious only
of the desolate solitude, as though I were standing alone and
isolated on one of those cakes.

What would I do now if my engine failed? How could a pilot
land on such a surface? Well, God and gravity would take care of
that. If an essential part of my engine broke, I'd be down in
thirty seconds. I'd have only time to bank left into wind, cut the
switch, pull my stick back, and pancake onto ice. The landing
gear would be wiped off the moment it hit a cake's edge. But
possibly the fuselage would skid along without smashing up too
badly and, with real good luck, end up on ice instead of water.

What then? There'd certainly be no rescue ships steaming
through an ice field. I might use fabric and framework from the
plane to erect a shelter, if the wind didn't blow too hard. Ribs,
engine oil, and spar splinters would make a good fire. But staying
with the wreckage would mean only a few more days of life. I'd
have to start traveling as soon as my clothes were dry.

I'd cut a strip of covering from the wing to wrap up in at
night. I'd cut a second strip to catch rain or snow for extra drink-
ing water. I'd lash my equipment on my back, and hold the raft
in front of me so I could fall on top of it if footing gave way. My
eyes pick out the best routes to follow as I imagine walking over
the ice field. There's a quarter-mile stretch where cakes are

jammed together without a crack of water in between. By travelling straight north I should strike the coast of Newfoundland within a hundred miles. For sustenance, I have with me five quarts of water, lacking a few swallows, five sandwiches, and five eight-ounce cans of Army rations. Possibly I could make ten miles a day on foot, using the rubber raft to cross patches of water.

But I'd have to ration food so carefully that each day would find me weaker. Suppose I reached the edge of the ice still many miles from land. There's little likelihood that a boat would pass and see my signal. No, I can't count on outside assistance. I've never planned on that. I'd launch my rubber raft, rig up a sail from the wing covering, and hope for a wind toward shore. At least then I could sit quietly, and I'd need less food.

But the wet and cold at night, without enough to eat – – – And suppose a storm came up and ground the cakes of ice together – – – Well, suppose the motor had cut out during take-off. It didn't. Every pilot knows the chance he takes at times; that's part of aviation. Ours is not a nation built on too much caution. I concluded that this flight over the Atlantic would be no more dangerous than flying mail for a single winter – – – Still, the idea that he would as likely have crashed in an Illinois forest wouldn't give much comfort to a man crawling across those ice cakes.

A winter on the mail, or a flight across the ocean — which involves the greater danger? From October through March — those are the worst months — each pilot makes about a hundred and twenty flights between St. Louis and Chicago. That totals close to thirty thousand miles, or about ten times the distance from New York to Paris. Well, I'd rather fly ten miles over Missouri and Illinois than one mile over this ice pack — or would I? How about that storm northeast of Peoria, last December?

There had been plenty of ceiling when I took my DH off from the mail field. The lights of the city formed a horizon as soon as I cleared the trees' dark masses. But a half hour's flight left me skimming two hundred feet over the ground, brushing the bottom of clouds with my wings, searching through thickening snow for

lights of the next village. I'd held on to the last dim glow behind
until I could see another on ahead. Then, I found myself circling
the center of a small city, my lower wing tips less than a hundred
feet above its street lamps. The blizzard had shut off all trace of
lights beyond. I can still see the path I followed in my bank. There's
the corner drug store, with a flat-fronted restaurant three doors
away. Two cars are parked against the curb, hazed by snowflakes.
There's the church, below me, with its black steeple merging into
night. There's the vaguely outlined street, lined with yarded houses.
There, the filling station. Again, the drug store and restaurant.
A dozen men and boys have run out onto the sidewalk to look
up, hands shielding their eyes against the snow.

I was like a moth circling its flame — blinded to more distant
objects, unable to break away. Suppose my engine had stopped
then, over those stores and houses – – – Yes, I'd as soon land on
the ice pack.

I'd found my way through to Chicago that night. The heavy
snow blew over enough for me to break away from my circle of
the city, and pick up farmhouse lights. I'd held my course partly
by instrument, partly by glowing windows, partly by lines of street
lamps, until I saw the Maywood beacon flash.

On our mail route, the pilots expect forced landings. We don't
average a hundred hours between them. There was the time my
throttle controls vibrated apart, a few miles north of Springfield —
engine running perfectly one moment, barely turning over the next.
I was no higher than I am now. Fortunately there was a clover
field ahead which I could reach with a shallow bank. I sideslipped
in over trees, and stalled down onto rain-soaked ground. The
wheels plowed ruts ten inches deep in places; but the tail was
heavy enough to keep my plane from nosing over.

On another flight, the metal tip of my propeller ripped off from
its wooden blade. I'd been daydreaming along at 1100 feet. Daydreaming – – – good Lord, that's what I'm doing now! I'm almost
10 degrees off course. I shake myself vigorously, skid the *Spirit of
St. Louis* back into position, and rub circulation through my
cheeks. There's a big gap below in the ice field. As I stare at it,

my mind wanders back to the mail route. All of a sudden, the DH's engine had started vibrating so violently that I thought it would jerk itself out of the plane before I could cut my switches. I avoided a crack-up that time by stalling into a twelve-acre field and ground looping just short of the fence corner.

Every month included incidents such as these. Yes, a winter on the air mail holds fully as much danger as a flight across the ocean. Whirlwind engines aren't like our old Liberties. They average thousands of hours between failures. The controls in the *Spirit of St. Louis* are new and carefully designed. There'll be no breakage of a throttle rod. And my propeller blades are made of metal, not of wood. They have no screwed-on tips to throw.

But I didn't start on this flight to Paris because of its relative safety. I used that argument only to bolster my decision, and to convince people that the hazard wasn't too great. I'm not bound to carry the night mail. I'm not bound to be in aviation at all. I'm here only because I love the sky and flying more than anything else on earth. Of course there's danger; but a certain amount of danger is essential to the quality of life. I don't believe in taking foolish chances; but nothing can be accomplished without taking any chance at all.

When I was a child on our Minnesota farm, I spent hours lying on my back in high timothy and redtop, hidden from passers-by, watching white cumulus clouds drift overhead, staring into the sky. It was a different world up there. You had to be flat on your back, screened in by grass stalks, to live in it. Those clouds, how far away were they? Nearer than the neighbor's house, untouch-able as the moon — unless you had an airplane. How wonderful it would be, I'd thought, if I had an airplane — wings with which I could fly up to the clouds and explore their caves and canyons — wings like that hawk circling above me. Then, I would ride on the wind and be part of the sky, and acorns and bits of twigs would stop pressing into my skin. The question of danger didn't enter my dreams.

One day I was playing upstairs in our house on the riverbank. The sound of a distant engine drifted in through an open window.

Automobiles had been going past on the road quite often that summer. I noticed it vaguely, and went on sorting the stones my mother and I had collected from the creek bed. None of them compared to the heart-shaped agate I'd found at the edge of a pool the week before — purple crystals outlined by stripes of red and white. Suddenly I sat up straight and listened. No automobile engine made that noise. It was approaching too fast. It was on the wrong side of the house! Stones scattered over the floor. I ran to the window and climbed out onto the tarry roof. It was an airplane!

Flying upriver below higher branches of trees, a biplane was less than two hundred yards away — a frail, complicated structure, with the pilot sitting out in front between struts and wires. I watched it fly quickly out of sight, and then rushed downstairs to tell my mother.

There had been a notice in the *Transcript,* my mother said, about an aviator who had come to our town. She'd forgotten to tell me about it. He was carrying passengers from a field over on the east side of the river. But rides were unbelievably expensive. He charged a dollar for every minute in the air! And anyone who went up took his life in his hands — suppose the engine stopped, or a wing fell off, or something else went wrong.

I was so greatly impressed by the cost and danger that I pushed aside my desire to go up in a plane. But I used to imagine myself with wings on which I could swoop down off our roof into the valley, soaring through air from one river bank to the other, over stones of the rapids, above log jams, above the tops of trees and fences. I thought often of men who really flew. From grown-up conversations, I heard and remembered the names of the Wright brothers, and Glen Curtiss, and Lincoln Beachey — they'd found a way to fly in spite of cost and danger.

As I grew older, I learned that danger was a part of life not always to be shunned. It often surrounded the things you liked most to do. It was dangerous to climb a tree, to swim down rapids in the river, to go hunting with a gun, to ride a horse, to drive my father's automobile. You could be killed as quickly on a farm as in an airplane. I had felt death brush past several times on our farm, and it was not as terrifying as I at first imagined.

I never felt safer, and never came closer to being killed than when a gangplow turned over behind my tractor. It was on one of those May days "when leaves on the oak trees are as big as squirrels' ears," and it was "time to plant corn." I was behind with plowing on the western forty, and working late into evening to catch up. It was an old field, with only a few stones left to hook a plowshare. The furrow lay straight behind, seven inches deep. I had just tripped the plow-lift and started to turn at the field's end when bright steel flashed by my head and thudded heavily on ground. The lift mechanism had jammed, upsetting the entire gangplow. If I hadn't turned my tractor at the moment I pulled the trip-lever, I would have been crushed on the seat. As it was, the share missed my head by less than six inches.

No, farm life isn't as safe as it's cracked up to be.

I center the earth-inductor compass needle, and drop down closer to the ice field.

When I was eleven years old, I learned to drive my father's Ford car, and at twelve I chauffeured him around the country. That car had seemed terribly dangerous at first. You could get your arm broken cranking the engine. You could skid off an embankment. You might collide with someone at any intersection. The Minneapolis paper carried stories about auto accidents each day. But as my driving experience advanced from a hundred miles to a thousand, and from one thousand to several, my confidence increased. There were foils against danger — judgment and skill. If you clasped your thumb and fingers on the same side of the crank handle, a backfiring engine wouldn't break your bones. If you adjusted speed to road conditions, skids and collisions could be avoided. Twenty miles an hour had seemed an excessive speed when I started driving. A decade later, sixty was safe enough on a clear stretch of pavement. I learned that danger is relative, and that inexperience can be a magnifying glass.

A drink of water would be good. I reach for my canteen. No, I'm not thirsty enough now. I've allowed only one quart for the flight, and I'll need it more tomorrow. The instruments? All readings are normal. I drain a few drops of gasoline from the Lunkenheimer sediment bulb — no sign of dirt or water. Fumes drift through the fuselage, and drift away.

When I was a sophomore at the University of Wisconsin, I decided to give up my course in mechanical engineering, and learn to fly. One of my closer friends, an upperclassman, tried to persuade me not to leave my studies. He said a pilot's life averaged only a few hours in the air, and cited wartime figures to prove his point. Why, he asked, did I want to enter so dangerous a profession? I argued that flying in peacetime was safer than flying in war, and that accidents could be reduced by care and judgment. He shrugged his shoulders and said it was far too dangerous anyway, but that my future was my own.

My friend was captain of the rifle team, and spoke in terms I understood. He was one of the initiated. He knew how to value danger. Hadn't we shot twenty-five-cent pieces out of each other's fingers at a range of fifty feet? His statement impressed me, but I'd grown tired of the endless indoor hours of university life. I longed for open earth and sky. The fascination of aircraft had mounted to form an irresistible force in my mind. Was a life of flying to be renounced because it shouldered danger? I chose a school in Nebraska, and enrolled for a course in the spring.

I'd never been near enough to a plane to touch it before entering the doors of the Nebraska Aircraft Corporation's factory. I can still smell the odor of dope that permeated each breath, like ether in a hospital's corridors. I can still see the brightly painted fuselages on the floor, still marvel at the compactness of the

Hispano-Suiza engine which turned the force of a hundred and fifty horses through its little shaft of steel.

Ray Page, the Corporation's president, took my check for tuition and welcomed me to his school. On April 9, 1922, at the age of twenty, I made my first flight. The plane had been hauled out from the factory the day before, wings stacked and padded carefully in a big truck, fuselage trailing behind, tail high and foremost. I stood on the air field all morning, watching riggers attach wings and "hook up" ailerons, flippers, and rudder; watching mechanics strain in fuel, drain the sediment bulb, tune up the engine; watching the engineer test cable tautness with his fingers and measure wing droop with his knowing eye.

Behind every movement, word, and detail, one felt the strength of life, the presence of death. There was pride in man's conquest of the air. There was the realization that he took life in hand to fly, that in each bolt and wire and wooden strut death lay imprisoned like the bottled genie — waiting for an angled grain or loosened nut to let it out. The rigger wound his copper wire with a surgeon's care. The mechanic sat listening to his engine and watching his gages as a doctor would search for a weakness in the human heart — sign of richness, blowing valve, or leaned-out mixture? An error meant a ship might crash; a man might die. I stood aside and watched the engine tested, watched the plane taxi out, take off, and spiral up through sky. I'd be on the next flight, if this test showed nothing wrong. I'd be a part of those wings, now no larger than a bird's, black against the clouds toward which they climbed.

How clearly I remember that first flight — I've lived through it again and again. Otto Timm was the pilot.

"CONTACT!"

The mechanic throws his leg and body backward as his arms jerk the propeller down.

"BOOSTER!"

There's a deep cough – – – vicious spitting. – – – The mechanic regains his balance – – – takes his place by the wing tip. Miraculously his fingers haven't been chopped off by that now invisible blade. The cylinders bark out their power – – – merge into a deep and constant roar. I am belted down in the front cockpit, goggles and leather helmet strapped tight on my head. Beside me is a younger boy, one of the workmen from the factory. He, too, has never flown before.

The roar grows louder. Wings begin to tremble. The engine's power shakes up my legs from the floor boards, beats down on my head from the slipstream, starts a flying wire vibrating. I twist about to look back at the pilot. His eyes study the instruments — no trace of a smile on his face. This is a serious business, flying.

The engine quiets. The pilot nods. A mechanic from each side ducks in and unchocks a wheel. We taxi downwind, bumping over sod clumps, to the end of the field. A burst of engine – – – the tail swings around into wind. There are seconds of calm while the pilot glances a last time at temperature of water, pressures of oil and air; checks again the direction of wind and clearness of field; makes a last slight adjustment to his goggles.

Now! – – – The roar becomes deafening – – – the plane lurches forward through a hollow in the ground – – – the tail rises – – – the axle clatters over bumps – – – trees rush toward us – – – the clatter stops – – – the ground recedes – – – we are resting on the air – – – Up, past riggers and mechanics – – – over treetops – – – across a ravine, like a hawk – – – The ground unfolds – – – we bank – – – it tilts against a wing – – – a hidden, topsy-turvy stage with height to draw its curtain.

Trees become bushes; barns, toys; cows turn into rabbits as we climb. I lose all conscious connection with the past. I live only in the moment in this strange, unmortal space, crowded with beauty, pierced with danger. The horizon retreats, and veils itself in haze. The great, squared fields of Nebraska become patchwork on a planet's disk. All the country around Lincoln lies like a relief map below — its lake, its raveled bend of river, its capitol, its offices and suburbs — a culture of men adhering to the medium of earth.

The world tilts again — another bank – – – we tighten in a spiral – – – My head is heavy – – – the seat presses hard against me – – – I become conscious of my body's weight, of the strength it takes to lift an arm – – – Fields curve around a wing tip – – – gravity is playing tag with space – – – Landing wires loosen — vibrate with the air. How can those routed wooden spars, how can that matchwork skeleton of ribs withstand such pressure? Those slender flying wires, hardly larger than an eagle's tendon — how can they bind fuselage to wings? On the farm, we used more metal to tie a wagon to a horse!

Why can't I keep the compass needle centered? I skid the Spirit of St. Louis *back onto course again.*

We made that flight at Lincoln five years ago last month. I was a novice then. But the novice has the poet's eye. He sees and feels where the expert's senses have been calloused by experience. I have found that contact tends to dull appreciation, and that in the detail of the familiar one loses awareness of the strange. First impressions have a clarity of line and color which experience may forget and not regain.

Now, to me, cows are no longer rabbits; house and barn, no longer toys. Altitude has become a calculated distance, instead of empty space through which to fall. I look down a mile on some farmer's dwelling much as I would view that same dwelling a horizontal mile away. I can read the contour of a hillside that to the beginner's eye looks flat. I can translate the secret textures and the shadings of the ground. Tricks of wind and storm and mountains are to me an open book. But I have never realized air or aircraft, never seen the earth below so clearly, as in those early days of flight.

I was the Nebraska Aircraft Corporation's only student that spring. Ira Biffle was my instructor — a dark-haired, face-creased man of the world and the sky. He'd soloed a lot of flyers for the Signal Corps during the war. But:

"Slim, you'd better watch your step," the factory workmen warned me. "The Army didn't have 'em any tougher."

Biff was impatient, quick, and picturesque of tongue, but not as hard-boiled as his reputation. We got along together well enough. But he'd lost the love of his art, and I found it hard to get time in the air. When rain was falling or wind blew hard, of course, flying was out of the question for a new student. On such days, I rode my motorcycle to the factory and spent hours watching the craftsmen show their skills. A would-be aviator had to learn how to care for his plane in the field. Tail skids and shock absorbers broke, ribs snapped, and wing covering ripped all too easily. Spark plugs needed cleaning out each week, and exhaust valves warped with regularity. You had to know how to lock-stitch, how to bind the ends of rubber rope, how to lap a propeller hub to its shaft. There were hundreds of details you had to learn; for as a barnstorming pilot, you were often your own helper, rigger, and mechanic.

But on mornings of calm, clear weather, I felt it was my right to receive the instruction I had paid for. And Biffle was often nowhere to be found. "The air's too turbulent at midday, Slim," he'd tell me when he arrived at the factory, later. "Meet me at the flying field when it smooths out this afternoon."

Around five o'clock, I'd park my motorcycle next the fence line, lie down under a wing, and watch the wind sock spin its tale of air — whipping, wilting, filling with the gusts. Sometimes Biff would come out with his roadster in time to make a half-dozen take-offs and landings before dusk. But often he didn't come at all. "Slim, it was just too rough," he might tell me the next morning, in his high-pitched voice, as he leaned against the Fokker's gold-varnished fuselage. "Let's try at sunrise tomorrow — that's the smoothest time of day."

Then the factory workmen who overheard would smile. *"Sunrise?"* they'd say later. "Ha, Biff *never* starts work before eleven. He's a damn good pilot," they'd usually continue, "but he's been different since Turk Gardner spun in. Biff took it hard. He knew Turk was good, too. They'd always been close friends."

Wherever aviation people gathered, talk of crashes arose. And yet the safety of flying had steadily increased. I could look forward to some nine hundred hours in the air as the average pilot's lifetime, I was told. I learned that most people thought of aviators as strange and daring men, hardly a human breed — men who had nerves of steel and supernatural senses; men who were wild with drink and women, and who placed no value on their lives. But of the aviators at Lincoln there was none who didn't want to live. The pilot I admired most had already spent more than two thousand hours in the air. He may not have held onto life as tightly, but he valued it as highly as anyone I knew. He didn't drink, and he didn't smoke. He flew for the love of flying. And above that, he flew to make enough money to marry his fiancée.

In factory and on flying field, I often worked with the boy who shared the cockpit with me on my first flight. He was four years younger than I, but our interest in aviation bridged the gap of time. Bud Gurney came from the sandhills of Nebraska, and he'd been hired by the Corporation a few months before I arrived at the school. He swept floors, lock-stitched wings, and acted as general handy man — anything to get a job, especially around aircraft.

Bud kept me posted on factory current events. He knew the character of each employee, sieved off their gossip from their facts. "You can trust Saully anywhere," he said. "He's *really* a good mechanic. But I don't know why Page keeps on paying N – – – . He's just a great big bluff. Watch out for him, Slim. He'll send you off to find a left-handed monkey wrench, or to get a quart of stagger."

The Spirit of St. Louis *has a tendency to gain altitude when I'm not watching carefully. I push the stabilizer adjustment forward a single notch, to change pressure on the stick.*

It was Bud Gurney, some days later, who warned me that the Corporation's training plane was being sold:

"Ray Page is making a deal with Bahl, Slim. I think he's the best flyer around Lincoln. But you'd better solo pretty soon or you won't have any plane to pilot."

"They can put dual controls in that silver job," I replied. "It's all ready to assemble."

"You're a week behind time. Page sold the silver job too."

I'd received about eight hours of flying instruction when Biff made it clear that his obligations as a teacher were fulfilled. Business, he said, was calling him away from Lincoln. "You can get up and down all right, as long as the air's not too rough. But you'll have to get Page to okay it, Slim, before I can turn you loose."

I lost no time getting to the factory and into the president's office. But Ray Page showed neither the confidence of his instructor nor the enthusiasm of his flying school's catalogue. "There isn't any question about your ability to fly," he said, after congratulating me. "But you understand we can't just turn an expensive airplane over to a student. Couldn't you put up a bond to cover our loss if you crack up?"

I didn't have enough money for a bond; and I knew that even if I soloed, there wouldn't be a pilot's job waiting for me. Owners of aircraft wanted experienced pilots, men with hundreds of hours of flying to their credit. They were like Ray Page. They weren't going to trust their lives or their machines to a newly graduated student. No, there were other steps that would have to be made between graduation and a pilot's job. Maybe I could get Bahl to take me with him, barnstorming.

Erold Bahl was a different type of pilot. Serious, mild-mannered, slender, there was no showmanship about him. He flew with his cap turned backward and in ordinary business clothes. He never wore an aviator's helmet and breeches like the rest of us. I waited until I found a chance to talk to him alone in one corner of the factory.

"You don't need somebody to help when you're out barnstorming, do you?" I asked. "I'd be glad to pay my own expenses – – – "

"I don't need any help where I'm going – – – " He started out to say no, in his soft but definite way. Then, hesitating a moment as he looked at me, he continued, "But if you want to go along badly enough to pay your own expenses, I'll take you."

We left on our first barnstorming trip in May. I kept the plane wiped clean, pulled through the propeller, and canvassed the crowds for passengers.

"You know, Slim," Bahl told me, after the first few days, "you're working hard, and you're making me extra money. From now on, I'm going to pay your expenses."

I felt secure flying with Bahl. He'd take off in weather that would keep most pilots on the ground; but he handled his plane perfectly, and he never did any silly stunts. "I think aviation can be safe," he told me. "And I intend to make it that way." Bahl believed that safety lay in judgment. He followed no frozen set of rules. I once suggested that we might draw a bigger crowd if I stood out on one of the wings while we flew over town. "You can climb out of the cockpit if you want to," he said, "but watch how you step on the spars, and don't go farther than the inner-bay strut the first time." Those simple instructions gave me my start as a wing walker.

After the trip with Bahl, my finances were getting low. I began working on odd jobs at the factory, at a wage of fifteen dollars every Saturday. And I left my twenty-dollar-a-month boarding house for a room I rented at two dollars and a quarter a week. I had several hundred dollars in the bank at home, accumulated slowly over many years; but I was determined to hold as much of it as I could in reserve for the day when I'd want to buy a plane of my own.

That June — it will be five years ago next month — a parachute maker came to Lincoln to demonstrate his product. His name was Charlie Harden. I watched him strap on his harness and helmet, climb into the cockpit and, minutes later, a black dot, fall off the wing two thousand feet above our field. At almost the same instant, a white streak behind him flowered out into the delicate, wavering muslin of a parachute — a few gossamer yards grasping onto air and suspending below them, with invisible threads, a human life, a man who by stitches, cloth, and cord, had made himself a god of the sky for those immortal moments.

I stood fascinated while he drifted down, swinging with the wind, a part of it, the 'chute's skirt weaving with its eddies, lightly, gracefully, until he struck the ground and all that fragile beauty wilted around him into a pile of earth-stained, wrinkled cloth.

A day or two later, when I decided that I too must pass through the experience of a parachute jump, life rose to a higher level, to a sort of exhilarated calmness. The thought of crawling out onto the wing, through a hurricane of wind, clinging on to struts and wires hundreds of feet above the earth, and then giving up even that tenuous hold of safety and of substance, left in me a feeling of anticipation mixed with dread, of confidence restrained by caution, of courage salted through with fear. How tightly should one hold on to life? How loosely give it rein? What gain was there for such a risk? I would have no pay in money for hurling my body into space. There would be no crowd to watch and applaud my landing. Nor was there any scientific objective to be gained. No, there was a deeper reason for wanting to jump, a desire I could not explain. It was the quality that led me into aviation in the first place, when safer and more profitable occupations were at hand, and against the advice of most of my friends. It was a love of the air and sky and flying, the lure of adventure, the appreciation of beauty. It lay beyond the descriptive words of men — where immortality is touched through danger, where life meets death on equal plane; where man is more than man, and existence both supreme and valueless at the same instant.

My search for the parachute maker ended in a corner of the factory where wing coverings were made. He and his young wife were busily engaged with sewing machine and shears, cutting and stitching the long, triangular strips of a new parachute. Folds and piles of white muslin lay all about them.

"You want to jump?" They both eyed me keenly.

"I'd like to make a double jump," I said.

"A double jump! You want to do a double jump the *first* time?" The tone was disapproving — I had to think fast. Why *did* I want to make a double jump the first time?

"I want to see what it's like – – – I want to learn how to do it – – – I — I might want to buy a parachute." (Yes, I might even become a parachute jumper myself. Maybe that was the best way to get out on barnstorming trips and really learn to fly.) "I've read about the multiple jumps you make. It isn't more dangerous with two 'chutes than with one, is it?"

Charlie Harden's handbills said that he had used as many as ten parachutes in one descent, and claimed the utmost reliability for the products he made and sold. My questioning of his parachutes' safety, and the prospect of a sale, had the effect I was after.

"It's not the danger. I just never knew anybody want to start with a double jump. All right; if Page will give you a plane, I'll let you use my 'chutes."

"How much does a parachute cost?" I asked.

"A hundred and twenty-five dollars for the twenty-eight-foot type. But if you really want to buy one, you can have it for a hundred dollars cash — harness, bag, and all."

Is that a small boat on ahead? No, of course not — just a shadow on a chunk of ice.

I watched with amazement the transition of my daydream into the reality of me, my mind, my body, in the front cockpit of an airplane climbing up through empty space into which I was to throw myself against the instincts of a thousand generations. The stiff, double-canvas straps of the harness dug into my legs and pressed down on my hipbones. The big parachute bag lay awkwardly out on the right wing, its top lashed to the inner-bay strut's steel fitting. To the uninitiated eye, it might have contained a bushel of potatoes. It was a long way out along that panel, but you had to be sure the parachute would clear the plane's tail surfaces as you jumped. How secure the cockpit of the airplane seemed! How strong wings, struts, and wires had become, now that I was giving up their citadel of safety for cords and cloth!

The sun was low in the west, the sky clear, the air smooth. The day's puffy wind had dropped. The plane's nose mounted high on the horizon, climbing. I looked down at the group of minute figures on the field — the president of the Corporation, the parachute maker and his wife, Bud Gurney, and a half dozen passers-by who had stopped to watch us prepare the 'chutes. How carefully that preparation had been made — just to think about it gave me confidence. We'd stretched the parachutes out full length on grass, their shroud lines running straight from skirt to ring. The canopies were packed in free, accordion folds. Each reversing turn of cord was separated by a paper sheet. Each lip of cloth was laid to grab the wind. Tangle? — there was no chance for those lines to tangle; once loosed, the 'chute must unfold, string out, billow on the air.

Those parachutes had been used before, time and time again, and they'd always brought their human freight to earth in safety. I should have confidence in them. I *must* have confidence in them, for I'm to jump when we reach two thousand feet. But it's hard to see safety inside that dirt-smeared canvas sack bulging on the wing. My heart races. My throat is dry. Minutes are long.

The nose drops, the wing lowers, the plane banks toward the field. The nose dips, rises, dips again. That's my signal. I look back. The pilot nods. Thank God, the waiting time is over! Un-buckle the belt – – – get a firm hold on center-section struts – – – rise in cockpit – – – leg over side – – – lean into the slipstream's blast – – – Air wedges between my lips, rushes down my sleeves, presses against the forward motion of my arm – – – A too-long strap on my helmet whips my throat – – –

The pilot throttles back a little more; that's better – – – Careful of the wing – – – I must keep my feet on the narrow walk next the fuselage – – – Now, out along the spar – – – Give up the safety of center-section struts – – – Nothing but wires to hold onto – – –

their slenderness gives no substance to the hand's grip, no confidence to flesh leaning over space – – – Heels off nose ribs – – – follow the spar with soles – – – fabric dents with a touch. The blast of air drops down – – – that's the slipstream's edge – – – I reach the inner-bay strut – – – Remember to hang on at top or bottom — never at the center, lest it snap.

The pilot opens his throttle. We've been losing altitude too fast – – – Pressure of air builds up again – – – I sink down on the wing — buttocks on spar — legs dangling on top of patchwork fields – – – I unsnap a parachute hook from the landing wire – – – snap it onto my harness – – – now the other – – – The parachute bag shifts forward on the wing – – – I look back – – – the pilot nods – – – I let myself down on drift and flying wires – – – they bite into my fingers – – – Nothing but space — terrible — beautiful – – – swinging free beneath the wing.

Now I *must* jump. It's impossible to get back on the plane. The flying field — I'd forgotten about it crawling out — is more than a mile ahead. It's too soon to jump. I'll have to wait till the pilot cuts his engine — that's to be the signal. I dangle under the varnished, yellow wing panel. Two ropes from my harness run up above my head and disappear into the parachute bag. A bowknot holds the bag's canvas lips together. It's like the knot I tied this morning on each boot. It's all that holds me to the plane. Eyes dry in wind. Clothes flutter against skin. I slant tailward over space, leaning on the turbulence of air.

The roar of the engine dies – – – the nose drops slightly – – – *Now!* – – – no hesitation – – – I force my hand to reach up and pull the bow's end – – – Tightness of harness disappears – – – the wing recedes – – – white cloth streaks out above me – – – I'm attached to nothing – – – I turn in space – – – I lose the sense of time – – – My body is tense in a sky which seems to have no place for tenseness – – –

Harness tightens on legs — on waist. My head goes down – – – muscles strain against it – – – tilt it back – – – The canopy is pear-shaped above me – – – It opens round and wide – – – There's the plane, circling – – – There's the field, below – – – I swing lazily, safely on the air. The sun is almost setting. Clouds have reddened in the west.

But there's a second jump to make. I must leave plenty of altitude. The ground has already risen — fields are larger. I reach over my head for the knife-rope; a pull, and it will cut the line lashing the second 'chute to the first. I glance at the earth – – – back at the 'chute – – – and — *yank* – – – The white canopy ascends – – – I'm again detached from old relationships with space and time – – – I wait – – – I turn – – – but my body is less tense – – – I have experience – – – I know what to expect – – – The harness will tighten – – – and – – – But why *doesn't* it tighten? – – – It didn't take so long before – – – Air rushes past – – – my body tenses – – – turns – – – falls – – – good God – – –

The harness jerks me upright – – – My parachute blooms white – – – Earth and sky come back to place – – – I'm controlled by gravity once more; I'd never realized the security of its oriented pressure. "Mother Earth" had been only a figure of speech to me before, a tongue's lightly tossed expression. Now, in a sense, she holds me as the arms of a mother hold a frightened child. I have disobeyed her laws, strayed too far, and yet I find a welcome on return.

Now, danger is behind. There are no more parachutes to open. And the ground is still several hundred feet below. I swing gently, the white canopy above me rippling, indenting, refilling with the air. I have a small camera in my pocket; I pull it out and photograph my 'chute's silhouette against the sky. There's still a little time to practice gliding. You must learn how to glide a parachute so you can miss trees and buildings. I reach up and take two groups of shroud lines in my hands – – – Pull – – – The skirt drops – – – the big canopy deforms and slips ahead – – – I swoop down – – – let go the shroud lines – – – cords burn across my palm – – – I swing up the other side – – – The ground is rising – – – must stop the swing – – – Pull down on top lines – – – glide the 'chute back overhead – – – too much – – – the other lines – – – too much again – – – no more time – – – I'm going to miss the flying field – – – I'll land on the golf course – – – so fast, these last few yards – – –

Sod rushes up – – – I brace to meet it – – – It clumps against my feet – – – I crumple sidewise – – – thigh and shoulder hit – – – earth presses hard against me – – – I feel its security — its strength.

Harden, Gurney, and two strangers come running up. Page is a little way behind.

"Slim! That was *some* jump!"

"Did you get much of a jerk?" Harden asks, out of breath.

"Not too bad," I reply, trying to appear calm.

"I sure didn't like the way that second 'chute came out," he continues. "I was afraid the break-cord was too light — but it's all we had. Well, it turned out all right. That's the longest fall I've ever seen one of my 'chutes take."

I learned later that Harden's usual procedure was to tie the vent of the second 'chute to the shroud ring of the first with a piece of twine. The idea was that the 'chute would string out its full length before the twine snapped; then it would leave the plane in the best possible position for a quick opening. But he'd forgotten to put twine in his pocket, and a hunt around the field produced only a piece of old white string. He used that, doubled two or three times, but it apparently broke during the packing. When I pulled the knife-rope, the second parachute came free in a wad, and several hundred feet of air were required to straighten it out.

"Slim, that was just grocery string," Bud told me as we rode back to Lincoln. "It was so rotten you could pull it apart with your finger. I cut off a piece to try."

How soundly I slept that night — as I always have after a jump! I simply passed out of mortal existence a few seconds after my head hit its pillow; and when I became conscious again, the sun had risen. There wasn't a dream in memory.

I push up, with legs and elbow, enough to shift my rubber seat-cushion an inch forward. Even this slight movement turns the Spirit of St. Louis *eight degrees off course.*

I believe parachute jumping had an effect on my dreams as well as on my sleep. At infrequent intervals through life I had dreamt of falling off some high roof or precipice. I'd felt terror and sickening fear as my body sank helplessly toward ground. It wasn't like that in a real parachute jump, I discovered. Real falling didn't bring horror to your mind or sickness to your belly. Such sensations stayed behind with the plane, as though they were too cowardly to make the final plunge. Strangely enough, I've never fallen in my dreams since I actually fell through air. That factual experience seems to have removed completely some illogical, subconscious dread.

Life changed after that jump. I noticed it in the attitude of those who came to help gather up my 'chute — in Harden's acceptance of me as a brother parachutist, in Page's realization that I'd done what he didn't dare to do. I'd stepped suddenly to the highest level of daring — a level above even that which airplane pilots could attain.

"Hi, Slim! Did you do it?"

"What was it like?"

The next morning I was giving information to the same experts who had previously been teaching me — I'd left my role of apprentice far behind. Saully might scrape his con-rod bearings to a thousandth of an inch, but I could tell him how it felt to pull the bowknot, to glide the canopy, to simmer down through air on a muslin bolt.

Science, freedom, beauty, adventure: what more could you ask of life? Aviation combined all the elements I loved. There was science in each curve of an airfoil, in each angle between strut and wire, in the gap of a spark plug or the color of the exhaust flame. There was freedom in the unlimited horizon, on the open fields where one landed. A pilot was surrounded by beauty of earth and sky. He brushed treetops with the birds, leapt valleys and rivers, explored the cloud canyons he had gazed at as a child. Adventure lay in each puff of wind.

I began to feel that I lived on a higher plane than the skeptics of the ground; one that was richer because of its very association with the element of danger they dreaded, because it was freer of the earth to which they were bound. In flying, I tasted a wine of the gods of which they could know nothing. Who valued life more highly, the aviators who spent it on the art they loved, or these misers who doled it out like pennies through their antlike days? I decided that if I could fly for ten years before I was killed in a crash, it would be a worthwhile trade for an ordinary lifetime.

I needed much more experience before I could fly a plane of my own with reasonable safety; but now I had found a way to get it. There were pilots barnstorming through the country who needed mechanics for their engines and parachute jumpers for their exhibitions at the county fairs. Surely some of them would be glad to carry a man who'd be as willing to climb out on a wing or make a parachute jump as to change a fouled spark plug. All these services I decided to render in payment for hours in the air.

By that time, the Corporation had assembled "the silver job." As Bud had warned me, it was already sold — to a wheat rancher from Bird City, in northwestern Kansas; "Banty" Rogers was his name. He hadn't learned to fly yet himself, but he'd teamed up with a pilot he introduced as "Cupid" Lynch — a jolly, chunky man who handled Lincoln-Standards with extraordinary skill. Page paid Lynch for giving me a few more instruction flights before the plane was taken away.

"I'd turn you loose for solo," Lynch said, "but Ray Page won't take a chance on your cracking up the plane. Say, how'd you like to go barnstorming with me this summer?"

"I can start any day," I replied, eagerly. Lynch was just the type of pilot I wanted to fly with.

Lynch grinned. "Well, I'll see what it's like when I get out to Bird City. My guess is that Banty'll be tied up with the harvest in a few more weeks. You know it's a tough job to pull a Hisso's bank alone, and you need somebody to help you taxi in those Kansas winds. You and I could put on a real show with a little wing walking and a parachute jump. Don't count on it, but I think I'll be sending you a telegram before long."

The school owed me about two more hours of instruction. In a three-cornered deal between Page, Harden, and myself, I traded these, the wages due me, my claim to the right to solo, and twenty-five dollars in cash, for a new muslin parachute.

I'm tired of holding my plane up off the ice. I shift the stabilizer adjustment back again.

I was the only parachute jumper on the field at Lincoln after Charlie Harden left. Just as people used to say, *"There's* a pilot," when Timm or Biff walked by, they'd speak of me as "the parachute jumper" in still lower tones. And following the example of the pilots, I pretended not to notice the prestige we all enjoyed.

If flying was considered dangerous, wing walking and parachute jumping were regarded as suicidal. On my safety standards of three months before, I would have refused to do either one. But then I was an outsider. The hazards of aviation loomed high in the night of ignorance and shrank with the dawn of knowledge. If you were careless, you would certainly be killed. But if you kept alert, studied the rules, and flew within your skill — well, Orville Wright, and Glenn Curtiss, and Eddie Stinson, and Ruth Law, and a dozen others showed what could be done. Right on the field at Lincoln there were Timm, Biffle, Bahl, and Slonniger, all old pilots, and all very much alive. Of course Turk Gardner had been killed, but he'd tried to land out of a tailspin — that was asking for a crash.

The same principle applied to parachute jumping. Parachutes never failed to open if they were properly made and packed. You could usually glide a parachute out of the way of trees; and even if you did land in branches you weren't likely to get hurt badly if you kept your legs together. Just as with airplanes, most accidents were caused by errors which could be avoided.

That jumper who had been killed in Kansas, for example, should never have used a parachute made of pongee silk. The old-timers said there was something about a pongee silk 'chute that kept it from opening quickly — static electricity, most of them thought. And the boy in Wyoming — he hadn't even worn a harness. He'd just hooked his arm through the shroud ring. Of course the jerk of opening tore him loose. His parachute was too small anyway — only eighteen feet at the skirt — a home-made affair of heavy rope and canvas. The pilot should never have taken him up. There was the jumper who had been killed in Nebraska, too. But his pilot circled and dove down so close to the parachute that the plane's slipstream blew the canopy inside out and got it all tangled up with shroud lines. Every one of those accidents could have been avoided. Look at a man like Charlie Harden — he knew his business; he'd made dozens of jumps and was still alive.

As for wing walking, it was almost as easy to hang on to the struts and wires of an airplane as to climb up through branches of a high tree with the wind blowing hard. Of course you had to get used to the slipstream's whipping blast; but it didn't reach out as far as the inner-bay struts. After you got there, it wasn't bad at all. You could hold on with one hand and look around quite comfortably.

There were lots of tricks in exhibition work — closely guarded secrets of professional circus flyers. Ownership of a parachute made me an apprentice in the craft, and gave me the right to be taught its skills. I'd made friends with a young mechanic called Pete, and carried him between factory and flying field many times on my motorcycle. In return, he handed me gems from his chest of aviation knowledge. It was from him I learned that a wing walker didn't really hang by his teeth from a leather strap attached to the landing gear's spreader-bar. He simply held the strap in his mouth while his weight was safely supported by a steel cable hooked to a strong harness underneath his coat. The cable was too thin for eyes on the ground to see, and the effect on the crowd was as good as though none were there. Certainly that didn't involve much danger, yet men who hung "by their teeth" from airplanes were called daredevils.

Of course in wing walking, as in parachute jumping, men had been killed; but here, too, it was usually due to avoidable mistakes. There was the performer who slid down under a Standard's lower panel to hang from its wing skid as his pilot flew over the heads of the crowd. Apparently the skid had been damaged in a recent landing. Anyway, his weight broke it off. Spectators told how he seemed to hurl it away in anger before his body hit the ground. The moral was that before you climbed down on a wing skid, you should tape a steel cable to it, with each end fastened firmly to a spar.

The day I stood on the top wing of an airplane while it looped, I was tied on as safely as though I'd been strapped in my cockpit. Dangerous as that stunt seemed to the man on the ground, there was really little danger involved. I had rigged up my own harness with several times the safety factors needed. I made metal heel cups. like those on roller skates, with straps to hold my feet in place. I wore a heavy leather belt around my waist, and attached it to four strong cables which ran to the wing-hinge pins. I might fall down (I did as we came out of the loop), but I could never fall off.

The tachometer needle is riding a shade too high. I bring it back to 1600.

As parachute jumper and wing walker, I again entered a new frame of values as far as danger was concerned. This occupation, that had seemed the sport of daredevils, could be carried on in reasonable safety if one used proper equipment and technique — and flew with an able pilot. The greatest danger lay in the choice of one's pilot; not in the leap off a plane into space, or in the wing walker's apelike stunt which appeared so death-defying to the fairground's crowd. Danger usually lay coiled in the hidden, in the subtle, not the obvious. I could choose and care for my own equipment. I could judge and control my own actions. But a single error on the pilot's part might easily end my life.

I studied every pilot who passed through Lincoln. Was he a "mechanical" flyer, or did he have the "feel" of his plane? How many hours had he logged? How many times had he crashed? What standards of maintenance did he hold? Was he afraid of wind and weather? Did he fly when he was drunk? Visitors who landed on our field never realized the care with which each detail of their lives was watched. And how we admired their qualities and criticized their defects: "He skids on his turns." "His tail's too high taking off." "He over-controls — did you see those ailerons flap when he was coming in to land?" "Boy, *he* always makes 'em three-point!" This man I would be willing to fly with; that man, I would not.

At last, I found my pilot and my airplane. In mid-July, 1922, the prophesied telegram arrived from Lynch, asking me to join him for the season, and to bring my parachute. I didn't expect to make much money, but I knew that all my expenses would be paid. And Lynch had skill and judgment, and a newly reconditioned plane. I settled my boarding-house bill, stored my motorcycle in the factory basement, packed up parachute and suitcase, and climbed on a hot, old, and grimy day coach that clanked slowly along the rails westward through Nebraska and Kansas. Bird City was almost at the end of the line — a few score houses, a few hundred people, completely surrounded by a sea of wheat.

Banty Rogers made a good living from wheat. He'd mechanized his ranch with tractor, gang plow, and combine. His profits had mounted until the summer of 1922 found him with enough surplus to buy an airplane. He and Lynch met my train at the station.

"You and I are going to barnstorm the towns nearby, Slim," Lynch said as we drove to the plane. "Have you tried out your new parachute yet?"

"No, I haven't had a chance."

"Say, how about startin' out with a jump at Bird City?" Rogers asked. "I'd like the people here to see you." He was grinning and enthusiastic.

"All right. Tonight?" I was anxious to get up into air again.

"No, let's make it tomorrow. I want to pass the word around."

"We've got a blowing valve to grind, Slim, before we do much flying," Lynch broke in. "I thought you and I might pull the block off in the morning."

I met another aviation enthusiast on Rogers' Ranch — his black-and-white smooth-haired fox terrier, Booster.

"That dog just naturally takes to flying," Lynch said as Booster leapt into the car, his clipped tail vibrating like a fly's wing.

"He's liked to ride in my car ever since he was a pup," Rogers added. "But he'll leave the car any day to ride on my tractor. He chases rabbits that jump out of the wheat — they're his greatest interest in life. What I can't understand is why he'll leave the tractor for the airplane. But he will — every time."

Booster became the mascot for our Standard. At first, he rode with me in the front cockpit on cross-country flights. Then, we fastened a rubber mat to the turtleback and bought him a harness so we could snap him loosely into place. As soon as we started the engine, he'd jump onto the stabilizer, run up to his mat, and hook his forepaws around the cockpit cowling. The pilot's head formed his windshield. The danger of flight didn't exist for him. He had no sense of altitude or fear. Once, when we were coming in to land, he tried to jump off fifty feet above the ground to chase some big jack rabbits. There was an unmistakable expression on Booster's face when he saw rabbits, and a tenseness to his body. At altitudes of a thousand feet or so, cows brought the same reaction. As far as animals were concerned, he never seemed able to relate altitude to size.

During the rest of that summer and the early weeks of fall, I was wing walker, parachute jumper, and mechanic. We flew over the golden fields of Kansas, across the badlands of Nebraska, along the Big Horns of Wyoming, to the rimrocks of Montana.

"DAREDEVIL LINDBERGH" — that's how I was billed, in huge black letters on the colored posters we threw out above towns and villages. People came for miles to watch me climb back and forth over wings, and finally leap off into space. Ranchers, cowboys, storekeepers in town, followed with their eyes as I walked by. Had I been the ghost of "Liver-Eating Johnson" I could hardly have been accorded more prestige. Shooting and gunplay those people understood; but a man who'd willingly jump off an airplane's wing had a disdain for death that was beyond them. I lived in a world of clouds and sky, and the great geographical expanses of the West. I had a powerful engine to work with, and an airplane to carry me aloft. I was learning more about aviation each day. Danger? Of course there was danger, yet during that entire year I didn't come as close to losing my life as I had back on our farm at home.

Five years have passed now since I learned to fly. I've spent almost two thousand hours in the air — twice that average flyer's lifetime back in 1922. But there've been close calls — many of them. Vivid images flash through my mind — treetops rushing toward my underpowered plane during a take-off in Minnesota; tangled shroud lines above Kelly; a rudder bar kicked off its post in a bank near the ground at St. Louis; the blur and bump of air from a fighter missed by inches in a Texas sky.

I feel the swoop on shroud lines, hear the pistol-like crack of my parachute skirt in blackest night. With a flash of lightning, I see the wet white canopy above me, bulging here, indented there by translucent, swirling cloud and air. I twist back and forth, down through the black, flashing belly of the storm. How can silk threads stand such whipping? What happens to a parachute that's churned and soaked with rain? If the canopy collapses, will it billow out again? And how much will weight of water increase my rate of fall? Does field or forest lie below? How strong is the wind on the ground? I've jumped from my mail plane, out of fuel, thirteen thousand feet above the earth.

Wing walking, parachute jumping, pursuit planes, the night mail, and now this flight across the ocean — I've never chosen the safer branches of aviation. I've followed adventure, not safety. I've flown for the love of flying, done the things I wanted most to do. I've simply studied carefully whatever I've undertaken, and tried to hold a reserve that would carry me through.

Why does one want to walk wings? Why force one's body from a plane just to make a parachute jump? Why should man want to fly at all? People often ask those questions. But what civilization was not founded on adventure, and how long could one exist without it? What justifies the risk of life? Some answer, the attainment of knowledge. Some say wealth, or power, is sufficient cause. I believe the risks I take are justified by the sheer love of the life I lead. Yes, just being in the air on a flight across the ocean, to Paris, warrants the hazard of an ice field below.

I look down. The ice field? — it angles off into the distance under my right wing. The sea ahead is covered with waves again, larger and colder, fit companions to the biting air and arctic sky. My shadow is becoming vague and far away. The wind, strong and almost west, blows me along swiftly. The horizon is still clear; no trace of fog. Only a dozen isolated clouds float high in the north. A few miles ahead lie the small French islands of Miquelon and Saint Pierre. Beyond, purple in the distance, the rugged mountains of Newfoundland are rising from the sea.

For thirty miles along Burin peninsula, my course parallels a coast of bare granite mountains, dented with bays and jutted with capes. A fishing schooner close to shore looks like a child's toy — a single pebble rolling down would swamp it. The sun is nearing the horizon. Why does it rush through those last degrees so fast, like a work horse trotting home to its oats after plodding slowly through the day? Already lengthening shadows cut sharp lines from cliff to cliff, and higher summits almost reach the sun.

I've never been as conscious of the minuteness of my plane or of the magnitude of the world. On my right, the ocean extends limitlessly, curving over the earth past a hundred horizons, and by some miracle, which seems beyond science's facile explanation, not spilling off the edges into space. On my left, sheer reddish walls of rock make the *Spirit of St. Louis* a speck against their background.

Nungesser and Coli may have crashed somewhere among those mountains. If they reached North America, it's barely possible they're still alive in a wilderness such as this. That crag rising high above the others — might they have struck it in a fog? Any one of those cliff-lined valleys could hold a shattered plane. Expeditions sent out to look for them haven't found a trace. But from the start it was almost a hopeless hunt. A plane is hard enough to find in the wilderness when you have some indication of where it crashed. Even then you may fly over the wreckage a dozen times without seeing it. For Nungesser and Coli, there was the northeastern corner of a continent to search, on the off chance that they hadn't gone down at sea. They might have flown, over clouds, far into Canada before running out of fuel. With no accurate clue to follow, searching was only a gesture, the payment of a debt felt by living men to their lost brothers who, by some miracle, might not be dead. When a plane is missing, you may convince yourself by logic that all hope for its crew is gone, yet the vision of injured and starving men haunts you into action, regardless of how futile it may be.

The gesture has been made. The searching parties have returned. Now if Nungesser and Coli are found, it will be through their own resources in reaching habitation, if they're alive; and by chance, if they're dead. If they crashed inland, they may still turn up at some lonely trapper's cabin; or a hunter in future years may stumble across rusting wires, white bones, and rotting spars. If they went down at sea, some floating fragment may reach a ship or beach in tragic confirmation.

I think of the day I saw Nungesser in St. Louis. He was clear of eye, quick of movement. He'd come to give an exhibition with his pursuit plane. I stood nearby, watching the great French ace, thinking of his deadly combats, of the enemies he'd killed, of the clashes from which he had so narrowly escaped. I wonder if *he* concluded that flying the ocean was less dangerous than, say, a single combat in the air.

THE ELEVENTH HOUR
Over Placentia Bay
TIME — 5:52 P.M.

WIND VELOCITY	20 *m.p.h.*	VISIBILITY	*Unlimited*
WIND DIRECTION	*W.*	ALTITUDE	300 *feet*
TRUE COURSE	70°	AIR SPEED	92 *m.p.h.*
VARIATION	30° *W.*	TACHOMETER	1600 *r.p.m.*
MAGNETIC COURSE	100°	OIL TEMPERATURE	37° *C.*
DEVIATION	0°	OIL PRESSURE	59 *lbs.*
COMPASS COURSE	100°	FUEL PRESSURE	3.5 *lbs.*
DRIFT ANGLE	7° *R.*	MIXTURE	2.5
COMPASS HEADING	93°	FUEL TANK	*Fuselage*
CEILING	*Unlimited*		

Only six o'clock in New York. It must be seven for the people at St. John's — or don't they go by daylight saving time? I've flown more than an hour eastward by the sun. Think of man competing with the speed of the earth's rotation! Think of covering an hour's sun travel since this morning. Why, if I flew a little farther north, the *Spirit of St. Louis* could move around the world as fast as the sun itself!

The rugged coast line fades northeastward. The time is 6:15. In the Mississippi Valley, our air-mail plane must be somewhere between St. Louis and Springfield. I wonder whether Love or Nelson has the run, and what the weather's like. Is the pilot dreaming along under an open sky, or might the tail end of that Nova Scotian storm extend westward to Missouri?

St. Louis! How far away it is from Placentia Bay in Newfoundland — a range of mountains lowering behind me; another, shouldering the sky ahead — yet how closely tied to my presence here at this moment. If it weren't for St. Louis, I'd probably still be barnstorming from some Midwestern pasture, or piloting an army plane as a lieutenant in the Air Corps.

What an amazing series of coincidences preceded this flight across the ocean. When I look back, the chance of their taking place seems impossibly remote, like flipping a coin a hundred times and having it always turn up heads. It was chance that took me to St. Louis in the first place. That was in 1923, the year of my solo flight. After a summer's barnstorming in Minnesota, I'd started following the season southward with my OX-5-powered Jenny. Circling above one town and then another, landing where I found good fields nearby, staying or leaving according to the crowds I drew, my route had wandered into the rich farm lands of southern Wisconsin. Passenger business wasn't good; the days were getting so chilly that people didn't like to ride in an open cockpit. Besides, some pilot had flown all through that section of the country during the summer, carrying passengers for half the standard rate of five dollars. I always gave a good ride, but I never cut the price. That lost me a lot of passengers in Wisconsin. After a few days of meager income, I pointed my plane toward Illinois.

I was in the air when I decided to fly to St. Louis. The earth below was cold, soft, and wet; good barnstorming pastures were getting hard to find. I was flying along day-dreaming. In my hotel the night before, I'd been glancing through the local paper. It carried an article about the International Air Races. They were being held that very week at Lambert Field.

Barnstorming, one seldom met other flyers, and never saw modern airplanes. A visit to an organized airport was a special event in a barnstorming pilot's life, and there I was, only a few hours' flight from the races. There'd be dozens of pilots, and the newest planes, and racers that could attain the incredible speed of over 200 miles an hour. What fun it would be to land on Lambert Field with my Jenny and view the show as an insider — as a pilot in my own right. There'd be much to see and learn.

For a day or two after my arrival over Lambert Field, I almost wished I hadn't come. Instead of gliding down onto a welcoming airport, I found one of the races under way. Large military planes were banking steeply around a brightly painted pylon in front of the crowd. Obviously, the airport was closed to common traffic. I had circled, high in the air, until I saw several other barnstorming planes — Standards, and Jennies like my own — sitting awkwardly on a hillside a mile or so away. I landed in the weeds beside them, and learned from their pilots that special hours were set aside for visiting aircraft to arrive at the races. Rules were strict in this respect, they said.

In late afternoon, I flew my Jenny over to Lambert and staked it down at the end of a long row of civilian planes. Wherever I'd been before, a pilot was accorded great prestige. Cars speeded out from town with offers of help and transportation; people assembled from nearby farms; often schools were let out so children could watch the flying. That, I soon realized, was because at a small town or county fair any airplane formed a center of attraction — even an old Jenny. Where there were dozens of planes and star performers, the ordinary pilot was not far ahead, in standing, of the layman in the crowd.

I bought a lunch of hamburgers, and wandered about the field alone, studying different types of aircraft, and growing more conscious of my unshined boots and unpressed clothes in contrast to the neatly tailored uniforms of military pilots. The small amount of baggage he can carry makes it difficult for a barnstorming pilot to keep a neat appearance, living in daily contact with oil, dust, and weather. When darkness came, I began looking for a place to spend the night; but every available room in the nearby towns of Anglum and Bridgeton had been rented. So with my bundle under one arm (I couldn't afford the weight or stiff-cornered bulk of a suitcase in my Jenny) I walked half a mile to the tracks, and boarded a streetcar for St. Louis.

The next day, I became completely absorbed in aircraft and flying — types I had never heard of, maneuvers I had never seen. I spent hours looking up into the sky, and walking from one plane to the next. I'd study first the streamlined wires of a Curtiss biplane, then the thick wing butt of a Fokker monoplane, trying to decide which kind of structure I liked best. I would have given my sum-

mer's barnstorming profits gladly for authority to fly a few of the
newer types. I was so fascinated by it all that I felt I must take my
Jenny into air when the field was thrown open to visiting pilots at
the end of the day's program; not for any good reason, but just
to be in the same sky with the others. I couldn't stay on the
ground any longer and watch all those airplanes overhead.

I unlashed the wings, blocked the wheels, set the throttle, and
swung through my propeller. The engine started with the first pull
on "contact." I felt highly professional as I climbed into my cockpit
and started the warm-up. Three minutes of idling – – – temperature
and pressure normal – – – I pushed the throttle wide open – – –
1410 r.p.m. – – – Everything was perfect. But as I throttled down
I heard shouts of rage behind me. I looked back to discover a
great cloud of dust thrown up by my slipstream. In it I could see,
vaguely, gesticulating pilots and a half dozen other planes. I'd
been used to flying from sod-covered pastures, not from a crowded
and newly graded airport, baked dry by Missouri's sun. It never
occurred to me that I was blowing dust on other people's aircraft.

An air race official emerged from the cloud, hanging onto his
hat with both hands, face and clothes yellow with dust. He outlined in no uncertain terms his opinion of my judgment as a pilot:

"God Almighty! Where did you learn to fly? Don't you know
enough to taxi out on the field before you warm up your engine?
Where do you come from? What's your name? How in hell did you
get here?" He spluttered out questions so fast I didn't have time to
answer any of them. "Get out and lift your tail around. Hold that
throttle down while you taxi! All right, damn it, go ahead!"

*I glance up at the compass mirror. Am I off course again?
No, it's just the compass variation. I must remember that Newfoundland's isogonic lines mark a difference of over 30 degrees
between true and magnetic north.*

1. *"Lambert Field lies in farming country – – –" (Page 20)*

Photograph taken in 1925; looking southwest, toward Bridgeton. National Guard hangars in foreground; air-race hangars in distance; Robertson Aircraft Corporation office and shops on right; take-off and landing area runs out of picture to the left.

2. Curtiss Jenny — JN4-D. (See Glossary)

3. De Haviland — DH-4, converted by the Robertson Aircraft Corp.,
for mail carrying.

4. "– – – *I stepped over the side of my cockpit, into space.*" *(Page 316)*

The wreck of Captain Lindbergh's mail plane.

5. *"– – – the wing in the loft created an unexpected problem." (Page 118)*
At the Ryan Airlines factory, San Diego.

6. *"Here is the ultimate in
lightness of weight and
power – – –" (Page 102)*

Wright Whirlwind J-5C engine; 220 hp. (See Appendix)

7. The *Spirit of St. Louis*, above Coronado Strand, California.

Underwood & Underwood

8. *"Yes, my cockpit is a little blind – – –" (Page 121)*
Captain Lindbergh, in the pilot's seat.

9. *"It's more like a funeral procession than the beginning of a flight to Paris."* (Page 178)

Start of the truck-tow from Curtiss Field; early morning of May 21, 1927.

10. *"The luminous dials of the instruments stare at me with cold, ghostlike eyes."* (Page 303)

The cockpit of the *Spirit of St. Louis*, with the camera's lens in the position of the pilot's eyes.

11. "– – – *a soft runway, a tail wind, an overload.*" *(Page 181)*
On Roosevelt Field, a few minutes before the take-off for Paris.

13. *"– – – the entire field ahead is covered with running figures." (Page 492)*

A typical scene on a field where the *Spirit of St. Louis* landed. This photograph was taken at Croydon Airdrome, England, where police lines gave way; May 29, 1927.

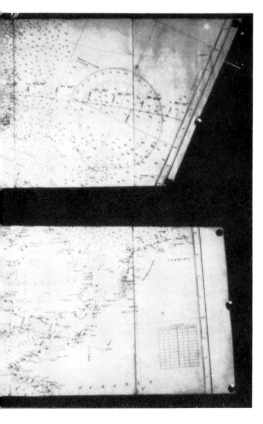

12. "— — — *that curving, polygonic line, cutting fearlessly over thousands of miles of continent and ocean."*
(Page 94)

The Mercator's charts, with the great-circle course laid out by Captain Lindbergh at San Diego.

The New York Times.

LINDBERGH SPEEDS ACROSS NORTH ATLANTIC, KEEPING TO SCHEDULE OF 100 MILES AN HOUR; SIGHTED PASSING ST. JOHN'S, N. F., AT 7:15 P. M.

EXTRA FINAL St. Louis Globe-Democrat. **EXTRA FINAL**

LINDBERGH SPEEDING ACROSS ATLANTIC WITH WIND AND WEATHER FAVORABLE

BIG WELCOME AWAITS DARING FLYER IN PARIS

Intrepid St. Louis Aviator's Trackless Route Across Atlantic from Western to Eastern Continent

ST. LOUISAN IS LAST SEEN AT ST. JOHN'S

LE FIGARO

30 CENTIMES · 30 CENTIMES

DIMANCHE 22 MAI 1927

DE NEW-YORK AU BOURGET EN AVION

Ayant traversé l'Atlantique en trente-cinq heures, Lindbergh a atterri hier soir à 10 heures 22

Une foule innombrable fait un accueil enthousiaste au pilote

The New York Times.

LINDBERGH DOES IT! TO PARIS IN 33½ HOURS; FLIES 1,000 MILES THROUGH SNOW AND SLEET; CHEERING FRENCH CARRY HIM OFF FIELD

COULD HAVE GONE 500 MILES FARTHER

CROWD ROARS THUNDEROUS WELCOME

Chicago Sunday Tribune

LINDBERGH LANDS IN PARIS

"Am I Here," He Asks, as City Goes Wild with Frenzy of Joy

AFTONBLADET

Söndagsnummer

Flygfältet i Paris stormades.

KONUNGEN LYCKÖNSKAR LINDBERGH. Dödsbapp från 3:e våningen.

FIRST INTERVIEW WITH CAPTAIN LINDBERGH IN PARIS

San Francisco Chronicle

LINDBERGH SAFELY IN PARIS 2½ HOURS AHEAD OF SCHEDULE

The Sunday Star.

PARIS WILDLY ACCLAIMS LINDBERGH

LA PRENSA

THE POST IS THE ONLY DENVER NEWSPAPER IN WHICH YOU GET ASSOCIATED PRESS NEWS

LINDBERGH LANDS IN PARIS

GREAT OVATION GREETS AIR HERO

GIGANTIC CROWD RUSHES ON FIELD AND PULLS HAGGARD FLYER FROM HIS AIRPLANE

THE DENVER POST
HOME

'WELL HERE WE ARE,' HE EXCLAIMS, EMERGING FROM 'DEATH CHAMBER'

YOUNG AMERICAN MAKES 3,600-MILE FLIGHT FROM NEW YORK IN THIRTY

und Handels-Zeitung

Lindberghs Flug geglückt.

Die Strecke New-York — Paris in 33 Stunden 47 Minuten durchflogen.

Die Grippe.

PARIS HONORS HERO

The Times-Picayune

THE WEATHER

NEW ORLEANS, SUNDAY, MAY 22, 1927

SINGLE COPY 3 CENTS

DELIRIOUS PARIS ACCLAIMS LINDBERGH

157,000 REFUGEES TO BE MOVED OUT FROM LOWER BASIN

Fight to Hold McCrea Levee May Be Won

On Road to Fame and Fortune

FRENCH CROWD NEARLY MOBS IDOL OF HOUR

AVIATOR SMILES AND WAVES WEARY ARMS AT THOUSANDS

The New York Times.

THE WEATHER

NEW YORK, SUNDAY, MAY 22, 1927

LINDBERGH'S OWN STORY OF EPOCHAL FLIGHT;
TEMPTED TO TURN BACK, KEEPS ON IN STORM;
ASKS FISHING BOAT: 'AM I ON ROAD TO IRELAND?'

IN FLOODED AREAS MAJORITY OFFERS AN EXTRA SESSION

CALLED LUCKY, BUT SAYS LUCK ISN'T ALL

Modestly Shares Credit With Plane and Engine Builders, Asking: 'I Hope I Made Good Use of What I Had.'

The New York Times.

THE WEATHER

FRANCE PINS ON LINDBERGH THE CROSS OF LEGION OF HONOR;
OTHER NATIONS AND RULERS OF EUROPE VIE TO ACCLAIM HIM;
HE NOW TALKS OF A VACATION FLYING ABOUT THE CONTINENT

CAPT. LINDBERGH'S TRIP HOMEWARD; A PAGE OF PICTURES—PAGE 5

The New York Times.

THE WEATHER

LINDBERGH LANDS AT CAPITAL TODAY FOR NATION'S WELCOME;
'GLAD TO BE HOME,' HE SAYS, AS THE MEMPHIS NEARS PORT;
MOTHER SHARES HONORS; HE WILL FLY HERE ON MONDAY

EXECUTIONS SPREAD TERROR IN RUSSIA; EUROPE IS SHOCKED

BERLIN CITY GIVES ITS MEDAL OF HONOR TO COLUMBIA FLIERS

37,000 Telegrams Arrive for Lindbergh With Flood on Wires Raging Unabated

Lindbergh

MEMPHIS PASSES CAPE

The New York Times.

NATION PAYS ITS HOMAGE TO LINDBERGH; ACCLAIMED BY 300,000 IN TRIUMPHAL RIDE; PRESIDENT PINS CROSS ON YOUNG AIR HERO

LINDBERGH'S SUNDAY IN WASHINGTON; A PAGE OF PICTURES ON PAGE 5

The New York Times.

NEW YORK IN HOLIDAY MOOD GREETS LINDBERGH TODAY; COMING IN HIS OWN SHIP, SHIFTS TO SEAPLANE IN HARBOR; HIS FINAL DAY IN CAPITAL ONE OF CONTINUOUS OVATION

THE CITY'S WELCOME TO LINDBERGH TOLD IN PICTURES—PAGES 5 AND 7

The New York Times.

MILLIONS ROAR WELCOME TO LINDBERGH IN CITY'S GREATEST TRIUMPHAL PAGEANT; GOVERNOR AND MAYOR PIN MEDALS ON HIM

The New York Times.

LINDBERGH LANDS IN MEXICO CITY WHILE THOUSANDS CHEER; EMBRACED BY CALLES; FLOWERS SHOWER TRIUMPHAL RIDE; FLIER TELLS STORY OF GOING ASTRAY IN 27-HOUR FLIGHT

14. *"It was like drowning in a human sea." (Page 496)*

The *Spirit of St. Louis,* after landing at Croydon. No similar photograph is available of the crowd surrounding the plane after its arrival on Le Bourget.

Brown Brothers

15. Farewell to St. Louis
Over Forest Park

In 1928, the *Spirit of St. Louis* was presented to the Smithsonian Institution, Washington, D. C., for permanent exhibition at the nation's capital.

The incident left me feeling like a forty-acre farmer stumbling through his first visit to the State Fair. I taxied carefully out and took off; but the joy was gone from wingovers, banks, and spirals. A crowded airport wasn't my environment. The sooner I could get back to the freedom of farm fields and open prairies, I decided, the better. Maybe I'd leave St. Louis in the morning.

That had been the lowest point. Not long after I landed, life began to brighten:

"Slim! When did you get here?" It was Bud Gurney.

"I came in yesterday."

"Got your Jenny?"

I pointed down the line, in answer. "Did you fly down from Lincoln, Bud?"

"No — couldn't get a ride — came on the train." He grinned as he looked at me. "And I didn't buy a ticket."

"I know what you mean," I said, "I got into a Colorado town last summer with fifteen cents in my pocket. I never rode a freight train – – – but I slept under a railroad station bench in Montana – – – and once I spent a night in a haystack, down in Tennessee." We laughed together. "Have you got your parachute with you?"

"I've got two of them — shipped 'em ahead by express. I won a spot-landing contest, Slim, and I came in second in the race to ground. I'm going to end the meet with a double jump."

"Who's going to drop you?" I asked.

"I haven't got a plane yet. Think you could do it, Slim?"

"I can if the Jenny will get enough altitude with a double 'chute on the wing."

"Say, a lot of the fellows are here. Let's go see some of them."

We walked over to a group of pilots, mechanics, and stunt men. Talk always wound around aircraft and flying. Which racer would win the Pulitzer prize — the Curtiss, the Verville, or the Wright? "Did you know H— was killed last summer? Stalled on take-off down in Texas — half spun into the ground — drunk, of course, as usual." Was I going to sell my Jenny at St. Louis? "There are a lot of buyers at the races." My plane might bring enough to pay for a newer one in the South with two or three hundred dollars profit left over, I was told. Also, there were people at the races who wanted to learn to fly. "You could sell your plane with a course of instruction thrown in." Barnstorming wasn't very good in the South that year — there were too many planes in Texas. "Everybody goes there for the winter." And fields were scarce in the other states. "You can't make enough to live on. Riddick got down to carrying passengers for a couple dozen eggs." "Why don't you stay at Lambert Field and do some instructing?"

That last question stuck in my mind. To be a flying instructor carried a prestige like one's twenty-first birthday. How I'd admired the older pilots who sat in the front cockpit — so experienced, so capable that they could grab a badly handled stick in time to stop a stall or crash; instilling confidence by their calmness in danger; guiding their students through the air by gestures — finger up for the stick back — palm motioning downward if you climbed too fast — hand to cheek to warn of slip or skid. A year and a half ago I'd been the student. Now, with two hundred and fifty hours in the air and a plane of my own, I had a chance to be *an instructor* — — — After all, why not?

"You don't need any license," I was told, on inquiring. "They expect you to know how to fly, and to use good judgment — that's all."

"Slim, I met a fellow who wants to buy a plane," Bud informed me while we were tying down for the night. "Maybe you could sell your Jenny. You'd have to teach him how to fly. Let's go over and talk about it."

Bud introduced me to a young Iowan who wanted to enter aviation as a profession. I set a price on my Jenny, with a solo flight guaranteed, that quickly closed the deal. In return for a down payment, I agreed to begin instruction flights as soon as the air meet was over.

Then I met Marvin Northrop, who'd come down from the Twin Cities and sold his Hisso-Standard. He asked me to instruct the man who bought it.

"You've got one student to teach. You might as well have two," he said. "It won't take you much longer. I'll pay enough to make it worth while."

Marvin Northrop never knew how glad I was to accept that job. I'd have taken it on regardless of what he paid me. It gave me a chance to spend more hours in the air, to gain experience as an instructor, to fly one of the powerful Hisso-Standards — in which I'd never soloed.

In the final hour of the program, I coaxed my Jenny up to 1700 feet, and Bud cut loose on the windward side of the field for his double drop. He had bad luck that afternoon. In landing, he broke his arm.

The Spirit of St. Louis *is three degrees off course. I drop the left wing slightly, and press left rudder. My throat's a bit dry. I can afford another swallow of water now, and still stay well within my ration.*

Lambert Field had changed in a few days from a beehive of activity to the home of a dozen civilian planes and a National Guard observation squadron which flew mostly on week ends. The field had the appearance of a circus lot after the circus has moved on — trampled ground, hundreds of pop bottles, thousands of bits of tinfoil and paper. It had the emphasized loneliness of a place recently deserted by a multitude of people.

I found an open welcome among the handful of pilots. Since I confined my activities to instructing my two students, I didn't compete for their sources of income, which were small enough at best. On the contrary, my instructing created additional flying activity. More planes in the air brought bigger crowds to the airport, and bigger crowds meant more people who would watch for a time and then gather courage to make a flight themselves — at five dollars a head.

When I taxied out with my first student in the rear cockpit, I was determined to combine in my teaching the best qualities of all the pilots I'd studied. For months I had praised and criticized others; now I had a chance to put into practice the ideas I'd preached. From T— I learned to inspect my plane carefully each morning before flight, but to avoid the puttering with details that made his students call him a timid pilot. From B— I learned that men who boasted the least might fly the best. I—'s bombastic methods taught me the value of patience with a student. S— was a wonderful acrobatic pilot, but he held no reserve for something going wrong; sooner or later he'd probably be killed. O— was so afraid to bank that he always skidded on his turns, and even leaned toward the high side of his cockpit. Each pilot I'd ridden with or watched added something to my philosophy of flight.

St. Louis is a city of winds, and the air above Lambert Field is usually rough, making it difficult to teach a new student how to land properly. Since turbulence is often least in early morning, we began our day, my pupil and I, by practicing take-offs and landings. After that, we worked on the Jenny, and made frequent trips to "Louie's" lunch stand. Pilots and mechanics gathered there for meals or coffee, and to comment on the flying.

When the wind died down, I would start instructing again: take-off and landing, take-off and landing, skid, slip, and stall. There were moments when I forgot my resolution to be patient, when I jerked the stick away roughly, and zoomed the Jenny as high as it would go.

I soon discovered that I was learning as much about flying as my students. A pilot doesn't understand the real limitations of his craft until he's instructed in it. Try as he may, he can never duplicate intentionally the plights that a student gets him into by accident. When you're flying yourself, you know in advance whether you're going to pull the stick back, push it forward, or cut the throttle. You think of a maneuver before you attempt it. But you're never sure what a student is going to do. He's likely to haul the nose up and cut the gun at the very moment when more speed is needed. If you check his errors too quickly, he loses confidence in his ability to fly. If you let them go too long, he'll crash you. You must learn the exact limits of your plane, and always keep him far enough within them so the wrong movement of a control will still leave you with the situation well in hand. You must learn not how high the tail *should* go in take-off, but how high it *can* go without disaster; not how to avoid a wind drift when you're landing, but how much drift there can be when the wheels touch, without a ground loop or blown tire resulting. And after you've learned how to keep a student out of trouble, you find that you've become a better pilot yourself. As you instruct your student in the primary art of flying, he instructs you in its advanced phases. In a gust of wind, or if the engine fails, or in any emergency, you handle your plane more skillfully than you ever did before.

Late in the fall of 1923 I soloed my Jenny student and rode with him, as check pilot, to his home town in Iowa. He planned on starting a flying service there the following summer. I took his note for final payment, wished him luck, and told him to keep plenty of altitude until he grew thoroughly familiar with the plane. "Don't fly below a thousand feet when you don't have to; and when you go over town, always stay high enough to glide to a field if your engine fails." But you can't pass on all the wisdom you have gained. A student absorbs only part of what his instructor tells him; often it seems a terribly small part. Cost what it may in damage or injury, the rest must be learned by trial. Possibly much of human progress stems from a refusal of the student to accept rules laid down by the instructor. At any rate, the last time I saw my Jenny it was flying in a farewell salute only two hundred feet above the railroad station where I was waiting for a train.

I found a number of odd piloting jobs on Lambert Field that fall, while I was waiting to take examinations for appointment as a flying cadet in the United States Army Air Service. I'd put my application in some weeks before, and been ordered to report at Chanute Field, Rantoul, Illinois, about January 1st. During December, I made more than my living expenses, but January was a poor month for flying. Snow and wind, freeze and thaw, discouraged the most enthusiastic aviators. For nearly three weeks after I returned from my examinations I didn't leave the ground. Then, one of the student pilots suggested that we fly south, in his OX-5 Canuck. He was a young automobile dealer named Leon Klink.

Why not barnstorm south with Klink's Canuck? He wanted to take a vacation, and at the same time learn to fly; while I wanted to make a living and keep my hand in at controls until I heard from the War Department. I was free until the flying school opened sometime in March, if I received an appointment; free an indefinite time if I didn't. We could fly each morning as far as the fuel in our tank would take us, and try to carry enough passengers in the afternoon to pay for the day's expenses. It would be great fun, and we'd learn a lot about the country and the people of the South.

It was the 25th of January, 1924, when we left Lambert Field. The hangar thermometer registered five degrees below zero Fahrenheit. All the wool clothing we could wear in our open cockpits didn't keep us warm. Air leaked in around firewall and fittings until our knees stiffened and our toes and fingers pained.

I had no plans, then, for returning to St. Louis. But a year and two months later, it was the destination on my day-coach ticket. I'd become a full-fledged second lieutenant in the United States Army Air Service Reserve. My olive-drab uniform with its wings and shining gold bars was folded carefully in the bottom of my foot locker. Rumors that the flying cadets would go on active duty after graduation had proved groundless. A cotton-dusting job in Georgia paid so low a salary that I turned it down — only two hundred dollars a month. Prices on barnstorming planes in Texas were too high for my cautious budget. They were asking a thousand dollars for a Jenny at Love Field! I had applied for authority to take examinations for a commission in the Regular Army Air Service, but the War Department hadn't answered.

"Why don't you come back to St. Louis after you get out of the Army?" Several of the pilots and mechanics at Lambert Field had extended that invitation, and it remained in the back of my mind during the year I spent in Texas, at Brooks and Kelly. There was a hospitality about St. Louis, a fellowship at Lambert Field, that I'd found nowhere else in my travels. Arriving at the races a complete stranger, I had left three and a half months later feeling that I was an accepted member of the city's little group of pilots. Now that I was in civilian life again, what better place to start looking for a job than St. Louis? With the summer season just ahead, there would almost certainly be students to teach and planes to take out barnstorming. At St. Louis they knew I could fly; they wouldn't hold it against me if I arrived by train and streetcar.

The compass needle is leaning. I rudder the Spirit *of St. Louis back onto course.*

There'd been plenty to do at Lambert Field — instructing, passenger-carrying, taxi flights, barnstorming trips. I found no trouble getting planes "on shares." New possibilities opened up each day. The Robertson Aircraft Corporation offered me the position of chief pilot if their bid for the St. Louis-Chicago air-mail route were accepted. I barnstormed through Missouri, Illinois, and Iowa, attended two weeks' Reserve training at Richards Field, near Kansas City, where I instructed on military aircraft, and dislocated my shoulder in an emergency 'chute jump over Anglum. August found me carrying passengers in a Curtiss Oriole at the National Guard encampment near Nevada, Missouri. There, I received a letter from the president of The Mil-Hi Airways and Flying Circus, at Denver, Colorado, offering me a flying job at four hundred dollars a month.

I'd always wanted to fly around mountains, and Denver was within gliding distance of the Rockies. That would give me a chance to explore the air currents around canyons, slopes, and ridges. I could study the effect of turbulence, about which aviators knew so little and speculated so much. The mail contract was not yet awarded. As soon as the encampment was over, I flew the Oriole back to St. Louis, and then boarded a train for the West.

On arriving at Humphrey's Field, outside of Denver, I found that The Mil-Hi Airways and Flying Circus consisted of one old Hisso-Standard, with a huge green dragon painted on each side of the fuselage. Closer examination showed it to be the same plane Lynch and I had barnstormed with three years before. Under its added coats of paint, it was "the silver job" that Page had sold to Rogers. Now, I had the role of pilot. The rear cockpit was mine. The inner-bay strut was for someone else's parachute, and the wings for someone else's feet.

Our contracts with fair officials usually called for daytime acrobatics and fireworks at night. What fun those fireworks contracts were. But how close one of them came to causing me a crash!

"Slim, whatever you do, don't get caught in the air after dark." One of the pilots at Lincoln had given me that warning when I was a student looking forward to my solo. "A fellow's crazy to fly at night. You're up there; you've got to land; and you can't see to do it."

Of course when you put on a night fireworks exhibition, you had to fly at night. The first time I tried it, I persuaded a dozen drivers to line their cars up along the edge of the field so I could take off and land across the beams from their headlights. It was more difficult with only one car for a marker on a dark night, but there were several occasions when that was all I could get. The patch of earth a single car illuminates seems awfully small as you glide down toward a strange stubble field or prairie.

Once, I got caught without any lights at all, circling a Colorado town I'd never seen before. That was really serious. We had a contract for night fireworks. But four passengers had come late to ride, at our previous location, and we'd stayed on after our planned departure time. That meant twenty extra dollars for the company. We'd still have gotten through before darkness if the engine hadn't run short of oil en route. It was only a half hour's flight. But I'd cut the margin close on that too, and my estimate was wrong. When the oil pressure gauge started fluctuating, I had to throttle down and land outside the nearest village.

By the time we found a car to take us to town, bought our oil, and got the cans back out, the sun had set. The president of Mil-Hi Airways, Wray Vaughn, was with me on that trip.

"Maybe we'd better tie down here," I'd suggested. "It's pretty hard to pick out a landing strip in dusk."

"We'll lose two hundred and fifty dollars," Vaughn argued. "It's the last night of the fair. I know right where the field is. It will only take us fifteen minutes to get there. There ought to be a little light left. Let's try it."

I was as anxious as he to make that money. I pushed the engine, and we flew low. The western sky was still bright when we reached the town and started circling, but you couldn't see much on the ground. It was essential to land right away. Vaughn was scanning the earth in all directions. After the third circle, I throttled my engine and shouted:

"Where's the field?"

"Right next the golf links," he replied anxiously.

"Well, where are the golf links?" I asked, as I eased on a little power.

"I don't know," he shouted. He said something else, but his words were lost in the engine's roar.

By that time, ditches and fences had merged with darkness. I'd done just what I'd been warned against as a student. I'd let night catch me in the air. I was up there. I had to land. And I couldn't see what was below. I headed away from the lighted streets, toward more open country. I'd simply have to throttle back, stall down, and cut the switches before I hit. On Colorado plains, there was a chance of not cracking up; but it wasn't very good.

The sky still reflected a little light, enough to show stubble field from pasture vaguely, like a cliff on early dawn. I throttled the engine again.

"Get your belt tight," I shouted. "We've got to land. Brace your arms against the cowling."

Vaughn nods, doesn't speak, follows my instructions calmly.

There's a big, dark area — probably a stubble field. There's a roundish patch near the center, not quite as dark — probably a strawstack. There are several blotches just beyond one end — probably trees. I bank and take my gliding distance, grateful for those meager scraps of information. Are there prairie dog holes, ditches, cows, or posts in that black area? We won't know until some substance touches our plane — until we hear a shattering of wood, or feel wheels clatter over ground – – –

"Well, we had luck that time," I say as we climb down from our cockpits and I dig my heels into the earth to see how soft it is.

"How far from town do you think we are?" Vaughn asks.

"Pretty close to five miles," I reply — not feeling at all sure.

"There's a car coming. I'll flag him down."

"Okay. I'll be there in a few minutes. I want to walk over the ground."

The field is smooth, and plenty big enough — I couldn't have picked a better one by day. I turn back. The lights have stopped. I hurry toward them.

"These men say they'll take us into town," Vaughn calls to me. "Maybe we can still put on the show. Our contract doesn't expire till midnight."

"There's not much wind. The plane'll be all right where it is." I climb into the back seat of the car.

"I'll locate the fireworks," Vaughan says. "You get the boards and hardware. It's not going to be easy — the stores will all be closed."

It's half past nine when we get back to the field, and we didn't stop for supper. We unload fireworks, boards, bail wire, hammer, saw, and nails. Stars are bright. The air is calm. I taxi the plane up close to the fence. Two automobiles turn on their lights to help us work. The owner of another takes me back and forth over the field to make doubly sure there aren't any posts or holes in the area I'll have to use.

It's half past eleven before we get the racks wired into place and the Roman candles fastened on. There are only thirty minutes to go, and I have two thousand feet to climb. All cars have left but one. We make a final check of terminals and lashings, and pause a moment to survey our efforts.

"You know these fireworks are going to be wasted," I say. "Everybody in town will be in bed."

"Our contract says 'midnight'," Vaughn replies firmly. "We've done our best, and we can't afford to lose that money."

"Where do you want me to throw my lights?" the car owner breaks in.

"Angle them down field so they just touch the edge of that strawstack," I say.

The Hispano starts smoothly. I warm it up for two minutes, and swing around for take-off. But what's the matter? Down field there are only two faintly glowing spots, like the eyes of a big animal. They're not pointed at the strawstack. They're moving back toward my plane. The car's battery must be going dead!

"Get him to drive you out so you can throw your flashlight on the strawstack," I call to Vaughn. "I've got to see *something* when I take off. Try to get another car before I land. If you can't, then flash your light up at me when I fly overhead after the show. Keep on flashing it right at the plane until I'm on the ground."

I taxi out a few feet, wait for Vaughn to reach his station, and open the throttle wide.

It's 11:40 when I get in the air and bank left in a steady climb. The city's pretty well asleep. More than half its lights are out. I've got to mark the stubble field's position in my mind. I'll be in a real jam, now, if I get lost. Let's see: that line of street lamps points about ten degrees northward. Four times its length projected southwest should about bring me overhead. I edge the throttle farther open. How slowly the Standard gains altitude with those racks tied on its wings!

Now it's 11:50. I'm over the fair grounds, at 1800 feet — high enough, and there's no more time. The bombs are in a box at my side. I pick one up, pull off the cap, rub the igniter, toss it over the cockpit's rim. One – – – two – – – three – – – four – – – five – – – six – – – green, red, and purple streamers arch out, fall, and fade.

That ought to attract attention down below. I toss a second bomb out; pick up a third. There are seven seconds between ignition and explosion. But don't count on more than five. Hang on tight after the fuse starts burning. If you let a bomb slip down into the fuselage, you'd be better off with the devil in hell. There, that's the last one – – – it bursts out brilliant red.

Now for the Roman candles. I turn eastward for position, nose down, and close the switch. Trails of flame stream backward, four below each upper wing. Colored sparklers blossom out between them. I pull up into a loop. My plane's brilliance blinds me to the stars, but the city's sprinkling of lights gives me a plane of reference which shows gravity's direction. There's my fiery trail below. I dive through it, loop again, bank over in a spiral. The candles sputter, fade into night. Now the flares ignite. They're so bright that people half a mile away can read a newspaper's printed page. For me, it's like driving a chariot of the sun. I can't even see the instruments in the cockpit. I shade my eyes with one hand and look straight down at the city's lights until the flares burn out.

My eyes adjust slowly to the blackness of the night. I pull the watch from my pocket – – – 11:57. We've completed our contract with three full minutes to spare. I ease back on power, find my row of street lamps, angle off at ten degrees. Down in the great dark sea ahead are only a half dozen pricks of light. Well, there'll be no flashes until my engine's heard.

I should be about over the stubble field now. I open my throttle and start to circle. Can that be the signal? There are regular blinks to the south — probably half a mile away. It must be the signal; but I didn't think an electric torch would show so dim. I glide lower. I circle at 500 feet. There's no longer a difference in shade between prairie and stubble. Even the strawstack is lost to human sight. The blinks continue. They're all I've got to land by. They seem as weak as the flame of a match. But we agreed that they would mark the strawstack. I can hold direction by the city and the stars. I straighten out on a southward heading, ease back the throttle, and sink down toward the hard, black

bottom of the night. Thank God for the length of Colorado
fields – – –

Winter found me back in St. Louis, instructing students, test
flying, and laying plans for the air-mail route to Chicago. The
Robertson Aircraft Corporation had been awarded the contract,
and had appointed me chief pilot, in charge of operations. Mail
flying was to start with good weather in the spring. There was
much to be done during the winter. I'd have to hire two other
pilots to help me. There was equipment to be selected. The route
had to be surveyed.

For the first time since I'd entered aviation, I had a permanent
home. I would be based at Lambert Field for months, possibly for
years. I could take part in activities that my nomadic life had
prevented in the past. I enlisted in the 110th Observation Squadron of the 35th Division, Missouri National Guard, and became
engineering officer for the squadron. Soon afterward I was pro-
moted to the rank of First Lieutenant. I instructed wartime pilots
in new techniques of flying, attended armory drill one night each
week, gave lectures on navigation, parachutes, aerodynamics, and
similar subjects. I attempted to pass on to officers and men as
much as I could of what I had learned both from civil experience
and from the Army schools at Brooks and Kelly.

My military work became so interesting that I managed to find
the hours needed. By cutting down on barnstorming trips, and
spending extra time with my flying students on weekdays, I could
usually have most of Sunday free to pilot the Hisso-Jennies of the
Guard. We'd schedule formation flights over St. Louis, practice
acrobatics, and send photographic missions to nearby towns. With
Army planes and parachutes, I could try maneuvers that were
too dangerous for our civil aircraft. One afternoon, I climbed my
Jenny to 14,000 feet, and brought it down in fifty consecutive
turns of a power spin.

It was during that winter I met the men who later joined with
me in *The Spirit of St. Louis* organization. Then there was Fonck's

crash, and that moonlit night in the mail cockpit when I conceived this flight across the ocean. And those were only a few of the coincidences it took to create the *Spirit of St. Louis,* flying, at this instant, across the center of Placentia Bay, on the great-circle route to Paris. There were other coincidences that ran through the difficult months of organization and finding a plane. There were all those that joined together to take me into aviation in the first place – – –

St. Louis! What time and space and incidents lie between us now! Only eight months ago — it seems as many years — I was sitting in the reality of my mail cockpit, dreaming of a plane that would fly across the sea. Now, I'm in the *Spirit of St. Louis,* on that very flight. The dream has become the reality; and the reality, the dream. Such things happen then in fact and not alone in fable. Aren't my silver wings fully as remarkable as those Daedalus made of wax and feathers? Placentia Bay — the strange — is my world, down there below me; and Illinois — the familiar — my object of imagination. Ideas are like seeds, apparently insignificant when first held in the hand! If a wind or a new current of thought drifts them away, nothing is lost. But once firmly planted, they can grow and flower into almost anything at all, a cornstalk or a giant red-wood — or a flight across the ocean. Ideas are even more wonder-ful than seeds, for they have no natural substance and are less restricted by hereditary form. Whatever a man imagines he can attain, if he doesn't become too arrogant and encroach on the rights of the gods.

Is aviation too arrogant? I don't know. Sometimes, flying feels too godlike to be attained by man. Sometimes, the world from above seems too beautiful, too wonderful, too distant for human eyes to see, like a vision at the end of life forming a bridge to death. Can that be why so many pilots lose their lives? Is man encroaching on a forbidden realm? Is aviation dangerous because the sky was never meant for him? When one obtains too great a vision is there some power that draws one from mortal life forever? Will this power smite down pilot after pilot until man loses his will to fly? Or, still worse, will it deaden his senses and let him fly on without the vision? In developing aviation, in making it a form of commerce, in replacing the wild freedom of danger with the civilized bonds of safety, must we give up this miracle of air? Will men fly through the sky in the future without seeing what I have seen, without feeling what I have felt? Is that true of all things we call human progress — do the gods retire as commerce and science advance?

I climb higher as I approach Avalon Peninsula. Bleak mountain summits glow coldly against a deepening sky. A thin layer of cloud burns molten gold. The wind lifts me up and carries me with it over the mountains, blowing hard and nearly on my tail, rocking my wings as it swirls past ridges and stirs in valleys. Each crevice fills with shades of gray, as though twilight had sent its scouts ahead to keep contact with a beaten sun. The empire of night is expanding over earth and sea.

Night has always affected the activities of men. To the farmer, it brings rest; to the marauder, action. The executive returns to his mansion. The watchman starts his vigil. For each person and each circumstance, night carries different meaning — safety or danger, home or adventure, revelry or prayer. To the pilot of an airplane without flares or landing lights, night has a meaning that no earth-bound mortal can fully understand. Once he has left the lighted airways there are no wayside shelters open to a flyer of the night. He can't park his plane on a cloud bank to weather out a storm, or heave over a sea anchor like the sailor and drag along slowly downwind. He's unable to control his speed like the driver of a motorcar in fog. He has to keep his craft hurtling through air no matter how black the sky or blinding the storm. To land without sight is to crash.

A plane in flight is dependent on the inertia of countless particles of air. Its wings must strike these particles suddenly, rest on them, deflect them, and leave them instantly behind in order to strike another mass. Where there is no speed, air seems to have no substance, and an airplane no more buoyancy than a rock.

I sometimes liken an airplane in flight to running over log jams on the Mississippi as a boy. Lumber companies were cutting virgin timber in the north, and each summer the river was filled with logs on their way to sawmills. Great numbers of them would pile up against boulders in the rapids until jams formed all the way to shore. The logs varied in size from huge, reddish butts of Norway pine to black, spindly top lengths of smaller timber. The neighbor boys and I often went out on these jams to fish and swim, and stretched naked in the sun on a warm, barkless surface of some larger butt log. Often we had to cross an area of freely floating top lengths, too small to hold up even a boy. Then we would leap so quickly from one to another that our weight was on the second before the first had time to sink, and on the third before the second was submerged. From the moment of leaving one big log until we could jump onto another, safety lay in speed. Fields remind me of butt logs; and air, of the top lengths in between.

All day, there have been "butt logs" of a sort along my route, places I could head for in emergency — a coast line to the west, fields and clearings, bays and lakes where one might land and swim ashore. Right now there's an area of thick young pine in the valley on my left. I'd bark my shins landing there all right, but I'd probably be able to walk away from the wreck.

At night, these "butt logs" disappear. Soon their existence will do me no good if a cylinder starts to miss. I won't be able to see them even if I turn back and reach a coast. To the eye, night equalizes mountains and meadows like ink spilled over the details of a map. If my engine should fail, I'd still have to keep on running, flying, touching swiftly the uniform particles of air, holding my speed and rhythm to the very instant of the blind, inevitable crash.

I never fully understood the value of sight until I lost my only parachute flare one night on the mail. I was caught in a storm, last

November. Clouds blanketed the earth behind me and shut it off ahead. I had used much of my fuel circling low over the city of Peoria, searching for its mail field. Twice I had tried to follow a line of street lamps toward the river, only to lose the ground in mist. Finally I climbed to 2,000 feet by instruments, and took up a course northeast. Unless the weather improved enough for me to pick up a beacon on the transcontinental route, my plane and its cargo of mail depended on the single parachute flare I carried. According to my calculations, 30 minutes of flying toward Chicago would put me over some of the flattest country within reach. At the end of that time I nosed down to 600 feet and found, as I had hoped, that there were frequent pockets in the clouds. But snow was falling and, even from that altitude, lights on the ground were dim.

I passed over a small town at less than 400 feet. Then, cloud shut off the earth again. But after a few minutes of blind flying I came to a large pocket of snow-hazed air. I pulled up, released the flare, and whipped the ship around to get under it before the parachute drifted to the ground. Clouds flashed as though with lightning against the night, as I hauled back on the stick. But instead of hanging in the sky above me, a point of dazzling fire catapulted toward the earth below. There were brilliant seconds — then total blackness.

I learned later that the rigger had put a new shoe on my tail skid before the flight. He'd left the end of the shoe projecting forward. That end hooked the flare's parachute and held it firmly, while the heavy flare jerked off and plunged to ground. But I had little interest in mechanical causes at the time. I was fully occupied with problems of survival. My plane was diving and banking, but I was so blinded by the flare that I couldn't see the instrument board to read my exact position. I lifted the down wing, pulled up the nose, and waited for dials to clarify — ready to throw myself out of the cockpit and yank the rip cord if sight were too long returning. Tense seconds broke through their cage of clocks; but vision came back in time. I levelled out the DH and climbed.

Landing lights had been installed on that plane only a few days before. One was set with a narrow beam to show obstructions far ahead. The other's beam was broadened to show the pilot nearby ground. I spiraled down as low as I dared over a large, black area between faintly glowing farmhouse windows, and switched on my lights. They were worse than useless. Snowflakes streaked the glare ahead. Farmhouse windows disappeared. I couldn't see a single object down below — not a fence post, tree, or building.

I switched off the landing lights, renounced the earth, and climbed. There was no more emergency equipment for me to rely on that night, except my parachute. My plane and engine were in perfect shape. There were plenty of fields below, large enough and hard enough to land on without damage. But it took sight to bring the one in contact with the other — a sound airplane; an open field. Between them, hidden like fortified lines of an enemy, stood trees and poles, hills and houses, fences and gullies.

I didn't have enough fuel to reach the dawn. That left me the choice of jumping out into darkness or of groping down blindly with my plane, to crash into whatever lay at the end of its glide-path – – – Then, in that mail plane, I had the choice; I had a parachute. Tonight, in the *Spirit of St. Louis*, I – – –

But why waste these minutes on thoughts of crashes or incidents that are past? This is my last hour of America and day. Whatever may come later, it shall be filled with life. I fly low across these last mountains, close to their granite summits, exploring ledges and crevasses no man has seen before. I skip over precipice and canyon, the ground now fifty feet, now a thousand feet beneath. I've never felt so carefree of terrain. Why should I concern myself with engine failure; I, who have flown above Nova Scotian forests and ice fields of a northern sea; I, who am about to take on the entire ocean and the night? What joy it is to fly past crags like an eagle, to glide fearlessly over the edge of these great cliffs. From now on, the explosion of the engine will be inseparable from the beat of my heart. As I trust one, I'll trust the other.

THE TWELFTH HOUR

Over Newfoundland

TIME — 6:52 P.M.

WIND VELOCITY	30 *m.p.h.*	VISIBILITY	10 *miles*
WIND DIRECTION	*W.*	ALTITUDE	700 *feet*
TRUE COURSE	68°	AIR SPEED	98 *m.p.h.*
VARIATION	31° *W.*	TACHOMETER	1650 *r.p.m.*
MAGNETIC COURSE	99°	OIL TEMPERATURE	37° *C.*
DEVIATION	0°	OIL PRESSURE	59 *lbs.*
COMPASS COURSE	99°	FUEL PRESSURE	3.5 *lbs.*
DRIFT ANGLE	7° *R.*	MIXTURE	2
COMPASS HEADING	92°	FUEL TANK	*Fuselage*
CEILING	*Unlimited*		

Hazy in the light of sunset, a great finger of water points down between the ridges on my left. The gray mass behind it, scarcely perceptible in the distance, is Conception Bay. Skirting the coast line timidly, a scratch of man across this tremendous wilderness, lies the winding track of a railroad. Looking at bay and mountains, I become aware of the roadbed as one notices a thread lying on a parlor floor.

I've covered 1100 miles in 11 hours. That's an average of exactly 100 miles an hour in spite of the detours I had to make around storms in Nova Scotia. I must be making a mile every 30 seconds now, with this wind on my tail. That would put St. John's just over a quarter hour's flight ahead. How surprised people there will be when they see the *Spirit of St. Louis* swoop down from the western sky, and head straight out into the Atlantic and the night!

No plane en route to Europe ever flew over Newfoundland before without landing. Commander Read used it as a refueling point for his transatlantic flight. It was in 1919, and also in the month of May, that his pilots pulled the overloaded NC-4 off the water. For them, this island was a steppingstone to Europe. Three of the Navy's big multiengined flying boats left Newfoundland; but only the NC-4 arrived at the Azores the next morning. Their four engines hadn't helped much when they ran into low visibility and fog; but their boat hulls helped a lot. The weather forecast had been wrong. The NC boats encountered an area of storm. Destroyers, stationed every 50 miles along the line of flight, flashed beacons and shot up star shells to guide the Navy pilots through the night; but after daybreak all three flying boats lost their bearings.

The NC-1 and the NC-3 landed in open ocean and were damaged too badly to take off again, but they stayed afloat. The crew of the NC-3, under Commander Towers, managed to sail through heavy seas for more than 200 miles, to Ponta Delgada. The NC-1, after drifting for several hours, was found and taken in tow by a ship. It sank later, but everyone on board was rescued. The NC-4 reached the island of Fayal, and landed off a lee shore to pick up its exact position. Then Commander Read and his crew flew to Horta's harbor.

I remember the chief mechanic at Lincoln telling about it; he'd been a member of the expedition. There were emergencies, forced landings, and engine trouble all along the route, he said. To begin with, four boats were going to make the flight; but there'd been a storm in which the NC-1 had been so badly damaged that the NC-2 was cannibalized to put it back in shape. Then, there was a hangar fire which caused more problems. On the flight north from New York, propellers began to crack, and had to be replaced with a new, less efficient type. Commander Read had so much difficulty flying up the American coast that the others thought he might not get to Newfoundland in time to start on the Azores leg. It was skill, determination, and a hard-working, loyal crew that carried him through to Lisbon and the completion of the first transatlantic flight.

How secure those naval aviators must have felt, when they started out, inside their big hulls. But they paid heavily in range for what they gained in seaworthiness. That was why they took off from Newfoundland and headed for the Azores. With flying boats they couldn't have gotten into the air with enough gasoline to make a nonstop flight between New York and Paris. Beacons and rescue ships — well, only the Navy can afford such things; for me, it's like wishing for the moon. No, I had to choose a land plane and go without rescue ships or not make the flight at all. But there are advantages on my side, too. When I stop to think about it logically, I know that I've got a better chance of reaching Europe in the *Spirit of St. Louis* than the NC boats had of reaching the Azores. I have a more reliable type of engine, improved instruments, and a continent instead of an island for my target.

I'm certainly better off than Alcock and Brown — and they got across the ocean in their twin-engined Vickers bomber after burrowing through hundreds of miles of fog and storm. It was a wonderful flight they made, for the year 1919. They took off from Newfoundland a month later than Commander Read, and crash-landed in an Irish bog.

Of course Hawker and Mackenzie Grieve went down in mid-Atlantic with their land plane when its engine overheated. But they found a Danish ship out there, and they too were rescued.

Those flights took place only eight years ago. What leaps forward aviation has made since then! It's amazing that pilots could get across the ocean at all with wartime engines and aircraft, even from island to island. Why, I've already flown over 1100 miles, and I still have fuel in my tanks for more range than they were able to take off with.

I come upon it suddenly — the little city of St. John's, after skimming over the top of a creviced granite summit — flat-roofed houses and stores, nestled at the edge of a deep harbor. It's almost completely surrounded by mountains. Farther ahead, the entrance to the harbor is a narrow gap with sides running up steeply to the crest of a low coastal range which holds back the ocean. Fishing boats are riding at buoys and moored at wharves.

Twilight deepens as I plunge down into the valley. Mountains behind screen off the colors of the western sky. For me, this northern city is the last point on the last island of America — the end of land; the end of day.

There's no time to circle, no fuel to waste. It takes only a moment, stick forward, engine throttled, to dive down over the wharves (men stop their after-supper chores to look upward), over the ships in the harbor (a rowboat's oars lose their rhythm as I pass), and out through the gap, that doorway to the Atlantic. Mountain sides slip by on either wing. Great rollers break in spray against their base. The hulk of a wrecked ship lies high upon the boulders. North America and its islands are behind. Ireland is two thousand miles ahead.

Here, all around me, is the Atlantic — its expanse, its depth, its power, its wild and open water. Is there something unique about this ocean that gives it character above all other seas, or is this my imagination? Flying swiftly through that gap in the mountains was like diving into a cold pool. One moment you look on water from the warm dryness of land. The next, you look at land from the enveloping wetness of water. In a few seconds your standards, your sensations, your viewpoint, have all undergone a major change. You've stepped suddenly into a different frame of life and values. A minute ago, I was a creature of the land, thinking of the ocean ahead, stripping for that final plunge. Now, I'm a creature of the ocean, sensing the exhilarating coolness of the water, thinking of the continent behind. This feeling penetrates my mind and body as though I'd actually made a dive, as though there were a major change in time, in air, in existence, between one side of that narrow gap and the other.

Now, I'm giving up both land and day. Now, I'm heading eastward across two oceans, one of night and one of water. From the ocean of water, I may still turn back to that receding coast; but I can't turn back to the shore of day. Even in an airplane I could never reach it.

I look at the black silhouette of the mountains behind me. On Avalon Peninsula, fields exist where I could land with little damage, now that a third of my fuel is gone—but never after nightfall. I've been holding on to such fields with my mind — holding on to the field at Long Island when mists looked thick ahead; holding on to the Maine coast, just over the horizon to my left; holding on to Newfoundland as a final point of refuge on my route. Now, the last of these is slipping from my grasp. The last gate is closing behind me. I study the face of each instrument. I switch off first one magneto and then the other. The tachometer needle barely moves. There's no sign of roughness. If I were landing from a test flight, I could suggest no adjustment to the most meticulous mechanic.

Suppose that in another hour the engine does begin to miss or the oil pressure drop? Of course I'd turn back. There'd be no sensible alternative. And the engine might keep going until I reached St. John's. But what then? A scattering of lights on the black earth below, the vague outline of mountains against the stars; beyond that, night would cover cliffs and boulders as water covers shoals. It would be a crash wherever I came down — on land or on sea.

I look back again at the lowering silhouette of the mountains, still sharp against the western sky. That is America. What a strange feeling — America at a distance! It's as though I were saying: "That's the earth" — far away, like a planet. There are no more reassuring islands ahead; no more test stretches of salt water. I've given up a continent and taken on an ocean in its place — irrevocably.

I've reached the point where real navigation must begin. Now that the fun of diving down on St. John's is over, I wish I were back on route. Now, I'll have to pay for that luxury. And I'm a little ashamed of having left my course so far. I'm 90 miles south of the great circle. All the way to Ireland, I'll have this extra factor to consider in setting my compass heading. The figures on my chart are no longer exact. In addition to wind drift and magnetic variation, I'll have to compensate for starting so far south. Not that it's a complicated matter — only a case of subtracting a few degrees. Then why should I be concerned with such a minor point? It's because I'm tired; that's it. I must realize I'm tired. That seems obvious enough; but at times my mind is too stubborn to admit it.

I look down at the ocean. Wind streaks are hard to see in the dusk — gray threads raveling across black water. This will be my final estimate. The figures I use now will have to last all through the night. The surface velocity looks close to 30 miles an hour. I wish I had some experience in estimating wind from waves. The direction is about west. I'll angle 10 degrees northward to compensate for drift. Another 5 degrees should carry me slowly back onto my great-circle route. Ideally, I want to strike it again at the southern tip of Ireland.

A change in navigation would be easy enough on a chart board, with its protractor and straight-edged rule; but in this breezy, narrow cockpit, there's no way to spread charts and lay out courses. I must estimate new angles roughly with my eye; and it's better to err north than south so I'll be sure of reaching land.

How will the wind blow during the night? Most of the afternoon it's source has shifted slowly toward the west. Will it hold from that direction? Will it continue to box the compass? Will it increase in velocity? There's no way of knowing. I can only calculate my heading from these last vague streaks on the water, and correct it at the break of dawn.

I crank the new heading into the earth-inductor dial, pull the throttle back to 1600 r.p.m. and lean out the mixture until my engine roughens slightly.

Suddenly I become aware of a white pyramid below me — an iceberg, lustrous white against the water. I've never seen anything so white before. Like an apparition, it draws my eyes from the instruments and makes me conscious of a strange new sea. Ahead and on each side are several more. So that's why surface ships stay south in warmer waters! Well, I'm flying high enough to miss these drifting crags. Here and there a wisp of fog hangs, low-lying, above the waves.

Soon there are icebergs everywhere — white patches on a blackened sea; sentries of the Arctic. The wisps of fog lengthen and increase in number until they merge to form a solid layer on ahead; but, separating as I pass above them, they leave long channels of open water in between — stripes of gray fog and black water across my course. With every minute I fly, these channels narrow; until finally all the ocean is covered with a thin, undulating veil of mist. At first it doesn't hide the denser whiteness of the icebergs, but makes their forms more ghostlike down below. Then, the top of the veil slopes upward toward the east — real fog, thick, hiding the ocean, hiding the icebergs, hiding even the lights of ships if there are any there to shine. I ease the stick back slightly, take five miles from my speed, and turn it into a slow and steady climb.

The last time I climbed over a fog like this was that night on the air-mail route, northeast of Peoria, when I jumped from my plane. It was a low fog that night, too, and I encountered it at almost the same time of evening, the sky still bright in the west. I'd wondered then what I would land on after I left my cockpit. Thoughts of windmills, and railroad tracks, and big chimneys with fires at the bottom, had all skipped through my mind as I hung, rocking gently, under the parachute's silk canopy, waiting for the hard impact of substance on my feet. Tonight, I know what's down there — wet, deep, and freezing water, with the nearest land already beyond the horizon. No, a parachute would be no good tonight. I was wise not to carry one.

Here I've left the coast of Newfoundland under the best conditions I ever hoped for — on schedule, plenty of fuel, and a tail wind. Up to now, my every wish has been fulfilled; my plans have meshed together with the utmost smoothness — except for the lack of sleep. But that night on the mail I'd been on schedule too, with plenty of fuel, or so I thought. Some days after the crash, I discovered that a mechanic had found a leak in the DH's 110-gallon gasoline tank. He'd taken it out, put an 83-gallon tank in its place, *and forgotten to tell the pilots*. We must have flown tranquilly into Chicago many times, during those weeks, with the main tank almost dry, and so close to the ground that there wouldn't have been time to shift to reserve if the engine had cut.

I won't run out of fuel over the ocean tonight. It was measured too carefully, and nobody's changed a tank in the *Spirit of St. Louis* without telling me. But what other unforeseen troubles may arise? The flight of a plane depends on the careful preparation of thousands of details. Has any one slipped by?

THE THIRTEENTH HOUR
Over the Atlantic
TIME — 7:52 P.M.

WIND VELOCITY	*Unknown*	VISIBILITY	*5 miles*
WIND DIRECTION	*Unknown*		*above fog*
TRUE COURSE	65°	ALTITUDE	*800 feet*
VARIATION	32°	AIR SPEED	*90 m.p.h.*
MAGNETIC COURSE	97°	TACHOMETER	*1625 r.p.m.*
DEVIATION	0°	OIL TEMPERATURE	*36° C.*
COMPASS COURSE	97°	OIL PRESSURE	*59 lbs.*
DRIFT ANGLE	10° *R.*	FUEL PRESSURE	*3.5 lbs.*
COMPASS HEADING	87°	MIXTURE	*2.5*
CEILING	*Unlimited above fog*	FUEL TANK	*Fuselage*

Twelve hundred miles behind. Two thousand four hundred miles to go. One-third of the flight completed. A third is a satisfying fraction — only twice that much again to Paris. I recheck the earth-inductor against the liquid compass, and drain another tablespoon of fuel from the Lunkenheimer trap, enjoying the pungent odor of gasoline. Let's see, I've flown an hour and a quarter from each of the outer wing-tanks, and a quarter hour from the center wing-tank. I'll run through the night on fuselage and nose tanks, leaving the gasoline in the wing-tanks for reserve. If anything goes wrong with the fuel pump, I can feed from the wings by gravity alone; and in case the big fuselage tank should spring a leak, every hour I use from it will be that much ahead.

Instrument readings are all normal. The engine sounds smoother than at the beginning of the flight. Possibly it's the night air; possibly it's simply the smoothness a well-cared-for engine gains during the early hours of its life. Whatever the cause, there's something in its rhythm that assures me, and gives me confidence with which to enter the unknown space ahead — to climb up over the fog, over the sea, and into the night.

For some unmeasurable time in memory — the mechanical hands of the clock say only twenty minutes, but they must lie — I've been climbing slowly to stay above the top of the fog bank, watching a light haze form in the air around me, wondering how thick it will grow. Now, I find myself looking at stars overhead. Day — I glance back — has almost vanished; just a trace of it left, a wash on the western sky, only enough to illumine the gray mist rollers beneath my plane. The fog, the icebergs, and the gathering haze caused me to neglect the sky. Here it's risen on the breaking crest of darkness to claim the night for its own. Those few faint stars, twinkling down through the window above me, seem more important than all the world below.

You fly by the sky on a black night, and on such a night only the sky matters. Sometime near the end of twilight, without realizing when it happens, you find that the heavens have drawn your attention subtly from earth, and that instead of glancing from the compass down toward ground or sea, your eyes turn upward to the stars.

I wonder if man ever escapes from worldly bonds so completely as when he flies alone above clouds at night. When there's no cloud layer beneath him, then, no matter how high he may ascend, he is still conscious of the surface of the earth by day and of its mass by night. While flying over clouds in daytime, there's something about the motherly warmth and light of the sun which imparts a feeling of the earth below. You sense it down there underneath, covered only by a layer of mist which may draw apart at any moment to leave the graceful contours of land or the flat, sparkling sea, clear and naked in sunlight.

By day, or on a cloudless night, a pilot may drink the wine of the gods, but it has an earthy taste; he's a god of the earth, like one of the Grecian deities who lived on worldly mountains and descended for intercourse with men. But at night, over a stratus layer, all sense of the planet may disappear. You know that down below, beneath that heavenly blanket, *is* the earth, factual and hard. But it's an intellectual knowledge; it's a knowledge tucked away in the mind; not a feeling that penetrates the body. And if at times you renounce experience and the mind's heavy logic, it seems that the world has rushed along on its orbit, leaving you alone, flying above a forgotten cloud bank, somewhere in the solitude of interstellar space.

How many icebergs are floating on the ocean's surface? I no longer care about them. The stars, the gathering haze, and the rising top of the fog bank are all-important to my mind. The air speed has dropped to 85 miles an hour, and the altimeter shows 2000 feet; but stars are getting dimmer, and the fog is climbing, ramplike, as fast as my plane.

Well, let the haze thicken; let the fog climb! What does it matter? I've checked my course on the Newfoundland coast; I've received all I asked for, all I hoped for, from the continent of North America. From the ocean, I never asked as much. It isn't essential that I see its surface. Maybe it's better to have a storm above the Atlantic. I can't expect good weather over all the 3600 miles between New York and Paris. If there's to be an area of fog and storm, this is probably the best place for it to begin. Much of my overload is gone; there's nothing ahead but ocean for almost 2000 miles, and the chance that a storm will be that large is slight.

If I fly through a storm over the Atlantic, it may propitiate the gods; and by the law of averages alone there should be less chance of striking another over Europe. If I make the whole flight without meeting anything worse than those scattered squalls in Nova Scotia, I'll feel as though I'd been cheating, as though I hadn't earned success, as though the evil spirits of the sky had disdained to sally forth in battle. A victory given stands pale beside a victory won. A pilot has the right to choose his battlefield — that is the strategy of flight. But once that battlefield is attained, conflict should be welcomed, not avoided. If a pilot fears to test his skill with the elements, he has chosen the wrong profession.

It's very dark. There's not a shade of twilight left to moderate the blackness of the night. Only a half-dozen of the brightest stars, directly overhead, pierce through the haze. The luminous dials of the instruments stare at me with cold, ghostlike eyes. The hands of the clock, which I haven't changed from their New York setting, show 8:35.

I glance at my altimeter — 5000 feet now, and still climbing. I look out through the window again. The cloud layer — you can hardly call it fog at this altitude — is dimly perceptible in the haze — an irregular, thicker substance, like a muddy ocean bottom to the mist. Its gray shoals are closer to my plane than before, uncomfortably close, less than 100 feet from my wheels. They've been rising faster than I.

Haze and night prevent my seeing what lies ahead in the distance. This slanted layer of clouds, like plains leading up to a mountain range, may go much higher. I'll either have to climb faster or give up the stars, withdraw into my cockpit, and follow instruments blindly through the night. I glance at the turn indicator, kicking rudder slightly as I do so. The needle jumps over to the side. Yes, it's working properly, and — my eyes run quickly from dial to dial — so are all the other instruments on the board.

But those glowing lines and dots seem so much less tangible, so much less secure, than the stars overhead. The stars have always been there. I watched them through the screen of my sleeping porch when I was a child; I drove under them on Minnesota roads with my father and mother; flew under them night after night with the mail. I can trust the stars; they're always the same — familiar constellations following each other slowly through the heavens. As long as I can hold onto them I'll be safe — no nuts to slip, no bearings to jam, up there. Besides, there may be ice inside the clouds; the air has become much colder.

My engine's only turning 1625 r.p.m.; there's plenty of extra power. With a strong tail wind, I'm gaining on my estimate of fuel; I can afford to spend a gallon or two for altitude. I open the throttle until the tachometer needle touches 1650, pull the nose a little higher, and reset the stabilizer. In the morning, I'll regain some of that fuel as I glide down.

I think again of the cautious phrases in Dr. Kimball's forecast. He knew that airmen's lives depended on the wording he used. "Most Atlantic coast stations report the fog clearing," it said, "and indications are that weather along the route will continue to improve." That has all come true. "A large high pressure area is forming over the North Atlantic," it continued, "and there are local storms off the coast of Europe."

A high pressure area over the North Atlantic. Then it's probably only a small storm ahead, nothing very high or dangerous. Possibly it will still turn out to be only a dense fog lying above the Grand Banks — they have a reputation for always being foggy.

But how high can white mist rise and still be fog? I wonder. I recall Dr. Kimball's warning that my route lay too far north to depend on the accuracy of his forecasts. The ship lanes may be clear at the same time the great-circle route is covered with fog and storm. Well, I can detour southward to the ship lanes if I have to. There's enough fuel in the tanks to do that, and still take me on to Paris.

I'm flying with my head thrown back, looking up through the skylight at the handful of stars above me, glancing down at intervals to make sure my compass heading is correct. When you can see stars close to the horizon it's easy to hold on course. They draw you toward them like a beacon on the earth. But looking straight up for guidance is like dangling at the end of a rope; it's almost impossible to keep from turning slightly.

The stars blink on and off as haze thickens in places and then thins out again. I hold on to them tightly, dreading the blind flying that lies ahead the moment I let them go, hoping I can climb above the haze into the crystal blackness of the higher night — hoping, climbing, and yet sinking deeper with every minute that I fly.

Soon haze becomes so thick that, except for those dim points of light, it might as well be cloud. At any moment those stars may blink their last and die, leaving me stranded thousands of feet below the surface, like a diver whose life line has been cut. I'd thought I could climb above the fog and leave it beneath me, a neat and definite layer. Now, I realize what a formidable enemy it is. Its forces have been in ambush all around me, waiting only for the cool of night to show their form.

Why try to hold on to those stars? Why not start in now on instruments? After all, they were put there so I could fly through fog. This game of hide and seek with a half-dozen stars is child's play. But if I start flying blind, God only knows how many hours of it lie ahead. It might go on through the entire night — the monotony of flying with my eyes always on the instrument board; the strain of flying by intellect alone, forcing the unruly senses of the body to follow the doubted orders of the mind — the endless bringing of one needle after another back to its proper position, and then finding that all except the one my eyes hold tight have strayed off again. The *Spirit of St. Louis* is too unstable to fly well on instruments. It's fast, and it has a greater range than any plane that flies; but it's high-strung, and balanced on a pin point. If I relax pressure on stick or rudder for an instant, the nose will veer off course.

And there's the question of staying awake. Could I keep sufficiently alert during long, monotonous hours of flying with my eyes glued to the instruments, with nothing more to stimulate my mind than the leaning of a needle? It was difficult enough to stay awake over the ice fields southwest of Newfoundland, when my eyes could travel the whole horizon back and forth, and with the piercing light of day to stir my senses. How would it be with fog and darkness shutting off even the view of my wing tips? It would be like a dream, motionless yet rocketing through space, led on and on by those will-o'-the-wisp needles, those glowing dials in front of me, always two feet away. A dream that could turn into a nightmare fully as alarming as engine failure. After I'd been flying for an hour or two or three, might I find myself struggling to keep upright, to hold my altitude, to bring my plane back under control (flapping my sleep-bound arms with superhuman effort in a vain attempt to stop the sickening fall)? Might I awake from my stupor to hear air screaming past my cockpit and see the turn indicator moving sluggishly, its venturi clogged with ice?

Then there would be no waking in a soft and comfortable bed. That fall would end – – – how would it end? What do you feel in the rending, crashing instant that must exist between life and violent death? Do you experience excruciating pain? Have you time to realize that life itself has ended? Is all consciousness forever blotted out, or is there an awakening as from a dream, as from a nightmare; an awakening that for some reason you can't communicate freely back to living men — just as you can't communicate freely from a dream? What waits after life as life waits at the end of a dream? Do you really meet your God, or does blank nothingness replace your being? – – –

I was once braced for the impact of death. I don't yet understand how it missed me. That was during my second emergency parachute jump, a few seconds after I left the cockpit. I had been running tests on a new type OXX-6-powered biplane, designed and built at Lambert Field. To gain passenger comfort the plywood-covered fuselage had been made unusually wide, and it was rather short in length. I'd been doing acrobatics at an altitude of about 2500 feet. In wingovers and banks, the plane answered its controls fairly well; but its stalls were mushy, and it had a tendency to fall off after certain maneuvers to the right.

Tailspins were the last items on my test list. I tried a right spin twice, unsuccessfully. The plane simply wouldn't fall into one. But it had snapped into a left spin, and snapped out just as quickly when I reversed controls. Then, I'd tried two full turns to the left, and found my controls useless — blanketed out by wings and fuselage. Full rudder and stick had no effect. Bursts from the engine did no good. The plane kept right on spinning, nose high, flat, lunging slightly.

I don't know how many revolutions it made all told — probably eight or ten. My mind was working too fast on other problems to count them. I rode it down for close to two thousand feet, fighting the controls. Then, a glance at the ground showed no more time. It was jump or crash.

I tripped my safety-belt buckle, got my feet beneath me, and rolled out over the high rim of the cockpit, pulling my rip cord the instant I passed under the stabilizer. Dizzy spinning pressures stopped. But the ground was right there, leaping at me. Trees and houses looked tremendous. There seemed scarcely enough room for a parachute to string out.

My 'chute opened quickly; but I'd dropped faster than the plane. I was under the periphery of the spin. The canopy had no more than billowed open to check my fall, when I looked up to see the plane less than a hundred feet away, pointed directly at me.

Usually the stroke of death either passes before you're aware of it, or your senses are occupied with the fight for life, or there's good reason to hope you'll escape. That time I saw it coming. I was helpless. No movement I could make would have effect. There didn't seem a chance for it to miss. I braced my body for the impact — propeller, wing, or whatever death's instrument might be. Every muscle, every nerve, was tensed for the tearing blow on flesh. Danger had swept all unessential detail from my mind — it was clear as a pane of glass. It had no thoughts of past or future, or of the swinging parachute, or of the closeness of the ground beneath my feet.

If the hand of death ever cracks the door that lets life's senses peek beyond life's walls, it should have cracked it then. In mind and body I'd arrived at the very second of impact. But that door stayed shut. The parachute's shroud lines had gotten twisted in the jump, and they swung me around awkwardly. In the fraction of time it took to turn my head from right to left, the plane passed.

and somehow missed my body and my 'chute. I wasn't over 350 feet high when I jumped, some of the pilots told me later.

You couldn't come much closer to death than that. And yet I've known times when the nearness of death has seemed to crack the door — times when I've felt the presence of another realm beyond – – – a realm my mind has tried to penetrate since child-hood – – –

It's Sunday in Little Falls. I press my stomach against a window sill of the yellow-brick Buckman Hotel and look out onto the dirt street, one story below. Several carriages are lined up in front, horses tied carelessly to the hitching rail. A farmer's heels click on the new cement sidewalk. The Minnesota sky is whitish blue. The morning is starting to get hot.

It's to be my first day in church. Mother has dressed me in a gray flannel suit, long black stockings, felt hat, and brown kid gloves — they're terribly uncomfortable. Now we are waiting for our own carriage to drive up. Church! How I dislike that word, although I'm not quite sure what it means. It's keeping me away from the farm, where we usually drive on Sunday mornings. Before our house burned down last summer we lived on the farm all the time.

Why do I have to go to church? Well, my father is going to be a Congressman in Washington. He's going to represent all the people of the town and of the country around it for miles and miles. It's a very important position, and the family of a man who holds such an important position is expected to go to church. Besides, when you're five years old it's time for you to learn something about a mysterious being called God. Church is the place where you learn about Him.

It's even hotter in church than behind our team of horses on the crunching road. There's no movement of leaves outside the window. No breath of air comes through. A smell of too many people weights the sticky dampness. My legs itch under their tight stockings, and stiff edges of my new suit press sharply against skin. The words of the preacher echo back and forth between high wood walls, merging with each other until all are meaningless to my ears. Now and then he mentions God, and death, and another life; but I can't understand him.

What the preacher says is religion. Good people are religious. But you have to be grown up to understand religion. When you don't understand it, it's awfully uninteresting. Two miles southward, the bank of the Mississippi lies cool under the branches of our farm's great pines, and a breeze almost always moves across the water. When church is over, we'll spend the rest of the day there. And in the carriage is a basket full of lunch. Meanwhile I can lean forward and run my thumbnail across the bottom of the pew's woven cane seat. It produces a unique and pleasantly tickling sensation.

Through the years of my childhood, church was an ordeal to be cautiously avoided. God remained vague and disturbing. You heard of Him in story books, in the cursing of lumberjacks, in the blessing of an old aunt. No one could tell you what He looked like, and He seemed to have a lot to do with people who died — there was nothing more disturbing than death. I pictured Him as a stern old man living in Heaven, somewhere off in the sky like clouds; knowing about and judging your every act. When you died, He might make you pay for all the things you did wrong, like staying home on Sunday, or scratching the bottom of a pew's seat.

On the sleeping porch of our new house, I lay awake in evenings, staring out at the sky, thinking about God and life and death. One might meet God after one died, I decided, but He didn't have much to do with life; no one I knew had ever seen Him, and the people who didn't believe in Him seemed to get along as well as those who did. If there were no God, then how could man have been created? But if there were a God, how did He begin? He couldn't very well have made Himself up out of nothing. But how did the universe begin — the stars, and space, and all the planets? It did. There it was. God wouldn't be more remarkable than that. But if God existed, why didn't He show Himself to people, so there'd be no argument about it? No, God was as remote as the stars, and less real — you could see the stars on a clear night; but you never saw God — — —

They are dim, blinking, gone — no, I can still see them. I rip through years of time, from a sleeping porch in Minnesota to a cockpit above the North Atlantic ocean. I feel a sudden desire to tear the pane out of the skylight, to remove all obstruction between my eyes and those points of light above. Glass forms too great a barrier between us. It seems to be holding me in, like prison bars. Through it, stars are but a picture on a flattened screen of air, devoid of true reality, unable to communicate their text. Seeing them through that window is like touching water through a rubber glove.

They blink off again. I open the throttle to 1700 r.p.m. It's best to get above the haze. After all, there must still be close to 300 gallons in the tanks, and in clear air I can make up in my own efficiency what I lose in fuel range by climbing. I may even gain a stronger tail wind at higher altitudes; but — that's what worries me most — maybe I won't; maybe there'll be a head wind aloft, or a side wind may drift the *Spirit of St. Louis* far off course and throw me south, or even north, of Ireland.

Subconsciously, without understanding the full significance of my action, I adopt a basic rule for the flight. Somewhere, in an unknown recess of my mind, I've discovered that my ability rises and falls with the essential problems that confront me. What I *can* do depends largely on what I *have* to do to keep alive and stay on course. If there were no alternative, I could fly blind through fog during all the night and day. The love of life is sufficient guarantee for that. But there *is* an alternative, the alternative of climbing faster; and that I choose.

My head is thrown back to look upward. My neck is stiff. But what of it? Hold on to those stars. Guide on them. Don't let them get away.

I was never convinced that going to church in Little Falls that Sunday had any effect on my father's job in Washington. I simply

accepted the fact that his election to Congress brought certain
changes in life for me, a number of which were disagreeable.
Among the most disagreeable were the winters my mother and I
spent at the nation's capital.

For me, the city formed a prison. Red brick houses replaced
the woodlands on our farm. Concrete pavement jarred against my
heels. The crystal light of sky crawled mangily into schoolrooms.
It was the clank of street cars, not the hoot of an owl, that woke
me at night. Through long winters, I counted the weeks and days
until spring when we would return to our Minnesota farm.

Surely my father found interest in his work in Washington. His
office was in a great marble building that covered an entire block.
I used to roller-skate around it. Congressmen were tremendously
important. People talked about how they were going to vote, and
treated them with great respect. Hadn't that man in the Navy Yard
given me a shaving from a cannon when he found out who my
father was? Hadn't a policeman let me walk along a railing in the
Capitol grounds when I told him I was a Congressman's son?

My father was often at his desk before dawn and late at night.
Sometimes he even slept on a black leather couch beside it. But
Congressmen's work seemed awfully boring to me. They spent
most of their days indoors, dictating letters, and talking to people
from home, and listening to long speeches on the floor of the
House. They seldom felt wind or rain on their faces. They even
had a tunnel built so they could walk back and forth to the Capitol
without being exposed to weather. My father didn't like that
tunnel. He used to take me for long walks outdoors whenever he
had time. Then we'd plan a camping trip for the summer, or he'd
tell stories about his boyhood on Sauk River. Sometimes we'd stop
in the House lobby on the way home, and I'd get a ten-cent glass
of apple cider, and we'd look at the weather map to see what the
day was like in Minnesota.

I spent many hours on the House floor with my father. There
were usually plenty of empty seats. Here laws for all the United
States of America were made. Here, the future of the nation was
decided. It was a wonderful opportunity for a boy to grow up in

such an atmosphere, surrounded by great men and great ideas. People often told me that. But the House reminded me of church. It was always too hot, and rather stuffy, and its speeches went on and on like sermons from a pulpit; only instead of talking about heaven and hell, like ministers, Congressmen were more interested in things like tariffs and trusts. Sometimes you got a headache as you listened – – –

A headache – – – Why does my head press against the sky-light's rib? It hasn't done that before. Something isn't right in the plane. Why is the cockpit too small for me? Certainly the dimensions haven't changed. Certainly I haven't grown any larger. But of course! — the air cushion I'm sitting on — it's been expanding as I climb to lower atmospheric pressures. I didn't notice how taut and hard it was getting. I open the valve for a few seconds, to lower my position and make sure the fabric won't burst.

Even in Washington there were interesting hours. I was six years old the first winter we arrived, and rented rooms in an apartment house. It hadn't taken me long to get outside, into the vacant lot next door. It was a marvelous place. No grown-up could understand the opportunities it offered. In it, I had early experiences in paleontology and aerodynamics. It held all kinds of imaginary adventures. There was a weed-screened pile of earth in one corner of the lot — a useless pile to anyone who didn't believe in buried treasures. But to one who did it offered days of work, and the reward — after patient digging with a stick — of a smooth and oval stone, split through the center to let out the perfect fossil of a fern leaf. Curving, brown, and glazed by time, that fossil was as graceful as it was old — millions of years old, my mother said.

And there were days in the lot when I encountered serious problems caused by a wind which blew away sheets of paper I brought out to play with. Of course one could weight them down with stones. Paper blew; stones didn't. It was like fire and water. One burned; one stopped burning. That was easy. But how about wood? A block of wood could hold down a sheet of paper, while a shingle, which felt heavier, might blow away all by itself. On windy days, I experimented with pieces of wood tossed high above my head. Cubes dropped straight back down, but shingles fluttered off at an angle. It was all very confusing. One must consider shape, as well as weight, in relationship to air. I concluded that it was best not to turn your back on an important sheet of paper weighted down with wood.

My happiest hours in Washington were outdoors, spinning tops, playing marbles "for keeps," and roller-skating over the asphalt streets. On clear and warm vacation days my mother and I visited the parks and buildings of the city. We usually started out from our boardinghouse by walking past Scott Circle. "General Winfield Scott was a relative of yours," my mother used to tell me, "a few generations back on the side of your grandfather Land." I climbed the Monument; watched the Treasury print our money; spent hours in the Smithsonian Institution. Sometimes we made trips through the country nearby, to places like Mount Vernon, or Potomac Falls, or Arlington Cemetery. Often we took a street car to Rock Creek Park, for a picnic in the woods and a walk through the zoo. It was seldom very crowded, and there were always things to do. You could float sticks down the creek, or climb its steep banks, or watch automobiles and horses on the drive while you ate your lunch. Lots of dignitaries passed by. If you were lucky, you might see the President himself. Once I watched Taft take exercise on that drive, walking behind his horse-drawn carriage.

Yes, I saw Teddy Roosevelt driving in his car. I stood near Woodrow Wilson, in the White House, while he signed a bill my father sponsored. I watched the "Suffragette Parade" on Pennsylvania Avenue. I met Champ Clark, and Bob LaFollette, and Knute Nelson of Minnesota. In Washington one lived with famous figures, saw history in the making. But one forgot about the sunsets, and lost the feel of branch to muscle.

It was near Washington that I attended my first air meet. Mother and I rode out of the city to Fort Myer, Virginia, where a half-dozen airplanes were lined up in front of the plank-built grandstand. We waited a long time while engines were tuned up and mechanics puttered around the wings. Then, one of the planes took off and raced a motor car around the oval track in front of us. You could see its pilot clearly, out in front — pants' legs flapping, and cap visor pointed backward to streamline in the wind. Another plane bombed the chalked outline of a battleship, with oranges thrown down by hand. A third had a forced landing in the woods half a mile or so away. I could see it banking as it dropped below treetops, and a lot of men began running toward the place where it went down.

The altimeter shows 7500 feet. Stars are brighter and there are more of them. That means I'm gaining on the storm. And the throttle isn't yet wide open; I still have a reserve of power. It's surprising how well the *Spirit of St. Louis* climbs at this altitude, with nearly 300 gallons in the tanks. Three hundred gallons is the biggest load I took off with during the test flights at Camp Kearney. It's 50 gallons more than I carried when I left North Island for the nonstop flight over the Rockies to St. Louis.

THE FOURTEENTH HOUR
Over the Atlantic
TIME — 8:52 P.M.

WIND VELOCITY	*Unknown*	VISIBILITY	*Night—*
WIND DIRECTION	*Unknown*		*heavy haze*
TRUE COURSE	66°	ALTITUDE	9300 *feet*
VARIATION	33° *W.*	AIR SPEED	85 *m.p.h.*
MAGNETIC COURSE	99°	TACHOMETER	1700 *r.p.m.*
DEVIATION	0°	OIL TEMPERATURE	35° *C.*
COMPASS COURSE	99°	OIL PRESSURE	60 *lbs.*
DRIFT ANGLE	10° *R.*	FUEL PRESSURE	3 *lbs.*
COMPASS HEADING	89°	MIXTURE	4
CEILING	*Unlimited above clouds*	FUEL TANK	*Nose*

Thirteen hundred miles behind. Two thousand three hundred miles to go. I finish the log entries and switch off the electric torch. Its light so blinded my night-accustomed eyes that minutes seem to pass before they see stars again. The clouds are still within a few hundred feet of my wheels. There's no doubt now that a storm area lies ahead. I keep climbing slowly, higher and higher, rising to meet it, thankful it didn't come before a third of my fuel's gone. What kind of storm will it be, how large, how high, how turbulent? Will my still overloaded plane have ceiling enough to climb above its clouds?

How high do storm clouds usually rise? We mail pilots often discuss that question, and ideas vary. To start an argument at the airport lunch stand or on a hangar evening, one need only to ask how high the average storm ascends.

"Higher than your plane can fly," a pilot will answer.

"At ten thousand feet you can get around most of them," claims another.

Somebody always expresses the opinion that a man's a fool to go up over them at all. "When a storm gets so bad you can't stay under it, you'd better find a field and land."

After the discussion is over, you go away with little more knowledge than you had when you arrived — and more respect for storms. The fact is that pilots seldom venture to fly above large areas of unbroken cloud. After all, mail planes have no radio, and their fuel ranges are short. When a pilot leaves ground contact far behind, the odds against him mount. Most of us can think of storms into which we ventured beyond prudence, and from which we escaped with narrow margins. We remember the times, too many of them, when someone took off into thick weather and never returned. Such incidents caution us against recurring boldness.

It's only a few months ago that the Detroit plane flew into a tornado, and told its story through the silent sky over the Chicago mail field when its arrival time came due. I flew in from the south that same evening, through storms and between layers of clouds. Ahead — black, tremendous, pyramided in the heavens, I saw the edge of the tornado. Those clouds had gone up more than 10,000 feet — more than 20,000; their tops had merged with thin cirrus tails that must have been five miles above the ground. But that was a tornado, and one expects tornados to do freak things.

I think of the stormy night in Illinois when I made my fourth emergency 'chute jump. The clouds were above 10,000 feet that time too. I'd climbed higher and higher, through lightning, turbulence, and whipping rain, running my fuel tanks dry to keep the mail from burning when it crashed, hoping to see the sky once more before I jumped. If I could see the stars, I'd thought, I wouldn't mind so much diving out into the storm. One gained such confidence from the stars. A single minute in their light was all I needed. But only once had I caught a glimpse of them, from the bottom of a giant funnel in the clouds. They'd blinked on for me one, two, possibly three seconds, and then were gone for good. The gray walls of that funnel had stretched upward to a hopeless height. The storm must have reached at least 20,000 feet above the ground that night; I never knew, for my reserve tank ran dry at 14,000 and I stepped over the side of my cockpit, into space.

How high should I climb tonight? When should I stop reaching for the stars, take fate as it comes, strike directly at the demons of the storm and plunge into their realm of misty blackness? I'll climb to 15,000 feet, I decide, and no higher. Above that altitude, air's too light to support efficiency of either plane or pilot. My engine would drop in power, my wings would grasp for substance, and lack of oxygen would dull perception when difficult flying required still more alertness.

No, if clouds rise above 15,000 feet, I'll throttle down again, reset my stabilizer, and sink into the body of the storm.

My eyes on the stars, I travel with their light-years back through time. I'm in the railroad station at Detroit. Escaping steam from the locomotive dampens my cheek as I wave good-by to its engineer and pass its great steel wheels and driving rods. There he is at the gate, a little to one side of the crowd, face beaming, familiar white mustache and gold-rimmed spectacles, an old black felt hat raised high in his hand to attract our attention—Grand-father! I can see the bald spot on his head where an organ grinder's monkey once tried to crack a peanut. He's not tall, and he never elbows his way to the front, but he's always there to meet us when we arrive. He takes a suitcase in each hand as he greets my mother, and we start toward the streetcar.

"Charles, we're having smelts for dinner," he says, "and you and I are going over to Canada this Sunday, to pick some flowers."

It's half a block from the car line to the gray frame house at 64 West Elizabeth Street. Lilac bushes by the steps are in full bloom, fresh against the city's carboned earth and sooty walls. We turn in off the flagstones and stop in front of the low porch, while my grandfather searches for his key ring. There's a metal plaque on the door, which says "C. H. LAND, DENTIST." The whole place is dwarfed, and partly hidden, by brick-walled apartments on each side.

Inside, I rush back to the kitchen to find my grandmother. There are the steps my tricycle once rolled down. There's the stuffed head of the big Rocky Mountain sheep that I use as a target for my unloaded rifle. Here's the safe which holds platinum foil and bright sheets of dental gold. And now I pass the cabinet full of polished stones and fossils. On one of its shelves there is a piece of a mammoth's tooth! Each wall and corner has its treasures, to be recounted through the days ahead. I'll get my uncle to open the box with the human skull, to fight with my cannon and leaden soldiers, to show me the latest rocks he's brought from his mining claim in Canada. There are my old toy fire engines, high on the back hallway shelf. There's Grandmother, smiling and getting up from the kitchen table, and at her feet my battle-scarred tomcat, Fluff.

Next, upstairs to wriggle out of my traveling suit and into clothes which can be rubbed against the black grime of central Detroit. My grandparents have struggled futilely against that grime. Years ago Grandfather invented an air-conditioning system for the house — big wooden frames of cheesecloth through which an elec-tric fan sucked air, scrubbing it clean of soot. But dirt soon clogged the layers of cloth, and seeped in through cracks with wind, until washing and dusting seemed to spread it rather than keep shelves and windows clean. As the city's factories increased in size and number, even the leaves on trees grew dark; and in spite of my grandmother's effort white lace curtains turned gray.

Grandfather is a scientist who invents all sorts of things, from baby-rockers to high temperature gas furnaces. His specialty is the development of porcelain dentistry. The basement and half the rooms on the ground floor of his house are filled with tools, machinery, and chemicals. The walls of these laboratories enclose a unique world. Here, I live amid turning wheels, the intense heat of muffle furnaces, the precise fashioning of gold and platinum, and talk about the latest discoveries of science.

My Grandfather is as wise as he is old, and he can make *any-thing* with his hands. Whether he's baking a delicate porcelain flower or building a bridge for the mouth of one of his patients, he's always ready to answer my questions and teach me the use of his tools. He has given me the freedom of his laboratories, restricting only the most delicate instruments and dangerous chemicals from my use. He shows me how to mix clay and make moulds, how to cast metal, to handle electrically charged wires, to polish my Minnesota carnelians on his dental wheels. The benches we work on are littered with forceps and plaster casts, patterns for gas furnaces, old teeth, blowpipes, and bottles with dust-covered labels. One always has to clear off a space in which to work. Grandmother just turns her back on the laboratory. She knows there's no use trying to keep it clean, and that Grandfather is happy there.

At dinner table, I listen to discussions of philosophy and the latest scientific theories. I can appreciate, even when I can't understand, the clear-cut language of science. It doesn't hum in my ears like a church sermon or a political speech. People have been preaching about God and arguing about government for hundreds of years, and still they don't agree about who's right and who's wrong. Science isn't like that. It confronts opinion with facts. In science men are measured by what they really do. There's no unfairness about it. It doesn't matter whether you believe in God, or whether you are a Republican or a Democrat. Your experiment works, or it doesn't. A machine will run, or it won't. You can't prove that the atheists are wrong, and you can't prove that the Democrats are wrong, but the arguments of science can't be denied when an airplane actually flies or a human voice is carried from one city to another without wires.

Science is a key to all mystery. With this key, man can become like a god himself. Science is truth; science is knowledge; science is power. With its telescopes it reaches out to the stars. With its microscopes it's learning the innermost secrets of life. By its growing proofs of evolution, it's confounding preachers with their fables of Adam and Eve. When I grow up maybe I'll become a scientist, too.

There are times when my grandfather is disturbed about science. He gives me nickels to go to the theater on Woodward Avenue where new "moving" pictures are replacing still slides on the screen. But he says the films may have a bad effect on boys and girls — for some reason they show life as it isn't, and as it shouldn't be. Detroit is becoming the automobile center of the world, he tells me proudly; but he's concerned about what automobiles will do to people and their homes. The time will come when every family will own a car, according to Henry Ford; but there are too many accidents on the streets — collisions, and men killed. Grandfather often passes by a wreck on his daily walks, and sometimes he brings back a broken spoke or a piece of glass to illustrate the story he tells about it. I remember him saying once, after he'd seen several accidents close together, that maybe evolution would limit the growth of the automobile. It might be, and he'd laughed a little when he said it, that automobile drivers would be killed off so fast there wouldn't be any left some day.

I don't understand evolution. It's all mixed up with dinosaurs and stone-age men. But science says it's true. And if it's true, that may prove there isn't any God. If men descended from apes, they didn't begin with Adam and Eve. The answer seems to depend on "the missing link." That's an old skull, half ape and half man. And Grandfather thinks that some day they'll find it. Then the Bible would be proved wrong. And if it lies about Adam and the Garden of Eden, how can one trust what it says about Heaven and hell, and God?

These problems continued to throb in my mind through years beyond childhood. Is there a God? Is there an existence after life? Is there something within one's body that doesn't age with years? There were times when I considered taking up the study of biology and medicine so I could explore the mysteries of life and death. But these sciences belonged to well-grounded, brilliant minds; their study was intricate, and my school marks were poor in the subjects they demanded as a background.

Our family travels made it difficult to be a good student. My mother and I always arrived in Washington after classes started in the fall, and left before they ended in the spring. Up to the time I entered college I had never completed a full academic year. It was true, too, that I didn't study very hard; and in class my mind was often far away from the subject being taught.

Of course if I'd been interested enough in biology, I suppose I'd have got down to business and passed my exams with better marks. After all, I came from a family of physicians on my mother's side. My grand-uncle Edwin was the doctor in attendance at my birth. He worried my mother by saying I had the biggest feet he'd ever seen. He took me for my first ride in an automobile, weaving back and forth marvelously through the streets of Detroit, between calls on his patients. He prescribed medicine for my colds, and bound up my hand when it was hurt.

My grand-uncle Gus was a doctor in Milford, Michigan. That was far enough away to make visiting difficult. But grand-uncle Albert lived only about three blocks distant, after my grandparents moved to Elizabeth Street. He was a huge man, muscular and gruff; but everybody liked him. I bicycled up to his office-home whenever I had the chance. He showed me his medical specimens, and gave me sugar pills. I never saw him when it happened, but Mother said he used to lose his temper on occasions. Once he was riding on a

Detroit streetcar and the motorman didn't pay attention when he rang the bell. The same thing had happened before, too often. Grand-uncle Albert walked to the front of the car, smashed the glass face of the fare register with his gloved fist, and said — as the astounded motorman jammed on brakes — "Maybe you'll stop the next time I ring." There was a note of admiration in my mother's voice whenever she told the story; but she usually added that it was wrong of my grand-uncle to do it.

Our family thought that Grand-uncle Albert inherited his quick temper from Great-grandmother Emma. She had been a beautiful girl, of southern Irish ancestry, whom Great-grandfather Edwin Lodge met and married in Canada.

We were all proud of Great-grandfather Edwin. He'd been one of the best doctors in Detroit, and a very active man. In addition to attending to a big practice, he ran a pharmacy, published the *Homeopathic Observer* and fathered eleven children in two marriages. He was extremely religious, our family thought. In his Bible he underlined all the words of Christ in red, and all those of the Disciples in blue. He used to write the Lord's Prayer on a piece of paper the size of a dime to entertain his grandchildren, and at the same time demonstrate his expert penmanship. Often on a Sunday he preached in a little wooden church on the shore of Orchard Lake, not far from a farm he purchased. My mother tells of seeing him wade out into the cold water to baptize new members of the congregation. No sprinkling on the head for him. He believed in ducking them right under.

Being a physician, Great-grandfather Edwin must have lived in close contact with both life and death. There didn't seem to be any conflict in his mind between science and God. His studies of biology didn't convince him that all existence ends with the flesh. He had faith in some quality that is independent of the body.

It's hard to be an agnostic up here in the *Spirit of St. Louis*, aware of the frailty of man's devices, a part of the universe between its earth and stars. If one dies, all this goes on existing in a plan so perfectly balanced, so wonderfully simple, so incredibly complex that it's far beyond our comprehension — worlds and moons revolving; planets orbiting on suns; suns flung with apparent recklessness through space. There's the infinite magnitude of the universe; there's the infinite detail of its matter — the outer star, the inner atom. And man conscious of it all — a worldly audience to what if not to God?

It's nine o'clock. I've reached an altitude of ten thousand feet. Clouds are still rising up to meet me, but the undulating plain they formed in early evening has given way to a foothill country of the sky. Passing over a misty summit, looking down onto a night-filled valley, I wonder what mountains lie ahead. It's cold at this altitude. I zip the flying suit up across my chest. It's cold enough for mittens and my wool-lined helmet, too, but not cold enough to put on flying boots, at least not yet — I'll let them go until later. Too much warmth would make me want, still more, to sleep.

I must straighten out my neck before it cramps permanently in this thrown-back position. I turn from the constellations of the stars to those of the instrument dials. I fix my eyes now on the glowing dots an arm's length before me, now on the points of fire millions of miles away. I travel with their vision back and forth. I feel first the compactness and detailed contents of my cockpit, my dependence on its instruments and levers, the personal proximity of its fabric walls; next, the unlimited expanse and solitude of space. Now, my plane is all-important, and life is vulnerable within it; now, neither it nor life is of any consequence at all, and consciousness seems unbound to either one.

As I fly through the body of night, haze lessens, and I discover that I'm among the cloud mountains themselves — great shadowy forms on every side, dwarfing my plane, dwarfing earthly mountains with their magnitude, awesome in their weird, fantastic shapes. Huge pillars push upward thousands of feet above the

common mass. Black valleys and chasms open below me to un-
fathomed depth.

There's no possibility of flying above those mountains. They
look higher than any clouds I ever saw before. How have I come
into their midst without knowing they were there? I must have
followed a great valley, blinded by the mist. Or did these sky
giants draw aside to entice me among them, and close in again
now that they have me hopelessly entrapped? Well, if I can't follow
the valleys, I'll have to challenge the mountains themselves. Flying through an occasional thunderhead will be less tiring than
spending hours on end down in the writhing body of the storm. A
few minutes of blind flying followed by relaxation under a star-
filled sky is nothing much to dread. It may even be a welcome
change, sharpen my dulled senses, break up the monotony of
routine flight.

Then I'll hold my course, stay above the stratus layer of the
storm, and tunnel through the thunderheads that rise directly on
my route.

A pillar of cloud blocks out the stars ahead, spilling over on
top like a huge mushroom in the sky. I tighten my belt, push the
nose down a bit, and adjust the stablizer for level flight. In the
seconds that intervene while I approach, I make the mental and
physical preparation for blind flying.

The body must be informed sternly that the mind will take
complete control. The senses must be drafted and lined up in
strictest discipline, while logic replaces instinct as commander. If
the body feels a wing dropping, and the mind says it is not (because
the turn indicator's ball and needle are still centered), the muscles
must obey the mind's decision no matter how wrong it seems to
them. If the eyes imagine the flicker of a star below where they
think the horizon ought to be, if the ears report the engine's tempo
too slow for level flight, if the nerves say the seat back's pressure
is increasing (as it does in a climb), the hands and the feet must
still be loyal to the orders of the mind.

It's a terrific strain on the mind also when it turns from long-proven bodily instincts to the cold, mechanical impartiality of needles moving over dials. For countless centuries, it's been accustomed to relying on the senses. They can keep the body upright on the darkest night. They're trained to catch a stumble in an instant. Deprived of sight, they can still hold a blind man's balance. Why, then, should they be so impotent in an airplane?

The mind must operate as mechanically as the gyroscope which guides it. The muscles must move as unfeelingly as gears. If the senses get excited and out of control, the plane will follow them, and that can be fatal. If the senses break ranks while everything is going right, it may be impossible, with the plane falling dizzily and needles running wild, to bring them back into line, reinstruct them, and force them to gain control while everything is going wrong. It would be like rallying a panicked army under the fire of an advancing enemy. Like an army under fire, blind flying requires absolute discipline. That must be fully understood before it starts.

Wings quiver as I enter the cloud. Air roughens until it jerks the *Spirit of St. Louis* about as though real demons were pulling at fuselage and wings. No stars are overhead now to help, no clouds are below. Everything is uniform blackness, except for the exhaust's flash on passing mist and the glowing dials in my cockpit, so different from all other lights. What lies outside doesn't matter. My world and my life are compressed within these fabric walls.

Flying blind is difficult enough in smooth air. In this swirling cloud, it calls for all the concentration I can muster. The turn and bank indicators, the air speed, the altimeter, and the compass, all those phosphorescent lines and dots in front of me, must be kept in proper place. When a single one strays off, the rest go chasing after it like so many sheep, and have to be caught quickly and carefully herded back into position again.

Remember that flight with the mail last winter — I don't want to go through anything like that up here. I was racing nightfall and a storm to Peoria. Both arrived ahead of me. Caught, skimming treetops, in snow so thick I couldn't see lights half a mile away, I had to decide between cutting the switches and crashing onto whatever lay below, and giving up the earth to climb into the storm. The ceiling wasn't high enough to drop a flare. If I'd been over an area of fields, I might have landed by the vague outlines of late dusk — taken the risk of gullies, scattered trees, and fences. But I was close to the Illinois River, where patches of woodland are thick. And DHs have a reputation for burning when they crash — "Flaming Coffins," they're called. A pilot has about a fifty-fifty chance of living through a landing under such conditions. But to pull up blindly into the storm was almost as dangerous.

I had in my DH a new device for blind flying — a gyroscopic pitch-and-turn indicator. One of the transcontinental pilots had been experimenting with it, and wished to replace it with a more recently constructed mechanism. I'd persuaded our Corporation to buy the instrument from him. Here was the emergency for which I'd wanted it. The trouble was that it had been installed in my plane only a few days before, and I'd had no chance to test it out.

Instrument flying was new. I'd never flown blind, except for a few minutes at a time in high clouds. Could I keep my plane under control? If I turned to the instruments, how could I make contact with the ground again? Night had closed in behind me as well as ahead, and there was a low ceiling over both Springfield and St. Louis. Besides, even if I found a hole in the clouds, even if I saw the lights of a village farther on, how could I tell where I was, how could I locate the Chicago airfield — unless the ceiling there were much higher? "A good pilot doesn't depend on his instruments," I was taught that when I learned to fly.

All these arguments had passed through my mind — harsh impact of earth, splintering wood, ripping fabric, bruised body; versus hurtling, dizzy blindness, lost in the storm. Suddenly, the vague blur of treetops rushing past at eighty miles an hour, a hundred feet below, jumped up in a higher mass — a hillside? I didn't wait to find out. I pulled the stick back, gave up the ground, and turned to my instruments — untrusted needles, rising, falling, leaning right and left.

At a thousand feet, my DH was out of control — skidding, and losing altitude. Altitude was the thing above all else I had to hold. I shoved the throttle wide open, pushed rudder toward the skid, and pulled the stick back farther. The altimeter needle slowed — stopped — started to climb; but air still rushed sideways across my cockpit. It seemed there were more needles than my eyes could watch. There wasn't time for my mind to formulate orders and pass them on to hands and feet. Finally I got the DH headed straight and the wings leveled out. I thought I was getting my plane in hand. The altimeter went up to 1500 feet. But then — she whipped! Loose controls — laboring engine — trembling wings — the final snap as the nose dropped. I shoved the stick forward, but it was too late. While I was concentrating on turn and bank, I'd let my air speed get too low, and the wings stalled.

A whipstall at 1500 feet, with nothing but needles by which to orient myself! Stick neutral – – – leave the nose down long enough to pick up control – – – throttle still wide open – – – let the air speed rise to 80 miles – – – Stick back firmly – – – not too fast – – – Watch the altimeter (before the needle touches zero, you'll be dead) – – – 900 feet – – – 800 feet – – – 700 feet (it steadies) – – – 700 – – – 750 – – – it starts to climb.

By then I'd learned that above all else it was essential to keep the turn indicator centered and the air-speed needle high. But in recovering I pulled the stick back too far and held it back too long. The DH whipped again, this time at only 1200 feet. But I made my recovery a little quicker. I'd decided to jump the moment the wings trembled in the stall, if my plane started to whip a third time. But I regained control after the second whip, and climbed slowly, and taught myself to fly by instruments that night.

It's cold up here at — I glance at the altimeter — 10,500 feet – – – *cold* – – – good Lord, there *are* things to be considered outside the cockpit! How could I forget! I jerk off a leather mitten and thrust my arm out the window. My palm is covered with stinging pinpricks. I pull the flashlight from my pocket and throw its beam onto a strut. The entering edge is irregular and shiny — *ice!* And as far out into darkness as the beam penetrates, the night is filled with countless, horizontal, threadlike streaks. The venturi tubes may clog at any moment!

I've got to turn around, get back into clear air — quickly! But in doing so those instrument needles mustn't move too far or too fast. Mind, not body, must control the turn. My bodily senses want to whip the *Spirit of St. Louis* into a bank and dive it out of the thunderhead, back into open sky:

"Kick rudder hard — no time to lose — the turn indicator's icing up right now."

But the mind retorts, "Steady, steady. It's easy enough to get into a steep bank, but more difficult to get out of one and on your course again. If you turn too fast, you'll lose more time than you save; the plane may get entirely out of control."

"If the turn indicator ices up, it'll get out of control anyway. There's no time — only a few seconds — quick — quick — harder rudder — kick it — — — "

"Don't do anything of the sort. I've thought all this out carefully and know just what's best to do. You remember, you are to obey my orders!"

"Yes, yes — but just a little faster, then — just a little — — — "

"No, no faster; turn just the right amount. You're to do exactly what I say; no more, no less!"

"Just a little!"

"No, none!"

I keep pressing rudder cautiously until the turn indicator's needle creeps a quarter-inch to the left. I push the stick over just enough to hold the proper bank — ball high — low — center again — slow and steady movements — mustn't let jerks from the turbulence throw me off — — — The air speed drops ten miles an hour — — — The altimeter shows a hundred foot descent — — —

"Turn faster! You see the air speed's dropping. It's ice doing that! Quick, or it'll be too late!"

"No, it's not ice — at least not very likely. It's probably just the normal slowing down in a bank."

"But the altimeter's dropping too! It's ice, I tell you!"

I open the throttle another 50 revolutions. I don't dare push the stick forward very much to gain speed. The *Spirit of St. Louis* is too close to the top of the main cloud layer. There were less than a thousand feet to spare when I entered the thunderhead. That endless stratus layer is probably full of ice too. If I drop down into it, I may never see the stars again.

The altimeter needle falls 200 feet – – – 300 feet – – – I push the throttle wide open – – – I *must* stay above that vast layer of cloud at the thunderhead's base – – – The bank indicator shows a skid — ball to right of center — a blast of air strikes my cheek — Ease up on the rudder – – – The air speed rises to 100 miles an hour – – – The pitch indicator points nose down – – – Stick back slightly – – –

I ought to be turned around now — Center the turn indicator — level out the plane — flashlight onto the liquid compass. (It's no time to trust the earth-inductor; it will be working backward anyhow, on a back-track heading.) No, not yet — about 30 degrees more to go — the card's swinging too much to read accurately.

I bank again and glance at the altimeter — 10,300 feet. Good — it's gone up a little. I throw my flashlight onto the wing strut. Ice is thicker!

The earth-inductor needle begins moving backward, jumping erratically – – – Level out wings – – – About the right heading this time. Now, if the turn indicator doesn't ice up for a few minutes more – – – I put my hand out the window again – – – the pinpricks are still there.

Steady the plane. Make the compass card stop swinging – – – but the air's too rough – – – Is the turn-indicator getting sluggish — icing? – – – It seems to move back and forth more slowly – – – Everything depends on its working till I get outside this cloud – – – Just two or three more minutes – – –

My eyes sense a change in the blackness of my cockpit. I look out through the window. Can those be the same stars? Is this the same sky? How bright! How clear! What safety I have reached! Bright, clear, safe? But this is the same hazy air I left, the same fraction of an earthly hour. I've simply been existing in a different frame of space and time. Values are relative, dependent on one's circumstance. They change from frame to frame, and as one travels back and forth between them. Here I've found security where I left danger, flying over a major storm, above a frigid northern ocean. Here's something I never saw before — the brilliant light of a black night.

I was in the thunderhead for ten minutes at most; but it's one of those incidents that can't be measured by minutes. Such periods stand out like islands in a sea of time. It's not the limitless vista of experience, not hours or years that are most important. It's the islands, no matter how small. They impress the senses as they draw the eye at sea. Against them, years roll in and break, as waves upon a coast.

How much ice has accumulated on the plane? I move my flashlight from one spot to another. There's none on the bottom surface of the wing; but a thin layer forward on the strut tells me that it's also clinging to the airfoil's entering edge. I can't see that from my cockpit. There's not enough weight to make much difference, but what about resistance? Will the change in contours have great effect on speed? The air-speed needle shows a five-mile drop. Is it because of ice on the Pitot tube, or the increased drag of the plane? Have those few minutes in the cloud cost me five miles an hour cruising? That seems a heavy penalty to pay.

I turn southward, skirting the edge of the cloud pillar. I'll have to fly around these thunderheads. But can I? There are more masses ahead, and fewer stars. Will they merge into one great citadel of storm? Will I follow up a canyon in the heavens, as I often have done on earth, to see it disappear against a mountain ridge? Or can I find real passes in these clouds, as I've found them in the mountains, where a plane can slip between the icy walls?

By day, I could set my course from the edge of one pillar directly to the next ahead, cutting down the angles of my zigzag route. But in the blackness of night, and in the haze that still cóntaminates the sky, one cloud merges into another miles behind it so I can't distinguish edge from center point. I have to bank as I approach, and follow around the vague wall of mist until I can again take up my compass heading.

Would it be wiser to change my course entirely, and try to fly around the whole storm area, as I'm now flying around its single columns? That's what my fuel reserve is for. Is this the emergency in which to use it? The ship lanes lie three hundred miles to the southward. Clear weather was reported there. But that report is getting old. It's almost fourteen hours since I took off from Roosevelt Field, and most of the weather messages were assembled some time before I left. They told of yesterday's weather, not today's. An unknown storm may have drifted over the ship lanes hours ago. "A high pressure area over the North Atlantic" can't last forever. Stars in the southern sky outline a ridge of cloud fully as high as lies ahead. And to the north? It's the same. I lean to the side of my cockpit and look back at the sky behind. It too is blocked out for thousands of feet above the level where I'm flying.

Great cliffs tower over me, ward me off with icy walls. They belong to mountains of another world, mountains with forms that change; with summits that overhang; mountains alluring in their softness. There'd be no rending crash if my wing struck one of them. They carry a subtler death. A crash against an earthly mountain is like a sword stroke; one flash and it's over. But to plunge into these mountains of the heavens would be like stepping into quicksand. They enmesh intruders. They're barbaric in their methods. They toss you in their inner turbulence, lash you with their hailstones, poison you with freezing mist. It would be a slow death, a death one would have long minutes to struggle against, trying blindly to regain control of an ice-crippled airplane, climbing, stalling, diving, whipping, always downward toward the sea.

For the first time, the thought of turning back seriously enters my mind. I can climb another five or six thousand feet. The canyons up there may be wider. If they're not, and I can find no passes east or southward, I'll have to turn back — back through the haze-filled valleys behind me, back over Newfoundland, over those ice fields, over Nova Scotia, over New England, over the stretches of ocean between them, back fourteen hundred miles to New York, back for another start from that narrow, muddy runway on Long Island. And when I got back, if I could find my way out through the maze of passageways I've entered, if fog hasn't re-formed along the American coast, if that other storm in Nova Scotia hasn't blocked my route, then, after bucking the wind which has been carrying me along so swiftly, I'd have been about thirty hours in the air — long enough to reach Ireland, if I can keep on heading eastward. Think of flying long enough to reach Ireland, and ending up at Roosevelt Field!

Of course I could try diving quickly to a lower level, where the air may be too warm for ice to form. My mind grasps at the thought of a secret portal to the storm, a passageway deep down in the clouds. Might it lead me through to safety and the light of day again? Hours of blind flying seem less formidable, now — if they're free of ice.

No, it would be a fool's chance; the danger is too great. As far north as Newfoundland and in the cold of night, icing conditions probably extend down to the waves themselves. There's no reason to believe I'd find a ceiling underneath the clouds; and once I got down into their lower levels, ice would clog my instruments long before I could climb back up again.

The pillars of cloud multiply and thicken. I follow narrow canyons between them, weaving in and out around thunderheads, taking always the southward choice for course, edging toward the ship lanes and what I hope is clearer weather. Dark forms blot out the sky on every side, but stars drop down to guide me through the passes.

THE FIFTEENTH HOUR
Over the Atlantic
TIME — 9:52 P.M.

WIND VELOCITY	*Unknown*	VISIBILITY	*Night—haze*
WIND DIRECTION	*Unknown*	ALTITUDE	10,500 *feet*
TRUE COURSE	66°	AIR SPEED	87 *m.p.h.*
VARIATION	33° *W.*	TACHOMETER	1700 *r.p.m.*
MAGNETIC COURSE	99°	OIL TEMPERATURE	35° *C.*
DEVIATION	0°	OIL PRESSURE	60 *lbs.*
COMPASS COURSE	99°	FUEL PRESSURE	3 *lbs.*
DRIFT ANGLE	10° *R.*	MIXTURE	4
COMPASS HEADING	89°	FUEL TANK	*Fuselage*
CEILING	*Unlimited above clouds*		

Fourteen hundred miles behind. Twenty-two hundred miles to go. All readings normal. I make the log entries and throw my flashlight onto the wing strut again. The coating of ice is thinner. It's evaporating slowly. When will it all be gone — in an hour, two, or five? I don't know. I've never picked up ice before on a flight long enough to consider its evaporation. When ice collected on our mail planes it stayed with us till we landed. Then we had either to wait until it melted, or peel it off the wings with our hands and beat it off the wires with a stick.

The haze continues to clear. I can see cloud formations farther away, fly closer to their walls, follow a straighter course through their valleys. There's another mushroomed column, miles ahead. Its top silhouettes against a star-brightening sky. I bank toward the southern edge, and settle back in my cockpit.

In keeping his heading by the stars, a pilot must remember that they move. In all the heavens, there is only one he can trust, only one that won't lead him off his course — Polaris, faint star of the northern pole. Those other more brilliant points of light, which at

first seem motionless too, sweep through their arcs so rapidly that
he can use them only as temporary guides, lining one up ahead,
letting it creep to the side, dropping the first to pick a second;
then the second for a third; and so on through the night.

As a child, I'd lie on my bed in Minnesota and watch the stars
curve upward in their courses — the box-like corners of Orion's
Belt — Sirius's piercing brilliance — rising over treetops, climbing
slowly toward our roof. I would curl up under my blankets and
web the constellations into imaginary scenes of celestial magnitude
— a flock of geese in westward flight — God's arrow shooting
through the sky. I'd make my wishes on the stars, and drift from
wakefulness to sleep as I desired. Dreams of day and dreams of
night could merge, while a planet's orbit had no effect on my
security. There was no roar of an engine in my ears, no sound
above the wind in leaves except the occasional whistle of a train,
far away across the river.

That whistle was the only note to break the peace of night,
to connect me to the modern world in which fate and my father's
business made me spend my winters. That train would carry me
back to Washington in September, as it carried me westward to
our farm in June. It followed the steel cords which tied marble
buildings and deliberative halls to my fields and rolling hills a
thousand miles away – – – Washington – – – Detroit – – – my
sleeping porch in Minnesota – – –

Wheels clatter on tracks. The tempo changes as our train
curves, and brakes across the bridge. Down river, over those long
stretches of white rapids, I see the great tops of Norway pine that
mark our farm. Our train slows, jerks, stops — "L-l-l-ittle-e-e
Fa-a-a-l-l-l-s." I jump after the conductor, down onto the board
walk, and turn to wait for my mother. Winter's school is over.
Summer has come; and with it, our Minnesota home.

It's a two-mile walk to our farm — past Martin Engstrom's
hardware store, past Wilsczek's butcher shop, past the swinging-
doored saloons. We stop at Ferguson's grocery to order food for

the week. Along with it, the one-horse delivery cart will bring our suitcases and trunk.

Our road bends south around the yellow brick church, still waiting for its steeple; then west to the Coultas home where my dog has spent the winter. From a flower-filled yard with picket gate he bounces out to meet me — red-haired, white-chested, barking, wriggling Dingo.

We start down the sandy street together. Soon I'll be out of city clothes — in overalls, barefooted. Here's the path through hazel brush — green leaves, ear-switching branches. Here's the short cut through the gravel pit where I sometimes find carnelians. Here we strike real country, for the telephone poles stop. There's where wagon wheels spoiled the bicycle path last summer; it's still sandy and soft. "La-a-l-l-y bo-o-o-s-s-y. La-a-l-l-y bo-o-o-s-s-y" — the Sandstrom girls are calling in their cattle. Here's the Johnson farm, with its pasture rolling over to the river — the brindle cow staked out in thick green grass.

Now, the road jogs away from the river to take in a strip of woodland. It widens and straightens for its half-mile stretch southward between the white-cedar fence posts of our farm. There's our gray barn, and the tenant's horses. Trees and flowering honeysuckle bushes screen our house. I throw open the iron gate, run under oaks and poplars along a deeply shaded footpath, feet kicking through last October's leaves. Short-tail, my pet chipmunk, scampers into his rock pile beside the back porch steps.

I turn the key in the padlock, jerk open the rusting hasp, push through our kitchen door. Dingo wedges past my legs, and Mother is close behind. A cool, musty smell surrounds us. There's been no one in the house all winter — unless some thieves have entered, as they did two years ago. I rush through rooms and basement, examining door and window locks. We throw everything wide open, let wind flood through our house. We light the cookstove, start unpacking boxes, closets, shelves. Between tasks I run out to see that the swing ropes have not been stolen, that the tree seat hasn't blown away, that the cave roof hasn't tumbled in, that I can still keep my balance on my stilts. There's the maidenhair patch to visit, the bluffs on the creek to slide down. There are neighbors' boys to swim and play with under noonday suns ahead. I have my guns to clean and hawks to hunt. Dingo has gophers to catch.

I bolt my mother's lunch of salad, preserves, and breaded round steak, and start up the river path toward Alex Johnson's home. Birds flutter out of grass and call from branches. A rabbit leaves its clump of brush for safer briers. Crows warn all the woods of my approach. This path the Chippewa once followed. These mounds of earth they may have built. With luck, one sometimes finds an agate arrowhead.

Mrs. Johnson, slight and wrinkled, waves from the kitchen, where she's planning supper for her family of seven. She offers me a pan of freshly baked sprits cakes. Mrs. Johnson still speaks with an "old country" accent. "I think Alex is cleaning out the barn," she says.

A blond-haired boy emerges from the red-plank building at the roadside, leaning steeply backward to balance the forkload of manure in his hands. I run down to meet him.

"Alex! Can ya go swimmin'?"

"Yah, I guess so, but I gotta clean the barn."

We finish the work together.

"Let's go pick up Bill."

Bill Thompson's house lies back in the woods, a quarter-mile to the west, in a stumpy clearing. It's a five-minute walk, if one hurries, along a grass-centered, little-traveled road. Alex captures a garter snake. I put it in my pocket.

Bill is in the yard, target-shooting with his older brother's rifle. The firing pin has been lost, but he's replaced it with a clipped-off shingle nail.

"How about goin' swimmin'?"

Bill runs in to stack his gun against the kitchen wall, and we start back toward the river.

"Let's go out to the log jam by the dryin' rock."

We push our way through cut-grass, and poke sticks under deadheads along the bank. Minnows and crayfish scuttle into deeper water. I almost catch a turtle.

We strip, swim down the current, roll logs, sun-dry, and dress. "Let's go to the creek!"

We climb up hill, crawl over four fences, run through the milk-cow herd, slow down to walk along the old, abandoned road – – –

"She's full up!" Pike creek, in early summer flood, churns against its gravel banks, carries our naked bodies down with its clear and brownish waters – – – Watch the rocks – – – stay away from snags – – – make the bank before the rapids. Pebbles press hard against winter-tendered feet as I pick my way back upstream to the sandbank, and slap a horsefly dead. Dingo yelps in a woodchuck's hole, backs up and sits on a thistle.

The sun is low when we cut across Williams' woods to leave Bill at his home. Ferns reach halfway to our heads. Thick leaves on basswood, oak, and ash shield off the sky. An owl quietly leaves its branch as a red squirrel chatters out our passing.

"A-a-a-lex!" It's Mrs. Johnson's voice.

"G-by. I gotta pump some water."

We lift our arms in parting gesture and I saunter toward the river. My feet ache from miles of walking. My clothes are sweaty from the sun. The water is cool and swift. I know the channel through the rapids; its wake-marked rocks create no threat. I wade out in shoes and clothes, and plunge downstream – – – Light is shallow – – – dark is deep – – – Keep well clear of log jams – – – angle into the current – – – angle back toward shore – – – sidestroke to check the depth.

Now it's twilight, after supper. I'm sitting on porch steps, in dry clothes, my hand on Dingo's velvet ear. Black swallows silhouette against the sky. Tomorrow we can finish our unpacking – – – tonight – – – I'm going to climb in bed – – – and sleep – – –

The earth-inductor compass needle is halfway to the peg! That constellation I've been following has drawn me south of course. I press left rudder, banking the *Spirit of St. Louis* toward its proper heading. The needle moves up slowly, fluctuating; then overshoots the lubber line and drops down on the other side. I kick right rudder. The needle falters upward. I've never seen it act like that before. Is the earth-inductor failing, or am I half asleep and flying badly?

I throw my flashlight on the liquid compass overhead. It, too, is swinging — probably because of the double change in heading. I center the turn-indicator, and hold my nose straight toward a star. But the earth-inductor needle is still top-heavy, and the liquid compass swinging doesn't stop.

Something's seriously wrong. I haven't depended too much on the earth-inductor compass. It's a new and complicated instrument, just past the experimental stage. If it failed completely, I wouldn't be surprised. But the liquid compass! — the whole flight is based on it. It's almost as essential for the liquid compass to work as for the engine to keep running. I never heard of *two* compasses giving out at the same time. The plane must still be turning. There must be something I've overlooked, some simple element I've neglected to consider. I've been sleepy — unobservant — my eyes must be tricking me. But the turn-indicator is centered, and the stars confirm that I'm flying straight.

I look at the liquid compass again, as though trying to steady is by concentration alone. The card is rocking through an arc of more than 60 degrees — more than 90 degrees at times. Is it possible that I'm entering a "magnetic storm"? Most pilots scoff at their existence. They say magnetic storms are figments of imagination, like air pockets — just an excuse for getting lost — an attempt to explain away mistakes in navigation. Do magnetic storms really occur, then? Have I found my way through a labyrinth of cloud only to be confronted with this new, unknown danger? How large are magnetic storms? How long do they last? How far off will they throw a compass card? Do they have a permanent effect on the magnets?

The earth-inductor is hopeless. The needle's wobbling back and forth from peg to peg. There's no use paying any attention to it. But the liquid compass hesitates between oscillations, and remains fairly steady for several seconds at a time. I set my heading by these periods of hesitation, and hold it by the stars — except when a thunderhead gets in the way. As long as the stars are there, I can hold a general easterly direction; but there'll be little accuracy to navigation. God only knows where I'll strike the European coast. But if the liquid compass gets any worse, and high clouds shut off the sky, I won't know whether I'm flying north, south, east, or west. I may wander around in circles.

It would be easier to set a course if I could read the liquid compass without a flashlight. But the luminous figures aren't bright enough for that. While the flashlight's on, I can't see the stars; and it's hard to watch the compass overhead and the instruments on the board at the same time.

On what delicate devices flight depends: a magnetized bar of steel, slender as a pencil lead, reaching for the North Pole thousands of miles away, swinging with each bump of air, subject to the slightest disturbance, barely strong enough to point; yet without its directive force the horsepower of the engine, the aerodynamic qualities of the plane, the skills of the pilot, become meaningless. Detouring thunderheads, flying in an unknown wind ten thousand feet above the water, trying to follow a compass that swings thirty degrees and more off course, what hope have I to make my landfall on the southern Irish coast? In fact, can I expect to find a coast at all?

Last night I couldn't go to sleep – – – Tonight I can barely stay awake – – – If only I could balance the one against the other – – – awake – – – asleep – – – which is it that I want to be? – – – But look – – – there's a great black mass ahead – – – It *necks out toward the route my compass points for me* – – – Its ears stick up – – – its jaws gape wide – – – It's a cloud – – – or – – – maybe it's not a cloud – – – It could be a dragon, or a tiger – – – I could imagine it into anything at all – – – What's that whitish object, moving just beyond the window of my room – – – no, my cockpit – – – no, my room – – – I push goggles up to see more clearly – – – No, they're bedsheets I'm peeking out between – – – I'm in the nursery of my Minnesota home, and I'm afraid of the dark! Yes, I know that jungle animals don't jump through windows in the North. I trust my mother and my father when they tell me. But what *is* *that,* moving slowly, there behind the table? Suppose it *did* leap forth!

Look! – – – it's turning! – – – it's crawling! – – – It's about to spring! Nerve and muscle tense against the terror – – – bed and nursery disappear. I raise my wing and kick left rudder, and watch the compass spin.

Dragons, tigers, jungle animals? How ridiculous! But it's true that I used to be fearful in the dark. It was years before I got completely over it. As a child, I could wander alone, tranquilly, through the most isolated places by the light of day. But at night my mind conjured up drowned bodies on the riverbank, and robbers behind every sumac clump. The reality of life was tame compared to my imagination's fantasies. It was what I couldn't see that frightened me — the python, slithering overhead, the face beyond the curtain. And most of all, the imaginary horrors that took no clear-cut form.

Stars drop lower. Valleys between thunderheads widen. I no longer have to look up through the window on top of the fuselage to find a stable point in space. Clouds tower and slant in bands and layers. Their outlines are sharp — too sharp for clouds at night; and the sky seems lighter. Can it be the first faint warning of the moon's approach? I turn to the south window — the night has a deeper shade. Yes, it must be the morning twilight of the moon — a luminous wash, barely perceptible, on the northeastern wall of night.

But so soon, and so far north! I thought it would rise on the other side of my plane. Have the swinging compasses turned me that many degrees off course? Am I heading for Africa instead of Europe? I hold the *Spirit of St. Louis* straight with the constellation overhead, and watch the liquid compass. No, if the compass is correct during its steady periods, I'm pointed about on course — maybe a little southward, but not over ten degrees, not enough to explain the moon's position unless — unless *both* compasses are *completely* wrong! Maybe the steady periods aren't caused by the magnets pointing toward the pole. Maybe they're the result of some freak vibration. But they can't be very far in error with the North Star in approximate position, high on my left.

I glance at the chart on my lap. Of course I've shortened the night by flying with the earth's rotation. And I've been bending more and more eastward as I follow the great-circle route, cutting each meridian at a greater angle than the last, changing course a degree or two clockwise every hour through the day and night. When I took off from New York, I pointed the *Spirit of St. Louis* northeast; and when the sky cleared, the morning sun beamed down on an angle from my right. But when I reach Paris, I'll be heading south of east, and heavenly bodies will be rising on my left. After all, it's late in May. That's probably where the moon should be for a pilot on the great-circle route.

I'd almost forgotten the moon. Now, like a neglected ally, it's coming to my aid. Every minute will bring improving sight. As the moon climbs higher in the sky, its light will brighten, until finally it ushers in the sun. The stars ahead are already fading. The time is 10:20. There have been only two hours of solid darkness.

Gradually, as light improves, the night's black masses turn into a realm of form and texture. Silhouettes give way to shadings. Clouds open their secret details to the eyes. In the moon's reflected light, they seem more akin to it than to the earth over which they hover. They form a perfect setting for that strange foreign surface one sees through a telescope trained on the satellite of the world. Formations of the moon, they are — volcanoes and flat plateaus; great towers and bottomless pits; crevasses and canyons; ledges no earthly mountains ever knew — reality combined with the fantasy of a dream. There are shapes like growths of coral on the bed of a tropical sea, or the grotesque canyons of sandstone and lava at the edge of Arizona deserts — first black, then gray, now greenish hue in cold, mystical light.

I weave in and out, eastward, toward Europe, hidden away in my plane's tiny cockpit, submerged, alone, in the magnitude of this weird, unhuman space, venturing where man has never been, irretrievably launched on a flight through this sacred garden of the sky, this inner shrine of higher spirits. Am I myself a living, breathing, earth-bound body, or is this a dream of death I'm passing through? Am I alive, or am I really dead, a spirit in a spirit world? Am I actually in a plane boring through the air, over the Atlantic, toward Paris, or have I crashed on some worldly mountain, and is this the afterlife?

For a moment the clouds give way, and the moon itself peers through a tremendous valley, flooding unearthly bluffs with its unearthly light, screening the eastern stars with its nearer, brighter glow, assuming mastery of the sky by night as does the sun by day.

Far ahead, a higher cloud layer is forming, thousands of feet above my level — glowing, horizontal strips, supported by thick pillars from the mass below — sculptured columns and arches to a temple of the moon. Has the sky opened only to close again? Will they finally merge, these clouds, to form one great mass of opaque air? Must I still turn back? *Can* I still turn back, or have I been lured to this forbidden temple to find all doors have closed? North, south, and west, clouds rise and tower; only the lighted corridors ahead are clear.

THE SIXTEENTH HOUR
Over the Atlantic
TIME — 10:52 P.M.

WIND VELOCITY	*Unknown*	VISIBILITY	*Unlimited*
WIND DIRECTION	*Unknown*		*outside of*
TRUE COURSE	69°		*clouds*
VARIATION	33° *W.*	ALTITUDE	10,200 *feet*
MAGNETIC COURSE	102°	AIR SPEED	86 *m.p.h.*
DEVIATION	0°	TACHOMETER	1675 *r.p.m.*
COMPASS COURSE	102°	OIL TEMPERATURE	33° *C.*
DRIFT ANGLE	10° *R.*	OIL PRESSURE	60 *lbs.*
COMPASS HEADING	92°	FUEL PRESSURE	3 *lbs.*
CEILING	*Unlimited*	MIXTURE	4
	above clouds	FUEL TANK	*Fuselage*

Fifteen hundred miles behind. Two thousand one hundred miles to go. I'm halfway to Europe; not halfway across the ocean or halfway to Paris, but halfway between New York and Ireland — and Ireland seems like Europe, though it's really an island lying well out in the Atlantic. If I can reach Ireland in daylight and in clear weather, it should be easy sailing from there on.

After I flew out through that gap in the mountains at St. John's, Ireland became, subconsciously, more of an objective than Paris in my mind. If I could reach Ireland, Paris would follow, I felt, just as I consciously always took for granted that if I could reach Paris, Le Bourget would follow. Now, I'm nearer to Ireland than to New York!

A long flight always divides up into such mileposts. They help pass time and distance — the first state, the first shore line, the first hundred miles, the first thousand — there's always some objective reached to give the feeling of accomplishment. My log of them is filling. In it I've placed the continent of North America, Newfoundland, three stretches of salt water, the first day, and the blackness of the first night. Next, still quite far away, will be the dawn.

There's the moon, a little higher, and too far north. I've let the plane veer off course again. If only those compasses would steady down, I could stop cramping my neck to see the stars, and rest. That's what I want most now — to rest. Why try to hold a steady course? There's no accuracy to navigation anyway, with the compasses swinging, and after all those detours of the night. If I keep the *Spirit of St. Louis* pointing generally eastward, that should be enough; that will bring me closer to Europe. Why bother with careful navigation when it's so much easier to sit quietly and rest? After the night has passed, I can hold a straight course. It will be easier when the sun's up. Until then why should I worry about a trivial five or ten degrees? – – – Ten degrees isn't much of an angle – – – I can't possibly miss the whole continent of Europe

— — — What difference does it make if I strike the shore line a little farther from course than I planned?

I shake myself violently, ashamed at my weakness, alarmed at my inability to overcome it. I never before understood the meaning of temptation, or how powerful one's desires can become. I've got to alert my mind, wake my body. I can't let anything as trifling as sleep ruin the flight I spent so many months in planning. How could I ever face my partners and say that I failed to reach Paris because I was sleepy? No matter how inaccurate my navigation, it must be the best I can carry on. Honor alone demands that. The more my compasses swing, the more alert I must stay to compensate for their errors. If my plane can stay aloft, if my engine can keep on running, then so can I.

I cup my hand into the slipstream, diverting a strong current of air against my face, breathing deeply of its gusty freshness. I let my eyelids fall shut for five seconds; then raise them against tons of weight. Protesting, they won't open wide until I force them with my thumb, and lift the muscles of my forehead to help keep them in place. Sleep overcomes my resistance like a drug.

My fingers are cold from the slipstream. I draw my mittens on again. Shall I put on flying boots? But I'd have to unbuckle the safety belt and take my feet off the rudder pedals, and do most of the work with one hand. The *Spirit of St. Louis* would veer off course and I'd have to straighten it out a dozen times before I got the boots on. It's too much effort. I'd rather be a little cold.

I draw the flying suit's wool collar across my throat. Should I put the windows in now? Why not shut off the world outside, relax in the warmth of a closed cockpit, and gain that last mile or two of speed from streamlining? Those windows, resting idly in their rack, pushing down on the plane with their three or four pounds of unused weight, still rankle in my mind—fifty miles of range thrown away. There's still time to save more than half of it, still time to make them pay a profit on their passage. But the same argument that kept them out before steps forward and wins its case again. If I shut myself off even partially from outside air and clouds and sky, the lure of sleep may prove beyond resistance. The coolness of the night is a guard against it; the clarity of moonlit clouds helps to overcome it; the exhaust of the engine, barking in through open windows, serves to ward it off.

How wonderful it would be if this really were a dream, and I could lie down on a cloud's soft, fluffy quilt and sleep. I've never wanted anything so much; never found anything more impossible to attain. I'd pay any price — except life itself. But life itself is the price. This must be how an exhausted sentry feels: unable to stay awake; yet knowing that if he's caught napping, he'll be shot.

I've *got* to do something to clarify my head. I've *got* to do a better job of navigation. This isn't a college problem with nothing but a grade mark in the balance. The entire flight — Europe — Paris — life or death — depends on the answer. How shall I compensate for the night's errors? When morning breaks, what estimate will I make of my position? I force my hands to unfold the chart on my knees and slant the flashlight's beam across its surface. The white paper glares back into my night-accustomed eyes as though it were reflecting a midday sun. The great-circle course runs off the edge. I pull the "Eastern Half of the North Atlantic Ocean" from the map pocket and join it to the western. Changing pressures on stick and seat warn me that the *Spirit of St. Louis* is climbing — yes, the air-speed needle's down to 80 – – – now 75 – – – now 70 miles an hour. I switch off the light and level out my plane.

This cockpit was never made for spreading out charts. The paper wrinkles. The ends hang down and flutter in swirls of air. I need four hands — one for the stick, one for the flashlight, and one for each strip of paper. I try holding the stick between my knees and the flashlight under my chin. It works for a moment; then comes that out-of-balance feeling which tells me the plane's veering off again. I clamp the charts firmly against my legs with one forearm, and throw the flashlight onto the instrument board — turn indicator's far to the right — air speed's up — altimeter's dropping. I shut off the light, pull the stick back, kick left rudder, and look out the window to find some plane of reference from which to level out. But the moon's covered. There's not even an approximate horizon. I look up through the skylight to find stars. There are none. The glaring whiteness of the chart has blinded me to such vague pinpricks.

Gradually sight returns. I find my stars, and straighten out on course — or rather what I estimate, from the oscillating compass, the course to be. I piece the charts together again, flying entirely by instruments, so that my wind-dried eyes work always in an even light. But the *Spirit of St. Louis* refuses to be left unattended for five seconds. As soon as I look down at the charts the plane starts cutting up like a spoiled child piqued at a moment's neglect.

Finally I give up trying to hold the charts, and decide to visualize them in my mind while I watch the moon and stars. I've worked over them until their features are as plain as a familiar face on memory's screen. I can see the outline of the European coast almost as clearly as though I were looking at the charts themselves. The finer details can wait until I learn the wind's direction after daybreak.

I'm in the sixteenth hour of flight, still angling slightly northward, but bending toward the east each hour. Far ahead and to the left should be Ireland; to the right, the tip of England and the westward point of France. It's better to err to the northward, in the direction of nearest land; yet fate's been pushing me farther and farther south — south to detour the storms in Nova Scotia; south to fly above St. John's; south around most of the thunderheads; south with the movement of the stars. The wind above the clouds may be drifting me southward too. I may be pointed at the Bay of Biscay instead of Ireland.

The Bay of Biscay! Its name strikes back in memory to my childhood in Minnesota, to a ditty my father used to sing as we drove along winding dirt roads on crystal summer nights, looking up at the moon and stars just as I'm looking up at them now. The words run through my mind, as though he were sitting at my side, singing them:

> "All through the Bay of Biscay,
>   That gallant vessel sailed,
>   Until one night among the sailors,
>   They raised a merry row – – – "

For me, that song has always been connected with night, stars — and sleep, for I was young and usually very sleepy when he sang. And here I am, at night, over the ocean, dependent on the same stars; flying, possibly, toward the Bay of Biscay itself. I may sail above it before another day has passed. I shout out the words as loudly as I can, trying to make them pierce the engine's roar. Singing may help to keep awake, and pass the hours until dawn. Maybe that's why my father used to sing, along those lonely Minnesota roads — to help keep awake, as I must keep awake tonight.

Lights! There are lights under my left wing. A ship on the ocean! Then the fog's broken, and it's clear below! There are men down there on that ship; I'm no longer alone. If my engine fails, there's help within reach. I could spiral down through that funnel in the clouds, glide past the captain on the bridge, and stall onto the water. They'd stop and pick me up – – –

What's the matter? – – – The lights are rising – – – They're too far apart for lights on a ship ten thousand feet below – – – They're gone all together — flashed off as they flashed on! I turn to the instruments; yes, I've been flying right wing low. I'm too far north of the ship lanes to be seeing boats. I must have been looking at some stars. Several of them dropped down through the clouds, unnoticed, to rest for a moment on the surface of the ocean, and I caught them there.

THE SEVENTEENTH HOUR
Over the Atlantic
TIME — 11:52 P.M.

WIND VELOCITY	*Unknown*	VISIBILITY	*Unlimited*
WIND DIRECTION	*Unknown*		*outside of*
TRUE COURSE	70°		*clouds*
VARIATION	33° *W.*	ALTITUDE	10,000 *feet*
MAGNETIC COURSE	103°	AIR SPEED	90 *m.p.h.*
DEVIATION	0°	TACHOMETER	1675 *r.p.m.*
COMPASS COURSE	103°	OIL TEMPERATURE	32° *C.*
DRIFT ANGLE	10° *R.*	OIL PRESSURE	60 *lbs.*
COMPASS HEADING	93°	FUEL PRESSURE	3 *lbs.*
CEILING	*Unlimited*	MIXTURE	4
	above clouds	FUEL TANK	*Fuselage*

It's midnight in New York, and I've covered about thirty degrees of longitude since take-off. That makes it two hours later local time. Here, it's two o'clock in the morning, if I think in daylight-saving terms. Dawn isn't many hours away. The moonlight is brilliant. Objects in my cockpit are taking form again; I can almost read the figures on the charts. Only corners and out of the way places remain hidden in darkness. Clouds are clear and sharp — the rolling, crevassed surface below; columns rising from it; high cirrus layers, floating miles above my altitude, lightly veiling the moon as they pass. From a distance these cirrus, cumulus, and stratus clouds had blocked the sky completely, except for corridors lit by the rising moon; but as I approach they separate into layers and isolated masses, with fields of stars between – – – no – – – yes – – – with fields of stars between – – – Why can't I stop my eyelids closing? – – – Yes, with fields of stars between – – –

See that gaping entrance to a cave of cloud – – – no, earth – – – See the moonlight gleaming on the mist – – – no, leaves in wind – – – I step down from my airplane's cockpit – – – no, it's my motorcycle that I leave behind – – – I'm in Kentucky, with two other Field Artillery cadets. This is Sunday. We're free of Camp

Knox's three-inch guns and classes. O'Connor and Drewary, in their streamlined "Bug," and I on my motorcycle, are out to judge the virtues of the state. At this spot, we'll stop to rest and eat a sandwich.

"You fellows been to Mammoth Cave?"

It's a local boy who comes up to ask us — grinning — high-school age.

"Yes, we just came from there," O'Connor answers. We'd spent hours walking through the damp, cool passages.

"Quite a place, isn't it?" the boy goes on.

"Sure is."

"This country's full o' caves," he tells us. "Ya know, we think we got a better one. Like to take a look at it? 'Tisn't far."

"Well – – – sure, let's go."

We've been hunting for caves ourselves, climbing along the banks of a river, and crawling under rocky ledges where an opening might be. Here's a chance to do some exploring with the help of an expert and inexpensive guide.

"My name's Homer Collins," the boy volunteers as we follow him. "We call ours 'Crystal Cave.' It's a lot purtier, an' mebbe it's bigger 'n Mammoth. Some o' the passages go further 'n we been."

We take lanterns and flashlights, and start in through the mouth. The temperature drops. The air is moist. Weird formations surround us, crystalline and white. Water drips in puddles. Our voices return strangely from the walls. We pick our way between stalagmites, duck down as Homer enters a tunnel where there is no trail. It's wet and slippery. In places, we have to crawl under stalactites on our knees. In others, our shoes sink down in muck.

"Have to watch this stuff," our guide tells us. "Sometimes it caves in."

Then the passage opens to a gallery, high, wide, white in our lantern light — it might well be a secret palace of the gnomes.

"Ya see that hole over there?" asks Homer, pointing to an archway in one wall, "Floyd — he's my brother — he tried to reach the end o' that; but he ran outa time an' food."

Time? Who knows what time it is inside this planet, shut off from sun and stars. Here, time is meaningless. There's no sign of earth's rotation, no direction, twilight, dawn, or day. It's the surface of the world that belongs to man. Above or below, he finds adventure, but not sustenance. To the surface of the earth he must return to live – – – to sleep – – – to wake – – – See the lanterns flicker on those crystal columns – – – no, it's moonlight on the mist – – – See the shadow in that passage slanting downward – – – no, it's another gaping chasm in the clouds – – –

I look up at the compass to check my heading. Good; it's in one of its steady periods – – – steadier than usual – – – or – – – yes, it's almost stopped oscillating! The earth-inductor needle, too, has regained some of its old precision — it no longer wobbles from one side to the other with every bump of air. Am I getting out of the magnetic storm? Will it remain behind with the haze and the night's black masses?

The haze is almost gone. The compasses are now reasonably steady. I throw my flashlight out onto the wing struts. There's no trace of ice remaining. It's warmer in the cockpit; pleasantly warm. My hands are warm too, and moist. I pull off my mittens and press an arm out against the slipstream. That air hasn't blown down from the arctic wastes of Canada. It has more the feel of a tropical sea. It's changed completely within the hour, like the clouds. It's friendly, relaxing air — no danger of ice; no pinpricks on the palm. I lay my mittens on the floor and zip down my flying suit.

The clouds are no longer impassable barriers of ice. They're only opaque masses of air. I can fly through them if the compasses hold steady, drop down into them, keep right on heading eastward though they rise Himalaya-high.

I'm about five hundred miles from Newfoundland. Maybe I've crossed the border of the Gulf Stream. Then the Labrador current is behind, with its icebergs and arctic climate. Down below, the water too will be warm. A man could live a long time in a rubber boat on the Gulf Stream — especially if it rained a little.

It's like crossing the ridge of a stormbound mountain range to find a sun-bathed valley just beyond. It reminds me of a flight I made to California, two years ago this fall. I'd been bucking a head wind all day with a slow and aged biplane, detouring summits, buffeted by turbulent air, struggling to gain altitude with the under-powered engine. Nevada's sky was dull and gray. Finally, the great Sierras had risen up, a sheer wall in front of me, black clouds lying sharp across their snowcapped peaks. I'd wondered then, as tonight, whether clouds and pillars would merge to form a solid mass. But a pass tunneled through them, narrow, winding, and windswept; bouldered too — the boulders deathlike in their immobility. It seemed that I'd followed the pass for hours, sandwiched between treetops and clouds, almost brushing precipices with one wing, leaving just room enough to pivot on the other and turn sharply back if storm met ground ahead. It was cold in that open cockpit. I hadn't dressed for such altitudes. Suddenly, as I turned a bend in the pass, earth and sky had opened like a stage. The storm remained on the mountains while I glided steeply down their western slopes, down from the chill of snowcapped ridges into the moist, welcoming warmth of the sun-flooded Sacramento Valley, carpeted with orchards and the lush green of irrigated farms.

Possibly I could glide down here too, if the moon were higher. Its slanting rays cut across great chasms in the clouds. Those chasms may extend all the way down to the waves, two miles beneath me.

But how could the warmth of water reach so great a height so quickly if a west wind is still blowing? I'm not sure exactly where the Gulf Stream runs out here; and even if it has drifted in below to warm the upper levels of the ocean, that would hardly account for a sudden change in air temperature at ten thousand feet above the surface. No, a change in air probably means a change in wind. Warmer air must come from the south. A wind from the south would drift me up toward my great-circle route. Then there'd be no need to angle back by compass. But air that originates in the south may not be blowing toward the north. Rules of meteorology aren't that simple. There are all sorts of possible circulations to consider.

The wind bothers me. I think of old pilots' stories about winds aloft that reach velocities of more than a hundred miles an hour, winds which start from one direction and veer around the entire compass rose as you ascend, winds that drift you hopelessly off your course, and sometimes even blow you backward.

Now, I've burned the last bridge behind me. All through the storm and darkest night, my instincts were anchored to the continent of North America, as though an invisible cord still tied me to its coasts. In an emergency — if the ice-filled clouds had merged, if oil pressure had begun to drop, if a cylinder had started missing — I would have turned back toward America and home. Now, my anchor is in Europe; on a continent I've never seen. It's been shifted by the storm behind me, by the moon rising in the east, by the breaking sky and warmer air, and the possibility that the Gulf Stream may lie below. Now, I'll never think of turning back.

I let the *Spirit of St. Louis* bore its way on eastward. Unless the clouds below me break too, there's nothing to do until the sun rises except hold my heading, shift fuel tanks, and fill in the log each hour. The mixture control is well advanced, and the engine's throttled down as far as it's advisable to go. There's no need to watch dials carefully. Earlier in the night if their needles had forecast trouble, the sooner I noticed it and turned back the better chance I had of reaching land. Now, no matter what the needles show, I'll continue on my course as long as engine can hold plane in air. Before, I'd been flying away from safety. Now, every mile I cover brings me closer to it.

THE EIGHTEENTH HOUR
Over the Atlantic
TIME — 12:52 A.M.

WIND VELOCITY	*Unknown*	VISIBILITY	*Unlimited*
WIND DIRECTION	*Unknown*		*outside of*
TRUE COURSE	72°		*clouds*
VARIATION	33° *W.*	ALTITUDE	9600 *feet*

THE EIGHTEENTH HOUR
Over the Atlantic
TIME — 12:52 A.M.

MAGNETIC COURSE	105°	AIR SPEED	88 *m.p.h.*
DEVIATION	1° *W.*	TACHOMETER	1625 *r.p.m.*
COMPASS COURSE	106°	OIL TEMPERATURE	34° *C.*
DRIFT ANGLE	10° *R.*	OIL PRESSURE	59 *lbs.*
COMPASS HEADING	96°	FUEL PRESSURE	3 *lbs.*
CEILING	*High thin*	MIXTURE	4
	overcast	FUEL TANK	*Fuselage*
	above clouds		

Seventeen hundred miles behind. Ninteen hundred miles to go. In one hour more I'll be halfway to Paris – – – if the wind is on my tail. I should be north of fifty degrees in latitude.

On a long flight, after periods of crisis and many hours of fatigue, mind and body may become disunited until at times they seem completely different elements, as though the body were only a home with which the mind has been associated but by no means bound. Consciousness grows independent of the ordinary senses. You see without assistance from the eyes, over distances beyond the visual horizon. There are moments when existence appears independent even of the mind. The importance of physical desire and immediate surroundings is submerged in the apprehension of universal values.

For unmeasurable periods, I seem divorced from my body, as though I were an awareness spreading out through space, over the earth and into the heavens, unhampered by time or substance, free from the gravitation that binds men to heavy human problems of the world. My body requires no attention. It's not hungry. It's neither warm nor cold. It's resigned to being left undisturbed. Why have I troubled to bring it here? I might better have left it back at Long Island or St. Louis, while this weightless element that has lived within it flashes through the skies and views the planet.

This essential consciousness needs no body for its travels. It needs no plane, no engine, no instruments, only the release from flesh which the circumstances I've gone through make possible.

Then what am I — the body substance which I can see with my eyes and feel with my hands? Or am I this realization, this greater understanding which dwells within it, yet expands through the universe outside; a part of all existence, powerless but without need for power; immersed in solitude, yet in contact with all creation? There are moments when the two appear inseparable, and others when they could be cut apart by the merest flash of light.

While my hand is on the stick, my feet on the rudder, and my eyes on the compass, this consciousness, like a winged messenger, goes out to visit the waves below, testing the warmth of water, the speed of wind, the thickness of intervening clouds. It goes north to the glacial coasts of Greenland, over the horizon to the edge of dawn, ahead to Ireland, England, and the continent of Europe, away through space to the moon and stars, always returning, unwillingly, to the mortal duty of seeing that the limbs and muscles have attended their routine while it was gone.

In a period of physical awakeness between these long excursions, I find the clouds around me covered with a whiter light. In the area of sky where my plane is flying, night is giving way to day. The night — so long — so short — is ending. This is the dawn of Europe, of Paris, of Le Bourget. But how dull appreciation is! Dawn — It's tremendously important. I've waited for it the whole night through. But my senses perceive it only vaguely, separately, indifferently, like pain through too weak an anaesthetic. It is intellectual knowledge, while my normal thoughts and actions are mechanical. In flesh, I'm like an automaton geared to a previously set routine.

The minute hand has just passed 1:00 a.m. It's dawn, one hour after midnight. But it's one hour after midnight only on the clock, and back at the longitude of New York where I set it before take-off in the morning — yesterday morning, it is, now. The clock simply shows the number of hours I've been in the air. It relates only to my cockpit and my plane, not to time outside. It no longer marks the vital incidents of day — dawn, and noon, and sunset. My flight is disconnected from all worldly measures. It passes through different frames of time and space.

With this faint trace of day, the uncontrollable desire to sleep falls over me in quilted layers. I've been staving it off with difficulty during the hours of moonlight. Now it looms all but insurmountable. This is the hour I've been dreading; the hour against which I've tried to steel myself. I know it's the beginning of my greatest test. This will be the worst time of all, this early hour of the second morning — the third morning, it is, since I've slept.

I've lost command of my eyelids. When they start to close, I can't restrain them. They shut, and I shake myself, and lift them with my fingers. I stare at the instruments, wrinkle forehead muscles tense. Lids close again regardless, stick tight as though with glue. My body has revolted from the rule of its mind. Like salt in wounds, the light of day brings back my pains. Every cell of my being is on strike, sulking in protest, claiming that nothing, nothing in the world, could be worth such effort; that man's tissue was never made for such abuse. My back is stiff; my shoulders ache; my face burns; my eyes smart. It seems impossible to go on longer. All I want in life is to throw myself down flat, stretch out — and sleep.

I've struggled with the dawn often enough before, but never with such a background of fatigue. I've got to muster all my reserves, all the tricks I've learned, all remaining strength of mind, for the conflict. If I can hold in air and close to course for one more hour, the sun will be over the horizon and the battle won. Each ray of light is an ally. With each moment after sunrise, vitality will increase.

Something's wrong on the instrument board — the compass needle — it's strayed ten degrees off course while I was making resolutions to hold it on its mark. I tense my muscles, shake my body, bounce up and down in the cockpit, bring the nose back onto its heading. I can't afford to waste time and fuel like this.

Why spend weeks studying navigation and laying out charts precisely, if I'm going to let my plane swing ten degrees off course? I simply *must* keep that compass needle in the center — good God, it's off again. This is like a feverish dream.

I've *got* to find some way to keep alert. There's no alternative but death and failure. *No alternative but death and failure,* I keep repeating, using the thought as a whip on my lagging mind; trying to make my senses realize the importance of what I'm saying. I kick rudder over sharply, skid back into position. But there's no use taking it out on the plane; that's unfair; it's not the plane's fault; it's mine. I try running fast on the floorboards with my feet for as many seconds as the *Spirit of St. Louis* will hold to course. Then, I clamp the stick between my knees while I simulate running with my hands. I push first one wing low and then the other, to blow fresh air through the cockpit and change pressures on my body. I shake my head until it hurts; rub the muscles of my face to regain feeling. I pull the cotton from my ears, fluff it out, and wad it in again. I must keep glancing at the turn-indicator, hold the needle in center with my feet.

I'll set my mind on the sunrise — think about that — watch the clouds brighten — the hands of the clock — count the minutes till it comes. It will be better when the full light of day has broken. It's always better after the sun comes up. As that dazzling ball of fire climbs into the sky, night's unpaid claims will pass. The desire for sleep will give way to waking habits of the day – – – That's always happened before – – – And yet, I'm not sure – – – It's never been like this before – – – I never wanted so badly – – – to sleep – – –

I'm leaning against my father's side. I hear the clump of horses' hoofs, smell their sweat-damped bodies. Wheels crunch through sand. It's still a long way to our farm. My mother pulls me over, rolls me up in the driving robe, lays me in a hammock formed by the folded carriage hood behind her. Half-turned in the seat, she sings softly:

"A Span-ish cav-a-lier stood in his re-treat, – – –"

The evening is black; the stars, bright; the carriage rocks on its springs – – –

"Say, dar-ling, say, when I'm far away, – – –"

Ah, if I could only sleep like that tonight; if I could only land on one of these clouds, even for a moment, and let its feathery billows cover me up. If I could give way to sleep for five minutes while the plane flew itself! What wouldn't I give for five minutes of sleep? Anything – – – except life – – –

Right rudder — twelve degrees!

My leg is cramped from holding the Ford's clutch in low. Wheels bump, spin, and stop. Water is steaming from the radiator. We step out into the mud — my father, his two friends, and I. Our car is mired to its hubcaps. All evening we've been grinding over wet, rough, and deeply rutted Minnesota roads. In this tamarack swamp the corduroy logs have rotted out.

I climb back into the driver's seat and push down on the clutch pedal, while the three men put shoulders to the car. We gain six inches, no more. We wade into the swamp to gather sticks and brush. One of the men gets a long pole to pry the wheels up while the rest of us fill the ruts beneath them. Twenty feet ahead is more solid ground.

We make it this time. The men scrape their feet on the running boards and climb in, splattered and muddy. We grind through another quarter mile, and get caught in another mire.

About midnight, we reach a crossroad with a house and country store. We've pushed, strained, and lifted until it's painful to move at all. And the nearest town is more than ten miles away, over the same kind of roads. I drive onto a higher bit of ground and switch off the engine. There's dead silence except for swamp cheepers. Our feet are wet, and it's much too cold to sleep in the car. My father makes his way to the dimly outlined porch. No light shows inside the house. My father's knocks are loud and clear. Minutes pass. There are flickers on glass. The door scrapes open. A lantern and legs appear.

It's a small house with only one bed for the storekeeper and his wife. But we're welcome to sleep on the parlor chairs. Or maybe we'd prefer sleeping in the store. There's plenty of room on the floor there, and we can have two new horse blankets for bedding. We choose the store.

It's hard, the rough plank floor, with only one blanket under us. Sleep is fitful. My father's friends are large men. One kicks, and the other snores. The top blanket, too small to cover four of us, moves constantly back and forth. I'm in between, and warm enough; but my clothes are sticky damp. I doze, and turn, and wake as heavy shoulders crowd against me and press my bones onto the floor — — —

It had seemed a hardship then, when I was thirteen years of age; but what luxury a bed like that would be in this mid-Atlantic dawn! I'd never feel the hardness of the boards, hear a sound, or notice movement, if I could only sleep — — —

Six degrees right rudder!

Girls' voices shrill out through open windows. Wheels splash in water. Our river boat throbs with its engine's beat. I wake, sway forward, lean back against the wall, and doze and wake again. I'm in a group of Field Artillery cadets off on a week-end leave, in the summer of '21. We move slowly up the Ohio. It's still more than an hour to our landing and a bed. If I didn't carry the dignity of a soldier's uniform, I'd lie down on deck and sleep soundly till we get there. All day long, before this excursion started, I was loading our Battery's guns on the range at Camp Knox, hooking up caissons, riding my wheel horse. Now, if I could even sit down, I'd close my eyes and sleep. But every bench is full. So I wake and doze and wake again, propped up against this wall.

I'd thought that was the ultimate in tiredness, to doze standing up against a wall. But how I'd welcome a wall tonight to sleep against! I hadn't appreciated the relaxation one can have, leaning against a wall, the freedom of mind, the security of body. One doesn't need comfort to sleep. Cushions and beds are unimportant. All one needs is the knowledge that one can — — — sleep — — — and — — — live — — —

Ten degrees right rudder!

I switch off the smoking engine, and brace my Excelsior motor-cycle upright with my legs. A truck is stalled in front of me, down to its axles in sand. I'm sweating all over in the damp heat of a Florida sun. It's been raining, on and off, for days.

"How far does this sand go west?" I ask.

"Brother, it goes further 'n where we all started from, an' we been goin' four days."

There are two farmers in the truck. Their faces are drawn. Their clothes are wet, spattered, wrinkled. One is sprawled back against the seat, staring at me dazedly. The driver speaks, his voice dull with fatigue.

"How fur does it go yer way?"

"There's about three miles of it," I answer.

"All like this?"

I nod my head. "All like this. A dozen cars are stuck between here and the end of the pavement."

A cow moos — there are three of them in the back of the truck.

"Three miles might as well be thirty, fur as we're concerned," the driver says. "Engine's so hot it's stuck tight. Can't crank it — — — Guess we better let the stock go, Jim." He motions toward the turpentine swamp. "They'll git somethin' to eat and drink out there."

Jim nods his head slowly, says nothing.

The driver opens the door, and steps down stiffly. He's so exhausted he can hardly keep his balance. He continues talking in the same monotone.

"We set out to market them critters. Had to sell 'em. Needed money – – – Nothin' to do about it now." He leans heavily against a fender, as though it were too difficult to stand alone. "We made six miles since yest'day mornin' — pushin' all night long – – – Not a wink o' sleep – – – Food's all gone, too – – – can't work without food – – – git weak – – –"

I have no food to give them, not even a chocolate bar in my pocket; and I've got barely enough money to get home — if I don't spend anything on hotels. I might help them get started, if their engine's not too far gone, but they'd be stuck again in fifty feet. They'll have to either get a team of horses to tow them or stay where they are till the rains stop.

"I passed a shack a mile or so back. Maybe you can get something to eat there," I suggest.

"Thanks, brother. We're goin' to rest fur a while. Then we'll start walkin'."

"I haven't got a bit of food with me," I say, embarrassed.

"On a motorcycle? Course ye hain't. We didn't expect none."

"I'd like to help you; but – – –"

"Thanks, brother, but ye can't help us now. If ye're goin' west, ye've got yer own problems. Ye're jist a damn fool fer tryin' it on a motorcycle. I'm tellin' ye, ye won't git five miles."

"Well – – – I'm going to try – – – Good-by."

"Try it if ye like. Ye're white an' free – – – G'by, brother."

I start on westward, walking astraddle my motorcycle to hold it upright as the tire churns wet sand. It falls over. I strain to raise it, start the engine, grind along the ruts. It tumbles again. I lift, and start, and waddle forward. I make a mile – – – five – – – ten – – – Tumble, lift, and tumble. Finally my limbs deny their orders. The weight's too much. The machine sinks back onto its side in the sand. I drop down next it on the road, stretch out, and lie still while my muscles rebuild strength – – –

Strength ‒ ‒ ‒ It's not strength I need tonight in the *Spirit of St. Louis* ‒ ‒ ‒ it's sleep ‒ ‒ ‒ sleep ‒ ‒ ‒ I take off my helmet ‒ ‒ ‒ rub my head ‒ ‒ ‒ pull the helmet on again ‒ ‒ ‒ I drink some water from the canteen ‒ ‒ ‒ that helps. Possibly if I eat a sandwich ‒ ‒ ‒ the grease-spotted bag lies unopened at my side. I've had nothing since breakfast yesterday; but my mouth wants no food, and eating might make me sleepier. Should I have taken along a thermos of coffee? Would that keep me awake? No, I don't want coffee either. It wouldn't do any good. It wouldn't have any effect when I'm feeling like this. Coffee may be all right for school pre-examination nights; but it would be worse than useless here.

If I could get down through the clouds and fly close to the waves, maybe that would help me stay awake. It did yesterday. But there isn't light enough yet. To glide down into those clouds would be like going back into night. Even if there's a ceiling underneath, it would be too dark to fly close to the water ‒ ‒ ‒ I'll have to wait another hour at least ‒ ‒ ‒ unless the clouds break up ‒ ‒ ‒ The crevasses are still black and bottomless ‒ ‒ ‒

There's a great, steep hollow in the mist ‒ ‒ ‒ No, not mist ‒ ‒ ‒ rock ‒ ‒ ‒ hard, reddish yellow walls ‒ ‒ ‒ broken, crumbling slopes, cupping a mile-wide crater. See the deep, blue sky above, through which a meteor once hurtled to make this giant pockmark on the earth. My mother, my uncle Charles, and I stand on the blasted rim, near Winslow, Arizona. A hot wind blows dust against our eyes, and whistles through stone crevices. Almost a thousand feet below us lies the brush-spotted desert floor, a group of abandoned mine buildings in its center. Far in the distance, a puff of dust marks another car's struggle with the sands. Beyond that, there's not a sign of life for as far as we can see.

It's late summer of 1916. I'm driving our Saxon car from Little Falls to California. We've been over thirty days on the road, and we've been pushing fairly hard. Weather and mechanical troubles have held us up — a worn-out timer-trigger in Iowa, mud in Missouri (oh, those dismal hotel rooms, where we waited for the roads to dry!), a broken spring-bolt in Kansas, a wheel shimmy that started on the Raton Pass. The list is long; we add new items almost every day, and we still have half a thousand miles to go. My uncle picks up a chunk of brownish rock. I wish we could find a fragment of the meteor – – – No, it's not rock – – – It's mist – – – soft, gray walls – – – billowing – – – sloping – – –

Shaking my body and stamping my feet no longer has effect. It's more fatiguing than arousing. I'll have to try something else. I push the stick forward and dive down into a high ridge of cloud, pulling up sharply after I clip through its summit. That wakes me a little, but tricks don't help for long. They're only tiring. It's better to sit still and conserve strength.

My mind strays from the cockpit and returns. My eyes close, and open, and close again. But I'm beginning to understand vaguely a new factor which has come to my assistance. It seems I'm made up of three personalities, three elements, each partly dependent and partly independent of the others. There's my body, which knows definitely that what it wants most in the world is sleep. There's my mind, constantly making decisions that my body refuses to comply with, but which itself is weakening in resolution. And there's something else, which seems to become stronger instead of weaker with fatigue, an element of spirit, a directive force that has stepped out from the background and taken control over both mind and body. It seems to guard them as a wise father guards his children; letting them venture to the point of danger, then calling them back, guiding with a firm but tolerant hand.

When my body cries out that it *must* sleep, this third element replies that it may get what rest it can from relaxation, but that sleep is not to be had. When my mind demands that my body stay alert and awake, it is informed that alertness is too much to expect under these circumstances. And when it argues excitedly that to sleep would be to fail, and crash, and drown in the ocean, it is calmly reassured, and told it's right, but that while it must not expect alertness on the body's part, it can be confident there'll be no sleep.

My eyes, under their weighted lids, seem completely disconnected from my body, to have within themselves no substance, to be conscious rather than to see. They became a part of this third element, this separate mind which is mine and yet is not, this mind both far away in eternity and within the confines of my skull, within the cockpit and outside of it at the same moment, connected to me and yet unlimited to any finite space.

During long ages between dawn and sunrise, I'm thankful we didn't make the *Spirit of St. Louis* a stable plane. The very instability which makes it difficult to fly blind or hold an accurate course at night now guards me against excessive errors. It's again a case of the plane and me compensating for each other. When I was fresh and it was overloaded, my quickness of reaction held its nose from veering off. Now that I'm dreaming and ridden by sleep, its veering prods my lagging senses. The slightest relaxation of pressure on either stick or rudder starts a climbing or a diving turn, hauling me back from the borderland of sleep. Then, I fix my eyes on the compass and determine again to hold it where it belongs.

There's no use; within a few minutes the needle swings over to one side. No mental determination within my control has more than fleeting value. That third quality has taken over. It knows and holds a limit I can't consciously define, letting my mind and body stay relaxed as long as the *Spirit of St. Louis* flies reasonably straight and level, giving the alarm to both when needles move too fast or far. So far, no farther, the nose can veer off course; so far, no farther, the plane can dive or climb. Then I react from my stupor, level out, kick the rudder back onto the compass heading, shake myself to half awakeness – – – and let the needle creep again. I'm asleep and awake at the same moment, living through a reality that is a dream.

The clock's minute hand shows quarter of two. It's almost time for my hourly routine of log and tanks and heading. Previously, I've looked forward to this as welcome diversion, as something to sharpen my senses, to force mental concentration, to bring movement to muscles cramped from the fixed position of long, straightforward flight. Now, the effort seems too much to bear. It's all I can do to rouse my senses sufficiently to pull out the pencil and lay the log sheet on my chart.

THE NINETEENTH HOUR
Over the Atlantic
TIME — 1:52 A.M.

WIND VELOCITY	*Unknown*	VISIBILITY	*Unlimited*
WIND DIRECTION	*Unknown*		*outside of*
TRUE COURSE			*clouds*
VARIATION		ALTITUDE	9000 *feet*
MAGNETIC COURSE		AIR SPEED	87 *m.p.h.*
DEVIATION		TACHOMETER	1625 *r.p.m.*
COMPASS COURSE		OIL TEMPERATURE	35° *C.*
DRIFT ANGLE		OIL PRESSURE	59 *lbs.*
COMPASS HEADING	96°	FUEL PRESSURE	3 *lbs.*
CEILING	*Unlimited*	MIXTURE	4
	above clouds	FUEL TANK	*Nose*

Eighteen hundred miles behind. Eighteen hundred miles to go. Halfway to Paris. This is a point I planned on celebrating out here over the ocean as one might celebrate a birthday anniversary as a child. I've been looking forward to it for hours. It would be a time to eat a sandwich and take an extra swallow of water from the canteen. But now all this seems unimportant. Food, I definitely don't want. And water — I'm no longer thirsty; why trouble to take another drink? I have as far to go as I've come. I must fly for eighteen endless hours more, and still hold a reserve for weather. Time enough for food and water after the sun rises and I wake; time enough after the torture of dawn is past.

Shall I shift fuel tanks again? I've been running a long time on the fuselage tank. I put another pencil mark on the instrument

board to register the eighteenth hour of fuel consumed. That wasn't
so difficult; it didn't require any thought — just a straight line, a
quarter inch long, one more in those groups of fives. But shall I
shift tanks? Let's see; how did I plan to keep the balance? Oh, yes;
it's best not to let the center of gravity move too far forward, so
the plane won't dive under the surface in case of a forced landing.
I turn on the nose tank, and shut off the flow from the fuselage
tank, instinctively.

There's one more thing — the change of course — each hour
it has to be done. But what difference do two or three degrees make
when I'm letting the nose swing several times that much to one side
or the other of my heading? And there are all the unknown errors
of the night. Sometime I'll have to figure them out — make an
estimate of my position. I should have done it before; I should do
it now; but it's beyond my ability and resolution. Let the compass
heading go for another hour. I can work it all out then. Let the
sunrise come first; with it, new life will spring. My greatest goal
now is to stay alive and pointed eastward until I reach the sunrise.

During the growth of morning twilight, I lose the sense of time.
There are periods when it seems I'm flying through all space,
through all eternity. Then the world, the plane, my whereabouts,
assume unearthly values; life, consciousness, and thought are different things. Sometimes the hands of the clock stand still. Sometimes they leap ahead a quarter-hour at a glance. The clouds turn
from green to gray, and from gray to red and gold. Then, on the
thousandth or two thousandth time I'm leveling out my wings and
bringing the nose back onto course, I realize that it's day. The last
shade of night has left the sky. Clouds are dazzling in their whiteness, covering all of the ocean below, piled up in mountains at my
side, and – – – That's why I've waked from my dazed compla-
cency – – – towering, a sheer white wall ahead!

I have only time to pull myself together, concentrate on the
instruments, and I'm in it — engulfed by the thick mist, covered
with the diffused, uniform light which carries no direction and

indicates no source. Mechanically, I hold my hand out into the slipstream. The temperature of air is well above freezing — no danger from ice.

Flying blind requires more alertness. And since alertness is imperative, I find it possible to attain. I'm able to accomplish that for which there's no alternative, but nothing more. I can carry on the essentials of flight and life, but there's no excess for perfection. I fly with instinct, not with skill.

The turn-indicator must be kept in center. That's the most important thing. Then the air-speed needle must not be allowed to drop or climb too far. The ball in the bank-indicator can wait until last; it doesn't matter if one wing's a little low, as long as everything else is in position. And at the same time, I have to keep the earth-inductor needle somewhere near its lubber line. Thank God it's working again. Altitude isn't so important. A few hundred feet up or down makes little difference now.

The knowledge of what would happen if I let those needles get out of control does for me what no amount of resolution can. That knowledge has more effect on my mind and muscles than any quantity of exercise or determination. It compresses the three elements of existence together into a single human being.

Danger, when it's imminent and real, cuts like a rapier through the draperies of sleep. The compass may creep off ten degrees without drawing my attention; but let the turn-indicator move an eighth of an inch or the air speed change five miles an hour, and I react in an instant.

It's not a large cloud. Within fifteen minutes the mist ahead brightens and the *Spirit of St. Louis* bursts out into a great, blue-vaulted pocket of air. But there are clouds all around — stratus layers, one above another, merging here, separating there, with huge cumulus masses piercing through and rising far above. Sometimes I see down for thousands of feet through a gray-walled chasm. Sometimes I fly in a thin layer of clear air sandwiched between layers of cloud. Sometimes I cut across a sky valley surrounded by towering peaks of white. The ridges in front of me turn into blinding flame, as though the sun had sent its fiery gases earthward to burn away the night.

Another wall ahead. More blind flying. Out in the open again. But only for minutes. The clouds are thickening. I'm down to nine thousand feet. Should I climb back up where valleys are wider? No, I've got to get under these clouds where I can see waves and windstreaks. I *must* find out how much the wind has changed. I *must* take hold — begin to grapple with problems of navigation. The rising sun will bring strength — it *must*. Half the time, now, I'm flying blind.

When I leave a cloud, drowsiness advances; when I enter the next, it recedes. If I could sleep and wake refreshed, how extraordinary this world of mist would be. But now I only dimly appreciate, only partially realize. The love of flying, the beauty of sunrise, the solitude of the mid-Atlantic sky, are screened from my senses by opaque veils of sleep. All my remaining energy, all the attention I can bring to bear, must be concentrated on the task of simply passing through.

THE TWENTIETH HOUR
Over the Atlantic
TIME — 2:52 A.M.

WIND VELOCITY	*Unknown*	VISIBILITY	*Variable*
WIND DIRECTION	*Unknown*	ALTITUDE	8800 *feet*
TRUE COURSE		AIR SPEED	89 *m.p.h.*
VARIATION		TACHOMETER	1625 *r.p.m.*
MAGNETIC COURSE		OIL TEMPERATURE	35° *C.*
DEVIATION		OIL PRESSURE	59 *lbs.*
COMPASS COURSE		FUEL PRESSURE	3 *lbs.*
DRIFT ANGLE		MIXTURE	4
COMPASS HEADING	96°	FUEL TANK	*Nose*
CEILING	*Flying between cloud layers*		

I change neither fuel tanks nor course.

This is morning — the time to descend and make contact with the ocean. I look down into the pit I'm crossing, to its misty gray bottom thousands of feet below. The bottom of that funnel can't be far above the waves. Then is the ocean covered with fog? Suppose I start down through these clouds, blind, where should I stop — at 2,000, at 1,500, at 1,000 feet? I reset my altimeter when I was flying close to the water, east of the Newfoundland coast. But that's almost eight hours back, now. Since then I've crossed an area of major storm. The barometric pressure has surely changed during the night. How much, there's no way of telling. I think of the Canadian pilot, caught in fog, who flew his seaplane into the water without ever seeing it. I'd be taking a chance to descend below a thousand feet on my altimeter dial. It would be cutting the margin close to fly blind even at that indicated elevation. No, I'll hold my altitude a little longer. The climbing sun may burn a hole through the clouds.

As sky draws attention from the earth at night, earth regains it with the day. Sometime unperceived, during this hour of morning twilight, I took back the earth and relinquished the sky. I no longer watch anxiously for stars in the heavens, but for waves on the sea. The height of cloud above is now less important than the depth of cloud below.

I've been tunneling by instruments through a tremendous cumulus mass. As I break out, a glaring valley lies across my path, miles in width, extending north and south as far as I can see. The sky is blue-white above, and the blinding fire of the sun itself has burst over the ridge ahead. I nose the *Spirit of St. Louis* down, losing altitude slowly, two hundred feet or so a minute. At eight thousand feet, I level out, plumbing with my eyes the depth of each chasm I pass over. In the bottom of one of them, I see it, like a rare stone perceived among countless pebbles at your feet — a darker, deeper shade, a different texture — the ocean! Its surface is splotched with white and covered with ripples. Ripples from eight thousand feet! That means a heavy sea.

It's one of those moments when all the senses rise together, and realization snaps so acute and clear that seconds impress themselves with the strength of years on memory. It forms a picture with colors that will hold and lines that will stay sharp throughout the rest of life — the broad, sun-dazzled valley in the sky; the funnel's billowing walls; and deep down below, the hard, blue-gray scales of the ocean.

I nose down steeply, resetting my stabilizer as pressure on the stick increases. Controls tighten – – – ribs press against fabric on the wings – – – the air-speed needle rises – – – 110 – – – 120 – – – 140 miles an hour. I close the mixture control and pull the throttle back still farther, letting the engine turn just fast enough to keep it warm and clear. Air crowding around the cowlings screams strangely in my deafened ears, the first different sound I've heard since take-off, yesterday.

A layer of cloud edges over the ocean. I turn sharply back to spiral through the open funnel. I forget about my plan to turn the altitude of night into distance during day. Those thousands of feet I've hoarded, I'll squander on the luxury of coming down with sight. Suppose I lose ten or fifteen miles in range. It's worth that to get down in safety to the wind-swept sea.

I bank again as another wall of cloud approaches. The shadow of my plane centers in a rainbow's circle, jumps from billow to billow as I spiral – – – The sun's rays flood through the fuselage window, cut across my cockpit, touch first this instrument, then that. Whitecaps sparkle on distant water – – – I'm banked steeply – – – I'm descending fast – – – My ears clear, and stop, and clear again from change in pressure – – – My air cushion wilts until I feel the hard wicker weaving of the seat – – – Wings flex in turbulence – – – Layer after layer of thin gray clouds slip by, merging here, broken there; mountains, caverns, canyons in the air.

Two thousand feet now — under the lowest layer of clouds. The sea is fairly writhing beneath its skin — great waves —

breakers — streaks of foam — a gale wind. From the northwest? I've been spiraling so long that I'm not certain of direction. I straighten out and take up compass course. Now I'll have the answer I wanted so badly through the night – – – I'm pointed obliquely with the waves – – – Yes, the wind's northwest – – – It's striking the *Spirit of St. Louis* at almost the same angle it blew off the coast of Newfoundland at dusk — but it's much stronger. A quartering tail wind! It's probably been blowing that way all night, pushing me along on my route, drifting me southward at the same time.

A tail wind! A tail wind across the ocean. That's what I've always wished for. How strong is it? I can judge better close to the surface. I ease the stick forward and begin a slow descent, translating my remaining altitude into extra miles toward Europe. The air's warmer and more humid — a different atmosphere than that above the clouds. It's like stepping through the door of a greenhouse full of plants.

I'm under a dark stratus layer of cloud. Only a spot of sun-brightened water behind marks the bottom of the funnel I spiraled through, as though the beam of a great searchlight had been thrown down from the heavens to guide me to the ocean's surface.

Curtains of fog hang down ahead and on each side, darkening the air and sea, shutting off the horizon. I nose down to 1000 feet – – – to 500 – – – to 50 feet above huge and breaking waves. The wind's probably blowing 50 or 60 miles an hour. It would have to blow with great force to build up a sea like that — to scrape whitecaps off and carry the spray ahead like rain over the surface. The whole ocean is white, and covered with ragged stripes of foam.

It's a fierce, unfriendly sea — a sea that would batter the largest ocean liner. I feel naked above it, as though stripped of all protection, conscious of the terrific strength of the waves, of the thinness of cloth on my wings, of the dark turbulence of the storm clouds.

This would be a hellish place to land if the engine failed. Still, it wouldn't be as bad as a forced landing during the night — gliding

blindly down through freezing mist and onto an ice-filled ocean.
Nothing that could happen now would be as bad as that. Now, at
least, I know which way the wind's blowing; I could head into it
and stall onto the water with almost no forward speed at all. I
could *see* what I was doing.

It would be awfully difficult to work down there with waves
breaking over the fuselage and whipped by a gale of wind. The
cockpit would probably fill up with water a few seconds after I
landed. I might have to hold my breath until I could crawl out
through the door and up on top of the plane. Then, I'd have to cut
through the roof of the fuselage to get at the raft, and hang on to
something while I pumped it up. After that, there'd be the problem
of getting my equipment unlashed from the steel tubes under water,
and getting it lashed again inside the raft.

Suppose I could get the raft pumped up and loaded. What
then? While I was in San Diego planning the flight, I considered
using the plane as a sea anchor and signal of distress if I were
forced down in the Atlantic. The silver wings would be more
likely than my small, black-rubber raft to attract the attention of
any ship that passed.

But there's not likely to be a passing ship at this latitude. Looking down on the wilderness of broiling water, I realize that mooring
my raft to the plane would cause the waves to break over it — if
the cord held in such a sea. It would be better to cut loose and
drift with the wind, southeast toward the ship lanes. At least then
I'd be going somewhere. That would be preferable to waiting in
one spot, watching an empty horizon, anchored to a sinking plane
up in this northern ocean.

But there are other things more important than imagining
forced landings; and now that I possess my senses, I must keep
them disciplined. It's essential to take stock of my position; to lay
out a definite plan of navigation for the day. The wind aloft is
probably stronger than it is down here. If it also is from the northwest, and if it didn't shift during the night, I must be well ahead
of schedule and south of my course. In that case, I should be about
over the middle of the ocean.

The middle of the ocean! I glance down at the chart — somewhere in that empty space between the continents, somewhere among those small black numerals which represent mountains and valleys under sea — 1600 fathoms — 2070 fathoms — 1550 fathoms, the figures read. Yes, there's ground down below, just as contoured and distinctive as the ground of which continents are made. Water is like fog, hiding the earth from human eyes. If I could see through it, I might locate my exact position from some submarine mountain range.

What wouldn't I give for a high cloud's shadow on the surface to tell me the wind drift aloft! Now, whatever estimate I make is just a guess, a probability on which I can base — only hope. But right or wrong, I've got to make some estimate. What *should* I allow for the wind, for the swinging of the compasses, for those detours around thunderheads? And what bothers me still more, how shall I allow for the inaccuracy of my navigation — for those swerves to right and left of course during innumerable minutes of unawareness? When I left Newfoundland, I set my heading ten degrees northward to compensate for drift. Should I now allow five degrees more? I look at the waves again. The wind streaks are really more tail than side — my route curved southward during the night. Fifteen degrees might be too much. Then for over an hour I haven't reset the compass at all. That leaves me headed an extra two degrees toward the north.

I have a strong feeling that I'm too far south to strike Ireland unless I change my heading. But there aren't enough facts to back it up. I must consider only the known elements in navigation. If I give way to feeling, that will remove all certainty from flight. Suppose I crank in five degrees to the earth-inductor compass, then if I don't make a landfall by – – –

The waves ahead disappear. Fog covers the sea. I have only time to reset the altimeter and start climbing. A hundred feet above water, in rough air, is no place for blind flying. Turbulence is severe. The safety belt jerks against me. Needles jump back and forth over dials until I can follow only their average indication with controls. I push the throttle forward, and hold 95 miles an hour until the altimeter shows 1000 feet. I watch the tachometer needle. It's steadier, and tells the position of my nose on the horizon more accurately than the inclinometer and the air-speed indicator put together. Problems of navigation fade into the immediate need of holding the *Spirit of St. Louis* level and on course. Adding and subtracting degrees, and keeping one result in my head while I consider some related factor, is too much. And to work with pencil and paper at the same time I watch those needles is out of the question. I'll figure it all out accurately after the fog has passed.

The fog doesn't pass. I go on and on through its white blankness. I'm growing accustomed to blind flying. I've done almost as much on this single trip as on all my flights before put together. Survival no longer requires such alertness. Minutes mass into a quarter-hour. A quarter becomes a half; then three-quarters. Still the waves don't appear. I'm flying automatically again through eyes which register but do not see – – –

No! No, I can't lie down and sleep! No! No, I can't get out and walk. Rub your eyes, shake your head. You're over the middle of an ocean!

But I'm not over the middle of an ocean. I'm not in an airplane flying through the sky. I'm – – –

"CHARLES!"

I hardly hear my nurse's voice above my heartbeat. I've slipped away from her guard to stare fearfully around the gray barn's corner.

"CHARLES, COME BACK!"

A huge column of smoke is rising from our house, spreading out, and blackening the sky. Then that's what the shouts and noise all meant. That's why I was jerked away from my play so roughly and rushed down the kitchen steps. Our house is burning down!

"CHARLES!"

A hand grasps my arm and pulls me behind the barn. "Charles, you *mustn't* watch!" My nurse is excited. She thinks it's too terrible for me to see. Where is my father — my mother — What will happen to my toys? – – –

Right rudder, five degrees.

"Father will build us a new house."

I hold Mother's hand tightly while she speaks, looking down on the still smoking ruins. It's the next day. Our entire house has sunk into the stone walls of its basement. I recognize our cook-stove, under pipes beside the furnace. Next to it are twisted bed-steads. There's the hot-water boiler. There's the laundry sink. Everything is covered with the gray snow of ashes. Right at my feet is a melted, green-glass lump that was once a windowpane. Out of the pit, smoke-smutted but sharp-cut against thick leaves and sky, rises our brick chimney, tall and spindly without a house around it. And on the chimney mantelpiece, midway up its height, where the big living room once ended, is Mother's Mexican idol — a small, red-clay figure — the only object to pass undamaged through the fire. Of course some clothes and books were saved, and the men carried out a few pieces of furniture. But my toys, and the big stairs, and my room above the river, are gone for-ever – – –

The compass needle is leaning again. I must swing the nose right with my rudder.

It was a dreary winter that came after the burning of our house, in 1906. We rented a small flat in Minneapolis. The crisp days of autumn were interesting enough — rustling leaves, bonfires, and games with children next door. But in icy weeks that began with

December, I missed the roomy freedom of my home on the farm. Why go outdoors when you're so heavily dressed you can hardly move? — when woolen layers bow your arms out from your body, when cold bites into your cheeks and pinches your ears, and you can't get your mittens off to blow your drippy nose. I spend hours on end in dry, heated rooms, with stuffy head and whitening skin. I grow tired of books and toys, and pressing my face against a frosted window. I move aimlessly about, experiment in strange new fields. Why can't I hold ten marbles between ten toes? How long can a cream-filled chocolate last if I eat it with a pin – – –

The nose is down, the wing low, the plane diving and turning. I've been asleep with open eyes. I'm certain they've been open, yet I have all the sensations of waking up — lack of memory of intervening time, inability to comprehend the situation for a moment, the return of understanding like blood surging through the body. I kick left rudder and pull the stick back cornerwise. My eyes jump to the altimeter. No danger; I'm at 1600 feet, a little above my chosen altitude. In a moment, I'll have the plane leveled out. But the turn-indicator leans over the left — the air speed drops — the ball rolls quickly to the side. A climbing turn in the opposite direction! My plane is getting out of control!

The realization is like an electric shock running through my body. It brings instant mental keenness. In a matter of seconds I have the *Spirit of St. Louis* back in hand. But even after the needles are in place, the plane seems to be flying on its side. I know what's happening. It's the illusion you sometimes get while flying blind, the illusion that your plane is no longer in level flight, that it's spiraling, stalling, turning, that the instruments are wrong.

There's only one thing to do — shut off feeling from the mind as much as your ability permits. Let a wing stay low as far as bodily senses are concerned. Let the plane seem to maneuver as it will, dive, climb, sideslip, or bank; but keep the needles where they belong. Gradually, when the senses find that the plane is continuing on its course, that air isn't screaming through the cowlings as it would in a dive, that wings aren't trembling as they would in a stall, that there's really no pressure on the seat as there would be in a bank, they recover from their confusion and make obeisance to the mind.

As minutes pass and no new incident occurs, I fall into the state of eye-open sleep again. I fly with less anguish when my conscious mind is not awake. At times I'm not sure whether I'm dreaming through life or living through a dream. It seems I've broken down the barrier between the two, and discovered some essential relationship between living and dreaming I never recognized before. Some secret has been opened to me beyond the ordinary consciousness of man. Can I carry it with me beyond this flight, into normal life again? Or is it forbidden knowledge? Will I lose it after I land, as I've so often lost the essence of some midnight's dream?

I'd had measles in Minneapolis that winter — drawn window shades — glasses of bitter medicine — four days in bed. It's the only time in my life I can remember having a doctor come to see me. The zero-cold months which followed left colorless space in my mind. It now seems that I spent most of them under a flowerpot, with Peter Rabbit, in Mr. McGregor's garden. When spring finally broke the weather, Mother and I made streetcar trips to the city parks, to the shores of Lake Minnetonka, to the falls of Minnehaha.

Summer found us back in our home town of Little Falls. The new house wasn't built yet. We had to live in a hotel. But Crook, our skittish driving horse, trotted us over the two miles of road to our farm almost every day. It was always an exciting ride, for he shied at rustling bushes and wind-blown bits of paper. Once he got so quivery that he just sat down between the shafts and snorted.

One of the carpenters working on our house made me a wooden ladder. It wasn't very long, but with it I could reach the lower scaffoldings, and climb over fresh-smelling piles of lumber. I watched Bolander, the architect, roll out his drawings from which a house would grow. I stood near Chelson, the mason, while he shaped his granite blocks with drill and hammer. I kept at a safe distance from Hendrickson, the farmer, while he swung his keen-edged scythe.

Lillian and Eva, my half sisters, were with me on the farm that summer. My father had been married before, and his wife had died. We often went to secret, violet-guarded dells where great pines strained wind through needles, and poplars filtered off the sun. The girls were a little big to play with, but they showed me lots of things, like making teacups out of acorns, and barnyards out of twigs. We'd sometimes go swimming together, and they'd blow up my water wings.

Father didn't have much use for water wings. He thought I'd try harder and learn more quickly without them. He'd often carry me on his back to a mid-river island, telling me to get down in the water and kick hard with my legs to help him buck the current.

I was with my father when I learned to swim. I was eight years old then. We were near our big, red granite "drying-rock," and stripped naked. We almost never wore bathing suits on the river bank, for there was rarely anybody within sight. One day, I waded out neck-deep on the slimy, smooth-stone bottom, and slipped into a hole that was over my head. When I broke surface and coughed in a breath of air, I was startled to find that my father wasn't running toward me. He just stood on shore and laughed. And then I realized that I was swimming by myself. The current quickly carried me to shallow water.

After that, Father and I often went on expeditions to rivers, creeks, and lakes. Now that I could both shoot and swim, I became his partner – – –

My senses tell me the left wing is low. Let them think so. Ball and needle are in center.

"How many do you want, Boss?"
My father dumps another turtle into the boat with his oar. It's

the summer of 1911. The lake is full of turtles, red, green, and yellow, sunning themselves on top of a thick growth of weeds. They try to dive as we approach, but some become entangled in the matted stems, and these we catch.

"Get that little one, Father!"

It flips in beside me. Sizes vary from summer-hatched babies to thick-shelled, snapping grandfathers. We'll let the big ones go before driving home; but I want the babies for my pen — a series of sandboxes, dishpans, and stone-islanded tubs that I've connected with special turtle walkways.

Father always calls me "Boss." I don't mind; but he's not fooling me. I know who's going to decide when we'll start home, and when we'll go on the next expedition. If I were really boss, we'd stay here tomorrow too, and go to Squaw Lake next week. Squaw Lake has the best fishing I've ever seen — just like the wilderness lakes of his boyhood, Father says.

Father taught me how to fish, just as he taught me how to handle turtles, and to swim and hunt. But it was Grandfather Land who started me off with a gun. He made me a present of a Stevens single-shot, .22-caliber rifle when I was six years old, and my Uncle Charles, just back from moose country, up in Canada, showed me how to shoot it at a special target in the basement. Whenever you'd hit the bull's-eye there was a clank and an iron bird jumped up. Father thought six was young for a rifle, but the next year he gave me a Savage repeater; and the year after that, a Winchester 12-gauge automatic shotgun; and he loaned me the Smith and Wesson revolver that he'd shot a burglar with. He'd let me walk behind him with a loaded gun at seven, use an axe as soon as I had strength enough to swing it, drive his Ford car anywhere at twelve. Age seemed to make no difference to him. My freedom was complete. All he asked for was responsibility in return — — —

The air speed's down to eighty miles an hour, and the nose is sixteen degrees off course!

I warn myself of relaxation's dangers. It's all very well, I argue, to go half asleep in high clear air, but flying blind at low altitude is a matter of life and death — life and death! It's no use. There's a power beyond my will's control which refutes these claims of my conscious mind, a power which knows exactly where the danger limit lies, and which realizes that as I become more skilled in using instruments, the need for concentration accordingly decreases. Simply telling myself that I must hold those needles on their marks has no effect. That power, that third being, has taken over the direction of my flight, knowing better than I how far down the wing or nose can drop before an emergency has to be declared and the alarm given to my ordinary senses.

I looked forward with great apprehension to long periods of flying blind under conditions of extreme fatigue. I was afraid that needles would jump around the cockpit more with each quarter-hour that passed, and that the plane might get completely out of control. Instead, the needles seem to quiet down. They stay reasonably well in place. The *Spirit of St. Louis* doesn't vary much in altitude, doesn't stray hopelessly far off course. Annoying as my compass errors are, they're no greater than they were above the clouds before I started flying blind. My errors seem to have certain definite limits, regardless of the condition of pilot, instruments, or air.

Witn each minute, my confidence increases. At first, my conscious mind didn't trust its ghostlike, newly made acquaintance. But now, when crises come, when sleep presses close and hard, it gives over command entirely, as an ailing man gives over a business he once thought no one else could run.

I climb to 1500 feet. If I fly higher I'm too likely to miss the pockets of clear air below the clouds. If I fly lower, more than half asleep, there'll be too much chance of crashing into water. I wish I could blow up the air cushion. But I can't fly blind with only my knees against the stick. The seat is hard and painful. Pain doesn't help to stay awake, as I once thought it would.

THE TWENTY-FIRST HOUR
Over the Atlantic

HOURS OF FUEL CONSUMED

NOSE TANK
¼ + ~~+~~~~+~~~~+~~ 1

LEFT WING	CENTER WING	RIGHT WING
¼ + 1	¼ +	¼ + 1

FUSELAGE
~~++++~~ ~~++++~~ 1

Four twenty! It's a half-hour late for instrument readings. But I can't control those needles at the same time I'm making entries in my log. It's not worth the effort anyway. I'll let it go until the air's clear again — let resetting the course go, too. I'll just mark the hour of fuel consumed. If I hadn't run thirty minutes over on timing, I'd shift to a wing tank. I reach forward and add one more line to the group under "nose tank." The altimeter moves up a hundred feet, and the turn-indicator leans over to the right as I put the pencil back. My route has curved eastward four degrees since I changed course. I offset that much on my compass.

Shall I go on blind, or climb above the clouds? The monotony of this changeless, opaque mist, and the overwhelming desire for sleep, create a longing for either sea or sky. Since I'm completely shut off from the sea, my mind grasps at the idea of giving up the frustrating hunt for its surface to climb back into sunlight and the crystalline upper world. Now I know which way the wind is blowing, now I've followed in body the excursion my mind made a hundred times during the night and early morning, why tunnel through this dismal fog when I have it in my power to reach the mountain peaks?

"It's clear up above."

"But you've been there all night long."

"It's better than this fog."

"The fog may lift at any moment. Then you'll have the sea."

"It's been an hour now and no lifting."

"It can't go on forever. Any second may bring the waves again."

I decide to continue blind for one hour more. There ought to be another clear spot by that time. If not, then I'll climb up above the clouds. At least the climb will be faster with every hour of fuel consumed.

I reach for the canteen. No, just reaching throws the plane off balance. I don't need water. What if my throat is a little dry? It's more important to keep the needles centered; every time I use an extra muscle they go jumping off.

Maybe if I dropped down to 1000 or 500 feet I'd find it clear right here below me. Maybe I'm flying in a layer of cloud lying well above the sea. Now that my altimeter's properly set, I know exactly how low I can fly in safety. But to do down through the mist, watching the altimeter needle so carefully, and at the same time keeping other instruments where they belong, between glances out to look for waves, seems a superhuman effort.

I continue boring through the fog at 1500 feet, while my mind weaves in and out through time and life – – –

EUROPE NEEDS FOOD!

CHILDREN STARVING!

CROPS CAN WIN THE WAR!

Every day new headlines appear in the papers. It's April, 1918, and our high school superintendent has offered full scholastic credit to students who leave classes to work on farms. I'd like to join the Army and fly a Scout, like Eddie Rickenbacker and the pilots of the Lafayette Escadrille; but I'm only sixteen — too young to enlist — so I'm going to help raise the crops to make the food we need to win the war. Father has bought a carload of Western heifers, and another of Western sheep. We'll make our hundred-and-twenty acres of field and woodland produce all the food they can.

I'm taking my books with me — mathematics, civics, English, history — for I'll graduate this spring; but it's a gesture; there won't be much studying after a full day's labor on the farm; not even our superintendent expects that. There'll be examinations, of course, but they won't be difficult to pass.

Father's going to buy a tractor too, so I can plow and seed our fields. He'll be away most of the time. He has a law office in Minneapolis, and business interests often take him East. I'll have charge of the detailed running of the farm. I must start right in and work hard, for there are fences to mend before the sheep come, and the barn needs fixing for cows – – –

Eight degrees right rudder.

B-b-b-a-a-a-a. The sound comes from a hazel-bushed hollow. I duck my head and scratch through dripping branches, glazed with sleet. B-b-a-a-a-a. It's weak and plaintive. I pick up the staggering lamb, sticky-wet from its mother's womb and the melting snow, and start back toward our house. Its legs hang awkwardly against my coat as it nuzzles around for milk. The sky's already darkening for night. I've spent over an hour searching, since the ewe came back with the flock, thin, bloody, and bleating. This lamb wouldn't have lived till morning. It's the fifth I've found abandoned, two of them dead; and more than half the flock must still give birth to offspring. These first-time mothers often leave their young.

It's a hard job keeping orphan lambs alive. You have to dry them off, keep them warm, and feed them cow's milk through a nipple at morning, noon, and night. It takes time, time you haven't got to give them when you're organizing a farm, breaking in new stock, and trying to get the ground prepared for crops in spring – – –

Twelve degrees right rudder.

Now it's mid-September.

"Sixty-four I'm bid. Sixty-four I'm bid. Who'll make it sixty-five? Make it sixty-five! – – – Fresh last month and going at sixty-four dollars! – – – She's worth ninety if she's worth a cent – – – going at sixty-four – – – going at sixty-four – – – sold to Charles Lindbergh at sixty-four dollars!" The auctioneer points his stick at me and turns to the next animal.

I'm buying cows for our milk herd. This roan is mixed as a mongrel dog. She's nothing to be proud of; but her udders are full and her veins are large. She'll run up our check from the creamery. The Western heifers Father bought won't help us much this winter. They're bred for beef, and only a few will even be worth milking.

Some day we hope to have an all-Guernsey farm. We're starting with a thoroughbred bull from the Williams herd, and one registered cow – – –

Five degrees right rudder.

Leaves flutter in the wind around us as we lift a barked poplar log, glistening with sap.

"Nay, he rubs in the center. Turn him half-vay 'round." Daniel Thompson scores a four-foot length with his axe, and wedges off the chips. We're building a log house for our Duroc-Jersey hogs. Next week I'll lay the roof and chink the cracks.

Thompson is a tremendous help around the farm. He was born in Norway about seventy years ago. When he first came to this country he worked in logging camps up north. Now he lives in a corner room of the vacant house that we used to rent to tenants. All he wants is a quiet place where he can spend his final years.

It's a month since September's killing frost warned us of a northern winter. The crops are in; our lofts are filled; we're working on the buildings. Walls must be thick and banked with earth. Our animals will have no stoves, and cold is ruthless in central Minnesota – – –

Seven degrees right rudder.

Light from my kerosene lantern throws soft shadows on the floor. The sun went down more than an hour ago. The year of 1919 is two weeks old. My fingers strip out last drops of milk. It's stuffy here in the barn. Air reeks of cows' breath, body, and manure. Tongues rasp up last scraps of bran. Teeth go on munching hay. I don't dare let in more air tonight. It's thirty-seven degrees below zero outside. Steam puffs out from nostrils, and windows are a half-inch thick with frost.

I separate cream, feed calves, check stock in the lower barn. There's Billy, one of my four pet rams. That quarter stick of dynamite he ate doesn't seem to have damaged him. Snow squeaks against my boots as I cross the road and follow the path to our chicken coop. Each breath of air puts frost on my nose hairs that melts when I exhale again. A tree cracks through the night's silence, like a rifle shot. A million stars light up the sky.

There's a honk as I shine my lantern into the goose house. Hooligan, Fanny, and Matilda stretch necks belligerently. No need to worry about them. Of all our animals and birds, they're the only ones that like such cold. Why, this afternoon when I brought them water, they splashed about and preened themselves till each feather was coated with ice.

I leave a lantern burning in the chicken coop, stack hardwood logs on the fire in our house's basement furnace, throw extra sticks in the stove upstairs, undress, and climb in between the blankets of my bed. Sheets are too cold in such weather. Wahgoosh, my fox terrier, jumps up and cuddles at my feet — — —

Swing the nose back south.

I slip teat cups on the last two cows and pull out my watch — half past four in the morning! Today, I'm taking a train to Minneapolis, a hundred miles away. At midnight I'll milk again. It will be a long wait for our animals, especially the fresher cows. But it's the only way I can make the trip and have enough time in the city. This afternoon I must interview prospective tenants for our farm. I've got to find someone who'll take charge of fields, machinery, and stock, for I'm to enter the University of Wisconsin in the fall. It's June of 1920. I don't like to think of giving up the animals I know so well, of strange hands moving the levers on my tractor. I may never farm again myself, for I'm going to be a mechanical engineer.

I didn't plan on running the farm permanently. I started because of the war, and kept on because I loved the life and our Minnesota home. But two years out of school are enough. Even now I may be too rusty to keep up in the strict classes of an engineering college. I have my high school diploma; but I haven't studied on the farm, and I've forgotten a lot about procedure, formulae, and rules.

I don't want to go to college very much. But Father and Mother went to the University of Michigan, and they think I ought to be a college graduate too. Everyone says it's important to have a diploma. "It helps you get along in later life."

Suppose I fail to get through the university? Even then I won't come back to the farm. And I'm not going to follow my father into law or politics. I've seen enough of life in Washington to know it's not for me. I'll never forget my father saying, "A lawyer's tied to his office and his desk." And then, after a pause, he added, "It isn't the kind of work you'd like."

Whether I graduate from the university or not, there are two things I want to do. I want to pilot an airplane, and I want to go to Alaska. Vilhjalmur Stefansson says Alaska is our modern frontier, like the West of a generation back. It holds adventure, and opportunity — and I'm not afraid of cold. Maybe someday I can learn to fly, and then fly to Alaska – – –

I'm twenty degrees off course!

I shake my head and thumb my eyelids open. It seems impossible to keep the earth-inductor needle centered. Is it going out of commission again? No, the liquid compass is steady and off in the same direction. Why does the needle insist on riding to the left of its lubber line? Time and again I've centered it with the rudder; but in a few seconds it's back where it was before. In the past my errors have averaged up; they've been as much one way as the other. Now, they have as definite a drift as the wind, and there's apparently nothing I can do about it. In moments of relative awareness this fact causes me much concern; but to the strange new apprehension I've developed, it seems of little import. Let the turn-indicator move excessively from center, and my muscles react to press the rudder; but ten degrees left on the compass causes them not the slightest stir.

THE TWENTY-SECOND HOUR

Over the Atlantic

HOURS OF FUEL CONSUMED

NOSE TANK

¼ + ┼┼┼┼   1 1

LEFT WING	CENTER WING	RIGHT WING
¼ + 1	¼ +	¼ + 1

FUSELAGE

┼┼┼┼ ┼┼┼┼ 1

Four fifty-two. I grope for the pencil in my pocket, and take my eyes from the turn-indicator long enough to add another mark to the group under "nose tank." There are an impressive number of those leaden marks now, on the instrument board — twenty of them — and an extra hour using up the top gallons from the tanks. I'm twenty-one hours from New York. I switch over to the right wing-tank — time to lighten it a bit. Log entries can go until the air's clear.

Will the fog never end? Does this storm cover the entire ocean? Except for that small, early morning plot of open sea, I've been in it or above it for nine hours. What happened to the high pressure area that was to give me a sunny sky? The only storms reported were local ones in Europe!

I remind myself again that I didn't wait for confirmation of good weather. Dr. Kimball said only that stations along the coast reported clearing, and that a large high-pressure area was moving in over the North Atlantic. He didn't say there'd be no storms. The weather's no worse than I expected when I planned this flight. Why should I complain of a few blind hours in the morning? If the fog lifts by the time I strike the European coast, that's all I should ask. The flight's been as successful as I ever hoped it would be. The only thing that's seriously upset my plans is the sleepless night before I started — those extra twenty-three hours before take-off.

Of course no one thought the weather would break enough to let me start so quickly. But why did I depend on what anyone thought? Why did I take any chance? I didn't have to go to a show that evening. I didn't have to go to New York. This is the price for my amusement, and it's too high. It imperils the entire flight. If this were the first morning without sleep instead of the second, blind flying would be a different matter, and my navigation on a different plane.

Sometimes, shut in by fog, the impression of movement ceases, and I seem to be just hanging in space — unrelated to any outside point of reference, hypnotized by the instruments, deluded by the noise and vibration of the engine into the belief that I'm flying rapidly across an ocean between two great continents of the world. How fantastic it is to think that if I just sit here long enough, juggling these needles, France will lie below — like a child's imaginary travels in a parlor chair.

Over and over again, I fall asleep with my eyes open, knowing I'm falling asleep, unable to prevent it; having all the sensations of falling asleep, as one does in bed at night; and then, seconds or minutes later, having all the sensations of waking up. When I fall asleep this way, my eyes are cut off from my ordinary mind as though they were shut, but they become directly connected to this new, extraordinary mind which grows increasingly competent to deal with their impressions — — —

Right rudder, twelve degrees.

The fog dissolves, and the sea appears. Flying two hundred feet higher, I wouldn't have seen it, for the overcast is just above me.

There's no sun; only a pocket of clear air. Ahead, is another curtain of mist. Can I get under it this time? I push the stick forward. Waves are mountainous — even higher than before. If I fly close to their crests, maybe I can stay below the next area of fog.

I drop down until I'm flying in salt spray whipped off whitecaps by the wind. I clip five feet above a breaker with my wheels, watch tossing water sweep into the trough beyond. But the fog is too thick. It crowds down between the waves themselves. It merges with their form. A gull couldn't find enough ceiling to fly above this ocean. I climb. The air's rougher than before, swirling like the sea beneath it. I open my throttle wider to hold a margin of speed and power.

Before I reach a thousand feet, waves show again, vaguely — whitecaps veiled and unveiled by low-lying scuds of fog. I nose down; but in a moment they're gone, smothered by mist. I climb.

The next clear area is larger, with a broken sky above. Strips and patches of blue open and close like shutters, while layers of clouds shuffle past one another. It looks as though the storm is really breaking. I pull out my air cushion, blow it up, stuff it back under me quickly, and straighten out the plane. There's not much time. More fog lies just ahead. I pour a little water down over the dryness of my throat. The canteen is still half full. I'm tempted to take long, cool swallows, but I must guard my supply in case I'm forced to land at sea.

Fog closes in. Again I try to stay below it. Again I have to climb. A light rain streaks by my windows, trickles over struts and wings, splashes through cracks and around corners into the cockpit. Flecks of cool water strike my face. Finding these pockets of clear air removes all question of climbing up above the clouds. Every glimpse I catch of the sea helps ward off sleep. And rain may be an indication of better weather close ahead.

While I'm staring at the instruments, during an unearthly age
of time, both conscious and asleep, the fuselage behind me becomes
filled with ghostly presences — vaguely outlined forms, trans-
parent, moving, riding weightless with me in the plane. I feel no
surprise at their coming. There's no suddenness to their appearance. Without turning my head, I see them as clearly as though in
my normal field of vision. There's no limit to my sight — my skull
is one great eye, seeing everywhere at once.

These phantoms speak with human voices — friendly, vaporlike shapes, without substance, able to vanish or appear at will,
to pass in and out through the walls of the fuselage as though no
walls were there. Now, many are crowded behind me. Now, only
a few remain. First one and then another presses forward to my
shoulder to speak above the engine's noise, and then draws back
among the group behind. At times, voices come out of the air itself,
clear yet far away, traveling through distances that can't be
measured by the scale of human miles; familiar voices, conversing
and advising on my flight, discussing problems of my navigation,
reassuring me, giving me messages of importance unattainable in
ordinary life.

Apprehension spreads over time and space until their old
meanings disappear. I'm not conscious of time's direction. Figures
of miles from New York and miles to Paris lose their interest. All
sense of substance leaves. There's no longer weight to my body,
no longer hardness to the stick. The feeling of flesh is gone. I
become independent of physical laws — of food, of shelter, of life.
I'm almost one with these vaporlike forms behind me, less tangible
than air, universal as aether. I'm still attached to life; they, not at
all; but at any moment some thin band may snap and there'll be
no difference between us.

The spirits have no rigid bodies, yet they remain human in
outline form — emanations from the experience of ages, inhabitants of a universe closed to mortal men. I'm on the border line of
life and a greater realm beyond, as though caught in the field of
gravitation between two planets, acted on by forces I can't control,

forces too weak to be measured by any means at my command, yet representing powers incomparably stronger than I've ever known.

I realize that values are changing both within and without my mind. For twenty-five years, it's been surrounded by solid walls of bone, not perceiving the limitless expanse, the immortal existence that lies outside. Is this death? Am I crossing the bridge which one sees only in last, departing moments? Am I already beyond the point from which I can bring my vision back to earth and men? Death no longer seems the final end it used to be, but rather the entrance to a new and free existence which includes all space, all time.

Am I now more man or spirit? Will I fly my airplane on to Europe and live in flesh as I have before, feeling hunger, pain, and cold, or am I about to join these ghostly forms, become a consciousness in space, all-seeing, all-knowing, unhampered by materialistic fetters of the world?

At another time I'd be startled by these visions; but on this fantastic flight, I'm so far separated from the earthly life I know that I accept whatever circumstance may come. In fact, these emissaries from a spirit world are quite in keeping with the night and day. They're neither intruders nor strangers. It's more like a gathering of family and friends after years of separation, as though I've known all of them before in some past incarnation. They're as different from men, and yet as similar, as the night's cloud mountains were to the Rockies of the West. They belong with the towering thunderheads and moonlit corridors of sky. Did they board my plane, unseen, as I flew between the temple's pillars? Have they ridden with me through sunrise, into day? What strange connection exists between us? If they're so concerned with my welfare, why didn't they introduce themselves before?

I live in the past, the present, and the future, here and in different places, all at once. Around me are old associations, bygone friendships, voices from ancestrally distant times. Vistas open up before me as changing as those between the clouds I pass. I'm flying in a plane over the Atlantic Ocean; but I'm also living in years now far away.

Whip-poor-will – – – *Whip-poor-will* – – – That's Father's whistle! He's coming down the icehouse road. I jump up from kitchen table, let the screen door slam, hop down steps to meet him. It's late afternoon. A cool breeze has followed midday's blistering sun. My father leans his bicycle against an oak tree, and we walk along the garden path. Here, tomato plants are growing. There, radishes are crisp and ripe. Under that stone pile, Spot, my hunting dog, is buried. I carried rocks for weeks to mark his grave.

Father and I eat radishes and lettuce, and talk of our plans, for next week, in this month of June, 1915, we start on a most important expedition. From the headwaters of the Mississippi, we are to make a rowboat voyage through forest, swamp, and rapids, until, after many nights of camping, we arrive again at the banks of our farm. Possibly in future years we'll drift all the way down to New Orleans — but that's a dream – – –

Six degrees right rudder.

Now, our train has jerked and whistled north to Bemidji. Now, our white, clinker-built rowboat is being towed by livery car over the forty miles of road to Lake Itasca. Now, our equipment is stowed in bow and stern, and only the painter holds us to the wharf.

My father rows along the shore, searching for the river outlet. Water is clear and satin smooth. Fish splash rings upon the surface. Turtles slither off their logs.

"Charles, you're young; you'll live to see great changes," my father tells me as we glide over the surface. "They may not come in my lifetime, but they will in yours."

Sometimes, when we're alone, Father talks to me about politics and economics, and the reforms our government ought to bring about. I don't make any answer, for I don't quite understand what he means, and it disturbs me to have him mention things that will take place after he is dead.

Ever since I can remember, Father has been concerned about what's going on in this country — tariffs, and monopolies, and the "Money Trust." I sometimes wonder if he doesn't spend too much time thinking about problems he doesn't have to solve. Maybe he makes them seem more serious than they really are. If such dangerous happenings lie ahead, why don't other men worry about them too? But of course my father isn't like other men. There are moments when I feel he can see into the future, as though he were living, today, in years ahead; as though it's my life to come that he dwells in rather than his own.

"Money can't draw such high interest rates indefinitely," Father continues. "A man who has a mortgage on his land at ten or twelve percent doesn't have a fair chance. If the farmers don't organize, big business will take everything they've got. This country belongs to the people, but they haven't learned how to run it yet. The trouble is that people don't have any way of getting at the truth."

Father's concerned about the war, too. He says special interests would like to get us in it, and that propaganda is already under way. "We're making too many foreign loans," he tells me; and, "the trouble with war is that it kills the best and youngest men."

We find the river — up here it's only a brook — and wind slowly down through grass banks, tamarack, and pine. Sun alternates with shower. There are noises in the brush.

Turn east, turn north, turn south, and west. You'd think a river had no purpose. But it's as certain as it is indifferent. We can trust the Mississippi. We know that regardless of where it wanders, it will finally take us to our farm. We portage around rapids. Clouds pinken in the west. Spaces between tree trunks darken. We ground our boat, pitch our teepee tent, and light the cooking fire – – –

Flames play with forest shadows. Two bass fry in the pan. An owl hoots in the distance. Water gurgles over stones. We stand in smoky air to keep mosquitoes away, and eat, and talk – – –

Our tent is dark. Frogs and crickets have the night. The day's work fades in mind – – – I'll wake at sunrise – – – know exactly where I am – – – One can't get lost – – – voyaging down a river – – –

Gray scales appear below, vague and misty. I nose down. But fog closes in before I drop a hundred feet. Were those waves real, or did I see a mirage in the mist? I'm not sure. I decide to fly at a thousand feet instead of fifteen hundred. There, I'll have a better chance of making contact with the water.

But I catch only tantalizing glimpses of the sea. Finally I give up searching for it, and resign myself to the cockpit, the instruments, and the strange passengers I carry. In them are solitude and companionship, proximity and distance, a call to death, a guidance to life. One or two, more prominent than the others, ride just behind my shoulder, close but never touching; communicating sometimes by voice and sometimes without the need of speaking.

Mist lightens — the *Spirit of St. Louis* bursts into brilliant sunlight, dazzling to fog-accustomed eyes — a blue sky — sparkling whitecaps. The ocean is not so wild and spray-lashed. It's less ragged with streaks of foam. The wind's strength has decreased, and it has shifted toward my tail.

The plane's shadow rushes in to meet me as I nose down closer to the waves. I last saw it centered in the rainbow, high up in morning clouds. Such a small shadow, skipping from crest to crest, all but losing itself in the troughs, seemingly fearful it won't catch up before I reach the surface.

Brilliant light, opening sky, and clarity of waves fill me with hope. I've probably passed through the great body of the storm. Clouds still lie ahead and on each side — some as fog on the water — some high above. But there are channels of clear air between. Not that I'll follow those channels, but future periods of blind flying should be shorter, and broken up by similar gemlike vistas of the sea. I'm free of the instruments. I can look around again. The gravitation of life is strong.

THE TWENTY-THIRD HOUR
Over the Atlantic

HOURS OF FUEL CONSUMED

NOSE TANK

¼ + ╫╫╫ 1 1

LEFT WING	CENTER WING	RIGHT WING
¼ + 1	¼ +	¼ + 1 1

FUSELAGE

╫╫╫ ╫╫╫ 1

Six zero five. For over three hours I've entered nothing in the log. What difference does it make? When one can sit still and warm in sun, and stare at such beauty, the clerklike details of a log are of trivial importance. Besides, I'll be in the next cloud before I can take down a set of readings — unless there's ceiling enough to fly beneath it.

There is no ceiling. I climb back to a thousand feet, and reset the wind drift from ten to five degrees.

I'm over ten hours out from Newfoundland. In less than eight hours more, if the wind holds and I'm not too far off course, I should strike the Irish coast. Eight hours isn't such a long flight — only one working day — only a little longer than the trip between St. Louis and New York. And then, in another six hundred miles, I'll be over Paris. In fourteen hours, the flight will be done. Fourteen hours is less time than it took to fly between San Diego and

St. Louis – – – *If* the weather clears – – – *If* the engine keeps on running – – – *If* I strike Ireland – – – Well, at least my plane will be light, and stall down slowly – – – Why think about a forced landing? Think about Ireland – – – Eight hours isn't such a long flight – – – only three times the length of the mail route between St. Louis and Chicago – – – I'm already biting into the eighth hour – – – In one more hour, only seven will be left – – – There's the sun again, beating down on another fog-shored lake of the ocean – – –

Sea, clouds, and sky are all stirred up together — dull gray mist, blinding white mist, patches of blue, mottling of black, a band of sunlight sprinkling diamond facets on the water. There are clouds lying on the ocean, clouds just risen from its surface, clouds floating at every level through twenty thousand feet of sky; some small, some overpowering in size — wisps, masses, layers. It's a breeding ground for mist.

I fly above, below, between the layers, as though following the interstices of a giant sponge; sometimes under a blue sky but over an ocean veiled by thick and drifting mist; sometimes brushing gray clouds with my wings while my wheels are almost rolling in the breakers' foam. It's like playing leapfrog with the weather. These cloud formations help me to stay awake. They give me something on which to fix my eyes in passing, but don't hold my stare too long. Their tremendous, changing, flashing world removes monotony from flight.

The wind continues to decrease. Angular rays from the sun spread through crevasses in clouds ahead. I climb to 500 feet. That keeps me above most areas of fog, and below most of the heavier cloud layers. Now and then I have to fly blind for a few minutes, but never for long.

A cloud arches above me, like a great bridge. If I pulled back on the stick, I could almost loop around it. That would help to keep awake. But looping bridges isn't part of a transatlantic flight – – –

"Come on folks, take an airplane ride with Captain Frank Dunn, the only man in the world who's ever looped-the-loop completely around a bridge over a navigable river! See your farm from the air! Tell the gals what it's like to fly! Only five dollars for a flight over town! Sure, take her up with ya. Who's next in line? Hi there! Stay away from that propeller!"

Captain Frank Dunn hasn't looped around any kind of a bridge, river below it navigable or not; he's a steady, cautious flyer. But it's a good line for the circus barker — extra mouthfuls of words — prestige for the pilot, bait for the crowd.

It's a summer week end, in 1925. Frank Dunn, Bud Gurney, and I have brought three planes to this pasture near St. Charles, Missouri. Bud learned to fly last year. He overhauled an engine to pay for his instruction, scraping in the bearings with a pocket knife. Now, he's one of the best pilots at Lambert Field. Our flying circus has been ballyhooed by press and handbills for a week. Business has been good all afternoon. Not a spark plug has fouled; not a tail skid has snapped. It's been a pleasant afternoon too — light wind, smooth air, and a field large enough to make each take-off and landing routine rather than adventure.

In order to attract passengers out to our rented pasture, we've advertised wing-walking and acrobatics. Now, the crowd is restless, demanding the show we promised. That means turning down good profits, but sunset's not far away.

"Ladies and gentlemen!" The barker's voice shrills through my idling exhaust. "Captain Lindbergh will now take the air for an exhibition of death-defying acrobatics. He flies upside down and rightside up! There's no stunt he will not do! Keep your eyes in the sky! Don't miss it! There he goes!"

I push the throttle open, zoom off the ground, climb, loop, spiral, and spin. I blow leaves off treetops with my slipstream, chandelle around the field, and land.

Now it's Dunn's turn. His engine has more power, so he's carrying the wing-walker. We pilots are concerned about the wing-walker. None of us has seen him perform, and he's to do a break-away. He says he's done them before; but he shows a slight uncertainty, a lack of sure technique that makes us wonder. I switch off my engine and walk over to his plane to make sure that his ladder is properly attached to the landing gear, that his harness strap is strong enough, that he understands the vital need of snapping on before he "breaks."

It's only a few weeks ago that R — — — lost his performer in a breakaway over a suburb of St. Louis. That man said he had experience, too; but he slipped off the wing with a slack ladder and a weak snap on his safety cable. The snap broke and his muscles gave way. He plunged down to his death.

I find the ladder's knots well tied. It's stretched taut along the wing. The performer's harness is ruggedly built. Its fittings are oversize. Yes, he knows about snapping on. "No need to worry," he says. There's nothing more I can do. I go back to my Standard. But no passenger steps forward. Every man and woman wants to see the show.

Captain Dunn takes off, banks, points back toward the crowd. A figure moves slowly from the fuselage, over the wing, to the outer-bay strut, waves as the plane passes overhead, climbs up to the cabane, crawls down onto the landing gear as the pilot circles. So far, so good. Now for the breakaway.

The Standard noses up to five hundred feet. The performer is sitting at the wing tip. He's a thousand yards away — — — five hundred — — — two hundred — — — one hundred — — — fifty — He falls off, swings in an arc beneath the plane, angles tailward with the force of air. That finishes our performance. Now, we can try to get a few more passengers before dark — — — But what's wrong? The performer dangles at the ladder's end. He should be halfway up. The plane turns back toward us. Was he injured in the jump? But the swing was smooth — there appeared to be no jerk.

Bud Gurney comes running up. "Dunn's only got twenty minutes of gas left in the tank."

"Can you cut him loose?" I ask. Bud's an expert wing-walker

"I can if you put him in the cockpit."

"Got a knife?"

"A pocket knife; but it's sharp."

"Pull the prop, then."

I open the throttle while Bud is climbing into my plane. No need to worry about *him* — clear head — steady nerves — agile as a monkey.

We're off the ground, banking, climbing. It's not going to be an easy job with my OX-5 Standard — no extra power for control; and I'll have to fit the front cockpit around the performer, and hold it there while Bud cuts through both ropes of the ladder with his knife.

But we're too late. Captain Dunn is gliding down to land. He's headed toward a cornfield next our pasture. I drop my wing to get a better view. The performer hangs limply in air — no sign of life – – – He's cleared the trees – – – he's cleared the fence – – – His body drags through tassels – – – through stalks – – – strikes the earth – – – plows a furrow along the ground – – – The plane stalls down ahead of him – – – bounces – – – ground-loops – – – stops with dead propeller – – – The pilot jumps out – – – runs back – – – helps the performer to his knees – – – to his feet – – –

Bud and I circle twice, and fly back and land on the pasture. Most of the crowd have rushed off to the cornfield. The sun is below the horizon. No more passengers will ride tonight.

It's nearly two hours before pilot and performer return, riding together in the back of an open car. Captain Dunn laughs as he steps out. "We took him to the hospital, just to make sure no bones were broken. The doctors say there's nothing wrong. He'll be a little stiff for a few days, that's all."

The performer limps out, smiling sheepishly. Purple bruises ring his eyes — "from the cornstalks."

"The ladder twisted around 'till he couldn't climb up," Dunn explains. "Ropes were too new, I guess. And" (a low-voiced aside to us) "I think he was badly scared, too. I could see him hangin' down there, lookin' up at me with his big eyes wide open. God, it was an awful feeling! Nothin' I could do to help him. Pretty short of fuel, too — thought I better land before I had a dead stick. Thought it would be softer for him in that cornfield — wouldn't drag him as far as on the pasture. I was afraid the tail skid would come down on top of him – – – but it didn't. How's my plane? Corn do much damage?" Dunn had rushed off to the hospital without even glancing at his ship.

"A few tears in the wing," I tell him. "We'll give you a hand patching 'em up in the morning."

"Say, how much did I clear that fence by? I wanted to be sure I didn't snag him on a wire."

"You had lots of room — twenty feet at least."

"Let's tie down for the night."

"Tie down for the night!" How lightly we said it at the end of a flying circus day. There was always a townsman's car to carry us to a hotel, always a warm supper, always a clean bed. And sleep was as certain as the sunset.

Sunlight flashes as I emerge from a cloud. My eyes are drawn to the north. My dreams are startled away. There, under my left wing, only five or six miles distant, a coastline parallels my course — purple, haze-covered hills; clumps of trees; rocky cliffs. Small, wooded islands guard the shore.

But I'm in mid-Atlantic, nearly a thousand miles from land! Half-formed thoughts rush through my mind. Are the compasses completely wrong? Am I hopelessly lost? Is it the coast of Labrador or Greenland that I see? Have I been flying north instead of east?

It's like waking from a sound sleep in strange surroundings, in a room where you've never spent a night before. The wallpaper, the bed, the furniture, the light coming in the window, nothing is as you expected it to be.

I shake my head and look again. There can be no doubt, now, that I'm awake. But the shore line is still there. Land in mid-Atlantic! Something has gone wrong! I couldn't have been flying north, regardless of the inaccuracy of my compasses. The sun and the moon both rose on my left, and stars confirmed that my general direction was toward Europe. I know there's no land out here in mid-ocean — nothing between Greenland and Iceland to the north, and the Azores to the south. But I look down at the chart for reassurance; for my mind is no longer certain of its knowledge. To find new islands marked on it would hardly be stranger than the flight itself.

No, they must be mirages, fog islands sprung up along my route; here for an hour only to disappear, mushrooms of the sea. But so apparently real, so cruelly deceptive! *Real* clouds cover their higher hills, and pour down into their ravines. How can those bluffs and forests consist of nothing but fog? No islands of the earth could be more perfect.

Did a wind of hurricane velocity blow me on toward Europe through the night? Have I been threading a tornado's corridors? That may be the coast of Ireland I'm passing. It would take less than five minutes to fly over and make sure. It can't be just fog — the pointed tops of spruce trees rise above the common mass; I can almost see their branches spreading out. How can it be all fog, when there are wisps of fog along the coast, when I can tell the difference between the fog and land? If it's not Ireland, it must be the shore line of some Atlantis.

I bank northward; then, before the *Spirit of St. Louis* turns ten degrees, I straighten out again. It's nonsense, pure nonsense, to be lured off course by fog islands in the middle of an ocean flight. I'll not allow myself such indulgence. I'll waste no time and gasoline on fanciful excursions which can only end in disillusionment and additional fatigue.

But if those islands aren't real land, if they are not of earth's substance, how can I distinguish land from air? How will I recognize Europe when I reach it? I see surf on the beaches and trees in the forests, yet my reason tells me that it all is fog!

An island lies across my route ahead, wooded and hilly. Now, curiosity can be satisfied without cost to conscience. As I fly toward it, my eyes almost convince my mind that it *is* land. Then, like the desert mirage that turns to burning sand, shades of gray and white and purple disappear. Boulders are only shadows next to sunlight. Trees and rolling hills become crevasses in the fog. Beaches are but wisps of mist; and the surf, a line of whitecaps on the sea.

Clouds break and lift as the angle of the sun increases. The horizon is now sharp and bright. I *must* get down to business. Navigation can't be neglected longer. If I keep putting it off for fifteen minutes at a time, the entire day will pass. Each apathetic hour adds hazard to my flight, becomes a blot on my record as a pilot, a depressant to morale. I feel shame at my lack of resolution, like dull internal pain. How disgusted I'll be with myself, after I'm rested and alert again. I've smiled at men who succeed only in the luxury of normal life. I've believed that fatigue and hardship are the real tests of character; and now, confronted by them, I'm failing. My body and my mind are dreaming; I'm flying as a somnambulist might walk, conscious of surrounding danger, yet unable to attain a woken state. I'm capable only of holding my plane aloft, and laxly pointed toward a heading I set some hours ago. No extra energy remains. I'm as strengthless as the vapor limbs of the spirits to whom I listen.

In San Diego, I'd planned on taking drift sights at dawn, and every hour through the day. Behind me in the fuselage, the drift-indicator is lying in its rack. The movement of an arm could slip it into the brackets on my window. I'd only have to line up its parallel hairs with the foam's apparent path. Then I could read off my exact angle of drift, and offset it on the compass. So simple. So impossible. Why did I ever think I could fly the *Spirit of St. Louis* straight while I lean out over the eyepiece of a drift-indicator? Why didn't I foresee the fatigue of morning after twenty-odd hours of flight? I could have traded the instrument's weight for another half gallon of fuel.

The sun is out half the time now. Its rays beat down through the top window. My flying suit is uncomfortably hot.

THE TWENTY-FOURTH HOUR

Over the Atlantic

HOURS OF FUEL CONSUMED

NOSE TANK

¼ + ̶1̶ ̶1̶ ̶1̶ ̶1̶ ̶1̶ 1 1

LEFT WING	CENTER WING	RIGHT WING
¼ + 1 1	¼ +	¼ + 1 1

FUSELAGE

̶1̶ ̶1̶ ̶1̶ ̶1̶ ̶1̶ ̶1̶ ̶1̶ ̶1̶ ̶1̶ ̶1̶ 1

The twenty-third hour is almost past. But I won't bother keeping the log any more. Its sequence has been broken, and the effort of filling in its columns is out of all proportion to any future value. The fuel valves can stay where they are, too — no need of shifting them each hour. I pencil one more score on the instrument board, for fuel, and go on struggling vaguely with my navigating problems.

Twenty-three hundred miles from New York. Thirteen hundred miles to Paris. I look down at the chart — then it's only 700 miles to Ireland — probably less than that — probably not over 600 with the tail wind that's been blowing. That 5 degrees I allowed for St. John's ought to have brought me north to my route by now. I reach down and remove it from my earth-inductor heading. And I should add 3 degrees for course change, too. But how about all the other factors? I must work with more precision.

Let's see, I'm making a little over 90 miles an hour on the indicator. Suppose the wind has added another 30 miles to my speed. Then for every hour I've flown since leaving Newfoundland I could add 20 miles to my estimated even 100. I'd be a long way ahead of the marks on the chart. I left Newfoundland – – – when did I leave Newfoundland? I seem no longer able to deal with figures. St. John's was 11¼ hours from New York, and I'm now 23 hours from New York — 11 from 23 is – – – twice 11 is 22 – – – then 11 and 12 make 23 – – – Twenty-three – – – what do I want with twenty-three? What am I going to use it for? I'll have to start again – – – in a minute or two – – – after my mind is clearer – – – I'll let my mind rest for a minute or two, and start again – – –

"Lindbergh, you do better in your sleep than most of the other fellows." It's Mr. Livermore, my university advisor, speaking. I'm a student again, in engineering. He shuffles through my practice lettering cards for drawing class. It's true that I've filled them out in midnight hours. "You'll get by on these. But what's the matter with your mathematics?"

"Well, sir, I can get the problems all right, but – – – "

"Lindbergh, your compositions are good, but why can't you learn to punctuate and spell?" Mr. Brosius, my instructor in freshman English, sits before me. He hands back the last essay I submitted. "I can't let you get by with commas where semicolons ought to be. You'd better put some extra study into the rules of construction – – –"

Why should one spend the hours of life on formulae, semicolons, and our crazy English spelling? I don't believe God made man to fiddle with pencil marks on paper. He gave him earth and air to feel. And now even wings with which to fly. I'd like to stop taking English, and concentrate on engineering. Then, maybe I could get my average grades up above the danger line. I wish I could take an aeronautical engineering course. I believe I'd be more successful in that. I could work hard to understand the magic in the contours of a wing. But the University of Wisconsin doesn't teach much aeronautics. The Massachusetts Institute of Technology is the best place one could go — but I couldn't pass the entrance requirements there.

I have not been a good student. My mind has been the partner of my body rather than its master. For so long, I can sit and concentrate on work, and then, willy-nilly, my body stands up and walks away — to the shores of Lake Mendota; to the gymnasium swimming pool; to my motorcycle and distant country roads.

Eleven different schools I've gone to, from the District of Columbia to Redondo Beach in California, and there's not one that I've enjoyed. Their memory chafes like a slipping rope against the flesh of childhood. A-B-C — make straight lines straight and curved lines smooth. D-E-F — copy big capital letters from the paper strip above the blackboard. G-H-I — I'm eight years old; it's my first week of school. After tutoring with my mother, I've started in Force's second grade. K-L-M — it's twenty minutes till lunch time. I stretch cautiously in the seat, and practice wiggling my ears. N-O-P — for each twelve breaths, one minute passes. Q-R-S — I can hold one deep breath for three full minutes. T-U-V – – –

Ten years of school were like that — mining for knowledge, burying life — studying in grade school so I could pass examinations to get into high school — studying in high school so I could pass examinations to get into college — studying in college so – – – but there I broke the chain. Why should I continue studying to pass examinations to get into a life I didn't want to lead — a life of factories, and drawing boards, and desks? In the first half of my sophomore year I left college to learn to fly.

Oh, I know that civilized progress depends on education. Without it, I'd have had no motorcycle to ride, no tractor to run on our farm; I wouldn't now be flying in an airplane above the North Atlantic Ocean. Of course one must have knowledge. But why can't we partake of it in moderation, balance it with other qualities in life? Why learn the mathematics of the planets if we lose appreciation of the earth?

But maybe if I'd been a better student I'd know what to do with the number "23". Maybe this is my punishment for not studying harder, for not training my mind on Latin verse, and memorizing those formulae of physics. "23" may be the key to Paris, and I don't know how to use it. "Failed his examination because he couldn't solve the problem when X equals 23."

Right rudder, fifteen degrees.

There was one exception. From the Army flying school in Texas I graduated top man in my class. There, I'd really gotten down to business, worked on my studies as I'd never worked before. I hadn't been much impressed by university diplomas. They seemed advantageous but essential bits of paper, not worth the sacrifices their award required. But an Air Service Pilot's wings were like a silver passport to the realm of light. With them went the right to fly all military airplanes. With them went a second lieutenant's bars. In pursuit, in bombardment, in observation, in attack, their owner could – – –

The sunbeams blink off in my cockpit. The waves are sheened with misty light between shadows of fast-drifting clouds. I must stop daydreaming — get back to navigation – – – I'm more than halfway across the ocean, still flying a haphazard course. I shift sideways in the seat, move joints, tense muscles, hunt for a pad of flesh my bones haven't half pushed through. Any change in feeling, any stimulation to the senses helps. It's less a question of pain or pleasure, than of attaining any feeling at all. I drink deeply from the canteen. Why conserve water for a forced landing when I need it so badly on the flight? I'll stake this water on getting through to Paris, rather than keeping alive a few extra days at sea. The best safeguard against disaster is to take what I need, now. Besides, I have a whole gallon put away for emergency.

It's much too hot in the cockpit. I zip open my flying suit, and cup a hand into the slipstream again to bring air against my face. I fly first with one arm and then with the other, stiffen and relax my body, shake my head and brain. These things I can do without taking my feet off the rudder pedals.

Now I'll start again. I left St. John's at 7:09. It's 7:20 on the clock. I'm 12 hours out from Newfoundland. At 100 miles an hour, that would put me less than 700 miles from the Irish coast. But the tail wind is stronger than I planned on. Suppose I've averaged 120 miles an hour since St. John's. 12 hours at 120 miles an hour – – – 10 hours at 120 miles an hour would be 1200 miles — 12 hours would make 1440 miles. 1440 from 1860 is about 400 miles. I may be within 400 miles of the Irish coast at this moment.

I may be closer! The wind aloft during the night might have been stronger. It might have been blowing 60 miles an hour. Suppose I averaged 150 miles during the night and 120 miles afterward. No, that's too much. I can't work it out. I don't want to bother with any more figures. It's better not to count on the wind. I'll calculate my course at an even 100 miles an hour and stay with my original estimate of navigation. I've got to be prepared for discouragement if I don't strike the coast of Ireland when my arrival time comes due. I have no reserve for disappointments. I can't afford to indulge in hopefulness and tail winds.

But what correction shall I make for drift, for the detours around thunderheads, for the hours I've been veering north of my headings? I'll rest a few more minutes and then figure out a solution for this problem too.

Right rudder, ten degrees.

It was in the Army flying schools that I learned the elements of navigation — how to swing a compass; how to lay a course. There, such words as "Mercator," "gnomonic," "polyconic," and "variation," lost their mystery — became clearcut pictures in my mind. Those schools had been a little like this flight — seemingly unattainable at first, then filled with obstacles too great for me to pass. But somehow I got through.

I was barnstorming in southern Minnesota when I first heard about the training fields of Brooks and Kelly. It was a summer evening in 1923. I was wiping off my Jenny's cowlings when a touring car drove up. The people in it were not passengers, as I had hoped. They came to watch, and talk of flying. The men wanted to show off a bit before the girls. Their voices were high and clearly pitched for me to hear that one of them had been in the Army Air Service. Finally two of the men stepped out and sauntered to the fence.

"How's business?"

"Not too good," I answered, going on with my work.

"This town's barnstormed out," one of the men continued. "There were three planes here last year. Where you going to stop next?"

"First town with a good field near it."

"It must be a hard way to make a living. Say, why don't you enlist in the Army as a flying cadet?"

"I've got a plane of my own. Why should I want to be a cadet?" I'd replied, laughing, but inwardly annoyed by the implication that I lacked experience as a pilot.

"Oh, you can barnstorm around with OX-5 Jennies all right; but the only way you'll get to fly the big ones is to join the Army. They train you on DHs with Liberty engines. You don't know what flying's like until you hold four hundred horses on your throttle. And you don't have to clean off your plane every night. The crew chiefs do that for you."

He'd used the right bait. Who wouldn't want to fly a Liberty engine? I hung my gasoline-soaked rag over the drift wire. "If a commercial pilot enlists, can't he fly army planes without going to cadet school?"

"No; you have to go through the whole course. Takes a year, but it's worth it. You get a lieutenant's commission if you graduate. Well, we've got to be going." They climbed back into the car. "Write a letter to the War Department. They'll tell you all about it."

I went on cleaning the fuselage. Think of zooming through the sky on the power of four hundred horses! Think of flying always on freshly covered wings with new and drum-tight fabric! An Army pilot had no makeshift splices in his spars, no bowed struts between them. His equipment was always up to date, and inspected every morning. And he didn't have to worry about the cost of repairs or gasoline. The government paid for that.

Of course when you joined the Army you lost the independence of a barnstorming pilot. You couldn't unlash your plane in the morning and point it north, south, east, or west. You didn't have the freedom of the birds, couldn't choose your pasture for the night, or drift across country with the seasons. You might gain freedom from financial worries, but didn't you have to follow orders all the time?

Right rudder, four degrees.

The lure of DeHavilands and Liberties won out. I'd written the letter, obtained two recommendations through my father, reported at Fort Snelling for an interview, and taken my entrance examinations at Chanute Field. How my heart had beaten under the flight surgeon's stethoscope. I couldn't hold it down at all. Suppose he found something wrong with my body? Suppose I failed to line up those little sticks that test the eyes? What about the mysterious Schneider Index, which all pilots seemed to fear? And the personal interviews with officers — would they judge my character as warranting a lieutenant's commission in the Air Service Reserve? Fortunately, my year and a half at the University of Wisconsin exempted me from taking academic examinations. I couldn't have passed them. I was much too rusty.

That was the month Leon Klink and I flew south with his Canuck. It was a trip of many stops, for the fuel tank held only twenty-three gallons — enough to fly for two and a half hours. If we left a half-hour in reserve for locating a field, which was often a difficult task, our plane had a range of a hundred and fifty miles in still air. But we had plenty of time. Klink wanted to gain experience in cross-country flying, while I wanted to learn the results of my examinations before making future plans.

We landed in Missouri, in Kentucky, in Tennessee, Mississippi, and Alabama. Barnstorming was poor all over the south that winter. We hardly took in enough money to pay our expenses.

"Why don't we try the West?" I suggested one evening. "We could work our way to the Atlantic coast, and then fly right across the United States to the Pacific. Whenever we find a place where a lot of people want to ride, we'll hold over and make some money."

Klink was always ready for adventure. The idea of a transcontinental flight appealed to him. "Do you think we can get across the mountains?" he asked.

"It won't do any harm to try," I said. "The mountains are lowest in the south, and we can hit the passes."

The following morning our project was under way. But Pensacola, Florida, turned out to be our farthest east. We landed on the Naval Air Station near that city. At the post office, I received my mail — the first since we left Lambert Field. In it was the long-hoped-for War Department envelope with its brief and stilted letter. I had passed my examinations satisfactorily. I was to report for enlistment in time to enter the March 15, 1924, class of flying cadets at Brooks Field, San Antonio, Texas.

It was a full month to the middle of March. Klink and I decided to cut short our stay in Florida. Then, if we averaged only one flight a day, there was time to make California. I could enlist on the coast, and take a train back to Texas.

The next morning, we started our engine with the intention of spending the night in Georgia. Before heading west I was to make good a ride we'd promised to the sister of our host. I followed my usual practice of taking off for a solo flight before putting the day's first passenger in the front cockpit. It didn't take much time or fuel, and gave me a chance to test sod, air, and engine. If anything weren't working properly I preferred to discover it when I was alone, with a lightly loaded plane.

My take-off direction was over the Bay. At two hundred feet, the engine cut out. We never found out why — probably a little water in the fuel line, although we'd checked the screen and drained the trap. I nosed down, banked left, and made shore. With another fifteen feet of altitude, I could have reached the field. As it was, I had to stall onto sand hillocks at its edge. The first mound crushed the landing gear, splintered the propeller, and drove the left wheel up through the lower wing's front spar.

I was hardly out of my cockpit when the Navy's sirens started screaming. That was a new experience for a barnstorming pilot. It was bad enough to crack up, without having sirens tell everybody about it. I stood, humiliated, and watched fire and wrecking trucks race toward me from the line of buildings.

There wasn't a great deal of damage done, and the Navy was grand about it. The station commander sent a crew of sailors to help move our Canuck back to the balloon hangar, ordered them to handle it with special care, and let us use parts from salvaged naval aircraft for repairs. We built a box splice around our broken spar, and the crew chiefs gave us enough dope and linen to patch up the wing's torn covering.

It was the twentieth of February before we were again ready to start west. That left just over three weeks to make the Pacific coast, and for me to get back to Texas. But with good breaks in weather, it was time enough. We decided to make longer flights after we left Pensacola. Landing for fuel sometimes wasted hours. At the Naval Air Station, we added ten gallons to our Canuck's gasoline capacity by lashing a cylindrical can, bought at a local hardware store, next to the fuselage on each lower wing. That gave us an hour more in the air. It cut down our speed, but added to our total range.

It was quite a job leaning out of my cockpit, into the slipstream, and unlashing one of those cans; and then, empty, lashing it back again. But with the aid of a steamhose slipped over the nozzle, I hardly spilled a drop. This improvised method extended our range so greatly that we were able to follow the Gulf of Mexico's coast all the way to Pascagoula, Mississippi, before we landed. On the next flight we made New Orleans; then Lake Charles; then Houston, Texas. At Rice Field, outside of Houston, we found a hangar full of surplus Army equipment. We bought three nine-gallon wing tanks, and attached them to our Canuck. With the regular fuselage tank and the two five-gallon cans, this gave us a cruising range of about four hundred miles.

At Brooks Field, San Antonio, our load-carrying troubles began. We'd filled both our cans and all our tanks with gasoline, and started our engine soon after sunrise. I never had a plane stick to the ground so long. Our Canuck must have run across a half-mile of sod before the wheels broke free. Fortunately, the field was both large and smooth.

I'd thought our problems would be over for a time after we got in the air; but the Canuck just couldn't climb. I made three wide circles around the field without getting as much as fifty feet above ground. There was no use going on that way. Like Alice through the looking-glass, we were doing all the climbing we could do "to keep in the same place." I landed, and we removed the five-gallon cans from the wings. We left one behind. Klink carried the other on his lap, to save air resistance.

The Canuck labored upward slowly, after our next take-off. Within fifteen minutes we were several hundred feet high, and making about fifty miles an hour against a quartering westerly wind. But a rising sun lowered the density of air, and the ground sloped upward faster than we could gain altitude through using up our fuel. An hour after leaving Brooks Field, our engine at full power, we were skimming mesquite and cactus in a country that had changed from plains to eroded, stony hills. Finally I had to nose down into a ravine, and signal Klink to heave his gas can overboard to keep us from running out of altitude completely. How he hated to give up the fuel we'd worked so hard to lift! I had to shout and motion twice before he'd let it go. After that, we struggled up over the hills in front of us.

Right rudder, ten degrees.

There were no good fields around Camp Wood, Texas, so being low on fuel, we landed in the town square. In spite of its poles,

wires, and rows of stores, it was the largest open area we could find
that was smooth enough to land on. People came running from all
directions as we taxied to a corner. Horses were hitched to posts;
stores were locked; school was let out. A crowd surrounded the
Canuck in no time at all. What was wrong? Why were we there?
Where were we going? Where had we come from? What were the
wings made of? Was there anything they could do to help?

All would have gone well if the wind hadn't veered southeastward through the night; but the next morning, buildings blocked
our take-off from the square. There was a possibility that I could
use one of the adjoining streets as a runway. Once in air, I could
fly six miles south and land on a clear and level strip of ground
some "old-timers" had told us about the night before.

I looked over the street carefully, walking up and down its
center. There was a depression a few hundred feet from the point
where I'd have to start; but my wheels should be clear before I
reached it, if I took off alone and with a light fuel load. After that
I'd have to brush my wing tips through some tree branches that
overhung the road, but they were little more than twigs. Then,
there'd be open miles of air in which to climb. But to get off before
the depression in the road I'd have to pass between two telegraph
poles, about fifty feet from my starting point, and only two or
three feet farther apart than the span of the upper wings.

Take-off conditions were certainly not favorable. But they
might not improve for days. After all, one drove a car regularly
between objects with only a few inches clearance. Why shouldn't
one do it with an airplane? I could mark the exact center of the
street between the poles, and imagine that I was in an automobile. We pushed our Canuck into position, and warmed up the
engine.

I thought I was rolling precisely along the center of the street,
but I failed by three inches to clear the right-hand telephone pole.
I jerked the throttle shut, but it was too late. The pole held my
wing, while the plane's momentum carried the fuselage around and
poked its nose right through the board wall of a hardware store.
The propeller was shattered, of course, and the engine stopped at

once. But pots and pans kept on crashing down inside the store for several seconds.

That did bring people running. The hardware dealer told us that he and his son thought an earthquake was taking place. But instead of being angry, he appeared quite pleased. When we tried to pay for the damage we'd done, he refused to accept a cent. It had been an interesting experience, he said, and the advertising value was worth much more than the cost of the few boards needed for repairs.

To my surprise, I could find nothing broken on our Canuck aside from the propeller and wing tip. We wired Houston for a new prop and a can of dope to be expressed to Camp Wood c.o.d. With the help of the crowd, we pushed our plane back into the square.

Three days later, we were ready to start again. The wind blew in the right direction that morning, and we took off with two of our wing tanks full. The Canuck flew as well as ever, except that it carried a little extra left rudder. By leaving the throttle wide open and following the valleys, we were able to hold an average altitude of several hundred feet.

A half-hour before sunset, we began looking for a place to come down for the night. There wasn't a town within sight; but beside the railroad ahead of us we saw a section house and three old boxcars which, we learned later, were dignified by the name of Maxon, Texas. A quarter-mile to the west lay a long, sloping, irregularly-shaped area of relatively smooth ground. It contained scattered clumps of cactus, but there was room for our wheels and wings to pass between them. There we landed, with an east wind.

The section boss and most of the Mexicans from the boxcars rushed over to meet us. They helped tie down our plane, and the "boss" invited us to stay at his house.

"Sure, there's an extra bed, an' ye'll be welcome company," he said. "I'm livin' here all alone — except fur the Mexicans. Don't see many people to talk to. It's thirty-two miles to the nearest store. Good thing ye stopped today, though; I'm goin' off fur a week t'morrow."

When we woke at Maxon, a westerly breeze was blowing down the slope of our prairie strip. A hill to the east prevented taking off downwind. There were no high obstructions toward the west; but rolling uphill, and without a stronger wind, it would take so long to get flying speed that we'd be in sagebrush and cactus before our wheels left the ground.

We hired some Mexicans to help us, and spent the entire morning cutting out a longer runway for our Canuck. There was room enough when we had finished, but the air was hot, and the wind still light. We decided to attempt an up-slope take-off with only the main fuel tank full. I got the Canuck to break free all right, with fifty yards to spare. But it had no extra power for climbing. The lower wings just rode on their ground cushion and held the wheels about four feet high. If I could have gotten up to eight feet and stayed there for a half-mile, we'd have been clear of obstructions and past the upward roll of earth. After that, the terrain slanted down. But our wheels began scraping through sagebrush. I couldn't get an extra foot of height.

We stalled over a gravelly wash, and slapped through a clump of cactus leaves on the far side. Then — I saw it coming thirty yards away — a Spanish bayonet stretched up above the foliage ahead. It was too late to land. I was too low to bank. I tried to zoom; but pulling the stick back did no good. As wing and trunk collided, I jerked my throttle closed, to crash. The six-inch trunk smashed fabric, nose, and spar. I'd expected it to shear right through our wing; but the bayonet planted itself in the middle of the panel, and rode on with us through the brush — green blades rising from the parchment-colored fabric like an orchid on a limb. The internal cross-brace wires had cut through the trunk like a machete.

There was no further shattering of structure, and our landing gear bumped along without collapsing. Sage and cactus brought us to a stop quickly. I'd already cut the switch. We climbed out to find our damage extraordinarily light. The propeller wasn't cracked; neither tire had blown out; struts were sound; the tail skid hadn't broken. Some turnbuckles needed tightening, and we had a few long tears in the fabric on the under surfaces of the wings; but except for the area the bayonet went through, not a single rib was shattered.

Our attention had been so concentrated on the crack-up and the plane that we didn't notice a freight train stopping on the tracks, a hundred yards away.

"NEED ANY HELP THERE?"

The fireman was running toward us, jumping over cactus. "We were afraid somebody got hurt," he added breathlessly as he came closer.

"Thanks, but I guess there's not much help you can give us," I said. "We'll just have to patch the plane up again, that's all."

"Won't you need to go to the city for repairs? Can't get anything out here, you know. We'll take you along in the cab if you like. But we gotta start right off — gotta get the track clear."

"Thirty-two miles to the nearest store," the section boss had said. And "the nearest store" certainly wouldn't have airplane dope on its shelves.

"You climb on board and get what material you can," I told my partner. "I'll stay and work on the plane."

Klink went all the way to El Paso to get a small can of pigmented dope, two lengths of crating board, some nails and screws, a can of glue, several balls of chalk line, and enough cotton cloth to repair our wings. We borrowed an axe, a butcher knife, a needle, and a spool of thread from the rancher, and started to make the Canuck airworthy once more. We hewed the crating boards down roughly to size with the axe, cut them into proper lengths with an old hack-saw blade from our engine's tool kit, and whittled off edges, thick spots, and splinters with the butcher knife which we'd whetted to the keenest edge its mediocre steel could hold. In a few hours we had the box splice completed. But in shrinking the cord wrapping we used up most of our dope. There was barely enough left to hold down the edges of the big cloth patch we put over the wing where the bayonet crashed through; the body of the patch, and the long rents in wing fabric which I'd sewed together while my partner was away, had to be left flabby and untreated.

I scraped up over the cactus on my next take-off attempt at Maxon. It was close, but a steady east wind helped, and the front cockpit was empty. We'd been on the ground for eight days. Our time had run out. Klink had decided to continue on to California by train, while I flew back to San Antonio and the Army Flying School's classes.

Right rudder, seven degrees.

The Canuck was in pretty sorry shape when I landed on Brooks Field. Undoped cloth had been unable to stand the air stream's whipping. It had worn away until several square feet of skeletal ribs and spars were exposed to view. The wing tip we'd repaired at Camp Wood drew one's eye like an awkwardly bandaged finger. The rips I'd sewed up were frayed and sagging. Box splices bulged on the spar. And one of the wheels had no tire — I'd pulled it off after a cactus-punctured inner tube had ripped beyond repair.

Crewmen on the line were amazed that the plane would fly, and still more amazed that anyone would fly it.

"How much right aileron do you have to hold to keep that wing up?"

"Does the resistance have much effect on your rudder?"

"Don't she want'a ground-loop with that tire off?"

Each mechanic had a different question. They'd never seen anything like it before, they said, as they tailed the Canuck into a back corner of a wooden, war-built hangar.

I'd hoped to repair and recondition our plane in spare hours, but the Commanding Officer held a different view. I was sitting on my barracks bunk when his messenger arrived. There were a dozen other cadets in the "bay." We were folding blankets, hanging up clothes, and packing newly issued equipment into our foot-lockers.

"Which one o' you fellers flies that plane that's out in the hangar?" he demanded.

"I do." I stood up as I spoke. All eyes turned on me — here was a cadet who was actually a pilot. I felt wise and proud.

"Major says, get that damn thing out'a his sight 'fore ya do anythin' else! Says he don't care what ya do with it, but git it off Brooks Field." The stern-faced corporal wheeled and left, heels clicking on the oiled-wood floor.

Army mechanics obligingly pushed the Canuck out on the line, and stopped their work to watch while I took off again on a tireless wheel, with aileron drooped to make up for missing fabric. Fortunately, there was a commercial airfield only a mile or two away, and at Stinson they were glad to have our plane. It meant more activity, more business, more income. There, any aircraft that could land was welcome — and any that wished to take off was encouraged to try.

On March 19, 1924, I enlisted in the Army. On that day, I became Cadet Lindbergh. I had to enlist for three years; but, I was informed, a cadet could resign at any time he wished, and receive his discharge within two weeks. It was implied, in fact, that you had to be pretty careful or you'd receive your discharge without resigning.

At Brooks Field "Pop" Sims, our barracks sergeant, told us they "separate men from the boys. We make ya into a soldier. If ya haven't got it in ya, we wash ya out." A huge man, tough in talk, kind in action, he put us to bed at night and woke us close to sunrise by methods of his own device, but with the firmness of a childhood nurse.

"R-R-R-I-I-I-S-E AND SHINE! R-R-R-I-I-I-S-E AND SHINE!" His voice came booming through our barracks every weekday morning, smothering the bugle notes. "Out of those bunks, you fellows, or I'll" – – –Scrape, thud – – –

"Pop" Sims waited on none of his charges. Any bunk still occupied when his clumping feet arrived was inverted with envied strength and skill. The resulting bumps, jibes, and bed-making argued strongly against a lazy head.

"Rise and shine!" I wish his voice would boom through my cockpit now. I wish he could dump me on the floor to bump my flesh and jar my bones. I need his firm insistence. If he could stand beside me, I think I'd wake – – –

Right rudder, three degrees.

Our flying training started in April of 1924. Along with six other cadets, I was assigned to a lanky sergeant named Bill Winston — good-natured, skillful, cautious — one of the finest pilots on Brooks field. The Hisso-Jennies the Army used for training were like the civil aircraft I'd been piloting, except that they were heavier and carried their throttles on the fuselage's left side. Since the war, I learned, all Army planes had been standardized with left-hand throttles.

A new plane, and changing hands on the stick, threw me off a little. My first landing was not three-point, as I'd expected it to be. But Master Sergeant Winston turned me loose for solo after three rounds of the field, and — a special honor — let me use his personal plane, JN6-H Number 326.

"You know how to fly all right," he said. "You've just got to get used to this Jenny. Later on I'll try you out in acrobatics."

Master Sergeant Winston had a human touch, wisdom, and humor that held the respect of his students aside from his pilot's skill. He usually gave us short talks before flying started in the morning — seven cadets grouped around him on the dew-wet grass:

"Now pretty soon you fellows are going to think you're pretty good. It happens to every pilot. Usually starts when he's had about twenty-five or thirty hours solo. I just want you to remember this: in aviation, it may be all right to fool the other fellow about how good you are — if you can. *But don't try to fool yourself.*"

When the marks from our examination in property accounting were posted, there was a 72 beside my name. Skimming through by two points wouldn't have worried me in high school or college. But at Brooks Field, that narrow margin was disturbing. Before,

I'd always gone to school because I had to go, because it was considered the proper thing to do. Here, I realized, I was going to school because I wanted to learn, to complete the course, to gain my Air Service bars and wings. I studied after classes, through the week ends, often far into the night. At times I slipped into my bunk with swimming head, but I had the satisfaction of watching my grade average climb slowly through the 80's and into the 90's, until I graduated second man at Brooks and first at Kelly.

In Texas, I was in the unique position of being both an army student and a civilian instructor. As soon as Klink returned from California, I began showing him the techniques he would have to use in getting the Canuck back to St. Louis. First came the solo flights; next, cautious sideslips and stall landings; then, picking out strange fields. I would spend a morning practicing acrobatics, sit through hours of ground school in the afternoon, instruct in the evening, and study at night.

There was so little contact between Army and civilian personnel in the area that I don't think the officers at Brooks knew I flew at Stinson. A mile of mesquite and cactus divided the two fields as though it were an ocean. And in many ways they seemed continents apart. At Brooks, there was extreme discipline. You walked erect, saluted, made sure every button on your uniform was properly inserted through its hole. The grounds were neat, the barracks swept, the hangars kept in perfect order. Then you took a winding, cactus-studded path — it was so hidden that you had to know exactly where it started — and ended up where there wasn't any discipline at all. Stinson's flyers wore what clothes they liked — new or old, clean or dirty. Only the most essential buttons were considered. Paper scraps and pop bottles littered hangar corners. Wrecks of airplanes lay around like unburied skeletons on the prairie grass.

At Brooks, your thoughts were channeled along precise, scientific lines. You followed a pattern for your landings; maneuvers were exact. Classes followed textbooks. Life was routined by military regulations. At Stinson, human nature had its freest play. You could land downwind or upwind, or come in between the trees.

There was no limit to your actions so long as they placed no limit upon others. You could drink if you wished. You could smoke on duty. The individualism of the place was stamped on both personnel and aircraft. There were planes like our Canuck, flight-scarred and patched. There were two or three in perfect shape — without a scratch — with drum-tight fabric. There were others in conditions in between. In one corner of an oily-floored hangar, an ornithopter reposed, coated with dust. Its strangly hinged and angled wings were supposed to carry it aloft by flapping like a bird. But the inventor's enthusiasm had been dulled by constant failure, and his last attempts at flight had been made some months before.

At Brooks, our ground school increased, with the summer's temperature, in toughness. By the end of June, nearly half of our class had faced the dreaded Benzine Board and been washed out. One after another, long faces had said good-by to classmates, and abandoned cots had been stacked away in storage until, as "Pop" Sims prophesied, our barracks were no longer crowded. Those of us who remained felt like veterans, though by no means secure. We knew that Benzine Boards would convene with regularity for close to eight months more, and we watched with apprehension each newly posted list of names.

Photography, motors, map-making, field service regulations, radio theory, military law – – – twenty-five courses we took in our first half-year of training. I spent as much as seven hours writing an examination. On one of the more difficult tests, I didn't get my paper completed until eleven o'clock at night. Somehow the schedule still dropped behind, so they worked us Saturdays too.

I'd thought our engineering classes severe, at the University of Wisconsin. But they'd never been like this. Lectures on navigation, meteorology, and rigging alternated with formations, transition, and cross-country flights. A student not only had to know his lesson, but his instructor's attitude as well. "Does he like you to glide in fast or slow? Tail skid high or tail skid low?" "Sergeant X will help you through as long as he thinks you're working." "Just make one slip with Captain Y, and boy, you'll be a goner!"

Eight degrees right rudder.

In September, thirty-three "veteran" cadets packed footlockers, piled into buses, and moved ten miles westward, from Major Royce's Brooks to Major Hickam's Keely, for "advanced training." We left Jennies behind. Kelly's students flew De Havilands. I was the only man left of the seven who started out with Master Sergeant Winston. Two had resigned; two had crashed; and two had been held over to the next class because of deficiency in flying.

I was assigned to Lieutenant Strickland for my first instruction at Kelly. He had that combination of ability and experience on which flying perfection must be based. Behind a caustic wit which cadet errors fed, he held a deep interest in his students. You felt he'd get you through the course if you had the "stuff" within you.

"Now just remember, DHs aren't built like Jennies," I remember his saying as we started out. "They got power to pull you through more; but if you once get 'em stalled, it takes a lot of altitude to recover. And you can't stunt 'em like a Jenny either — no rolls or loops. Their wings aren't tied on that strong; if you pull the stick back too hard, they're liable to leave you."

Most of our transition to DHs consisted of wing-overs, figure eights, spot landings, and hurdles. Of course there were days when "one-eightys," "three-sixtys," and "strange field approaches" were thrown in; but the system of training at Kelly was quite different from that at Brooks. For one thing, it was built around a much more formidable type of plane. For another, the instructors seemed to swap students every week or two. I flew with Lieutenants Canfield, Griffith, Richter, Chapman, Cannon, Guidera, Maughan, Reeves, Moon, and Moore.

"Keep the wing tip on that barn. Don't be afraid to haul her over!" My instructors insisted on precision. "That's what they put you through this school for. Any pilot can slop around the air." And they believed that Kelly's students should follow standardized procedures. "Now Lindbergh, don't you slip that plane," I remember being warned. "It may be all right later on; but we don't like it in the School. Don't come in so high. Cut your gun farther back. Get used to judging distance. And don't forget, no hedge-hopping here at Kelly. We wash you out for that!"

We were trained in gunnery, photography, and bombing. We were taught how to intercept enemy aircraft, how to get maximum performance from our planes. We learned to hold tight formations, to follow signals quickly in the air. Ground school continued in its strict routine.

Only six weeks remained before our graduation when the discipline relaxed. "You'll soon be commissioned officers," we were told. "You must learn to be responsible for your own conduct."

Each man was assigned to one of the Air Service's four branches — Pursuit, Bombardment, Observation, or Attack. For months I'd been working for Pursuit, and along with Collins, Love, and Stevens, I achieved it – – –

The sun blinks on again in my cockpit. The cloud's shadow has passed. The ocean stretches ahead to the horizon, bleak and endless as a desert. Its brilliance smarts against my eyes. According to all previous rules, this dawn-created stupor should have departed long ago. It should have vanished with the morning twilight, given over to woken habits of the day. Now the sun is almost overhead. Why can't I break these elastic bonds of sleep? It's seven-thirty in New York. That makes it about half past ten local time. The day will grow no brighter, and I'm still carrying on the vaguest kind of navigation. I'm losing time. I'm losing fuel — mixture control and throttle are only roughly set. My eyes close and stay shut for too many seconds at a time. No mental effort I exert can hold them open. I've lost command over their muscles.

Here it's well into midday and my mind's still shirking, still refusing to meet the problems it undertook so willingly in planning for this flight. Are all those months of hard and detailed work to be wasted for lack of a few minutes of concentrated effort? Is my character so weak that I can't pull myself together long enough to lay out a new, considered course? Has landing at Le Bourget become of so little import that I'll trade success for these useless hours of semiconscious relaxation? *No; I must, I will* become alert, and concentrate, and make decisions.

There are measures I haven't yet used — too extreme for normal times. But now it's a case of survival. Anything is justified that has effect. I strike my face sharply with my hand. It hardly feels the blow. I strike again with all the strength I have. My cheek is numb, and there's none of the sharp stinging that I counted on to wake my body. No jump of flesh, no lash on mind. It's no use. Even these methods don't work. Why try more?

But Paris is over a thousand miles away! And there's still a continent to find. I must be prepared to strike a fog-covered European coast hundreds of miles off course; and, if necessary, to fly above clouds all the hours of another night. How can I pass through such ordeals if I can't wake my mind and stir my body? But the alternative is death and failure. Can I complete this flight to Paris? Can I even reach the Irish coast? *But the alternative is death and failure! Death! For the first time in my life, I doubt my ability to endure.*

The stark concept of death has more effect than physical blow or reasoned warning. It imbues me with new power, power strong enough to communicate the emergency to my body's senses, to whip them up from their lethargy and marshall them once more — in straggling ranks, but with some semblance of order and coordination. *It's life, life, life itself at stake.* This time I'm not just saying so. *I know it.*

I shake my head and body harshly. I flex arms and legs, compress muscles of chest and stomach, stamp feet on floor boards, bounce up and down, jam the stick forward to throw my weight against the belt, jerk it back to press myself tightly to the seat and floor. *I'll break this spider web of sleep!* --- But ---but ---what I need most of all is breath---*b-r-e-a-t-h*---The instrument board is vague---like evening twilight---My brain swims---

Instinct tells me the key to life is air. I lean to the side of the cockpit, grip the sill, push my head dizzily out of the window – – – Am I gliding or climbing? – – – The sense of level flight has gone – – – Pull the stick back a little – – – not too much, or — a spin — a stall – – – Is one wing down? – – – Waves are gone from the ocean – – – There's no horizon to the sky – – – Consciousness is leaving – – – I'm passing out – – – Maybe it's carbon monoxide from the exhaust – – – I've been afraid of that – – –

The fresh blast of the slipstream washes over my face, rushes into my mouth and nostrils, forces my eyelids open, fills my lungs with breath. Can I hold on to consciousness? I must hold on – – – A single second would merge into eternity – – – I'm too close to the water to let go for an instant – – – less than a hundred feet – – – Breathe deeply – – – Force the eyes to see – – – Each gulp of air is medicine — but has it time to work? There's not enough area to my lungs – – – Sea, sky, and instruments merge in night – – – God give me strength – – –

No – – – I'm not going over the precipice – – – The ocean is green again – – – The sky's turning blue – – – Clouds are whitening – – – Instrument faces stare at me – – – Numbers come in focus – – – I've been hanging over the chasm of eternity, holding onto the ledge with my fingertips; but now I'm gaining strength, I'm crawling upward. Consciousness is coming back.

The *Spirit of St. Louis* is climbing slowly. I push the stick forward — and left to lift the wing. Left rudder to stop the turn. I keep my head in the slipstream, breathing deeply. Now, I see clearly. Now, my mind and my senses join. The seriousness of the crisis has startled me to awareness. I've finally broken the spell of sleep. The sight of death has drawn out the last reserves of strength.

I feel as though I were recuperating from a severe illness. When you're suffering from a disease, the time comes when you know the crisis has passed. The fever leaves; a sense of health returns, and you're increasingly able to use your normal mind and body. You become aware of life's quality again. I sit quietly, looking out of the open window, letting strength and confidence build up. How beautiful the ocean is; how clear the sky; how fiery the sun! Whatever coming hours hold, it's enough to be alive this minute.

The line of fog islands angles northward and disappears over the horizon. I take stock of my position. The greater portion of the ocean is behind me. There's plenty of fuel left in the tanks, and no indication of a defect in my plane or engine. Instrument needles are all exactly where they belong. I'm wide awake. It's almost noon of the day I'll land in Europe — *at Paris* — *on Le Bourget.*

In three minutes it will be 7:52, New York time. I watch the hand creep forward – – – 7:50 – – – 7:51 – – – 7:52 — exactly one day since take-off. At this moment yesterday, I'd just cleared the telephone wires at the end of the runway on Long Island.

THE TWENTY-FIFTH HOUR

Over the Atlantic

HOURS OF FUEL CONSUMED

NOSE TANK

¼ + ̶H̶H̶t̶ 1 1

LEFT WING	CENTER WING	RIGHT WING
¼ + 1 1 1	¼ +	¼ + 1 1

FUSELAGE

̶H̶H̶t̶ ̶H̶H̶t̶ 1

I shift back to the right wing-tank, and mark another line on the instrument board. Now to fill in the log – – – no, navigation is more important. I'll lay out plans while my mind is clear.

I have a strong impression that I've turned and drifted southward of my route, and I was ninety miles south when I left Newfoundland. But I've already compensated for my St. John's detour, so I must put that out of my mind entirely. I unfold the strip charts on my knees, and begin to estimate the southward factors.

First, the detours around thunderheads during the night. It seemed a long distance at the time, while I still held navigating accuracy to be of prime importance; but as I look back from the objectivity of day and sunlight, I remember that most of my detours were only fifteen or twenty degrees to the southward. After the moon rose, I made several to the north in partial compensation. Probably the distance I deviated from my route was somewhere between twenty-five and fifty miles.

The second factor is more difficult. I don't know how to estimate it. The compass swinging seemed as much one way as the other in the magnetic storm. I simply took for granted that the card was in its right position during the steadier periods. What else could I do? This second factor I'll have to class as an unknown, an X quantity in my equation.

And the stars lure a pilot southward with their movement through the heavens, when he follows them, no matter how stubbornly he tries to compensate by change in heading. I'll make an estimate of ten to twenty miles.

The fourth factor, which disturbs me most of all, is the direction and velocity of the wind aloft. I flew over clouds for seven hours, at high altitude, without any indication of the wind whatever. I have reasons to hope that a strong tail or quartering tail wind blew me far along during the night. Possibly it also drifted me many miles southward. Since there's no way of knowing, this too must be treated as an X quantity.

Now, the northward compensations. For the last seven hours I've been lax in changing compass headings. That would leave me somewhat north of the course on my chart, but probably not over five or ten miles. Much more important is the northward error caused by hours of lethargic and inaccurate flying, by the fact that the compass needle leaned so far and so frequently to the left of its lubber line. Sometimes I was two or three degrees off heading, sometimes ten, sometimes close to twenty. All I'm certain of is that the needle usually lay to the left of the center point, as though a stronger mind than mine were deciding its position. How far this carried me off course is as uncertain as the wind drift. But in this case it was definitely to the north. And since an estimate must be made, I'll put it at between 25 and 50 miles.

My equation contains southward errors of 35 to 70 miles, northward errors of 30 to 60 miles, and two X quantities. The most practical approach to a solution seems to lie in assigning probable maximum values to the X quantities — first in one direction and then in the other. That should bracket the extreme positions where my plane might be.

Suppose the wind aloft, during the night and morning, blew constantly from the north at 50 miles an hour. In 7 hours I would have drifted 350 miles southward. Adding 70 miles for thunderhead detours and star-steering errors would make 420 miles. If I allow 50 miles for compass swinging, it brings the total to 470 miles. From this must be subtracted the 25 miles estimated minimum error caused by faulty flying (by the compass needle riding always on the left). That leaves 445 miles. And finally, there's the estimated minimum of 5 miles I angled northward through not changing compass heading. The result gives me a probable maximum southward error of about 440 miles.

I look down at the chart. Four hundred and forty miles would take me off the edge of the strip. If I'm that far south and hold my present heading, I'll strike the coast of Europe where the Bay of Biscay scallops farthest into France — and after darkness. I'll have to fly over half a thousand more miles of ocean than if I make my landfall on the Irish coast. It will be hard to locate my position even if the moon shines down through a clear sky. If there are clouds, and the earth's so black that I can't recognize some coastal landmark or some foreign city, I'll have to throttle down and keep awake while I wait for another dawn. After that, I may not have enough fuel to reach Paris.

Maybe it would be better to turn twenty degrees northward, even though I strike Ireland well above my route. Then, I'll have a good chance of locating my position before darkness. If I can do that, and if fog doesn't hide the ground, I'll find my way to Paris through the blackest night.

But suppose a south wind blew at 50 miles an hour above the clouds last night. It's possible that the *Spirit of St. Louis* is north of course: 350 miles for wind, plus 50 miles for letting the compass needle wander, plus 50 miles for swinging (it might have turned me north instead of south), plus 10 miles for not changing my heading on time, makes a total of 460 miles. Subtracting 25 miles for detouring the thunderheads and 10 miles for following the stars (it must have been at least that), leaves 425 miles. If I'm that far north of route, I'll hit the Scottish coast. If I subtract another 20° from my heading, on a mistaken theory that I'm too far south, I may miss the British Isles entirely! That would mean striking the foggy, fjorded coast of Norway in the night.

Suppose an east wind blew at 50 miles an hour, and slowed my ground speed down to 50 miles. That would leave me nearly a thousand miles from Ireland at this moment. Then, a twenty degree change in compass heading would carry me close to Glasgow.

Suppose, which thank God is most probable of all, the wind aloft was both strong and tail. If it blew 50 miles an hour from the west, I'm within 300 miles of Ireland at this moment. Then there's no need to turn northward; even if I'm south of course, I'll strike the French coast before nightfall.

Three conditions argue against turning northward, and only one argues in its favor. Certainly any major change in heading involves a dangerous risk. It seems wisest to fall back on the basic plan of navigation I laid out in San Diego when my mind was fresh and there was more time to think. Sitting at the drafting table, with all my charts spread out, I'd decided that I would compensate only for known and highly probable factors until I estimated my position to be 100 miles east of the meridian cutting the western Irish coast. At that time, if land were still unsighted, I'd subtract thirty degrees from my heading. Then, regardless of how the winds blew or how faulty my navigation had been, I could hardly miss striking somewhere on the western coast of Ireland, or the southern end of England, or the northern coast of France.

I'll estimate that I've averaged 120 miles an hour since I left Newfoundland. That would put me 1560 miles to the eastward of St. John's. Suppose I lost an hour in climbing, detouring, compass swinging, and poor flying. I'd be 420 miles from Ireland. I'll let my known northward and southward errors cancel out. They're all estimates, and there's not enough difference between them to justify a change in course.

Now for wind drift. I look down at the waves. The streaks are nearly paralleling my course, and the velocity is probably about 30 miles an hour. The great circle on my chart, 400 miles from Ireland, calls for a magnetic course of 119°. Plus 1° for westerly deviation makes 120°. A 30-mile wind from 290° must drift me about 5° to the right. 5° from 120° leaves 115°. I reach down to adjust the earth-inductor compass – – – But that's almost exactly the heading I've been following! It calls for a shift of only 2°.

Then all those lethargic hours may not have been squandered. Maybe I haven't lost much efficiency by giving way to dreams and sleep. And by resting, I've built up strength to fit me for the day, afternoon, and night. I'm probably better off than if I could have forced myself to stay alert.

My navigating plans complete, I settle back with clear conscience, letting my eyes sweep leisurely over the sea and horizon on both sides. If I've drifted far south of my route, I may at any time see ships. At least it's worth while watching for them.

Suppose I sight a vessel on the sea. What will I do? That's pleasant to think about. If it's far to the north or south, I won't waste time and fuel detouring. But if it lies close to my route, a slight change in angle will cost only a minute or two. Possibly I could get a check on my heading from the direction in which it's steaming. Most ships will be on lanes that round the southern tips of Ireland and of England.

The people on board probably wouldn't notice the *Spirit of St. Louis* at first. Then, as I came closer, somebody would hear my engine and shout that a plane was approaching. I'd dive down past one side of the ship, about even with the bridge, and wave, and zoom up onto course again. How surprised the captain and the crew would be to see an airplane diving past them out here in the ocean. Everyone would run out on deck.

The sun is overhead, burning between clouds. I wish I could move over into the shade of a wing, the way I used to barnstorming, between flights. When no one was waiting to ride, I'd cut the engine, jump down from my cockpit, and stretch out on the grass. It's a sociable place, under a wing, and good for business, too. People like to come and sit beside you. They start asking questions about flying, and telling about their farms. Pretty soon they begin kidding each other into taking a flight over town. If you help them along a little, they're the best salesmen you could have.

Some of the pleasantest hours of my life have been spent in the shade of a wing — waiting for the Nebraska wind to calm when I was learning to fly; waiting for passengers on Kansas fields; waiting for a fuel truck to drive out from some Missouri town. There, one meets the extremes of human character — from bank presidents to tramps; from sheriffs to outlaws; from professors to idiots; from country preachers to town prostitutes — — —

I see a sun-baked plateau, near the city of Red Lodge in Montana. It's midafternoon. Our plane has been idle all day.

"It's too hot for anybody to fly now," I say. "Maybe we'll get some passengers this evening."

Lynch and I are sitting in the shade of the Standard's lower panel.

"Maybe we're going to get some passengers right now," he replies, pointing.

An open touring car has left the main road, and is curving upslope toward our strip of prairie. It is large, new, and brightly painted — good omens to the barnstorming profession. The car skids to a showy stop, a few yards from our Standard. A tanned, broad-hatted man springs out. He looks like a rancher, and he's the only occupant. Lynch and I get up on our feet to meet him, brushing dried bits of grass from our clothes. The stranger's eyes sparkle and his teeth show white as he strides toward us.

"Howdy! Turner's my name. Say, what'll ya charge to fly me over the town?" he asks.

"We'll give you a real good ride for ten dollars," Lynch replies. "That's a deal."

We strap our passenger down tightly in the front cockpit. I pull the propeller through, and Lynch takes off into the wind, between patches of prickly pear.

There isn't a square foot of shade, with the plane gone. It's too hot to sit down. I wander over the ground, keeping well clear of Spanish bayonet and kicking stones into prairie-dog holes. Whirlwinds of dust spiral in the distance.

Close to a quarter hour passes before the Standard returns. The rancher, beaming, jumps down from his cockpit, hands us a ten-dollar bill, walks jauntily to his car, and spins his wheels over the gravel to a skidding, jack-rabbit start.

"Slim, in all the years I been flying, I never had a ride like that." Lynch's face is half-humorous, half-serious, as we search for cactus-free ground under the wing. "I've heard about fellows like him, out here in the West, but I never met one before." We settle down as comfortably as we can. "After we got in the air, he twisted around and shouted something at me," Lynch continues. "I couldn't hear, of course, so I pulled the throttle. 'TAKE ME LOW DOWN THE MAIN STREET,' he yells. You know, Slim, I've always been an obliging cuss. He seemed to be having such a good time that I just couldn't say no. And we were charging him a pretty good price for the flight, too. I took a chance on the engine cutting, and flew him along the store fronts, about a hundred feet high. Everybody in town was running out into the street and looking up. First thing I know, when we were right smack over the business section, the son-of-a-bitch pulls two horse pistols out of that jacket of his and begins shooting past the wings. I was afraid he'd cut through one of the wires, but he had the guns empty before I could do a damn thing about it. God a'mighty, do you know what he says while we're taxiing in? He turns around with that grin all over his face and yells, 'I SHOT THIS TOWN UP A'FOOT, AN' I SHOT THIS TOWN UP A'HOSSBACK, AN' NOW I SHOT THIS TOWN UP FROM A AIRPLANE.' And he just laughs and laughs! Well, that sure ought to bring the passengers out if there are any. God a'mighty, I hope none of those bullets hit anybody!"

THE TWENTY-SIXTH HOUR

Over the Atlantic

HOURS OF FUEL CONSUMED

NOSE TANK

¼ + ~~11111~~ 1 1

LEFT WING	CENTER WING	RIGHT WING
¼ + 1 1 1	¼ +	¼ + 1 1 1

FUSELAGE

~~11111~~ ~~11111~~ 1

Twenty-five hours from New York. High cumulus clouds dot the sky. I'm cruising at 1575 r.p.m., with mixture control pulled back slightly from the point of roughness. The air speed shows 93 miles an hour.

In 25 hours the engine has burned about 300 gallons of fuel. The *Spirit of St. Louis* is light enough to throttle down still farther. It should fly nicely at 1550, possibly even at 1525 r.p.m. To obtain maximum range, it's necessary to take a little less power from the engine with every hour that passes. I reach for the throttle, but spectres of fog and darkness rise in my mind. With the tail wind that's been blowing, I hope to reach the coast of Europe before dark. If I throttle down, I may not.

Which is more valuable, fuel or time? If I'm south of course I'll miss Ireland entirely; but I might still strike land by sunset. Fifty r.p.m. could make the difference between day and night. Shall I build up a fuel reserve against the possibility that I'll have to spend the entire night over a fog-covered continent? Or shall I draw on my reserves now to increase the probability of a daylight landfall? Security and caution demand the conservation of fuel. Success and adventure argue for a higher speed. With plenty of fuel, I can get down without a crack-up, regardless of the weather. Flying faster will give me a better chance of finding Paris and Le Bourget.

But if security were my prime motive, I'd never have begun this flight at all — I'd never have learned to fly in the first place. Security is a static thing; and without adventure, lifeless as a stone. I open the throttle to 1650 r.p.m., reset the mixture control, and watch the indicator needle rise 7 miles an hour. It seems very little extra speed for such a sacrifice, but it will add up to 50 miles by sunset.

How satisfying it is just to sit still and fly eastward toward Europe; with the engine running smoothly; with my course set, and navigating problems no longer pressing on my mind. The hours of afternoon stretch out, empty, warm, and safe, like the limitless sky ahead. Whatever may come later, these sun-filled hours are mine. I'll take advantage of them, rest in them, enjoy them, push worry off my shoulders until either I see land or the dangers of night draw near.

Reaching into my flying-suit pocket for a fresh handkerchief, my fingers touch a small object, hard and thin. I hadn't noticed it before, mixed in with hunting knife, pencils, and flashlight. There's a little chain attached. I pull it out, hold it in my palm. It's a St. Christopher medal. Silvered Saint and staff and Child, from whom did this gift come? Man or woman; young or aged — whose hand slipped it in my pocket? It was a person who asked for no thanks, who cared for no credit. It was sent with me like a silent blessing or a prayer.

Sunbeams are moving in the cockpit. The nose is veering north. I push right rudder. I've been daydreaming; I must be more careful. I certainly can't afford to lose control again.

The sunbeams are a great help. Their movements catch my eye more quickly than the compass needle or the turn-indicator.

I shake my mind back to alertness, and begin studying the sea. Am I allowing enough for drift? The waves themselves form no stable point of reference; but the foam from a breaking crest remains almost stationary on the water's surface, a patch of white, uninfluenced by succeeding rollers, riding over ridge and trough. I select a spot of foam three hundred yards ahead, and estimate an angle five degrees to the southward. Do I follow that imaginary line of drift as I approach, or do I edge right or left? If a man walks three miles an hour, am I drifting twice as fast as a man walks? If a man runs fifteen miles an hour, am I drifting southward as fast as a man runs?

Is there something alive down there under my wing? I thought I saw a dark object moving through the water. I search the surface, afraid to hope, lest I lose confidence in vision. Was it a large fish, or were my eyes deceiving me? After the fog islands and the phantoms, I no longer trust my senses. The *Spirit of St. Louis* itself might fade away without causing me great surprise. But – – – yes, there it is again, slightly behind me now, a porpoise — the first living thing I've seen since Newfoundland. Fin and sleek, black body curve gracefully above the surface and slip down out of sight.

The ocean is as desolate as ever. Yet a complete change has taken place. I feel that I've safely recrossed the bridge to life — broken the strands which have been tugging me toward the universe beyond. Why do I find such joy, such encouragement in the sight of a porpoise? What possible bond can I have with a porpoise hundreds of miles at sea, with a strange creature I've never seen before and will never see again? What is there in that flashing glimpse of hide that means so much to me, that even makes it seem a different ocean? Is it simply that I've been looking so long, and seeing nothing? Is it an omen of land ahead? Or is there some common tie between living things that surmounts even the barrier of species?

This ocean, which for me marks the borderland of death, is filled with life; life that's foreign, yet in some strange way akin;

life which welcomes me back from the universe of spirits and makes me part of the earth again. What a kingdom lies under that tossing surface! Numberless animals must be there, hidden from my sight. It's a kingdom closed to man, one he can fly above all day and never recognize. How blind our normal senses are. We look at a star, and see a pin point of light; a forest is a green carpet to a flyer's eye; the ocean, a tossing mass of water. Inner vision requires a night alone above the clouds, the sight of deer in a clearing, the leap of a porpoise far from land.

My eyes sweep over the waves again, and I climb to a hundred feet. How far from the coast do porpoises swim, I wonder? Do they travel all the way across the ocean, or do they stay near shore and fishing banks? In laying plans for the flight, I didn't think about studying salt water life as a part of navigation. If I look carefully, there may be other things to see. But the evenness of the horizon is unbroken by ship or sail or smoke. Scan the surface as I may, I find no second spark of life.

Can it be that the porpoise was imaginary too, a part of this strange, living dream, like the fuselage's phantoms and the islands which faded into mist? Yet I know there's a difference, a dividing line that still exists between reality and apparition. The porpoise *was* real, like the water itself, like the substance of the cockpit around me, like my face which I can feel when I run my hand across it.

THE TWENTY-SEVENTH HOUR

Over the Atlantic

HOURS OF FUEL CONSUMED

NOSE TANK
¼ + ~~1111~~ 1 1

LEFT WING	CENTER WING	RIGHT WING
¼ + 1 1 1	¼ +	¼ + 1 1 1

FUSELAGE
~~1111~~ ~~1111~~ 1 1

Nine fifty-two on the clock — twenty-six hours since take-off. I put the twenty-fifth pencil line on the board in front of me. Sunbeams are moving again; the compass needle leans toward one side. I nose back onto course. Somehow I still can't keep the plane from swinging left, from following my instinctive feeling that Ireland lies to the northward. I can't force my senses to accept my reasoned plan of navigation. I decide to do nothing but watch the compass needle. I'll make it stay in center through pure concentration. I should be awake enough to do that now.

It works for a few minutes. Then I find myself staring at the cockpit's details — the stitches in the fabric covering, the undoped edges where it's cut and joined, the scrape marks my heels have made on the floor board's varnish. And soon the nose is edging north again.

It's like the first cross-country flight I made as pilot of my own airplane. I was so busy studying my map and trying to make it correspond to the ground below, that I let my plane veer off course just as the *Spirit of St. Louis* is veering now. And I ended up by not knowing my position over the land, just as I now don't know my position over the water. But I was an amateur pilot then. There was excuse for my inaccuracy in navigation.

That was in May, 1923. I was on my way home to Minnesota with a Jenny I'd bought at Souther Field in Georgia. That trip would be simple for me now, just routine, several days of professional effort. But then, it was at least as hazardous as this flight across the ocean. I'd gone to Souther Field with a few hundred dollars in my pocket, in checks and cash. "That's a good place to buy Jennies cheap," I'd been told the year before.

I'd paid five hundred dollars for my Jenny. It was more than I planned on, but only half the price first asked; and I had my choice from over a hundred planes. Also, I got a brand-new Curtiss OX-5 engine in the trade, a fresh coat of olive drab dope on all surfaces, and an extra twenty-gallon tank installed in the fuselage. The tank doubled my fuel capacity and more than doubled my practical range; but of course it increased the weight of the plane, and Jennies were overweight in the first place.

My father had helped me buy the Jenny, so I still had money left for the trip home; and I hoped to make at least out-of-pocket expenses by carrying passengers from the towns where I landed. I saved a few dollars by living alone on the field while my plane was being assembled and painted. Souther had been abandoned by the Army after the war ended. It was like a ghost city. During the day, three or four civilian mechanics worked in one of the dozen hangars, reconditioning planes which had been sold. Occasionally a car from Americus would drive out. But in the evening, usually there wasn't a sign of human life. Then, I'd explore big wooden warehouses, and roam along weed-lazy streets between barracks where thousands of men once lived.

When my Jenny was assembled and the paint all dry, I faced my greatest problem; for I hadn't flown in six months, and I'd *never* soloed. Everybody at Souther Field took for granted that I was an experienced pilot when I arrived alone to buy a plane. They didn't ask to see my license, because you didn't have to have a license to fly an airplane in 1923. There were no instructors on the field, and anyway I didn't want to spend more money on instruction.

"Well, she's ready. When are you going to test her out?" The chief mechanic, a young man of about twenty, handed me my plane graciously with word and gesture. It was obvious that he expected me to say, "Let's push her out on the line." So that's what I said. After all, I knew the theory of flying. I'd had eight hours of instruction from Ira Biffle just one year before. I'd had a little "stick time" flying with Bahl, and a little more with Lynch. Souther Field was big and smooth. I thought I ought to be able to get my Jenny into the air and down again without cracking up. I climbed into the cockpit, warmed up the engine, and taxied downwind to the farthest corner of the field.

How I wished I'd had my training in Jennies instead of Standards! I'd flown in a Jenny for only thirty-five minutes at the flying school, only enough to realize that it had quite a different feel, especially in landing. "And you have to be careful of them in the air too," I remembered one of the pilots at Lincoln saying. "They just haven't got the power."

I knew there wasn't any halfway about flying. It wasn't like starting to drive a new automobile. You couldn't loaf along while you were learning, and stop if anything went wrong. Once you decided to take the air, you needed all the speed and power you could get. But I could taxi across the field a few times before I actually took off. That would give me a little practice and a better feel of controls. Then, I could lift the wheels two or three feet off the ground, cut the throttle, taxi back, and try again. It wouldn't matter if I bounced a little. After I gained confidence in my landing ability, I'd climb straight ahead and make a full circle of the field.

I headed directly into wind and opened the throttle — cautiously. The Jenny swerved a little. I kicked opposite rudder. It swerved the other way. I straightened out — opened the throttle more – – – The tail lifted up — a bit too high – – – I pulled back on the stick – – – The tail skid touched – – – I pushed forward – – – pulled back – – – Before I knew it, I was in the air! – – – I cut the throttle – – – dropped too fast – – – opened it wide – – – ballooned up, right wing low – – – closed the throttle – – – yanked back on the stick – – – bounced down on wheel and wing skid.

Nothing broke, but it was a hard landing, much too rough for the safety of frail wooden structure. Had I hit a puff of wind, or was it all bad flying? I didn't want to repeat that experience. What an exhibition I'd made! And they'd probably been watching me from the line, too. They'd know now that I'd never soloed. I was sweating all over. I needed time to think. I decided to wait for an hour in which the air was completely calm. I wished I could have switched off the engine and stayed right there in the middle of the field; but of course the mechanics would have driven out in their cars to ask what the trouble was. I turned and taxied slowly back toward the hangars.

A stranger sauntered out to meet me — young, heavy-set, and smiling — dressed in typical pilots' costume of breeches and boots. Henderson, he said his name was. It was the first time I'd seen him on the field.

"Why don't you let me jump in the front cockpit before you try that again?" he asked.

I could feel my cheeks turning red, and sweat broke out again. "The air's a little rough, and I haven't flown since October," I replied, hesitant to lay my troubles bare before a stranger. "I'm going to wait until it's not so rough."

"Lots of pilots are in the same spot," he said, laughing. "It's pretty hard to make expenses through the winter. I'll give you some time while I'm waiting for the ship I bought. Are the dual controls hooked up?"

"They've never been disconnected," I answered. "But – – – "

"Why don't we make a few rounds right now?" he asked. "Don't worry, it won't cost you anything. I haven't much to do for the next day or two."

"I'd – – – I'd like to – – – but – – – "

But he was already stepping into the front cockpit. I taxied out onto the field again and plunged up into air. It was a lot easier when I knew someone was there to check any serious errors I might commit. I made a big circle and came down to a two-point, bouncy landing. After a half-dozen take-offs and landings, my new friend pulled back the throttle and said, "You won't have any trouble. You're just a little rusty from not flying for so long. Why don't you wait until the wind dies down this evening and then make a few hops yourself?"

Three degrees right rudder.

It was nearly five o'clock when I started the engine again. The air was almost calm. There was no one on the field except an old Negro, who wandered in and stood at a respectful distance, looking at my plane.

"Suh, could Ah ask if you all goin' up in the sky dis aft'noon?" he'd said.

"Yes, I'm going to take off in a few minutes," I'd answered, not paying much attention.

"Well suh, if you all don't object, Ah'll jist stand right heah an' watch, suh."

I'd taxied out, taken a last look at the instruments, and opened the throttle.

No matter how much training you've had, your first solo is far different from all other flights. You are completely independent, hopelessly beyond help, entirely responsible, and terribly alone in space. For the first time, you're free of an instructor's wishes. No one else knows whether you bank with slip or skid. There's no hand to motion the nose down before a stall, no other head to check your fuel or watch your r.p.m. You can choose your point of the compass, and fly on as long as you like. But if you get lost from your field, the penalty is more severe than words of reprimand and laughter.

I kept climbing that day, higher and higher, over red plowing, green forests, and shanty homes of Georgia. There was the city of Americus unfolding in the distance. There was Souther Field, with its lines of buildings, shrinking in size below me. I held the rocker arms above the horizon until my altimeter needle covered the dot at 4500 feet. I might not have stopped climbing then, but the sun was almost touching earth, and dusk makes landing difficult for the amateur's eyes.

"Boss, you sho' are a great flyah!"

The old Negro had been waiting for me all the time I was in the air. He walked up close to the fuselage after I cut the switch; and stood there staring at me admiringly.

"Dese other aviators jist fly 'bout low-down like. They ain't nuthin' compared to a man like you. Boss, you all was so-o high Ah could *jist* see you. You looked like a bird up thar. Not a smidge bigger; no, suh. Ah'm sho' glad Ah come out here to see you, Boss. Yes, *suh*."

I knew well enough that the altitude I reached had required no excess skill, and that my old instructor Biff would have cursed each one of my landings. But there was something about the aged Negro's praise and courtesy that gave me confidence. It was pleasant to listen to such an appreciative audience. And besides that, I was happy to have finished my first solo flight without cracking up.

I spent a week at Souther Field, practicing take-offs and landings. Then I felt it was time to start barnstorming. I'd built up nearly five hours of solo, and my funds were getting lower each day. It was important to find a location where I could offset the cost of flying training with an income from passenger-carrying. I decided to work west, through the Southern states, to Texas, and then north to Minnesota. Why detour as far as Texas? Why not fly direct? Well, every barnstorming pilot I knew had flown in Texas. They all talked about Texas. Texas seemed to be a badge of the profession. Now that I had a chance to fly there in my own plane, why miss it?

"You're heading over some of the worst territory in the South," a local pilot told me when he heard of my plans. "If you're bound to go to Texas, I'd advise you to follow the Gulf coast. That's not so bad."

But my engine was new; and my inexperience great. I'd not be bluffed by a few swamps and hills. Surely, with more than four hours of fuel in my tanks, I'd be able to find good fields, large enough to land on. It would be interesting to see what the South's worst flying territory was like.

I sent my suitcase home by railway express. Then I rolled up an extra shirt, a pair of breeches, a toothbrush, some socks, spark plugs, tools, and other spare equipment in a blanket, and strapped the bundle down in the front cockpit with the seat belt. At ten o'clock on the morning of May seventeenth, I took off, circled once above the hangars to say good-by, and set my course directly toward Montgomery, Alabama.

I made Meridian, Mississippi, before sunset, and headed west again the following morning. That was the day I became so badly lost. The sky was full of great white clouds; the horizon, broken by local storms. For almost half an hour, I saw no check point on the ground that conformed with the small-scale map I had purchased from an Americus drug store. Then I placed too much significance in the angling tracks of a railroad, and changed my course to the right. I kept on flying in a direction I thought was westward. There was no compass in my Jenny. I'd bought a compass, discolored by age, the day before I left Souther Field. But in my hurry to get started I'd wrapped it up in my blanket roll, planning to install it sometime when weather held me on the ground. Now it was out of reach.

The territory below grew wilder — mostly swamp and timber. Storms became thicker and heavier. After an hour had passed, I decided to land, ask where I was, and fill up my tanks. The fields below were small, hilly, and most of them plowed. To land in plowing meant an almost sure nose-over for a Jenny; and one could never get off again — even when the ground was dry. At last I found a pasture that contained two well-sodded slopes, with a small meadow between. That would give me an upgrade for the end of my landing roll, and a downgrade for the start of my take-off — an ideal combination. The territory all around was pretty rough. Engine failure on take-off would mean a nasty crack-up. But that was true most places in the South. I circled several times, studying the surface of the ground, made the shortest landing I had yet accomplished, coasted down the near slope, across the meadow, and stopped rolling halfway up the slope on the far side. I felt highly professional.

A small but dark storm area was drifting in my direction, and only a mile or two away. I wanted to get my plane into a grove of pine trees at one side of the slope behind me, and tie the wings down before strong wind gusts arrived. So I opened my throttle, blew the tail around, and taxied across the little meadow at the highest speed I dared. It was too late to stop or ground-loop when I saw a ditch ahead, almost completely hidden by grass. I had barely time to pull the throttle shut. There was the crash of wood as my wheels dropped in and the propeller struck the ground. The tail rose, like a seesaw run amuck, until it was almost vertical in air. I thought my Jenny was turning upside down. Then it settled back to an angle of some forty-five degrees.

I climbed out of the cockpit down to the wing, and then to the ground, and surveyed my damaged plane. It was splattered with mud, but I could find nothing broken aside from the propeller. If I'd followed my landing tracks, or if I'd even been ten feet farther over, I wouldn't have hit the ditch at all. Raindrops began to patter on fabric. Northwest treetops were boiling in the wind. The rudder drummed against the flippers with a heavy puff. Several men and boys came running up.

"What's the name of the nearest town?" I asked.

"Well suh, if you go nawtheast, you come to the city of Maben. If you go sauthwest, you come to the city of Mathiston. When you all landed, you jist about split the difference between 'em."

"What's the closest big city?"

"Well suh, if you go 'bout a hundred miles sauth, you come to Meridian. That's about the biggest un we got 'round heah."

Meridian, Mississippi! That's where I'd started from — I'd flown *north* instead of west! I thought they were going to say I was in Louisiana.

By that time a crowd was assembling in spite of the rain — whites and Negroes, grandfathers, daughters, babies, and dogs. We hauled down the fuselage and pushed my Jenny out of the ditch, into the grove of pines. I tied wings to trees, and rode into Maben with a storekeeper who had locked up his place of business when he heard of my landing and driven out to see for himself what had happened.

Before leaving Souther Field, I'd invested twenty dollars in two extra propellers as a safeguard for my summer's barnstorming. I telegraphed for one of them to be expressed to Maben. Then I engaged a room at the old Southern Hotel. The next afternoon, I installed the compass in my cockpit.

Four degrees right rudder.

Three days later, the new propeller arrived at the railway station. I lapped it onto the engine shaft between showers. A large part of the population of Maben, Mathiston, and the surrounding country came to watch me work and test the plane.

On the test flight, my take-off was easy, and my landing fairly good; but constant rains had kept the field soft. Wheels and tail skid left shallow ruts behind. I taxied back carefully around the ditch end, and announced that I was ready for passengers. While I was waiting for the propeller, I had talked half-a-dozen towns-men into promising to fly with me. Most of them were right there, gathered around my plane.

"Hank, climb in; you all been talkin' all mornin' 'bout the flight you're going to take!"

"Oh, Ah – – – Ah'm goin' up all right; but how 'bout all you fellers that was fightin' for first ride? Sol, you was speakin' mighty big few minutes ago. Don't hear nuthin' from you now."

"Seemed a lot safer yest'day when that plane couldn't really fly."

It took several minutes of persuasion to get the first Mississip-pian into my cockpit. After that, they came fast. I stopped my engine only when it was necessary to pour gasoline in the tanks. I kept the fuel level low, to make take-offs easier. That day, I took in enough money to pay for new propeller, gasoline, and hotel bills, and leave me a profit besides. At last, my flying was on a paying basis. Hours in the air put dollars into my pocket instead of taking them out. I was earning enough to live, and for the upkeep of my plane; that was all I asked.

"Bill, you'll nevah know what your place is like till you look down on it from up 'bove. Say, you ought'a see the chickens ta-a-ke for cover. Costs money, but it's sho' worth it!"

"Mose, how'd you feel strapped in 'tween them wings?"

"Boss, Ah'd go but Ah ain't got no money."

"Well, Ah'll chip in fifty cents to give Mose a ride. Boys, who'll go 'long with me?"

"Ah'll put up half a dollar."

"We'll pay his fare if you'll give him a flip-flop, mister. Mose, how 'bout a flip-flop?"

"Yes, suh. Ah ain't feared o' nothin' that man wants to do."

Mose, delighted by the attention and encouraged by a dozen fellow Negroes, was willing to take on anything at all. I showed him where not to step on the wing as he climbed in, and belted him tightly down in the cockpit. But his attitude of confidence melted when I snapped the buckle and he realized he was committed to the air. His face grew serious.

"Mose, Ah bet you wish you hadn't spoke up so quick now. You look 'most white already."

"Sho' a scared nigger sittin' in that place."

"Shucks, who's scared? Ain't nobody scarin' me. Ah know that aviator ain't goin' to kill hisself, and Ah'm stayin' right with him."

"Mose, that airplane won't no sooner git off the ground than you goin' to duck yo head down 'tween your knees an nevah bring it up agin." Everybody laughed.

"Huh! Scared? why, man, Ah'm goin' to enjoy myself up thar. Ah'll be a-laughin' an' a-wavin' all the time."

"Wavin'— why, man, you goin' to have your hands so full of airplane you won't be able a get 'em high as yo' nose."

"Mose, don't you let them rascals skeer you. Jist hold your handk'chief out an' show 'em you can wave."

"Course Ah kin wave." Out came a huge red and rather dirty bandanna.

There was a cheer as I opened the throttle and taxied off. I climbed to two hundred feet, banked steeply, dove on the field, pulled up in a cautious zoom. Mose grasped the rim of his cockpit with one hand until his knuckles whitened; but he held the bandanna resolutely aloft with the other while dozens of faces looked up at us.

But I'd promised flip-flops. Zooming around the field wouldn't satisfy the sponsors of the flight. They expected much more in return for their fifty-cent pieces, and I intended to give it to them. The main problem was that I'd never had any training in acrobatics. I'd been in the front cockpit once when Bahl looped his Hisso-Standard, and once when he spun it; and I'd stood on top of his wing once while he looped. But I'd never handled the controls during any kind of stunt. However, I'd listened to older pilots talk, and I'd stunted in my mind, working out theoretically the movements of stick and rudder.

"You don't have to dive much," I'd been told. "Just nose her down and let her pick up speed." That advice, I realized later, concerned a Hisso-Standard — not my underpowered Jenny.

It took me close to fifteen minutes to get up 3000 feet. I wasn't sure where to hold my nose on the horizon to get the best angle of attack, and I didn't want to overwork the engine climbing. Three thousand feet seemed high enough for safety, even with inexperienced feet and hands. I splashed around in the air for a few minutes to get the feel of controls — wingovers, sideslips, and two steep spirals, all of them pretty sloppy and with the earth quite out of place.

Mose had ducked his head down between his knees in the first bank; but he kept his handkerchief high above the cockpit, although no one could possibly see it from the ground.

I was still over 2000 feet high when I finished the last spiral and leveled out. It was time to loop. I pushed the nose down and waited a few seconds. Wing fabric bulged between ribs. Controls stiffened. Noises took on a higher pitch. It seemed we were going awfully fast. I pulled the stick back slowly and opened the throttle wide. My body sank into the cockpit's seat. The earth drifted rearward, behind my trailing edges. Two landing wires fuzzed against the sky. White clouds took on an awkward tilt. How much strain would the fittings stand? I didn't dare use more muscle on the stick. At forty-five degrees, the engine began to labor. At sixty degrees, the wings were trembling. At ninety degrees, my Jenny hung motionless in air.

At that instant, Mose must have thought the flip-flops were over, for his head reappeared above the cockpit's rim. I kicked full right rudder, but I'd waited too long. It had no effect. She whipped. Air rushed backward past the fuselage. The tail jerked up. The nose jerked down. Strange things happened to clouds and ground — A plowed field was where the sky had been, and it was getting bigger fast. All trace of Mose had disappeared, including the bandanna.

It was easy enough to come out of the dive, and I held the nose high to gain back a little altitude. Then I climbed for three or four minutes and tried another loop, with almost the same result. The Jenny would have whipped again, but I kicked rudder sooner on the second try and tipped her over on one wing. Something was wrong with my technique; that was clear enough. I gave up any more attempts at looping, and brought Mose down in dives, zooms, and spirals. It wasn't until I throttled the engine for the final glide that the bandanna rose again, followed by his face. He peeked out, drew his head in like a startled turtle, then straightened up and looked around.

As I taxied back to the laughing, shouting crowd, the bandanna was flying as high as the top wing.

"Hi, Mose, was it worth it?"

"Shucks, it was won'erful! Ah'd like to go right back up agin." Mose was warming up as I guided his foot onto the walkway to keep him from stepping through the wing covering. "Ah wouldn't take nuthin' for that trip. Boy, you don't know what you're missin'." As soon as he got onto the ground, he was surrounded by Negroes and whites, all talking and joking, and paying almost no attention to what was being said.

I stayed in Maben for two weeks, and carried close to sixty passengers. People flocked in from the surrounding country. Some traveled for fifteen miles in oxcarts, just to see my Jenny fly. One old Negro woman came up to me with serious face and asked, "Boss, how much you all charge fo' to take me up to Heaven an' leave me dah?"

I could have carried many more passengers, but the rains continued, and each flight rutted the meadow until the OX-5 engine didn't have enough power to pull its Jenny through the mud. Every time I landed I had to ask several men to push on the wings before I could get back to the harder ground of the take-off slope. I had looked over the surrounding country for a better field; but there was none. I said good-by to my Southern friends, and headed west again, for Texas.

How simple it was, flying above ground! If you got lost, you landed and inquired; if you were short of fuel, you phoned the nearest oil company to send out a truck. If you were tired, you stretched out on the grass; and if you wanted to sleep, you slept – – –

I'm five degrees off course again. I've got to be more careful.

At Marshall, Minnesota, I joined my father. He was running as a candidate for the United States Senate that year, in a special election called because of Knute Nelson's death. I had suggested that he make some of his campaign trips in my Jenny, and he agreed to go. Father had never liked the idea of my flying. It was too dangerous an occupation, he said, and I was his only son. He told me there would always be a position open for me in his office; and he outlined several business projects we might start together. But when he found that I was determined to follow the profession of an airplane pilot, he helped me in every way he could. "You're your own boss," he'd said finally. And that time he really meant it. Now, I was to take him for his first ride in an airplane.

If Father had any fear of flying, he didn't show it, although I thought his lips were tighter set than usual when I gave him helmet and goggles, and strapped him down. He began his aerial campaign that day by throwing out printed circulars above the town. I hadn't thought to tell him to let the slipstream catch a few dozen sheets at a time, so when I nodded the signal to cut them loose a block of five hundred banged against the stabilizer. Father looked a bit startled at that. But our handbills hit the town; and he enjoyed the ride, and started plans immediately for going up again.

Flying has often made me conscious of the relativity of time. I felt it more than ever that morning, with my father's head in

front of my windshield. He'd fled in an oxcart from savages, at the
speed of two miles an hour; and now, in this same state of Minnesota, he was riding through the air on wings, at the speed of a
mile a minute. My father's lifetime spanned more change in the
environment of man than man had experienced in the previous
thousand years.

That was the summer I landed at our Minnesota farm. I'd
looked forward to bringing my own airplane home ever since I
began flying. It was a luxury to which I'd promised to treat myself
as soon as I'd made a little extra money and developed sufficient
skill. By early fall I felt I'd amassed enough of both. I barnstormed
my way north, past Minneapolis, past St. Cloud; and pointed my
nose one morning in the direction of Little Falls – – –

There it is, lying nakedly below me, river and creek, fields and
woodlands — our farm. It has never fully exposed itself to my eyes
before. How well I know each detail! How little I've understood
the whole! In the past, I've seen our farm as a surgeon views his
patient — all parts hidden but the one on which he works. Now, I
embrace its entire body in sight and consciousness at once — in a
realization which previous generations assigned to birds and God.
How delicately Pike Creek ravels through its valley! How stal-
wartly the pines stand up, like guards for lower timber! I see the
bare curves of our western hill, the dells of our eastern-twenty.
Cow trails tie barn to pasture, gate to gate, wind in and out
through trees. The Lunds' house is closer, the Williams woods is
smaller, than I thought either one to be.

I learn the wind's direction from silvered poplar leaves, stall
over the fence, land tail skid first, stop rolling with plenty of room
to spare. I open the throttle enough to swing the tail around and
taxi slowly. The ground is soft. The take-off won't be easy. If it
rains tonight, I'll probably have to wait for the earth to dry again.

"Nay doggone, the man that invented these things vas quite a
feller!"

Daniel Thompson stands looking at my Jenny, axe at an angle
on his shoulder.

"Aye never thought Aye'd live to see such a contraption," he continues, looking first at the plane, and then at me, and then chuckling in a sort of bewilderment. Of course he knows I learned to fly last year, and he's used to seeing me drive cars, and my motorcycle, and all sorts of farm machinery; but the airplane resting here where we used to unhitch our hay wagon is almost too much for him.

"How's the farm, Thompson?" My eyes sweep over the neglected field.

"All in veeds."

Yes, it's true. There are no crops in the fields, no wheel marks on the road that crosses the creek, no fresh cow dung on the path we follow. The tenants I selected failed to make a living on the farm. There weren't enough acres under plow, the pastures were too wooded, the buildings were too far apart. It was one problem after another until finally they left. Well, that's the price I pay for flying. One can't direct a farm from an airplane hundreds of miles away.

"They're starting to cut timber in the valley," Thompson volunteers, as we walk toward our padlocked house.

Yes, I know, the survey for the new Pike Rapids dam showed that our valley would be flooded, so all the trees will have to go — the great white-oak where my father and mother camped while the first house was being built, the little crab-apple orchard by the river bank, the tall linden whose branches filtered up the rising stars. In the future, my rapids will become a lake; my drying-rock, a slippery, submerged stone.

I knew that day that childhood was gone. My farm on the Mississippi would become a memory, of which, sometime, I'd tell my children, just as my father told me of his fields and forests on Sauk River. As the modern railroad came to divide his family homestead, a modern dam would submerge the valley acres of our farm — — —

It's twenty-six and a half hours since I took off. That's almost twice as long as the flight between San Diego and St. Louis: and that was much the longest flight I ever made. It's asking a lot of an engine to run twenty-six hours without attention. Back on the mail, we check our Liberties at the end of every trip. Are the rocker-arms on my Whirlwind still getting grease? And how long will it keep on going if one of them should freeze?

I shift arms on the stick. My left hand — being free, and apparently disconnected from my mind's control — begins aimlessly exploring the pockets of the chart bag. It pulls the maps of Europe halfway out to reassure my eyes they're there, tucks my helmet and goggles in more neatly, and fingers the shiny little first-aid kit and the dark glasses given me by that doctor on Long Island. Why have I let my eyes burn through the morning? Why have I been squinting for hours and not thought of these glasses before? I hook the wires over my ears and look out on a shaded ocean. It's as though the sky were overcast again. I don't dare use them. They're too comfortable, too pleasant. They make it seem like evening — make me want to sleep.

I slip the glasses back into their pocket, pull out the first-aid kit, and idly snap it open. It contains adhesive tape, compact bandages, and a little pair of scissors. Not enough to do much patching after a crash. Tucked into one corner are several silk-covered, glass capsules of aromatic ammonia. "For use as Smelling Salts," the labels state. What did the doctor think I could do with smelling salts over the ocean? This kit is made for a child's cut finger, or for some debutante fainting at a ball! I might as well have saved its weight on the take-off, for all the good it will be to me. I put it back in the chart bag – – – and then pull it out again. If smelling salts revive people who are about to faint, why won't they revive people who are about to fall asleep? Here's a weapon against sleep lying at my side unused, a weapon which has been there all through the morning's deadly hours. A whiff of one of these capsules should sharpen the dullest mind. And no eyes could sleep stinging with the vapor of ammonia.

I'll try one now. The fumes ought to clear my head and keep the compass centered. I crush a capsule between thumb and fingers. A fluid runs out, discoloring the white silk cover. I hold it cautiously, several inches from my nose. There's no odor. I move it closer, slowly, until finally it touches my nostrils. I smell nothing! My eyes don't feel the slightest sting, and no tears come to moisten their dry edges. I inhale again with no effect, and throw the capsule through the window. My mind now begins to realize how deadened my senses have become, how close I must be to the end of my reserves. And yet there may be another sleepless night ahead.

I lean out into the slipstream again, to breathe the fresher air. I nose down next to the water, gliding along tail high, swiftly, with lightened load and faster turning engine. I force the wheels as close as I dare to the waves, playing with their crests to stimulate my senses. I sharpen the blade of skill on the stone of danger.

Now, I fly in tight formation with my shadow, less than ten feet above the waves. Now, I let the *Spirit of St. Louis* rise to masthead height while I sink back to rest within the cockpit. At times I'm tempted to touch my tires on the water to break monotony and see spray fly up.

I did this once on the Mississippi River at St. Louis, racing with a speedboat. There was a regatta that day. The shores were lined with spectators, and the competition between boat and airplane was a star attraction. Our course lay around the piers of two bridges a half-mile or so apart. My old Standard biplane was so much faster than the speedboat that it was more an exhibition than a race. I throttled down to keep from gaining too many laps on my adversary. I flew under the bridge spans with him to give the crowd an extra thrill. I ran my tires through the wave tops — they were ripples compared to these out here — and flew so low over a launch that one of the crewmen jumped overboard when he saw my plane approaching. The crowd enjoyed it immensely. But the president of the company for whom I flew was not so impressed by my skill. He said he'd expected to see me crash into the water at any moment, and that the man who jumped overboard telephoned him the next morning, cursing and threatening suit.

No, I won't clip the top off a whitecap out here, hundreds of miles from shore. It wouldn't be like swimming halfway across the Mississippi and paying for a five-hundred-dollar airplane if I misjudged my height!

The Mississippi River — how it has wound in and out through my life, like the seasons! I grew up on its banks, swam through its rapids, portaged its headwaters with my father. From Montana to Alabama, from Wisconsin to Texas, I've barnstormed through its valley. Each flight on my mail route took me over its junction with the muddy Missouri. Now, the movement of the ocean waves below, extending on to the straight line of the horizon, reminds me of the river's wheatfields. They too bent and rippled in the wind. I've flown mile after mile above their golden tassels, in Kansas, no higher than I'm flying now above the Atlantic. Sometimes I saw a coyote loping away from my plane, just as I saw the porpoise here at sea.

Is that a piece of driftwood? No, it's moving, it's a bird, a gull, wheeling low over the waves. A second sign of life! I twist around to watch the flapping wings pass behind my tail. There's another gull in the distance, a speck rising and lowering against the southern sky. This is becoming a populated ocean. What are gulls doing here so far from land? I've heard that they follow ships all the way from America to Europe, dropping down to pick up scraps of refuse. Then have I drifted south to the ship lanes? Are these birds simply waiting for the next liner to pass by? But there's not a ship in sight; not a sign of refuse on the surface — no spar, no floating box, no orange peel.

Those gulls may have been resting on the water. How fortunate they are! Maybe they can sleep — head tucked under wing and floating on the swells. They are really children of ocean and air, while I am an intruder where I don't belong. Gulls fly by nature, by God's design; I stay aloft by man's witchcraft. It takes no more than a stuck valve or a cracked pipe line to break the spell of my flight. If my engine failed at this altitude of fifty feet, I'd scarcely have time to bank left into the wind, pull the stick back, and stall onto the water. Within half a minute, I'd be submerged in it, feeling its wetness, tasting its salt.

Of course the *Spirit of St. Louis* would float a long time with two-thirds of the fuel gone — for hours — perhaps for days. The sea is light. There'd be no rush about getting the raft out — I could take my time pumping it up and loading in the equipment. I'd have a fair chance of being rescued, too — in these European waters, especially if I'm on the ship lanes. With the sun overhead, beating down through a clear sky, it wouldn't be so very cold after I got the raft inflated and bailed out. I'd moor to the wreckage of the plane, curl up on the rubberized canvas bottom, and give way to sleep. I'd forget about all my problems. Nothing would matter until I'd slept — — —

Is that a spout rising from the sea, a half-mile ahead? Are there whales too out here, a few feet below those waves? I fix my eyes on the area and wait, as one waits for the second flash of an airway beacon at night. But it doesn't appear again. Probably I imagined that I saw a spout. At least I'll charge it to imagination. There must be no question about what is real and what is not. I'm still too close to the border line where one merges with the other.

Far away, in the northeastern sky, a layer of clouds is forming. Does that mean another storm ahead? It looks like a single stratus layer, several thousand feet above the ocean. But — I study it carefully — possibly broken cumulus clouds have bunched together to appear as a layer at a distance.

Europe — I know from maps and newspapers and books it's there, somewhere over the horizon, as tangible and earthlike as America; but my senses will be skeptical of its existence until my eyes actually see it down below, until I fly close and find that its land does not dissolve into mist and shadow.

It must be there. The charts show it. They didn't lie about Nova Scotia. They told the truth about Newfoundland. I've measured them accurately. Europe *must* be there too. I know people who have been to Europe. Geographies and histories confirm its existence. Flying eastward from Newfoundland, it's impossible to miss. All I have to do is hold my course, and sooner or later I'll be bound to strike land — as I struck Nova Scotia — as I struck Newfoundland.

But how endlessly the ocean stretches out ahead. How mythical the European countries seem. Ireland, England, France, what lands of fable, how far away from home — vague countries of my mother's people. They are there. They've got to be there. They're not like the cloud islands. They're like the porpoise and the gulls. By evening I should strike one of their coasts. In three hours, if I haven't sighted land, I'll turn thirty degrees to the north.

The shadows in my cockpit have assumed a different angle. The sun is lower. The wind has decreased. There are no longer foam streaks on the sea. Cumulus clouds mirror white on the deep blue water. A light haze replaces midday's crystal clarity. Gray areas in the distance mark scattered squalls.

During the hours of brilliant sunlight there seemed no need to concern myself greatly with problems of European weather. I could afford to fly lazily along, now aware of my surroundings, now far away in dreams. Why accuse such clear air of harboring a storm; why be suspicious of such an open sky? But those squalls ahead can no longer be shut out by blinders of the mind. They're real. They're not many miles away. They require a definite plan of action.

I've already spent fuel to increase my chance of a daylight landfall, so it's essential to stay underneath the clouds. I'll climb above them only as a last resort. Even if the sky becomes completely overcast the cloud base may stay high. If I can see only a few miles when I strike the coast line, I should be able to locate my position in daylight.

If vision is cut down by haze, I'll fly low over the first town I come to, and let the signboards tell me which country I'm in. Maybe I can read the name of the town itself on the railroad station, as I've done so often on cross-country flights at home. But you must be cautious flying over a land you don't know. I re-member a day near New Orleans when my eye caught slender, vertical lines of steel ambushed in the haze and extending into the clouds above my Canuck. They were a few seconds of flight away, but I had to look carefully to see them, for they showed only a shade darker than the haze itself. Interconnected and held erect by an invisible maze of wires, those radio towers formed a great spider web for aircraft. Any one of their wires would have cut through a wing as scissors cut through paper. Such hazards aren't marked on the best maps one can buy.

The greatest test of my navigation will come if I make a land-fall in darkness, when hills merge into valleys and railroad inter-sections are impossible to see. Then, I'll have to keep a sharp watch ahead to avoid flying into some hill or mountain before I know I'm leaving the ocean behind. Then, I'll have to establish my position from the general contour of the coast — the bays, the peninsulas, the harbors, the meandering shore line. Then, I'll set a compass course from the lights of one major city to those of another, checking the distance between them against the air speed and the clock. If I find my position to be on the coast of northern Ireland, for instance, I'll set course first for Dublin, then for Birmingham, next London, and finally for Paris. All four cities are so large that I should be able to find them if there's any ceiling at all beneath the clouds. The lights of ground traffic will help, too. In Europe, as in America, it must be true that "all roads lead to Rome."

My mind goes back to other nights; to submarine oceans of darkness, under a surface of thick clouds, over shoals of hills and trees. Many a night on the mail I've bored into one of those shallows, guided only by an occasional village and the dim lights of farmhouse windows. On such nights, ground and air are cloaked in a blackness that leaves no shade for horizon, no shadow for perception. Sometimes, when the mail was late, the lights in the windows blinked out, one after another, until there'd be only a single farmhouse as a beacon. Then I'd hope that some forgotten chore would keep the housewife busy for an extra minute, until I'd passed.

I used to search the ground below for the most meager scraps of guidance. The lights of a motorcar were diamonds of information. Fence posts, in wintertime, were black pearls strung out to lead me on. I remember Love saying that one murky night he had crossed the river at Peoria by following cracks in the ice. The black network of water showing through helped him to judge his vital hundred feet of altitude.

There'll be no ice cracks to follow in Europe at the end of May, and no snow to accentuate trees and fences. But there will be shore lines with village lights on one side and not on the other, and roads with motorcars running along them. And in extreme emergency, there may be a softer shade of blackness to mark a clearing.

I'm flying along dreamily when it catches my eye, that black speck on the water two or three miles southeast. I realize it's there with the same jerk to awareness that comes when the altimeter needle drops too low in flying blind. I squeeze my lids together and look again. A boat! A small boat! Several small boats, scattered over the surface of the ocean!

Seconds pass before my mind takes in the full importance of what my eyes are seeing. Then, all feeling of drowsiness departs. I bank the *Spirit of St. Louis* toward the nearest boat and nose down toward the water. I couldn't be wider awake or more keenly aware if the engine had stopped.

Fishing boats! *The coast, the European coast, can't be far away!* The ocean is behind, the flight completed. Those little vessels, those chips on the sea, are Europe. What nationality? Are they Irish, English, Scotch, or French? Can they be from Norway, or from Spain? What fishing bank are they anchored on? How far from the coast do fishing banks extend? It's too early to reach Europe unless a gale blew behind me through the night. Thoughts press forward in confused succession. After fifteen hours of solitude, here's human life and help and safety.

The ocean is no longer a dangerous wilderness. I feel as secure as though I were circling Lambert Field back home. I could land alongside any one of those boats, and someone would throw me a rope and take me on board where there'd be a bunk I could sleep on, and warm food when I woke up.

The first boat is less than a mile ahead — I can see its masts and cabin. I can see it rocking on the water. I close the mixture control and dive down fifty feet above its bow, dropping my wing to get a better view.

But where is the crew? There's no sign of life on deck. Can all the men be out in dories? I climb higher as I circle. No, there aren't any dories. I can see for miles, and the ocean's not rough enough to hide one. Are the fishermen frightened by my plane, swooping down suddenly from the sky? Possibly they never saw a plane before. *Of course* they never saw one out so far over the ocean. Maybe they all hid below the decks when they heard the roar of my engine. Maybe they think I'm some demon from the sky, like those dragons that decorate ancient mariners' charts. But if the crews are so out of contact with the modern world that they hide from the sound of an airplane, they must come from some isolated coastal village above which airplanes never pass. And the boats look too small to have ventured far from home. I have visions of riding the top of a hurricane during the night, with a hundred-mile-an-hour wind drift. Possibly these vessels are anchored north of Ireland, or somewhere in the Bay of Biscay. Then shall I keep on going straight, or turn north, or south?

I fly over to the next boat bobbing up and down on the swells. Its deck is empty too. But as I drop my wing to circle, a man's head appears, thrust out through a cabin porthole, motionless, staring up at me. In the excitement and joy of the moment, in the rush of ideas passing through my reawakened mind, I decide to make that head withdraw from the porthole, come out of the cabin, body and all, and to point toward the Irish coast. No sooner have I made the decision than I realize its futility. Probably that fisherman can't speak English. Even if he can, he'll be too startled to understand my message, and reply. But I'm already turning into position to dive down past the boat. It won't do any harm to try. Why deprive myself of that easy satisfaction? Probably if I fly over it again, the entire crew will come on deck. I've talked to people before from a plane, flying low with throttled engine, and received the answer through some simple gesture — a nod or an outstretched arm.

I glide down within fifty feet of the cabin, close the throttle, and shout as loudly as I can:

"WHICH WAY IS IRELAND?"

How extraordinary the silence is with the engine idling! I look back under the tail, watching the fisherman's face for some sign of understanding. But an instant later, all my attention is concentrated on the plane. For I realize that I've lost the "feel" of flying. I shove the throttle open, and watch the air-speed indicator while I climb and circle. As long as I keep the needle above sixty miles an hour, there's no danger of stalling. Always before, I've known instinctively just what condition my plane was in — whether it had flying speed or whether it was stalling, and how close to the edge it was riding in between. I didn't have to look at the instruments. Now, the pressure of the stick no longer imparts its message clearly to my hand. I can't tell whether air is soft or solid.

When I pass over the boat a third time, the head is still at the porthole. It hasn't moved or changed expression since it first appeared. It came as suddenly as the boats themselves. It seems as lifeless. I didn't notice before how pale it is — or am I now imagining its paleness? It looks like a severed head in that porthole, as though a guillotine had dropped behind it. I feel baffled. After all, a man who dares to show his face would hardly fear to show his body. There's something unreal about these boats. They're as weird as the night's temples, as those misty islands of Atlantis, as the fuselage's phantoms that rode behind my back.

Why don't sailors gather on the decks to watch my plane?

Why don't they pay attention to my circling and shouting? What's the matter with this strange flight, where dreams become reality, and reality returns to dreams? But these aren't vessels of cloud and mist. They're tangible, made of real substance like my plane — sails furled, ropes coiled neatly on the decks, masts swaying back and forth with each new swell. Yet the only sign of crew is that single head, hanging motionless through the cabin porthole. It's like "The Rime of the Ancient Mariner" my mother used to read aloud. These boats remind me of the "painted ship upon a painted ocean."

I want to stay, to circle again and again, until that head removes itself from the porthole and the crews come out on deck. I want to see them standing and waving like normal, living people. I've passed through worlds and ages since my last contact with other men. I've been away, far away, planets and heavens away, until only a thread was left to lead me back to earth and life. I've followed that thread with swinging compasses, through lonely canyons, over pitfalls of sleep, past the lure of enchanted islands, fearing that at any moment it would break. And now I've returned to earth, returned to these boats bobbing on the ocean. I want an earthly greeting. I deserve a warmer welcome back to the fellowship of men.

Shall I fly over to another boat and try again to raise the crew? No, I'm wasting minutes of daylight and miles of fuel. There's nothing but frustration to be had by staying longer. It's best to leave. There's something about this fleet that tries my mind and spirit, and lowers confidence with every circle I make. Islands that turn to fog, I understand. Ships without crews, I do not. And that motionless head at the porthole — it's no phantom, and yet it shows no sign of life. I straighten out the *Spirit of St. Louis* and fly on eastward.

Land *must* be somewhere near. Those boats were too small to be anchored far at sea — or were they? When I first saw them, navigating problems seemed past, as though their bows pointed my direction like signposts, saying: "This way to Paris." But as I leave them behind, a few black dots on an endless waste of ocean — about to vanish, as birds vanish into distant air — reason argues that I know nothing more about my latitude than I did before. They might be north of Scotland; they might be south of Ireland. They might be anywhere along the coast. There's no way to tell. And it's dangerous to take for granted that land is very near; even small boats sometimes venture far to sea. The Grand Banks of Newfoundland run hundreds of miles offshore. For all I know, similar shallows may extend from the European side. What can I do but continue on the course I set before, and follow the same plan of navigation?

Patches of blue sky above me are shrinking in size. To the north, heavier storm clouds gather.

THE TWENTY-EIGHTH HOUR

Over the Atlantic

HOURS OF FUEL CONSUMED

NOSE TANK
¼ + ~~++++~~ 1 1

LEFT WING	CENTER WING	RIGHT WING
¼ + 1 1 1	¼ +	¼ + 1 1 1

FUSELAGE
~~++++~~ ~~++++~~ 1 1 1

Ten fifty-two a.m. Twenty-seven hours behind me. If I've covered sixty degrees of longitude since leaving New York, it's four hours later here — or about three o'clock in the afternoon. I reset my heading and bring the compass needle back to center.

I keep scanning the horizon through breaks between squalls. Any one of those rain curtains may hide a ship or another fishing fleet. The air is cool, fresh, and pleasantly turbulent. I fly a hundred feet or so above the ocean — now under open sky, now with rain streaming over wings and struts.

Is that a cloud on the northeastern horizon, or a strip of low fog — or — — — *can it possibly be land?* It looks like land, but I don't intend to be tricked by another mirage. Framed between two gray curtains of rain, not more than ten or fifteen miles away, a purplish blue band has hardened from the haze — — — flat below, like a waterline — — — curving on top, as though composed of hills or aged mountains.

I'm only sixteen hours out from Newfoundland. I allowed eighteen and a half hours to strike the Irish coast. If that's Ireland, I'm two and a half hours ahead of schedule. Can this be another, clearer image, like the islands of the morning? Is there something strange about it too, like the fishing fleet and that haunting head? Is each new illusion to become more real until reality itself is meaningless? But my mind is clear. I'm no longer half asleep. I'm awake — alert — aware. The temptation is too great. I can't hold my course any longer. The *Spirit of St. Louis* banks over toward the nearest point of land.

I stare at it intently, not daring to believe my eyes, keeping hope in check to avoid another disappointment, watching the shades and contours unfold into a coast line — — — a coastline coming down from the north — — — a coast line bending toward the east — — — a coast line with rugged shores and rolling mountains. It's much too early to strike England, France, or Scotland. It's early to be striking Ireland; but that's the nearest land.

A fjorded coast stands out as I approach. Barren islands guard it. Inland, green fields slope up the sides of warted mountains. This *must* be Ireland. It can be no other place than Ireland. The fields are too green for Scotland; the mountains too high for Brittany or Cornwall.

Now, I'm flying above the foam-lined coast, searching for

prominent features to fit the chart on my knees. I've climbed to
two thousand feet so I can see the contours of the country better.
The mountains are old and rounded; the farms small and stony.
Rain-glistened dirt roads wind narrowly through hills and fields.
Below me lies a great tapering bay; a long, bouldered island; a
village. Yes, there's a place on the chart where it all fits — line
of ink on line of shore — Valentia and Dingle Bay, *on the south-
western coast of Ireland!*

I can hardly believe it's true. I'm almost exactly on my route,
closer than I hoped to come in my wildest dreams back in San
Diego. What happened to all those detours of the night around the
thunderheads? Where has' the swinging compass error gone? The
wind above the storm clouds must have blown fiercely on my tail.
In edging northward, intuition must have been more accurate than
reasoned navigation.

The southern tip of Ireland! On course; over two hours ahead
of schedule; the sun still well up in the sky; the weather clearing!
I circle again, fearful that I'll wake to find this too a phantom, a
mirage fading into mid-Atlantic mist. But there's no question about
it; every detail on the chart has its counterpart below; each major
feature on the ground has its symbol on the chart. The lines correspond exactly. Nothing in that world of dreams and phantoms was
like this. I spiral lower, looking down on the little village. There
are boats in the harbor, wagons on the stone-fenced roads. People
are running out into the streets, looking up and waving. This is
earth again, the earth where I've lived and now will live once more.
Here are human beings. Here's a human welcome. Not a single
detail is wrong. I've never seen such beauty before — fields so
green, people so human, a village so attractive, mountains and
rocks so mountainous and rocklike.

One senses only through change, appreciates only after absence. I haven't been far enough away to know the earth before.
For twenty-five years I've lived on it, and yet not seen it till this
moment. For nearly two thousand hours, I've flown over it without
realizing what wonders lay below, what crystal clarity — snow-

white foam on black-rock shores — curving hill above its valley — the hospitality of little houses — the welcome of waving arms. During my entire life I've accepted these gifts of God to man, and not known what was mine until this moment. It's like rain after drought; spring after a northern winter. I've been to eternity and back. I know how the dead would feel to live again.

I circle a third time, straighten out, and spread the chart across my knees. Only six segments more to fly, only six hundred miles to Paris. There are golden hours of the afternoon still left, and the long evening twilight. I'll cover most of that six hundred miles before darkness. There'll be less of night to Paris than on a single flight over my air-mail route in December. One round trip on the mail route would almost span the remaining distance to Paris. Now I'm dealing with distances and methods of navigation I can measure in terms of past experience — two flights over the mail route — and if the squalls are no worse than this, night flying will be easy.

I look ahead at the weather. But – – – Is it after all a nightmare? – – – Have I lost ability to distinguish fact from fancy? There's only water ahead where land has been, and storms instead of breaking sky! Where is the coast? What's happened? What's wrong again? The compass needle almost centers on its mark, and I've not changed the setting on the dial. Phantoms, mist islands, haunted fishermen; and now, is this perfect landfall also an illusion? It's too much. Hope has leapt too high to live with nothing to sustain it. But again, it's too wrong; so terribly wrong that there must be a simple answer. There always is a simple answer when life seems as wrong as this. The mountains, the coast, the rocks, the village — all Ireland *couldn't* disappear! Collect thoughts — blink eyes — shake head — start again.

There *is* a simple answer. I look back; and there behind me, less than a mile away, lies Valentia and the Irish coast. I was watching first the earth and then the chart with such intentness that I lost all sense of direction; and in straightening out, I took up the reverse heading to my course. I'm pointed back over the ocean, a hundred and eighty degrees from Paris. The storms ahead are only the scattered squalls through which I've come. And the earth-inductor compass, naturally, is reading backward on a back-track heading. Just to convince myself, I kick left rudder and watch the needle lean over toward the right.

I bank steeply around and set my course southeastward, cutting across the bouldered fjords, flying low over the hilltop farms, the rock fences, and the small, green fields of Kerry. Now, I can check the engine – – – All cylinders hitting on the left switch – – – all cylinders hitting on the right – – – And all instrument readings are normal.

Sheep and cattle graze on their sloping pastures. Horse-drawn carts crawl along their shiny roads. People move across walled-in barnyards, through doorways of the primitive stone buildings. It must be a hard place to gain a living from the soil. And it would be worse than New England for a forced landing.

Even the wish to sleep has left, and with it the phantoms and voices. I didn't notice their absence before; but now, as I settle down for the last six hundred miles to Paris, I realize that they remained behind with the fishing fleet. They vanished with that first strange touch of Europe and of man. Since I sighted those specks on the water, I've been as wide awake as though I started the flight this morning after a warm breakfast and a full night's sleep. The thought of floating off in a bed of feathers has lost its attractiveness.

Time is no longer endless, or the horizon destitute of hope. The strain of take-off, storm, and ocean, lies behind. There'll be no second night above the clouds, no more grappling with misty walls of ice. There's only one more island to cross — only the narrow tip of an island. I look at England's outline on my map. And then, within an hour, I'll see the coast of France; and beyond that, Paris and Le Bourget. As Nova Scotia and Newfoundland were stepping-stones from America, Ireland and England are stepping-stones to Europe. Yesterday, each strip of sea I crossed was an advance messenger of the ocean. Today, these islands down below are heralds to a continent.

It's as though a curtain has fallen behind me, shutting off the stagelike unreality of this transatlantic flight. It's been like a theater where the play carries you along in time and place until you forget you're only a spectator. You grow unaware of the walls around you, of the program clasped in your hand, even of your body, its breath, pulse, and being. You live with the actors and the setting, in a different age and place. It's not until the curtain drops that consciousness and body reunite. Then, you turn your back on the stage, step out into the cool night, under the lights of streets, between the displays of store windows. You feel life surging in the crowd around you, life as it was when you entered the theater, hours before. Life is real. It always was real. The stage, of course, was the dream. All that transpired there is now a memory, shut off by the curtain, by the doors of the theater, by the passing minutes of time.

Striking Ireland was like leaving the doors of a theater — phantoms for actors; cloud islands and temples for settings; the ocean behind me, an empty stage. The flight across is already like a dream. I'm over villages and fields, back to land and wakefulness and a type of flying that I know. I'm myself again, in earthly skies and over earthly ground. My hands and feet and eyelids move, and I can think as I desire. That third, controlling element has retired to the backgroud. I'm no longer three existences in one. My mind is able to command, and my body follows out its orders with precision.

Ireland, England, France, Paris! The night at Paris! *This* night at Paris — less than six hours from now — *France and Paris!* It's like a fairy tale. Yesterday I walked on Roosevelt Field; today I'll walk on Le Bourget.

I'm angling slowly back onto my great-circle route. I must have been within three miles of it when I sighted Ireland. An error of fifty miles would have been good dead reckoning under the most perfect conditions. Three miles was – – – well, what was it? Before I made this flight, I would have said carelessly that it was luck.

Now, luck seems far too trivial a word, a term to be used only by those who've never seen the curtain drawn or looked on life from far away.

That little lighthouse down below, so white against gray rock and water, what security it offers! Tonight, its beam would guide me back to Ireland if England should be blanketed with fog, and I could circle with it until dawn. If my engine failed, I could stall down into the waves beside it and find helping hands to pull my rubber raft ashore. My eyes follow the coast as it bends back northward, half hidden by a squall. Beyond those distant mountains, among the stones and fields of Tipperary, some of my ancestors lived — three generations ago, on my mother's side. They sailed for weeks to reach America. I've returned to their old world in less than thirty hours.

Ireland — the land of banshees, ghosts, and fairies. I've never believed in apparitions; but how can I explain the forms I carried with me through so many hours of this day — the voices that spoke with such authority and clearness — that told me – – – that told me – – – but what did they tell me? I can't remember a single word they said.

THE TWENTY-NINTH HOUR

Over St. George's Channel

HOURS OF FUEL CONSUMED

NOSE TANK

¼ + ҇҇҇҇҇ 1 1

LEFT WING	CENTER WING	RIGHT WING
¼ + 1 1 1	¼ +	¼ + 1 1 1

FUSELAGE

҇҇҇҇҇ ҇҇҇҇҇ 1 1 1 1

It's eleven fifty a.m. on the clock. I pull my watch from my pocket — eleven forty-nine and three quarters. Yes, they check. I hold the watch in my palm for a moment. It always stirs old memories, for it belonged to my grandfather. He used to let me touch it with my fingers as a child, guess at the time from its hands, see how far away my ears could hear it tick. When my grandfather died my uncle gave the watch to me, and we've passed through many an interesting hour together. We've spilled off my motorcycle, stunted in my planes, made — let's see — eighteen parachute jumps all told; and now we've flown across an ocean. Once a year I spend a dollar to have it cleaned, and it's always carried on accurately and snugly, in its little nickel-alloy case, unmindful of the changing time and space through which it passes.

Now it's 11:52. I run my eyes over the instruments, put the twenty-seventh score on the board, and shift to the nose tank. I'll leave the nose tank on until it runs dry, so the center of gravity will be well to the rear if I'm forced down on some field along the coast. The heavier the tail, the less chance of nosing over. Also, I want to get a check on fuel consumption. None of the tanks has run dry yet, and I'm still figuring gallons per hour by theory instead of actual timing. The nose tank has already lasted longer than I expected. Judging from it, I should have enough fuel left to fly through the night and well into daylight, even though I've been using a higher cruising speed.

The wind is strengthening, and tail. Cumulus clouds mottle the sea with their shadows. Scattered squalls, one after another, emerge from the haze — light squalls, light haze, a clearing sky. I can see almost to the horizon. Some man-imagined line below me divides the Atlantic Ocean from St. George's Channel. Ahead, less than two hours away, lies England's Cornish coast.

It's a pleasant sky, neither dull nor dangerous. The mellowness of late afternoon blends with the approaching termination of my flight. The heavy chores of the day — the great difficulties of the flight — are over. The remaining hours are downgrade, simply routine to be completed without excessive effort. There are ships to be seen for the looking — four of them in sight at this moment. I have plenty of fuel, plenty of power. Every major obstacle is behind.

It's incredible that so much weight can be moved through the air so far. The gasoline left in my tanks when I reach France will weigh more than all the mail one of our DHs can carry between St. Louis and Chicago. Why, if I landed and refueled at an airport in Newfoundland, and then refueled again in Ireland, I could have brought thousands of letters to Paris. Let's see, that would have let me transform 1700 miles of fuel into mail sacks. At, say, 10 gallons to 100 miles, that would be 170 gallons, or more than 1000 pounds of fuel. And there'd be the saving in tank weight, too. By landing twice en route, I could have carried a huge pay load!

What limitless possibilities aviation holds when planes can fly nonstop between New York and Paris! The year will surely come when passengers and mail fly every day from America to Europe. Of course flying will cost much more than transportation by surface ship; but letters can be written on light-weight paper, and there'll be people with such pressing business that they can afford the higher price of passage. With multiengined flying boats, the safety of operation should be high. Weather will be the greatest problem. We'll have to find some way to fly through sleet and land in fog.

Planes may even replace automobiles someday, just as automobiles replaced horses. Possibly everyone will travel by air in another fifty years. I'm not sure I like the idea of millions of planes flying around overhead. Of course I want to see aviation develop into important branches of industry and commerce. But I love the sky's unbroken solitude. I don't like to think of it cluttered up by aircraft, as roads are cluttered up by cars. I feel like the western pioneer when he saw barbed-wire fence lines encroaching on his open plains. The success of his venture brought the end of the life he loved.

What is aviation leading to? What effect will it have on the lives of men? That it will bring revolutionary changes seems certain. There are moments when I fear the conditions aircraft will create. Sometimes, in lazy weather on the mail route, these problems stir uncomfortably in my mind ―――

The engine jerks against its mounting! I stiffen as though I'd had an electric shock. Irregular spluttering replaces the exhaust's sharp rhythm. Thoughts rush back into the cockpit, traveling, in a fraction of a second, back from aviation's future, back from my ancestors in Ireland, back from the scattered squalls ahead, to a tense and waiting body, a body which instinctively pushed forward on the stick at the first sound of engine failure, and which now sits rigidly, waiting for command, anxious for instant action.

This is the start of a real forced landing. This is no idle speculation, no aimless wandering of the mind. Am I to be forced down on this trivial arm of ocean? Have I grown too confident, too arrogant, before my flight is done?

But of course! Nothing serious is wrong. The nose tank simply ran dry, as I intended it to. That's why I'm flying at a thousand feet instead of closer to the water. There's no reason to be startled. I turn on the center wing-tank, shut off the nose-tank valve, close the throttle and mixture control, and begin working the hand wobble pump. Meanwhile my eyes sweep the horizon for ships, and my mind notes down the essential elements for a forced landing at sea ― just in case the engine doesn't pick up again ―――

There are two ships in sight ― but miles away ― far beyond gliding range. They wouldn't even see the splash from my plane hitting the water ― might as well forget about them. The wind is still a little north of tail. That means a left turn ― not quite 180 degrees. I ought to fasten my safety belt, but that takes two hands more than I can spare.

The jerking and coughing stop. I ease the throttle forward. Power surges through the plane. The engine smooths out. The air speed rises. I take up course.

THE THIRTIETH HOUR

Over St. George's Channel

HOURS OF FUEL CONSUMED

NOSE TANK

¼ + ~~++++~~ 1 1 1

LEFT WING	CENTER WING	RIGHT WING
¼ + 1 1 1	¼ +	¼ + 1 1 1

FUSELAGE

~~++++~~ ~~++++~~ 1 1 1 1

It's 12:52 p.m., New York time; about 5:30 here. I'm just over four hours from Paris. By turning the engine faster, I can reach France before darkness. If there should be a thick haze beneath low clouds over the English Channel it would be difficult to cross at night, for there'll be few lights, and no differences in shading between air and water. But if I can reach the French coast in daylight, then only fog or violent storms can hold me back from Le Bourget.

I close the mixture control, open the throttle to 1725 r.p.m., and watch the air speed mount to 110 miles an hour. That will take me to England well before sunset, and leave just enough time to get back to Ireland by dark if Cornwall is covered with fog.

Of course a return to Ireland would probably mean giving up a nonstop flight to Paris. There'd hardly be enough fuel left to circle through the night and then fly on for 600 miles after the fog cleared in the morning — if it did. A half-hour ago, in the joy of my landfall, I felt that nothing would induce me to lose contact with the surface of the earth again. I decided that if England were covered with fog I'd turn back to Ireland and land, and that if I found France covered with fog, I'd circle the lights of some English city through the night and try to reach Le Bourget after sunrise. Then, the security I'd regained seemed more important than any success I could achieve. But with each passing minute the idea of turning back becomes more repulsive. I begin reconsidering my decision not to climb above a fog. There may be fog over England and the Channel while the continent beyond is clear. Everyone has read about the London fogs. After flying over storms and ocean, I'm not going to be defeated by a narrow strip of weather. How ashamed I'd feel if I turned back to Ireland when above Le Bourget there'd been an open sky. No, I won't let a little fog frighten me now. I'll fly over Paris by dead reckoning if need be, and then decide whether to go on or turn back.

Judging from the nose tank, I have enough fuel to reach Rome. I can certainly get that far if this tail wind keeps blowing. How surprised people back home would be if I cabled them from Rome instead of Paris! I unfold the map of Europe. Rome is about 700 miles beyond Paris, and not far south of my great-circle route extended eastward. It's a shame to land with nearly a thousand miles of fuel in the tanks. Why waste all that gasoline after carrying it across the ocean? I'm not sleepy any more. I've gained a second wind. I can sit here and fly on indefinitely. *Why not* throttle down again and fly eastward through another night? I could coax every mile of distance from the remaining fuel. I could circle Paris, if it's clear, dip my wings, and fly on to Italy and Rome. Think of it: a flight of almost forty-three hundred miles nonstop.

And if I can reach Rome, I can reach the dawn. I wouldn't have to worry about finding a place to land at night. But is my estimate of fuel correct? I haven't followed the power curves we laid out at San Diego. All I'm sure of is that the center wing-tank holds a twenty-five-gallon reserve. What if I run short over the mountains of Switzerland or northern Italy in darkness? I'd have to find some city and circle its lights, hoping it had an airport with a beacon and that someone would hear me and turn it on.

I did that once, over Cleveland. I was delivering a Hisso-Standard from St. Louis. Mechanical troubles had held me down at Ft. Ben Harrison, in Indiana, and I arrived at my destination after nightfall. Since Cleveland was an air-mail stop, I expected to find a revolving beacon marking its airport. But the only flashes were along the lake front. They were clearly timed for ships.

I'd kept circling over the outskirts of the city, searching for dark areas on the earth large enough to hold an airport. There wasn't much gasoline left in my tanks, and I had to keep enough of that in reserve to reach the farm lands south of the city. To give up the lines of street lights and turn south meant an almost certain crack-up; but I'd have a good chance of getting through unhurt. If I stayed too long hunting for the airport and ran out of fuel, I'd have to stall down among telephone poles and houses. Then, I'd be lucky if I weren't killed. The Standard wasn't equipped for night flying. It had no lights and no flares – – – But neither has the *Spirit of St. Louis*.

I remember banking over two vacant city blocks large enough to land on. Lamps along a sidewalk showed small semicircles of grass that gave me some perspective. But a street divided the area in half, and even if the ground I couldn't see were smooth I'd have broken my landing gear rolling across it.

Suddenly there was a flash from the ground about two miles to the west. I straightened out the wings and waited. Another flash. I banked toward it. Yes, it was the mail field. Floodlights blinked on as I approached.

"Say, do you make a practice of flying around unannounced after dark?" the chief postal clerk had asked after I landed.

"I thought mail beacons were turned on all night," I'd countered.

"No sir, not ours. When there aren't any planes coming in we turn it off. What's the use wasting electricity?"

"How did you happen to turn it on?" I asked.

"Some fellow up the line telephoned the post office. He said there was a plane flying around overhead and he thought the pilot was lost. Well, guess we might as well turn it off again now."

I don't want to find myself low on fuel tonight, circling some European city with the *Spirit of St. Louis*. No, this flight is from New York to Paris; I planned and organized it with the intention of landing at Paris. I didn't start out to see how far I could fly. If Paris is covered with fog, that's different; then I can go on with a clear conscience. But first I must exert every effort to land at the destination I set.

All readings are normal. The sky is broken, the sea light, the horizon veiled in haze. Without even bending forward, from my altitude of 1500 feet, I count half-a-dozen ships. At any moment now England's shore line will be in sight.

How different from that long uncertainty of waiting for the Irish coast, not knowing either my latitude or longitude, or whether the course I followed lay across it. Here, it's a matter of minutes at most. There's no question, no longer the slightest doubt in my mind. Within the next ten minutes, England will rise to view. It will be no mirage. It will have no tantalizing islands made of mist.

For aviators approaching from the sea, a coast line chooses between two methods of appearing. When air is crystal clear it announces itself delicately, subtly, as a fine, dark line, barely breaking the evenness of the horizon; rising, growing, flowering gradually, giving one plenty of time to adjust to its presence, its shades of color, its intricacies of character and shape. But in heavy haze or fog it can loom up with terrifying suddenness, not even leaving time to turn from its crushing impact. On one day, it uses the curvature of the earth as a cloak. On another, it veils itself with different shades of mist and weather. Welcoming hills in sunlight are deadly bluffs in storm; and a summit higher than the rest may be either a flyer's beacon or his grave. Therefore the first sight of land is an omen of great significance.

The coast of England is well above the horizon when I see its outline, pale and whitish in the haze. Then there's no fog over Cornwall. I can let go of Ireland completely, and move forward another notch in the ratchet of my mind. No matter what happens now, I'll not return to those hilly, bouldered fields for safety, or land in the waves beside some Celtic lighthouse keeper's home. If by any dwindling chance I still have to turn back from Paris, I now have England for a haven.

Above the sheer Cornish cliffs, rising straight up out of the sea, farm fields break off abruptly where their soil has tumbled down into encroaching waves. As a schoolboy I read of the slowly changing surface of the earth, of clam fossils found on hilltops, of glaciers building and melting, of land masses that disappeared, of drifting continents and dried-up seas. But all these things were measured on a time scale that made little impression on my mind — hundreds of centuries — ages before the Sphinx was built. Here, I see the earth actually in the modeling, changing in terms of time I understand. The signs below are fresh, unmistakable. The road, and little houses and barns on top of the cliff, are all set back from the precipice, leaving a strip of green fields along the edge, a few generations' worth of land to delay the inevitable collapse into sea — an offering to the god of the ocean.

THE THIRTY-FIRST HOUR

Over England

HOURS OF FUEL CONSUMED

NOSE TANK

¼ + ⫲⫲⫲ 𝟙𝟙𝟙

LEFT WING	CENTER WING	RIGHT WING
¼ + 𝟙𝟙𝟙	¼ +	¼ + 𝟙𝟙𝟙

FUSELAGE

⫲⫲⫲ ⫲⫲⫲ ⫲⫲⫲

One fifty-two p.m., Eastern daylight time. Almost thirty-three hundred miles from New York. The twenty-ninth score goes up on the instrument board.

Cornwall is more populated and prosperous than Ireland, and less rugged. How foreign — how different from America it is, with its neat, miniature farms all divided off by hedge and stone fences, and its narrow, sod-walled roads running crookedly between slate-roofed villages! How can a farmer make his living from fields so small? He'd barely get started with a plow before the hedge at the far end would turn him back. No wonder there are so many one-horse carts. It wouldn't pay to buy modern machinery for such acreage. A hundred of these fields would fit into a single Kansas wheat ranch.

It was from such farms and villages as these that Englishmen set out to build a new life in America. The men and women down below are children of those who stayed at home, still carrying on the traditions of our forefathers. I'm a child of those who left — flying back three generations later. Most of my mother's forebears came from England. Early Lands and Lodges were subjects of the King. How strange it is to realize that this ground below me is ruled by a monarch.

Lodge family legend brings an ancestor to England in the train of William the Conqueror. We know next to nothing about the British generations. But my great-great-grandfather, William Gibbon Lodge, sailed to America soon after the War of 1812. He became a lawyer in New York. Our written records begin with his wife, Harriet Clubb, of Tunbridge, Kent. She had reservations in regard to Americans, if one judges from entries in her diary: "We walked about in the Battery Gardens," she wrote, soon after arriving in this country, "and had a sight of the fireworks as well as a good look of the American ladies, who are anything but pretty. They are small women without hips, lanky, scraggy, pale, and Lantern Jaw'd and rather prudish looking. At any rate they look very modest. Nature does not appear to have done so much for them as for the vegetation which is luxuriant in the extreme. The men are likewise far from being so good looking or gentlemanly as the English." How often our family has laughed over that paragraph!

Well, now it's *my* turn to get a first impression of the *English*. I drop down to five hundred feet. People raise their heads as I fly

over them. What do they think when they see my plane? Do any of
them realize I've flown across the Atlantic Ocean, or do they regard
me as simply a British pilot on a local flight? Do they know they're
looking at the *Spirit of St. Louis* — a plane which has traveled
from the United States to England in thirty hours? But even if
they heard of my take-off from their local radio or press, they
wouldn't expect me to fly through their particular sky, or think I
could have made the trip so soon.

Inland hills are higher, and air becomes slightly turbulent again.
To the north, real mountains rise halfway to clouds. A mellow
country, it seems, in the long shadows and soft light of late afternoon. The sun is setting slowly, but it's probably a full hour above
the horizon. English daylight is long in the month of May. I'll reach
the coast of France by darkness. It's only another hour's flight.
One more hour to the coast of France!

There's the English Channel already — shore line darkening
against pale gray of distant water. It's through this very channel
that the Spanish Armada sailed. And all around me, just as tangible
and real and earthlike as the states in America, are the countries
of Europe. They're no longer colored portions of a paper map, no
longer at the end of a rainbow. The Channel coast of England is
gliding range ahead; the coast of France, an hour's flight beyond.
Memories of school texts and childhood stories flood my mind.
These are the countries of Robin Hood and King Arthur, of Henry
the Eighth and the Redcoats, of Joan of Arc and Lafayette and
Napoleon. Farther up this Channel, where it narrows down near
Dover, Bleriot made his famous flight. And somewhere beyond that
lies the hill from which Lilienthal launched himself on early wings.
    I've crossed England so quickly! It seems so small! — in keep-
ing with the miniature farms below. Why, I'll be over the sea again
within twenty minutes of the time I struck the Atlantic Cornish

coast! Of course it's really the tip of England I'm crossing, the narrow peninsula that runs down to Land's End and the Scilly Islands. But it's only three hours since I sighted Ireland, and now I'm about to leave England behind. I can't accustom myself to the short distances of the Old World. I look down at my map. All England is no larger than one of our Midwestern states.

There, on my left, is Plymouth, and the same harbor from which the *Mayflower* once sailed, against weeks of adverse winds and hardships. Yesterday, I flew almost over Plymouth Rock, on the coast of Massachusetts. Today, my course takes me above the mother city in England — a gray city, curving around its ship-filled harbor, smoke from its chimneys drifting leisurely along my line of flight; a low city compared to the steel-skeletoned sky-scrapers we build in America. Beyond, the green, indented, rolling coast parallels my course for another thirty miles.

Only three hundred miles to Paris. The horizon is sharpening, and the sky ahead is clear.

From Start Point of England to Cape de la Hague of France is eighty-five miles. In the past, I would have approached an eighty-five-mile flight over water, in a land plane, with trepidation. It would have appeared a hazardous undertaking. This evening, it's just part of the downhill glide to Paris. Why, I should be able to paddle halfway across the Channel with my hands if I were forced down. What's eighty-five miles in contrast to an ocean — or to that space above the clouds at night? It's not even as long as the little bay of water between Cape Cod and Nova Scotia. It's less than that short hop across the ice fields between Cape Breton Island and Newfoundland. And here the ocean is no wilderness; it's a populated country, filled with ships. Dozens of them ply back and forth along the coast — fishing smacks to ocean liners — dots all over the surface, as far as I can see. Probably some of them have come from New York, too; churning through the water for days to make their crossing.

How safe the people on those ships have been, but how little they know the air and ocean! Security and luxury shield one off from life. You never see the sky until you've looked upward to the stars for safety. You never feel the air until you've been shaken by its storms. You can never understand the ocean until you've been alone in its solitude. To appreciate fully, you must have intercourse with the elements themselves, know their whims, their beauties, their dangers. Then, every tissue of your being sees and feels, then body, mind, and spirit are as one.

The men who sailed in open boats a thousand years ago — they knew. They were at the mercy of the storm wind. They felt the wet, salty closeness of the ocean. They hadn't bought tickets under colored posters, or been assured return from voyage started. But for the passengers on those liners down below, life is insulated; and the senses are dulled by the very luxuries they pay for. Storms and fog and freezing gales may hold them back a day in reaching port; that's all. A high sea simply means closed portholes and less pleasantness in eating, sleeping, and walking. Only in some rare instance, in some extreme and unforeseen condition, would an emergency open life to view. For them, this evening's sky is simply picturesque and clear; how can they know it forms an archway in the air to France and Paris?

Haze slowly covers up the Channel coast behind. Only a few ships are left in sight. There are none ahead. I start climbing — — — to one thousand — — — to two thousand feet. The sun behind me is low, only a few diameters above the horizon. This is the last water, this little strip of ocean. In less than half an hour I'll be in sight of France.

THE THIRTY-SECOND HOUR

Over the English Channel

HOURS OF FUEL CONSUMED

NOSE TANK

¼ + ̶1̶ ̶1̶ ̶1̶ ̶1̶ 1 1 1

LEFT WING	CENTER WING	RIGHT WING
¼ + 1 1 1	¼ +	¼ + 1 1 1

FUSELAGE

̶1̶ ̶1̶ ̶1̶ ̶1̶ ̶1̶ ̶1̶ ̶1̶ ̶1̶ ̶1̶ ̶1̶ ̶1̶ ̶1̶ 1

A strip of land, ten miles or so in width, dents the horizon — Cape de la Hague. The coast of *France!* It comes like an outstretched hand to meet me, glowing in the light of sunset. From this very coast, thirteen days ago, Nungesser and Coli set out for the westward flight across the ocean. They took off from Le Bourget, where I am soon to land. How far did they fly? Why were they lost? Was it engine failure, storm, or fuel shortage? Were they caught at night in a mountainous cloud of ice? Could they have flown off through starlit passageways, and lost the thread of earth entirely? Or are they still alive, somewhere in the wilderness of North America? They too rode on a magic carpet, but somehow the magic was lost.

Yes, aviation has great power, but how fragile are its wings! When all goes well in flying, one can soar through the sky like a god, letting the planet turn below — remaining aloof or partaking of its life as one desires. But how slight an error can bring one tumbling down; how minute are the pitfalls of the air — a microscopic flaw in a fitting, a few crystals of ice in a venturi tube, the lack of an hour's sleep.

The sun almost touches the horizon as I look down on the city of Cherbourg, embracing its little harbor. Here is France, two thousand feet underneath my wing. After three thousand, four hundred miles of flying, I'm over the country of my destination. I've made the first nonstop airplane flight between the continents of America and Europe. There'll not be another night above the clouds. There's no longer any question of turning back across the water. No matter what happens now, I'll land in France. It's only two hundred miles to Paris, and half of that will be in twilight.

I slip my Mercator's projection into its pocket for the last time, and draw out the map of France. Ahead, the sky is clear. On my left, several ships punctuate the sea. On my right, smoke from little factory chimneys points toward Paris. My route passes over ten or fifteen miles of land and then parallels the coast of Normandy to Deauville.

Hitherto, I haven't dared plan beyond landing on Le Bourget, as though in a sense that were the end of life itself. Now, time stretches on again. There are days and weeks and years ahead.

What *will* I do after I land at Le Bourget? First, of course, I'll get the *Spirit of St. Louis* put away in some hangar. Then, I'll send a cable home, giving my time of landing. The speed I've made will surprise everyone back there — nearly three hours ahead of schedule — an average of more than a hundred miles an hour all the way from New York to Paris. After that, I'll find some place to spend the night. Everything else can go until morning.

These arrangements would be simple enough back home. They'll be more difficult in a foreign country — in France, when I don't speak a word of French. I didn't get a visa before I took off — I wonder how much trouble that will cause. I'm so far ahead of schedule that I may not find anybody waiting for me on the field. But one of the pilots or mechanics will probably speak a little English.

The first two or three days will be taken up by routine arrangements and meetings. There'll be newspaper interviews and photographs to get over with. And a lot of people will come out to the airport to see the *Spirit of St. Louis*. That will be fun. I like showing off the plane. In between times, I'll check over the engine and measure the fuel. I'll have to buy a new suit of clothes, and a half-dozen odds and ends. I haven't brought even a toothbrush or an extra shirt with me. Later on, I'll take a day or two off to walk through the streets and buildings of Paris.

Possibly I can make a flying tour through other European countries. Why not? It wouldn't be very expensive — mostly hotel bills and gasoline and oil. Aside from a routine inspection and a few minor adjustments, my engine ought to be good for thousands of miles of flying. It shouldn't even need a top overhaul for two or three hundred hours. That's enough to take me the rest of the way around the world!

People over here will surely want to see the plane that's flown nonstop all the way from the United States to France. I can probably get permission to land wherever I want to go. I could fly to England, spend a day or two at London, and then hop over to Ireland — something draws me back to those green fields and boulders. I might go up to Scotland. I glance down at the chart. For the *Spirit of St. Louis*, Glasgow and Dublin are only two hours' flight apart. I could visit Sweden and Denmark and Norway, and stop off in Germany on the way. After that, there's still Russia — and Italy and Spain and Africa, and all those Balkan countries. Why hurry back home? New adventures open endlessly ahead. There's nothing I can't do with the *Spirit of St. Louis*. It's truly a magic carpet, as though it came directly out of the tale of the Arabian Nights to take me anywhere at all. When I'm ready to leave Europe, I can step into its cockpit again and fly on around the world, through Egypt, and India, and China, until I reach the West by flying east. There's no place on earth I can't go.

As a matter of fact, how *will* I return home? *Why not* fly on around the world? The scarcity of airports in Asia is no problem for a plane that can fly four thousand miles nonstop. If I crossed the Pacific in the north, between Siberia and Alaska, I probably wouldn't ever need to take off with more than a half load of fuel. And what if there are no airports in some places where I'd want to land? Haven't I barnstormed for weeks at a time without seeing an airport?

Flying on around the world would show again what modern

airplanes can accomplish. Besides, it's beneath the dignity of the *Spirit of St. Louis* to return to the United States on board a boat. Rather than that, I'll make the westward flight back over the route I've just followed. There'd be head winds, of course, flying westward, and the danger of striking fog over Newfoundland and Canada. But I could take off from Ireland instead of France. That would cut down the distance back by almost six hundred miles. If I started from Ireland, I might fly all the way to St. Louis nonstop. It would be great fun to take off from Europe one day and land at home, on Lambert Field, the next. I can see the pilots and mechanics running up to my plane.

"Where did you come from?"

"I came from Ireland."

"From Ireland – – – when did you leave?"

"I left yesterday."

I would say it all casually, just as though I'd landed on a routine mail flight from Chicago.

THE THIRTY-THIRD HOUR

Over France

HOURS OF FUEL CONSUMED

NOSE TANK

¼ + ɫɫɫɫ ɪ ɪ ɪ

LEFT WING	CENTER WING	RIGHT WING
¼ + ɪ ɪ ɪ	¼ +	¼ + ɪ ɪ ɪ

FUSELAGE

ɫɫɫɫ ɫɫɫɫ ɫɫɫɫ ɪ ɪ

Almost thirty-five hundred miles from New York. I've broken the world's distance record for a nonstop airplane flight. The fuselage tank must be almost empty; and now there's no need to run it dry. I turn on the right wing-tank. In one hour more I should see the lights of Paris.

The sea is calm. Southward, just out of gliding range, lies the dusk-touched coast of Normandy. Little boats sail in toward shore, apparently motionless on the surface, leaving only their wakes as signs of movement to an airman's eye. A faint point of land, far ahead on my left, marks the location of Le Havre. The expanse of water, extending on eastward below it, is the estuary of the Seine.

I cross the coast again exactly on course, over Deauville. All the east foreshadows night. Day now belongs only to the western sky, still red with sunset. What more I see of France, before I land, will be in this long twilight of late spring. I nose the *Spirit of St. Louis* lower, while I study the farms and villages — the signs I can't read, the narrow, shop-lined streets, the walled-in barnyards. Fields are well groomed, fertile, and peaceful — larger than those of England. It's not hard to see how French farmers make a living; and there are plenty of places where I could land in emergency without cracking up.

People come running out as I skim low over their houses — blue-jeaned peasants, white-aproned wives, children scrambling between them, all bareheaded and looking as though they'd jumped up from the supper table to search for the noise above their roofs. Four-twenty on the clock. That's nine-twenty here. Why, it's past suppertime! I hold the stick with my knees, untwist the neck of the paper bag, and pull out a sandwich — my first food since take-off. The *Spirit of St. Louis* noses up. I push the stick forward, clamp it between my knees again, and uncork the canteen. I can drink all the water I want, now — plenty more below if I should be forced down between here and Paris. But how flat the sandwich tastes! Bread and meat never touched my tongue like this before. It's an effort even to swallow. I'm hungry, because I go on eating, but I have to wash each mouthful down with water.

One sandwich is enough. I brush the crumbs off my lap. I start to throw the wrapping through the window — no, these fields are so clean and fresh it's a shame to scatter them with paper. I crunch it up and stuff it back in the brown bag. I don't want the litter from a sandwich to symbolize my first contact with France.

All details on the ground are masking out in night. Color is gone. Only shades remain — woods darker than fields; hedgerows, lines of black. Lights twinkle in villages and blink in farmhouse windows. My instruments are luminous again. The rest of the flight will be in darkness. But I can't miss Paris, even if I find no other check point on my route. I'm too close. The sky's too clear. The city's too large.

I ease back on the stick and climb – – – to five hundred – – – to a thousand – – – to two thousand feet. A light flashes from the darkness, miles ahead. Could it be – – – I stare at the area from which it came, and wait. On our mail route at home, you count eleven between flashes – – – Another flash. Yes, it's an air beacon! And there are two more, blinking dimly in the distance, to the left. It must be the airway between London and Paris! Nobody told me it had lights.

From now on everything will be as simple as flying in to Chicago on a clear night. That line of beacons is converging with my course. Where the two lines meet — the beacons and my course — less than a hundred miles ahead — lies Paris. I can project them over the horizon, into the night, and already see the city in my mind's eye. Within half an hour, its glow will lighten the southeastern sky.

Down under my left wing, angling in from the north, winding through fields submerged in night, comes the Seine, shimmering back to the sky the faint remaining light of evening.

With my position known and my compass set, with the air clear and a river and an airway to lead me in, nothing but engine failure can keep me now from reaching Paris. The engine is running perfectly — I check the switches again.

The *Spirit of St. Louis* is a wonderful plane. It's like a living creature, gliding along smoothly, happily, as though a successful flight means as much to it as to me, as though we shared our experiences together, each feeling beauty, life, and death as keenly, each dependent on the other's loyalty. *We* have made this flight across the ocean, not *I* or *it*.

I throw my flashlight on the engine instruments. Every needle is in place. For almost thirty-three hours, not one of them has varied from its normal reading — except when the nose tank ran dry. For every minute I've flown there have been more than seven thousand explosions in the cylinders, yet not a single one has missed.

I'm leveled off at four thousand feet, watching for the luminosity in the sky ahead that will mark the city of Paris. Within the hour, I'll land. The dot on my map will become Paris itself, with its airport, hangars, and floodlights, and mechanics running out to guide me in. All over the ground below there are clusters of lights. Large clusters are cities; small ones, towns and villages; pin points are buildings on a farm. I can image that I'm looking through the earth to the heavens on the other side. Paris will be a great galaxy lighting up the night.

Within the hour I'll land, and strangely enough I'm in no hurry to have it pass. I haven't the slightest desire to sleep. My eyes are no longer salted stones. There's not an ache in my body. The night is cool and safe. I want to sit quietly in this cockpit and let the realization of my completed flight sink in. Europe is below; Paris, just over the earth's curve in the night ahead — a few minutes more of flight. It's like struggling up a mountain after a rare flower, and then, when you have it within arm's reach, realizing that satisfaction and happiness lie more in the finding than the plucking. Plucking and withering are inseparable. I want to prolong this culminating experience of my flight. I almost wish Paris were a few more hours away. It's a shame to land with the night so clear and so much fuel in my tanks.

I'm still flying at four thousand feet when I see it, that scarcely perceptible glow, as though the moon had rushed ahead of schedule. Paris is rising over the edge of the earth. It's almost thirty-three hours from my take-off on Long Island. As minutes pass, myriad pin points of light emerge, a patch of starlit earth under a starlit sky — the lamps of Paris — straight lines of lights, curving lines of lights, squares of lights, black spaces in between. Gradually avenues, parks, and buildings take outline form; and there, far below, a little offset from the center, is a column of lights pointing upward, changing angles as I fly — the Eiffel Tower. I circle once above it, and turn northeastward toward Le Bourget.

THE THIRTY-FOURTH HOUR

Over France

HOURS OF FUEL CONSUMED

NOSE TANK

¼ + ┼┼┼┼ 1 1 1

LEFT WING	CENTER WING	RIGHT WING
¼ + 1 1 1	¼ +	¼ + 1 1 1 1

FUSELAGE

┼┼┼┼ ┼┼┼┼ ┼┼┼┼ 1 1

Four fifty-two on the clock. That's 9:52, Paris time. Le Bourget isn't shown on my map. No one I talked to back home had more than a general idea of its location. "It's a big airport," I was told. "You can't miss it. Just fly northeast from the city." So I penciled a circle on my map, about where Le Bourget ought to be; and now the *Spirit of St. Louis* is over the outskirts of Paris, pointed toward the center of that circle.

I look ahead. A beacon should be flashing on such a large and important airport. But the nearest beacon I see is fully twenty miles away, and west instead of east of Paris. I bank slightly, so I can search the earth directly ahead. There's no flash. But I'm flying at four thousand feet. The beacon may be sweeping the horizon. I'm probably far above its beam. It's probably like the beacons on our mail route, set low to guide pilots wedging underneath clouds and storm, not for those who fly high through starlit nights. From my altitude, I shouldn't be hunting for a beacon, but for a darkened patch of ground, bordered by straight-lined, regularly spaced points of light, with a few green and red points among the yellow; that's how a landing field should look from four thousand feet.

Yes, there's a black patch to my left, large enough to be an airport. And there are lights all around it. But they're neither straight nor regularly spaced, and some are strangely crowded together. But if that's not Le Bourget, where else can it be? There's no other suitable grouping of lights — unless the location I've marked on my map is entirely wrong. I bank left to pass overhead. Are those floodlights, in one corner of the dark area? If they are, they're awfully weak. They're hardly bright enough to be for landing aircraft. But don't I see the ends of hangars over at one side? Or are they just the buildings of some factory?

It looks like an airport. But why would an airport be placed in such a congested section? There are thousands of lights along one side. They probably come from a large factory. Surely Le Bourget wouldn't have a factory that size right next to it. I'm almost overhead now. I can see no warning lights, no approach lights, and no revolving beacon. Looking straight down on a beacon, one can see the diffused light from its beam sweeping the ground under the tower. But those *are* floodlights, and they show the edge of a field. Maybe the French turn out their beacons when no planes are due, like that air-mail field at Cleveland. And even the people who think I have a chance of reaching Paris won't expect me here so soon. But why leave floodlights burning, and not the boundary lights and beacon? Of course I must remember I'm over Europe, where customs are strange.

This is right in the direction where Le Bourget ought to be; but I expected to find it farther out from the city. I'll fly on northeast a few miles more. Then, if I see nothing else that looks like an airport, I'll come back and circle at lower altitude.

Five minutes have passed. Only the lights of small towns and country homes break the blackness of the earth. I turn back on my course, throttle down slightly, and begin a slow descent.

The altimeter shows two thousand feet when I approach the lights again. Close to a large city in an unknown country, it's best not to fly too low. There may be hills with high radio towers on top of them. There are bound to be radio towers somewhere around Paris. I point my pocket flashlight toward the ground, and key out a message. There's no response.

I circle. Yes, it's definitely an airport. I see part of a concrete apron in front of a large, halfopen door. But is it Le Bourget? Well, at least it's a Paris airport. That's the important thing. It's Paris I set out for. If I land on the wrong field, it won't be too serious an error — as long as I land safely. I look around once more for other floodlights or a beacon. There are none — nothing even worth flying over to investigate. I spiral lower, left wing down, keeping close to the edge of the field. There aren't likely to be any radio towers nearby. I'll give those lights along the southern border a wide berth when I come in to land. There may be high factory chimneys rising among them.

From each changed angle, as I bank, new details emerge from night and shadow. I see the corners of big hangars, now outlined vaguely, near the floodlights — a line of them. And now, from the far side of the field, I see that all those smaller lights are automobiles, not factory windows. They seem to be blocked in traffic, on a road behind the hangars. It's a huge airport. The floodlights show only a small corner. It *must* be Le Bourget.

I'll drag the field from low altitude to make sure its surface is clear — that no hay-making machinery, cattle, sheep, or obstruction flags are in the way. After that, everyone down there will know I want to land. If they have any more lights, they'll switch them on. I shift fuel valves to the center wing-tank, sweep my flashlight over the instrument board in a final check, fasten my safety belt, and nose the *Spirit of St. Louis* down into a gradually descending spiral.

I circle several times while I lose altitude, trying to penetrate the shadows from different vantage points, getting the lay of the land as well as I can in darkness. At one thousand feet I discover the wind sock, dimly lighted, on top of some building. It's bulged, but far from stiff. That means a gentle, constant wind, not over ten or fifteen miles an hour. My landing direction will be over the flood-lights, angling away from the hangar line. Why circle any longer? That's all the information I need. No matter how hard I try, my eyes can't penetrate the blanket of night over the central portion of the field.

I straighten out my wings and let the throttled engine drag me on beyond the leeward border. Now the steep bank into wind, and the dive toward ground. But how strange it is, this descent. I'm wide awake, but the feel of my plane has not returned. Then I must hold excess speed — take no chance of stalling or of the engine loading up. My movements are mechanical, uncoordinated, as though I were coming down at the end of my first solo.

I point the nose just short of the floodlights, throttle half open, flattening out slightly as I approach. I see the whole outline of the hangars, now. Two or three planes are resting in the shadows. There's no time to look for more details. The lighted area is just ahead. It's barely large enough to land on. I nose down below the hangar roofs, so low that I can see the texture of the sod, and blades of grass on high spots. The ground is smooth and solid as far as the floodlights show its surface. I can tell nothing about the black mass beyond. But those several pin points in the distance look as though they mark the far border. Since Le Bourget is a major airport, the area between is probably also clear — I'll have to take a chance on that; if I land short, I may stop rolling before I reach it.

I open the throttle and start a climbing turn. I don't dare pull the nose up steeply. I don't dare chandelle around the hangars to celebrate my arrival, as I often do coming in with the night mail at Chicago. I must handle the *Spirit of St. Louis* as I'd teach a student to fly.

I climb to a thousand feet. There are the lamps of Paris again, like a lake of stars. There's the dark area below, just as it was before. No one has turned on more lights. I level off for the downwind stretch. The wind sock hasn't changed — still bulged and angling across the line of hangars. The motorcars are still jammed in traffic. There's no sign of movement on the ground.

I'm a quarter-mile downwind now — — — Back on throttle — — — Bank around for final glide. Is my nose down far enough? Yes, the air speed's at ninety miles an hour. I'll overshoot if I keep on at this rate — — — Stick back — — — trim the stabilizer back another notch — — — close the throttle — — — I can hardly hear the engine idling — is it too slow? — It mustn't stop now — The silence is like vacuum in my ears. I open the throttle for a quick burst — But I'm going much too fast.

In spite of my speed, the *Spirit of St. Louis* seems about to stall. My lack of feel alarms me. I've never tried to land a plane without feel before. I want to open the throttle wider, to glide faster, to tauten the controls still more. But — I glance at the dial — the needle points to eighty miles an hour. The *Spirit of St. Louis* is lightly loaded, with most of its fuel gone. Even at this speed I'll overshoot the lighted area before my tail skid strikes the ground. No, I'll have to pull the nose higher instead of pushing it down. I'll have to depend on the needle, on judgment more than instinct. I kick rudder and push the stick to one side, just to be sure — yes, controls are taut, there's plenty of speed. And feeling is not completely gone. I still have a little left. I can feel the skid and slip. But the edge of perception is dull, very dull. It's better to come in fast, even if I roll into that black area after I land. And it's better to come in high — there may be poles or chimneys at the field's edge — Never depend on obstruction lights — especially when you don't see any.

It's only a hundred yards to the hangars now — solid forms emerging from the night. I'm too high — too fast. Drop wing — left rudder — sideslip — — — Careful — mustn't get anywhere near the stall. I've never landed the *Spirit of St. Louis* at night before. It would be better to come in straight. But if I don't sideslip, I'll be too high over the boundary to touch my wheels in the area of light. That would mean circling again – – – Still too high. I push the stick over to a steeper slip, leaving the nose well down – – – Below the hangar roofs now – – – straighten out – – – A short burst of the engine – – – Over the lighted area – – – Sod coming up to meet me – – – Deceptive high lights and shadows — Careful — easy to bounce when you're tired – – – Still too fast – – – Tail too high – – – Hold off – – – Hold off – – – But the lights are far behind – – – The surface dims – – – Texture of sod is gone – – – Ahead, there's nothing but night – – – Give her the gun and climb for another try? – – – The wheels touch gently — off again — No, I'll keep contact — Ease the stick forward – – – Back on the ground — Off — Back — the tail skid too – – – Not a bad landing, but I'm beyond the light —can't see anything ahead — Like flying in fog — Ground loop? — No, still rolling too fast — might blow a tire — The field *must* be clear — Uncomfortable though, jolting into blackness — Wish I had a wing light — but too heavy on the take-off – – – Slower, now – – – slow enough to ground loop safely — left rudder — reverse it — stick over the other way – – – The *Spirit of St. Louis* swings around and stops rolling, resting on the solidity of earth, in the center of Le Bourget.

I start to taxi back toward the floodlights and hangars – – – But the entire field ahead is covered with running figures!

AFTERWORD

AFTERWORD

MY RECEPTION by the French people, in 1927, cannot be compressed into a final chapter of this book. After the warnings I had been given in America, I was completely unprepared for the welcome which awaited me on Le Bourget. I had no idea that my plane had been so accurately reported along its route between Ireland and the capital of France — over Dingle Bay, over Plymouth, over Cherbourg. When I circled the aerodrome it did not occur to me that any connection existed between my arrival and the cars stalled in traffic on the roads. When my wheels touched earth, I had no way of knowing that tens of thousands of men and women were breaking down fences and flooding past guards.

I had barely cut the engine switch when the first people reached my cockpit. Within seconds my open windows were blocked with faces. My name was called out over and over again, in accents strange to my ears — on this side of my plane — on that side — in front — in the distance. I could feel the *Spirit of St. Louis* tremble with the pressure of the crowd. I heard the crack of wood behind me when someone leaned too heavily against a fairing strip. Then a second strip snapped, and a third, and there was the sound of tearing fabric. That meant souvenir hunters were going wild. It was essential to get a guard stationed around my plane before more damage was done.

"Are there any mechanics here?" I asked.

I couldn't understand a single word that came back in answer — from a half-dozen different mouths.

"Does anyone here speak English?" I shouted.

The noise and excitement made a reply impossible. There were rips of fabric every few seconds, and I could feel my tail skid inching back and forth across the ground. I was afraid the *Spirit of St. Louis* might be seriously injured. The thought entered my mind that the longerons would buckle if enough men climbed on top; and I knew the elevators wouldn't stand much of any pressure without bending. I decided to get out of the cockpit and try to find some English-speaking person who would help me organize a guard to hold back the crowd.

I opened the door, and started to put my foot down onto ground. But dozens of hands took hold of me — my legs, my arms, my body. No one heard the sentences I spoke. I found myself lying in a prostrate position, up on top of the crowd, in the center of an ocean of heads that extended as far out into the darkness as I could see. Then I started to sink down into that ocean, and was buoyed up again. Thousands of voices mingled in a roar. Men were shouting, stumbling. My head and shoulders went down, and up, and down again, and up once more. It was like drowning in a human sea. I lost sight of the *Spirit of St. Louis*. I heard several screams. I was afraid that I would be dropped under the feet of those milling, cheering people; and that after sitting in a cockpit-fixed position for close to thirty-four hours, my muscles would be too stiff to struggle up again.

I tried to sit up – – – to slip down into the crowd – – – to roll over onto my hands and knees. It was useless. I was simply wasting strength that I might need for a final effort to save myself, if my head angled beneath my feet too far. It seemed wisest to relax as much as I could, and let time pass. I realized that the men under me were determined that no matter what happened to them, I would not fall.

After the lapse of minutes whose number I cannot judge, I felt my helmet jerked from my head. Firmer hands gripped on my body. I heard my name more clearly spoken. And suddenly I was standing on my feet — on European ground at last. With arms linked solidly in mine, I began moving slowly, but unnoticed, through the crowd.

In the week I spent at Paris, between ceremonies and engagements which crammed almost every hour of each day, I pieced together the story of what happened that Saturday night at Le Bourget. Regardless of the skepticism which existed about my flight, the French authorities had prepared for my reception. Extra guards were detailed to the aerodrome; and when reports of my plane being sighted over Ireland, England, and Normandy, brought automobiles pouring out from Paris by the thousands, two companies of soldiers were sent to reinforce the civil police. It was intended that, after I landed, my plane would be guided to a position near the Administration building, where I was to be met by a reception committee of French and American officials. Press photographers and reporters were assigned to appropriate positions.

When the crowd broke down steel fences and rushed out onto the field, all these arrangements collapsed. Police and soldiers were swept away in the rush which followed. Two French aviators — the military pilot Detroyat and the civil pilot Delage — found themselves close to me in the jam of people. Delage grabbed Detroyat's arm and cried, "Come. They will smother him!" Detroyat, being in uniform, and tall, was able to exercise some authority over the men who had me on their shoulders. Once my feet were on the ground, it was too dark for my flying suit to be very noticeable. I soon became an inconspicuous member of the crowd. Meanwhile my helmet had somehow gotten onto the head of an American reporter. Someone had pointed to him and called out, *"There is Lindbergh! There is Lindbergh!"* The crowd had taken over the reporter and left me free.

I might have had difficulty walking when I first tried to step out of the cockpit after landing, but my muscles were well limbered up by the time my feet actually touched French soil. Delage rushed away to get his little Renault car, while Detroyat maneuvered me to the outskirts of the crowd. When the car arrived, I said that before leaving I wanted to be sure a guard had been placed around the *Spirit of St. Louis.* Communication was difficult, because my ears were still deafened from the flight. I spoke no word of French; my new friends, but little English; and in the background were the noises of the crowd. My plane was being taken care of, they told me. I should not try to go back to it. They were determined about that — there was no mistaking their tones and gestures. They laughed and shook their heads as I protested, and kept pointing to the car.

We drove into a big hangar, and I was taken to a small room on one side. My friends motioned me to a chair and put out most of the lights — so I would not be discovered by the crowd. Did I need food, drink, the attention of a doctor? Would I like to lie down? they asked. I had only to tell them what I wanted. France was mine, they said. It was easier for me to understand them indoors, with everyone speaking more slowly.

I didn't feel like lying down, and I had no need whatever for a doctor; but I was greatly worried about my plane, even though I received assurances that everything possible was being done to take care of it. I suggested that we drive back out onto the field to make certain, but the two French pilots pursed their lips and shook their heads again. I then asked what customs and immigration formalities I had to go through. I was a little worried about that, since I had no visa. But I received mostly smiles and laughter in reply. I decided that the best thing for me to do was just to wait and let events develop. Was there any word of Nungesser and Coli? I asked. Faces lengthened. No, no news had come.

I remained with Delage while Detroyat went to search for an officer of higher rank. At first, he could find no one. Then, in the midst of the crowd, he came upon Major Weiss of the Bombardment Group of the 34th A.F. Regiment. The Major could not believe that I was sitting in a hangar's darkened room. "It is impossible," he told Detroyat. "Lindbergh has just been carried triumphantly to the official reception committee." Probably he had seen the reporter with my helmet, who had been taken, struggling, to the American Ambassador before the mistake in identity was finally established. But Major Weiss followed Detroyat, and on seeing me insisted that I be taken to his office on the military side of Le Bourget — about a mile away. So we climbed into the

Renault again, and drove across the field. Then, it was Major Weiss's turn to go out and search for higher officers.

It must have been an hour later when I heard American voices, and someone said that the Ambassador of the United States was outside. In a moment the door opened, and I was introduced to the Honorable Myron T. Herrick, to his son Parmely, and to his daughter-in-law Agnes. The room soon filled with people.

Ambassador Herrick was an extraordinary man. He had a combination of dignity, perception, and kindness, which few in public life possess. After extending a welcome and inquiring about my welfare, which he judged through his eyes more than through my answer, he said he was going to take me back with him to the Embassy. I accepted gladly; but I asked to see the *Spirit of St. Louis* before we left the field.

Ambassador Herrick nodded. "Of course we'll take you to your plane," he said, "if we can get there." A discussion in French followed, with several people taking part. I was assured that it was unnecessary for me to think more about the *Spirit of St. Louis* that night, because it had not been badly damaged, and it had been placed in a locked hangar, under a military guard. I needed to sleep, it was suggested. There would be time enough to see the plane after that.

"Well, how do you feel about it, Captain?" Ambassador Herrick asked.

I couldn't put the cracking wood and ripping fabric from my mind that easily. I was anxious to find out for myself what repairs would have to be made. I didn't know, then, that the French authorities wished to have all repairs completed before I saw my plane. I argued that I wanted to get some items from the cockpit, and to show the mechanics how to put the windows in. Inserting the windows required a special technique, I explained.

After more conversation which I could not understand, we climbed into Delage's car and drove back to the Air-Union hangar which we had left an hour earlier. In the meantime, my *Spirit of St. Louis* had been placed inside. It was a great shock to me to see my plane. The sides of the fuselage were full of gaping holes, and some souvenir hunter had pulled a lubrication fitting right off one of the rocker-arm housings on my engine. But in spite of surface appearances, careful inspection showed that no serious damage had been done. A few hours of work would make my plane airworthy again.

It was then time for me to rejoin Ambassador Herrick and drive with him to Paris. But my escorts were unable to locate the Ambassador. After hunting for a quarter-hour, they decided to take me to the American Embassy themselves — by a special route to avoid the heavy jam of traffic. So the four of us started out — Weiss, Delage, Detroyat, and I — all in the little Renault. Nobody looked twice at our car as we wound about through the crowd. I settled back in the seat to rest, to see what I could through the window, and to try to understand the English sentences at which my escorts laughed and struggled.

We traveled over bumpy side roads, toward the outskirts of Paris, stopping once to ask our way. We passed Dugny, Stains, Saint Denis, and entered through the Saint Ouen gate. Soon we were driving between rows of close-packed brick and stone houses with no yards between. It was tremendously different from America. Then came the heart of the city — "Place de l'Opera," Detroyat said. When we reached the end of a long avenue, Delage parked at the curb of a circular area in the center of which was a great stone arch. The surfaces of the arch were sculptured and softly lighted. My friends took me through the arch, and I found myself standing silently with them at the tomb of France's Unknown Soldier, with its ever-burning flame. They wanted my first stop in Paris to be at the Arc de Triomphe, they said.

We arrived at the American Embassy far ahead of Ambassador Herrick. He had searched for me all over Le Bourget. And then his car had become involved in the traffic jam between aerodrome and city. Neither his driver nor his escort of motorcycle police knew about the side roads the French pilots took me over. It was three o'clock when the Ambassador reached his home at No. 2 Avenue d'Iena. I was waiting for him, after eating a supper which his staff very considerately provided in spite of the early hour. By that time a small crowd — mostly newspapermen — had assembled in the street outside. At Herrick's suggestion they were invited in, and I spent a few minutes answering questions and telling them about my flight. Paris clocks marked 4:15 in the morning before I went to bed. It was sixty-three hours since I had slept.

I woke that afternoon, a little stiff but well rested, into a life which could hardly have been more amazing if I had landed on another planet instead of at Paris. The welcome I received at Le Bourget was only a forerunner to the welcome extended by France, by Belgium, by England — and, through messages, by all of Europe. It was a welcome which words of appreciation are incompetent to cover. But the account of my experiences abroad, of my homecoming to the United States, and of my gratitude to the peoples of Europe and America, belongs to a different story.

APPENDIX

THE LOG OF THE *Spirit of St. Louis*

CHARLES A. LINDBERGH, *Pilot*

(except as noted)

April 28 Dutch Flats, San Diego, California
1927

First test flight	0 hrs. 20 min.
Second test flight	0 hrs. 05 min.

April 29 Dutch Flats

Three test flights	0 hrs. 20 min.

May 3 Dutch Flats

One test flight, carrying Donald A. Hall (Designing Engineer)	0 hrs. 10 min.
One flight, carrying Major Erickson (Photographer)	0 hrs. 10 min.
One flight, for photographs from other plane	0 hrs. 15 min.

May 4 Dutch Flats to Rockwell Field, North Island (Landed, because of fog, at 5:50 a.m.) — 0 hrs. 10 min.

Rockwell Field to Dutch Flats	0 hrs. 05 min.
Dutch Flats to Coronado Strand speed course to Camp Kearney parade grounds (Tests)	1 hr. 10 min.
Three test flights, starting with 38 gallons of gasoline	0 hrs. 10 min.
One test flight, with 71 gallons	0 hrs. 15 min.
One test flight, with 110 gallons	0 hrs. 05 min.
One test flight, with 150 gallons	0 hrs. 05 min.
One test flight, with 200 gallons	0 hrs. 10 min.
One test flight, with 250 gallons	0 hrs. 10 min.
One test flight, with 300 gallons	0 hrs. 05 min.

May 5 Camp Kearney parade grounds to Dutch Flats, carrying Major Erickson — 0 hrs. 15 min.

May 8 Dutch Flats to North Island, carrying A. J. Edwards (Sales Manager) — 0 hrs. 05 min.

North Island to Dutch Flats, carrying A. J. Edwards	0 hrs. 10 min.

Total flying time: **4 hrs. 15 min.** Total flights: **23.**

[503]

May 10 Dutch Flats to North Island, carrying Mr. McNeal (Final Assembly Dept.)	0 hrs.	05 min.

Rockwell Field, North Island, California, to Lambert Field, St. Louis, Missouri, and circle of St. Louis   **14 hrs. 25 min.**
(Took off, North Island, 3:55 p.m. Pacific time. Over Lambert Field at 8:00 a.m., May 11, Central time. Landed at 8:20 a.m. Central. Serious engine-missing over desert mountains at night. Probably due to lack of carburetor air heater.)

May 12 Lambert Field, St. Louis, to Curtiss Field, Long Island, New York   **7 hrs. 20 min.**
(Took off, Lambert Field, 8:13 a.m., Central Standard. Landed Curtiss Field, 5:33 p.m., Eastern Daylight.)

May 13 Curtiss Field

One test flight, carrying Brice Goldsborough (Instrument expert)   **0 hrs. 10 min.**

May 14 Curtiss Field

One test flight   **0 hrs. 10 min.**

One test flight, carrying Kenneth Boedecker (Whirlwind expert)   **0 hrs. 20 min.**

One test flight, carrying Edward Mulligan (Whirlwind expert)   **0 hrs. 15 min.**

May 15 Curtiss Field

One test flight, carrying Brice Goldsborough   **0 hrs. 15 min.**

One test flight, carrying Kenneth Boedecker   **0 hrs. 10 min.**

Total flying time: **27 hrs. 25 min.** Total flights: **32.**

May 20 Roosevelt Field, Long Island, New York, to Le Bourget Aerodrome, Paris, France   **33 hrs. 30 min.**
(Took off, Roosevelt Field, 7:52 a.m. Eastern Daylight time. Landed, Le Bourget, 10:22 p.m. French time, May 21st.)

(Fuselage fabric badly torn by souvenir hunters. Also, fairing strips broken and one grease reservoir torn off engine. Fuselage repaired and recovered at Le Bourget.)

May 28 Le Bourget Aerodrome, Paris, to Evere Aerodrome, Brussels, Belgium   **2 hrs. 15 min.**
(Circled Paris, Senlis, Valenciennes.)

May 29 Evere Aerodrome, Brussels, to Croydon Aerodrome, London, England   **2 hrs. 35 min.**
(Flew via Waereghem, Belgium.)

One flight around Croydon Aerodrome   0 hrs. 05 min.
(Took off before end of landing roll, to avoid injuring crowd, which broke through police lines.)

(Stabilizer damaged by pressure of crowd. Repaired at Croydon.)

May 31   Croydon Aerodrome, London, to Gosport   0 hrs. 50 min.

Total flying time: **66 hrs. 40 min.** Total flights: **37.**

(At Gosport, the *Spirit of St. Louis* was dismantled by the Royal Air Force, crated, and placed on board the U.S. cruiser *Memphis* for its return voyage to the United States. It was reassembled at Bolling Field, Washington, D.C.)

June 16   Bolling Field, Washington, D.C., to Roosevelt Field, Long Island, New York   2 hrs. 35 min.

Roosevelt Field, Long Island, to Mitchel Field, Long Island   0 hrs. 05 min.

June 17   Mitchel Field, Long Island, to Lambert Field, St. Louis, Missouri   9 hrs. 20 min.
(Flew via Paterson, N.J.; Columbus, Dayton, Ohio; Indianapolis, Terre Haute, Ind.; St. Elmo, Scott Field, Ill.)

June 18   Lambert Field
One flight, over Forest Park and return   0 hrs. 30 min.

July 1   Lambert Field, St. Louis, to Selfridge Field, Mt. Clemens, Michigan   5 hrs. 10 min.
(Flew via Ft. Wayne, Ind.; Toledo, Ohio; Detroit, Mich.)

Major Lanphier, Commanding Officer of Selfridge Field, piloted the *Spirit of St. Louis* on one flight in the vicinity of the field   0 hrs. 10 min.

July 2   Selfridge Field, Mt. Clemens, to Ottawa, Ontario, Canada   4 hrs. 10 min.

July 3   Ottawa

One flight, over funeral of Lieutenant Johnson   1 hr. 10 min.
(The tail was cut off of Lt. Johnson's pursuit plane in a mid-air collision. He was a member of a twelve-plane escort which had accompanied me from Selfridge Field to Ottawa.)

July 4   Ottawa to Teterboro Airport, New Jersey   3 hrs. 50 min.
(Circled Ottawa for 35 minutes before leaving.)

| July 19 | Teterboro Airport to Mitchel Field, Long Island | 0 hrs. | 30 min. |

July 20 Mitchel Field, L.I., to Hartford, Connecticut   1 hr.   35 min.
(Flew via Niantic, Conn.)

July 21 Hartford to Providence, Rhode Island   1 hr.   35 min.
(Flew via Springfield, Mass.)

July 22 Providence to Boston, Massachusetts   1 hr.   35 min.
(Flew via Bristol, Conn.; Pawtucket, Woon-
socket, R.I.; Worcester, Mass.)

July 23 Boston to Concord, New Hampshire   5 hrs.   00 min.
(Flew via Lynn, Lowell, Mass.; Nashua, N.H.;
Portland, Me. Circled vicinity of Portland for
two and a half hours, in fog, attempting to find
flying field.)

July 24 Concord to Portland, Maine   2 hrs.   45 min.
(Circled vicinity of Portland for one and a half
hours, in fog, hunting for flying field. Finally
landed on Orchard Beach.)

July 25 Orchard Beach to Portland Airport   0 hrs.   30 min.
(Flew via Portland.)

Portland to Concord, N.H.   2 hrs.   20 min.
(Flew via South Poland, Me.; Mt. Hope, White
Mountains, Lake Winnepesaukee, Manchester,
N.H.)

July 26 Concord to Springfield, Vermont   2 hrs.   10 min.
(Flew via Lebanon, Hanover, N.H.; Rutland,
Vt.; Claremont, N.H.)

July 27 Springfield to Albany, N.Y.   2 hrs.   45 min.
(Flew via Plymouth, Vt.; Keene, N.H.; Brattle-
boro, Bennington, Vt.; Catskill Mountains,
N.Y.)

July 28 Albany to Schenectady, N.Y.   1 hr.   45 min.
(Flew via Troy, Glen Falls, Lake George, N.Y.)

Schenectady to Syracuse, N.Y.   2 hrs.   15 min.
(Flew via Little Falls, Utica, Rome, N.Y.)

July 29 Syracuse to Rochester, N.Y.   1 hr.   15 min.

Rochester to Buffalo, N.Y.   2 hrs.   00 min.
(Flew via Batavia, Lockport, Niagara Falls,
N.Y.; Niagara Falls, Ont.)

Aug. 1   Buffalo to Cleveland, Ohio   2 hrs.   15 min.
(Flew via Jamestown, Chattauqua, N.Y.; Erie,
Pa.)

Aug.	**3**	Cleveland to Pittsburgh, Pennsylvania (Flew via Gates Mills, Akron, Massillon, Canton, Alliance, Youngstown, Ohio; Newcastle, Pa.)	2 hrs.	30 min.
Aug.	**4**	Pittsburgh to Wheeling, West Virginia (Flew via East Liverpool, Steubenville, Ohio.)	1 hr.	45 min.
Aug.	**5**	Wheeling to McCook Field, Dayton, Ohio (Flew via Columbus, Ohio)	2 hrs.	25 min.
		McCook Field to Wilbur Wright Field	0 hrs.	10 min.
		Wilbur Wright Field to McCook Field	0 hrs.	15 min.
Aug.	**6**	McCook Field, Dayton, to Cincinnati, Ohio (Flew via Franklin, Middletown, Hamilton, Ohio.)	1 hr.	15 min.
Aug.	**8**	Cincinnati to Louisville, Kentucky (Flew via Lawrenceburg, Aurora, Rising Sun, Vevay, Ind.)	1 hr.	35 min.
		Lieutenant Philip R. Love piloted the *Spirit of St. Louis* on one flight in the vicinity of the field	0 hrs.	10 min.
Aug.	**9**	Louisville to Indianapolis, Indiana (Flew via Camp Knox, Ky.)	2 hrs.	25 min.
Aug.	**10**	Indianapolis to Ford Airport, Detroit, Michigan (Flew via Kokomo, Ft. Wayne, Ind.; Toledo, Ohio.)	4 hrs.	10 min.
Aug.	**11**	Ford Airport		
		One flight, carrying Henry Ford (This was Henry Ford's first flight in an airplane.)	0 hrs.	10 min.
		One flight, carrying Edsel Ford	0 hrs.	10 min.
Aug.	**12**	Ford Airport, Detroit, to Grand Rapids, Mich. (Flew via Saginaw, Lansing, Ionia, Mich.)	2 hrs.	05 min.
		One flight, carrying Mother	0 hrs.	20 min.
Aug.	**13**	Grand Rapids to Chicago, Illinois (Flew via Kalamazoo, Benton Harbor, St. Joseph, Mich.)	2 hrs.	15 min.
Aug.	**15**	Chicago to Springfield, Ill. (Flew via Moosehart, Aurora, Joliet, Peoria, Ill.)	2 hrs.	35 min.
		Springfield to St. Louis, Mo.	1 hr.	30 min.
Aug.	**17**	St. Louis to Kansas City, Mo. (Flew via Chamois, Jefferson City, Mo.)	3 hrs.	45 min.

Aug. 18	Kansas City to Wichita, Kansas (Flew via Osawatomie, Ft. Scott, Girard, Chanute, Kan.)	3 hrs. 15 min.
Aug. 19	Wichita to St. Joseph, Mo. (Flew via Junction City, Ft. Riley, Ft. Leavenworth, Kan.)	3 hrs. 10 min.
	St. Joseph to Moline Airport, Tri-Cities (Flew via Ottumwa, Muscatine, Ia.)	3 hrs. 30 min.
Aug. 20	Moline Airport to Milwaukee, Wisconsin (Flew via Dixon, Rockford, Ill.; Beloit, Wis.)	2 hrs. 35 min.
Aug. 22	Milwaukee to Madison, Wis. (Flew via Waukesha, Fond du Lac, Oshkosh, Wis.)	2 hrs. 50 min.
Aug. 23	Madison to Minneapolis, Minnesota (Flew via Portage, La Crosse, Wis.; Winona, Red Wing, Minn.)	4 hrs. 00 min.
Aug. 25	Minneapolis to Little Falls, Minn. (Flew via Savage, Shakopee, St. Cloud, Melrose, Sauk Center, Minn.)	2 hrs. 20 min.
Aug. 26	Little Falls to Fargo, North Dakota (Flew via Lake Itasca, Minn.)	2 hrs. 50 min.
Aug. 27	Fargo to Sioux Falls, South Dakota (Flew via Aberdeen, Redfield, Huron, Mitchell, S.D.)	4 hrs. 30 min.
	Sioux Falls to Sioux City, Iowa	1 hr. 15 min
Aug. 29	Sioux City to Des Moines, Iowa (Flew via Battle Creek, Ia.)	2 hrs. 20 min.
Aug. 30	Des Moines to Omaha, Nebraska (Flew via Ft. Des Moines, Ia.)	2 hrs. 00 min.
Aug. 31	Omaha to Denver, Colorado (Flew via Columbus, Lincoln, Hastings, Kearney, Lexington, McCook, Neb.; Bird City, Kan.; Imperial, Neb.)	7 hrs. 45 min.
Sept. 1	Denver to Pierre, S.D. (Flew via Rocky Mountain National Park, Long's Peak, Greeley, Col.; Scotts Bluff, Neb.)	6 hrs. 35 min.
Sept. 2	Pierre to Cheyenne, Wyoming (Flew via Philip, Hermosa, President Coolidge's summer home, Rapid City, Spearfish, Deadwood, S.D.)	5 hrs. 30 min.

Sept. 3	Cheyenne to Salt Lake City, Utah (Flew via Laramie, Parco, Rawlins, Wy.; Craig, Col.; Mt. Pleasant, Ut. Took plane up to 19,800 feet indicated altitude, en route.)	7 hrs.	35 min.
Sept. 4	Salt Lake City to Boise, Idaho (Flew via Bingham, Ogden, Ut.; Oakley, Twin Falls, Id.)	4 hrs.	30 min.
Sept. 5	Boise to Butte, Montana	3 hrs.	35 min.
Sept. 6	Butte to Helena, Mont. (Flew via Swan Lake Camp, Highgate, Mt. Cleveland, Glacier National Park, Blackfoot, Sweetgrass, Mon.; Milk River, Alb.; Great Falls, Mon.)	6 hrs.	45 min.
Sept. 7	Helena to Butte, Mon. (Flew via Billings, Mon.; Yellowstone Lake, Old Faithful Geyser, Wy.)	6 hrs.	05 min.
Sept. 12	Butte to Spokane, Washington (Flew via Anaconda, Bonner, Missoula, Mon.; Wallace, Id.)	3 hrs.	50 min.
Sept. 13	Spokane to Seattle, Wash. (Flew via Walla Walla, Pasco, Yakima, Renton, Wash.)	5 hrs.	15 min.
Sept. 14	Seattle to Portland, Oregon (Flew via Tacoma, Ft. Lewis, Olympia, Aberdeen, Centralia, Chehalis, Home Valley, Wash.)	4 hrs.	45 min.
Sept. 16	Portland to San Francisco, Cal. (Flew via Vancouver, Wash.; Silverton, Chemawa, Salem, Corvallis, Eugene, Crater Lake, Medford, Ore.; Mt. Shasta's peak, Anderson, Red Bluff, Cal.)	7 hrs.	05 min.
	One flight, around Mills Field	0 hrs.	05 min.
Sept. 17	San Francisco to Oakland, Cal. (Flew via Mt. Tamalpais; Golden Gate.)	1 hr.	25 min.
	Oakland to Sacramento, Cal. (Flew via Livermore, Lathrop, Stockton, Cal.)	1 hr.	35 min.
Sept. 19	Sacramento to Reno, Nevada (Flew via Livermore, Cal.)	3 hrs.	35 min.
Sept. 20	Reno to Los Angeles, Cal. (Flew via Carson City, Nev.; Yosemite Park, Death Valley, Cal.)	7 hrs.	00 min.
Sept. 21	Los Angeles to San Diego, Cal. (Flew via Pomona, Cal.)	2 hrs.	25 min.

Sept. 23	One flight, carrying B. Franklin Mahoney	0 hrs.	05 min.
	San Diego to Tucson, Arizona (Flew via El Centro, Cal.; Mexicali, Mexico; Yuma, Ariz.)	5 hrs.	05 min.
Sept. 24	Tucson to Lordsburg, New Mexico (Flew via Silver City, Ft. Bayard, N.M.)	3 hrs.	10 min.
	Lordsburg to El Paso, Texas (Flew via Chihuahua, Mexico.)	2 hrs.	25 min.
Sept. 25	El Paso to Santa Fe, New Mexico (Flew via Las Cruces, Albuquerque, N.M.)	4 hrs.	05 min.
Sept. 26	Santa Fe to Abilene, Tex. (Flew via Crosbyton, Roaring Springs, Stamford, Tex.)	5 hrs	45 min.
	Abilene to Ft. Worth, Tex. (Flew via Jacksboro, Bridgeport, Tex.)	2 hrs.	50 min.
Sept. 27	Fort Worth to Dallas, Tex. (Flew via Alvarado, Hillsboro, Waxahachie, Tex.)	2 hrs.	00 min.
Sept. 28	Dallas to Oklahoma City, Oklahoma (Flew via Denton, Tex.; Ardmore, Sulphur, Pauls Valley, Okla.)	3 hrs.	00 min.
Sept. 30	One flight, carrying Donald E. Keyhoe	0 hrs.	05 min.
	Oklahoma City to Tulsa, Okla. (Flew via Stillwater, Pawhuska, Okla.)	2 hrs.	35 min.
Oct. 1	Tulsa to Muskogee, Okla.	1 hr.	00 min.
	Muskogee to Little Rock, Arkansas (Flew via Ft. Smith, Van Buren, Booneville, Ark.)	2 hrs.	40 min.
Oct. 3	Little Rock to Memphis, Tennessee (Flew via Pine Bluff, Helena, Ark.)	3 hrs.	00 min.
Oct. 4	One flight, carrying Earl C. Thompson	0 hrs.	25 min.
Oct. 5	Memphis to Chattanooga, Tenn. (Flew via Florence, Muscle Shoals, Sheffield, Tuscumbia, Ala.)	4 hrs.	40 min.
	Chattanooga to Birmingham, Alabama	2 hrs.	30 min.
Oct. 7	Birmingham to Jackson, Mississippi (Flew via Columbus, Starkville, Maben, Mathiston, Miss.)	3 hrs.	35 min.

Oct.	8	Jackson to New Orleans, Louisiana (Flew via Columbia, Miss.; Franklinton, La.)	2 hrs. 55 min.
Oct.	10	Two flights, searching for Navy pilot, near New Orleans flying field	0 hrs. 40 min.
		New Orleans to Jacksonville, Florida (Flew via Pensacola, Tallahassee, Fla.)	5 hrs. 30 min.
Oct.	11	Jacksonville to Atlanta, Georgia (Flew via McRae, Vidalia, Millen, Ga.)	5 hrs. 45 min.
Oct.	12	Atlanta to Spartanburg, South Carolina (Flew via Athens, Ga.; Greenwood, S.C.)	2 hrs. 40 min.
Oct.	14	Spartanburg to Greensboro, North Carolina (Flew via Gaffney, S.C.; Kings Mountain, Salisbury, Lexington, N.C.)	2 hrs. 25 min.
		Greensboro to Winston-Salem, N.C.	0 hrs. 45 min.
Oct.	15	Winston-Salem to Richmond, Virginia (Flew via Danville, South Boston, Va.)	2 hrs. 50 min.
Oct.	16	Richmond	
		One flight, carrying Governor Harry F. Byrd	0 hrs. 10 min.
		One flight, carrying Harry F. Guggenheim	0 hrs. 10 min.
		One flight, carrying C. C. Maidment (Whirlwind expert)	0 hrs. 05 min.
Oct.	17	Richmond to Washington, D.C.	1 hr. 15 min.
Oct.	18	Washington to Baltimore, Maryland	0 hrs. 55 min.
Oct.	19	Baltimore to Atlantic City, N.J.	2 hrs. 00 min.
Oct.	21	Atlantic City to Wilmington, Delaware (Flew via Mays Landing, Salem, N.J.)	1 hr. 50 min.
Oct.	22	Wilmington to Philadelphia, Pa. (Flew via Chester, Media, Pa.)	0 hrs. 55 min.
Oct.	23	Philadelphia to Mitchel Field, L.I. (Flew via Trenton, N.J.; New York City, N.Y.)	1 hr. 50 min.
Oct.	25	Mitchel Field, L.I., to Teterboro, N.J., carrying Milburn Kusterer	0 hrs. 40 min.
Dec.	5	Teterboro	
		One test flight	0 hrs. 15 min.
Dec.	7	Teterboro to Bolling Field, Washington, D.C.	3 hrs. 15 min.

Total flying time: **359 hrs. 05 min.** Total flights: **148.**

Dec. 13 Bolling Field, Washington, D.C., to Valbuena Airport, Mexico City, Mexico   27 hrs.   15 min.
(Took off, Bolling Field, 12:25 p.m. Eastern
Standard time. Landed, Mexico City, 3:40 p.m.
Eastern Standard time, December 14th. Flew via
Texas coast of Gulf of Mexico. Lost position
flying over fog between Tampico and Valley of
Mexico. Climbed after fog cleared, and located
approximate position from the direction of
watersheds. Located exact position from sign on
hotel wall at Toluca.)

Dec. 21 Valbuena Airport

One exhibition flight   0 hrs.   25 min.

Dec. 22 Valbuena Airport
One flight, escorting Ford trimotored plane
which brought Mother from Detroit   1 hr.   00 min.

Three short flights, made to avoid injuring anyone in crowd which overran field   0 hrs.   15 min.
(Took off before end of first and second landing rolls. Then landed in adjoining field to
attract crowd. Took off before first people
reached my plane. Returned to Valbuena Airport, and taxied *Spirit of St. Louis* into
hangar.)

Dec. 28 Valbuena Airport, Mexico City, to Guatemala
City, Guatemala   7 hrs.   05 min.

Dec. 30 Guatemala City to Polo Field, Belize, British Honduras   3 hrs.   20 min.

Jan. 1 Polo Field, Belize, to San Salvador, Salvador   2 hrs.   50 min.
1928

Jan. 3 San Salvador to Tegucigalpa, Honduras   2 hrs.   05 min.

Jan. 5 Tegucigalpa to Managua, Nicaragua   2 hrs.   35 min.
(Flew via Leon, Nicaragua.)

Jan. 7 Managua to San Jose, Costa Rica   3 hrs.   25 min.

Jan. 9 San Jose to Panama City, Panama   4 hrs.   05 min.
(Flew via shore of Mosquito Bay.)

Jan. 12 Panama City to France Field, Colon, Canal Zone   0 hrs.   45 min.

Jan. 22 France Field

One test flight   1 hr.   15 min.
(Flew over Gatun Lake; San Lorenzo; San
Colon.)

Jan. 26 France Field, Colon, to Cartagena, Colombia   4 hrs.   30 min.
(Flew via coast of Gulf of Darien.)

Jan. 27   Cartagena to Madrid Field, Bogota, Colombia   **6 hrs.   05 min.**
(Circled over Bogota.)

Jan. 29   Madrid Field, Bogota, to Maracay Field, Caracas, Venezuela   **10 hrs.   50 min.**
(Detoured storm to Caribbean coast, about 150 miles east of Caracas. Followed coast most of way back to Maracay Field.)

Jan. 31   Maracay Field, Caracas, to golf grounds, St. Thomas, Virgin Islands   **10 hrs.   15 min.**
(Flew via islands of Lesser Antilles.)

Feb. 2   Golf grounds, St. Thomas, to San Juan, Porto Rico   **2 hrs.   10 min**
(Flew via St. Croix.)

Feb. 4   San Juan to Santo Domingo, Dominican Republic   **3 hrs.   50 min.**

Feb. 6   Santo Domingo to Port au Prince, Haiti   **3 hrs.   30 min.**
(Flew via Santiago; Christophe's Citadel; Cape Haitien; St. Marc.)

Feb. 8   Port au Prince to Havana, Cuba   **9 hrs.   20 min.**
(Carried three sacks of mail, including one sack from Santo Domingo.)

Feb. 13   Havana to Lambert Field, St. Louis, Mo.   **15 hrs.   35 min.**
(Both compasses malfunctioned over Florida Strait, at night. The earth-inductor needle wobbled back and forth. The liquid compass card rotated without stopping. Could recognize no stars through heavy haze. Located position, at daybreak, over Bahama Islands, nearly 300 miles off course. Liquid compass card kept rotating until the *Spirit of St. Louis* reached the Florida coast.)

Feb. 14   Lambert Field

One flight, over St. Louis and vicinity   **3 hrs.   00 min.**

April 30   Lambert Field, St. Louis, to Bolling Field, Washington, D.C.   **4 hrs.   58 min.**
(Tail wind. Distance 725 miles.)

TOTAL FLYING TIME: **489 hrs. 28 min.** TOTAL FLIGHTS: **174.**

The official time of the flight of the *Spirit of St. Louis* from New York to Paris, on May 20–21, 1927, recorded by the National Aeronautic Association, under the rules and regulations of the Fédération Aéronautique Internationale, is 33 hours, 30 minutes, 29.8 seconds.

The flight to Ottawa, Ontario, Canada, on July 2, 1927, was made in response to an invitation from the Canadian Government, extended by Premier W. L. Mackenzie King.

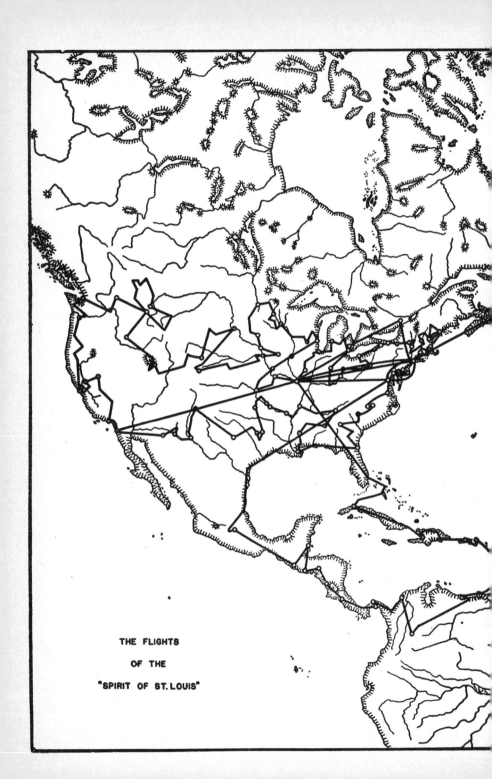

THE FLIGHTS

OF THE

"SPIRIT OF ST. LOUIS"

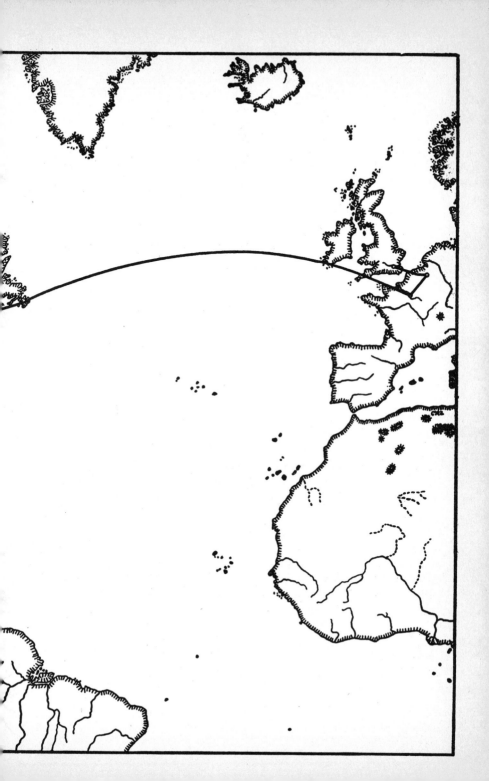

The tour of the United States, starting at Mitchel Field, Long Island, New York, July 20, 1927, and ending at Mitchel Field on October 23, 1927, was sponsored by the Daniel Guggenheim Fund for the Promotion of Aeronautics. The excessive time spent in flying between many of the cities visited on this tour was caused by requests from other cities whose inhabitants wished to see the *Spirit of St. Louis* circle overhead. Also, extra time was usually allowed for the possibility of encountering head winds and having to detour weather areas en route. On several occasions, long "exploration" detours were made over interesting portions of the country. The tour consumed 260 hours and 45 minutes of flying time, and covered about 22,000 miles. Eighty-two stops were made. The *Spirit of St. Louis* arrived late only once (at Portland, Maine, because of fog).

The flight from Washington, D.C., to Mexico City, on December 13 and 14, 1927, was planned at the suggestion of Ambassador Dwight W. Morrow, and made in response to an invitation issued by President Plutarco Elias Calles.

The flights through Central and South America and the islands of the West Indies were made in response to invitations sent by the governments of the countries visited.

At Bolling Field the *Spirit of St. Louis* was presented to the Smithsonian Institution. It was dismantled, and reassembled in the museum in Washington, where it now rests, in permanent exhibition, with the Kitty Hawk biplane of Orville and Wilbur Wright.

EMERGENCY EQUIPMENT CARRIED IN THE *Spirit of St. Louis*
ON THE FLIGHTS BETWEEN SAN DIEGO AND PARIS

1 air raft, with pump and repair kit
1 canteen of water—4 quarts
1 Armbrust cup
5 cans of Army emergency rations
1 hunting knife
1 ball of cord
1 ball of string
1 large needle
1 flashlight
4 red flares, sealed in rubber tubes
1 match safe with matches
1 hack-saw blade

THE CRUISER *Memphis*

By direction of President Coolidge, the United States Navy sent the Cruiser *Memphis* to carry Capt. Lindbergh and the *Spirit of St. Louis* back to the United States from France. This was the flagship of Vice Admiral Guy H. Burrage, with Capt. Henry Ellis Lackey in command. The *Memphis* sailed from Cherbourg on June 4th, and arrived at Washington, D. C., on June 11th, 1927.

DECORATIONS, AWARDS, TROPHIES, AND GIFTS PRESENTED TO CAPTAIN LINDBERGH IN CONNECTION WITH THE FLIGHTS OF THE *Spirit of St. Louis*

By Esther B. Mueller
CURATOR OF THE LINDBERGH COLLECTION
OF THE MISSOURI HISTORICAL SOCIETY

Most of the items listed here are on permanent file or exhibit at the Jefferson Memorial Building, Forest Park, St. Louis, Mo.

UNITED STATES: Messages of congratulation from President Coolidge and from Secretary of State Kellogg; Congressional Medal of Honor, presented by President Coolidge; Gold Medal of the Congress, presented by President Hoover; Distinguished Flying Cross (first Cross ever awarded), presented by President Coolidge; Commission of Colonel in the U.S. Army Air Corps Reserve, presented by Secretary of War Davis; Scroll authorizing the use of Naval Aircraft; First impression of air-mail stamp depicting the *Spirit of St. Louis* (the first time a living American was honored by a U.S. stamp), presented by Postmaster General New; Gold thermos bottle from the Assistant Secretaries of Aeronautics in Army, Navy, and Commerce Departments (Davison, Warner, MacCracken), engraved "For Unparalleled Service to American Aviation"; Memorial volume of diplomatic exchanges between the United States and foreign governments, relating to the flights of the *Spirit of St. Louis* —compiled by the State Department and presented by Secretary of State Kellogg.

FRANCE: Messages of congratulation from President Doumergue, Foreign Minister Briand, and War Minister Painlevé; Chevalier Cross of the National Order of the Legion of Honor, presented by President Doumergue; Testimonial Scroll, from the Senate; Special Gold Medal, from the Administration de Monnaies et Médailles.

BELGIUM: Messages of congratulation from King Albert and from the Government of Belgium; Order of Chevalier of the Royal Order of Leopold, presented by King Albert.

ENGLAND: Messages of congratulation from King George V, from Secretary of State for Air Sir Samuel Hoare, and from the Royal Air Force; Air Force Cross, presented by King George V.

ARGENTINA: Message of congratulation from President Alvear.

BULGARIA: Message of congratulation from King Boris.

GERMANY: Message of congratulation from the Government of Germany.

GREECE: Message of congratulation from the Naval College.

HOLLAND: Message of congratulation from the Government of the Netherlands.

IRELAND: Message of congratulation from President Cosgrave.

ITALY: Message of congratulation from Premier Mussolini.

PERU: Message of congratulation from the Government of Peru.

POLAND: Message of congratulation from Prime Minister Pilsudski and the Government of Poland.

PORTUGAL: Message of congratulation from the Government of Portugal.

ROUMANIA: Aviation Cross and Testimonials, from King Carol.

SPAIN: Message of congratulation and decoration of Plus Ultra Vires, from King Alfonso XIII.

SWEDEN: Message of congratulation from King Gustav V.

URUGUAY: Message of congratulation from President Campisteguy.

CANADA: Messages of congratulation from Prime Minister Mackenzie King and from the Royal Canadian Air Force; Gold Confederation Medal and Album.

MEXICO: Cross of the Order of Merit and Valor, presented by President Calles; Gold Medal of Homage from the Senate; Gold Medal of Homage from the Chamber of Deputies; Gold Medal from the Director of Mail Service; Album from the Military College.

GUATEMALA: Message of congratulation from President Chacón; Gold Medal from the Government, presented by President Chacón; Gold Medal of the Grand Order of the Guatemalan Army; Silver desk set, from the Guatemalan Army; Gold pocket watch, from the Aviation Section; Native-woven linen scarfs and girdles; Decorative gourds

SALVADOR: Special Gold Medal of Homage, presented by President Bosque.

HONDURAS: Special Gold Medal of Honor, presented by President Baraona; Testimonial; Watch, hidden in a U.S. $20 gold piece, from the Department of the Treasury.

NICARAGUA: Gold Medal of Merit and Valor, presented by President Diaz; Testimonial; Native-made hammock.

COSTA RICA: Gold Medal and set of books, from the Department of

Labor; Set of specially-printed Lindbergh stamps, presented by President Jiminez and the Director of Posts.

PANAMA: Message of congratulation from President Chiari; Gold Medal of Honor, presented by President Chiari; Gold Simon Bolivar Centenary Medal.

CANAL ZONE: Large gold Indian idol to the Eastern Sun, and two smaller gold idols, from the citizens of the Canal Zone.

COLUMBIA: Decoration of the Cross of Boyaca, presented by President Mendez; Gold Testimonial Plaque, from the War Department; Gold Commemorative Plaque, from the School of Military Aviation.

VENEZUELA: Message of congratulation from the Government of Venezuela; Commander's Order of Busto-del Liberator with Star, presented by President Gomez; Jewelled billfold and set of men's jewelry.

PORTO RICO: Gold Medal of Homage and resolution conferring citizenship of Porto Rico, from the Legislative Assembly.

DOMINICAN REPUBLIC: Message of congratulation from President Vasquez; Gold Medal of Homage, presented by President Vasquez; Native gold-nugget brooch.

HAITI: Medal of Honor and Merit, presented by President Borno.

CUBA: Message of congratulation from President Machado; Gold Cross of the Order of Miguel de Cespedes with Star, presented by President Machado.

STATE OF NEW YORK: Medal of Valor, presented by Gov. Alfred E. Smith.

STATE OF CONNECTICUT: Gold Sesquicentennial Medal; Gold inspector's badge, from the Aviation Dept.

STATE OF RHODE ISLAND: Testimonial.

STATE OF MASSACHUSETTS: Gold Commemorative Medal and Testimonial.

STATE OF NEW HAMPSHIRE: Fragment of native granite set with gold medal.

STATE OF VERMONT: Bronze Testimonial Plaque.

STATE OF MICHIGAN: Gold honorary-membership badge, from the State Police.

STATE OF ILLINOIS: Testimonial resolutions from the 55th General Assembly.

STATE OF MISSOURI: Commission of Colonel of the Missouri National Guard.

STATE OF MINNESOTA: Gold Commemorative Medal.

STATE OF SOUTH DAKOTA: Testimonial from the Legislative Assembly.

STATE OF COLORADO: Painting of Lindbergh Peak, from the children of the Rocky Mountain Region.

STATE OF NEW JERSEY: Gold Honorary Special-Inspector's Badge, from the Dept. of Motor Vehicles.

STATE OF PUEBLO, MEXICO: Three large glazed-china vases, one showing the Aztec calendar.

PARIS, FRANCE: Gold Medal of the City of Paris, commemorating New York to Paris flight; Gold Key of the City.

ALSACE, FRANCE: Silver Medal of the City.

LYONS, FRANCE: Large silk U.S. Flag.

VALENCIENNES, FRANCE: Medal of Homage.

BRUSSELS, BELGIUM: Gold Medal; Lace shawl and linens for Capt. Lindbergh's mother.

LONDON, ENGLAND: Gold Keys of the City of London.

LIMERICK, IRELAND: Irish lace shawl for Capt. Lindbergh's mother.

HAMBURG, GERMANY: Engraved gold dress sword.

DEBRECEN, HUNGARY: A Kulacs, from the citizens.

MALTA ISLAND: Gold pin.

WEST BELFAST, IRELAND: Linens.

NEW YORK CITY, N.Y.: Gold Medal of the City; Testimonial; Gold Honor Legion Medal, from Police Dept.; Gold photograph, from citizens of the Borough of Bronx; Sterling silver trays, from citizens of the Borough of Brooklyn; Gold Commemorative Medal, from school children of Brooklyn.

ST. LOUIS: Key of the City; Gold Commemorative Medals from the Chamber of Commerce; Gold chest, depicting St. Louis-New York-Paris flights; Testimonials.

HAMILTON, CANADA: Key of the City.

HARTFORD, CONN.: Cane carved of wood from a tree in the Mark Twain Garden.

PROVIDENCE, R.I.: Chest of 197 pieces of sterling silver flatware.

BOSTON, MASS.: Original bronze statuette of "Appeal to the Great Spirit," by C. E. Dallin.

CAMBRIDGE, MASS.: Piece of Washington Elm.

CHELSEA, MASS.: Gold Key of the City.

PLAINFIELD, MASS.: Specially designed mesh bag, for Col. Lindbergh's mother.

SPRINGFIELD, VT.: Gold Commemorative Medal.

SYRACUSE, N.Y.: Set of 140 pieces of Syracuse chinaware.

ROCHESTER, N.Y.: Pen and pencil set; Testimonial.

BUFFALO, N.Y.: Gold Medal; Key of the City; Commemorative medals.

PATCHOGUE, N.Y.: Gold thimble, set with diamonds, for Col. Lindbergh's mother, from the children of Patchogue.

WATERTOWN, N.Y.: Scroll of Welcome.

PITTSBURGH, PA.: Gold Medal of the City; Gold commemoration medal.

JOHNSTOWN, PA.: Gold fountain pen, set with diamonds.

PITTSTON, PA.: Gold Honorary Police Lieutenant's badge.

READING, PA.: Silver cup; Scroll naming Lindbergh Viaduct.

DAYTON, OHIO: Wright Brothers' Memorial Medals; Testimonial.

CINCINNATI, OHIO: Rockwood pottery jar; Testimonial.

INDIANAPOLIS, IND.: Scroll of Welcome; Commemorative coins.

KOKOMO, IND.: Dirigold plaque.

DETROIT, MICH.: Gold pocket watch; Gold commemorative medal, from the Board of Education.

CHICAGO, ILL.: Testimonial; Honorary Membership Certificate, from the Junior Assn. of Commerce; Gold Honorary Police badge.

CAIRO, ILL.: Scroll of Welcome.

COOK COUNTY, ILL.: Leather-bound Resolution.

LINCOLN, ILL.: Bronze plaque of Abraham Lincoln, from the school children of Lincoln.

SPRINGFIELD, ILL.: Gold pocket watch; Commemorative Air-mail Medal.

COLUMBIA, MO.: Scroll of Welcome.

WICHITA, KAN.: Gold Key of the City; Testimonial.

MOLINE, EAST MOLINE, and ROCK ISLAND, ILL., and DAVENPORT, IA.: Silver commemorative ring; Desk set.

LITTLE FALLS and MORRISON COUNTY, MINN.: Gold locket, containing photographs of Col. Lindbergh's parents.

DULUTH, MINN.: Scroll of Welcome.

FARGO, N.D.: Pair of gold cuff links.

SIOUX CITY, IA.: Scroll of Welcome.

OMAHA, NEB.: Scroll of Welcome.

SALT LAKE CITY, UTAH: Gold Key of the City.

BOISE, ID.: Gold Key of the City.

BUTTE, MONT.: Smoking set, made of native copper.

HELENA, MONT.: Gold Commemorative Medal.

PENDLETON, ORE.: Indian blanket.

SEATTLE, WASH.: Gold monogrammed amethyst ring, from the citizens of Seattle.

SAN FRANCISCO and SAN MATEO COUNTY, CAL.: Gold Honorary Citizenship Medal.

SACRAMENTO, CAL.: Gold watch fob, from the City Council and citizens of Sacramento; Scroll naming Lindbergh Field.

RENO, NEV.: Testimonial Scroll.

LOS ANGELES, CAL.: Gold Medal; Gold Plaque of Welcome; Scroll naming Lindbergh Beacon.

SAN DIEGO, CAL.: Sterling-silver replica of the *Spirit of St. Louis,* from the citizens of San Diego; Scroll.

TUCSON, ARIZ.: Scroll of Welcome.

FORT WORTH, TEX.: Oil portrait of Col. Lindbergh's mother, from the citizens of Fort Worth.

DALLAS, TEX.: Scroll of Welcome.

EL PASO, TEX.: Serape, sombrero, and hand-carved cane, from the citizens of El Paso.

TULSA, OKLA.: Testimonial.

MUSKOGEE, OKLA.: Pair of silver wings.

MEMPHIS, TENN.: Scroll of Welcome.

CHATTANOOGA, TENN.: Testimonials.

NASHVILLE, TENN.: Testimonial, and gold-headed cane made from wood of a tree planted by Andrew Jackson.

BIRMINGHAM, ALA.: Scroll of Welcome.

FLORENCE, ALA.: Scroll of Welcome.

NEW ORLEANS, LA.: Bronze and silver aviation map of the City of New Orleans.

ORLANDO, FLA.: Scroll of Welcome.

PENSACOLA, FLA.: Scroll of Welcome.

SARASOTA, FLA.: Scroll of Welcome.

TAMPA, FLA.: Gold Testimonial Plaque.

WINTER HAVEN, FLA.: Scroll of Welcome.

STONE MOUNTAIN, GA.: Silver Cup.

COLUMBIA, S. C.: Scroll of Welcome.

GREENVILLE, S. C.: Scroll of Welcome.

GREENSBORO, N. C.: Set of 13 bound books by O. Henry, from the citizens of Greensboro.

RICHMOND, VA.: Gold medal.

BALTIMORE, MD.: Amethyst ring, from the citizens of Baltimore.

ATLANTIC CITY, N. J.: Gold Medal; Key of the City; Testimonial; Gold Honorary Special Detective's badge; Gold Honorary Special Investigator's badge.

MEXICO CITY, MEXICO: Gold Keys to the City; Testimonial; Handmade silver chandelier, for Col. Lindbergh's mother.

TAMPICO, MEXICO: Gold Guest-of-Honor Medal; Gold Key of the City; Testimonials.

GUATEMALA CITY, GUATEMALA: Gold Medal; Scroll, making Col. Lindbergh the city's first adopted son.

BELIZE, BRITISH HONDURAS: Flags and Testimonials.

TEGUCIGALPA, HONDURAS: Key of the City.

COMAYAGUELA, HONDURAS: Key of the City.

MANAGUA, NICARAGUA: Gold Medal of Homage; Key of the City; Gold-headed cane.

SAN JOSE, COSTA RICA: Silver testimonial plaque, from the Chamber of Commerce.

PANAMA CITY, PANAMA: Gold Medal of Homage; Gold Key of the City; Gold filigree necklace and earrings, and Chinese shawl, for Col. Lindbergh's mother.

CARTAGENA, COLOMBIA: Album of the City.

BOGOTA, COLOMBIA: Gold Medal.

BARRANQUILLA, COLOMBIA: Gold Key of the City; Testimonials.

MADRID, COLOMBIA: Silver commemorative plaque.

ST. THOMAS, VIRGIN ISLANDS: Guest-of-Honor Scroll, from the Colonial Council; Inlaid drop-leaf table made by the natives; Testimonial, from the citizens.

ST. CROIX, VIRGIN ISLANDS: An 1830 St. Croix sword.

SAN JUAN, PORTO RICO: Testimonial, from the Municipal Assembly of the City; Testimonial and set of monogrammed table linens, from the Chamber of Commerce.

SANTO DOMINGO, DOMINICAN REPUBLIC: Gold Key of the City.

PORT-AU-PRINCE, HAITI: Honorary Citizenship Certificate; Resolution naming Lindbergh Avenue; Mahogany paper weight set with piece of iron from the anchor of Columbus' flagship *Santa Maria*.

HAVANA, CUBA: Gold Medal of Honor, from the Province of Havana; Gold Key of the City of Havana; Linens.

RAYMOND ORTEIG TRUSTEES: Gold Medal and Resolution awarding the twenty-five thousand dollar prize for the first nonstop flight between New York City and Paris.

WOODROW WILSON FOUNDATION: Wilson Medal and twenty-five thousand dollar award for contributions to international friendship, presented by Norman H. Davis.

SMITHSONIAN INSTITUTION: Gold Langley Medal, for the increase and diffusion of knowledge among men, presented by ex-President William Howard Taft.

THEODORE ROOSEVELT MEMORIAL ASSOCIATION: Gold Medal for distinguished service in the leadership of youth and development of American character.

NATIONAL GEOGRAPHIC SOCIETY: Gold Hubbard Medal, for heroic service to the science of aviation, presented by President Calvin Coolidge.

GEOGRAPHIC SOCIETY OF FRANCE: Great Medal of Gold of the Society.

GEOGRAPHIC SOCIETY OF CUBA: Gran Medallo de Oro.

PACIFIC GEOGRAPHIC SOCIETY: Honorary Life-Membership Certificate.

CENTRAL SWEDISH SOCIETY, SWEDEN: Gold Medal.

U.S. FLAG ASSOCIATION: Cross of Honor investing the title of Knight of the Flag, and Life Membership in the Order of the Flag, presented by Charles Evans Hughes.

LE COMITÉ DE L'UNION INTERNATIONALE: Bronze Membership Medal, presented by Marshal Ferdinand Foch.

UNIVERSITY OF WISCONSIN: Honorary Degree of Doctor of Laws.

WASHINGTON UNIVERSITY, ST. LOUIS: Honorary Degree of Master of Science.

NEW YORK UNIVERSITY: Honorary Degree of Master of Aeronautics.

NORTHWESTERN UNIVERSITY: Honorary Degree of Doctor of Laws.

PRINCETON UNIVERSITY: Honorary Degree of Master of Science.

ST. JOSEPH'S COLLEGE, PHILADELPHIA: Honorary Degree of Master of Arts in the Science of Aeronautics.

MASONIC KEYSTONE LODGE NO. 243, ST. LOUIS, MO.: Gold life membership card.

AERONAUTICAL CHAMBER OF COMMERCE OF AMERICA: Gold Medal; Aviation clock, depicting the New York-Paris flight.

FÉDÉRATION AÉRONAUTIQUE INTERNATIONALE: Grand Gold Medal, for the greatest achievement in aviation in 1927.

AERONAUTICAL LEAGUE OF FRANCE: Silver Medal.

AERO CLUB OF FRANCE: Gold Medal; Bronze memorial representing flight.

ESCADRILLE LAFAYETTE: Medal and Scroll.

LAFAYETTE FLYING CORPS: Bronze Honorary Membership Medal.

ROYAL AERO CLUB OF BELGIUM: Gold Honorary Membership Medal.

LIGUE INTERNATIONALE DES AVIATEURS (*Harmon Award*): Grand Medal of Gold of the King of the Belgians for the world's champion aviator for 1927; Médaille d'Honneur as U.S. champion aviator for 1927; Honorary Life Membership; Insignia, stickpin, and scroll.

NATIONAL AERONAUTIC ASSOCIATION: Life Membership Insignia; Testimonial.

FEDERATION AERONAUTICAL ASSN. OF MEXICO: Gold membership Insignia.

AERO CLUB OF SWEDEN: Gold Membership Medal.

AVIATION LEAGUE OF TURKEY: Gold and diamond brooch, conferring membership.

AERO CLUB OF CZECHOSLOVAKIA: Marble and bronze plaque, Membership.

AERO CLUB OF THE NETHERLANDS: Commemorative Medal.

LIGA INTERNATIONAL DE AVIADOR (*Central American Section*): Gold Medal of Honor.

35TH DIVISION FLYING CLUB, ST. LOUIS: Gold and silver globe; ring.

LONG BEACH, CALIF. FLYING CLUB: Gold membership Plaque.

Spirit of St. Louis ASSOCIATION: Memorial Plaque; Fifteen display cases.

VETERANS OF FOREIGN WARS OF U.S., DEPT. OF STATE OF NEW YORK: Special Gold Medal of Honor.

AMERICAN LEGION, NATIONAL EXECUTIVE COMM.: Testimonial.

BOY SCOUTS OF AMERICA: Award of the Silver Buffalo; Membership and Statuettes.

UNITED STATES JUNIOR CHAMBER OF COMMERCE: Scroll of Testimonials.

OLD GUARD OF NEW YORK CITY: Membership Scroll.

SEVENTY CHURCHES OF ALL DENOMINATIONS IN NEW YORK CITY: Framed Testimonial.

BIBLE SOCIETY OF NEW YORK CITY: Red Letter Bible.

INTERNATIONAL OLYMPIC COMMITTEE: Diploma for Outstanding Achievement.

MISSOURI ATHLETIC CLUB, ST. LOUIS: Gold Membership Card.

AUTO CLUB OF MUNICH, GERMANY: Grand Gold Sport Medal.

UNIVERSITY OF OKLAHOMA CITY: Resolution establishing a Chair of Commercial Aeronautics in honor of Col. Lindbergh.

AMERICAN SOCIETY OF MECHANICAL ENGINEERS: Silver cigarette case.

LOUIS BLERIOT: Fragment of his plane which made the first flight across the English Channel, in 1909.

RYAN AIRLINES, INC.: Five-place, high-wing, cabin monoplane.

WRIGHT AERONAUTICAL CORP.: Whirlwind J-5C, 220 hp. engine.

PIONEER INSTRUMENT CO.: Complete set of airplane instruments.

STANDARD STEEL PROPELLER CO.: Adjustable metal propeller.

CANADIAN NATIONAL RAILWAYS CO.: Gold lifetime pass.

PENNSYLVANIA RAILROAD: Documents naming the *Spirit of St. Louis* train.

EX-PRESIDENT OBREGON, MEXICO: Serapi.

WILLIAM RANDOLPH HEARST: Pair of celestial and terrestial spheres, silver, made in 1700—only known pair in existence.

GOLD MINES OF HONDURAS: Gold chest of native gold nuggets.

NATIONAL PRESS CLUB: Gold pocket watch and leather-bound testimonial.

VACUUM OIL COMPANY: Twenty-five thousand dollar award.

LONDON DAILY MAIL: Gold cup.

SHUBERT THEATRE CORP.: Gold and diamond lifetime pass, to all theaters in the United States and Europe, for Col. Lindbergh and his family.

FRANKLIN AUTOMOBILE CO.: Four-door sedan, with air-cooled engine.

HENRY FORD: Four-door sedan for Col. Lindbergh's mother.

CADILLAC-LA SALLE MOTOR CO.: Two-door convertible.

NATIONAL ASSOCIATION OF PROFESSIONAL BASEBALL LEAGUES: Gold lifetime pass to all games.

NATIONAL LEAGUE OF PROFESSIONAL BASEBALL CLUBS: Gold lifetime pass to all games.

STANDARD OIL CO. OF CAL.: Shares of stock in the company.

MOTION PICTURE FRATERNITY: Autographed gold cup.

MATADOR JOSE ORTIZ: Silk and gold embroidered capote.

ELITCH GARDENS, DENVER, COL.: Silver pass.

DONOR UNKNOWN: German Shepherd police dog.

DONOR UNKNOWN, PANAMA: Large pearl for Col. Lindbergh's mother.

DONOR UNKNOWN: Stickpin, with *Spirit of St. Louis* cut from a single diamond.

Space limitations prevent listing everything presented to Col. Lindbergh in connection with his flights. Only items directly related to the *Spirit of St. Louis* are carried here, and even of these many have had to be omitted. In addition to hundreds of thousands of letters and telegrams, more than fifteen thousand articles from sixty nine countries have been presented to Col. Lindbergh since May 21, 1927, in recognition of his flights. The selections are as varied as the donors, whose personality radiates in many. The collection's greatest value is human, reflecting the admiration of cross sections of the world. Many items are typical products of the localities from which they came, or the occupations of the donors; some are of historic or religious significance; and in some cases the gift represents the sacrifice of a highly valued possession.

The gifts range from specially-cut diamond stickpins to wall paper made in Sweden to commemorate the flight. There are portraits done in gold, tapestry, oil, water colors, pen and ink, charcoal, crayon, and on cameo by artists in all age brackets and stages of excellence; sculptured pieces, many of which are busts of Col. Lindbergh, made of bronze, pure silver, ivory, plaster, and soap; airplane models of solid gold as well as fragile silk; handicrafts from finished artisans to that of primitive native weavers, carvers, metal workers, etc.; books covering many subjects, from Mother Goose to a copy of the Gutenberg Bible—most contemporary volumes being autographed by their authors; bound volumes of newspapers in many languages; thousands of poems and songs, including one by George M. Cohan, inspired by the flight; aviator's equipment and wearing apparel of every imaginable sort; sporting equipment, from an ivory inlaid billiard cue to fishing flies; phonograph recordings of songs and receptions; air baggage labels and coins from many countries; first-flight and first-day covers; stamps, both singles and in sheets, some of which were issued by foreign countries in honor of Col. Lindbergh; handmade linens, bedspreads, quilts, and pillows; jewelry; toilet articles; religious objects; photographs; and good luck tokens of every variety.

Many offers made were declined. These included a home in Flushing Meadows, a live monkey, a fifty thousand dollar offer for a cigarette endorsement, and several motion picture contracts—one of which carried a figure of five million dollars. A 150,000-franc gift from Mme. de la Meurthe, presented through the Aero Club of France, was returned with thanks, and the request that it be used for the families of men who lost their lives in aviation. Similarly, a gift of 5,351.62 crowns, sent by the Stockholm newspaper *Svenska Dagbladet* from its readers, was returned with the request that it be used for aviation purposes. On record in the files of the Missouri Historical Society, in addition to items listed previously, are medals, plaques, testimonials, scrolls, life memberships, and gifts from the following groups and organizations:

Natl. Assn. of Letter Carriers; Missouri Soc. of the Dist. of Columbia; Clemenceau War Orphans' Home, Fr.; Aero Club of Austria; Aero Club of Switzerland; San Diego Pilots of U.S. Army; Silversmiths of Belgium; Bricklayers Local 9 and AF of L, Sacramento; Indians of New Mexico; Ottawa Rowing Club, Can.; Walkers League of the World; GAR of Seattle; Internatl. Brotherhood of Magicians; North Side Boys Club, St. Louis; Christian Endeavor Soc. of Havana; Women of Santo Domingo; Colt Firearms Mfg. Co.; Lindbergh Hotel, Bogota; Aeronautic Club of Alton, Ill.; Unione Veterani Ciclisti, It.; Order of Owls; Men's Bible Class of Westminster Presbyterian Church, New Orleans; Tarpon Club, Panama, C.Z.; United Spanish War Veterans; Engineers' Club, N.Y. City; Aero Club of Czechoslovakia at Prague; Aero Club of Italy; Aero Club of Norway; St. John's College,

Br. Honduras; Filipino Federation of America; Pilots of Imperial Airways, Eng.; League of German War Fliers, Ger.; Natl. Educational Assn.; Boy Scouts of Panama; Sigma Phi Fraternity; A.C. Spark Plug Co.; Enlisted Reserve Corps of Service Squad 381, Cal.; American Woman's Club, Toronto, Can.; Aero Club, Portland; Veterans Organizations in the Dist. of Columbia; Union League Club, Chicago; Aero Club of Germany; Aero Club of Denmark; Aero Club of Spain; Imperial Aero Society of Japan; American Residents of Mexico City; Naval Hospital Patients, Chelsea, Mass.; Swedish Cultural Soc., St. Louis; New York *Times*; Natl. Glider Assn.; Masons of Panama; Sisters of Notre Dame, Porto Rico; Pittsburgh Press Club; American Assn. of Engineers; American Legion, through Crosscup-Pishon Post 281 of Boston; YMCA, Sacramento; Lindbergh Club No. 1, San Francisco; Aero Club of Yugoslavia; Dutch Royal Air Club; Aerial Naval Society of Hungary; American Chamber of Commerce of Cuba; Columbia Broadcasting System; American Legion Post 14, St. Petersburg; Fédération Interalliée des Combattants, Fr.; Society of Marine Flyers of Germany; Aero Club of Poland and League of Aerial Defense; Gruen Watch Guild; Daughters of the Union Veterans of the Civil War, Chicago; Lodge No. 10 of the Order of Elks, Boston; Mexican Assn. of Football; Federation of Mexican Mothers' Clubs; Kansas City Reserve Air Corps; Société Française de St. Louis; N.J. Hudson County Blvd. PBA; School Children of Kearney, Neb.; U.S. Naval Veterans and Aux., Geo. Fitz Randolph Ship No. 1 of N.J.; United Bowling Clubs, N.Y. City; Soc. of Russian Refugees, Wolomin, Pol.; Normal School of Panama; Racquet Club, Washington, D.C.; Elks Lodge No. 6, Sacramento; Boys Club of Hay Island Ranch, Can.; American Information Bur.; Vienna Club, Aus.; Sciots, Long Beach, Cal.; West Coast Theaters; YMCA of Mexico City; Lions' Club, Little Falls, Minn.; GAR Circle No. 62, St. Louis; Rotary Club, San Jose, C.R.; Venezuelans in Costa Rica; Far Western Travelers Assn.; The Sport and General Press Agency, Ltd., London; Military Casino of Guatemala; Chicago Chapter of the DAR; Flying Club of Wichita, Kan.; Willy Coppens Memorial, Belgium; San Diego Athletic Club; Federation of Mexican Workmen; Los Maestros del Tribunal Paramendres, Mex.; Detroit Coin Club; Detroit Athletic Club; St. Paul Assn. of Public and Business; Motor Corps of America; Société des Femmes de France de New York; Citizens and the Aero Club, Fargo, N.D.; Pan-American Union; Society of the Chagres, Panama Canal Zone; Aero Club of Penn.; Masons of Porto Rico; Remington Arms Co.; Scabbard and Blade; Rifle Club, Univ. of Wis.; Citizens and Businesses of the Kings Highway Sec., Brooklyn; Sun Club, N.Y. City;

Paris Chapter of the Natl. Aeronautic Assn. of the U.S.A.; DAR of
Peoria, Ill.; Columbian Club of Indianapolis; Masons of New Orleans;
U.S. Veterans Hospital, Jefferson Barracks, St. Louis; Natl. Air Race
Comm.; Fraternal Order of Orioles; Irvin Air Chute Co.; WCTU of
Peoria, Ill.; Sociedad Bolivian, Bogota; Rotary Club, Barranquilla;
Mecca College of Chiropractic, Wilmington; Ontario Educational
Assn.; Lindy League of the Playground Assn., San Francisco; Active
Club Internatl.; Chauffeurs Assn., in Bogota; Columbia Phonograph
Co.; American Colony in Costa Rica; Boy Scout Troops in Arizona,
California, Indiana, Michigan, Missouri, Ohio, and Washington; Auto-
moto Club de Schaerbeck, Belgium; U.S. Fleet Reserve Assn., Chicago;
Masons of Santo Domingo; Sigma Lambda Fraternity of the State
College, Cal.; The Club of Barranquilla, Col.; American Colony in
Bogota; Hotel del Prado, Barranquilla; Commerce Prudence Industry,
Winnipeg; Women's Committee of Welcome of the Dist. of Columbia;
Optimist Club, Chicago; Jack and Jill Club, Chicago; High Noon Club,
Chicago; School Children of St. Louis; American War Mothers Chap-
ter, Kansas City; United Commercial Travelers of America No. 143,
Detroit; *Christian Science Monitor*, Boston; Strangers Club, Colon;
Gold Mines in Panama; Natl. Museum in Philadelphia; Aero Club of
Pittsburgh; Mettmana, Den.; Benrus Watch Co., Switz.; Lt. Louis
Bennett League,, Weston, W. Va.; Army and Navy Club, N.Y. City;
Order of Northern Lights, Providence; Bulova Watch Co.; Roth
Cadillac Club, Erie, Pa.; Penn Athletic Club; Society of Medalists;
U.S. Naval Hospital, San Diego; San Diego Press Club; Masons of
Costa Rica; Centro Syrio, Santo Domingo; Social Club of Havana;
Cuban American Telephone and Telegraph Co.; Loyal Order of Moose,
Lodge No. 70, Baltimore; Navy Yards, Boston; Svenska Krigarefor-
bund, Chicago; Medallic Art Co.; St. Louis *Post-Dispatch*; New York
Sun; Sport Press of France; Russian Invalids of France; Société de
Hospitaliers Sauveteurs, Fr.; Veterans of Foreign Wars Post 390 of
Greater Atlanta, Ga.; Fraternal Order of Eagles; Advertising Club,
Portland; Prensa Ilustrada y La Semana, Panama; Boy Scouts of Porto
Rico; BPOE of San Juan, P.R.; Masonic Lodge No. 356, St. Thomas,
V.I.; Wheel of Progress; General Alumni Assn., Univ. of Wis.; United
Ancient Order of Druids, Cal.; Club Deportivo de Seybo, Dominican
Repub.; American Residents in Santo Domingo; Swedish Natl. Soc.,
St. Louis; Nassau County Camp 115 of USWV of Long Island; VFW
Ridgewood Post No. 123, N.Y. City; Natl. Federation of Post Office
Clerks; American Scenic and Historic Preservation Soc., N.Y. City;
Casino Espanol, Rio Piedras, P.R.; Camp Oreilles, Hayward, Wis.;
USWV Manial King Camp No. 1 of Natl. Military Home; Commodore

Athletic Club, N.Y. City; Natl. American War Mothers and the Vet
erans of Foreign Wars; Women of the Dist. of Columbia; San Gabriel
Mission Parochial School, Cal.; Universal Safety Congress; Liberty
Memorial Assn., Kansas City; Russell Lobe Parachute Co. and the
Natl. Aeronautic Assn. of San Diego; Mexican Postal Employees.

In the summer of 1927, Col. Lindbergh was asked by the Missouri
Historical Society to allow his trophies to be exhibited in the Jefferson
Memorial Building, at Forest Park. To this he agreed, with the understanding that it should be for a period of ten days, beginning June 25th.
During that time approximately 80,000 people visited the exhibit. Col.
Lindbergh then consented to the request that the trophies remain on
display for an indefinite period. The first year 1,495,000 people visited
the collection. By the winter of 1928, display cases containing the
trophies occupied practically the entire first floor of the west wing of
the Jefferson Memorial Building.

The members of the Spirit of St. Louis Organization refused to
accept any share in the awards made to Col. Lindbergh in connection
with the flights of the *Spirit of St. Louis*. In 1935, Col. and Mrs. Lindbergh, and Col. Lindbergh's mother, Evangeline L. L. Lindbergh,
executed a deed of gift presenting the entire collection to the Missouri
Historical Society, for permanent exhibition in St. Louis. Col. Lindbergh also presented the Society with a stone carving, by the sculptor
Walker Hancock, dedicating the exhibit to his partners in the Spirit
of St. Louis Organization.

THE RAYMOND ORTEIG PRIZE

On May 22, 1919, Raymond Orteig, of New York City, offered a
prize of twenty-five thousand dollars "to be awarded to the first aviator
who shall cross the Atlantic in a land or water aircraft (heavier-than-
air) from Paris or the shores of France to New York, or from New
York to Paris or the shores of France, without stop." After June 1,
1925, it was stipulated that the flight be made under the rules of the
National Aeronautic Association of the United States of America, and
the Fédération Aéronautique Internationale of Paris, France.

On Mr. Orteig's request, the sixty-day advance notification requirement was waived by the Trustees of the prize fund, and the prize was
officially awarded to Col. Lindbergh on June 16, 1927, at Hotel
Brevoort, New York City.

ENGINEERING DATA ON THE *Spirit of St. Louis*

By Donald A. Hall

CHIEF ENGINEER OF RYAN AIRLINES, INC., in 1927

These data are compiled from or based on original records, some of which are in Technical Note No. 257 of the National Advisory Committee for Aeronautics, Washington, D.C., July 1927, entitled "Technical Preparation of the Airplane *Spirit of St. Louis*" by Donald A. Hall.

The company model designation for the *Spirit of St. Louis* was "NYP" (New York-Paris).

SECTION A—DESIGN CHARACTERISTICS
GENERAL

Span	46 ft. 0 in.
Overall length	27 ft. 8 in.
Overall height	9 ft. 10 in.
Wing chord	7 ft. 0 in.
Airfoil	Clark Y
Wing incidence	0°
Wing aspect ratio	6.6

AREAS

Wing	319 sq. ft.
Ailerons, each	8.0 sq. ft.
Horizontal tail	36 sq. ft.
Vertical tail	11.3 sq. ft.

POWER PLANT

Engine—Wright J-5C, "Super inspected."
    Rated power—1800 RPM—sea level   223 BHP
    Maximum power—1950 RPM at max. air speed—sea
        level   237 BHP

Propeller—duralumin—Standard Steel Propeller Co.   8 ft. 9 in. dia.

Fuel capacity—designed   425 gal.
    Main fuselage tank (under wing)   200 gal.
    Nose (forward fuselage) tank   80 gal.
    Three wing tanks   145 gal.

Oil capacity   25 gal.

NOTES—

    RPM = engine propeller shaft speed in revolutions
        per minute.
    BHP = brake (actual) horse power output of engine
        to propeller.
    The capacity of the fuel tanks as built came out over-
        size at 210, 88 and 152 gal. respectively, totaling
        450 gal.

LANDING GEAR

Tread—no load   8 ft. 9 in.

Tread—fully-deflected shock absorbers   10 ft. 0 in.

Wheel rise with fully deflected shock absorbers   8.5 in.

Tire size   30 in. x 5 in.

WEIGHTS AND LOADINGS

See Sec. F for weight data upon leaving New York for
    Paris.

Empty weight complete with equipment and instruments   2150 lb.

Useful load
    Pilot   170 lb.
    Miscellaneous   40 lb.
    Fuel—425 gal. Calif. gasoline at 6.12 lb./
        gal.   2600 lb.
    Oil—25 gal. at 7.0 lb./gal.   175 lb.

    TOTAL   2985 lb.

Design gross weight—fully loaded—start of flight   5135 lb.

Lightly loaded gross weight—end of flight—without
fuel and food—10 gal. oil left   2415 lb.

Wing loading
     Design gross weight—start of flight   16.1 lb./sq. ft.
     Lightly loaded—end of flight   7.6 lb./sq. ft.

Power loading—rated
     Design gross weight—start of flight   23.0 lb./BHP
     Lightly loaded—end of flight   10.8 lb./BHP

CALCULATED CENTER OF GRAVITY LOCATIONS
AT SEVERAL LOADING CONDITIONS

LOADING CONDITION	GROSS WEIGHT lb.	C. G. LOCATION RELATIVE TO WING CHORD	
		LONGITUDINAL Aft of wing leading edge	VERTICAL Below chord (base) line
Design gross weight —start of flight	5135	28.4%	19.2%
Normal most forward C. G. —200 gal. main tank fuel and 8 gal. oil used	3845	25.8%	15.5%
Normal most aft C. G. —10 gal. oil, food, and all fuel except 145 gal. wing fuel, used	3340	*29.6%	15.2%
Lightly loaded—end of flight —no fuel and food—10 gal. oil remaining	2415	27.6%	19.7%
Design gross weight—without fuel, oil, and food	2345	**29.0%	19.2%

* If the 80 gallons of fuel in the nose tank were used first, the center of gravity (C.G.) would move aft to 31.6% wing chord with a consequent reduction in longitudinal stability. In all of his long distance flights with the NYP, Lindbergh decided to sacrifice stability to a more rearward C.G. position in case of a forced landing, thus reducing the tendency to nose over. He therefore used fuel from the nose tank before the main fuselage tank was dry.

** This C.G. location was measured by balancing the airplane in three positions (Lindbergh in pilot's seat and miscellaneous useful load properly located). The intersection of the weight vectors located the C.G. This checked the calculated C.G. location, both longitudinal and vertical, within .15 in.

SECTION B—CALCULATED PERFORMANCE AT SEA LEVEL

Maximum Air Speed (Figs. 2 and 7)
    Design gross weight—start of flight   120 MPH
    Lightly loaded—end of flight   124.5 MPH

Minimum Air Speed (Fig. 2)
    Design gross weight—start of flight   71 MPH
    Lightly loaded—end of flight   49 MPH

Range with Zero Wind and 425 Gal. Fuel (Figs. 5 to 8)
    Ideal economic air speeds of 97 MPH at start and 67 MPH
        at end   4110 miles
    Practical economic air speeds of 95 MPH at start and 75
        MPH at end   4040 miles

NOTES—

MPH = miles per hour in statute miles of 5280 feet.

Maximum air speed is in level flight without benefit of gravity in descending flight.

Minimum air speed or stalling speed is the lowest possible speed relative to the air that an airplane is capable of flying. This is also called landing speed, but airplanes are rarely landed as slow as their minimum speeds because of the stalling danger.

Economic air speed is the speed of best fuel economy.

The conservatively calculated and measured performance figures given here for the *Spirit of St. Louis* should not be confused with the extravagant claims of performance which were often released by manufacturers of small airplanes.

SECTION C—FLIGHT TEST PERFORMANCE
MAXIMUM AIR SPEED AT SEA LEVEL

Clocked test over 3 km. course (average of three runs in each
    direction)—25 gal. fuel and 5 gal. oil (Fig. 7)   129 MPH

Design gross weight with 425 gal. fuel—developed from cal-
    culated and clocked speeds plotted as curves of max. speed
    vs. gross weight in Fig. 7   124.5 MPH

TAKE-OFF DISTANCE

Take-off tests were made at abandoned World War I Camp Kearney, 11 miles north of the City of San Diego and .8 mile south of the present U.S. Naval Air Station, Miramar. This field, located on a mesa, was 12,000 ft. long in the direction of the prevailing west wind, had a constant downward slope of 6 ft. in 1000 ft. toward the west, and a natural surface of hard-packed clay and rock.

The take-off runs started near the east end of the field at a 485 ft. elevation. A series of seven take-off tests were made with fuel loads from 36 to 301 gal. In Fig. 9, the take-off distances were plotted against the gross weight to produce the solid-line curve. The approximate take-off distance for hard ground, with zero wind, at 485-ft. elevation for 5135 lb. design gross weight (425 gal. fuel), determined by extrapolation of the test curve was 2250 ft.

SECTION D—NOTES ON DESIGN PROCEDURE

After intensive preliminary design analyses of aerodynamics, structures, and weights, of various configurations of the proposed airplane, it was concluded that a redesign of the production model 3-seater, open-cockpit, Ryan M-2 could not make the 3600 mile flight between New York and Paris with ample reserve fuel, and that a new design development was necessary. The short time of two months provided in the order, dated Feb. 25, 1927, which Lindbergh placed for the NYP, precluded incorporating major design features not well proven by actual service on airplanes. The next decision was to utilize as many parts of the M-2 design as practicable to save time and cut costs.

Among major considerations involved in freezing the NYP basic design were the following:

1. *Gross weight.* In order to carry the heavy fuel and oil load required for the proposed flight, the M-2 gross weight of 2500 lb. had to be practically doubled in the first weight estimates.

2. *Wing.* The 36 ft. span of the M-2 was changed to 46 ft. to increase both the wing area (33%) and the aspect ratio for good take-off characteristics and for improved range. Fortunately the wing chord did not have to be changed, so the excellent M-2 wing rib was incorporated. Throughout the entire wing it was not possible to use any other M-2 part, due to both dimensional and structural load differences.

3. *Effects of new wing on basic design.*
   a. FUSELAGE. The empennage was moved aft 24 in., which, in combination with a more forward C.G. requirement, made it necessary to move the engine forward 18 in. The 42 in. increase in fuselage structure length, in addition to the increased gross weight, prevented utilizing any M-2 fuselage part.
   b. LANDING GEAR. The 6 ft. 0 in. wheel tread of the M-2 (at no load) was widened to 8 ft. 9 in. to secure good ground stability with the increased wing span and doubled gross weight. The NYP landing-gear design, with its fairly high wheel rise for good shock absorption, was adapted from a successful commercial single-engine transport.

4. *Empennage.* The M-2 empennage, comprising horizontal and vertical tail surfaces, was used with a minimum of change. The forward movement of the C.G. of the NYP (about 5% wing chord), combined with the 24 in. aft movement of the empennage, improved the longitudinal and directional stability, while doubling the gross weight and enlarging the wing reduced both. It was anticipated that the resulting stability would be ample for the take-off at New York and the flight across the Atlantic, but not for commercial purposes.

5. *Power Plant Installation.* The fuel and oil systems obviously could not utilize any of the M-2 design. The M-2 fuel capacity was approximately 50 gal., while the NYP was designed to carry 750% more fuel.

FINAL CONFIGURATION

The final configuration of this strut-braced high-wing monoplane (refer to three-view drawing in Fig. 1) was a composite of the best design features of successful military and commercial airplanes.

SECTION E—TYPICAL FEATURES

Wing. The I-section spars were made of spruce, comprising four flange members casein glued to web members. The wood ribs utilized the Warren-truss principle. Drag bracing comprised double piano wire, with compression ribs made by reinforcing standard ribs with spruce compression members. Relatively small ailerons (20% less area than on the M-2) were located 38 in. inboard of the wing tips, to avoid excessive wing structural loads in the full load condition. The lateral control with these ailerons proved to be ample. The external struts used to brace the wing were SAE 1020 mild carbon steel tubes, streamlined with balsa wood.

Fuselage. The fuselage was built of SAE 1020 mild carbon steel tubes, welded together to form horizontal and vertical trusses.

Empennage. The vertical and horizontal surfaces were made of SAE 1020 mild carbon steel tubes to form structure and ribs. The horizontal stabilizer was adjustable from the cockpit for maintaining longitudinal balance (trim) in flight at any speed or loading condition.

Landing gear. Wide-tread, split-axle type. Each of the dual axles, as well as the tail skid, were made of chrome molybdenum (SAE 4130) steel tubes heat-treated to 180,000 lb. per sq. in. and streamlined with balsa wood. The "trombone" type of shock absorber utilized shock absorber cord of eight individual links in tension to give 6½ in. compressive deflection of the unit.

Power plant installation. The oil tank, located immediately behind the engine, filled practically the entire fuselage cross section, to perform effectively the additional function of a firewall. The fuel and oil tanks were made of a soft sheet steel called "ternplate," to reduce the danger of leaks developing from vibration. Each of the five fuel tanks was connected to a distribution system in the cockpit, so that fuel could be transferred by hand pumping from any tank to any other tank. Two independent fuel lines ran from the cockpit distribution system to the engine. In case the engine fuel pump in one line failed, fuel could be hand wobble-pumped from either of the fuselage tanks to one of the wing tanks, where it could then flow to the engine by gravity. The cowling and propeller spinner were made of soft aluminum. The duralumin propeller blades, which were adjustable on the ground, were set at 16¼° pitch.

Covering. The wing, empennage, fuselage, external struts, axles, and tail skid were covered with grade A cotton fabric finished with cellulose acetate dope.

Streamlining. In relation to standard practices of the period, unusual emphasis was placed on streamlining the *Spirit of St. Louis.* As a result, in the lightly loaded condition, the maximum speed obtained was about 10 MPH higher than the maximum speed of the Ryan M-2, with the same engine, while the minimum air speed was about 8 MPH lower than that of the M-2.

1. The accuracy of the airfoil contour of the wing was increased by:
   a. Wing ribs spaced 11 in. apart instead of the conventional 14 to 15 in.
   b. Plywood completely around the leading edge to the front spar.
   c. Wing tips formed of balsa wood planking with airfoil contour in plan and faired spanwise sections.
2. At the juncture of external struts with wing, fuselage, horizontal stabilizer, etc., aluminum fairings were made to enclose strut ends and fittings to reduce the interferential resistance.
3. Each landing gear shock absorber unit was covered by a streamlined aluminum enclosure. The wheels were streamlined with doped fabric laced to the tires at their maximum width.
4. The engine and forward fuselage cowling were carefully faired into the remainder of the fuselage.

Safety of pilot's location. The location of the pilot behind the main fuel tank, as well as all other tanks, had the following advantages:

1. Pilot could not be crushed by the weight of tank and fuel in a crack-up.
2. The C.G. of the design fuel load was close to the airplane C.G. for improved longitudinal stability in the critical first part of the flight.

SECTION F—CHARACTERISTICS OF THE *Spirit of St. Louis*
UPON LEAVING NEW YORK FOR PARIS

WEIGHTS

Summary

Empty, complete with equipment and instruments	2150	lb.

Useful load

Pilot	170 lb.	
Miscellaneous	40 lb.	
*Fuel, 450 gal. (actual)	2750 lb.	
Oil, 20 gal.	140 lb.	

TOTAL	3100	lb.

Gross weight, fully loaded	5250	lb.

* At New York, Lindbergh decided to exceed the design fuel load by completely filling all tanks (see Sec. A).

Equivalent net weight empty

Assume that a fuel capacity of 60 gal. and an oil capacity of 5 gal. is sufficient for ordinary flying. Then the weight of excess tanks, special equipment, and special instruments not required in ordinary flying is	450	lb.
Equivalent net weight empty (2150 minus 450)	1700	lb.

Weight efficiency

Equivalent useful load (5250 minus 1700)	3550	lb
Ratio of equivalent useful load to equivalent weight empty	2.1	
Ratio of gross weight to equivalent weight empty	3.1	

LOADINGS

Wing loading	16.5 lb./sq. ft.
Power loading, rated	23.6 lb./BHP

MINIMUM STRUCTURAL LOAD FACTORS
(5250 lb. Gross Weight)

Wing structure in high incidence condition	3.3
Wing structure in low incidence condition	2.3
Landing gear in three-point landing condition	4.0

CALCULATED PERFORMANCE AT SEA LEVEL
WITH 450 GAL. FUEL

(Based on calculated performance of Sec. B and Figs. 2 to 8)

Maximum air speed (Fig. 7)	119.5	MPH
Minimum air speed	72	MPH
Range at economic air speeds with zero wind		
Practical air speeds of 95 MPH at start and 75 MPH at end	4210	miles

PROBABLE MAXIMUM AIR SPEED AT SEA LEVEL

Developed from calculated and clocked speeds (Fig. 7)	124	MPH

TAKE-OFF DISTANCE WITH 450 GAL. FUEL

Estimated for hard ground with zero wind at 485 ft. elevation by extrapolation of Sec. C test data plotted in Fig. 9	2500	ft.

SECTION G—TOTAL POSSIBLE RANGE BY USING FUEL REMAINING IN TANKS WHEN *Spirit of St. Louis* REACHED PARIS

Fuel remaining in tanks	85	gal.
Additional range available with zero wind—practical economic air speeds	1040	miles
Total range		
Practical economic air speeds for remaining fuel (3610 plus 1040)	4650	miles

SECTION H — MAN HOURS TO DESIGN AND BUILD THE *Spirit of St. Louis*

ENGINEERING

Total time spent by the engineer (Hall) on design, weight and balance analysis, stress analysis, drawings, inspection, performance analysis, and flight test engineering—Feb. 25 to May 10 (Lindbergh left San Diego)	775	man hrs.
The purchasing agent (Locke) assisted in the weight and balance analysis, and the factory manager (Bowlus) assisted in the fuel and oil system layout	75	man hrs.
TOTAL ENGINEERING	850	man hrs.

CONSTRUCTION

Total time in the construction and assembly but not including the shop superintendent's and factory manager's time	3000	man hrs.

SECTION I—CONCLUDING REMARKS

A combination of factors associated with the design and construction of the *Spirit of St. Louis* made it possible to complete the project in two months. One of these was the almost constant availability of Lindbergh to discuss the problems which arose. Normally, the purchaser of a custom-built airplane did not stay at the factory during its development, and this required the engineer to maintain an extensive correspondence. Rather complete preliminary design drawings and data had to be specially prepared and forwarded to the purchaser for study and comment. Such work and correspondence took a large part of the engineer's time. Fortunately, this was not necessary for the NYP.

The presence of Charles Lindbergh, with his keen knowledge of flying, his understanding of engineering problems, his implicit faith in the proposed flight, and his constant application to it, was a most important factor in welding together the entire factory organization into one smoothly running team. This group was unusually conscientious, co-operative, and hard working.

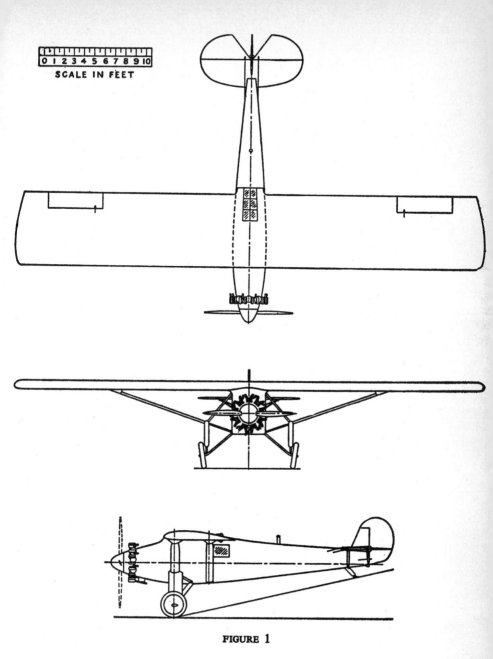

SCALE IN FEET

FIGURE 1

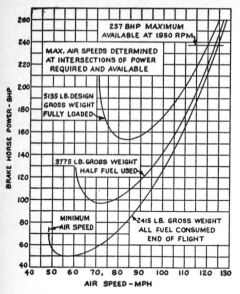

FIGURE 2

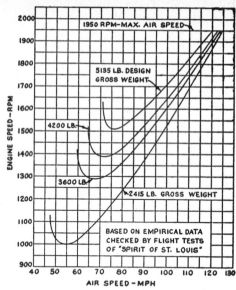

FIGURE 3

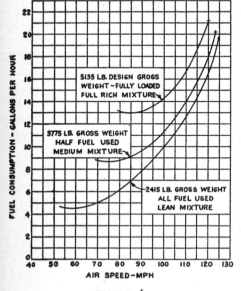

FIGURE 4

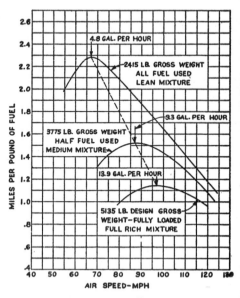

FIGURE 5

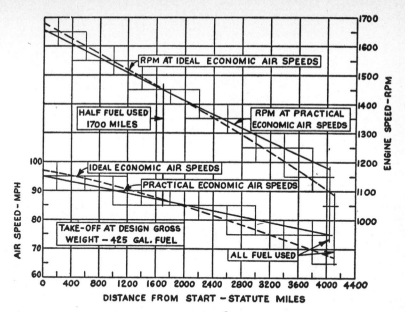

FIGURE 6

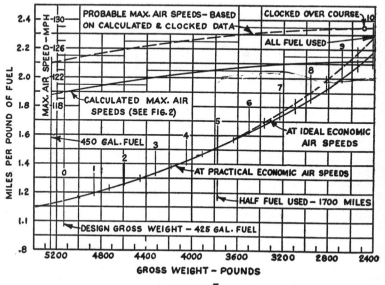

FIGURE 7

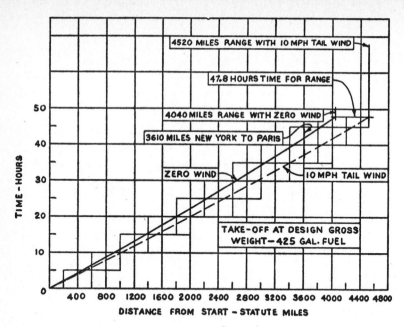

FIGURE 8

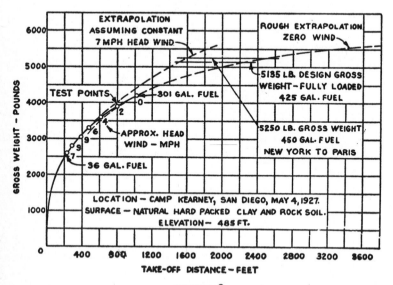

FIGURE 9

WRIGHT WHIRLWIND AVIATION ENGINE
MODEL J-5C

SPECIFICATIONS AND GENERAL DESCRIPTION

By Kenneth M. Lane

CHIEF AIRPLANE ENGINEER OF WRIGHT AERONAUTICAL
CORPORATION IN 1927

Wright Whirlwind J-5C, Serial No. 7331,
powered the *Spirit of St. Louis*

Specifications

Horsepower, sea level	220 hp
Normal operating speed	1800 rpm
Bore	4.5 in.
Stroke	5.5 in.
Displacement	788 cu. in.
Compression ratio	5.2
Weight, dry	500 lb.
Overall diameter	45 in.
Overall length, with Eclipse starter	40 5/32 in.
Fuel consumption @ 200 H.P. @ 1800 rpm	.53 lb./hp./hr.
Oil consumption, not over	.035 lb./hp./hr.
Magnetos, two	Scintilla AG9D
Spark plugs, two per cylinder	AC Type N
Carburetor	Stromberg NA-T4
Ignition timing	30° b.t.c.
Valve timing	
intake opens	8° b.t.c.
intake closes	60° a.b.c.
exhaust opens	60° b.b.c.
exhaust closes	8° a.t.c.

GENERAL DESCRIPTION

The Wright Whirlwind aviation engine, Model J-5C, is a nine-cylinder, air-cooled, radial, operating on the four-stroke cycle.

The cylinder consists of a cast aluminum alloy head, screwed and shrunk onto a forged steel barrel. Head cooling fins are cast; those on the barrel are machined. A flange on the barrel serves for attachment to the crankcase. Bronze valve seats, bronze spark-plug bushings, bronze intake valve guides, and tungsten steel exhaust guides are provided in the head.

The crankcase is built up of five sections of cast aluminum alloy, joined by means of studs and nuts. The one-piece crankshaft is machined from a chrome-nickel steel forging and is fully counterbalanced. The shaft runs in four bearings—a ball thrust bearing in the nose, two main roller bearings, and a plain bearing in the rear section.

The connecting-rod system comprises a master rod and eight link rods. The master rod is in two sections, main and cap, each carrying four link rods. The master rod bearing is steel-backed babbitt, while the knuckle and wrist pin bushings of the link rods are bronze. Pistons are permanent mold aluminum alloy castings, with two compression rings, one scraper ring above the wrist pin, and a compression ring at the bottom of the skirt. The low tungsten steel intake valve and the sodium-cooled cobalt-chromium (or high tungsten) steel exhaust valve are both of the tulip type. These valves are operated by rocker-arms journaled in rocker boxes attached by studs on the cylinder heads. These rocker-arms are actuated, through enclosed push rods, by a disk cam having two tracks (one for intake and one for exhaust) having four lobes each. The cam is driven at one-eighth crankshaft speed and in the reverse direction.

The Wright fuel pump is of the Viking internal gear type, and is provided with an adjustable pressure relief valve and a by-pass valve to enable the operator to hand-pump fuel around the gear pump to the carburetor. The Stromberg NA-T4 carburetor is a three-barrelled type, each barrel supplying fuel-air mixture to three cylinders, through appropriate passages in the rear portion of the main crankcase section, terminating in three ring-type manifolds, from which the individual intake pipes conduct the mixture to the cylinder-head intake ports.

Dual ignition is provided by two Scintilla AG-9D magnetos mounted on the front section of the crankcase, the righthand magneto serving the front spark plugs and the lefthand magneto the rear plugs.

The lubrication system is of the full pressure type except that cylinder walls, wrist pins, and accessory drive gears are lubricated by "splash," *i.e.*, by oil spraying out of the ends of the adjacent bearings, and the rocker-arm bearings are greased. For general service this greasing is accomplished periodically through a pressure-gun fitting, but for long range service—such as the New York to Paris flight—a magazine type attachment is substituted for the pressure-gun fitting, the grease in the magazine being fed to the bearing slowly but continuously throughout the flight. The engine is of the dry sump type, oil being drawn from a tank and fed by a pressure pump through the hollow crankshaft to the various bearings, the oil escaping from the bearings ultimately draining to the sump, whence a scavenge pump returns it to the tank.

The engine is equipped with a heater for the carburetor intake air. The necessary heat is provided by leading the hot exhaust gases from two cylinders through the heater, which is attached to the carburetor intake.

We

Soon after landing the *Spirit of St. Louis* at Paris, I adopted a suggestion that I take part in publishing a book about my flight and life. I was then under the impression that the account would be written in the third person, through interviews, over someone else's name, and that I would confirm its authenticity and contribute a foreword. Instead, a "ghost-written" manuscript, in the first person, was submitted to me for approval, and rejected.

Since the project had already been announced publicly, I felt under obligation to carry it through. I wrote the manuscript for a short book at the home of my friends, Harry and Carol Guggenheim, near Port Washington, Long Island. This was brought out, in 1927, under the title of *We*. With the exception of a few pages, the writing had to be, and was, completed in about three weeks. To stay within this time limit, I made no attempt at a second draft. Frequently I did not reread the sentences I penned. I had little experience in writing, limited facilities for research, and no extra hours to work on shading or balance. Being young, and easily embarrassed, I was hesitant to dwell on my personal errors and sensations. Also, believing in aviation's future, I did not want to lay bare, through my own experience, its existing weaknesses. For reasons such as these, I left out of my story much of greatest interest—which I am now, twenty-five years later, attempting to portray in *The Spirit of St. Louis*.

OTHER BOOKS, MAGAZINE ARTICLES, AND PRESS ACCOUNTS

Mention should be made here of other books, and the thousands of newspaper and magazine articles, which carry statements connected with my life and flights. A number of these accounts have been carefully written, but most are riddled with errors—some caused by carelessness, some by ignorance, some put there by intent. A study of their contents quickly brings out their fallibility. In childhood, I did not gain my desire to fly by a careful study of birds' wings, or by sitting on a bicycle lashed in the high branches of a tree. (In fact, I never saw such a contrivance.) While I was in San Diego, before starting on the flight for Paris, I did not go for long walks training myself "to stay awake for periods of thirty to forty-nine hours" (I slept for part of every night that I was there). I was not separated from a wife and family. I had not been engaged to several different girls (nor even one). I did not have a kitten as a mascot for the *Spirit of St. Louis*, nor did I carry the wishbone of a chicken across the ocean to bring me luck.

Before taking off from Roosevelt Field, I did not say that entering my cockpit was like entering a death chamber (if I had believed that, I would never have started on the flight). I was not escorted across the Channel by a squadron of English planes. (After the Oriole turned back above Long Island Sound, I saw no other plane until I was low enough for my eyes to penetrate the hangars' shadows on Le Bourget.) When I landed at Paris, I did not announce my name, or request a cigarette or a glass of milk, or say "Well, I made it," or inquire as to whether I had landed at Paris. I was not clubbed on the back of the head by "a good samaritan," and a group of French doctors did not rub my legs and force bits of chocolate into my mouth to give me nourishment. (After being swept away by the crowd, many of the reporters on the aerodrome sent back to their organizations partly imaginary accounts of my landing. There was considerable difference of opinion as to what took place and what my words were likely to have been.) The *Spirit of St. Louis* was not down to twenty gallons of gasoline when I cut its engine switch on the 21st of May. (At the instigation of some newspaper reporters, a mechanic had tried to measure the plane's remaining fuel without my knowledge. The fuel system was complicated, and he failed to drain all five tanks. Actually, eighty-five gallons of gasoline and fourteen and a half gallons of lubricating oil remained on board after the flight from New York— enough to have carried the *Spirit of St. Louis* more than a thousand miles farther eastward, under existing wind conditions.) Even in some of the newspaper articles which appeared under my name, inaccuracy was high, for the first several were "ghost written" after short interviews, and the demands on my time were so great that I found no opportunity to correct, or even read, the story which was cabled home.

Little is to be gained by recording here more of the erroneous statements that have been printed about my life and activities. The list is long. Few articles touching the subject have been written which do not at least in some degree conflict with fact and the story in these chapters of *The Spirit of St. Louis*. No work is infallible; desire, records, and memory, combined cannot produce exactness in every instance; but sufficient effort has been expended on the pages of this book to warrant that in the majority of cases where there is conflict, accuracy will rest with the account carried herein.

C. A. L.

GLOSSARY

NOTE: The maximum and landing speeds listed by the manufacturers of airplanes often varied appreciably from the speeds accurately measured. Listed speeds are used throughout this glossary.

ace · A combat pilot with five or more victories.

aileron · Usually a hinged section of a trailing-edge area of a wing, controllable by the pilot for the purpose of raising or lowering the wing during flight.

airfoil · A surface shaped for movement through the air in order to obtain a desired reaction. (Wing, rudder, stabilizer, etc.)

air pocket · A term once used to describe turbulent air. Some people were under the impression that "pockets" existed in the atmosphere, in which an airplane fell toward the ground like a rock.

air speed · The speed of an aircraft in relation to the air. It is unaffected by wind velocity.

air-speed indicator · An instrument for showing the relative speed of an aircraft's movement through the air.

altimeter · An instrument, similar to an aneroid barometer, graduated to indicate the altitude at which an airplane is flying above sea level or above a set reference level.

analysis, balance · The analytical determination of the center of gravity of an aircraft.

analysis, stress · The analytical determination of the dynamic forces acting on a structure (wing, fuselage, empennage, landing gear, etc.), the loads and stresses acting on its component parts, and the structural design of such parts.

analysis, weight · The analytical determination of the weight of an aircraft, by calculating the weight of all components and subsidiary parts.

approach lights · Green lights indicating the best direction of approach for landing aircraft.

aspect ratio · The ratio of the span to the mean chord of an airfoil (wing length divided by wing width).

Attack · The branch of the Army Air Service which specialized in the development and operation of aircraft for relatively short-range and low-altitude missions, such as the support of ground troops and the destruction of tactical objectives.

azimuth · An arc of the horizon, measured clockwise from north.

ball (*bank indicator*) · The steel ball which rolls through liquid in a curved glass tube and indicates whether the wings are level in straight flight, or properly inclined in a turn.

balloon (*in landing*) · To let the plane rise, unintentionally, after levelling off for contact with the ground.

bank (*engine*) · A row of cylinders. The 150 hp. and 180 hp. Hispano-Suiza engines had two banks of four cylinders each.

bank · The position of an airplane when its wings are tilted laterally to prevent skidding while turning.

bank indicator (*Spirit of St. Louis*) • A steel ball in one instrument, and an air bubble in another instrument, which showed when the wings were level in straight flight, or properly inclined in a turn.

barnstorm • To travel around the country, carrying fare-paying passengers on local flights (usually from farm fields or prairies).

bay (*wing*) • A portion of the wing span bounded by interplane bracing members of (Jennies, Standards, DHs) a biplane.

Benzine Board • The name applied by flying cadets to a board of officers which convened to act on the cases of cadets who were being dropped from the school.

biplane • An airplane with two main supporting surfaces (wings), placed approximately one above the other.

blackout • Temporary loss of vision and dulling of senses caused by a steep bank or a quick pull-out from a dive during which blood is forced downward from the head.

Bombardment • The branch of the Army Air Service which specialized in the development and operation of bombing aircraft for relatively high-altitude and long-range missions.

booster • A magneto, turned by hand, for the purpose of creating a hotter spark while starting a gasoline engine. The command given when it is desired to have the booster magneto operated.

breakaway • An acrobatic stunt used in flying exhibitions, in which the wing-walker slips off the tip of a lower wing and swings down under the airplane at the end of a rope ladder or cable attached to the landing gear.

break cord, parachute • The cord or heavy string used to hold the vent of certain types of parachutes to the plane until the canopy and shroud lines are strung out during the initial stage of the jump.

breather • A vent in the crankcase of an engine, which allows gases to escape and keeps crankcase pressure approximately equal to atmospheric.

bubble (*bank indicator*) • The air bubble which floats in liquid in a curved glass tube and indicates whether the wings are level in straight flight, or properly inclined in a turn.

bubble sight • A sextant observation in which a bubble floating in liquid is used to replace the natural horizon.

cabane strut (*as used in this book*) • A strut in the system of trussing used for supporting the overhang of an upper wing, located above the outer-bay wing struts.

cannibalize • To remove a part from one airplane for the purpose of using it on another.

canopy (*parachute*) • The main cloth (umbrella-shaped when open) portion of a parachute.

Canuck • A Canadian modification of the Curtiss JN4 (Jenny). More lightly built and with slightly higher performance.

carburetor • An apparatus used on internal combustion engines, in which passing air is charged with gasoline.

cartographer • A maker of charts or maps.

ceiling (*absolute*) • The maximum height above sea level at which an airplane can maintain horizontal flight under standard atmospheric conditions.

ceiling (*weather*) • The bottom of a cloud layer. Also the distance between the ground and the bottom of a cloud layer.

center of gravity • The point about which an aircraft will balance, irrespective of its attitude.

chamois • The process of filtering (gasoline) through a chamois skin.

chandelle • An abrupt climbing turn which makes use of the momentum of the airplane to gain altitude.

chord • The longitudinal dimension of an airfoil section (wing width).

cirrus • A thin, white, featherlike cloud which forms at altitudes of 20,000 to 40,000 feet.

club propeller • A propeller with relatively wide blades and blunt tips.

cockpit • A portion of an airplane in which one or more members of the crew, or sometimes passengers, are seated.

compass button • The button, usually located at the end of the stick, with which the pilot turns on the compass light momentarily.

compass card • A circular dial, marked in degrees, attached to the magnets of a compass.

compass heading • The compass reading to be followed in maintaining the desired direction of flight. The compass heading includes compensation for variation, deviation, and wind drift.

compass rose • A circle, graduated in degrees, printed on charts to simplify measuring courses and directions.

con rod (*engine*) • A connecting rod. A steel rod or bar, connecting a piston to the crankshaft.

contact • The command given when it is desired to have the engine switch turned to the "on" position.

contact flying • Flying in which the pilot maintains visual contact with the ground or water.

controls (*airplane*) • The stick and rudder, by means of which the pilot controls the attitude of his airplane in relation to the three axes, *i.e.*, all positions of the wings and nose.

course, compass • The compass reading to be followed in maintaining the desired direction of flight when there is no wind drift. The compass course includes compensation for variation and deviation. When there is no wind drift, the compass course is the same as the compass heading.

course, magnetic • The direction of flight in relation to magnetic north, measured clockwise in degrees between magnetic north and the desired path of the airplane over the ground.

course, true • The direction of flight in relation to true north, measured clockwise in degrees between true north and the desired path of the airplane over the ground.

cowling • A removable metal covering on the nose of a fuselage or nacelle, used to house the engine and to reduce its air resistance.

crab • To head an airplane at an angle into a cross wind in order to keep from drifting to the leeward of the desired course.

crack-up • An accident in which the airplane is damaged. Usually used to imply less seriousness than is indicated by the term "crash."

crankcase • The metal covering of the crankshaft of an engine.

crankshaft • The steel shaft driven by the pistons acting through the connecting rods, at one end of which the propeller is attached in the case of direct-drive aircraft engines.

crash • An accident in which the airplane is seriously damaged.

cumulo-nimbus • A mountainous, billowy storm cloud, accompanied by rain and often by violent air currents.

cumulus • A billowy white cloud, varying in size from small to mountainous.

cylinder (*engine*) • The chamber in which the combustion takes place and the piston moves back and forth.

dead stick • A propeller which has stopped turning during flight. Often used to describe the condition when a propeller is still turning but no longer exerting useful thrust because of engine trouble.

De Haviland (*DH-4B*) • A two-place, tandem-cockpit, tractor biplane, powered by one Liberty 400 hp. engine. Built primarily for observational purposes in World War I. Max. speed 124 mph. Landing speed 55 mph. (See photograph.)

deviation (*compass*) • The angular difference between the compass indication and the magnetic heading of the plane. Caused by magnetism in iron and steel parts, and by magnetic fields created by electric circuits.

direct drive engine • An engine in which the crankshaft is attached directly (not through gears) to the propeller.

dolly • A wheeled handcart, placed under the tail skid, to assist in moving an airplane by hand, on the ground.

dope • A cellulose acetate or cellulose nitrate material used to shrink and strengthen the cloth surfaces of aircraft and to make them impervious to air and water.

drag the field • To fly over a field at very low altitude in order to observe its surface, usually with the intent of landing.

drift • The angular movement of an aircraft in relation to the ground, to one side or the other of its heading, caused by a cross wind.

drift angle • The angle at which an airplane must be headed into the wind in order to avoid being drifted off the desired course.

drift indicator • An instrument for determining the angle of drift of an airplane flying in a cross wind. This is usually accomplished by observing the apparent motion of objects on the ground along the wires of a grid incorporated in the instrument.

drift wire (*also called "drag wire"*) • A steel cable running (Jennies, Standards, DHs) from a forward inner-bay strut fitting to the nose of the fuselage, resisting the tendency of the wing to bend backward.

earth-inductor compass • A compass which depends for its indications on the current generated in a coil revolving in the earth's magnetic field.

elevator (*also called "flipper"*) • An airfoil, usually hinged to the back of the stabilizer, which is controllable by the pilot for the purpose of inclining the longitudinal axis of the airplane in relation to the horizon (climbing, gliding, etc.).

empennage • The tail surfaces of an airplane, including stabilizing and control surfaces.

exhaust, engine • The escape of the gas, after combustion in the cylinders.

fair it in • To shape the contours in a manner resulting in smooth outline and decreased air resistance.

fin • The vertical stabilizing surface (Jennies, Standards, DHs) above the fuselage, forward of the rudder.

fitting • A part, usually a small part, of a plane, engine, etc.

flare (*parachute*) • A stick of combustible material, attached to a parachute, which ignites automatically on dropping and burns with an intense light.

flip-flops • A term sometimes used to describe acrobatics.

flippers • A term which was sometimes used for the elevators.

flying speed • Any normal speed above stalling speed.

flying wire • A wire or cable running angularly between upper and lower wings (Jennies, Standards, DHs), which transmits the lift on the outer portion of the wings in toward the fuselage.

Fokker Trimotor F VII-3M (*Commercial model*) • A full-cantilever, high-wing, 10-place, cabin monoplane with tapered, plywood-covered wings, and a welded steel-tube, fabric-covered fuselage. Powered by three Whirlwind tractor-engines. Max. speed 122 mph. Landing speed 62 mph. Built at Hasbrouck Heights, N.J.

freeze (*controls*) • To hold the stick and rudder rigidly.

fuselage • The approximately streamline body of an airplane.

gnomonic projection (*chart*) • A projection in which the eye is imagined to be at the center of the sphere. The projection, by radials from the center, of the surface of a sphere on a plane tangent to the sphere. Great circles on the earth's sphere project as straight lines, but areas are greatly distorted.

great circle • Any portion of the line cut on the surface of the earth by a plane surface which passes through the center of the earth. The shortest surface distance between any two points on a hemisphere.

ground loop • An uncontrollable turn while an airplane is rolling over the ground at a speed too low for the rudder to be effective.

ground school • A school which gives instruction in various subjects to students undergoing flight training.

ground speed • The speed of an aircraft in relation to the ground. It is affected by wind velocity.

gun • A term often used for the throttle.

gyroscopic turn-indicator • An instrument, actuated by a gyroscope, for showing whether an airplane is remaining on its heading or veering right or left, and the approximate rate of any turn.

hedge-hopping • Flying so low over the ground that it is necessary to pull up to clear trees and other obstructions.

Hispano-Suiza (*Model A*) • An eight-cylinder, direct-drive, vee-type, water-cooled, engine, rated at 150 hp. at 1450 rpm. Dry weight 445 lbs.

hp (*horsepower*) • A unit of power equal to a rate of 33,000 foot-pounds of work per minute.

hurdles • The artificial obstructions over which a cadet is sometimes required to land his plane during flying training.

Immelmann • A half-roll on top of a half-loop, reversing the direction in which the airplane was flying before the maneuver was started.

inclinometer (*fore-and-aft*) • A device for showing the inclination of the longitudinal axis of an aircraft to the horizontal, *i.e.,* to show whether the nose is on the horizon or pointing up or down.

inner bay • The area and structure of the wings between (Jennies, Standards, DHs) the fuselage and the nearest pair of wing struts.

inner-bay strut • One of either pair (Jennies, Standards, DHs) of the upper-to-lower wing struts nearest the fuselage.

isogonic lines • Imaginary lines on the earth's surface, at all points on which the magnetic variation is the same.

Jenny (*Curtiss JN4-D*) • A two-place, open tandem-cockpit, tractor biplane, powered by an OX-5 engine. Used for training in World War I. Max. speed 75 mph. Landing speed 45 mph. (See photograph.)

Jenny Immelmann • A half-loop after a half-roll, reversing the direction in which the plane was flying when the maneuver was started, but with a loss of altitude.

Keystone Pathfinder (*Commercial model*) • A trimotored, fabric-covered, cabin biplane, powered by Wright Whirlwind tractor-engines. Max. speed 120 mph. Landing speed 56 mph. Built at Bristol, Pa.

knife rope, parachute • The rope attached to the hinged knife-blade which cuts the lashing cord and releases the parachute (certain types) for the jump.

Laird (*OX-5 engine*) • An open tandem-cockpit, tractor biplane with fabric-covered wings and fuselage. One pilot, two passengers. Max. speed 95 mph. Landing speed 40 mph. Built at Wichita, Kan.

landfall • The sighting of land after a sea voyage.

landing wire • A wire or cable running angularly between upper and lower wings (Jennies, Standards, DHs) which opposes the flying wire, and resists forces in the opposite direction to that of normal flight.

lean out (*the mixture*) • To reduce the amount of gasoline which is mixed with the air passing through the carburetor.

Liberty • A twelve-cylinder, direct-drive, vee-type, water-cooled engine, developing 400 hp. at 1700 rpm. Dry weight 844 lbs. Designed and built for use in World War I.

Lincoln Standard Tourabout (*Hispano-Suiza A engine*) • A converted World War I training, tractor biplane. One pilot, two passengers; open tandem-cockpits; fabric-covered. Max. speed 90 mph. Landing speed 45 mph. Converted at Lincoln, Neb.

line (*"on the line"*) • The area of a flying field on which airplanes in active use are parked between flights.

line of position • A part of a circle (for practical purposes, a straight line) obtained by plotting on a chart a sextant observation of a heavenly body. An accurate line of position passes through the point of observation; therefore the intersection of two lines of position, with compensation for time difference in observation, establish a location on the earth's surface within the limits of the navigator's skill and the steadiness of flight.

liquid compass • A compass in which the magnets and cards are immersed in liquid in order to damp out oscillation.

loading up (*engine*) • The condition of an engine when too much gasoline is being accumulated in the cylinders.

lock stitch • To attach the cloth covering to the ribs of an airfoil by means of heavy thread passed, with a long needle, around the rib.

longeron • One of the main longitudinal members forming the framework of the fuselage.

lubber line • The line on a compass, corresponding to the longitudinal axis of the airplane, in relation to which the readings are taken from the compass card.

Lunkenheimer • A fitting containing fuel valves, dirt screen, water trap, and drain cock, placed in the fuel line between gasoline tanks and engine.

Lunkenheimer trap • A reservoir at the bottom of the Lunkenheimer, for the purpose of removing small amounts of water which might pass into the fuel line from the tanks.

magnetic course • See course, magnetic.

magnetic storm • A major disturbance of the earth's magnetic conditions.

magneto • A small dynamo, geared to an internal combustion engine for the purpose of generating and distributing high-tension current for ignition.

Mercator's projection (*chart*) • A projection in which the meridians and the parallels of latitude are straight lines, intersecting each other at right angles. Distortion increases rapidly with latitude, but compass courses can be taken directly from the chart.

mixture control • The control, operated by the pilot, which regulates the ratio of gasoline to air before the mixture is drawn into the engine cylinders.

monoplane • An airplane with only one main supporting surface (wing).

m.p.h. • Miles per hour.

nacelle, engine • The approximately streamlined enclosure of an engine.

navigation lights • The colored lights which show the position and direction of movement of an airplane at night. (Green at right wing tip; red at left wing tip; yellow on tail.)

NC-4 • A biplane flying boat, specially modified for transatlantic flight; fabric-covered wings; wood hull; powered by four 400 hp. Liberty engines (three tractors and one pusher). Crew of five men. Max. speed 85 mph. Landing speed 62 mph. Range, economical—1690 statute miles.

needle • The indicating hand of an instrument in the cockpit (altimeter, air speed, turn indicator, etc.).

north, magnetic • The direction indicated by the needle of a compass unaffected by local magnetic attraction.

North Magnetic Pole • A point in northern Canada where a freely suspended magnet would point vertically (latitude about 71° north; longitude about 96° west).

north, true • The direction of the north pole of the earth's axis.

Observation • The branch of the Army Air Service which specialized in the development and operation of aircraft used primarily for observational purposes (photography, direction of artillery fire, reconnaissance, etc.).

obstruction lights • Red lights placed on poles, towers, buildings, and other obstructions in the vicinity of an airport to warn pilots of objects which must be cleared in landing and taking off.

one-eighty • A training maneuver in which the cadet closes his throttle as he flies above a field, executes a 180-degree turn with his plane, and lands without the further use of power.

on shares • An agreement made between the owner and the pilot of a plane, in regard to dividing the revenue from flying activities.

Operations • The place, usually on the edge of an airport, from which flying activities are directed.

Oriole (*Curtiss*) • An open tandem-cockpit, tractor biplane with fabric-covered wings and wood monocoque fuselage. One pilot, two passengers. Powered by one Curtiss C-6 160 hp. engine. Max. speed 98 mph. Landing speed 50 mph.

ornithopter • A flying machine with wings that flap; designed in an attempt to copy the flight of a bird.

outer bay • The area and structure of the wings between (Jennies, Standards, DHs) the inner and outer pairs of struts.

outer-bay struts • One of either pair (Jennies, Standards, DHs) of the upper-to-lower wing struts nearest the wing tip.

OX-5 (*Curtiss*) • An eight-cylinder, direct-drive, vee-type, water-cooled, engine, rated at 90 hp. at 1400 rpm. Dry weight 390 lbs.

OXX-6 (*Curtiss*) • An eight-cylinder, direct-drive, vee-type, water-cooled, engine, rated at 100 hp. at 1400 rpm. Dry weight 401 lbs.

pancake • To hit the ground hard with an airplane after levelling off too high for a proper landing. The wings are in a stalled but approximately horizontal position.

panel • A separately constructed portion of the wing surface of an airplane.

parachute bag • The canvas bag in which certain types of parachutes are placed in preparation for a jump, or for storage afterward.

parachute flare • See flare.

pay load • The load (passengers, mail, express, etc.) which produces revenue.

peg • The point on an instrument dial beyond which the indicating needle is mechanically prevented from moving.

physical (*pilot's*) • An examination, given by a flight surgeon, to determine fitness for flying duty.

pitch indicator • An instrument for showing whether the nose of an aircraft is remaining in position relative to the horizon or moving up or down, and the approximate rate of change.

pitot tube • A cylindrical tube with the open end pointed into the air stream to measure impact pressure, used in connection with a static tube so that the difference in pressures can be translated into air speed on an indicator's dial.

pockmarked valve seat • A valve seat which has become pitted with use, and therefore subject to leakage.

polyconic projection (*map*) • A projection based on the development of a series of cones, each one tangent to and having a common axis with the earth. The distortion of area is reduced.

power spin · A spin with the throttle partly or fully open, during which the engine is exerting power, thereby making the spin more violent.

propeller hub · The metal fitting incorporated in or with a propeller for the purpose of mounting it on the engine shaft.

Pursuit · The branch of the Army Air Service which specialized in the development and operation of fighting planes, *i.e.*, airplanes whose primary mission is to find and shoot down enemy aircraft.

pusher engine · An engine with the propeller in the rear.

quartering wind · A wind blowing from an angle of approximately forty-five degrees to the course a plane is following.

radial engine · An engine with stationary cylinders arranged radially around a common crankshaft, like spokes around the hub of a wheel.

rev (*engine*) · Turn (from "revolution").

rib (*wing*) · A fore-and-aft member of a wing, stabilizer, or similar structure, which gives the section its form and transmits the load from skin to spars.

rigger · A specialist in assembling and aligning aircraft, as distinct from engine mechanic, instrument expert, etc.

ring, parachute · A ring of wood above the jumper's head, to which the shroud lines and harness ropes were attached in certain exhibition types of parachutes. An old automobile steering-wheel was often used for the purpose.

rip cord · The cable which the jumper pulls to release a parachute from its container.

rocker-arm · A part of the valve-operating mechanism on an engine equipped with overhead valves. Its purpose is to reverse the direction of thrust of the valve push-rods.

roll (*barrel roll*) · A snap maneuver in which the airplane makes a complete rotation around its longitudinal axis, ending with the plane heading in the same direction it was flying when the maneuver started.

rpm · Revolutions per minute.

rudder · The hinged vertical airfoil on the tail of most airplanes, controllable by the pilot for the purpose of turning the airplane around its vertical axis, *i.e.*, right or left.

rudder bar · The bar, hinged at the center and moved by the pilot's feet, which operates the rudder.

runway · A long and narrow strip, usually hard-surfaced, maintained for the take-off and landing runs of airplanes.

Ryan M-2 · An externally-braced, high-wing, open tandem-cockpit, tractor monoplane with fabric-covered wings and fuselage. Powered by either one Wright Whirlwind or one Hispano-Suiza engine. Max. speed with Wright engine 133 mph.; with Hispano-Suiza engine 128 mph. Landing speed 47 mph. Built at San Diego, Cal.

screen oil · To pour the engine oil through a screen to remove any foreign material, such as lint, dirt, etc.

sediment bulb · A dirt and water trap in the fuel line.

sextant · A portable instrument used for measuring the angular distance between a heavenly body (sun, moon, star) and the earth's horizon or an artificial horizon. The latitude and longitude of the observer can be computed from sextant observations.

sextant sight · An observation made with a sextant.

shock absorbers (*as used in this book*) · A system, incorporating loops of rubber rope, for the purpose of cushioning the jolts received by the wheels and tail skid in taking off, landing, and taxiing.

shroud line (*parachute*) · One of the cords, to which the cloth of the canopy is sewn, running from the vent around to the skirt and then down to the shroud ring.

sideslip · To slide an airplane sideways, in a downward direction, usually for the purpose of losing altitude without gaining forward speed.

Sikorsky (*Fonck's transatlantic S-35*) · A specially constructed, fabric-covered biplane, powered by three, tractor, Gnome-Rhone-Jupiter 425 hp., air-cooled, radial engines. Max. speed 143 mph. Landing speed 60 mph. Built at Westbury, Long Island, N.Y.

skid · To slide outwardly, away from the direction in which an airplane is turning. The opposite of a slip. Caused by too fast a turn in relation to the angle of bank.

skin · The outside covering of an airplane (fabric; metal; plywood).

skirt, parachute · The rim of the canopy.

slip · See sideslip.

slipstream · The stream of air driven aft by the propeller.

span · The straight-line distance between wing tips.

spar (*wing*) · One of the main transverse structural members of a wing, to which the ribs are attached.

spin · A maneuver consisting of a combination of roll and yaw, in which the airplane remains in a stalled attitude although the nose is usually pointed steeply downward. The position of controls is normally with the stick back and full rudder in the direction of spin. The airplane descends in a helix of large pitch and small radius.

spinner · A fairing which is fitted coaxially with the propeller hub to reduce air resistance and improve appearance. It revolves with the propeller.

spiral · A maneuver in which an airplane ascends or descends while in a more or less uniform bank, the air speed usually being well above the stalling point.

spot landing · A landing made, usually without the use of power, in an attempt to stop the airplane rolling at a mark placed or chosen on the landing field.

spreader bar · The fixed, horizontal, structural member on a landing gear, parallel (Jennies, Standards, DHs) to the wheel axle.

stability · That property of a body which causes it, when disturbed from a condition of equilibrium or steady motion, to develop forces or moments which tend to restore the body to its original condition.

stabilizer · An airfoil—usually a horizontal airfoil located on the tail—whose primary function is to give stability to an aircraft.

stall · The condition of an airplane when it has lost the air speed necessary for support or control.

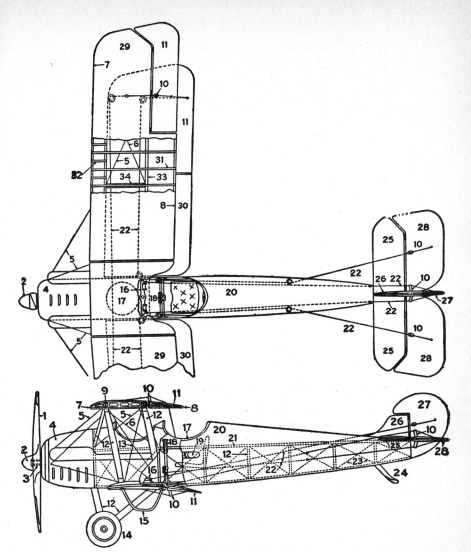

Airplane. Plan and elevation (both partly sectional) of a Biplane, showing: 1 Propeller Blade; 2 Spinner; 3 Propeller Hub; 4 Cowling; 5 Drag Wire; 6 Antidrag Wire; 7 Leading Edge; 8 Trailing Edge; 9 Wing Spar (front); 10 Horn; 11 Aileron; 12 Strut; 13 Stagger Wires; 14 Landing Gear; 15 Wing Skid; 16 Rudder Bar; 17 Cockpit; 18 Control Stick; 19 Exhaust Pipe; 20 Fuselage; 21 Longeron; 22 Control Wires; 23 Stays; 24 Tail Skid; 25 Stabilizer; 26 Fin; 27 Rudder; 28 Elevator; 29 Upper Wing or Plane; 30 Lower Wing or Plane; 31 Wing Rib; 32 Wing Rib Former, or False Rib; 33 Wing Spar (rear); 34 Drag Strut.

By permission. From Webster's New International
Dictionary, Second Edition
Copyright, 1934, 1939, 1945, 1950, 1953
by G. & C. Merriam Co.

stall landing • A landing in which the airplane has made the latter portion of its approach to the ground with its wings at an angle of attack close to the stalling point.

Standard (*OX-5*) • A converted, World War I, training, tractor biplane; one pilot, one passenger; open tandem-cockpits; fabric-covered. Max. speed 70 mph. Landing speed 42 mph.

stick • The vertical lever in the cockpit by means of which the pilot operates ailerons and elevator, thereby controlling the horizontal inclination of the wings, and the longitudinal inclination of the fuselage.

stick load • The load impressed by the control surfaces (ailerons and elevator) on the pilot's stick.

strut • See wing strut.

stuck valve (*engine*) • A valve which has become sluggish or frozen so that it does not follow the movement of the operating cam.

sump (*engine*) • The portion of an engine crankcase which serves as a reservoir for lubricating oil.

sun line • A line of position resulting from a sextant observation of the sun.

tachometer • An instrument which shows the revolutions per minute of an engine.

tail skid • A skid or runner which supports the tail of certain types of airplanes when in contact with the ground, acting also as a brake.

tail spin • See spin.

tail surfaces • The stabilizing and control surfaces at the tail end of an aircraft (stabilizer, fin, elevator, rudder).

tandem cockpits • Cockpits placed one behind the other.

taxi • To move an airplane over the ground or water under its own power.

three-point landing • A landing in which the wheels and tail skid touch ground at the same moment.

three-sixty • A training maneuver in which the cadet closes his throttle as he flies above a field, executes a 360-degree turn with his plane, and lands without the further use of power.

throttle • The hand lever in the cockpit, which regulates the flow of the fuel-air mixture to the engine cylinders.

ticking over (*engine*) • Revolving so slowly that the individual cylinder exhausts are heard separately and distinctly.

top off • To fill to the point of overflowing.

tractor engine • An engine with the propeller in front.

Travel Air biplane (*OXX-6 engine*) • An open tandem-cockpit, tractor biplane with fabric-covered wings and fuselage. One pilot, two passengers. Max. speed 96 mph. Landing speed 38 mph. Built at Wichita, Kan.

Travel Air monoplane • An externally-braced, high-wing, cabin monoplane with fabric-covered wings and fuselage. Powered by one Whirlwind tractor-engine. Max. speed 123 mph. Landing speed 55 mph.

trick it up • Improve the performance by means of unusual techniques.

true course • See course, true.

turbulence • Roughness of air, caused by wind, convection currents, etc.

turnbuckle • A sleeve which turns on a right-hand screw thread at one end and a left-hand screw thread at the other end, used for adjusting the tension on wires, tie-rods, etc.

turn indicator • See gyroscopic turn indicator.

turtleback • The approximately streamline cover over the aft portion of the fuselage, behind the cockpit.

valve seat (*engine cylinder*) • The circular, smooth-ground, fixed surface on which the valve rests when in the closed position.

variation (*magnetic*) • The angular difference between true north and magnetic north.

vent, parachute • The small opening at the top of the canopy, for the purpose of decreasing swinging during descent by allowing the gradual escape of air.

venturi tube • A short tube with flaring ends and a constriction between them into which a side tube enters. When the axis of the venturi tube is in, and parallel to, an airstream, a negative pressure is created in the side tube which may be used to operate certain instruments—such as a gyroscopic turn-indicator.

vertical reversement • An acrobatic maneuver in which the airplane is snap-rolled from a steep bank in one direction to a steep bank in the opposite direction.

Vickers Vimy (*Rolls-Royce 350 hp. liquid-cooled engines*) (*the type converted for the transatlantic flight by Alcock and Brown*) • A twin-engine, fabric-covered, biplane bomber, designed for use in World War I. Max. speed 103 mph. Landing speed 56 mph. Built in England.

visibility • The transparency and illumination of the atmosphere as affecting the distance at which objects can be seen.

Waco 9 (*OX-5 engine*) • An open tandem-cockpit, tractor biplane with fabric-covered wings and fuselage; one pilot, two passengers. Max. speed 92 mph. Landing speed 32 mph. Built at Troy, Ohio.

wallow • Roll about heavily.

washout (*crash*) • A crash which leaves the airplane in an unrepairable condition.

washout (*Flying Cadets*) • A man who has been or is being dropped from the flying school; to flunk out of the flying school.

whip-stall • In a whip-stall the airplane falls, out of control, from a stalled position with the nose pointing steeply upward. The tail whips up during the fall, and when the pilot's controls become effective again the nose is pointing steeply downward.

wind direction • The direction from which the wind is blowing.

wind rose • A diagram which shows, by radial arrows, the relative frequency and average strength of winds from different directions, at a given place and altitude and over a stated period of the year.

wind sock • A conically-shaped fabric bag, open at both ends. One end is attached to a metal hoop which is free to pivot while the sock bulges out with any wind that may be blowing, thereby indicating direction, turbulence, and velocity.

wing hinge • A fitting for one of the points of attachment of a wing.

wingman • A pilot who has been assigned to fly his airplane in formation, off the wing of, and relative to, a leading airplane.

wing-over • A maneuver in which the airplane is pulled up in a climbing turn until the stalling point is approached. The nose is then allowed to drop while the turn is continued, until the plane is pointing in the opposite direction to which it was flying when the wing-over began.

wing span • See span.

wing strut • A structural member between the upper and lower wings (Jennies, Standards, DHs) of a biplane. One of the struts on an externally-braced (*Spirit of St. Louis*) monoplane, which runs from the base of the fuselage diagonally up to the wing.

Wright-Bellanca (*J-5*) • A cabin type, externally-braced, high-wing monoplane with fabric covering, powered by one Wright Whirlwind tractor-engine. Max. speed 130 mph. Landing speed 47 mph. Built at Paterson, N.J.

zero zero • No ceiling and no visibility—as in dense fog.

zoom • A maneuver in which an airplane makes use of its kinetic energy to climb, for a limited time, at an angle greater than its engine's power can maintain in steady flight.